JANAKIRAM J. UGPSN 09102
REXT 3060 + REXT 6190
REXT 6190
W04
W04
W06

Dec. 2003.

Everyday Encounters

Second Canadian Edition

UNIVERSITY OF GUELPH LIBRARY

3 1188 01657156 0

P9-CAU-978

Everyday Encounters
Second Canadian Edition

An Introduction to Interpersonal Communication

Julia Wood
University of North Carolina, Chapel Hill

Angela Henry
Camosun College

NELSON
™
THOMSON LEARNING

Australia • Canada • Mexico • Singapore • Spain • United Kingdom • United States

NELSON

™

THOMSON LEARNING

Everyday Encounters: An Introduction
to Interpersonal Communication
by Julia T. Wood and Angela Henry

Editorial Director and Publisher:
Evelyn Veitch

Executive Editor:
Chris Carson

Marketing Manager:
Murray Moman

Developmental Editor:
Rebecca Rea

Production Editor:
Natalia Denesiuk

Production Coordinator:
Helen Locsin

Copy Editor:
Karen Rolfe

Proofreader:
Joan Rawlin

Interior & Cover Designs:
Suzanne Peden

Cover Image:
Jackie Besteman

Compositors:
Alicja Jamorski, Susan Calverley

Printer:
Transcontinental

COPYRIGHT © 2002 by Nelson
Thomson Learning, a division of
Thomson Canada Limited. Nelson
Thomson Learning is a registered
trademark used herein under
license.

Printed and bound in Canada
1   2   3   4   04   03   02   01

For more information contact
Nelson Thomson Learning,
1120 Birchmount Road,
Scarborough, Ontario, M1K 5G4.
Or you can visit our internet site at
www.nelson.com

ALL RIGHTS RESERVED. No part of
this work covered by the copyright
hereon may be reproduced,
transcribed, or used in any form or
by any means—graphic, electronic,
or mechanical, including
photocopying, recording, taping,
web distribution or information
storage and retrieval systems—
without the written permission of
the publisher.

For permission to use material
from this text or product, contact
us by
Tel 1-800-730-2214
Fax 1-800-730-2215
www.thomsonrights.com

**National Library of Canada
Cataloguing in Publication Data**

Wood, Julia T.
Everyday encounters : an
introduction to interpersonal
communication

2nd Canadian ed.
Includes bibliographical references
and index.
ISBN 0-17-616911-3

1. Interpersonal communication.
2. Interpersonal relations.
 I. Henry, Angela, 1945– . II. Title.

BF637.C45W66 2001   153.6
C2001-903503-9

Brief Table of Contents

Table of Contents

PART TWO   WEAVING COMMUNICATION INTO RELATIONSHIPS

Preface

Everyday Encounters: An Introduction to Interpersonal Communication, Second Canadian Edition, offers a distinct alternative to existing textbooks for the introductory course in interpersonal communication. The book is unique in its emphasis on theories, research, and skills that are anchored in the field of communication and in its attention to significant trends in Canadian social life as we navigate through the first years of a new millennium. The Canadian adaptation of the American text brings the obvious changes that distinguish Canada from the United States, namely spelling, currency, economic, geographical, demographic, and political changes, but it also includes changes in language that represent the more subtle differences in values and approaches that mark Canadians. The cultural diversity of Canada is represented in the many voices in the text. Familiar Canadians, whether in research, art, media, politics, or sport give the text a unique flavour. But unfamiliar voices of the common folk also provide a regional perspective. The Canadian adaptation also provides added pedagogical supports that make it very accessible to students and very helpful to teachers. *Everyday Encounters* is highlighted with a unique cartoon series that punctuates each chapter and takes us humorously through everyday experiences.

....

FOCUS ON COMMUNICATION

RESEARCH AND THEORY

In the 1970s, when interpersonal communication was a very young intellectual area, research was limited. Because theoretical and research foundations for courses were not abundant, the content of most texts and courses either extended general principles of communication to interpersonal contexts or relied primarily on research in fields other than communication.

Although interpersonal communication continues to draw from other disciplines, by now it is a substantive field in its own right, complete with a base of knowledge, theories, and research founded in communication. The maturation of interpersonal communication as an intellectual area is evident in the substantial original research published in academic journals, as well as in the steady stream of scholarly books. It is clear that interpersonal communication is no longer a derivative field.

Textbooks for introductory communication courses no longer need to rely primarily on research and theories developed by scholars outside the communication field. *Everyday Encounters* reflects a strong focus on research in the communication discipline. Woven into each chapter, for example, are discussions on relationships that highlight the extensive research on relational dialectics, the emergent knowledge of differences in communication that are influenced by gender, economic class, sexual orientation, ethnicity, and race. Communication scholars' strong interest in ethics is also woven into this book. Ethical issues and choices are integral to the discussion of the range of topics that are part of interpersonal communication. These and other topics in current communication inquiry are integrated into this book. As a result, students who read it will gain an appreciation of the scope and depth of scholarship in the field of communication.

ATTENTION TO SIGNIFICANT SOCIAL TRENDS

Social diversity is not merely a timely trend, a new buzzword, or a matter of political correctness. Instead, social diversity is a basic fact of life in Canada, a country (like many others) enriched by a cornucopia of people, heritages, customs, and ways of interacting. *Everyday Encounters* reflects and addresses social diversity by weaving it into the basic fabric of interpersonal communication.

Addressing diversity adequately requires more than tacking paragraphs on gender or race to conventional approaches to topics. Awareness of race, economic class, gender, age, and sexual orientation are woven into discussions of communication theory and skills. For example, in exploring self-concept, detailed attention is given to race, gender, and sexual orientation as core facets of identity that shape how individuals communicate and interpret the communication of others. In examining patterns of interaction in families, research on families that are not White and middle class is included. Discussion on romantic relationships includes research on gay and lesbian relationships as well as heterosexual ones. Rather than highlighting the attention to diversity with diversity boxes or separate features, diverse social groups, customs, and lifestyles are blended into the book as a whole.

Social diversity is not the only significant social trend that affects and is affected by interpersonal communication. *Everyday Encounters* addresses communication challenges, confusions, and issues that are part of personal and social life in our era. There is attention to friendships, which have assumed enlarged importance in the face of increasing numbers of broken marriages and geographically dispersed families. Discussion on romantic relationships addresses abuse and violence between intimates, managing long-distance relationships, and the use of communication to negotiate safer sex in an era shadowed by HIV and AIDS. The workplace chapter examines current topics in workplace health such as how to bring soul to the workplace, sexual harassment, dealing with difficult people, and untraditional jobs for men and women.

SPECIAL FEATURES OF *EVERYDAY ENCOUNTERS: AN INTRODUCTION TO INTERPERSONAL COMMUNICATION*, SECOND CANADIAN EDITION

The emphasis on communication research and theories and attention to social diversity are two distinctive features of the book. In addition to those features, there are other facets of the book that are designed to make it engaging and useful to students and helpful to teachers.

First, the authors have adopted a conversational tone so that students are invited to interact with ideas on a personal level. Every chapter begins with a cartoon of our communications heroine, "Chloe." Her escapades through everyday experiences underscore the concepts of each chapter in a humorous and engaging way. Each chapter is also enhanced by commentaries written by students in interpersonal communication classes. Their voices add a broader perspective to the scholarly material and remind the reader that the topic of interpersonal communication is about the lives of real people.

Everyday Encounters also includes pedagogical features that promote development of interpersonal communication skills. Each chapter includes several Apply the Idea exercises, which encourage students to apply concepts and principles discussed in the text to their own lives. Coupled with these exercises are Reflective Exercises that help promote reflective thinking and personal examination. Each chapter also includes a number of Communication Notes features, which highlight interesting research and examples of interpersonal communication in everyday life. Many of these are drawn from the Canadian landscape and offer a snapshot of communication ideas, foibles, and challenges in Canada. Clusters of concepts are highlighted and brought into the sidebar for quick reference, review, and summary. These sidebars are called Concepts at a Glance and Review Boxes. These pedagogical features allow the student to capture key concepts in point form, which will assist study and recall. Interspersed in each chapter are photographs of people in everyday interactions. Most photographs have captions that pose questions or invite reflection. This becomes particularly helpful for the visual learner to capture the salient concepts of the chapter and to augment the denseness of the written text. Following each chapter are several questions that invite students to engage in further reflection and discussion of ideas covered in the reading. For most chapters, at least one question focuses specifically on ethical issues in interpersonal communication, and at least one question suggests an activity using InfoTrac College Edition, which can be bundled with this text. For more information on this special offer, please contact your local Nelson Thomson Learning sales representative.

ADDITIONAL RESOURCES FOR INSTRUCTORS

Accompanying *Everyday Encounters* are many instructional resources:

An extensive Instructor's Resource Manual supplements the textbook. The manual discusses philosophical and pragmatic considerations involved in teaching the introductory course in interpersonal communication. It also includes suggestions for course emphases, sample syllabi, exercises and films appropriate for each chapter, masters for overheads of diagrams from the text, a correlation chart for the CNN Interpersonal Communication Video, a list of net resources, journal items, panel ideas, and a bank of test items.

A text-specific PowerPoint presentation includes professionally created text and images to illustrate important concepts in this book—plus a built-in flexibility that lets you add your own materials. These PowerPoint slides can be downloaded from the text Web site—www.everydayencounters.nelson.com

The InfoTrac® College Edition Student Activities Workbook for Interpersonal Communication 1.0 can also be bundled with the text. This workbook features extensive individual and group activities that focus on specific interpersonal communication course topics and make use of InfoTrac. The workbook also includes guidelines for faculty and students that describe how to maximize the use of this resource.

Nelson Thomson Learning will also provide qualified instructors who adopt this book with a videotape produced by CNN that demonstrates everyday applications of principles and skills covered in this book. There are four CNN videotapes in total. Please contact your local Nelson Thomson Learning representative for further details.

The Media Guide for Interpersonal Communication is a 200-page guide containing media resource listings that provide compelling examples of interpersonal communication in an engaging format. The guide generates student interest and motivates learning through the use of film, books, plays, Web sites, and journal articles.

InterLink: A Multimedia Presentation Tool for Interpersonal Communication 2.0 is an additional presentation tool that provides searchable databases of Microsoft® PowerPoint® slides; text, photos, and art from a number of Wadsworth Interpersonal Communications texts; embedded Web links; and cued CNN video clips.

Finally, the Service Learning in Communication Studies handbook is an invaluable resource for integrating a service learning component in your course. It contains guidelines for connecting service learning work with classroom concepts and offers advice for working effectively with agencies and organizations. The handbook also provides model forms and reports and a directory of online resources.

JULIA WOOD'S ACKNOWLEDGMENTS

Many people have contributed to this book. I am especially indebted to Deirdre Cavanaugh, my editor at Wadsworth. From start to finish, she has been a full partner in this project, and her interest and insights have greatly enhanced the book. Deirdre was also most generous in providing personal support, enthusiasm, and encouragement to me.

Also essential to the birth of this book were members of the publishing team who transformed an unembroidered manuscript into the final book that you are holding. Specifically, I thank Cathy Linberg, project editor; Barbara Britton, print buyer; Bob Krauser, permissions editor, whose detective skills were put to the test (they passed) in tracking down materials that required permissions; Megan Gilbert, assistant editor, who took charge of the ancillary materials for this book; and Matt Lamm, editorial assistant, who kept all of the team on track and in touch; Jennifer Gordon, who copyedited this book with unusual patience and skill; Cecile Joyner of The Cooper Company, who oversaw production of the book; Norman Baugher, who created the beautiful interior and cover designs; and Judy Mason, who was in charge of photo research.

In addition to the editorial and production team at Wadsworth, I am grateful to the many students and teachers who reviewed versions of the manuscript and whose comments and suggestions improved the final content of the book. For the first edition, I thank Patricia Amason, University of Arkansas; Lucinda Bauer, University of North Carolina at Chapel Hill; Betsy W. Bach, University of Montana; Cherie L. Bayer, Indiana University; Kathryn Carter, University of Nebraska, Lincoln; Joseph S. Coppolino, Nassau Community College; Laverne Curtis-Wilcox, Cuyahoga Community College; Michelle Miller, University of Memphis; John Olson, Everett Community College; William Foster Owen, California State University, Sacramento; Nan Peck, Northern Virginia Community College, Annandale Campus; Mary Jo Popovici, Monroe Community College; Sharon A. Ratliffe, Golden West College; Susan Richardson, Prince George's Community College; Cathey S. Ross, University of North Carolina, Greensboro; Kristi A. Schaller, Georgia State University; Michael Wallace, Indiana University/Purdue University at Indianapolis; and the students at North Virginia Community College, Annandale Campus, and University of Arkansas who class-tested the book.

For the second edition, thank you to reviewers Lynn Badertscher, Fresno City College; Diane Boynton, Monterey Peninsula College; Larry Nadler, Miami University of Ohio; John Olson, Everett Community College; Sally Planalp, University of Montana; Valerie Randhawa, Harrisburg Area Community College; and Susan Richardson, Prince George's Community College.

Writing this book was not only a professional activity but also a personal engagement that benefited from the generous support of individuals who make up my family of choice. At the top of that list is Robbie Cox, my partner in love, life, and adventure for 25 years. He cheered me on when writing was going well and bolstered my confidence when it was not. He provided a critical ear when I wanted a sounding board and privacy when I was immersed in writing. Along with Robbie, I am fortunate to have the support of my sister Carolyn and my special friends Nancy and Linda Becker. And, of course, I must acknowledge the four-footed members of my family—Madhi, Sadie Ladie, and Wicca. Unlike my two-footed companions, these three willingly keep me company when I am writing at 2 or 3 in the morning.

ANGELA HENRY'S ACKNOWLEDGMENTS

I am indebted to several people whose assistance made the Second Canadian Edition of *Everyday Encounters* possible. First, I am honoured to be working with such a fine manuscript from Julia Wood. Her extensive research and attention to scholarship has been a joy to work with. The breadth and depth of the topics on interpersonal communication in the first edition is what drew me to the text for my own students several years ago. I was delighted when Kelly Torrance and Evelyn Veitch approached me to do the Canadian adaptation of the second U.S. edition. Julia Woods's commitment to the field of communication is evident in the quality of her own research and the attention she pays to her students. It has been a great pleasure doing the Canadian adaptation of her work.

Second, I would like to thank Ron Sept and Jane Duncan for the material of their workplace chapter from the first Canadian edition of *Everyday Encounters*. It provided the basis of the revisions in chapter 11.

Third, I have the highest regard and appreciation for the team at Nelson Thomson Learning: Rebecca Rea, a wonderful and exceedingly patient developmental editor; Kelly Torrance, who could turn granite to gold with her laugh and encouragement; Rebecca Hull for photo research and the arduous permissions; Stephen Lee for his enchanting and cryptic cartoons; Karen Rolfe for such careful and insightful copy editing; and the dedicated production editor, Natalia Denesiuk, who worked on such a tight schedule to complete this work.

Fourth, my heartfelt gratitude to the many reviewers in colleges and universities across Canada who provided insightful suggestions, critical commentary, and fine detail that enhanced the quality and readability of the text.

Finally and most importantly, I thank my dear family and beloved friends who endured a year of supporting me through the highs and lows of writing. In particular, I wish to thank my life-mate, my husband, Gil Henry, for his unjudgmental support, humour, and creativity in managing a year bereft of my relationship best. I would also like to thank my daughter, Tasha, for her soul-wisdom, my son Damon for technical and artistic support, my niece, Tristesse, and her partner, Dave, for graphic design and film consultation, my sisters and brother and my dear friend and colleague Pearl Arden, all of whom cheered me on, counselled, cajoled, and contributed ideas and critical review. Thanks go also to all those who either generously donated photographs or patiently posed for photographs for the text. A special thank you goes to Monique Salez for many hours of patient and detailed work proofing, photographing, typing, and running errands. My last acknowledgments go to my wonderful students in my communication classes. Their response to my teaching has always provided me with a profound source of personal reflection and joy. Their critical review of the text provided guidance for changes and their humour and candor provided much of the material for the Student Voices. A project of this magnitude is never done alone. I extend my heartfelt appreciation to you all.

The Fabric of Interpersonal Communication

A First Look at Interpersonal Communication

Everyday Encounters
By Stephen Lee

Chloe is the heroine of Everyday Encounters. She has just been confronted with all the kinds of noise that get in the way of clear communication. Do they look familiar? Her experiences, like yours, are part of what we encounter everyday. This book examines the interpersonal communication of our everyday lives. Let's begin our look at interpersonal communication by considering the importance of it in our lives. Consider the following scenario. You've been interviewing for two months, and so far, you haven't gotten a single job offer. After another interview that didn't go well, you run into a close friend who asks what's wrong. Instead of just offering quick sympathy, your friend suggests the two of you go to lunch and talk. Over sandwiches, you disclose that you're starting to worry you won't find a job, and you wonder what's wrong with you. Your friend listens closely and lets you know he cares about your concerns. Then he tells you about other people he knows who also haven't received job offers. Suddenly you don't feel so alone. Your friend reminds you how worried you felt last term when you were struggling with that physics course and then you made a B on the final. Listening to him, your sagging confidence begins to recover. Before leaving, he helps you come up with new strategies for interviewing. You feel hopeful again by the time you leave.

This scenario reveals the importance of interpersonal communication in our everyday lives. We count on others who are special to us to care about what is happening in our lives and to help us sort through problems and concerns. We want them to share our worries, as well as our joys. Good listeners allow us to sort through the powerful impact of our feelings so that we can make decisions. In addition, we need others to encourage our growth. Friends and romantic partners who believe in us often enable us to overcome self-defeating patterns and to become more the selves we want to be. And sometimes we just want to hang out with people we like and trust. Interpersonal communication is common to the many ways close relationships contribute to our lives.

Interpersonal communication is the foundation of personal identity and growth, and it is a primary basis of building connections with others. Effective communication broadens us as individuals and enhances the quality of relationships, whereas ineffective communication diminishes us personally and can poison, or even destroy, our relationships. We engage in communication to develop identities, establish connections, deepen ties over time, and work out problems and possibilities. In short, interpersonal communication is central to our everyday lives and our happiness. It is the lifeblood of meaningful relationships.

In this chapter, we take a first look at interpersonal communication. We'll start by considering how communication meets important human needs. We will then distinguish interpersonal communication from communication in general. Next, we will identify principles and skills of effective interpersonal communication. After reading this chapter, you should understand what interpersonal communication is (and is not), why it matters in our lives, and the skills and principles of competent interpersonal communication.

Concepts at a Glance

Good listeners

- Help us sort through problems
- Share our feelings
- Facilitate our growth

THE INTERPERSONAL IMPERATIVE

Have you ever thought about why we communicate with others? There are many reasons we seek interaction, and there are many human needs we meet by communicating. Abraham Maslow (1968), a psychologist, described a hierarchy of human needs; according to Maslow, basic needs must be satisfied before we can focus on those that are more abstract (Figure 1.1). As we will see, communication is a primary means of meeting our needs at each level in the hierarchy.

PHYSICAL NEEDS

At the most basic level, humans need to survive, and communication helps us meet this need. To survive, babies must alert others when they are hungry or in pain. And others must respond to these needs, or babies will die.

Beyond surviving, children need interaction to thrive. Linda Mayes (2000), a physician at the Child Study Center at Yale University, reports that children can suffer lasting damage if they are traumatized early in their lives. Trauma increases the stress hormones that wash over infants' fragile brains. One result is inhibited growth of the limbic system, which controls emotions. Adults who suffered abuse as children often have reduced memory ability, anxiety, hyperactivity, and impulsiveness (Begley, 1997). Noted Canadian researcher Dr. Fraser Mustard (1994) has tied infant brain development to social and physical environments, stressing the impact of early infant care on learning, behaviour, and health across the life span.

As we grow older, we continue to rely on communication to survive and thrive. We discuss medical problems with doctors in order to stay well, and our effectiveness in communicating affects what jobs we get and how much we earn to pay for basic needs such as medical care, food, and housing. Further, researchers have amassed impressive evidence to document the close link between physical health and relationships with others.

At times we all rely on others. We might need assistance to understand difficult material in courses, fix a short in our stereo, learn a new computer program, or develop effective interviewing strategies. In each case, we communicate to gain assistance. Through communication we meet basic needs—

Figure 1.1
Maslow's Hierarchy of Needs

whether those are gaining food and water or engaging in sex, which Maslow considered a basic human need. It may be easy to meet our needs or it may be difficult. Sometimes we may have to persuade or convince others to comply with our requests by explaining why they should. This too requires communication skill.

Student Voices

Navita:

It's funny, but it's harder to talk about sex than to have it. I'm having to learn how to bring up the topic of safety and how to be assertive about protection. I used not to do that because it's embarrassing, but I'd rather be embarrassed than dead.

SAFETY NEEDS

We also meet safety needs through communication. If your roof is leaking or termites have invaded your apartment, you must talk with the property manager or owner to have the problem solved so that you have safe shelter. If someone is threatening you, you need to talk with law enforcement officers to gain protection. If your friend has been drinking and you take the car keys and say, "I'll drive you home," you may be saving a life. In an era under the shadow of AIDS, couples have to talk with each other about safer sex. Being able to discuss private and difficult issues surrounding sex is essential to our safety, although it may be embarrassing, as Navita comments.

Communication skills also allow us to protect ourselves from damaging, or even deadly, products. When foods are determined to be a health threat, news media inform the public of the danger. Car makers send owners recall messages when defects in a model are found. Communication is also required to protect ourselves from environmental toxins. Residents in communities with toxic waste dumps have to communicate with officials and media to call attention to environmental toxins that endanger their physical survival and safety. Later, the officials and media may communicate to compel corrective action from those responsible for dumping toxic wastes. We need only witness the staggering effects of the Walkerton water contami-

When in your life have you felt unsafe? How did it affect communication?

Photo: A. Henry

nation in Ontario in May and June 2000 to recognize how crucial it is to have effective and timely communication. When safety needs are not being met, it is almost impossible to focus on the higher needs of belonging, self-esteem, or self-actualization. This will explain why, for example, a student will be unresponsive to romantic advances when next week's rent isn't secured or why a single parent can't focus on career opportunities while struggling with the financial devastation of a leaky condo.

BELONGING NEEDS

The third level in Maslow's hierarchy is belonging, or social, needs. Most humans seek others to be happy, to enjoy life, and to enrich experiences. We want others' company, acceptance, and affirmation, and we want to give acceptance and affirmation to others. The alternative is loneliness, which can be very painful. Interaction with others provides us with a sense of social fit so that we feel we're part of various groups. Communication also allows us to structure time effectively—talking with others, watching films together, and working on projects are ways we interact to meet belonging needs. As well, interpersonal communication introduces us to perspectives that broaden our own views. Perhaps after talking with someone about an issue you've thought, "I never saw it that way before," or "Gee, that really changes my attitude." Chad notes how important this type of communication is in his commentary.

Student Voices

Chad:

I never had a label for it before, but a lot of my communication is for belonging needs. When I feel down or bored, I find one of my friends and we hang out. It doesn't matter what we do, or whether we do anything, really. Sometimes it's just important to have somebody to hang with.

The connection between good relationships and well-being is demonstrated by a great deal of research. For instance, one study found that people who lack strong social ties are 200 to 300 percent more likely to die prematurely (Narem, 1980). Another report concluded that heart disease is far more prevalent in people lacking strong interpersonal relationships than in those who have healthy connections with others (Ruberman, 1992). Researchers have also found a significant link between having few friends and problems such as depression, anxiety, and fatigue (Hojat, 1982; Jones & Moore, 1989). Perhaps you've been through periods when all of your friends were unavailable, either because they were involved with their own priorities or because they moved away. Did you feel more lonely, less satisfied during those times? Most of us do feel less optimistic and less valued when we don't have good friends with whom we can interact and who let us know we matter to them.

A particularly dramatic finding is that people who are deprived of interaction often hallucinate, lose physiological coordination, and become depressed and disoriented (Wilson, Robick, & Michael, 1974). Two extreme cases demonstrate the effects of social isolation. Sociologist Kingsley Davis (1940, 1947) documented the cases of Anna and Isabelle, two girls, unrelated to one another, who received minimal human contact and care during the first six years of their lives. Both children were born out of wedlock, which may explain why they were rejected and removed from normal family life. Authorities who discovered the children reported that both girls lived in dark, dank attics. Anna and Isabelle were so undeveloped intellectually that they behaved like six-month-old children. Anna was startlingly apathetic and unresponsive to others. She did not progress well despite care, contact, and nutrition. She died four years after she was discovered. Isabelle fared better. When she was found, she communicated with grunts and gestures and was responsive to human interaction. After two years in systematic therapy, Isabelle approached normal intelligence levels for her age.

This research confirms that isolation is one of the cruellest forms of punishment and helps explain why isolation is considered an effective torture. Most people are better able to withstand hunger and physical pain than social isolation. How do we explain the difference between these two isolated children and what happened to them? There was one major difference. Anna was left alone all of the time and had no human contact. Food was periodically put in her room, but nobody talked to her or played with her. Isabelle, on the other hand, shared her space with her mother, who was deaf and mute. The family renounced both of them and sequestered them together. Although Isabelle didn't have the advantage of normal family interaction, she did have contact, apparently with a mother who loved her. Because the mother was deaf and mute, she couldn't teach Isabelle to speak, but she did teach Isabelle to interact with gestures and sounds that both of them understood. Thus, Isabelle suffered far less extreme deprivations than Anna.

The need for social contact continues throughout our lives. Even people who have been raised with normal social interaction can be affected if it is withdrawn later in life. British sociologist Peter Townsend (1962) reported that many institutionalized elderly people have few opportunities for social interaction. The result, according to Townsend, is progressive depression, resignation, and apathy.

SELF-ESTEEM NEEDS

Moving up the hierarchy, we find self-esteem needs, which involve being valued by others and ourselves. We want others to respect us, and we want to respect ourselves. As we will see in Chapter 2, communication is the primary way we figure out who we are and who we can be. We gain our first sense of self from others who communicate how they see us. Parents and other family members tell children they are pretty or plain, smart or slow, good or bad, helpful or difficult. As family members communicate their perceptions, children begin to form images of themselves.

This process continues throughout life as we see ourselves reflected in others' eyes. In elementary school, how our teachers interact with us influences how we perceive ourselves. Our peers also express evaluations of us—how smart we are, how good we are at soccer, how attractive we are. Later, in professional life, our co-workers and supervisors communicate in ways that suggest how much they respect us and our abilities. Through all the stages in our life, our self-esteem is shaped by how others communicate with us. People who lack strong interpersonal communication skills are unlikely to rise to the top in their fields, and many of them will suffer lowered self-esteem as a result.

The story of "Ghadya Ka Bacha," the "wolf boy," demonstrates that communicating with others is essential to self-concept—and even to human identity (Shattuck, 1980). Ramu was a feral child, a child raised with little or no human contact. As a result, he did not have a high sense of his worth as a person, if indeed he had a sense of himself as a person at all. His self-concept and self-esteem were shaped by those with whom he interacted—presumably wolves.

SELF-ACTUALIZATION NEEDS

According to Maslow, the most abstract human need is self-actualization. By this, he meant that each of us wants to have peak experiences that allow us to grow throughout life and to realize our unique potential. As humans, we seek more than survival, safety, belonging, and esteem. We also thrive on growth. Each of us wants to cultivate new dimensions, enlarge our perspectives, engage in challenging and different experiences, and learn new skills. We want to become our fullest selves by realizing our unique potential.

Communication fosters our growth as individuals. It is often in interaction with others that we first recognize possibilities for who we can be—possibilities that hadn't occurred to us. Perhaps you can recall someone who first noticed you had a talent and encouraged you to cultivate it. Who was that person? What messages did you receive that encouraged you to pursue your talents?

Others also help us grow by introducing us to new experiences and ways of thinking. Conversations can enrich our perspectives on ourselves, values, relationships, events, and situations. As a result, we are enlarged. Mother Teresa was well known for inspiring others to be generous, compassionate, and giving. She had the ability to see the best in others and to help them see it in themselves. Although she died in 1997, her influence on others continues through the work she inspired them to do.

Communication Notes

Ghadya Ka Bacha

In 1954, a young naked boy who was starving found his way to the hospital at Balrampur, India. He showed no ability to interact with people and had heavy calluses as if he moved on all fours. In addition, there were scars on the boy's neck as if he had been dragged by animals. The boy, named Ramu by the hospital staff, spent most of his time playing with a stuffed animal as a wild animal might in its lair. He showed no interest in communicating; indeed, he seemed to feel no connection with other people. Only twice did Ramu seem excited: when he was taken to see wolves at a zoo and when he saw a dog.

Ramu would howl when he smelled raw meat in the hospital kitchen over 100 yards from his room—far too great a distance for the human sense of smell to detect a scent. Ramu also didn't eat like a human: He tore meat apart and lapped milk from a container. Most of the doctors and scientists who examined Ramu concluded he was a "wolf boy" who had grown up in the wild and been socialized by wolves. He had no concept of himself as a person. Instead, he saw himself as a wolf and was more interested in interacting with animals than humans, who were not "his kind." Thus, doctors referred to Ramu as "Ghadya Ka Bacha," Indian for "wolf boy."

Source: Shattuck, T. (1980). *The forbidden experiment: The story of the wild boy of Aveyron.* New York: Farrar, Straus & Giroux.

Another way that we seek personal growth is by experimenting with new versions of ourselves. For this too we rely on communication. Sometimes we talk with others about goals and challenges we are embracing. At other times we try out new styles of identity without calling explicit attention to what we're doing. We see how others respond and decide whether we like the effects of the new identity or whether we need to go back to the drafting board. We could not assess changes in ourselves in isolation. We need to interact with others to get feedback on our identities and actions.

Others also help us self-actualize through inspiration and teaching. Gandhi, for instance, was a model of strength who didn't depend on aggression. Seeing him embody passive resistance with grace and impact inspired thousands of Indians to define themselves as passive resisters. Religious leaders such as Lao-tzu, Confucius, Jesus, Muhammad, and Buddha also inspire people to grow personally. Consider the Canadians that inspire us and help create a Canadian identity: people such as Pierre Trudeau, Margaret Atwood, Emily Carr, and Wayne Gretzky to name a few. As we interact with

Our friends are mirrors. They invite us to examine ourselves.

Photo: © Photodisc

teachers and leaders who inspire us, we may come to understand their visions of the world and of themselves and may weave those into our own self-concepts.

PARTICIPATING EFFECTIVELY IN A DIVERSE SOCIETY

To the needs Maslow identified, we must add a sixth. As we navigate in this new millennium, we need to know how to live effectively in a richly diverse society. Our world includes people of different ethnicities, genders, social classes, sexual orientations, ages, and abilities. Canada is particularly diverse. Geographically, it spans an area rivalled only by Russia, China, and the United States. Socially and economically, there are vast differences from north to south and east to west. The aboriginal cultures across Canada are also as diverse as the geography. Many job applications describe routinely, "Must be able to work in a cross-cultural environment." To function effectively in a world such as this, marked by diversity, we rely on communication. Through interaction with others, we learn about experiences and lifestyles that differ from our own; in addition, we share our experiences and values with people who seem unlike us in certain ways. Through interaction, diverse individuals come to understand their differences and similarities, and this recognition fosters personal growth.

Participating effectively in a diverse social world is critical to success in professional life, and the multicultural mosaic of Canadian life brings many communication challenges. A study of the most sought-after employability skills in the Canadian workforce ranks communication skills and particularly "the recognition and respect for people's diversity and differences" highest (Corporate Council on Education 1992). Canada is one of the few countries in the world that has a *Multicultural Act.* Passed in 1988, it is devoted to the preservation and enhancement of multiculturalism in Canadian communities. Like the other needs in Maslow's hierarchy, living in a diverse world becomes salient to us when we meet more basic needs. As long as we need food, shelter, and a sense of belonging, engaging diversity may not be an issue to us. When more basic needs are met, however, we recognize the importance of appreciating diversity. It's also the case that learning to engage diversity may help us meet some of our more basic needs. For example, our safety may depend on communicating with someone from a different culture, and we may meet belonging needs by joining groups with people who represent a range of ethnicities, religions (see "Religions around the World" on page 12), sexual orientations, and so forth. One of the most vital functions of communication in the new millennium is helping us understand and participate in a diverse world.

Apply the Idea

Communication and Your Needs

How do the needs we've discussed show up in your life? To find out, try this:

- *First, keep a diary of your communication for the next three days. Note the people you talk to, what is said, and how you feel about each interaction.*

- *After you've completed a three-day diary, go back and classify each interaction according to one of the six needs we discussed. How much of your communication focuses on each need?*

☐ physical survival ☐ self-esteem

☐ safety ☐ self-actualization

☐ belonging ☐ participating effectively in a diverse society

Review

- Our communication is driven by the needs we are trying to meet.
- It is very difficult to focus on higher needs when lower needs are not being met.

DEFINING INTERPERSONAL COMMUNICATION

So far we've seen that interpersonal communication is a primary way to meet a range of human needs. We now want to clarify what interpersonal communication is so that we have a shared understanding of what it includes and means.

WHAT DISTINGUISHES INTERPERSONAL COMMUNICATION?

When asked to distinguish interpersonal communication from communication in general, many people say that interpersonal communication involves fewer people, often just two. Although much interpersonal communication does involve only two or three individuals, this isn't a precise way to define interpersonal communication. If it were, then an exchange between a shopper and a salesclerk would be interpersonal, but a family conversation wouldn't be. Clearly, the number of people involved is not a good criterion for defining interpersonal communication.

Some people suggest that intimate contexts define interpersonal communication. Using this standard, we would say that a couple on a first date in a romantic restaurant engages in more interpersonal communication than an established couple in a shopping mall. As this illustration shows, context doesn't tell us what is unique about interpersonal communication.

What distinguishes interpersonal communication is a special quality of interaction. This emphasizes what happens between people, not where they

Communication Notes

Religions around the World

Christianity is the majority religion in the West, but around the world a number of religions are vital and growing.

Buddhism was founded by Prince Siddhartha Gautama (called the Buddha) in southern Nepal in the sixth century BCE. Buddhism emphasizes the interdependence of all living beings and seeks to reduce suffering in the world. By overcoming selfish desires, human beings attain the freedom of nirvana. There are more than 307 million Buddhists.

Confucianism, founded by Confucius, a Chinese philosopher, in the sixth century BCE, stresses the relationships among individuals, families, and society based on *li*, or proper behaviour, and *jen*, or sympathetic attitudes. It is difficult to estimate the number of Confucians because many people in China follow the teachings of Buddhism, Confucianism, and Taoism at the same time. However, it is estimated that there are nearly 160 million Confucians.

Hinduism dates back to 1500 BCE when indigenous religions of India combined with Aryan religions. Hindus believe in a strict caste system, which ranks people into different classes that one progresses through in a series of reincarnations. Today there are nearly 700 million Hindus.

Islam was founded early in the seventh century CE by the prophet Muhammad who received the holy scriptures of Islam (the *Koran*) from Allah. Islam teaches that Muhammad was the last in a long line of holy prophets including Abraham, Moses, and Jesus. Islam is an Arabic word that means "submission to God." Observant Muslims pray five times each day while facing Mecca, give money to the poor, follow dietary restrictions including not consuming pork and alcohol, and fast during the holy month of Ramadan, which is the ninth month in the Muslim year. At least once in their life, Muslims make a pilgrimage to Mecca (in Saudi Arabia). Today, there are nearly 900 million followers of Islam.

Judaism, the oldest of the world's living religions, teaches that the human condition can be bettered by following the teachings of the Jewish, or Hebrew, *Bible*. The *Torah*, the first five books of the *Bible*, is especially revered. Today there are approximately 18 million followers of Judaism.

Taoism was founded in China by Lao-tzu, born about 604 BCE. Taoism encourages living simply, spontaneously, and in harmony with nature. The number of Taoists today is thought to be close to 30 million.

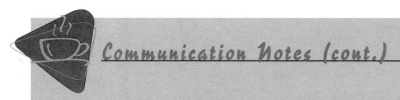

Communication Notes (cont.)

Shintoism is an ancient indigenous religion of Japan that has been traced to the sixth century BCE. Shintoists believe in veneration of multiple spiritual beings and ancestors, called *kami*. Shintoism is characterized by a lack of formal dogma. There are approximately 3.5 million Shintoists today.

Source: *New York public library desk reference*. (1989). New York: Simon & Schuster/Songstone Press, pp. 189–91.

are or how many are present. For starters, then, we can say **interpersonal communication*** is a special type of interaction between people.

A COMMUNICATION CONTINUUM

We can begin to understand the special character of interpersonal communication by tracing the meaning of the word "interpersonal." It is derived from the prefix "inter" meaning "between" and the word "person," so interpersonal communication literally occurs between persons. In one sense, all communication happens between persons, yet actually many interactions don't involve us personally. Communication exists on a continuum from impersonal to interpersonal (Figure 1.2).

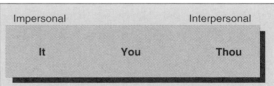

Figure 1.2
The Communication Continuum

Sometimes we don't acknowledge others as persons at all but treat them as objects. In other instances, we interact with others in stereotypical or role-bound ways but don't deal with them as distinct persons. And with a select few, we communicate in deeply personal ways. These distinctions were captured in poetic terms by the philosopher Martin Buber (1970) who distinguished among three levels of communication: I–It, I–You, and I–Thou.

I–It Communication

In an I–It relationship, we treat others very impersonally, almost as objects. In **I–It communication** we do not acknowledge the humanity of other persons; we may not even affirm their existence. Salespeople, servers in restaurants, and clerical staff are often treated not as people but as instruments to take orders and produce what we want. We also tend not to have personal conversations with phone solicitors. In the extreme form of I–It relationships, others are not even acknowledged. When a homeless person asks for money for food, some

---

* Boldface terms are defined in the glossary at the end of the book.

people do not even respond, but look through and beyond the person as if she or he isn't there. In dysfunctional families, parents may ignore children, thereby treating the children as its, not as unique individuals. Students on large campuses may also feel they are treated as its, not as persons.

Student Voices

Jason:
When I left the career program I was in at the college, and went to the university, I was constantly aware of how alone I felt. No one knew me or asked how I was doing. I was a student I.D. number only, an it.

I–You Communication

The second level that Buber identified is **I–You communication**, which accounts for the majority of our interactions. I–You communication is midway between impersonal and interpersonal communication. People acknowledge one another as more than objects, but they don't fully engage each other as unique individuals. For example, suppose you go shopping and a salesclerk asks, "May I help you?" Chances are you won't have a deep conversation with the clerk, but you might treat him or her as more than an it. Perhaps you say, "I'm just browsing today. You know how it is at the end of the month—no money." The clerk might laugh and commiserate about how money gets tight by the end of each month. In this interaction, you and the clerk treat each other as more than its: The clerk doesn't treat you as a faceless shopper, and you don't treat the clerk as just an agent of the store.

I–You relationships may also be more personal than interactions with salesclerks. For instance, we talk with others in our classes and on our sports teams in ways that are somewhat personal. Interaction is still guided by our roles as peers, members of a class or team, and students. Yet we do affirm their existence and recognize them as individuals within those roles. Teachers and students often talk personally yet stay within their social roles and don't reveal their private selves. In the workplace, the majority of our relationships are I–You. We interact with peers, supervisors, and subordinates within our job roles. Most of our co-workers are not strangers, but neither are they intimates. We communicate in less depth with most people in our social circles than with those we love most. Casual friends, work associates, and distant family members typically engage in I–You communication.

I–Thou Communication

The rarest kind of relationship involves **I–Thou communication.** Buber regarded this as the highest form of human dialogue because each person affirms the other as cherished and unique. When we interact on an I–Thou level, we meet others in their wholeness and individuality. Instead of dealing with them as occupants of social roles, we see them as unique human beings whom we know and accept in their totality. Also, in I–Thou communication we don't mask ourselves; instead, we open ourselves fully, trusting others to accept us as we are with virtues and vices, hopes and fears, strengths and weaknesses.

Buber believed that only in I–Thou relationships do we become fully human, which for him meant we discard the guises we use most of the time and allow ourselves to be completely genuine in interaction (Stewart, 1986). Much of our communication involves what Buber called "seeming," in which we're preoccupied with our image and careful to manage how we present ourselves. In I–Thou relationships, however, we engage in "being," in which we reveal who we really are and how we really feel. For Buber, only I–Thou communication is fully interpersonal, for only in I–Thou encounters do we meet each other as whole, existential persons.

I–Thou relationships are not commonplace, because we can't afford to reveal ourselves totally to everyone all of the time. We also don't want to be completely open or to form deeply personal ties with everyone. Thus, I–Thou relationships and the communication in them are rare and special. They represent fully interpersonal relationships.

Review

Buber distinguishes "seeming" from "being."

Apply the Idea

Communicating in Your Relationships

Consider how Buber's theory of communication applies to your life. Identify someone with whom you have each kind of communication: I–It, I–You, I–Thou. Describe what needs and values each relationship satisfies.

How does communication differ among the relationships? What don't you say in I–It and I–You relationships that you do say in I–Thou relationships? How do different levels of communication affect the closeness you feel with others?

Realizing that interpersonal communication is a matter of degree is a first step in understanding. Yet, we still don't have an appreciation of all that's involved in the process of interpersonal communication. To gain that, we'll now examine three models of interpersonal communication to see how it differs from public or social interaction.

MODELS OF INTERPERSONAL COMMUNICATION

Models are attempts to represent what something is and how it works. Over the years, scholars in communication have developed a number of models of interpersonal communication. Early models were simplistic, but later models offer sophisticated insight into the process of interpersonal communication.

LINEAR MODELS

In 1948, Harold Laswell developed an initial model of communication. According to Laswell's **linear model,** communication is a linear, or one-way, process in which one person acts on another person. Laswell didn't use a visual diagram to represent his view of communication. Instead, he provided a verbal model that consisted of five questions describing a sequence of acts that make up communication:

1. Who?
2. Says What?
3. In What Channel?
4. To Whom?
5. With What Effect?

A year later, Claude Shannon and Warren Weaver (1949) revised Laswell's model. In collaboration, they developed a model that portrays communication as the flow of information from a source to a destination. Their model extended Laswell's idea with the addition of noise. In their model, noise is anything that causes a loss of information as it flows from source to destination. Noise might be static in a phone line or activities going on that distract the sender or receiver of information.

Figure 1.3 shows Shannon and Weaver's model. Although early models, such as those by Laswell and Shannon and Weaver, are useful starting points in thinking about what interpersonal communication is and how it works, these linear models have three serious shortcomings. First, they portray communication as flowing in only one direction—from a sender to a receiver. This suggests that listeners only listen; they never send messages. Also, it suggests that speakers only speak; they never listen or receive messages from listeners.

The second weakness of linear models is that they suggest that listeners passively absorb senders' messages and do not respond. Listeners aren't represented as active participants in interpersonal communication. Clearly, this isn't how communication occurs. Listeners affect what speakers do. Listeners nod, frown, smile, look bored or interested, and so forth. All of these types of nonverbal communication influence what speakers say and do. In other words, what others do affects how we communicate, and what we do and say affects their communication.

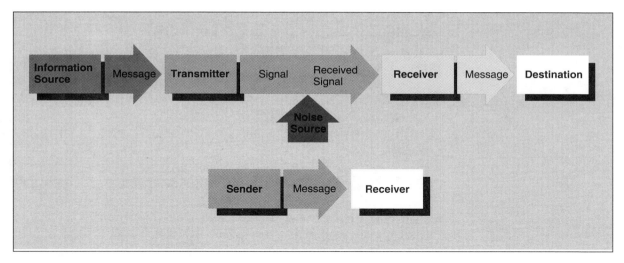

Figure 1.3
Linear Model of Communication (Adapted from Shannon & Weaver, 1949)

The third deficiency of linear models is that they represent communication as a sequential set of actions in which one step (listening) follows an earlier step (talking). In reality, communication is dynamic with interactions occurring simultaneously. As you talk to friends, you notice whether they seem engaged or bored. If they nod, you're likely to continue talking; if they yawn or turn away from you, you might stop. At any moment in the process of interpersonal communication, all participants are sending and receiving messages and adapting to one another.

INTERACTIVE MODELS

Awareness that listeners respond to speakers led to **interactive models,** which portray communication as a process in which listeners are involved in sending messages back to speakers. A key feature of interactive models is **feedback,** which is responses to a message (Weiner, 1967). Feedback may be verbal, nonverbal, or both, and it may be intentional or unintentional.

The best-known interactive model was advanced by Wilbur Schramm (1955), who depicted feedback as a second kind of message in the communication process. In addition, Schramm pointed out that communicators create and interpret messages within personal fields of experience. The more communicators' fields of experience overlap, the better they can understand each other. With the additional factor of fields of experience added to the model, we can see why misunderstandings may occur. You jokingly put a friend down, and he takes it seriously and is hurt. You offer to help someone, and she feels patronized. Sandy's commentary gives an example of this type of misunderstanding.

Sandy:
When I moved from the West Coast to Toronto to go to York University, I was surprised at how my friendliness was misinterpreted. The women in my classes wouldn't speak to me. At Simon Fraser, everyone spoke to each other and greeted each other even if we were strangers. At York, I was a pariah. The women regarded me as a threat.

Adding fields of experience and feedback allowed Schramm to develop a model that portrays communication as an interactive process in which both senders and receivers participate actively (Figure 1.4).

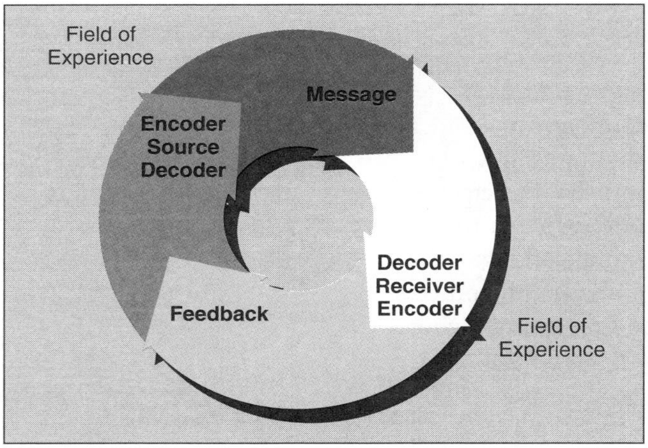

Figure 1.4
Interactive Model of Communication

Although interactive models are an improvement over linear ones, they don't fully capture the dynamism of human communication. A serious limitation of interactive models is that they portray communication as a sequential process and designate one person as a sender and another as a receiver. In reality, everyone who is involved in communication both sends and receives messages at the same time. When you are talking with someone you just met, you pay attention to how he or she responds to you. Does he look at you? Does he seem interested in you? Does he ask questions or make comments that invite further interaction?

Another shortcoming of the interactive model is that it doesn't capture the fact that interpersonal communication is a dynamic process. To do this, a model would need to show that communication changes over time as a result of what happens between people. For example, two people communicate more openly and casually after months of seeing each other than they do on their first date. What they talk about and how they talk have changed as a result of interacting.

TRANSACTIONAL MODELS

To overcome the weaknesses of interactive models, we need a model that emphasizes the dynamism of interpersonal communication and the multiple roles people assume during the process. An accurate model would include the factor of time and would depict other aspects of communication—such as messages, noise, and fields of experience—as varying over time, rather than as constant. Figure 1.5 is a **transactional model** of communication that highlights these features and others we have discussed.

The transactional model includes the strengths of earlier models and overcomes their weaknesses. The transactional model recognizes that **noise** is always present in interpersonal communication. Noise is anything that interferes with the intended communication. This can be external to the communicators or internal. In addition, this model emphasizes that interpersonal communication is a continuously changing process. The feature of time underlines this by reminding us that how people communicate varies over time.

The outer lines in the transactional model emphasize that communication occurs within systems that affect what and how people communicate and what meanings are created. Those systems, or contexts, include shared systems of both communicators (shared campus, town, and culture) as well as the personal systems of each person (family, religious association, friends).

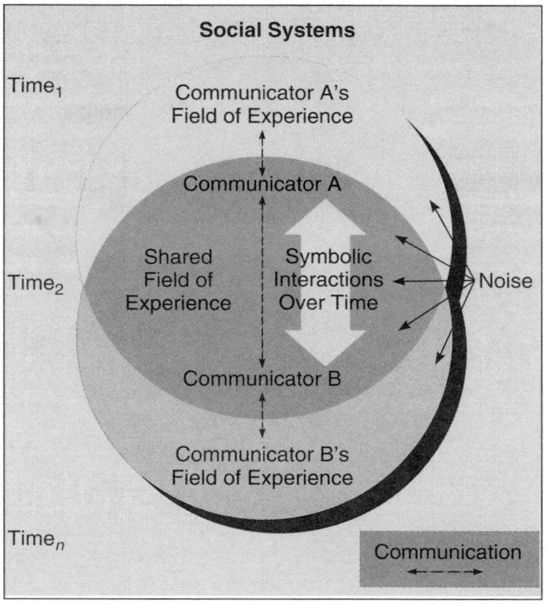

Also notice that the transactional model, unlike previous ones, portrays each person's field of experience and the shared field of experience between communicators as changing over time. As we encounter new people and have new experiences that broaden us personally, we change how we interact with others. As we get to know others over time, I–It relationships may progress to I–You and sometimes to I–Thou relationships. Finally, our model doesn't label one person a "sender" and the other a "receiver." Instead, both individuals are defined as communicators who participate equally, and often simultaneously, in the communication process. This means that at a given moment in communication, you may be sending a message (speaking or nodding your head), receiving a message, or doing both at the same time (interpreting what someone says while nodding to show you are interested). Because communicators continuously affect each other, there are strong ethical implications to interpersonal communication. Our verbal and nonverbal behaviours can enhance or diminish others, just as their communication can enhance or diminish us. As we shall see in future chapters, *you cannot not communicate!*

Now that we have examined models of interpersonal communication and learned what is involved in the process, we're ready to develop a precise definition.

Figure 1.5
Transactional Model of Communication

DEFINITION OF INTERPERSONAL COMMUNICATION

Interpersonal communication is a selective, systemic, unique, and ongoing process of interaction between individuals who reflect and build personal knowledge of one another and create shared meanings.

This seems like a weighty definition, but we'll discuss each of the key terms in this definition so that we have a common understanding of interpersonal communication.

SELECTIVE

First, as we noted above, fully interpersonal communication is not something we engage in or desire with everyone. Instead, we invest the effort and take the risks of being genuinely open with only a few people. As Buber realized, the majority of our communication is relatively superficial and occurs on I–It or I–You levels. This is fine, because I–Thou relationships require more time, energy, and courage than we want to offer to everyone.

SYSTEMIC

Interpersonal communication is also **systemic,** which means it takes place within various systems. All communication occurs in contexts that influence what happens and the meanings we assign to communication. The ways people communicate also vary across cultures. Whereas North Americans tend to communicate assertively and look at one another, in many Asian societies assertion and eye contact are considered rude. First Nations people are traditionally less verbal than Canadians of European heritage.

Consider an example of the systemic character of communication. Suppose Ian gives Cheryl a solid gold pendant and says, "I wanted to show how much I care about you." What do his words mean? That depends in large part on the systems in which he and Cheryl interact. If Ian and Cheryl just started dating, an extravagant gift means something different than if they've been married for 20 years. On the other hand, if they don't have an established relationship and Cheryl is engaged to Sacha, Ian's gift may mean something else. What if Ian beat Cheryl the day before? Perhaps then the gift is to apologize, not to show love. If Ian is rich, a solid gold pendant may be less awesome than if he is short on cash. Systems that affect what this communication means include Cheryl and Ian's relationship, their socioeconomic classes, cultural norms for gift-giving, and Cheryl's and Ian's personal histories. All of these contexts affect their interaction and what it means.

Because interpersonal communication is systemic, situation, time, people, culture, personal histories, and so forth interact to affect meanings. We can't just add up the various parts of a system to understand their impact on communication. Instead, we have to recognize that all parts of a system interact, so that each part affects all others. In other words, elements of communication systems are interdependent; each is tied to all of the others.

Recall also that all systems include **noise,** which is anything that distorts communication or interferes with individuals' understandings of one another. Noise in communication systems, just like other kinds of noise, complicates understanding. Also, like other kinds of noise, noise in communication systems is both inevitable and unavoidable. We should simply be aware that it exists and try to compensate for the difficulties it causes.

There are three kinds of noise. **Physical noise** includes extreme temperatures, hunger that interferes with concentration, fatigue, or crowded conditions. **Psychological noise** occurs in us and affects how we communicate and how we interpret others. For instance, if you are preoccupied with a problem, you may be inattentive. Likewise, prejudice, cultural differences, and defensive feelings can interfere with communication. Our needs may also affect how we interpret others. For example, if we really need affirmation or love, we may be predisposed to perceive others as communicating more commitment than they really do. Finally, **semantic noise** exists when words themselves are not mutually understood. Authors sometimes create semantic noise by using jargon or unnecessarily technical language.

When we say that communication is systemic, then, we mean three things. First, all communication occurs within multiple systems that affect meanings. Second, all parts and all systems of communication are interdependent, so they affect one another. Finally, all communication systems have noise that may be physical, psychological, or semantic.

UNIQUE

Interpersonal communication is also unique. In relationships that go beyond social roles, every person is unique and, therefore, irreplaceable. We can substitute people in I–It and even I–You relationships (one clerk can ring up purchases as well as another; we can get another racquetball buddy), but we can't replace intimates. When we lose intimates, we may find new friends and romantic partners, but they aren't interchangeable with the ones we lost.

Just as every person is unique, so is each friendship and romantic relationship. Each develops its own distinctive patterns and rhythms and even special vocabulary that are not part of other interpersonal relationships. In the process of becoming close, people work out personal roles and rules for interaction, and these may deviate from general social rules and roles. With one friend you might go in-line skating and get together for athletic events and insult each other in jest. With a different, equally close friend you

Concepts at a Glance

There are three kinds of noise:

1. Physical
2. Psychological
3. Semantic

Communication Blooper

"Communication can be egregiously obstructed by phenomena extrinsic to an exchange that actuate misrepresentations and symbolic incongruities." This is an accurate but unclear statement filled with semantic noise.

Student Voices

Syki:

I wish professors would learn about semantic noise. I really try to pay attention in class and to learn, but the way some faculty talk makes it impossible to understand what they mean, especially if English is not a first language. I wish they would remember that we're not specialists like they are, so we don't know all the technical words.

How is your uniqueness defined?

Photo: J. Torrance

might talk openly about feelings. Within one family, siblings can have different communication styles. For example, you may be very close and playful with one particular sibling and more aloof with another. In other words, interpersonal communication involves persons in relation to each other.

ONGOING PROCESS

Interpersonal communication is an ongoing, continuous **process.** This means, first, that interpersonal communication evolves over time, becoming more interpersonal as individuals interact. Friendships and romantic relationships gain depth and significance over the course of time, and they may also decline in quality over time. Because relationships are dynamic, they don't stay the same, but continuously change just as we do.

An ongoing process also has no discrete beginnings and endings. Figure 1.5 (on page 19) highlights this by including time as a dynamic feature that changes. Suppose a friend stops by and confides in you about a troubling personal problem. When did that communication begin? Although it may seem to have started when the friend came by, earlier interactions may have led the friend to feel it was safe to talk to you and that you would care about the problem. We can't be sure when this communication began. Similarly, we don't know where it will end. Perhaps it ends when the friend leaves, but perhaps it doesn't. Maybe your response to the problem helps your friend see new options. Maybe what you learn changes how you feel toward your friend. Because communication is ongoing, we can never be sure when it begins and ends, as Kate illustrates.

Because interpersonal interaction is a process, what happens between people is linked to both past and future. In our earlier example, the meaning of Ian's gift reflects prior interactions between him and Cheryl, and their interaction about the gift will affect future interactions. All of our communication occurs in three temporal dimensions—past, which affects what happens now; present; and future, which is moulded by what occurs in this moment (Dixson & Duck, 1993). How couples handle early arguments affects how they deal with later ones; what happened in a relationship last week shapes interaction today. Past, present, and future are always interwoven in communication.

The ongoing quality of interpersonal communication also suggests that we can't stop the process, nor can we edit or unsay what has been said. In this sense, communication is irreversible—we can't take it back. Interpersonal communication is always evolving, changing, moving ever onward.

Kate:

It's really true about not knowing where communication stops. I'm a peer supporter at my college, and last year a student stopped me in the library. I started to ask her to come back later, because I was trying to finish a paper, but she looked so upset that I put it aside. She asked me what I planned to do when I got out of college and if things ever got so rough I just wanted to call it quits. I couldn't figure out what was bothering her, but I felt like I needed to keep listening. After an hour or so, she thanked me for my time and left. A few months later, her best friend told me that she'd been considering killing herself and talking with me was what stopped her.

INTERACTION

Interpersonal communication is a process of interaction between people. In interpersonal communication, each person both sends and receives communication. As you speak to a friend, your friend smiles; while a teacher explains an idea, you nod to show you understand; as your parent scolds you, you wrinkle your brow resentfully. In interpersonal encounters, all parties communicate continuously and simultaneously.

The interactive nature of interpersonal communication implies that responsibility for effectiveness is shared among communicators. We often say, "You didn't express yourself clearly" or "You misunderstood me," as if understanding rests with a single person. In reality, responsibility for good communication is shared: The person speaking should use language carefully and be sensitive to others' responses both during and after speaking; at the same time, the person listening should try to understand and to give feedback to the speaker. Alone, neither person can make interaction successful. Because interpersonal communication is an ongoing, interactive process, all participants share responsibility for its effectiveness.

INDIVIDUALS

From Buber we learned that fully interpersonal communication involves engaging others as individuals, unlike any other persons. Interpersonal communication involves more than speaking from social roles (teacher–student, boss–employee, customer–salesclerk). Instead, to engage in interpersonal communication, we must treat others and be treated by them as individuals. This is possible only if we learn who they are and they come to understand us as distinct individuals, unlike anyone else. We can't automatically communicate

Review

The goal of communication is to understand and be understood. This takes commitment from all parties.

with others as full, unique individuals because we don't know them personally when we first meet. Instead, we come to understand the unique fears and hopes, problems and joys, needs and abilities of persons as we interact with them meaningfully over a period of time. As trust builds, people disclose personal information that allows insight into their unique selves.

PERSONAL KNOWLEDGE

Interpersonal communication creates personal knowledge of others. To connect as unique individuals, we have to get to know others personally. You can't interact with someone as a full person until you know something about that person. Over time, as we move toward more fully interpersonal relationships, our communication is based increasingly on personal knowledge (see "Pillow Talk").

Interpersonal communication also creates personal knowledge. As our relationships with others deepen, we build trust and learn how to communicate in ways that make each other feel comfortable and safe. In turn, the personal knowledge that allows us to do this encourages us to self-disclose further: We share secrets, fears, and experiences that we don't tell to just anyone. This is part of what Buber meant by "being" with others. Personal knowledge is a process—one that grows and builds on itself over time as people communicate interpersonally.

Sometimes we may even feel that our closest friends know us better than we know ourselves, as Lizelle explains.

Sharing personal information and experiences highlights the ethical dimension of interpersonal communication. We confront ethical choices about what to do with personal information about others. We can use our inside knowledge to protect people we care about. We can also use it to hurt those people—for example, personal knowledge allows us to attack vulnerabilities others have revealed to us. Ethical communicators choose not to exploit personal information about others.

Student Voices

Lizelle:

What I like best about long-term relationships is all the layers that develop. I know the friends I've had since high school in so many ways. I know what they did and felt and dreamed in high school, and I know them as they are now. They have the same kind of in-depth knowledge of me. We tell each other everything, so it sometimes seems that my deepest friends know me better than I know myself.

Communication Notes

Pillow Talk

Counsellors have discovered what couples have long known—that private codes of communication are part and parcel of intimacy. Recent studies indicate that most intimate partners develop private vocabularies to express themselves to each other in unique ways. Couples report having private nicknames for one another ("the redhead," "noodle brain"), special codes for indicating they want to make love ("want to read in bed tonight?"), and teasing routines and mock insults used to show affection.

What researchers also discovered is that closeness between partners seems linked to how extensive a private language they have developed. Thus, it may be that communication is not only the messenger of loving feelings but also the creator.

Source: Public pillow talk. (1987, October). *Psychology Today*, p. 18.

MEANINGS

The heart of interpersonal communication is shared meanings between people (Duck, 1994a, 1994b). We don't just exchange words when we communicate. Instead, we create meanings as we figure out what each other's words and behaviours stand for, represent, or imply. Meanings grow out of histories of interaction between unique persons. Most close friends and romantic partners develop vocabularies that have meaning only to them.

Reflective Exercise

What is an example of a unique language that you share with another person?

You might have noticed that we refer to meanings, not just one meaning. This is because all interpersonal communication has two levels of meaning (Watzlawick, Beavin, & Jackson, 1967).

The first level, called the **content meaning,** deals with literal or denotative meaning. Content meanings concern information. If a parent says to a five-year-old child, "Clean your room now," the content meaning is that the room is to be cleaned.

The second level of meaning is the **relational meaning.** This refers to what communication expresses about relationships between communicators.

Concepts at a Glance

All interpersonal communication has two levels of meaning:

- Content (literal)
- Relational (relationship)

The relational meaning of "Clean your room now" is that the parent has the right to order the child—they have an unequal power relationship. If the parent had said, "Would you mind cleaning your room?" the relational meaning would have suggested a more equal relationship. Assume a friend says, "You're the only person I can talk to about this," and then discloses something that is worrying him. The content level includes the actual issue itself and the information that you're the only one with whom he will discuss this issue. But what has he told you on the relationship level? He has communicated that he trusts you, he considers you special, and he perhaps expects you to care about his troubles.

Scholars have identified three general dimensions of relational-level meanings (Wood, 1994d). The first dimension is responsiveness, and it refers to how aware of others and involved with them we are. Perhaps you can remember a conversation you had with someone who shuffled papers and glanced at a clock. If so, you probably felt she wasn't interested in you or the conversation. Low responsiveness is communicated on the relationship level of meaning when people don't look at us or when they are preoccupied with something other than talking with us. Higher responsiveness is communicated by eye contact, nodding, and feedback that indicates involvement.

A second dimension of relational meaning is liking, or affection. This concerns the degree of positive or negative feeling that is communicated. Although liking may seem synonymous with responsiveness, the two are actually distinct. We may be responsive to people we don't like but have to pay attention to, and we are sometimes preoccupied and unresponsive to people we care about. We communicate that we like or dislike others by what we actually say as well as by tone of voice, facial expressions, how close we sit to them, and so forth.

Power or control is the third dimension of relational meaning. This refers to the power balance between communicators. A parent may say to a five year old, "Clean your room because I say so, that's why." This communicates that the parent has greater power than the child—the power to tell the child what to do. Friends and romantic partners sometimes engage in covert power struggles on the relationship level. One person suggests going to

Concepts at a Glance

Three Dimensions of Relational Meanings

1. Responsiveness
2. Liking or affection
3. Power or control

Student Voices

Ana:

My father needs to learn about relational meanings. Whenever I call home, he asks me if anything's wrong. Then he asks what the news is. If I don't have news to report, he can't understand why I'm calling. Then Mom gets on the phone, and we talk for a while about stuff— nothing important, just stuff. I don't call to tell them big news. I just want to touch base and feel connected.

movie X and then to dinner at the pizza parlour. The other responds by saying she doesn't want to see that movie and isn't in the mood for pizza. They could be arguing on the content level about their different preferences for the evening. If arguments over what to do are recurrent and heated, however, chances are the couple is negotiating power. In interpersonal relationships, the relationship level of meaning is often the most important, for it sets the tone for interaction and for how people feel about each other.

Apply the Idea

Levels of Meaning

For the next 48 hours, focus on relational meanings in your communication. Record examples of the following:

- *communicating responsiveness*
- *communicating lack of responsiveness*
- *expressing liking*
- *expressing dislike*
- *announcing superiority*
- *showing subordination*
- *expressing equality*

    What does this tell you about the relationship issues being negotiated and expressed in your relationships?

Review

We have seen that communication exists on a continuum, ranging from impersonal to interpersonal. We've also learned that it is best understood as a transactional process, not a linear exchange or an interaction. Based on the transactional model, we have also defined interpersonal communication as a selective, systemic, unique, and ongoing process of interaction between individuals who reflect and build personal knowledge of one another as they create meanings. Meanings, we have seen, reflect histories of interaction and involve both content and relationship levels. Building on this definition, we're now ready to identify basic principles of interpersonal communication.

PRINCIPLES OF INTERPERSONAL COMMUNICATION

The definition of interpersonal communication and our discussion of reasons we communicate suggest eight basic principles. Understanding these will help you communicate more effectively in a variety of contexts.

WE CANNOT NOT COMMUNICATE

Whenever people are together, they communicate. We cannot avoid communicating when we are with others, because they interpret what we do and say as well as what we don't do and don't say. Even if we choose to be silent, we're communicating. What we mean by silence and how others interpret it will depend on cultural backgrounds. Silence communicates.

What is the power balance here?

Photo: © Corel

Eight Principles of Interpersonal Communication

1. We cannot not communicate.
2. Communication is irreversible.
3. Interpersonal communication involves ethical choices.
4. Meanings are constructed in interpersonal communication.
5. Metacommunication affects meanings.
6. Interpersonal communication develops and sustains relationships.
7. Interpersonal communication is not a cure-all.
8. Interpersonal communication effectiveness can be learned.

We cannot not communicate.

Photo: © Corel

Although others sometimes misunderstand what we mean, they still respond to our presence and what we do and don't do and do and don't say. Even when we don't intend to communicate, we do so. We may be unaware of a grimace that gives away our disapproval or an eye roll that shows we dislike someone, but we are communicating nonetheless. Unconscious communication particularly occurs on the relationship level of meaning as we express feelings about others through subtle, often nonverbal communication. Regardless of whether we aim to communicate and whether others understand our intentions, we continuously, unavoidably communicate.

COMMUNICATION IS IRREVERSIBLE

Perhaps you have been in heated arguments in which you lost your temper and said something you later regretted. It could be that you hurt someone or revealed something about yourself you meant to keep private. Later, you might have tried to repair the damage by apologizing, explaining what you said, or denying what you revealed. But you couldn't erase your communication; you couldn't unsay what you said. The fact that communication is irreversible means that what we say and do matters. It has impact. Once we say something to another person, that becomes part of the relationship. Remembering this principle keeps us aware of the importance of choosing when to speak and what to say—or not say!

INTERPERSONAL COMMUNICATION INVOLVES ETHICAL CHOICES

Ethics is a branch of philosophy that focuses on moral principles and codes of conduct. Ethical issues concern what is right and what is wrong. Because interpersonal communication is irreversible and affects others, it always has ethical implications. What we say and do affects others—how they feel, how they perceive themselves, how they think about themselves, and how they think about others. Thus, responsible people think carefully about moral guidelines to direct their communication. They also recognize ethical choices that arise in interaction. For instance, in an argument with a friend, should you lie to defuse the anger? Whether or not to lie is an ethical choice. Should you not tell someone something that might make him less willing to do what you want? That is also an ethical choice. Do you judge others' communication from your own individual perspective and experience? Or do you try to understand their communication on their own terms and from their perspective? In these and many other instances, we face choices that have ethical implications.

Reflective Exercise

What ethical choices have you had to make recently? What did you learn from this experience?

Because interpersonal communication affects us and others, ethical considerations always underlie our interactions. Throughout this book we'll note ethical issues that arise when we interact with others. As you read, consider what kinds of choices you make and what moral principles guide your choices.

MEANINGS ARE CONSTRUCTED IN INTERPERSONAL COMMUNICATION

Human beings construct the meanings of their communication. The significance of communication doesn't lie in words and nonverbal behaviours. Instead, meaning arises out of how we interpret one another. This calls our attention to the fact that humans use **symbols,** which sets us apart from other creatures (Mead, 1934; Wood, 1992a).

As we will see in Chapter 5, symbols such as words have no inherent or true meanings. Instead, we have to interpret symbols. What does it mean if someone says, "You're crazy"? To interpret the comment, you have to consider the context (a counselling session, a party, after a daredevil stunt), who said it (a psychiatrist, a friend, an enemy), and the words themselves, which may mean various things (a medical diagnosis, a compliment on your zaniness, disapproval).

In interpersonal communication, people continuously interpret each other. Although typically we're not aware that we assign meanings, inevitably we do so. Someone you have been dating suggests you need some time away from each other; a friend starts turning down invitations to get together; your supervisor at work seems less open to conversations with you than in the past. The meanings of such communications are neither self-evident nor inherent in the words. Instead, we construct their significance. In close relationships, partners gradually coordinate meanings so that they have shared understandings of issues and feelings important to their connection. When a relationship begins, one person may regard confrontation as healthy, and the other may avoid arguments. Over time, partners come to share meanings for conflict—what it is, how to handle it, and whether it threatens the relationship or is a path to growth. The meaning of conflict, as well as other aspects of communication, is shaped by cultural backgrounds.

Even one person's meanings vary over time and in response to experiences and moods. If you're in a good mood, a playful jibe might strike you as funny or as an invitation to banter, but the same remark might hurt or anger you if you're feeling down. The meaning of the jibe, like all communication, is not preset or absolute.

METACOMMUNICATION AFFECTS MEANINGS

We use communication not only to discuss people, feelings, ideas, events, and objects; we also use communication to discuss our communication. The word metacommunication comes from two root terms: *meta*, which means "about," and "communication." Thus, **metacommunication** is communication about communication. Whenever we discuss how we are talking to each other or how we are treating each other, we are metacommunicating. Metacommunicating is a tool to check out what is going on between you and another person. It shifts focus from the content level of meaning to the relational level. When you say "I would like to wait until we are alone before we discuss this," or "I love the way you support me in front of our friends," you are talking about the way you communicate. Metacommunication deepens a relationship and can solve conflicts. It may comment on the verbal or nonverbal behaviours of our partners. If an argument between Joe and Marc gets out of hand, and Joe makes a nasty personal attack, Joe might say, "I didn't really mean what I just said. I was just so angry it came out." This metacommunication may soften the hurt caused by the attack. If Joe and Marc then have a productive conversation about their differences, one might conclude by saying, "This has really been a good talk. I think we understand each other a lot better now." This comment metacommunicates about the conversation that preceded it. Metacommunication is important to effective interpersonal interaction. When you develop skill in communicating about your and others' messages, you can increase the chance of creating shared understanding. For instance, teachers sometimes say, "The next point is really important." This comment signals students to pay special attention to what follows. A co-worker might say "I hope I'm not intruding, please tell me if I am." The comment tells the co-worker how to interpret the message and invites comment about their relationship. A manager tells a subordinate to take a comment seriously by saying, "I really mean what I said. I'm not kidding." On the other hand, if we're not really sure what we think about an issue and we want to try out a stance, we might say, "I'm thinking this through as I go, and I'm not really stuck to this position, but what I tend to believe right now is ..." This preface to your statement tells listeners not to assume what you say is set in stone.

We can also metacommunicate to check on understanding: "Was I clear?" "Do you see why I feel like I do?" "Is what I said logical?" "Can you see why I'm confused about the problem?" Questions such as these allow you to find out if another person understands what you intend to communicate. You may metacommunicate to understand more clearly what another person expresses to you. You may even say, "I don't understand what you just told me. Can you say it another way?" This question metacommunicates by letting the other person know you did not grasp her message. You may also metacommunicate to shift the direction of an uncomfortable conversation. "I'm uncomfortable having this conversation right now, could we meet after work to continue?" or "Let's confine our conversation to what happened today only."

Apply the Idea

Improving Your Metacommunication

For each of the scenarios described below, write out a verbal metacommunication that would be appropriate to express your feelings about what has been said or how it was said. Remember, you are trying to draw focus to your relationship and away from the content of a message.

1. *You are arguing with a person who seems more interested in winning the argument than in working things through so that both of you are satisfied. You want to change how the argument is proceeding.*

METACOMMUNICATION

_____

_____

_____

2. *Your manager at work routinely gives you orders instead of making requests. You resent it when she says to you, "Take over the front room," "Clean up the storeroom now," and "I want you in early tomorrow." You want to change how your manager expresses expectations for your performance.*

METACOMMUNICATION

_____

_____

_____

3. *You are volunteering as an aide in an elementary school, and one parent constantly wants to talk to you about her child's work habits when the child is within earshot. You are very uncomfortable discussing this in the child's presence.*

METACOMMUNICATION

_____

_____

_____

_____

Effective metacommunication also helps friends and romantic partners express how they feel about their interactions. Linda Acitelli (1988, 1993) has studied what happens when partners in a relationship talk to each other about how they perceive and feel about their interaction. She reports that both women and men find metacommunication helpful when there is a conflict. Both sexes seem to appreciate knowing how the other feels about their differences; they are also eager to learn how to communicate to resolve those differences. During a conflict, one person might say, "I feel like we're both being really stubborn. Do you think we could each back off a little from our positions?" This expresses discontent with how communication is proceeding and offers an alternative. Following conflict, one partner might say, "This really cleared the air between us. I feel a lot better now." Tara explains this type of metacommunication in her commentary.

Acitelli also found that women are more likely than men to appreciate metacommunication when there is no conflict or immediate problem to be resolved. While curled up on a sofa and watching TV, a woman might say to her male partner, "I really feel comfortable snuggling with you." This comments on the relationship and on the nonverbal communication between the couple. According to research by Acitelli and others (Wood, 1997, 1998), men in general may find talk about relationships unnecessary unless there is an immediate problem to be addressed. Understanding this gender difference in preferences for metacommunication may help you interpret your partner more accurately.

| Student Voices |

Tara:

I never feel like an argument is really over and settled until Andy and I have said that we feel better for having thrashed out whatever was the problem. It's like I want closure, and the fight isn't really behind us until we both say, "I'm glad we talked," or something to say what we went through led us to a better place.

Reflective Exercise

What is your metacommunication like with friends and intimate partners? Are there differences in metacommunication behaviours between your male friends and partners and your female friends and partners?

INTERPERSONAL COMMUNICATION DEVELOPS AND SUSTAINS RELATIONSHIPS

Interpersonal communication is the primary way we build, refine, and transform relationships. Communication is not merely a mechanism we use to convey preexisting meanings; instead, it is a creative process of generating meanings. Partners talk to work out expectations, understandings of how to act with each other, which topics and styles of communicating are appropriate and which are off-limits, and what the relationship itself is. Is it a friendship or a romantic relationship? How much and in what ways can we count on each other? How do we handle disagreements—confront them, ignore them, or use indirect strategies to restore harmony? What are the bottom lines—the "shalt not" rules for what counts as unforgivable betrayal? What counts as caring—words, deeds, both? What do certain responses, words, and strategies mean? Because communication has no intrinsic meanings, we must generate our own in the course of interaction. Steve Duck (1994a, 1994b), a relationship scholar, maintains that communication is relationships—that interaction is the crux of what a relationship is and what partners mean to each other.

Communication also allows us to construct, or reconstruct, individual and joint histories. For instance, when people fall in love, they often redefine former loves as "mere infatuations" or "puppy love," but definitely not the "real thing." Although marriage may be defined as a joining of two individuals, in many societies, marriage is regarded as a union of two families or communities. In some societies, marriage is not an individual choice, but a relationship arranged by parents. When something goes wrong in a relationship, partners may work together to define what happened in a way that allows them to continue. Marriage counsellors report that couples routinely work out face-saving explanations for affairs so that they can stay together in the aftermath of infidelity (Scarf, 1987). As partners communicate thoughts and feelings, they generate shared meanings for themselves, their interaction, and their relationship.

Student Voices

Lynda:

The key to the success of my long-term relationship is that we learned early on how to talk to each other and how to fight well. We don't say things we don't mean anymore, and we don't let more than 24 hours go by without talking if one of us is upset.

Communication is also the primary means by which intimates construct a future for themselves, and a vision of shared future is one of the most powerful ties that link people (Dixson & Duck, 1993). Romantic couples often dream together by talking about the family they plan and how they'll be in 20 years. Likewise, friends discuss plans for the future and promise reunions if they must move apart. Communication allows us to express and share dreams, imaginings, and memories and to make all of these part of the joint world of relational partners.

INTERPERSONAL COMMUNICATION IS NOT A CURE-ALL

As we have seen, we communicate to satisfy many of our needs and to create relationships with others. Yet it would be a mistake to think communication is a cure-all. Often, it can help us work out problems and disagreements, but it isn't a panacea for everything that ails us and our relationships. Many problems can't be solved by talk alone. Communication by itself won't end hunger, abuses of human rights around the globe, racism, or physical diseases. Neither can words alone bridge irreconcilable differences between people or erase the hurt of betrayals. Although good communication may increase understanding and help us find solutions to problems, it is not a cure-all. We should also realize that the idea of "talking things through" is distinctly Western. Not all societies think it's wise or useful to communicate about relationships or to talk extensively about feelings. Just as interpersonal communication has many strengths and values, it also has limits, and its effectiveness is shaped by cultural contexts.

INTERPERSONAL COMMUNICATION EFFECTIVENESS CAN BE LEARNED

One of the most important principles of interpersonal communication is that we can become more effective if we invest personal effort in learning and practising good communication skills. It is erroneous to believe that effective communicators are born, that some people just have a natural talent and others don't. Although some people have extraordinary talent in athletics or music, all of us can become competent athletes and respectable musicians. Likewise, some people may seem naturally gifted at communicating, but all of us can become competent communicators. This book and the course that you are taking should sharpen your understandings of how interpersonal communication works and should help you learn skills that will enhance your effectiveness in relating to others.

The eight principles we have identified clarify what interpersonal communication is and is not and suggest ways to become more skillful in our own communicative endeavours. Building on all we have covered, we turn now to guidelines for becoming competent in interpersonal communication.

GUIDELINES FOR INTERPERSONAL COMMUNICATION COMPETENCE

Sometimes we handle interactions well, whereas in other cases we are ineffective. What are the differences between effective and ineffective communication? Scholars define **interpersonal communication competence** as the ability to communicate in ways that are effective and appropriate. Effectiveness involves achieving the goals we have for specific interactions. In different situations, your goals might be to explain an idea, comfort a friend, stand up for your position, negotiate a raise, or persuade someone to change behaviours. The more effectively you communicate, the more likely you'll be competent in achieving your goals.

Competence also emphasizes appropriateness. This means that competent communication is adapted to particular situations and individuals. Language that is appropriate at a party with friends may not be appropriate in a job interview. Somewhat reserved communication is appropriate with people with whom we have I–You relationships, whereas more open communication is appropriate in I–Thou relationships. Appropriateness also involves contexts. It may be appropriate to kiss an intimate in a private setting but not in a classroom. Similarly, many people choose not to argue in front of others, but prefer to engage in conflict when they are alone. Five skills are closely tied to competence in interpersonal communication.

Concepts at a Glance

Guidelines for Interpersonal Communication Competence

1. Develop a range of skills.
2. Adapt communication appropriately.
3. Engage in dual perspective.
4. Monitor your communication.
5. Commit to effective and ethical communication.

DEVELOP A RANGE OF SKILLS

No one style of communication is best in all circumstances, with all people, or for dealing with all issues. Because what is effective varies, we need to have a broad repertoire of communication behaviours. Consider the different skills required for interpersonal communication competence in several situations: To comfort someone, we need to be soothing and compassionate. To negotiate a good deal on a car, we need to be assertive and firm. To engage constructively in conflict, we need to listen and defuse defensive climates. To support a friend who is depressed, we need to affirm that individual, demonstrate we care, and encourage the friend to talk about problems. To grow closer to others, we need to know how and when to disclose personal information and how to express our caring in ways others appreciate. Sometimes it's effective to accommodate another person, yet in other cases we need to compromise or work out mutual solutions. Because no single set of skills composes interpersonal communication competence, we need to learn a range of communicative abilities.

ADAPT COMMUNICATION APPROPRIATELY

When might humour be inappropriate?

Photo: © Corel

Being able to communicate in a range of ways doesn't make us competent unless we also know which kinds of communication are suitable at specific moments. For instance, knowing how to be both assertive and deferential isn't useful unless we can figure out when each style of communication is appropriate. Although there isn't a neat formula for adapting communication appropriately, it's generally important to consider personal goals, context, and the individuals with whom we communicate.

Your goals for communication are a primary guideline for selecting appropriate behaviours. If your purpose in a conversation is to give emotional support to someone, then it isn't effective to talk at length about your own experiences. On the other hand, if you are trying to let someone understand you better, talking in depth about your life is effective. If your goal is to win an argument and get your way, it may be competent to assert your point of view, point out flaws in your partner's ideas, and refuse to compromise. If you want to work through conflict in a way that doesn't harm a relationship, however, other communication choices might be more constructive. As Mary Margaret notes, she is still learning how to select appropriate behaviours.

Context is another influence on decisions of when, how, and about what to communicate. It is appropriate to ask your doctor about symptoms during an office exam, but it isn't appropriate to do so when you see the doctor in a social situation. Timing is an important aspect of context, because there are often better and worse times to bring up various topics. When a friend is feeling low, that's not a good time to criticize, although at another time criticism might be constructive. Children are geniuses at timing, knowing to wait until parents are in a good mood to ask for favours or new toys.

Remembering Buber's discussion of the I–Thou relationship, we know it is important to adapt what we say and how we say it to particular individ-

|Student Voices|

Mary Margaret:

I think I need to work on figuring out when to be assertive and when not to be. For most of my life I wasn't at all assertive, even when I should have been. Last spring, though, I was so tired of having people walk all over me that I signed up for a workshop on assertiveness training. I learned how to assert myself, and I was really proud of how much more I would stand up for myself. The problem was that I did it all the time, regardless of whether something really mattered enough to be assertive. Just like I was always passive before, now I'm always assertive. I need to figure out a better way to balance my behaviours.

uals. As we have seen, interpersonal communication increases our knowledge of others. Thus, the more interpersonal a relationship is, the more we can adapt our communication to unique partners. Abstract communicative goals such as supporting others call for quite distinct behaviours in regard to specific individuals. What feels supportive to one friend may not to another. We have to learn what our intimates need, what upsets and pleases them, and how they interpret various kinds of communication. Scholars use the term **"person-centredness"** to refer to the ability to adapt messages effectively to particular individuals (Bernstein, 1974; Burleson, 1987; Zorn, 1995). Appropriately adapted communication, then, is sensitive to goals, contexts, and others.

ENGAGE IN DUAL PERSPECTIVE

Central to competent interpersonal communication is the ability to engage in **dual perspective**, which is understanding both our own and another person's perspective, beliefs, thoughts, or feelings (Phillips & Wood, 1983; Wood, 1992a). When we adopt dual perspective, we understand how someone else thinks and feels about issues. To meet another person in genuine dialogue, we must be able to realize how that person views himself or herself, the situation, and his or her thoughts and feelings. We may personally see things much differently, and we may want to express our perceptions. Yet we also need to understand and respect the other person's perspective.

People who cannot take the perspectives of others are egocentric. They impose their perceptions on others and interpret others' experiences through their own eyes. Consider an example. Robert complains that he is having trouble writing a paper for his communication class. His friend Raymond responds, "All you have to do is outline the theory and then apply it. That's a snap." "But," says Robert, "I've always had trouble writing. I just block when I sit down to write." Raymond says, "That's silly. Anyone can do this. It just

Student Voices

Asha:

Sometimes it's very difficult for me to understand my daughter. She likes music that sounds terrible to me, and I don't like the way she dresses sometimes. For a long time, I judged her by my own values about music and dress, but that really pushed us apart. She kept saying, "I'm not you. Why can't you look at it from my point of view?" Finally, I heard her, and now we both try to understand each other's point of view. It isn't always easy, but you can't have a relationship on just one person's terms.

took me an hour or so." Raymond has failed to understand how Robert sees writing. If you have trouble writing, then composing a paper isn't a snap, but Raymond can't get beyond his own comfort with writing to understand Robert's different perspective.

As Asha says, engaging in dual perspective isn't necessarily easy, because all of us naturally see things from our own point of view and in terms of our own experiences. Yet, like other communication skills, we can learn how to do it.

Three guidelines can help you increase your ability to take the perspective of others. First, be aware of the tendency to see things from your own perspective, and resist that inclination. Second, listen closely to how others express their thoughts and feelings so that you gain clues of what things mean to them and how they feel. Third, ask others to explain how they feel, what something means to them, or how they view a situation. Asking questions and probing for details communicates on the relationship level that you are interested and that you want to understand. Making a commitment to engage in dual perspective and practising the three guidelines just discussed will enhance your ability to recognize and respond to others' perspectives.

Concepts at a Glance

Guidelines for Dual Perspective

- Remember there is more than one perspective.
- Listen closely.
- Ask others for clarification.

Apply the Idea

Developing Dual Perspective

Practise the guidelines for improving dual perspective. During the next two days, do the following in conversations:

- *Identify your own perspective on issues that others talk about. What do you think about the issues?*

- *Try not to impose your thoughts and feelings. Suspend them long enough to hear others.*

- *Pay close attention to what other people say. How do they describe feelings, thoughts, and views? Listen carefully to others without translating their communication into your own language.*

- *Ask questions. Ask, "What do you mean?" "How does that feel to you?" "How do you see the issue?" "What do you think about the situation?"*

- *Notice what you learn by suspending your own perspective and working to understand others.*

MONITOR YOUR COMMUNICATION

The fourth ability that affects interpersonal communication competence is **monitoring**, which is the capacity to observe and regulate your own communication (Wood, 1992a, 1995c). Most of us do this much of the time. Before bringing up a touchy topic, you remind yourself not to get defensive and not to get pulled into counterproductive arguing. During the discussion, your partner says something that upsets you. You think of a really good zinger but stop yourself from saying it because you don't want to hurt the other person. Later, you're feeling defensive, so you prompt yourself to stay open. In each instance, you monitored your communication.

Monitoring occurs both before and during interaction. Often, before conversations we indicate to ourselves how we feel and what we do and don't want to say. During communication, we stay alert and edit our thoughts before expressing them. Our ability to monitor allows us to adapt communication in advance and gauge our effectiveness as we interact.

Of course, we don't monitor all of the time. When we are with people who understand us or when we are talking about unimportant topics, we don't necessarily need to monitor communication with great care. Sometimes, however, not monitoring can result in communication that hurts others or that leads us to regard ourselves negatively. In some cases, failure to monitor results from getting caught up in the dynamics of interaction. We simply forget to keep a watchful eye on ourselves, and so we say things we shouldn't. In addition, some people have poorly developed monitoring skills. They have limited awareness of how they come across to others. Communication competence involves learning to attend to feedback from others and to monitor the impact of our communication as we interact with others.

COMMIT TO EFFECTIVE AND ETHICAL INTERPERSONAL COMMUNICATION

The final requirement for interpersonal competence is commitment to effective and ethical communication. Without a firm decision to try to meet another in honest, genuine dialogue, all of the other skills are insufficient.

To commit to interpersonal communication means four things. First, it means you care about a relationship and are willing to invest energy in communicating ethically with your partner. This requires you to think about the moral implications of what you say and do and how that may affect others. Second, you must commit to the other as a unique and valuable individual. This implies you can't dismiss the other's feelings as wrong, inappropriate, or silly. Instead, you must honour the person and the feelings he or she expresses, even if you feel differently. Third, commitment involves caring about yourself and your ideas and feelings. Just as you must honour those of others, so too must you respect yourself and your own perspective. Finally, competent communicators are committed to the communication process itself. They realize that it is interactive and always evolving, and they are willing to deal with that complexity. In addition, they are sensitive to multiple levels of meaning and to the irreversibility of communication. Commitment, then, is vital to relationships, others, ourselves, and communication.

Concepts at a Glance

To Monitor Communication

- Stay alert.
- Note feelings.
- Edit thoughts.
- Note others' reactions.

Concepts at a Glance

Committing to Interpersonal Communication

- Invest energy in ethical communication.
- Honour the other.
- Respect yourself.
- Deal with communication complexity.

Review

Interpersonal communication competence is the ability to communicate in ways that are interpersonally effective and appropriate. Five requirements for competence are developing a range of communication skills; adapting them appropriately to goals, others, and situations; engaging in dual perspective; monitoring communication and its impact; and committing to ethical interpersonal communication.

Apply the Idea

Improving Communication Competence

Are you satisfied with your proficiency at each skill?

- *How competent are you in various communication skills?*
- *Describe communication situations in which you don't feel you are as competent as you'd like to be.*
- *How well do you adapt your communication to different goals, situations, and people?*
- *How consistently and effectively do you engage in dual perspective when interacting with others? How can you tell when you really understand another's point of view?*
- *How well do you monitor your communication so that you gauge how you come across to others?*
- *Describe your commitments to others, relationships, yourself, and the interpersonal communication process.*

Consider which aspects of communication competence you would most like to improve, and make a contract with yourself to work on those during this course.

Chapter Summary

In this chapter, we launched our study of interpersonal communication. We began by noting that communication is essential to our survival and happiness. Communicating with others allows us to meet basic needs for survival and safety, as well as more abstract human needs for inclusion, esteem, self-actualization, and effective participation in a socially diverse world.

We learned that not all communication is interpersonal and that communication exists on a continuum that ranges from impersonal (I–It) to interpersonal (I–Thou). Fully interpersonal communication occurs when individuals engage each other as full, unique human beings who create meanings on both content and relational levels.

To define interpersonal communication more precisely, we looked at three different models of the process. The best model is the transactional one, because it both emphasizes the dynamic nature and the systemic quality of interpersonal communication and recognizes

that people simultaneously send and receive messages. This model is the foundation for our definition of interpersonal communication as a selective, systemic, unique, and ongoing process of interaction between individuals who reflect and build personal knowledge and create meanings.

We discussed eight principles of interpersonal communication. First, it is impossible not to communicate. Whether or not we intend to send certain messages and whether or not others understand our meanings, communication always occurs when people are together. Second, communication is irreversible because we cannot unsay or undo what passes between us and others. Third, interpersonal communication always has ethical implications. The fourth principle maintains that meanings don't reside in words but rather in how we interpret them. Fifth, metacommunication affects meanings in interpersonal interaction. Sixth, we use communication to develop and sustain relationships. In fact, communication is essential to relationships because it is in the process of interacting with others that we develop expectations, understandings, and rules to guide relationships. Seventh, although communication is powerful and important, it is not a cure-all. The final principle is that effectiveness in interpersonal communication can be learned through committed study and practice of principles and skills.

Competent interpersonal communicators interact in ways that are effective and appropriate. This means that we should adapt our ways of communicating to specific goals, situations, and others. Effectiveness and appropriateness require us to recognize and respect differences that reflect personal and cultural backgrounds. Guidelines for doing this include developing a range of communication skills, adapting communication sensitively, engaging in dual perspective, monitoring our own communication, and committing to effective and ethical interpersonal communication. In later chapters, we will focus on developing the skills that enhance interpersonal communication competence.

Key Concepts

- content meaning
- dual perspective
- ethics
- feedback
- I–It communication
- interactive models
- interpersonal communication
- interpersonal communication competence

- I–Thou communication
- I–You communication
- linear models
- metacommunication
- models
- monitoring
- noise
- person-centredness

- physical noise
- process
- psychological noise
- relational meaning
- semantic noise
- symbols
- systemic
- transactional model

For Further Thought and Discussion

1. Use each of the three models presented in this chapter to describe an interpersonal communication encounter. What does each model highlight? What does each model neglect or ignore? Which model best explains the process of interpersonal communication?

2. Interview a professional in the field you plan to enter. Ask him or her to explain the communication skills necessary to succeed and advance in the field. Which of the skills do you now have? Which ones do you need to develop or improve? Write out a personal action plan for how you will use this book and the course it accompanies to enhance your effectiveness in interpersonal communication.

3. Go to the employment office on your campus and read descriptions of job openings. Record the number of job descriptions that call for communication skills. Share your findings with others in your class.

4. Identify a relationship of yours that has become closer over time. Describe the earliest stage of the relationship. Was it an I–It or an I–You relationship at that time? During that early stage of the relationship, what did you talk about? Were there topics or kinds of talk you avoided? Now describe the current relationship. What do you now talk about? Can you identify differences over time in shared fields of experience between you and the other person?

5. Use your InfoTrac College Edition to locate two articles that focus on ethical issues in communication. You might enter key words such as "ethics, communication" or "morality, interaction" or "impact on others." With classmates, identify basic ethical principles that you think could serve as good general guidelines for interpersonal communication.

Communication and the Creation of Self

Babe

Jock

Academic

Well Sparks, I bet it's easy for a dog not having to make so many choices.

Can we go for that walk now?

Who am I? Throughout our lives we ponder this question. We answer it one way at one time, then change our answer as we ourselves change. At the age of five, perhaps you defined yourself as your parents' daughter or son. That view of yourself implicitly recognized sex, race, and social class as parts of your identity. In high school, you may have described yourself in terms of academic strengths ("I'm good at math and science"), athletic endeavours ("I'm a forward on the team"), leadership positions ("I'm president of the Photography Club"), friends and romantic partners ("I'm going steady with Cam"), or future plans ("I'm starting college next year"; "I'm going to be a lawyer"). Now that you're in college or university, it's likely you see yourself in terms of a major, a career path, and perhaps a relationship you hope will span the years ahead. You've probably also made some decisions about your sexual orientation, spiritual commitments, and political beliefs.

As you think about the different ways you've defined yourself over the years, you'll realize that the self is not a constant entity that is fixed early and then remains stable. Instead, the **self** is a process that evolves and changes continuously. The self emerges and is reborn throughout our lives. The influences that shape who we are include interactions with others and our reflections on them. In this chapter, we will explore how the self is formed and changed in the process of communicating with others.

WHAT IS THE SELF?

The self arises in communication and is a multidimensional process that involves "importing" and "acting" from social perspectives. Although this is a complicated definition, as we will see, it directs our attention to some important propositions about what, in fact, *is* very complicated—the self.

THE SELF ARISES IN COMMUNICATION WITH OTHERS

Communication is essential to developing a self. Infants aren't born with clear understandings of who they are and what their value is. Instead, we develop selves in the process of communicating with others who tell us who we are. Just as countries sometimes import materials from other countries, individuals import ideas about themselves from the people and culture around them. As we import others' perspectives inside ourselves, we come to share their perceptions of the world and ourselves.

From the moment we enter the world, we interact with others. As we do, we learn how they see us, and we take their perspectives inside ourselves. Once we have internalized the views of others, both "the particular others and the generalized other," we engage in internal dialogues in which we

Concepts at a Glance

Defining the Self

- The self arises in communication with others.
- The self is multi-dimensional.
- The self is a process.
- The self internalizes social perspectives.
- Social perspectives on the self are constructed and variable.

remind ourselves of social perspectives. Through the process of internal dialogues, or conversations with ourselves, we enforce the social values we have learned and the views of us that others communicate. How we perceive ourselves reflects the image of us that is reflected in others' eyes.

Self-Fulfilling Prophecy

Concepts at a Glance

The Self-Fulfilling Prophecy

• Originates with us

• Originates with others

One particularly powerful way in which communication shapes the self is **self-fulfilling prophecy,** which is acting in ways that bring about our expectations or judgments of ourselves. If you have done poorly in classes where teachers didn't seem to respect you, and done well with teachers who thought you were smart, then you know what self-fulfilling prophecy is. Robertson and Jacobson (1992) describe this very phenomena in their research called "Pygmalion in the Classroom" where teacher expectation and not pupil abilities mediated educational outcomes. The prophecies that we act to fulfill are usually first communicated by others. However, because we import others' perspectives into ourselves, we may label ourselves as they do and then act to fulfill our own labels. We may try to live up or down to the ways others define us and the ways we define ourselves. We may perceive that something is forbidden to us because others have said we can never attain it. This is examined in "Challenging the Definition of Dancer."

Many of us believe things about ourselves that are inaccurate. Sometimes labels that were once true aren't any longer, but we continue to believe them. In other cases the labels were never valid, but we are trapped by them anyway. Unfortunately, children are often called "slow" or "stupid" when they have physiological difficulties such as impaired vision or hearing or if they are from another culture and are struggling with a second language.

Communication Notes

Challenging the Definition of Dancer

Internationally acclaimed British Columbia choreographer Lynda Raino created "Big Dance," a modern dance class for large people. All of the participants believed that they could never dance because of how they saw themselves and how "dancer" is portrayed in our culture. Raino describes the overwhelming transformation that occurs in the women when they don dance leotards and celebrate their large bodies in movement instead of hiding in shame. Raino says these women have to reinvent themselves as dancers and their journey challenges the definition of "dancer" for all of us. "It is a renovation of the spirit that takes place, and it is truly awesome to witness" (personal communication 10 March 2001).

Even when the true source of difficulty is discovered, it may be too late if the children have already adopted a destructive self-fulfilling prophecy. If we accept others' negative judgments, we may fulfill their prophecies.

As Sidonie's comment shows, how others define us affects how we see ourselves. Yet not all others affect us equally. Communication with three kinds of others is especially influential in shaping self-concept.

Communication with Family Members

For most of us, family members are the first and most important influence on how we see ourselves. Because family interaction dominates our early years, it usually sculpts the foundations of our self-concepts. Parents and other family members communicate who we are and what we are worth through

- direct definitions
- scripts
- attachment styles.

Direct Definition

Direct definition, as the name implies, is communication that explicitly tells us who we are by labelling us and our behaviours. Parents and other family members define us by how they describe us. For instance, parents might say "You're my little girl," or "You're a big boy" and thus communicate to the child what sex it is. Having been labelled "boy" or "girl," the child then pays attention to other communication about boys and girls to figure out what it means to be a certain sex. Family members guide our understandings of gender by instructing us in what boys and girls do and don't do. The gender

Big Dance, Victoria, BC. How do you respond to this picture of dancers?

Photo: J. Hoadley

Concepts at a Glance

Three kinds of Others that shape self-concept

- Family members
- Peers
- Society

Student Voices

Sidonie:

I now see that I labelled myself because of others' perspectives. Since I was in first grade, my grandmother said I was fat and that I would never lose weight. Well, you can imagine what this did to my self-esteem. I felt there was nothing I could do about being fat. At one point I weighed 82 kg—pretty heavy for a girl who's 160 cm tall. Then I got with some other people who were overweight and we convinced ourselves to shape up. I lost 22 kg, but I still thought of myself as fat. That's only started to change lately as friends and my family comment on how slim I am. Guess I'm still seeing myself through others' eyes.

What risk is involved in being different?

Photo: © Corel

stereotypes of parents and caregivers are typically communicated to children, so, in traditional families, daughters may be told "Good girls don't play rough," "Be nice to your friends," and "Don't mess up your clothes." Sons, on the other hand, are more likely to be told "Go out and get 'em," "Stick up for yourself," and "Don't cry." As we hear these messages, we pick up our parents' and society's gender expectations.

Family members provide direct communication about many aspects of who we are through statements they make. Positive labels enhance our self-esteem: "You're so smart," "You're sweet," "You're great at soccer." Negative labels can damage children's self-esteem: "You're a trouble-maker," "You're stupid," and "You're impossible" are messages that demolish a child's sense of self-worth.

Family members also offer us direct definitions of our ethnic identities. Most Canadians define themselves in two ways, first as Canadian and second as an ethnic subgroup. The challenge of modern parenting lies in not only helping children identify with their unique cultural heritage, such as Metis or Scottish or Pakistani, but also providing them with the skills to function in diverse communities.

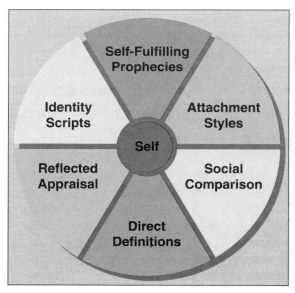

Figure 2.1

Influences on the Self-Concept

Direct definition also takes place as family members respond to children's behaviours.

If a child clowns around and parents respond by saying "What a cutup; you really are funny," the child learns to see herself or himself as funny. If a child dusts furniture and receives praise ("You're great to help me clean the house"), being helpful to others is reinforced as part of the child's self-concept. From direct definition, children learn what parents value, and this shapes what they come to value.

Through explicit labels and responses to our behaviours, family members provide direct definitions of who we are and—just as important—who we are supposed to be. Parents and other family members boost or retard children's self-esteem by how they respond to children's behaviour. Especially important is responding with enthusiasm to a child's accomplishments. When a baby masters walking, she or he will show a look of delighted accomplishment. For that feeling to be complete, however, the child needs positive responses from others. Family members need to smile and say, "Wow, you did it." Pediatrician T. B. Brazelton claims that how a child is treated in the first eight months of life sets an expectation of success or failure (1997). If the child's accomplishments are noticed and praised, the child gains progressive

Communication Notes

Emotional Abuse

Andrew Vachss is an attorney and author who has devoted his life to helping children who have been abused. He has worked with children who have been sexually assaulted, physically maimed, abandoned, starved, and otherwise tortured. Yet, Vachss regards emotional abuse as the worst harm of all. He says, "of all the many forms of child abuse, emotional abuse may be the cruellest and longest-lasting of all. Emotional abuse is the systematic diminishment of another. It may be intentional or subconscious (or both), but it is always ... designed to reduce a child's self-concept to the point where the victim considers himself unworthy—unworthy of respect, unworthy of friendship, unworthy of the natural birthright of all children: love and protection .... [T]here is no real difference between physical, sexual, and emotional abuse. All that distinguishes one from the other is the abuser's choice of weapons" (p. 4).

Source: Vachss, A. (1994, August 28). You carry the cure in your own heart. *Parade*, 4–6.

self-confidence and will undertake increasingly difficult challenges. If, on the other hand, the child's achievements are not noted and approved, the child is a candidate for low self-expectations and a defeating self-fulfilling prophecy. These negative messages are examined in "Emotional Abuse."

Identity Scripts

Identity scripts are another way family members communicate who we are. Psychologists define identity scripts as rules for living and identity (Berne, 1964; Harris, 1969). Like the scripts for plays, identity scripts define our roles, how we are to play them, and basic elements in the plots of our lives. Think back to your childhood to identify some of the principal scripts that operated in your family. Did you learn "We are responsible people," "Save your money for a rainy day," "Always help others," "Look out for yourself," or "You have to work twice as hard to get ahead because you're female or aboriginal"? These are examples of identity scripts people learn in families.

What messages did you receive as a child?

Photo: © Photodisc

Grace:

In my family, intelligence was a primary value: To be smart was good, and to be less than smart was unacceptable. I was great at outdoor activities such as building tree houses and leading "jungle expeditions" through the woods behind our home. Yet my parents were indifferent to my aptitudes for adventures and physical activity. What they stressed was learning and reading. I still have vivid memories of being shamed for a B in reading on my first-grade report card. Just as intensely, I recall the excessive praise heaped on me when I won a reading contest in fourth grade. By then I had learned what I had to be to get approval from my family.

What were your family scripts?

Photo: © Photodisc

Most psychologists believe that the basic identity scripts for our lives are formed very early, probably by age five. This means that fundamental understandings of who we are and how we are supposed to live are forged when we have virtually no control. We aren't allowed to co-author or even edit our initial identity scripts. Adults have the power, and children unconsciously internalize the scripts that others write. As adults, however, we are no longer passive tablets on which others can write out who we are. We have the capacity to review the identity scripts that were given to us and to challenge and change those that do not fit the selves we now choose to be.

Reflective Exercise

Your Identity Scripts

To take control of our own lives, we must first understand influences that shape it currently. Identify identity scripts your parents or caregivers taught you.

1. First, recall explicit messages your parents or caregivers gave you about "who we are" and "who you are." Can you hear their voices telling you codes you were expected to follow?

2. Next, write down the scripts. Try to capture the language your family used in teaching the scripts.

3. Now review each script. Which ones make sense to you today? Are you still following any that are irrelevant to your present life? Do you disagree with any of them?

4. Finally, commit to changing scripts that aren't productive for you or that conflict with values you hold.

We *can* rewrite scripts once we are adults. To do so, we must become aware of what our families taught us and take responsibility for scripting our own lives.

Attachment Styles

Attachment styles are the third way parents or caregivers communicate who we are. Attachment styles are patterns of parenting that teach us who we and others are and how to approach relationships. From extensive studies of interaction between parents and children, John Bowlby (1973, 1988) developed a theory that we learn attachment styles in our earliest relationships.

Most children form their first human bond with a parent, usually the mother, because women do more of the caregiving in our society (Wood, 1994e). Clinicians who have studied attachment styles believe that the first bond is especially important because it forms expectations for later relationships (Ainsworth, Blehar, Waters, & Wall, 1978; Bartholomew & Horowitz, 1991; Miller, 1993). Four distinct attachment styles have been identified, as shown in Figure 2.2.

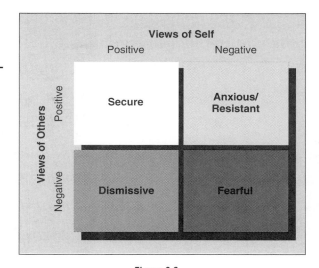

Figure 2.2
Styles of Attachment

Secure   A **secure attachment style** is the most positive. This style develops when the caregiver responds in a consistently attentive and loving way to the child. In response, the child develops a positive sense of self-worth ("I am lovable") and a positive view of others ("People are loving and can be trusted"). People with a secure attachment style tend to be outgoing, affectionate, and able to handle the challenges and disappointments of close relationships without losing self-esteem. Equally important, people who have secure attachment styles are comfortable with themselves when they are not involved in close relationships. Their security makes them able to engage in intimacy with others without depending on relationships for their self-worth.

Fearful   A **fearful attachment style** is cultivated when the caregiver in the first bond communicates in negative, rejecting, or even abusive ways to the child. Children who are treated this way often infer that they are unworthy of love and that others are not loving. Thus, they learn to see themselves as unlovable and others as rejecting. Not surprisingly, people with a fearful attachment style are apprehensive about relationships. Although they often want close bonds with others, they fear others will not love them and that they are not lovable. Thus, as adults they may avoid others or feel insecure in relationships.

Dismissive   A **dismissive attachment style** is also promoted by caregivers who are disinterested, rejecting, or abusive toward children. Yet, people who develop this style do not accept the caregiver's view of them as unlovable. Instead, they dismiss others as unworthy. Consequently, children develop a

Zondi:

In South Africa where I was born, I learned that I was not important. Most daughters learn this. My name is Zondomini, which means between happiness and sadness. The happiness is because a child was born. The sadness is because I am a girl, not a boy. I am struggling now to see myself as worthy.

positive view of themselves and a low regard for others and relationships. Those with a dismissive attachment style often develop a defensive view of relationships and regard them as unnecessary and undesirable.

Anxious-Resistant   A final pattern is the **anxious/resistant attachment style,** which is the most complex of the four. Each of the other three styles results from some consistent pattern of treatment by a caregiver. The anxious/resistant style, however, is fostered by inconsistent treatment from the caregiver. Sometimes the adult is loving and attentive, yet at others she is indifferent or rejecting. The caregiver's communication is not only inconsistent but also unpredictable. He may respond positively to something a child does on Monday and react negatively to the same behaviour on Tuesday. An accident that results in severe punishment one day may be greeted with indulgent laughter another day. Naturally, this unpredictability creates great anxiety for the child who depends on the caregiver (Miller, 1993). Because children tend to assume adults are always right, they believe they are the source of any problem—they are unlovable or deserve others' abuse. In her commentary, Noreen explains how inconsistent behaviours from her father confused and harmed her as a child.

In adult life, individuals who have an anxious/resistant attachment style tend to be preoccupied with relationships. On one hand, they know others can be loving and affirming. On the other hand, they realize that others can

Noreen:

When I was little, my father was an alcoholic, but I didn't know that then. All I knew was that sometimes he loved me and played with me and sometimes he would shout at me for nothing. Once he told me I was his sunshine, but later that same night he told me he wished I'd never been born. Even though now I understand the alcohol made him act that way, it's still hard to feel I'm okay.

hurt them and be unloving. Reflecting the pattern displayed by the caregiver, people with an anxious/resistant attachment style are often inconsistent themselves. One day they invite affection; the next day they rebuff it and deny needing closeness.

Our probability for developing a particular attachment style is affected by socioeconomic class, as clinical psychiatrist Robert Karen reports (in Greenberg, 1997). Poor families face serious hardships brought on by poverty: lack of adequate and nutritious food, poor shelter or homelessness, and inadequate medical care. These hardships can preoccupy and depress parents, making it difficult for them to be as responsive and loving to children as parents who have more material resources (Greenberg, 1997).

The attachment styles we learned in our first close relationship tend to persist (Bartholomew & Horowitz, 1991; Belsky & Pensky, 1988; Bowlby, 1988). As a result, we tend to choose romantic partners that parallel the relationship style to which we are accustomed.

However, this is not inevitable. We can modify our attachment styles by challenging unconstructive self-perceptions communicated in our early years and by forming relationships that foster secure connections as Thomas did.

Student Voices

Thomas:

I couldn't count on my parents. They divorced when I was young. I was raised on a farm by my father who was away a lot. I spent a lot of time alone. I can see that I developed an anxious/resistant attachment with all my girlfriends until I met my future wife whose family was very supportive and present in our lives. They became the parents I never had. I've changed. I no longer act clingy and no longer need constant assurance that I'm O.K.

Apply the Idea

Determining Your Attachment Style

Using the four descriptors below taken from Griffin and Bartholomew (1994), choose the relationship style that most accurately describes you in your romantic relationships.

A. It is easy for me to become emotionally close to others. I am comfortable depending on others and having others depend on me. I don't worry about being alone or having others not accept me.

B. I am uncomfortable getting close to others. I want emotionally close relationships, but I find it difficult to trust others completely, or to depend on them. I worry that I will be hurt if I allow myself to become too close to others.

C. I want to be completely emotionally intimate with others, but I often find that others are reluctant to get as close as I would like. I am uncomfortable being without close relationships, but I sometimes worry that others don't value me as much as I value them.

D. I am comfortable without close emotional relationships. It is very important to me to feel independent and self-sufficient, and I prefer not to depend on others or have others depend on me.

A = Secure; B = Fearful; C = Preoccupied (or Anxious/Resistant); D = Dismissing

What accounts for the relationship style you chose?

Reflective Exercise

Consider the lines from this Canadian songwriter.

> It's not love that brings me back to these shores.
>
> It's just something that I've never found.
>
> It's not love that brings me back to these shores.
>
> The past is rising fast and I'm searching for high ground.

Essig, David. (1998). "High Ground." From *Redbird Country and High Ground.* **[CD]** Appaloosa.

Our pasts influence the present. The words of David Essig capture how our pasts influence the present. Water is such a fine metaphor for examining the depths of our psyche. What elements of your past might have you "searching for high ground"?

Communication with Peers

A second major influence on our self-concepts is communication with peers.

Reflected Appraisal

From childhood playmates to work associates, friends, and romantic partners, we interact with peers throughout our lives. As we do, we gain information about how others see us, and this affects how we see ourselves. The term **"reflected appraisal"** refers to the idea that we reflect the appraisals that

Concepts at a Glance

There are two ways that we receive information from our peers:

- Reflected appraisal
- Social comparison

others make of us. This concept is also called the looking-glass self, based on Charles Cooley's poetic comment, "Each to each a looking glass/Reflects the other that doth pass" (1961, p. 5). If others communicate that they think we are smart, we are likely to reflect that appraisal in how we act and think about ourselves. If others communicate that they see us as dumb or unlikable, we may reflect their appraisals by thinking of ourselves in those ways.

Peers also use reflected appraisals to let us know when our behaviours are not acceptable. This is one of the primary ways we learn social norms. The importance of peers' reflected appraisals is illustrated by Laurel's story.

Student Voices

Laurel:

When my son went to kindergarten, he was still sucking his thumb. His teacher was a wonderful man. He drew Rowan aside and said, "The other children might laugh at you if you suck your thumb here. Can you wait 'til you get home?" Rowan stopped sucking his thumb in public that day. That teacher saved my son from the crushing jeers of his peers.

How others see us inevitably affects how we see ourselves. Reflected appraisals of peers join with those of family members and shape the images we have of ourselves.

Social Comparison

A second way in which communication with peers affects self-concept is through **social comparison,** which involves comparing ourselves with others to form judgments of our own talents, abilities, qualities, and so forth. Whereas reflected appraisals are based on how others view us, social comparisons are our own use of others as measuring sticks for ourselves.

We gauge ourselves in relation to others in two ways. First, we compare ourselves to others to decide whether we are like them or different from them. Are we the same age, colour, religion? Do we hang out with the same people? Do we have similar backgrounds, political beliefs, and social commitments? Assessing similarity and difference allows us to decide with whom we fit. Research has shown that people generally are most comfortable with others who are like them, so we tend to gravitate toward those we regard as similar (Pettigrew, 1967; Whitbeck & Hoyt, 1994). This can, however, deprive us of perspectives of people whose experiences and beliefs differ from our own. When we limit ourselves to people like us, we impoverish the social perspectives that form our own understandings of the world.

We also use social comparison to gauge ourselves in relation to others. Because there are no absolute standards of beauty, intelligence, musical

Review

Reflected Appraisals
- How others view us

Social Comparisons
- Our own use of others to measure ourselves

Ricky:

For years I thought something was wrong with me because I didn't have ambitions like other guys. In high school I babysat a lot, because I really love kids. I thought I would like to become a kindergarten teacher, but the guys I hung out with really put me down for that. They wanted to become doctors and lawyers and accountants. They let me know that what I wanted to be was wrong or somehow not good enough. I would also like to be a stay-at-home dad, but I don't dare tell that to my guy friends. My girlfriend understands and that's cool with her because she wants kids but doesn't want to have to stay home with them. She makes me feel like I'm really special because I want to care for children. I like who I am in her eyes.

talent, athletic ability, and so forth, we measure ourselves in relation to others. Am I as good a batter as Hendrick? Do I play the guitar as well as Sam? Am I as smart as Serena? Am I as attractive as Jana? Through comparing ourselves to others, we crystallize a self-image based on how we measure up on various criteria. This is normal and necessary if we are to develop realistic self-concepts.

However, we should be wary of using inappropriate standards of comparison. It isn't realistic to judge our attractiveness in relation to stars and models or our athletic ability in relation to Olympic athletes.

Review

We use others to determine

- Where we fit
- How similar or different we are

Apply the Idea

Reviewing Your Social Comparisons

Find out if your social comparisons are realistic. First, write "I am" six times. Complete the first three sentences with words that reflect positive views of yourself. Complete the fourth through sixth sentences with words that express negative views of yourself. For example, you might write, "I am kind," "I am smart," "I am responsible," "I am clumsy," "I am selfish," and "I am impatient."

Next, beside each sentence write the names of two people you use to judge yourself for each quality. For "I am kind," you would list people you use to measure kindness. List your social comparisons for all self-descriptions.

Now, review the names and qualities. Are any of the people unrealistic comparison points for you? If so, whom might you select to make more realistic social comparisons?

Communication with Society

The third influence on our self-concepts is interaction with society in general. As members of a shared social community, we are influenced by its values, judgments, and perspectives.

What subculture do you identify with?

Photo: © Corel

The perspectives of society (generalized other) are revealed to us in two ways. First, they surface in interactions with others who have internalized cultural values and pass them on to us. In the course of conversation we learn how society regards our sex, race, ethnicity, and class and what society values in personal identity. As we interact with others, we encounter not just their particular perspectives but also the perspective of the generalized other as they reflect it.

Second, broadly shared social perspectives are also communicated to us through media and institutions that reflect cultural values. For example, when we read popular magazines and go to movies, we are inundated with messages about how women and men are supposed to look and act. In Western culture, desirable women are invariably thin, beautiful, and deferential. Yet different ideals of femininity exist in non-Western cultures, as "Femininity—Muslim Style" shows. Attractive men are strong, in charge, and successful (Faludi, 1991). Communication from media and institutions infuses our lives, telling us over and over again how we are supposed to be and providing us with a basis for assessing ourselves. Media can also represent culture. In Canada, the Canadian Radio-television and Telecommunication Commission (CRTC) established a policy that 60 percent of broadcast material on TV must be Canadian content, and 35 percent of AM/FM radio content must be Canadian in order to stimulate Canada's cultural production.[1] The institutions that organize our society further convey social perspectives by the values they uphold. For example, our judicial system reminds us that as a society we value laws and punish those who break them. The institution of Western marriage communicates society's view that when people marry they become a single unit, which is why joint ownership of property is assumed for married couples. In other societies, marriages are arranged by parents, and newlyweds become part of the husband's family. Our great numbers of schools and levels of education inform us that as a society we value learning. At the same time, institutional processes reflect prevailing social prejudices. For instance, we may be a lawful society, but wealthy defendants can often buy better "justice" than poor ones. Similarly, although we claim to offer equal educational opportunities to all, students from families with money have a better chance at completing postsecondary education than students from families without such resources. These and other values are woven into the fabric of our culture, and we learn them with little effort or awareness. Reflecting carefully on social values allows us to make conscious choices about which ones we will accept for ourselves.

Concepts at a Glance

We communicate with our society through interaction with

- People who hold the values of the culture
- Media and institutions that reflect the culture

[1] For more information see www.media-awareness.ca/eng/issues/cultural/issues/cancon.htm

Communication Notes

Femininity—Muslim Style

The standards of feminine beauty aren't the same worldwide, so we shouldn't judge the appearance of women in one culture by the standards of femininity in another. U.S. citizens are quick to criticize Muslim women as oppressed because many prefer the hijab that covers them. However, Muslims may see their modest form of dressing as less oppressive than U.S. women's quest for beauty. This observation appeared in a 1984 issue of *Mahjubah: The Magazine for Moslem Women*:

> If women living in western societies took an honest look at themselves, such a question [why Muslim women cover themselves] would not arise. They are the slaves of appearance and the puppets of a male chauvinistic society: Every magazine and news medium tells them how they should look and behave. They should wear glamorous clothes and make themselves beautiful for strange men to gaze and gloat over them. So the question is not why Muslim women wear hijab, but why the women in the West, who think they are so liberated, do not wear hijab.

Source: Cited in Ferrante, J. (1992). *Sociology: A global perspective.* Belmont, CA: Wadsworth.

Apply the Idea

Identifying Social Values in Media

Select four popular Canadian magazines. Record the focus of their articles and advertisements. What do the articles and ads convey about what is valued in Canada? What themes and types of people are emphasized?

If you have a magazine aimed primarily at one sex, consider what cultural values it communicates about gender. What do articles in it convey about how women or men are regarded and what they are expected to be and do? Ask the same questions about advertisements. How many ads aimed at women focus on being beautiful, looking young, losing weight, taking care of others, and attracting men? How many ads aimed at men emphasize strength, virility, success, and independence?

To extend this exercise, scrutinize the cultural values that are conveyed by television, films, billboards, and news stories. Pay attention to who is highlighted and how different genders, ethnic groups, and professions are represented. Examine U.S. magazines and determine what values we in

Canada share with the United States and in what way we differ.

Photo: © Corel

We have seen that the self arises in communication. From interaction with family members, peers, and society as a whole, we are taught the prevailing values of our culture and of particular others who are significant in our lives. These perspectives become part of who we are. We'll now discuss more briefly other premises about the self.

THE SELF IS MULTIDIMENSIONAL

There are many dimensions, or aspects, of the human self. You have an image of your physical self—how large, attractive, and athletic you are. In addition, you have perceptions of your cognitive self including your intelligence and aptitudes. You also have an emotional self-concept. Are you sensitive or not? Are you easily hurt? Are you generally upbeat or cynical? Then there is your social self, which involves how you are with others. Some of us are extroverted, enjoy people around and dominate interactions, whereas others prefer to be less prominent and seek solitary activities. Our social selves also include our social roles—daughter or son, student, worker, parent, or partner in a committed relationship. Finally, each of us has a moral self consisting of our ethical and spiritual beliefs, the principles we believe in, our overall sense of morality, and our beliefs about how we are connected to the world. Although we use the word "self" as if it referred to a single entity, in reality the self is made up of many dimensions.

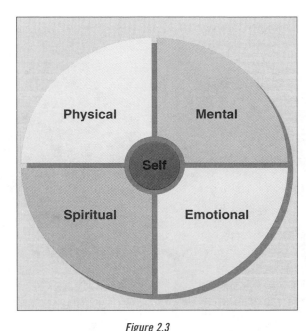

Figure 2.3
The Dimensions of the Self

THE SELF IS A PROCESS

Virtually all researchers and clinicians who have studied human identity conclude that we are not born with selves, but instead we acquire them. George Herbert Mead, a distinguished social psychologist, was among the first to argue that humans do not come into the world with a sense of themselves. Babies literally have no **ego boundaries,** which define where an individual stops and the rest of the world begins (Chodorow, 1989). To an infant, being held by a mother is a single sensation in which it and the mother are blurred. A baby perceives no boundaries between its mouth and a nipple or its foot and the tickle by a mother. As infants have a range of experiences and as others respond to them, they gradually begin to see themselves as distinct from the external environment. Both mothers and fathers help children define their identities. "The Unique Role of Fathers in Socializing Children" explains distinctions between how mothers and fathers typically contribute to children's self-development. This is the beginning of a self-concept—the realization that one is a separate entity.

Within the first year or two of life, as infants start to differentiate themselves from the rest of the world, the self begins to develop. Babies, then toddlers, then children devote enormous energy to understanding who they are. They actively seek to define themselves and to become competent in the identities they claim (Kohlberg, 1958; Piaget, 1932/1965). For instance, early on, little girls and boys start working to be competent females and males, respectively. They scan the environment, find models of females and males, and imitate and refine their performances of gender. In like manner, children figure out what it takes to be smart, strong, attractive, and responsible, and they work to become competent in each. Throughout our lives, we continue the process of defining and presenting our identities. The ways we define ourselves vary as we mature. Struggling to be a swimmer at age four gives way to being popular in high school and being a successful professional and partner in adult life.

Some people feel uneasy with the idea that the self is a process, not a constant entity. We want to believe there is some stable, enduring core that is our essence—our true, unchanging identity. Of course, we all enter the world with certain biological abilities and limits, which constrain the possibilities of who we can be. Someone without the genes to be tall and coordinated, for instance, is probably not going to be a basketball superstar, and a person who is tone deaf is unlikely to perform in The Ford Centre. Beyond genetic and biological limits, however, we have considerable freedom in sculpting who we will be. The fact that we change again and again during our lives is evidence of our capacity to be self-renewing and ever-growing beings.

How has fatherhood changed?

Photo: P. Arden

THE SELF INTERNALIZES SOCIAL PERSPECTIVES

In studying how infants acquire selves, Mead (1934) realized that we take social perspectives inside ourselves to form views of who we are. He spoke of this as "importing" social perspectives to indicate that we take into ourselves views that originally come from others. We rely on two kinds of social perspectives to define ourselves and to guide how we think, act, and feel.

Communication Notes

The Unique Role of Fathers in Socializing Children

For years, mothers have been regarded as essential in children's development. We've all heard about the maternal instinct and about mothers' intuition. Yet, mothers are only half of the picture. It turns out that fathers too play important roles in children's development, and the roles they play are distinct from those of mothers.

Fathers seem more likely than mothers to challenge and stretch children to achieve more. Fathers urge children to take initiative, tolerate risks, and experiment with unfamiliar activities and situations. Fathers also tend to focus on playing with their children, and fathers' play is generally physically stimulating. Roughhousing with fathers seems to develop courage and a willingness to take risks in children.

Mothers, in contrast, seem to specialize in giving children emotional reassurance and in protecting them. Mothers, more than fathers, accept children at their current levels and don't push them to go further. Mothers also spend more of their time with children in caretaking activities than in play.

Consider a typical family outing in a playground. A two-year-old girl is on the swings. The father pushes his daughter and cheers her on as she swings higher and higher. The mother watches apprehensively and says, "Careful, honey, don't go too high." Differences like this showed up in studies of how men and women parent. Again and again, researchers noted that mothers emphasized protection and reassurance, and fathers emphasized challenge and stimulation.

Researchers who have studied parents' interactions with children conclude that fathers and mothers typically contribute in unique and valuable ways to their children's development and self-esteem. Fathers seem especially prepared to help their sons and daughters develop confidence, autonomy, and high expectations for themselves. Mothers are more likely to provide children with a sense of self-acceptance and a sensitivity to others.

Researchers conclude that both mothers and fathers make substantial contributions to the full development of children. They emphasize, however, that fathers don't do mothering. They do fathering, and that's different.

Sources: Popenoe, D. (1996). *Life without father*. New York: Free Press; Stacey, J. (1996). In *the name of the father: Rethinking family values in a postmodern age*. Boston: Beacon.

Particular Others

The first perspectives that affect us are those of **particular others.** As the term implies, these are specific individuals who are significant to us. Mothers, fathers, siblings, and often daycare providers are particular others who are significant to most infants. In addition, some families include aunts, uncles, grandparents, and others who live with the family and may be perceived by the infant as particular others.

As babies interact with particular others in their world, they learn how others see them. This is the beginning of a self-concept. Notice that the self starts from outside—from others' views of who we are. Recognizing this, Mead said that we must first get outside ourselves to get into ourselves. By this he meant that the only way we can see ourselves is from the perspectives of others. We first see ourselves in terms of how particular others see us. If parents communicate to children that they are special and cherished, the children will come to see themselves as worthy of love. On the other hand, children whose parents communicate that they are not wanted or loved may come to think of themselves as unlovable.

Earlier in this chapter, we discussed this process as reflected appraisal and the "looking-glass self." Reflected appraisals are not confined to childhood but continue throughout our lives. Sometimes a teacher first sees potential that students have not recognized in themselves. When the teacher communicates that students are talented in a particular area, the students may come to see themselves that way. Later, as you enter professional life, you will encounter co-workers and bosses who reflect their appraisals of you—you're on the fast track, average, or not suited to your position. The appraisals of us that others communicate shape our sense of who we are. Thus, reflected appraisals can lead to self-fulfilling prophecies—with positive or negative effects on our self-esteem.

Student Voices

Clark:

My brother Alan was really significant in my life. He was four years older than me, and I thought he was perfect. I wanted to be just like him, and I remember imitating what he did and how he talked so that I could be manly. When he said I did something well, I was so proud, and when Alan made fun of me I worked harder to get it right. I think I still see myself through his eyes a lot.

Tanya:

I can still hear my grandmother's voice saying, "If you get a fat belly, you'll never lose it!" That's what she said all the time. She said it if I was eating cookies after school or if I had second helpings at dinner or if I wanted ice cream on hot summer days. Now when I reach for a cookie, her voice echoes in my head—I can't get that voice, that message, out of my mind.

Apply the Idea

Reflecting on Reflected Appraisals

To understand how reflected appraisals have influenced your self-concept, try this exercise.

1. *Make two columns.*

2. *In the first column, list five words that describe ways you see yourself. Examples are responsible, ambitious, unattractive, clumsy, funny, intelligent, shy, and athletic.*

3. *In the second column, identify the particular individuals who have been and are especially significant in your life. Try to list at least five individuals who matter to you.*

4. *Now, think about how these special people communicated to you about the traits you listed in Step 1. Connect the traits with the people. How did they express their appraisals of what you defined as important parts of yourself?*

   Can you trace how you see yourself to the appraisals reflected by particular others in your life?

Generalized Others

The second social perspective that influences how we see ourselves is called the **perspective of the generalized other.** The generalized other is the collection of rules, roles, and attitudes endorsed by the whole social community in which we live (Mead, 1934). In other words, the generalized other represents the views of society. The process of socialization is one in which individuals internalize the perspective of the generalized other and thus come to share that perspective.

Concepts at a Glance

Four Aspects of our Social Communities That Are Central to Personal Identity

- Race and ethnicity
- Gender
- Sexual orientation
- Socioeconomic status

Photo: © Photodisc

In Canadian culture, the perspective of the generalized other views murder, rape, robbery, and embezzlement as wrong, and each of us learns that as we participate in the society. In addition, we learn which aspects of identity society considers important, how society views various social groups, and, by extension, how it views us as members of specific groups. Researchers have identified four elements that are central to personal identity in modern Western culture: race and ethnicity, gender, sexual orientation, and socioeconomic status (Andersen & Collins, 1992; James, 1999; Wood, 1995b, 1996).

Race and Ethnicity

Race and ethnicity are considered primary aspects of personal identity. The word "race" has often been used to categorize and identify the peoples of the world. Seen in the four colours of red, white, black, and yellow, race focused upon skin colour as the defining measure. Now, with our multicultural communities, the distinctions between colour are blurred and so is the importance placed upon those differences. The

Communication Notes

The Construction of Race in North America

The word "White" wasn't used to describe race or identity until Europeans colonized the United States. They invented the label "White" as a way to increase solidarity among European settlers who actually had diverse ethnic backgrounds. By calling themselves "White," these diverse groups could gloss over differences among them and use their common skin hue to distinguish themselves from people of colour. White, in other words, is a term that was created to legitimize slavery.

During the time when slavery was an institution in the United States, Southern plantation owners invented a system of racial classification known as "the one-drop rule." According to this system, a person with as little as one drop of African blood was classified as Black. Thus, racial divisions were established, though arbitrarily.

Social demographer William Petersen says that ethnicity is incredibly difficult to measure reliably. One problem is that increasing numbers of people have multiple racial and ethnic identities. For example, if a woman is one-fourth Black, one-fourth Chinese, one-fourth Thai, one-eighth White, and one-eighth First Nations, what race is she?

Sources: Bates, E. (1994, fall). Beyond black and white. *Southern Exposure*, pp. 11–15; Petersen, W. (1997). *Ethnicity counts*. New York: Transaction.

uniqueness of our ethnic communities, however, is cause to celebrate. It may be seen in the Chinese New Year in Vancouver or a ceilidh in Nova Scotia. Rich and diverse cultural customs are part of the fabric of Canadian life. The large cosmopolitan cities of Toronto and Vancouver are clear examples of multicultural communities, while in smaller communities, an ethnic majority may still predominate the social landscape. Wherever we live, our ethnicity is one way to define ourselves. "The Construction of Race in North America" explores the origins of race and ethnicity.

Student Voices

Leona:

I was a child of the adoption scoops of the 50s and 60s in B.C. and Alberta. I was taken from my First Nations home and raised by white adoptive parents. When I became an adult, I not only began my search for my biological parents as so many adopted children do, I also began my search for my ethnic identity. In finding my family and ancestors, I reclaimed my aboriginal roots and redefined my ethnicity. I am a First Nations woman!

Gender

Gender is another important category in Western culture. Historically, men have been more valued and considered more rational, competent, and entitled to privilege than women. In the 1800s, women were not allowed to own property, gain professional training, or vote. It was considered appropriate for a husband to beat his wife; the phrase "rule of thumb" comes from the law that stated a man could beat his wife as long as he used a stick no larger than the size of his thumb. On October 18, 1929, the Privy Council of England, at the time Canada's highest court, decided that women were "persons" under Section 24 of the *B.N.A. Act*. This case came to be known as the Persons Case brought forward by five Canadian women who challenged the interpretation of "person" as "he." These courageous women—Emily Murphy, Nellie McClung, Irene Parlby, Louise Mckinney, and Henrietta Muir Edwards—became known as the Famous Five. Even now, at the beginning of the 21st century, women and men are still not considered equal in many societies. Some scholars argue that gender is the most important aspect of personal identity in Western culture (Fox-Genovese, 1991). From the pink and blue blankets hospitals wrap around newborns to differential salaries earned by women and men, gender is a major facet of identity. Given the importance our society places on gender, it is no wonder that one of the first ways children learn to identify themselves is by their sex (Wood, 1996).

Western cultures have had strong gender prescriptions. Girls and women were expected to be caring, deferential, and cooperative, whereas boys and men were supposed to be independent, assertive, and competitive (Wood, 1994d). Consequently, women who asserted themselves or competed were likely to receive social disapproval, be called "bitches," and otherwise reprimanded for violating gender prescriptions. Men who refused to conform to social views of masculinity and who were gentle and caring risked being labelled "wimps." Views on gender prescriptions are changing, but there is still great variability in how the roles of men and women are perceived. Our gender, then, makes a great deal of difference in how others view us and how we come to see ourselves.

Student Voices

Allison:
When I was really young, I was outside playing in a little swimming pool one day. It was hot, and my brothers had their shirts off, so I took mine off too. When my mother looked up and saw me, she went berserk. She told me to get my shirt back on and act like a lady. That's when I knew that girls have to hide and protect their bodies, but boys don't.

Sexual Orientation

Sexual orientation is the third aspect of identity that is salient in our culture. Historically, heterosexuality was viewed as the normal sexual orientation, and lesbians, bisexuals, and gays were regarded as abnormal. Society continues to communicate this viewpoint not only directly in some cases but also through privileges given to heterosexuals but denied to gays, lesbians, and bisexuals. For example, a woman and man who love each other can be married and have their commitment recognized religiously and legally. However, two men or two women who love each other and want to be life partners are denied social and legal recognition (Wood, 1995c). Heterosexuals can cover partners on insurance policies and inherit from them without paying taxes, but people with other sexual orientations cannot. To be homosexual or bisexual in modern Western culture is to be socially devalued. However, many gays and lesbians reject negative social views of their identity; instead they form communities that support positive self-images.

Socioeconomic Status

Socioeconomic status is a fourth important aspect of identity in our society. Even though Canada is relatively open with regard to class, as examined in "Creating Class," the strata of society we belong to affects everything from

Communication Notes

Creating Class

Societies around the world have created systems of classifying people. Open systems, such as the system in Canada, allow interaction among different socioeconomic groups and assume individuals can move from one group to another. We still use terms such as "middle class" and "working class" to describe socioeconomic status, but the British origins of class have largely fallen away. In contrast, caste classifications are closed systems that assume individuals are locked into the social status ascribed to them at birth. These strongly discourage interaction among members of different castes.

Apartheid, an Afrikaans word that means "apartness," has prevailed in South Africa for hundreds of years and was made the official policy of the country in 1948. When the Nationalists, a conservative White political party, seized power in the 1940s, they legislated hundreds of laws to enforce rigid racial separation in virtually every area of life and to support domination of the country by the White minority.

In 1990, South Africa abolished the *Separate Amenities Act*, which had mandated separate and unequal cemeteries, parks, trains, hotels, hospitals, and so forth for Whites and Blacks. Other discriminatory practices and laws are gradually being dismantled in South Africa.

Sources: Ferrante, J. (1992). *Sociology: A global perspective*. Belmont, CA: Wadsworth; Wren, C. S. (1990, October 16). A South Africa color bar falls quietly. *The New York Times*, pp. Y1, Y10.

Student Voices

David:

I'm gay, and many people think that gay is all I am. Once they find out I'm gay, nothing else about me seems relevant to them. They can't see all the ways in which we are alike and that we have more similarities than differences. They don't see that I am a student (just like them), that I am working my way through school (just like them), that I worry about tests and papers (just like them), that I love hockey (just like them). All they see is that I am gay, and that I am not like them.

how much money we make, to the kinds of jobs and lifestyle choices we see as possibilities for ourselves. Class, as defined by Langston (1992) is difficult to point to because, unlike sex and ethnicity, it is not visible. Class isn't just the amount of money a person has. It's a basic part of how we understand the world and how we think, feel, and act. Class affects which stores, restaurants, and schools are part of our life. It influences who our friends are, where we live and work, and even the kind of car we drive.

Reflective Exercise

Do you think class is evident in your community? In what way are you affected by the demarcations between people in your job, at your school? Is the difference largely one of available money and resources, or is it a deeper difference? Is "class" alive and well in Canada?

In 1995 Barney Dews and Carolyn Law edited a book titled *This Fine Place So Far from Home: Voices of Academics from the Working Class.* Although the academics who contributed to this book have entered a middle-class world, they say that they don't feel at ease or fully accepted. Many report wrenching identity conflicts as they interact with their working-class families and their middle-class colleagues. "Torn between two worlds and two identities" is how they describe themselves. The values and self-concepts that they grew up endorsing are at odds with the values and identities regarded as appropriate where they now live and work.

Class influences which needs we focus on in Maslow's hierarchy. For example, people with economic security have the resources and leisure time to contemplate higher-level needs such as self-actualization. They can afford therapy, yoga, spiritual development, and elite spas to condition their bodies. These are not feasible for people who are a step away from poverty. Members

|Student Voices|

Geneva:

I may be in a first-class university, but I don't fit with most of the folks here. That hits me in the face every day. I walk across campus and see girls wearing shoes that cost more than all four pairs I own. I hear students talking about restaurants and trips that I can't afford. Last week I heard a guy complaining about being too broke to get a CD player for his car. I don't own a car. I don't know how to relate to these people who have so much money. I do know they see the world differently than I do.

of the middle and upper classes assume they will attend college or university and enter good professions, yet these are often not realistic options for working-class people (Langston, 1992). Guidance counsellors may encourage academically gifted working-class students to go to work or pursue vocational education after high school, whereas middle-class students of average ability are routinely steered toward good colleges and status careers. In patterns such as this, we see how the perspective of the generalized other shapes our identities and our concrete lives.

Ethnicity, gender, sexual orientation, and class dominate our society's views of individuals and their worth. In thinking about these four social constructions of identity, it's important to realize they intersect with one another. Ethnicity interacts with gender, so that First Nations women experience double oppression and devaluation in our culture. Class and sexual orientation also interact: Homophobia, or fear of homosexuals, is particularly pronounced in the working class, so a lesbian or gay person in a poor community may be socially ostracized (Langston, 1992). Class and gender are also interlinked, with women being far more likely to exist at the poverty level than men (Stone, 1992). All facets of our identity interact.

Although ethnicity, gender, sexual orientation, and socioeconomic class are especially salient in social views of identity and worth, there are many other views of the general society that we learn and often internalize. For instance, Western societies clearly value intelligence, ambition, individualism, and competitiveness. People who do not conform to these social values receive less respect than those who do. Another value our society endorses is slimness, particularly in women. Being slim (and beautiful) is considered very important, and those who don't measure up are often shunned and regarded as less worthy than those who do. Because society places such emphasis on slenderness in women, eating disorders are epidemic. Society imposes physical requirements on men as well. Strength and sexual prowess are two expectations of "real men," which may explain why increasing numbers of men are having pectoral implants and penis enlargement surgery. People not born with bodies favoured by society may feel compelled to construct them!

Apply the Idea

Internalizing the Generalized Other

Which views of the generalized other have you internalized?

- *How do you evaluate women? How important is physical appearance to your judgments?*
- *How do you evaluate men? To what extent do strength and ambitiousness affect your judgments?*
- *What were you taught about First Nations people, Francophones, Anglophones, or members of Asian cultures? Which of those views have you imported into yourself?*

- *How do you see heterosexuals, bisexuals, gays, and lesbians? How did you develop these views?*

Are there social perspectives and attitudes that you hold but don't really respect or like? If so, consider challenging them and reforming those parts of yourself.

As we interact with the significant people of our lives (the particular others) and participate in general social life (the generalized other), we learn what and whom our society values. Social perspectives, however, do not remain outside us. In most cases, we import them into ourselves, and we thus come to share the views and values generally endorsed in our society. In many ways this is useful, even essential, for collective life. If we all made up our own rules about when to stop and go at traffic intersections, car accidents would skyrocket. If each of us operated by our own code for lawful conduct, there would be no shared standards regarding rape, murder, robbery, and so forth. Life would be chaotic.

Yet not all social views are as constructive as traffic rules and criminal law. The generalized other's unequal valuing of different ethnic groups, genders, and sexual orientations fosters discrimination against whole groups of people whose only fault is not being what society defines as normal or good. Each of us has a responsibility to exercise critical judgment about which social views we personally accept and use as guides for our own behaviours, attitudes, and values. This leads to a third proposition about the self.

SOCIAL PERSPECTIVES ON THE SELF ARE CONSTRUCTED AND VARIABLE

We have seen that we gain a sense of personal identity and an understanding of social life by encountering and internalizing social perspectives of particular others and the generalized other. This could lead you to think that our self-concepts are determined by fixed social values. As we will see, however, this isn't the case. Social views are constructed and variable, so they can be changed. An example of the variability of social values is examined in "A Cross-cultural Look at Sexual Identity."

Constructed Social Views

Social perspectives are constructed in particular cultures at specific times. What a society values does not reflect divine law, absolute truth, or the natural order of things. The values that are endorsed in any society are arbitrary and designed to support dominant ideologies or the beliefs of those in power. For example, it was men's advantage to deny women the right to vote, because doing so preserved men's power to control the laws of the land. Similarly, it was to the European settlers advantage to force the aboriginal people of Canada onto reserves. By approving of heterosexuality and not

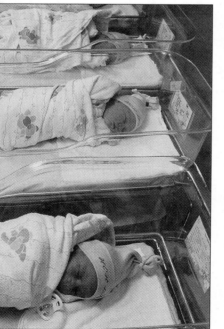

Photo: © Lori Adamski Peek/Tony Stone Images, Inc.

Communication Notes

A Cross-cultural Look at Sexual Identity

In Canada, First Nations peoples confer a special name to gay, lesbian, or bisexual members. They are called "Two-Spirited." "The aboriginal concept of gender assignment and identity is somewhat more complex than the binary opposites of male and female in Anglo-American Society" says Gordon de Frane, who addresses the nature and limitations of the term "Two-Spirited" (2000, p.3). Today, the term applies not only to sexual orientation but also to a larger more encompassing view of the world, or a truer integration of the male and female in all of us. Two-spirited members of tribes were revered and exalted to the status of shaman because of the gift they bore.

homosexuality, the culture supports a particular, arbitrary family ideal. When we reflect on widely endorsed social values, we realize that they tend to serve the interests of those who are privileged by the status quo.

Differing Social Views

The constructed and arbitrary nature of social values becomes especially obvious when we consider how widely values differ from culture to culture. For example, in Sweden, Denmark, and Norway, same-sex marriages are allowed and are given full legal recognition. Prescriptions for femininity and masculinity also vary substantially across cultures. In some places, men are emotional and dependent, and women are assertive and emotionally controlled.

The individualistic ethic so prominent in the West is not valued or considered normal in many other countries, particularly Asian and African ones (Gaines, 1995). There are also countries in which heterosexuality is not the only sexual orientation regarded as normal. Some cultures even recognize more than two genders!

Social meanings also vary across time within single cultures. For example, in the 1700s and 1800s, women in Europe and the West were defined as too delicate to engage in hard labour. During the World Wars, however, women were expected to do "men's work" while men were at war. When the men returned home, society once again decreed that women were too weak to perform in the labour market, and they were reassigned to home and hearth. The frail, pale appearance considered feminine in the 1800s gave way to robust, fleshy ideals in the mid-1900s, as embodied by Marilyn Monroe. Today, a more athletic body is one of the ideals prescribed for

Hannah:

Because I'm an older student, I have a good understanding of how views change in society. Forty years ago when I first started college, women were not taken very seriously. I had no female professors, and there wasn't a women's studies department at my college. Our teachers, and all of us, just expected that most women at the college would become wives and mothers who either worked little part-time jobs or didn't work outside the home. Any woman who said she wanted to pursue a full-time career was considered kind of strange. Attitudes on campus are so different today. There are lots of female professors, who are role models to young women—they are living proof that women can have careers and families. And this generation of students doesn't assume women are going to school to get their "Mrs. degrees." A majority of the female students I know have serious career ambitions, and most of the male students seem to assume their female classmates and girlfriends will work full-time for most of their lives. What a difference 40 years has made in how women are viewed.

women. Magazines reflect and encourage the current view that strength and athletic ability are feminine.

Social prescriptions for men have also varied. The rugged he-man who was the ideal in the 1800s relied on his physical strength to farm wild lands. After the Industrial Revolution, physical strength and bravado gave way to business acumen, and money replaced muscle as a sign of manliness. Today, as our society struggles with changes in women, men, and families, the ideals of manhood are being revised yet again. Increasingly, men are expected to be involved in caring for children and to be sensitive as well as independent and strong.

Apply the Idea

Social Definitions of Masculinity and Femininity

To find out how society in general (the generalized other) defines ideals for women and men today, review five current popular Canadian magazines. You may review them in the library or on-line, using your InfoTrac College Edition. Select magazines that aim at postsecondary-age readers. While reviewing the magazines, answer the following questions:

- *How many females are shown actively involved in pursuits such as sports or manual labour?*

How has femininity changed in the new millennium?

Photo: G. Lee

- *How many females are shown in passive roles such as relaxing, eating, or waiting for others?*
- *How many females are shown in domestic settings or engaged in domestic activities such as preparing meals and caring for children?*
- *How many males are shown actively involved in pursuits such as sports or manual labour?*
- *How many males are shown in passive roles such as relaxing, eating, or waiting for others?*
- *How many males are shown in domestic settings and/or engaged in domestic activities such as preparing meals and caring for children?*
- *How many females are slender and thin?*
- *How many males are muscular and strong?*
- *How many members of minorities are shown?*
- *How many members of the minorities shown have features that are more typical of Caucasians than their ethnic groups?*

The meaning of homosexuality has also been revised over time in Western culture. Until fairly recently, our society strongly disapproved of gays, lesbians, and bisexuals, so most non-heterosexuals did not publicly acknowledge their sexual orientation. Although much prejudice still exists, it is gradually diminishing.

Marriage in Canada is administered by the provinces. British Columbia has recognized gay and lesbian partnerships by setting up a parallel system to heterosexual marriage, and homosexuals there have rights equivalent to married couples. Some same-sex spousal rights have been granted in Ontario. In mid-1999, the Supreme Court of Canada found that the existing legislation concerning couples who live together without being married is discriminatory. The court required the Government of Ontario to change its laws so that both heterosexual and homosexual couples are treated equally. As social views of homosexuality change, more and more gays and lesbians are openly acknowledging their sexuality.

The meaning our society assigns to different ethnic groups has also varied markedly over our history as a nation. Although ignorance and prejudice still haunt our nation, they are lessening. Today, inclusive curricula in schools recognize and celebrate the strengths of students of various abilities and ethnic origins. Professional development conferences for teachers frequently have a focus of "Diversity and Multiple Perspectives." As the generalized other's perspective on diverse ethnicities enlarges, people of all strata of society gain more positive reflected appraisals of their identity than was the case years ago. "The Reality of Race" discusses the issue of race as a social, not biological, reality.

Other socially constructed views are also variable. In the 1950s and 1960s, people with disabilities were often kept in their homes or put in

Communication Notes

The Reality of Race

For centuries, race has been used as a primary way of classifying people. Yet, most scientists now reject the concept of race as a valid means of defining individual and group identities. According to Jonathan Marks, a biologist at Yale University, "race has no biological reality."

Increasingly, scientists assert that race is only a socially constructed category. DNA research reveals that there is no scientific basis for the racial categories widely used in society. According to DNA studies, there is actually far more genetic variation within a single African population than in all non-African populations together. Loring Brace, an anthropologist at the University of Michigan, reports that intelligence is one human trait that doesn't vary from population to population. According to Brace, the differences among people grouped into different races that show up on intelligence tests reflect environmental and cultural factors, including differing levels of nutrition and quality of education, and don't reflect innate intellectual capacity.

Source: Boyd, R. (1996, October 9). Notion of separate races rejected. *Raleigh News and Observer*, pp. 1A, 15A.

institutions. Today, many schools endorse inclusion, which places students with physical or mental disabilities in regular classrooms. Sensitivity to people who have special needs grows as fully-abled students become familiar with people with disabilities.

The meaning of age has also varied throughout our history. In the 1800s, the average lifespan was less than 60 years, and it was not uncommon for people to die in their 40s or 50s. Then, unlike today, 50 was considered old. The average lifespan today is nearly 80, making 50 seem considerably less old. In the 1800s, people typically married in their teens, and they often had five or more children before reaching 30. Today, many people wait until their 30s to begin having children, and parents in their 40s aren't considered "too old."

Changing Social Views

Social perspectives are changeable and, in fact, have changed significantly over time. Social perspectives are fluid and respond to individual and collective efforts to weave new meanings into the fabric of social life. Each of us has the responsibility to speak out against social perspectives that we perceive as wrong or harmful. By doing so we participate in the ongoing process of refining who we are as a society.

Michiko:

After the internment of the Japanese in British Columbia during World War II, my parents were afraid to openly demonstrate any of our Japanese customs. We only ate rice and used chopsticks at home and only if no one would witness it. It's taken a long time for my parents to trust that their Japanese customs and heritage are once again valued. I am gradually changing the way they think by voicing my views. It's wonderful to see my father proud once again to be a Japanese-Canadian in public.

In sum, meanings for facets of identity are socially created. Because the meanings are arbitrary constructions, they vary over time and across cultures. This highlights the power of individuals and groups to shape social understandings that make up the generalized other. Just as our culture shapes who we are, we too shape our culture. In the final section of this chapter, we consider guidelines for improving self-concept.

GUIDELINES FOR IMPROVING SELF-CONCEPT

So far, we have explored how we form our self-concepts through interaction with others and participation in society. Although this information helps us understand how we developed our current views of ourselves, it doesn't tell us a great deal about how we might transform aspects of our self-concepts that are unconstructive and hold us back. As we will see, there are ways to strengthen our identities.

MAKE A FIRM COMMITMENT TO CHANGE

The first principle for changing the self-concept is the most difficult and most important: You must make a firm commitment to cultivating personal growth. This isn't as easy as it might sound. A firm commitment involves more than saying "I want to be better" or "I want to like myself more." Saying these sentences is simple. What is more difficult is actually investing energy and effort to bring about change. A firm commitment requires that we keep trying. From the start, you need to realize that changing how you think of yourself is a major project.

Concepts at a Glance

To Improve the Self-Concept

- Make a firm commitment to change.
- Gain knowledge to assist personal change.
- Set realistic goals.
- Create a context that supports personal change.

It is difficult to change the self-concept for two reasons. First, doing so requires continuous effort. Because the self is a process, it is not formed in one fell swoop, and it cannot be changed in a moment of decision. We have to be willing to invest effort in an ongoing way. In addition, we must realize at the outset that there will be setbacks, and we can't let them derail our resolution to change. Last year, a student said she wanted to be more assertive, so she began speaking up more often in class. When a professor criticized one of her contributions, her resolution folded. Changing how we see ourselves is a long-term process.

A second reason it is difficult to change the self-concept is that the self resists change. Morris Rosenberg (1979), a psychologist who has studied self-concept extensively, says that most humans tend to resist change and that we also seek esteem or a positive view of ourselves. The good news is that we want esteem or a positive self-image; the bad news is that we find it difficult to change, even in positive directions. Interestingly, Rosenberg and others have found that we are as likely to hold onto negative self-images as we are positive ones. Apparently, consistency itself is comforting. If you realize in advance that you may struggle against change, you'll be prepared for the tension that accompanies personal growth. Because change is a process and the self resists change, a firm commitment to improving your self-concept is essential.

GAIN KNOWLEDGE TO ASSIST PERSONAL CHANGE

Commitment alone is insufficient to bring about constructive changes in who you are. In addition, you need several types of knowledge. First, you need to understand how your self-concept was formed. In this chapter, we've seen that much of how we see ourselves results from socially constructed values. Based on what you've learned, you can exercise critical judgment about which social perspectives to accept and which to reject. For instance, you may not wish to go along with our society's evaluations of ethnicity, gender, sexual orientation, and class.

Second, you need to know what changes are desirable and how to bring them about. Often, our ideas about changing ourselves are too vague and abstract to be useful. For instance, "I want to be more skillful at intimate communication" or "I want to be a better friend" are very abstract objectives. You can't move toward such fuzzy goals until you know something about the talk that enhances and impedes intimacy and what people value in friends. Books such as this one will help you pinpoint concrete skills that facilitate your own goals for personal change. Someone who wants to be a better friend might focus on developing empathic listening skills and creating supportive communication climates. The goal of being adept at intimate communication requires learning how to self-disclose appropriately, manage conflict constructively, and engage in dual perspective. In later chapters, we will discuss these and other specific skills that advance interpersonal communication competence in particular relationships and settings.

Jacquie:
One of my teachers was particularly good at not getting caught up in gender-biased statements. Because it was an Outdoor Recreation Program, there was a lot of lifting and moving of heavy equipment. She never called for men only. She always said things like, "I need six brawny people over here to help move these kayaks." I loved the way she saw women and men equally in that environment. The truth was, several of the women were, pound for pound, stronger than the men. She was a great role model for women in alternative jobs.

In addition to reading this book and learning from your class, there are other ways to gain knowledge to help you set and achieve goals of personal improvement. One very important source of knowledge is other people. Talking with others is a way to learn about relationships and what people want in them. Others can also provide useful feedback on your interpersonal skills and your progress in the process of change. Finally, others can provide models. If you know someone you think is particularly skillful in supporting others, observe her or him carefully to identify particular communication skills. You may not want to imitate this person exactly, but observing will make you more aware of concrete skills involved in supporting others. You may choose to tailor some of the skills others display to suit your personal style.

SET GOALS THAT ARE REALISTIC AND FAIR

Although it is true that willpower can do marvelous things, it does have limits. We need to recognize that trying to change how we see ourselves works only when our goals are realistic. If you are shy and want to be more extroverted, it is reasonable to try to speak up more and socialize more often. On the other hand, it may not be reasonable to aim at being the life of the party you're going to next week.

Realistic goals require realistic standards. Often, dissatisfaction with ourselves stems from unrealistic expectations. In a culture that emphasizes perfectionism, it's easy to be trapped into expecting more than is humanly possible. If you define a goal of being a totally perfect communicator in all situations, you are setting yourself up for failure. It's more reasonable and constructive to establish a series of realistic small goals that can be met. You might focus on improving one of the skills of communication competence we discussed in Chapter 1. When you are satisfied with your ability at that skill, you can move on to a second one. Remembering our discussion of social comparison, it's also important to select reasonable measuring sticks for ourselves. It isn't realistic to compare your academic work to that of a certified genius. It is reasonable to measure your academic performance against others who have intellectual abilities similar to your own. Setting realistic goals and selecting appropriate standards of comparison are important in bringing about change in yourself.

Student Voices

Kyle:

I really got bummed out my first year of university. I had been the star of my high school theatre company, so I came to university expecting to be a star here too. The first day of auditions, I saw a lot of guys who were better than I was. They were incredible. I felt like nothing. When I got back home that night, I called my mom and told her I was no good at theatre here. She told me I couldn't expect to compete with guys who had been involved in theatre for years. She asked how I stacked up against just the other first-year students, and I said pretty good. She told me they were the ones to compare myself to.

Being realistic also involves making fair assessments of ourselves. This requires us to place judgments in context and to see ourselves as in process. To assess ourselves effectively, we need to understand not only our discrete qualities and abilities but also how all of our parts fit together to form the whole self. One of the ways we treat ourselves unfairly is to judge particular abilities out of context. We have to appreciate our particular skills and weaknesses in the overall context of who we are. For example, if an accomplished young writer compares herself to only national literary greats such as Margaret Atwood or Ann-Marie MacDonald, she will never recognize her own achievements in writing. Her self-assessment is unrealistic because she compares herself to people who are extremely successful in particular spheres of life, yet she doesn't notice that her models are not especially impressive in other areas. As a result, she mistakenly feels she is inadequate in most ways. In our efforts to improve self-concept, then, we should acknowledge our strengths and virtues as well as parts of ourselves we wish to change.

A key foundation for improving self-concept is accepting yourself as in process. Earlier in this chapter, we saw that one characteristic of the human self is that it is continuously in process, always becoming. This implies several things. First, it means you need to accept who you are now as a starting point. You don't have to like or admire everything about yourself, but it is important to accept who you are today as a basis for going forward (Wood, 1992a). The self that you are results from all of the interactions, reflected appraisals, and social comparisons you have made during your life. You cannot change your past, but neither do you have to be bound by it forever. Only by realizing and accepting who you now are can you move ahead.

|Student Voices|

Tiriel:

I've really struggled at school. It's very important to me that I do well in school. I've felt badly when I make Bs and Cs and others in my classes make As. For a long time, I said to myself, "I am not as smart as they are if they make better grades." But I work 35 hours a week to pay for school. Most of the others in my classes either don't have to work or work fewer hours than I do. One student was complaining of only getting an A on an assignment and I know that he lives at home and his mother makes him lunch everyday and does his laundry. He has a lot more time to spend writing papers and studying for tests than I do. I think better of my academic abilities when I compare myself to other students who work as much as I do and who live alone. That is a more fair comparison than comparing myself to students who don't work and who have lots of support.

Second, accepting yourself as in process also implies that you realize you can change. Who you are is not who you will be in five or ten years. Because you are in process, you are always changing and growing. Don't let yourself be hindered by defeating self-fulfilling prophecies or the mindtrap that you cannot change (Rusk & Rusk, 1988). You can change if you set realistic goals, make a genuine commitment, and then work for the changes you want. Remember that you are not fixed as you are; you are always in the process of becoming.

CREATE A CONTEXT THAT SUPPORTS PERSONAL CHANGE

Just as it is easier to swim with the tide than against it, it is easier to change our views of ourselves when we have some support for our efforts. You can do a lot to create an environment that supports your growth by choosing contexts and people who help you realize your goals.

First, think about settings. If you want to improve your physical condition, it makes more sense to go to recreation centres than to hang out in bars. If you want to lose weight, it's better to go to restaurants that serve healthy foods and offer light choices than to go to fast food outlets where everything is fried. If you want to become more extroverted, you need to put yourself in social situations rather than in libraries. But libraries are a better context than parties if your goal is to improve academic performance.

Who we are with has a great deal to do with how we see ourselves and how worthy we feel we are. This means we can create a supportive context by consciously choosing to be around people who believe in us and encourage our personal growth. It's equally important to steer clear of people who pull us down or say we can't change. In other words, people who reflect positive appraisals of us enhance our ability to improve who we are.

Student Voices

Bob:

I never drank much until I got into this one group at school. All of them drank all the time. It was easy to join them. In fact, it was pretty hard not to drink and still be one of the guys. This year, I decided I was drinking too much, and I wanted to stop. It was hard enough not to keep drinking, because the guys were always doing it, but what really made it hard was the ways the guys got on me for abstaining. They let me know I was being uncool and made me feel like a jerk. Finally, to stop drinking, I had to get a different apartment.

One way to think about how others' communication affects how we feel about ourselves is to realize that others can be one of the following:

- uppers
- downers
- vultures

Uppers are people who communicate positively about us and who reflect positive appraisals of our self-worth. They notice our strengths, see our progress, and accept our weaknesses and problems without discounting us. When we're around uppers, we feel more upbeat and positive about ourselves. Uppers aren't necessarily unconditionally positive in their communication. A true friend can be an upper by recognizing our weaknesses and helping us work on them. Instead of putting us down, an upper believes in us and helps us believe in ourselves and our capacity to change.

Downers are people who communicate negatively about us and our self-worth. They call attention to our flaws, emphasize our problems, and put down our dreams and goals. When we're around downers, we tend to feel down about ourselves. Reflecting their perspectives, we're more aware of our weaknesses and less confident of what we can accomplish when we're around downers.

Vultures are an extreme form of downers. They not only communicate negative images of us but also attack our self-concepts just as actual vultures prey on their victims (Simon, 1977). Sometimes vultures initiate harsh criticism. They say, "That outfit looks dreadful on you," or "You really blew that one."

In other cases, vultures pick up on our own self-doubts and magnify them. They find our weak spots and exploit them; they pick us apart by focusing on sensitive areas in our self-concept. They might say, "You're the most unproductive person I've ever known. You're a waste of space. Your output doesn't justify your salary." That harangue typifies the attack on self-worth that vultures enjoy. By telling us we are inadequate, vultures demolish our self-esteem.

Reflective Exercise

Choose two people who are uppers in your life. Now, choose two people that are downers. Are there any vultures in your life? Reflect on how you feel about yourself when you're with uppers, downers, and vultures. Can you see how powerfully others' communication affects your self-concept? You might also think about the people for whom you are an upper, downer, or vulture.

Others aren't the only ones whose communication affects our self-concepts. We also communicate with ourselves, and our own messages influence our esteem. One of the most crippling kinds of self-talk we can engage in is **self-sabotage**. This involves telling ourselves we are no good, we can't do something, there's no point in trying to change, and so forth. We may be repeating judgments others made of us or may be inventing negative self-fulfilling prophecies ourselves. Either way, self-sabotage defeats us because it undermines belief in ourselves. Self-sabotage is poisonous; it destroys our motivation to change and grow. We can be downers or even vultures, just as others can be. In fact, we can probably do more damage to our self-concepts than others can because we are most aware of our vulnerabilities and fears. This may explain why vultures were originally described as people who put themselves down.

We can also be uppers for ourselves. We can affirm our strengths, encourage our growth, and fortify our sense of self-worth. Positive self-talk builds motivation and belief in yourself. It is also a useful strategy to interrupt and challenge negative messages from yourself and others. The next time you hear yourself saying "I can't do ..." or someone else says "You'll never change," challenge the self-defeating message with self-talk. Say out loud to yourself, "I can do it. I will change." Use positive self-talk to resist counterproductive communication about yourself.

Review

To Change the Self-Concept

- Spend time around uppers.
- Avoid downers and vultures.
- Avoid self-sabotage.
- Use positive self-talk.

Before leaving this discussion, we should make it clear that improving your self-concept is not facilitated by uncritical positive communication. None of us grows and improves when we listen only to praise, particularly if it is less than honest. The true uppers in our lives offer constructive criticism as a way to encourage us to reach for better versions of ourselves.

Apply the Idea

Improving Your Self-Concept

1. *Define one change you would like to make in yourself. It might be a behaviour or a self-fulfilling prophecy or anything about yourself you would like to alter.*

2. *Write down the change you desire to make. Use strong, affirmative language to motivate yourself. For example, "I will listen more carefully to friends," or "I will start speaking up in classes."*

3. *Refine your general goal by making sure it is realistic and fair. Write out your refined goal using specific language. For example, "I want to show my two best friends that I am paying attention when they talk to me," or "I want to make one comment in each meeting of one class this week."*

4. *Place the card or paper where you will see it often. Each time you see the card, repeat the message aloud to yourself. This should help sustain your commitment to making the change.*

5. *Observe others who are models for what you want to be. Write down what they do. Use specific language to describe how they communicate. For example, "Tracy nods a lot and repeats back what others say so they know she is listening," or "James provides examples of concepts in class so that the ideas are more concrete."*

6. *Select contexts that assist you in reaching your goal. For example, "I will talk with my friends in private settings where there aren't distractions that interfere with listening well," or "I will begin speaking up in class in my Communication course because it is the most discussion-oriented and because other students make a lot of comments there. Later I will speak up in my sociology course, which is more lecture-oriented."*

In sum, improving your self-concept requires being in contexts that support growth and change. Seek out experiences and settings that foster belief in yourself and the changes you desire. Also, recognize uppers, downers, and vultures in yourself and others, and learn which people and which kinds of communication assist you in achieving your own goals for self-improvement.

Chapter Summary

In this chapter, we explored the self as a process that evolves over the course of our lives. We saw that the self is not present at birth but develops as we interact with others. Through communication, we learn and import social perspectives, both those of particular others and those of the generalized other, or society as a whole. Reflected appraisals, direct definitions, and social comparisons are communication processes that shape how we see ourselves and how we change over time. The perspective of the generalized other includes social views of aspects of identity, including ethnicity, gender, sexual orientation, and class. These, however, are arbitrary social constructions that we may challenge once we are adults. When we resist counterproductive social views, we promote change in society.

The final section of the chapter focused on ways to improve self-concept. Guidelines for doing this are to make a firm commitment to personal growth, acquire knowledge about desired changes and concrete skills, set realistic goals, assess yourself fairly, and create contexts that support the changes you seek. Transforming how we see ourselves is not easy, but it is possible. We can make amazing changes in who we are and how we feel about ourselves when we embrace our human capacity to make choices.

Key Concepts

- anxious/resistant attachment style
- attachment styles
- direct definition
- dismissive attachment style
- downers
- ego boundaries
- fearful attachment style
- identity scripts
- particular others
- perspective of the generalized other
- reflected appraisal
- secure attachment style
- self
- self-fulfilling prophecy
- self-sabotage
- social comparison
- uppers
- vultures

For Further Thought and Discussion

1. Complete the last Apply the Idea exercise in this chapter. Set a specific, fair, realistic goal for improving your interpersonal communication. For the next two weeks, focus on making progress toward that goal, following the guidelines in this chapter. Share the results of your work with others in your class.

2. Talk with one man and one woman who are in their 40s. Talk with one man and one woman who are in their 60s. In each conversation, ask them to describe how women and men were expected to act and dress when they were 20 years old. Ask them to explain what behaviours, goals, and attitudes were considered inappropriate for women and men when they were 20 years old. Compare their responses to views held by 20-year-olds today.

3. Think about a time when you tried to create some change in yourself and were not successful. Review what happened by applying the four principles for improving self-concept presented in the last section of this chapter. Now that you understand these principles, how might you be more effective if today you wanted to create that same change in yourself?

4. Use your InfoTrac College Edition to locate one article in a journal that discusses the concept of race. What did you learn from reading this article about the relationship between race and personal identity?

Perception and Communication

Everyday Encounters
By Stephen Lee

Chloe's response reminds us that we all perceive the world around us differently. This chapter focuses on meaning, which is the heart of communication. To understand how humans create meanings for themselves and their activities, we need to explore relationships between perception and communication. As we will see, these two processes interact so that each affects the other in an ongoing cycle of influence. In other words, **perception** shapes how we understand others' communication and how we ourselves communicate. At the same time, communication influences our perceptions of people and situations. The two processes are intricately intertwined in the overall quilt of perception. Before reading further, try to connect the nine dots at right. You may use no more than four lines, the lines must be straight, and the lines must be connected to one another.

To understand how perception and communication interact, we will first discuss the three-part process of perception. Next, we'll consider factors that affect our perceptions. Finally, we will explore ways to improve our abilities to perceive and communicate effectively.

Before we get into those topics, let's return to the nine-dots problem. Could you solve it? Most people who have trouble solving the problem are stymied because they label the nine dots a "square," and they try to connect the dots staying within the boundaries of a square. However, it's impossible to connect the dots with four straight lines if you define them as a closed square. One solution appears at the end of the chapter, on page 119.

This exercise makes an important point about the topics we'll consider in this chapter. The label "square" affects how you perceive the nine dots. In the same fashion, our words affect how we perceive others, situations, and ourselves. At the same time, our perceptions, which are always incomplete and subjective, shape what things mean to us and the labels we use to describe them. As long as we perceive the nine dots as a square, we won't be able to solve the problem. Similarly, we communicate with others according to how we perceive and define them, and we may miss opportunities when our labels limit what we perceive. In the pages that follow, we want to unravel the complex relationships between perception and communication.

Concepts at a Glance

Perception and Communication

- Perception shapes communication.
- Communication influences perception.

Labels limit what we perceive.

Photo: © Corbis/Magma

....

THE PROCESS OF HUMAN PERCEPTION

When we talk about perception, we're concerned with how we make sense of the world and what happens in it. Perception is an active process of creating meaning by selecting, organizing, and interpreting people, objects, events, situations, and activities. The first thing to notice about this definition is that perception is an active process. We are not passive receivers of what is "out

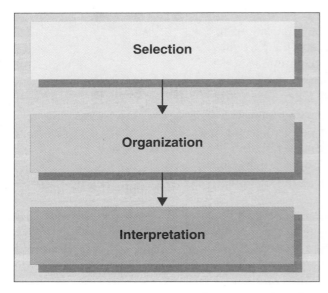

Figure 3.1
The Process of Human Perception

there" in the external world. Instead, we actively work to make sense of ourselves, others, and our interactions. To do so, we select only certain things to notice, and then we organize and interpret what we have selectively noticed. What anything means to us depends on which aspects of it we attend to and how we organize and interpret what we notice. Thus, perception is not a simple matter of recording external reality. Instead, we actively interact with the world to construct what it means to us (Figure 3.1).

Perception consists of three processes—selecting, organizing, and interpreting. These processes are continuous, so they blend into one another. They are also interactive, so each of them affects the other two. For example, what we select to perceive in a particular situation affects how we organize and interpret the situation. At the same time, how we organize and interpret a situation affects our subsequent selections of what to perceive in the situation.

SELECTION

Stop for a moment and notice what is going on around you right now. Is there music in the background or perhaps several different kinds of music from different places? Is the room warm or cold, messy or clean, large or small, light or dark? Is there laundry in the corner waiting to be washed? Can you smell anything—food being cooked, the stale odour of cigarette smoke, traces of cologne? Who else is in the room and nearby? Do you hear other conversations? Is the window open? Can you hear muted sounds of activities outside? Now think about what's happening inside you: Are you alert or sleepy, hungry, comfortable? Do you have a headache or an itch anywhere? On what kind of paper is your book printed? Is the type large, small, easy to read? How do you like the size of the book, the colors used, the design?

Chances are that you weren't conscious of most of these phenomena when you began reading the chapter. Instead, you focused on reading and understanding the material in the book. You narrowed your attention to what you defined as important in this moment, and you were unaware of many other things going on around you. This is typical of how we live our lives. We can't attend to everything in our environment, because there is simply far too much there, and most of it isn't relevant to us at a particular time.

We select the stimuli we attend to based on a number of factors. First, some qualities of external phenomena draw attention. For instance, we notice things that STAND OUT because they are larger, more intense, or more unusual than other phenomena. So we're more likely to hear a loud voice than a soft one and to notice someone in a bright shirt than someone in a drab one. Change also compels attention, which is why we may take for granted all of the pleasant interactions with a friend and notice only the tense moments.

Sometimes we deliberately influence what we notice by indicating things to ourselves (Mead, 1934). In fact, in many ways education is a process of learning to indicate to ourselves things we hadn't seen. Right now you're learning to be more conscious of the selectiveness of your perceptions, so in the future you will notice this more on your own. In literature courses, you learn to notice how authors craft characters and use words to create images. Women's studies classes heighten awareness of the consistent absence of women in conventional accounts of history. In every case, we learn to perceive things we previously didn't recognize. Take a look at Figure 3.2. What do you see? Do you see a vase, or do you see two faces?

Suzanne illustrates how we can use selective perception to our advantage.

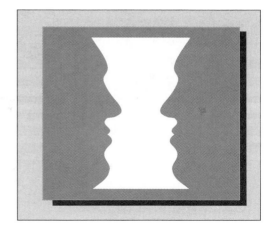

Figure 3.2
Perception: What do you see?

|Student Voices|

Suzanne:

I decided to use the information about selective attention to stop smoking. Usually when I smoked, I noticed how relaxing it was to puff a cigarette and how much I liked the flavour. But this week when I lit up, I would focus on the burning smell of the match. Then I would notice how the smoke hurt my eyes when it rose from the cigarette. I also noticed how nasty ashtrays look with butts in them and how bad a room smells when I've been smoking in it. Once I really paid attention to everything I disliked about cigarettes, I was able to stop. I haven't had one in six days!

What we select to notice is also influenced by who we are and what is going on in us. Our motives and needs affect what we see and don't see. If you've just broken up with a partner, you're more likely to notice attractive people at a party than if you are in an established relationship. Motives also explain the oasis phenomenon in which thirsty people stranded in a desert see an oasis although none really exists. Our expectations further affect what we notice. We are more likely to perceive what we expect to perceive and what others have led us to anticipate. All of us have had this experience when someone tells us that we are going to love or hate an experience before we have it. This explains the self-fulfilling prophecy that we discussed in

Chapter 2; a child who is told she is unlovable may perceive herself that way and may notice only rejecting but not affirming communication from others.

Cultures also influence what we selectively perceive. Assertiveness and competitiveness are encouraged and considered good in individualistic cultures such as Canada, so we don't find it odd when people compete and try to beat each other. By contrast, collectivist cultures emphasize group loyalty, cooperation, and not causing others to lose face. Thus, in many Asian societies competitive individuality is noticed and considered negatively. In Korea, for example, age is a very important aspect of individuals—the older a person is, the more he or she is to be respected. Koreans also place a priority on family relations. Consequently, Koreans learn to selectively perceive the age and family role of people to whom they are speaking. Korean language reflects the cultural value placed on age and family ties by including distinct words to refer to people of different ages and different family status: *gahndah* is used to refer to a teenage peer; *gah*, to a parent; and *gahneh*, to a grandparent (Ferrante, 1995; Park, 1979). Our perceptions are influenced by the cultural milieu in which we live. Consider the influences on your selection process as a result of living in Canada.

Review

Selection *is the process of focusing on*

- The phenomena around us
- Our self-interest
- The culturally familiar

ORGANIZATION

Once we have selected what to notice, we must make sense of it. We don't simply collect perceptions and string them together randomly; instead, we organize them in meaningful ways. The most developed and useful theory for explaining how we organize experience is **constructivism,** which states that we organize and interpret experience by applying cognitive structures called schemata. Originally developed by George Kelly in 1955, constructivism has been elaborated by scholars in communication, psychology, and education. We rely on four schemata to make sense of interpersonal phenomena: prototypes, personal constructs, stereotypes, and scripts (Figure 3.3).

Prototypes

Prototypes are knowledge structures that define the clearest or most representative examples of some category (Fehr, 1993). For example, you probably have a prototype of great teachers, boring teachers, true friends, and perfect romantic partners. Each of these categories is exemplified by a person who is the ideal case—that's the prototype. We use prototypes to place others in categories: Jane is a confidante, Burt is someone to hang out with, Corina is a romantic interest,

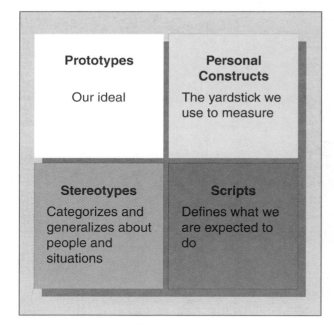

Figure 3.3
Cognitive Schemata Used to Organize and Interpret Experience

Camille:

The person who is my ideal of a friend is my sister Jaden. When my relationship broke up, I was devastated. She stayed by me making sure I ate, got outside once in a while, and listened endlessly to my crying and negativity. She reminded me that yes it is wonderful to have someone to sweep you off your feet but it's also good to have someone to sweep the floor occasionally. I eventually began to feel like life as a single woman wasn't intolerable. She stood by me.

Elfrida is an enemy. Each category of people is exemplified by one person who best represents the whole group.

We also have prototypes for relationships; we have models for the ideal friendship, family, business group, or romantic relationship. Communication scholar Beverly Fehr and her colleagues (Fehr, 1993; Fehr & Russell, 1991) report that the prototype of romantic relationships comprises five qualities: trust, caring, honesty, friendship, and respect. Although passion may come to mind when we think of love, it seems less central to our prototype of love than companionship and caring.

Prototypes define categories by identifying ideal cases. We classify people by asking which of our prototypes they most closely resemble. Prototypes organize our perceptions by allowing us to place people and other phenomena in broad categories. We then consider how close they are to the prototype, or exemplar, of that category.

Personal Constructs

Personal constructs are "mental yardsticks" we use to measure people and situations along bipolar dimensions of judgment (Kelly, 1955). Examples of personal constructs are intelligent–unintelligent, kind–unkind, interesting–boring, arrogant–modest, assertive–passive, and attractive–unattractive. To size up an individual, we measure her or him by personal constructs that we use to distinguish among people. How intelligent, kind, or attractive is this person? Whereas prototypes help decide into which broad category a person or event fits, personal constructs let us make more detailed assessments of particular qualities of phenomena we perceive.

The personal constructs we rely on fundamentally shape our perceptions, because we define something only in the terms of the constructs we use. Notice that we structure what we perceive and what it means by the constructs we choose to use. Thus, we may not notice qualities of people that aren't covered by the constructs we apply.

Nai Lee:

One of the ways I look at people is by whether they are independent or related to others. That is one of the first judgments I make of others. In Korea, we are not so individualistic or independent as people in the West. We think of ourselves more as members of families and communities than as individuals. The emphasis on independent identity was the first thing I noticed when I came to this country, and it is still an important way I look at people.

Apply the Idea

Changing Constructs—Changing Perceptions

Use the left-hand column below to list five adjectives that are important in how you perceive potential romantic partners. These are your personal constructs.

1. _____   1. _____
2. _____   2. _____
3. _____   3. _____
4. _____   4. _____
5. _____   5. _____

Now use the right-hand column to list five other constructs that you could use when you are perceiving potential romantic partners.

How would using the constructs on the right alter or enlarge your perceptions of people you are considering as romantic partners?

Stereotypes

Stereotypes are predictive generalizations about people and situations. Based on the category in which we place someone or something and how it measures up against personal constructs we apply, we predict what it will do. For instance, if you define someone as right wing, you might stereotype her or him as likely to vote Alliance, hold traditional family values, and so forth. You may have stereotypes of artists, athletes, and people from other cultures. The stereotypes you have don't necessarily reflect actual similarities among people. Instead, stereotypes are based on our perceptions of similarities among people or on widely held stereotypes we've internalized.

Social critic Eric Bates (1994) claims that grouping people into racial categories and basing expectations on race may perpetuate racist stereotypes.

Phyllis:

I'll tell you what stereotype really gets to me: the older student. I'm 48 and working on my degree, and everyone at this college treats me like their mother, not a peer. They believe I'm dabbling in courses like a hobby instead of seriously planning a career. They expect I won't understand what the workplace is like nowadays. It's as if I was from another planet instead of another generation.

Our personal constructs create a kind of picture frame through which we view every new person we meet. If they don't fall within the boundaries of our "frame" we may not notice them.

Photo: J. Liburd

Bates also believes that racial categories are no longer accurate for describing people with increasingly multiracial heritages, as discussed in "I'm Cablinasian!" on page 90. Statistics Canada has moved away from the term "race" and instead categorizes people in terms of their ethnic origins. But this is problematic also. Is the term "Asian," for instance, useful for describing people from varied cultures including Japan, Malaysia, and China? Mahicans asks a similar question about the term "First Nations."

Mahicans:

People have a stereotype of First Nations people. Non-aboriginals think we are all alike—how we look, how we act, what we believe, what our traditions are. But that isn't true. The Coast Salish and Cree are as different as people from Kenya and Winnipeg. Some tribes have a history of aggression and violence; others have traditions of peace and harmony. We pray to different spirits and have different tribal rituals and customs. All of these differences are lost when people stereotype us all into one group.

Key Concepts

We may perceive similarities that others don't, and we may fail to perceive commonalities that are obvious to others.

Stereotypes may be accurate or inaccurate. In some cases, we have incorrect understandings of a group, and in other cases individual members of a group don't conform to the behaviours typical of a group as a whole. Although we need stereotypes in order to predict what will happen around us, they can be harmful if we forget that they are based on our perceptions, not objective reality.

Scripts

The final cognitive schemata we use to organize perceptions is **scripts**, which are guides to action based on our experiences and observations of interaction.

What stereotype and personal constructs would you have of the people in this photo?

Photo: J. Liburd

Scripts consist of a sequence of activities that define what we and others are expected to do in specific situations. Many of our daily activities are governed by scripts, although we're often unaware of them. You have a script for greeting casual acquaintances as you walk around campus ("Hey, how's it goin'?" "Fine—can't complain," "See ya"). You also have scripts for dating, managing conflict, talking with professors, dealing with clerks, and hanging out with friends. Scripts organize perceptions into lines of action. ("A Script for Romance" on page 93 describes the commonly held ideas of romance in our culture.)

We use these schemata to make sense of what we notice and to determine how we and others will act in particular situations. All four cognitive schemata reflect the perspectives of particular others and the generalized other. As we interact with people, we internalize our culture's ways of classifying, measuring, and predicting phenomena and its norms for acting in various situations.

Social perspectives are not always accurate or constructive, so we shouldn't accept them blindly. For instance, if your parents engaged in bitter, destructive quarrelling, you may have learned a script for conflict that will undermine your relationships. Similarly, cultural views of groups that are not mainstream are often negative and inaccurate, so we should assess them criti-

Review

We use four cognitive schemata to organize our thinking about people and situations:

- Prototypes
- Personal constructs
- Stereotypes
- Scripts

Communication Notes

I'm Cablinasian!

Tiger Woods firmly, but politely, rejects it when others label him "African American" or "Asian." I'm both and more, he says. As a young boy he made up the term Cablinasian to symbolize his ethnic heritage. He is part Caucasian (Ca), part Black (bl), part Indian (in), and part Asian (asian).

Tiger's not alone in embracing his multiracial identity. Keanu Reeves defines his ethnicity as Hawaiian, Chinese, and White. Mariah Carey identifies herself as Black, Venezuelan, and White. Johnny Depp is Cherokee and White.

As more and more people reflect multiple ethnic heritages, stereotypes of ethnic groups will prove to be very unreliable bases for perceptions of individuals.

Sources: Leland, J., & Beals, G. (1997, May 5). In living color. *Newsweek*, pp. 58–60; Strege, J. (1997). *Tiger: A biography of Tiger Woods.* New York: Bantam Doubleday.

cally before using them to organize our own perceptions and direct our own activities.

Apply the Idea

Sizing Up Others

Pay attention to the cognitive schemata you use the next time you meet a new person. First, notice how you classify the person. Do you categorize her or him as a potential friend, date, bureaucrat, neighbour? Next, identify the constructs you use to assess the person. Do you focus on physical characteristics (attractive–unattractive), mental qualities (intelligent–unintelligent), psychological features (secure–insecure), and/or interpersonal qualities (eligible–committed)? Would different constructs be prominent if you used a different prototype to classify the person? Now, note how you stereotype the person. What do you expect him or her to do based on the prototype and constructs you've applied? Finally, identify your script—how you expect interaction to unfold between you.

INTERPRETATION

Interpretation is the third stage of perception. Even after we have selectively perceived people, interactions, and situations, and we have organized our perceptions, what they mean is not clear. There are no intrinsic meanings in phenomena. Instead, we assign meaning by interpreting what we have noticed and organized.

Interpretation is the subjective process of explaining perceptions in ways that let us make sense of them. To interpret the meaning of another's actions, we construct explanations for what she or he does. The best way to examine the process of interpretation is to discuss attributions.

Attributions

Attributions are explanations of why things happen and why people act as they do (Heider, 1958; Kelley, 1967). Attributions have four dimensions, as shown in Figure 3.4. The first is internal/external locus, which attributes what a person does to either internal factors (he's got a mean personality) or external factors (the traffic jam frustrated him). The second dimension is stable/unstable, which explains actions as the result of stable factors that won't change (she's a Type A personality) or temporary occurrences (she acted that way because she just had a fight with the boss). Global/specific is the third dimension, and it defines behaviour in terms of what activated it. The behaviour may be the result of a general pattern (he's an angry person) or a specific instance (he gets angry about sloppy work). Finally, there is the dimension of responsibility, which attributes behaviours to either factors people can control (she doesn't try to overcome her depression) or to those

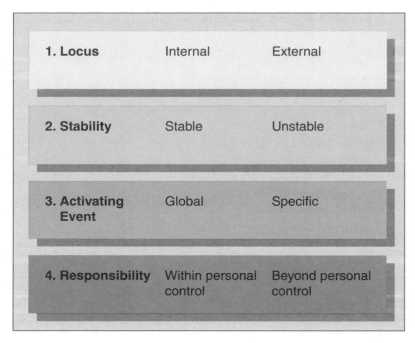

1. Locus	Internal	External
2. Stability	Stable	Unstable
3. Activating Event	Global	Specific
4. Responsibility	Within personal control	Beyond personal control

Figure 3.4
Dimensions of Attributions

they cannot (she is depressed because of a chemical imbalance). In judging whether others can control their actions, we decide whether to hold them responsible for what they do. How we account for others' actions affects our feelings about them and our relationships with them. We can be more or less positive toward others depending on how we explain what they do. "Attributional Patterns and Relationship Satisfaction" on page 95 discusses the connection between attributions couples make and how they feel about their partner.

Our attributions critically influence the meanings we attach to others and their behaviours. For example, how do you account for the fact that a 157 cm woman weighs 91 kilograms? Is she an undisciplined glutton (internal, stable attribution for which the person has control)? Or does she have a hormonal imbalance (internal, not necessarily stable attribution over which the person doesn't have control)? Or is she in a period of severe stress (external, unstable attribution for which control may be arguable)? Each of the three attributions invites a distinct overall view of the individual who weighs 91 kilograms.

Attributional Errors

Concepts at a Glance

Two Common Attributional Errors

1. Self-serving bias
2. Fundamental attribution error

Researchers who have studied the ways that humans explain behaviours have identified two common attributional errors. The first is the **self-serving bias.** As the name implies, this is a bias to favour ourselves and our interests. Research indicates that we tend to construct attributions that serve our personal interests (Hamachek, 1992; Sypher, 1984). Thus, we are inclined to make internal, stable, and global attributions for our positive actions and our successes. We're also likely to claim good results come about because of personal control we exerted. For example, you might say that you did well on a test because you are a smart (internal and stable) person who is always responsible (global) and studies hard (personal control).

The self-serving bias also works in a second way. We tend to avoid taking responsibility for negative actions and failures by attributing them to external, unstable, and specific factors that are beyond personal control. To explain a failing grade on a test, you might say that you did poorly because the professor (external) put a lot of tricky questions on that test (unstable, specific factor) so that all of your studying didn't help (outside personal control). In other words, our misconduct results from outside forces that we can't help, but all the good we do reflects our personal qualities and efforts. This self-serving bias can distort our perceptions.

In a 1996 interview with *Newsweek*'s John McCormick and Sharon Begley, Tiger Woods described how his father taught him to accept responsibility for his bad shots in golf. When he was a preschooler and hit a bad shot, he slammed his club on the ground. His father would ask him, "Who's responsible for that bad shot? The crow that made the noise during your backswing? The bag somebody dropped? Whose responsibility was that?"

Communication Notes

A Script for Romance

Researchers Christine Bachen and Eva Illouz wanted to know how much mass media influence young people's ideas about romance. To find out, they asked students in Grades Three, Four, Ten, and Eleven to pick three out of six photos shown to them that represented a man and a woman who were in love. They then asked the students to select the single photo that best exemplified a man and a woman in love. Next, the researchers asked the students to use their own words to describe a romantic dinner and to describe what happens on a typical first date. Finally, the researchers asked the students to tell an ideal love story.

There was high consensus among students. For the first task, they overwhelmingly chose pictures of couples in exotic locales who were looking directly at each other and touching or kissing. For the second task, the majority of students selected a photo showing a couple on a boat—the most exotic of the pictures they were shown. Descriptions of romantic dinners emphasized atmosphere and visual features of settings—soft lighting, music, exquisite food. Students also agreed on the script for a first date: going out to dinner, although not necessarily a romantic dinner, and/or a movie. Most interesting to the researchers was what students offered as ideal love stories: The stories involved falling in love and getting married, but that wasn't the end. The final focus of students' stories was having children and acquiring material goods to give them comfortable lives.

After analyzing the data, Bachen and Illouz concluded that students' perceptions of love and romance reflect media ideals. Advertising and broadcast media link romance to leisure, consumption, and exotic places and activities—the very things that students associate with love and romance.

Source: Bachen, C., & Illouz, E. (1996). Imagining romance: Young people's culture models of romance and love. *Critical studies of mass communication*, 13, 279–308.

(p. 55). Tiger learned to say it was his responsibility. As he took responsibility for his bad shots, Tiger Woods learned that he could control his skill.

|*Student Voices*|

Jens:

When I do badly on a test or paper, I usually say either the professor was unfair or I had too much to do that week and couldn't study like I wanted to. But when my friends do badly on a test, I tend to think they're not good in that subject or they aren't disciplined or whatever.

The second kind of attributional error is so common it is called the **fundamental attribution error.**

This involves overestimating the internal causes of others' undesirable behaviours and underestimating the external causes. Conversely, we are likely to underestimate the internal causes of our own misdeeds and failures and overestimate the external causes. Consider the following personal account.

The fundamental attributional error was obvious in a legal case in 1997. A woman sued her employer for transferring her. She alleged that he did so because her boss was biased against women. Her boss denied being biased against women. He claimed that he transferred her because he needed someone at another office location, and her poor performance made her the most expendable person in his department. Written records, such as yearly performance reviews, and the woman's own testimony revealed that she had not met all of her job responsibilities and had been told this repeatedly. Further, her boss's record of hiring and promotions proved that nearly 50 percent of his hires and promotions over the past decade had gone to women and minorities. At the trial, the plaintiff was asked if she had considered her performance or the need for new staff at another location to have influenced her boss's decision to transfer her. "No, he did it because he doesn't want to work with women," she replied. Thus, she totally discounted external factors that could explain his decision and placed full responsibility on internal qualities—his alleged gender bias. When asked if she thought her performance might have made her more expendable than others who worked in her former department, she said, "No, the only problems with my performance were due to interruptions and lack of cooperation from others." Thus, she discounted any personal responsibility for errors in her work and laid full responsibility on circumstances beyond her control. In court, an expert witness explained the fundamental attribution error to the jury and showed how it surfaced in the woman's testimony. The jury came back with a judgment against the woman who had sued.

We've seen that perception involves three interrelated processes. The first of these, selection, involves noticing certain things and ignoring others. The second process is organization, whereby we use prototypes, personal constructs, stereotypes, and scripts to order what we have selectively perceived. Finally, we engage in interpretation to make sense of the perceptions we have gathered and organized. Attributions are a primary way we explain what we and others do.

Although we discussed selection, organization, and interpretation separately, in reality they may occur in a different order or simultaneously. Thus, our interpretations shape the knowledge schemata we use to organize experiences, and the ways we organize perceptions affect what we notice and interpret. For instance, in her commentary earlier in this chapter, Nai Lee's interpretations of Westerners' individualism were shaped by the schemata she learned in her homeland of Korea. Also, reliance on the construct of individualistic–communal shaped what she noticed about Westerners. Now

Communication Notes

Attributional Patterns and Relationship Satisfaction

Investigations have shown that happy and unhappy couples have distinct attributional styles. Happy couples make relationship-enhancing attributions. Individuals attribute nice things a partner does to internal, stable, and global reasons. "He got the film for us because he is a good person who always does sweet things for us." Unpleasant things a partner does are attributed to external, unstable, and specific factors. "She yelled at me because all of the stress of the past few days made her not herself."

Unhappy couples employ reverse attributional patterns. They explain nice actions as results of external, unstable, and specific factors. "She got the tape because she had some extra time this particular day." Negative actions are seen as stemming from internal, stable, and global factors. "He yelled at me because he is a nasty person who never shows any consideration to anybody else."

Negative attributions fix pessimistic views and undermine motivation to improve a relationship. Whether positive or negative, attributions may be self-fulfilling prophecies.

Sources: Bradbury, T. N., & Fincham, F. D. (1990). Attributions in marriage: Review and critique. *Psychological Bulletin*, 107, 3–33;. Fletcher, G. J., & Fincham, F. D. (1991). Attribution in close relationships. In G. J. Fletcher & F. D. Fincham (Eds.), *Cognition in close relationships*. Hillsdale, NJ: Erlbaum, pp. 7–35.

that we understand the complex processes involved in perception, we're ready to consider a range of factors that influence what and how we perceive.

INFLUENCES ON PERCEPTION

Concepts at a Glance

There are several factors that influence our perceptions.

- Physiology
- Age
- Culture
- Social roles
- Cognitive abilities
- The self

Consider the following eyewitness account.

There was a frightening fire at the campus during the construction of one of the new buildings a few years ago. An acetylene tank blew up during the tarring of the roof. After the event was over, people were astonished at the various reports of what had occurred.

- There was one big explosion!
- There were two explosions!
- All the windows of Ewing Building were blown out!
- Three windows were broken!
- It was terrifying!
- It was cool!

One student climbed to the top of an adjacent building to film it. He was an applied communications student. His age and experience led him to perceive the event in terms of the visual spectacle it provided. He was awed by the incredible colour and height of the fireball. On the ground, teachers were more concerned with who was in the building, and students were concerned with getting their newly purchased expensive gear out of the classroom they'd just vacated.

As this example illustrates, not everyone perceives situations and people in the same way. In this section, we consider some of the influences on our perceptions.

PHYSIOLOGY

One reason perceptions vary among people is that we differ in our sensory abilities and physiologies. The five senses are not the same for all of us. Music that one person finds deafening is barely audible to another. Salsa that is painfully hot to one diner may seem mild to someone else. On a given day on a Canadian campus, students might wear everything from shorts and sandals to jackets, indicating they have different sensitivities to cold. Some people have better vision than others, and some are colourblind. These differences in sensory abilities affect our perceptions.

Our physiological states also influence perception. If you are tired or stressed, you're likely to perceive things more negatively than you normally would. For instance, a playful insult from a friend might anger you if you're feeling down, but wouldn't bother you if you felt good. Also, you might attribute a stressed friend's behaviours to unstable and specific causes rather than to enduring personality. Each of us has our own biorhythm, which influences the times of day when we tend to be alert or fuzzy. Morning people are alert and creative early in the day and may not notice detail in the afternoon and evening as their energy declines. Medical conditions are another physiological influence on perceptions. If you've ever taken drugs that affected your thinking, you know how dramatically they can alter perceptions of time and experiences. Doctors who prescribe drugs to treat various conditions report that they can alter patients' perceptions radically. People may become severely depressed, paranoid, or uncharacteristically happy under the influence of hormones and other drugs. Changes in our bodies due to medical conditions may also affect what we selectively perceive. A person with a serious back ailment will be far more aware of stairs, uneven ground, and any activities that require bending than someone without back pain.

Are you a morning, afternoon, or evening person?

Photo: © Photodisc

AGE

Age is another factor that influences our perceptions. The older we get, the richer our perspective for perceiving life and people. Thus, compared to a person of 20, a 60-year-old has a more complex fund of experiences to draw on in perceiving situations and people.

Reflective Exercise

Consider the cost of these ordinary purchases:

- A cup of coffee
- A glass of beer
- Parking
- Bus fare
- A litre of milk
- The cost of a movie

Now ask a person in his or her 40s to remember the cost of these when he or she was 20. Ask the same of people in their 60s and 80s. How do these people perceive the cost of living today? Does that perception alter what they choose to do with their money? How does having a point of comparison alter their decisions? Does it alter yours?

Age and the wealth of experiences it brings can also change our perceptions of social life and its problems. The extent of discrimination still experienced by women and minorities understandably discourages many. In the past, few laws protected women and minorities against discrimination in hiring, pay, and advancement. The substantial progress made in the last 50

How does age affect our perceptions?

Photo: A. Henry

years might lead a 75-year-old woman to perceive the current employment climate as open, flexible, and equitable. On the other hand, her experience may also lead her to perceive that nothing is static, and what appears to be progress is only temporary. How different that perception might be from that of a young woman today battling for equal pay in the workplace whose age does not provide her with a point of comparison.

CULTURE

A **culture** consists of beliefs, values, understandings, practices, and ways of interpreting experience that are shared by a number of people. It is a set of assumptions that form the pattern of our lives and that guide how we think, feel, and act. The influence of culture is so pervasive that it's hard to realize how powerfully it shapes our perceptions. Perhaps the best way to recognize the assumptions of our own culture is to travel to places where values, understandings, and codes of behaviour differ.

Consider a few aspects of modern Western culture that influence our perceptions. One characteristic of our culture is the emphasis on technology and its offspring: speed. We expect things to happen quickly—almost instantly. Whether it's instant photos, five-minute copying, or one-hour dry-cleaning, we live at an accelerated pace (Wood, 1995c). We send letters by express mail, jet across the country, and microwave meals. Social commentators suggest that the cultural emphasis on speed may diminish patience and thus our willingness to invest in long-term projects, such as relationships (Toffler, 1970, 1980). In countries such as Nepal and Mexico, life proceeds at a more leisurely pace, and people spend more time talking, relaxing, and engaging in low-key activity. However, in Germany, citizens spend little time on small talk because they tend to regard it as boring and useless.

Canada is largely an individualistic culture in which personal initiative is expected and rewarded. Other cultures, particularly many Asian ones, are more collectivist, and identity is defined in terms of one's family, rather than as an individual quality. Because families are more valued in collectivist cultures, elders are given greater respect and care in those cultures. The difference between collectivist and individualistic cultures is also evident in child-care practices. More communal countries have policies that reflect the value they place on families. In every developed country except the United States, new parents, including adoptive parents, are given at least six weeks of paid parental leave (Wood, 1994d). In Canada, since December 31, 2000, maternity leave has been extended to 50 weeks (15 weeks maternity and 35 weeks parental). Parental leave can be shared by the parenting partners.

Check out the Government of Canada Web site for particulars at <www.hrdc-drhc.gc.ca/ae-ei/pubs/in201_e.shtml#new>

Apply the Idea

Cultural Values

How do values in Western culture affect your everyday perceptions and activities? See if you can trace concrete implications of these cultural values:

Example: Competition. This value is evident in concrete practices such as competitive sports, grading policies, and attempts to get the last word in casual conversations.

- *Productivity*
- *Individualism*
- *Speed*
- *Youth*
- *Wealth*

Discuss with classmates the impact of cultural values on your day-to-day perceptions and activities.

At the University of British Columbia and McMaster University, medicine is taught in a setting of problem-based learning. This new approach to learning in a very traditional and formal discipline such as medicine is refreshing. One of the inclusions in the curriculum is an awareness of the culture a patient comes from and the beliefs and values around healing that the culture advocates. This alters the approach the doctor takes in communication, diagnosis, and treatment. Because culture affects perception, the Western doctor uneducated in the values of other cultures may misdiagnose or be inappropriate in his or her treatment or communication. A Chinese-Canadian living in Vancouver might be taking shark cartilage supplements for the treatment of arthritis, and an insensitive doctor may dismiss the patient as ignorant or superstitious if he or she was not familiar with alternate views of healing. David Suzuki's account of being a Japanese-Canadian (page 100) also illuminates some of the assumptions we make about culture and the impact culture has on our perceptions.

Photo: © Corel

Standpoint

In recent years, scholars have realized that we are affected not only by the culture as a whole but also by our particular location within the culture (Haraway,

Communication Notes

A Japanese-Canadian Perspective
by David Suzuki

My genes can be traced in a direct line to Japan. I am a pure-blooded member of the Japanese race. And whenever I go there, I am always astonished to see the power of that biological connection. In subways in Tokyo, I catch familiar glimpses of the eyes, hairline, or smile of my Japanese relatives. Yet when those same people open their mouths to communicate, the vast cultural gulf that separates them from me becomes obvious: English is my language, Shakespeare is my literature, British history is what I learned, and Beethoven is my music.

Each time I visit Japan, I am reminded of how Canadian I am and how little the racial connection matters. I first visited Japan in 1968 to attend the International Congress of Genetics in Tokyo. For the first time in my life, I was surrounded by people who all looked like me. While sitting in a train and looking at the reflections in the window, I found that it was hard to pick out my own image in the crowd. I had grown up in a Caucasian society in which I was a minority member. My whole sense of self had developed with that perspective of looking different. All my life I had wanted large eyes and brown hair so I could be like everyone else. Yet on that train, where I did fit in, I didn't like it.

Source: John Borovilos, ed., (1990). *Breaking through: A Canadian literary mosaic.* Scarborough, Ontario: Prentice-Hall, pp. 181–82. Reprinted with permission.

1988; Harding, 1991). Standpoint refers to your point of view as it is influenced by your social circumstances.

Standpoint theory claims that a culture includes a number of social groups that distinctively shape perceptions, identities, and opportunities of members. As we saw in Chapter 2, ethnicity, gender, class, and sexual orientation are primary ways that Western culture groups people. Our society attaches differential value to different social groups. The way we perceive the world and ourselves is shaped by our experiences as members of the particular groups to which we belong.

In an early discussion of standpoint, the philosopher Georg Hegel (1807) pointed out that standpoints reflect power positions in social hierarchies. To illustrate, he noted that the institution of slavery is perceived very differently by masters and slaves. Extending Hegel's point, we can see that those in positions of power have a vested interest in preserving the system that gives them privileges. Thus, they are unlikely to perceive its flaws and inequities. On the other hand, those who are disempowered by a system are able to see inequities and discrimination (Harding, 1991).

Women and men, as social groups, have different standpoints, although not every individual man and woman shares the standpoint typical for his or her sex. For instance, the caregiving we generally associate with women is not due to maternal instinct but rather to the social role of mother, which teaches women to care for others, notice who needs what, and defer their own needs (Ruddick, 1989). Other researchers have discovered that men who are in caregiving roles become nurturing, accommodative, and sensitive to others' needs as a consequence of being in the social role of caregiver (Kaye & Applegate, 1990).

Gendered standpoints are also evident in marital conflict. Researchers have found that conflict lessens wives' love for husbands more than it lessens husbands' love for wives (Huston, McHale, & Crouter, 1985; Kelly, Huston, & Cate, 1985). This makes sense when we realize that husbands generally exercise more power over decision-making, so they usually prevail in conflict. Naturally, the winners of conflicts are more satisfied with relationships than the losers!

Gendered standpoints are also obvious in the effort that women and men in general invest in maintaining relationships. Socialized into the role of relationship expert, women are expected by others and themselves to take

Student Voices

Janice:

I'll vouch for the idea of standpoint affecting how we communicate. I was always a pretty independent person. Some people even thought I was kind of selfish, because I really would prioritize myself. Then I had my first baby, and I stayed home with him for a year. I really changed—and I mean in basic ways. I believed that my most important job was to be there for Timmy, and so my whole day focused on him. He was the person I thought about first, not myself. I learned to hear the slightest difference in his cries, so I could tell when he was hungry or needed his diapers changed or wanted company. When I went back to work after a year, a lot of my former colleagues said I was different—much more attentive and sensitive to what they said and more generous with my time than I had been. I guess I developed new patterns of communication as a result of mothering.

Who's taking care of business in this boat?

Photo: © Corel

care of relationships (Tavris, 1992; Wood, 1993, 1994d, 1998). They are supposed to know when something is wrong and to resolve the tension. This may explain why women tend to be more aware than men of problems in relationships (Brehm, 1992; Wood, 1998).

Other standpoints also influence our perceptions. Ethnicity, for example, affects how we perceive ourselves and our families. As we noted previously, many cultures are less individualistic than the majority of Canadians. Yet, even within this country, there are differences among distinct social groups. These differences exhibit in our perceptions of how we care for our children, our elderly, and our sick. Ethnicity will dictate the kind of attention we pay and the responsibility we feel to families.

Apply the Idea

Exploring Standpoints

To become more aware of diverse perspectives on social life, talk with someone whose standpoint differs from your own. Discuss how you and the other person think about families, careers, and attending college. Explore how the individual perceives his or her relationship with his or her family, the financing of his or her education, the expectations on him or her upon graduation. How do these perceptions differ from your own? Does interaction with this person give you new perspectives on familiar things in your life?

Both our membership in an overall culture and our standpoint as members of particular social groups shape how we perceive people, situations, events, and ourselves.

SOCIAL ROLES

Our perceptions are also shaped by our social roles. Both the training that we receive to fulfill a role and the actual demands of the role affect what we notice and how we interpret and evaluate it. Your teacher's perception of your class will likely focus on how interested students seem, whether they appear to have read the material, and whether what they're learning is useful in their lives. Students' perceptions are likely focused on the number and difficulty of tests, whether papers are required, and whether the teacher is interesting. We have different perspectives on what classes are. Some professions, such as police work and the military, require emotional detachment and objectivity. This training influences not only the perception of events and people but also the response to them. We'll discuss the relationship between social roles and communication about emotions more fully in Chapter 4.

|*Student Voices*|

Rebecca:

I was stunned at the impact training can have on the way we take part in the simplest things. I was at the beach with my friend Stan last summer, and his eyes kept darting around the waterfront. At one point he jumped up and ran into the water, reached down and pulled up a coughing, sputtering toddler, much to the shock and gratitude of the parent standing a metre away. Stan is a lifeguard and, although he wasn't on duty that day, he is trained to notice the subtle changes in the splashing water and the look on people's faces. Me, I was just taking in a beautiful scene at the beach and focusing on the sun, the colour of the water, and the sailboats. I hadn't even noticed the distressed child.

COGNITIVE ABILITIES

In addition to physiological, cultural, and social influences, perception is also shaped by our cognitive abilities. How elaborately we think about situations and people, and our personal knowledge of others, affect how we select, organize, and interpret experiences.

Cognitive Complexity

People differ in the number and type of knowledge schemata they use to organize and interpret people and situations. **Cognitive complexity** refers to the number of constructs (remember, these are bipolar dimensions of judgment) used, how abstract they are, and how elaborately they interact to shape perceptions. Most children have fairly simple cognitive systems: they rely on few schemata, focus more on concrete categories than abstract and psychological ones, and often are not aware of relationships among different perceptions. For instance, toddlers often call any and every adult male "Daddy," because they haven't learned more complex ways to distinguish among men.

Concepts at a Glance

There are two aspects of our cognitive abilities that affect communication.

- Cognitive complexity
- Person-centredness

Adults also differ in cognitive complexity, and this affects the accuracy of our perceptions. If you can think of people only as nice or mean, you have a limited range for perceiving the motives of others. Similarly, people who focus on concrete data tend to have less sophisticated understandings than people who also perceive psychological data. For example, you might notice that a person is attractive, tells jokes, and talks to others easily. These are concrete perceptions. At a more abstract, psychological level, you might reason that the concrete behaviours you observe reflect a secure, self-confident personality. This is a sophisticated explanation because it provides a rich perception of why the individual acts as she or he does.

What if you later find out that the person is very quiet in classes? Someone with low cognitive complexity would have difficulty integrating the new information into prior observations. Either the new information would be dismissed because it doesn't fit or the most recent data would replace the former perception and the person would be redefined as shy. A more cognitively complex person would integrate all of the information into a coherent account concluding that the person is very confident in social situations but less secure in academic ones.

Research has shown that cognitively complex individuals are flexible in interpreting complicated phenomena and are able to integrate new information into how they think about people and situations. Individuals who are less cognitively complex are likely to ignore discrepant information that doesn't fit with their impressions or to throw out old ideas and replace them with new impressions (Crockett, 1965; Delia, Clark, & Switzer, 1974). Either way, they fail to recognize the nuances and inconsistencies that are human nature. The complexity of our cognitive systems affects how intricately we perceive people and interpersonal situations.

Person-Centredness

Person-centredness is related to cognitive complexity because it requires abstract thinking and a breadth of schemata. As discussed in Chapter 1, person-centredness is the ability to perceive another as a unique and distinct individual apart from social roles and generalizations based on the person's membership in groups. Our ability to perceive others as unique depends, first, on how well we make cognitive distinctions. People who are cognitively complex rely on more numerous and more abstract schemata to interpret others. Second, person-centred communicators base their interactions on knowledge of particular others. Thus, they use vocabulary and nonverbal behaviours that suit those with whom they interact, and they tailor the content of what they say to the experiences, values, and interests of others. The result is communication that is centred on a specific person.

Recalling the discussion of I–Thou relationships in Chapter 1, you may remember that these are relationships in which people know and value each other as unique individuals. To do so, we must learn about another, and this requires considerable time and interaction. As we get to know another better, we gain insight into how she or he differs from others in a group ("Rob's not obsessive like other political activists I've known," "Ellen's more interested in people than most computer science majors"). The more we interact with another and the greater the variety of experiences we have together, the more insight we gain into her or his motives, feelings, and behaviours. As we come to understand others as individuals, we fine-tune our perceptions of them. Consequently, we're less likely to rely on stereotypes to perceive them. This is why we often communicate more effectively with people we know well than with strangers or casual acquaintances.

Student Voices

Steve:

You really have to know somebody on an individual basis to know what she or he likes and wants. When I first started dating Sherry, I sent her red roses to let her know I thought she was special. That's the "lovers' flower," right? It turns out that was the only flower her father liked, and they had a million red roses at his funeral. Now they make Sherry sad because they remind her he's dead. I also took her chocolates once, then later found out she's allergic to chocolate. By now, I know what flowers and things she likes, but my experience shows that the general rules don't always apply to individuals.

Person-centredness is not the same as empathy.

Empathy is the ability to feel with another person—to feel what she or he feels in a situation. Feeling with another is an emotional response that some scholars believe we cannot fully achieve. Our feelings tend to be guided by our own emotional tendencies and experiences, so it may be impossible to feel exactly what another person feels. What we can do is realize that another is feeling something and connect as well as we can based on our own, different, experiences. A more realistic goal is to learn to adopt dual perspective so that we adapt our communication to other people's frames of reference (Phillips & Wood, 1983; Wood, 1982, 1995a, 1995c). With commitment and effort, we can learn a lot about how others see the world, even if that differs from how we see it. This knowledge, along with cognitive complexity, allows us to be person-centred communicators.

When we take the perspective of others, we try to grasp what something means to them and how they perceive things. This requires suspending judgment at least temporarily. We can't appreciate someone else's perspective when we're imposing our evaluations of whether it is right or wrong, sensible or crazy. Instead, we have to let go of our own perspective and perceptions long enough to enter the world of another person. Doing this allows us to understand issues from another person's point of view, so that we can communicate more effectively with her or him. At a later point in interaction we may choose to express our own perspective or to disagree with another's views. This is appropriate and important in honest communication, but voicing our own views is not a substitute for the equally important skill of recognizing another's perspective.

SELF

The self influences perception.

Photo: L. Raino

A final influence on our perceptions is ourselves. What we selectively perceive and how we organize and interpret phenomena are shaped by many aspects of our selves. Attachment style, which we discussed in Chapter 2, is one obvious influence on interpersonal perceptions. Consider how differently people with the four attachment styles would perceive and approach close relationships. People with secure attachment styles assume that they are lovable and that others are trustworthy. Thus they tend to perceive others and relationships in positive ways. In contrast, people with fearful attachment styles perceive themselves as unlovable and others as not loving. Consequently, they may perceive relationships as dangerous and potentially harmful. The dismissive attachment style inclines individuals to perceive themselves positively, others negatively, and close relationships as undesirable. Individuals who have anxious/resistant attachment styles are often preoccupied with relationships and perceive others in unpredictable ways.

Implicit personality theory also helps explain how the self influences interpersonal perceptions. Implicit personality theory is unspoken and sometimes unconscious assumptions about how various qualities fit together in human personalities (Schneider, 1973). Most of us think certain qualities go together in people. For instance, you might think that a person whom you have observed being outgoing and friendly is also confident and fun. The assumptions that the person is confident and fun are not based on direct knowledge of the person; instead, they are inferences based on your observation that she or he is outgoing and friendly, coupled with your implicit personality theory of what qualities usually accompany outgoingness and friendliness.

Apply the Idea

Discovering Your Implicit Personality Theories

Below are three descriptions of people. After reading each one, list other qualities that you would expect to find in the person described.

- *Jane is highly intelligent and analytical, and she is planning for a career as a trial attorney. She loves to argue issues and enjoys being with others who have sharp reasoning and verbal skills.*

- *Andrew is a loner. He spends a lot of his time in his room reading or surfing the Net. At first, others in his classes invited him to parties, but he never went, so they quit asking him. He is always polite and pleasant to others, but he doesn't seek out company.*
- *Pat loves jokes, including pranks. Those around Pat have learned to expect practical jokes and, also, that Pat enjoys being the recipient of pranks. Pat studies enough to get decent grades, but academics aren't a priority. Seldom seen alone, Pat is a sociable person who likes to have a good time.*

In the Apply the Idea exercise above, you made inferences about Jane, Andrew, and Pat based on what you already knew about them. What is the basis of your inferences? If you're like most people, the basis is others you have known or observed. Thus, how you perceive Jane, Andrew, and Pat reflects as much about you and your experiences as about those individuals. This underlines the fact that how we perceive others and relationships is based not only on what is external to us but also on what is internal.

In sum, we've seen that many factors influence perception and account for differences among people in perceptions. Differences based on physiology, culture and standpoint, social roles, cognitive abilities, and ourselves affect what we perceive and how we interpret others and experiences. In the final section of the chapter, we consider ways to improve the accuracy of our perceptions.

GUIDELINES FOR IMPROVING PERCEPTION AND COMMUNICATION

Perception is a foundation of interpersonal communication. Yet, as we have seen, many factors influence how we perceive others and situations. To be a competent communicator, it's important to form perceptions carefully and check their accuracy. We'll discuss seven guidelines for improving the accuracy of perceptions and, ultimately, the quality of interpersonal communication.

RECOGNIZE THAT ALL PERCEPTIONS ARE PARTIAL AND SUBJECTIVE

What you've read so far makes it clear that our perceptions are inevitably partial and subjective. Each of us perceives from a particular perspective that is shaped by our physiology, culture, standpoint, social roles, cognitive abilities, and aspects of ourselves and our personal experiences. This means that what we perceive is always partial and subjective. It is partial because we cannot perceive everything but instead select only certain aspects of phenomena

Concepts at a Glance

Seven Guidelines for Improving the Accuracy of Perceptions

- Recognize that perceptions are partial and subjective.
- Avoid mindreading.
- Check perceptions with others.
- Distinguish between facts and inferences.
- Guard against the self-serving bias.
- Guard against the fundamental attribution error.
- Monitor labels.

to notice. We then organize and interpret those selected stimuli in personal ways that are necessarily incomplete. Perception is also subjective because it is influenced by individual background and physiology and our personal modes of interpretation.

Objective features of reality have no meaning until we notice, organize, and interpret them. It is our perceptions that construct meanings for the people and experiences in our lives. An outfit perceived as elegant by one person may appear cheap to another. A teacher one student regards as fascinating may put another student to sleep. A weekend camping trip may be a joy to a person who loves the outdoors and an ordeal to an individual not accustomed to roughing it. It is difficult, if not impossible, to determine the truth or falsity of perceptions, because they are not objective descriptions. Instead, perceptions represent what things mean to individuals.

The subjective and partial nature of perceptions has implications for interpersonal communication. One implication is that when you and another person disagree about something, neither of you is necessarily wrong or crazy. It's more likely that you have attended to different things and that there are differences in your personal, social, cultural, and physiological resources for perceiving. A second implication is that it's wise to remind ourselves that we profoundly influence how we perceive others. As we have seen, our perceptions are based at least as much on ourselves as on anything external to us. If you perceive another person as domineering, there's a chance that you are feeling insecure in your ability to interact. If you perceive others as unfriendly toward you, it may be that you think of yourself as unworthy of friends. Remembering that perceptions are partial and subjective curbs the tendency to think our perceptions are the only valid ones or that they are based exclusively on what lies outside of us.

Student Voices

Joelle:

So this girl I met a few weeks ago said she was having a party, and it would be lots of fun with some cool people. She asked if I wanted to come, so I said, "Sure—why not?" When I got there everybody was drinking—I mean seriously drinking. They were playing this weird music—sort of morbid—and they had a horror flick going nonstop. They got so loud that the neighbours came over and told us to hold it down. In a couple of hours most of the people there were totally wasted. That's not my idea of fun. That's not my idea of cool people.

AVOID MINDREADING

Because perception is subjective, people differ in what they notice and in what it means to them. One of the most common problems in interpersonal communication is **mindreading,** which is assuming we understand what another person thinks or perceives. When we mind read, we don't check with another person to see what he or she is thinking. Instead, we act as if we know what's on another's mind, and this can get us into considerable trouble. John Gottman and his colleagues identify mindreading as one of the behaviours that contributes to interpersonal tension (Gottman, 1993; Gottman, Notarius, Gonso, & Markman, 1976). The danger of mindreading is that we may misinterpret others and have no way of checking on the accuracy of our perceptions. Sometimes we do understand one another, but sometimes we don't.

Consequently, for the most part mindreading is more likely to harm than help interpersonal communication. Consider a few examples. One person might say to her partner, "I know you didn't plan anything for our anniversary, because it doesn't matter to you." Whether or not the partner made plans, it's impossible to guess motives or to know why the partner forgot, if indeed he did. A supervisor might notice an employee is late for work several days in a row and say, "Obviously, you're no longer committed to your job." One friend might say to another, "You were late coming over because you're still mad about what happened yesterday." The speaker is guessing reasons for the friend's tardiness and could well be wrong. Mindreading also occurs when we say things such as "I know why you're upset" (Has the person said she or he is upset?) or "You don't care about me anymore" (maybe the other person is too preoccupied or worried to be as attentive as usual). We also mind read when we tell ourselves we know how somebody else will feel or react, or what he or she will do. The truth is, we don't really know—we're only guessing. When we mind read, we impose our perspectives on others instead of allowing them to say what they think. This can cause misunderstandings as well as resentment, because most of us prefer to speak for ourselves.

CHECK PERCEPTIONS WITH OTHERS

The third guideline follows directly from the first two. Because perceptions are subjective and partial, and because mindreading is an ineffective way to figure out what others think, we need to check our perceptions with others. In the first example above, it would be wise to ask, "Did you forget our anniversary?" If the partner did forget, then the speaker might ask, "Why do you think you forgot?" The person may not know why, or the reasons may not be satisfactory, but asking is a better way to open a productive dialogue than attributing bad motives to another.

Adriana:

Mindreading drives me crazy. My boyfriend does it all the time, and he's wrong as often as he's right. Last week he got tickets to a concert because he "knew" I'd want to go. Maybe I would have if I hadn't already planned a trip that weekend, but he never checked on my schedule. A lot of times when we're talking, he'll say something, then before I can answer he says, "I know what you're thinking." Then he proceeds to run through his ideas about what I'm thinking. Usually he's off base, and then we get into a sideline argument about why he keeps assuming what I think instead of asking me. I really wish he would ask me what I think.

Concepts at a Glance

There are three steps to perception-checking:

1. State what it is that you have observed.

2. Give one or two possible interpretations of the behaviour.

3. Request clarification or confirmation of the behaviour.

Perception-checking is an important communication skill because it helps people arrive at mutual understandings of each other and their relationships.

An example of a perception check might look like this. If your partner seems less attentive than usual, you might say:

"You seem distracted when we talk" (observable data). "Are you worried about something, or are you losing interest in our relationship?" (possible interpretations). "What's going on for you these days?" (request for clarification).

When checking perceptions, it's important to use a tentative tone, rather than a superior or accusatory one. This minimizes defensiveness and encourages good discussion. Just let the other person know you've noticed something and would like him or her to clarify his or her perceptions of what is happening and what it means.

Apply the Idea

Checking Perceptions

I. Reflective Exercise

To gain skill in perception-checking (and all communication behaviours), you need to practise. Try these exercises:

* *Monitor your tendencies to mindread, especially in established relationships in which you feel you know your partner well.*

* *The next time you catch yourself mindreading, stop. Instead, perception-check. Describe what you are noticing, interpret the behaviour in two plausible ways, and invite her or him to explain how she or he perceives what's happening.*

- *Engage in perception-checking for two or three days so that you have lots of chances to see what happens. When you're done, reflect on the number of times your mindreading was inaccurate.*
- *How did perception-checking affect interaction with your friends and romantic partners? Did you find out things you wouldn't have known if you'd engaged in mindreading?*

II. Practical Exercise

Provide a good perception check for the following scenarios.

You pass a good friend in the hall, you smile and say hi. Your friend looks at you and keeps walking without responding.

_____

_____

_____

You lend your car to a friend with the request to fill it up upon return. You jump in your car the next morning to find the gas tank empty.

_____

_____

_____

You clearly tell your friends that you do not want to be set up on a blind date. You arrive for dinner at their house to find a stranger, completing a cozy foursome. You wait until you are alone with your friends and you say:

_____

_____

_____

Communication Blooper

Perception-checking using loaded, aggressive language will backfire! For example:
"You seem distracted lately. What's the matter, has early Alzheimer's settled in, or are you cheating on me?" This caustic response will surely create a defensive response in your partner. Check perceptions with a real desire to understand your partner.

DISTINGUISH BETWEEN FACTS AND INFERENCES

Competent interpersonal communication also depends on distinguishing facts from inferences. A fact is an objective statement based on observation. An inference involves an interpretation that goes beyond the facts. For example, a student consistently comes to class late and sits at the back of the room, sometimes dozing off during discussions. The teacher might think, "That student is rude and unmotivated." The facts are that the student comes late, sits toward the rear of the classroom, and sometimes falls asleep.

Defining the student as rude and unmotivated is an inference that goes beyond the facts. The fact might be that the student is tired because he or she has a job that ends right before the class.

It's easy to confuse facts and inferences because we sometimes treat the latter as the former. When we say, "The student is rude," we've made a statement that sounds factual, and we may then regard it that way ourselves. To avoid this tendency, substitute more tentative words for is. For instance, "The student seems rude" or "This student may be being rude" are more tentative statements that keep the speaker from treating an inference as a fact. "The Truth, the Whole Truth, and Nothing but the Truth" explores the influence of language on our perceptions. Our implicit personality theories consist of inferences—assumptions beyond what we have observed about others. Inferences aren't necessarily bad. In fact, we must make inferences to function in the world. Yet, we risk misperceptions and misunderstandings if we don't distinguish our inferences from facts. Learning to make the distinction is an important interpersonal communication skill.

Communication Notes

The Truth, the Whole Truth, and Nothing but the Truth

Research indicates that eyewitness testimony may not be as accurate as we often assume. Studies show that witnesses' perceptions are shaped by the language attorneys use.

In one experiment, viewers were shown a film of a traffic accident and then were asked, "How fast were the cars going when they smashed into each other?" Other viewers were asked how fast the cars were going when they bumped or collided. Viewers testified to significantly different speeds depending on which word was used in the question.

In a separate experiment, viewers were shown a film of a traffic accident and then filled out a questionnaire that included questions about things that had not actually been on the film. Viewers who were asked, "Did you see the broken headlight?" more frequently testified they saw it than did viewers who were asked, "Did you see a broken headlight?"

The accidents that viewers "saw" were shaped by the words used to describe them.

Source: Trotter, R. J. (1975, October 25). "The truth, the whole truth, and nothing but ..." *Science News*, 108, 269.

Apply the Idea

Using Tentative Language

To become more sensitive to our tendencies to confuse facts and inferences, pay attention to the language you use for the next 24 hours when you describe people and interactions. Listen for words such as "is" and "are" that imply factual information. Do you find there are instances in which more tentative language would be more accurate?

Now extend your observations to other people and the language they use. When you hear others say, "she is," "they are," or "he is," are they making factual statements or are they making inferences?

GUARD AGAINST SELF-SERVING BIAS

Earlier in this chapter, we discussed the self-serving bias, which involves attributing our successes and positive behaviours to internal and stable qualities in us that we control and attributing our failures and negative behaviours to external, unstable factors beyond our control. Because this bias can distort perceptions, we need to monitor it carefully. Try to catch yourself in the act of explaining away your failures or adverse behaviours as not your fault and taking personal credit for accomplishments that were helped along by luck or situational factors. The self-serving bias also inclines us to notice what we do and to be less aware of what others do. Obviously, this can affect how we feel about others, as Janet illustrates in her comments.

Monitoring the self-serving bias also has implications for how we perceive others. Just as we tend to judge ourselves generously, we may also be inclined to judge others too harshly. Monitor your perceptions to see whether you attribute others' successes and admirable actions to external factors beyond their control and their shortcomings and blunders to internal factors they can (should) control. If you do this, substitute more generous explanations for others' behaviours and notice how that affects your perceptions of them.

GUARD AGAINST FUNDAMENTAL ATTRIBUTION ERROR

A second error in interpretation that we discussed is the fundamental attribution error. As you recall, this occurs when we overestimate the internal causes and underestimate external causes for undesirable behaviour from others and when we underestimate the internal causes and overestimate the external causes for our own failings or bad behaviours. Engaging in the

Janet:

For years, my husband and I have argued about housework. I am always criticizing him for not doing enough, and I have felt resentful about how much I do. He always says to me that he does a lot, but I just don't notice. After studying the self-serving bias in class, I did an "experiment" at home. I watched him for a week and kept a list of all the things he did. Sure enough, he was—is—doing a lot more than I had thought. I never noticed that he sorted laundry or walked the dog four times a day or wiped the kitchen counters after we'd finished fixing dinner. I noticed everything I did but only the big things he did like vacuuming. I simply wasn't seeing a lot of his contributions to keep our home in order.

fundamental attribution error distorts perceptions—both of ourselves and others. Thus, we want to guard against it in our interpersonal interactions.

To reduce your chances of falling victim to the fundamental attribution error, you can prompt yourself to look for external causes of behaviours from others that you don't appreciate. Instead of assuming the unwanted behaviour reflects the other's motives or personality, ask yourself, "What factors in the person's situation might lead to this behaviour?" You can ask the converse question to avoid underestimating internal influences on your own undesirable actions. Instead of letting yourself off the hook by explaining a misdeed as due to circumstances you couldn't control, ask yourself "What inside of me that is my responsibility influenced what I did?" Looking for external factors that influence others' communication and internal factors that influence your communication checks our tendency to engage in the fundamental attribution error.

Apply the Idea

Guarding against the Fundamental Attribution Error

For each scenario described below, write out an alternate explanation based on *external* factors that might account for the other person's behaviour.

- *The person you've been dating for a while is late to meet you. It is the third time this month you've had to wait, and you are angry that your date is so inconsiderate.*

- *You're talking with a friend about your serious concerns about what you will do after you graduate. You notice that your friend seems uninterested and keeps looking at her watch. You think to yourself, "If you are so self-centred you can't make time for me, I don't need you for a friend."*

For each scenario described below, write out an alternate explanation based on *internal* factors that could influence your behaviour.

- *You are running late, so when a friend stops by to chat, you don't invite him in and don't encourage conversation. Your friend says, "You're being a real jerk." You think to yourself, "This has nothing to do with me. It has to do with all of the pressures I'm facing."*

- *During an argument with your roommate about who is going to do grocery shopping, you get really angry. Without thinking, you blurt out, "With all of the weight you've gained, you should stop thinking about groceries." Your roommate looks hurt and leaves the room. Afterward, you think, "Well, I wouldn't have said that if she hadn't been so belligerent."*

MONITOR LABELS

Words crystallize perceptions. Until we label an experience, it remains nebulous and less than fully formed in our thinking. Only when we name our feelings and thoughts do we have a clear way to describe and think about them. But just as words crystallize experiences, they can also freeze thought. Once we label our perceptions, we may respond to our own labels rather than to actual phenomena. If this happens, we may communicate in ways that are insensitive and inappropriate.

Consider this situation. Suppose you get together with five others in a study group, and a student named Andrea monopolizes the whole meeting with her questions and concerns. Leaving the meeting, one person says, "Gee, Andrea is so selfish and immature! I'll never work with her again." Another person responds, "She's not really selfish. She's just insecure about her grades in this course, so she was hyper in the meeting." Chances are these two people will perceive and treat Andrea differently depending on whether they label her "selfish" or "insecure." The point is that once the two people have labelled Andrea's behaviour based on their subjective and partial perceptions, they may not respond to Andrea herself, but to the words they use to label their perceptions of her.

Effective communicators realize that the words they use influence their perceptions. In Chapter 5, we consider in depth how language affects perception. For now, remember that when we engage in interpersonal communication, we abstract only certain aspects of the total reality around us. Our perceptions are one step away from reality, because they are always partial and subjective. We move a second step from reality when we label a perception. We move even further from the actual reality when we respond not to behaviours or our perceptions of them but instead to the label we impose. This process can be illustrated as a ladder of abstraction (Figure 3.5, on page 117), a concept emphasized by one of the first scholars of interpersonal communication (Hayakawa, 1962, 1964).

We should also monitor our labels to adapt our communication to particular individuals. Competent interpersonal communicators choose words that are sensitive to others and their preferences. This is especially important when we are talking with or about identities. Many adult females resent being called "girls," so it is better to address and refer to them as "women." Most gays and lesbians reject the label "homosexual," and they may resent hearing themselves described by that label. A great many people who have disabilities do not want to be called "disabled persons." Many feel this label suggests they are disabled as persons simply because they have some physical or mental condition. Most of them refer to themselves as "persons with disabilities," and that is how they prefer others to refer to them (Braithwaite, 1996).

Is effective, sensitive communication possible when there are no universal guidelines for what to call people? Yes, if we are willing to invest thought and effort in our interactions. We begin by assuming we may not know how others want to be labelled and that not all members of a group have the same preferences. Just because one of your friends wants to be called "Black," you shouldn't assume others share that preference. It's appropriate to ask others how they identify themselves. Asking shows that we care about their preferences and want to respect them. This is the heart of person-centred communication.

Perceiving accurately is neither magic nor an ability that some people just naturally have. Instead, it is a communication skill that can be developed and practised. Following the seven guidelines we have discussed will allow you to make more careful and accurate perceptions in interpersonal communication situations.

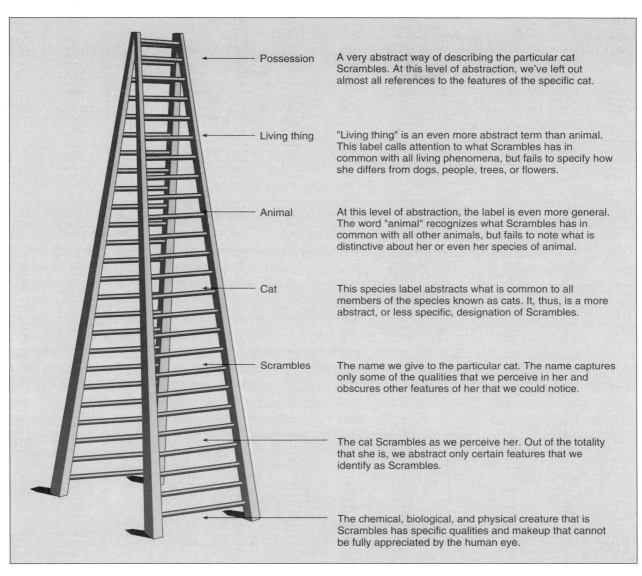

Possession — A very abstract way of describing the particular cat Scrambles. At this level of abstraction, we've left out almost all references to the features of the specific cat.

Living thing — "Living thing" is an even more abstract term than animal. This label calls attention to what Scrambles has in common with all living phenomena, but fails to specify how she differs from dogs, people, trees, or flowers.

Animal — At this level of abstraction, the label is even more general. The word "animal" recognizes what Scrambles has in common with all other animals, but fails to note what is distinctive about her or even her species of animal.

Cat — This species label abstracts what is common to all members of the species known as cats. It, thus, is a more abstract, or less specific, designation of Scrambles.

Scrambles — The name we give to the particular cat. The name captures only some of the qualities that we perceive in her and obscures other features of her that we could notice.

The cat Scrambles as we perceive her. Out of the totality that she is, we abstract only certain features that we identify as Scrambles.

The chemical, biological, and physical creature that is Scrambles has specific qualities and makeup that cannot be fully appreciated by the human eye.

Figure 3.5
Labels, Perception, and Influence

Chapter Summary

In this chapter, we've explored human perception, a process that involves selecting, organizing, and interpreting experiences. These three processes are not separate in practice; instead, they interact so that each one affects the others. What we selectively notice affects what it is that we interpret and evaluate. At the same time, our interpretations become a lens that influences what we notice in the world around us. Selection, interpretation, and evaluation interact continuously in the process of perception.

We have seen that perception is influenced by many factors. Our sensory capacities and our physiological condition affect what we notice and how astutely we recognize stimuli around us. In addition, our cultural backgrounds and standpoints in society shape how we see and interact with the world. Social roles are another influence on perception. Thus, our professional training and our roles in families affect what we notice and how we organize and interpret it. Interpersonal perception is also influenced by cognitive abilities including cognitive complexity, person-centredness, and perspective-taking. Finally, our perceptions are shaped by who we are and what experiences we have had. Thus, interpersonal perceptions reflect both what is inside us and what is outside us.

Understanding how perception works provides a foundation for improving our perceptual capacities. We discussed seven guidelines for improving the accuracy of perceptions. First, realize that all perceptions are subjective and partial, so there is no absolutely correct or best understanding of a situation or a person. Second, because people perceive differently, we should avoid mindreading or assuming

we know what others are perceiving and what their actions mean. Third, it's a good idea to check perceptions, which involves stating how you perceive something, providing possible interpretations, and asking for clarification. A fourth guideline is to distinguish facts from inferences. Avoiding the self-serving bias is also important, because it can lead us to perceive ourselves too charitably and to perceive others too harshly. We should also guard against the fundamental attribution error, which can undermine the accuracy of our explanations for how we and others communicate. Finally, it's important to monitor the labels we use. This requires us to be aware that our labels reflect our perceptions of phenomena and to be sensitive to the language others prefer, especially in describing their identities. Just as we can't see how to solve the nine-dots problem if we label the dots "a square," so we cannot see aspects of ourselves and others when our labels limit our perceptions. Realizing this encourages us to be more sensitive to the power of language and to make more considered word choices.

Perception is a process of abstracting in which we move further and further away from the concrete reality as we select, organize, interpret, evaluate, and label phenomena. We need to know when we are making factual descriptions and when we are making inferences that require checking.

What we have covered in this chapter allows us to understand how we perceive others and situations and how we might improve our perceptual skills. In the next chapter, we explore the power of language in greater depth, and we will see how what we say affects our interpersonal relationships.

Key Concepts

- attributions
- cognitive complexity
- constructivism
- culture
- empathy
- fundamental attribution error
- implicit personality theory
- interpretation
- mindreading

- perception
- personal constructs
- prototypes
- scripts
- self-serving bias
- standpoint theory
- stereotypes

For Further Thought & Discussion

1. To understand how your standpoint influences your perceptions, try visiting a social group that is different from your own. If you are Christian, you could go to a Jewish synagogue or a Buddhist temple. While in the unfamiliar setting, what stands out to you? Attend a meeting of International students. What verbal and nonverbal communications do you notice? Do these stand out because they are not present in your usual settings? What does your standpoint highlight and obscure?

2. Think of two situations: one in which you perceive that the majority of people are like you (same sex, ethnicity, sexual orientation, age) and one in which you perceive that you are a minority. How does your sense of being a majority or minority in each setting influence your perceptions of others who are present?

3. Identify an example of the self-serving bias in your interpersonal perceptions. Describe how you explained your and others' behaviours. Then, revise your explanation so that the self-serving bias is eliminated.

4. Identify an example of the fundamental attribution error in your interpersonal perceptions. Describe how you explained your and others' behaviours. Then, revise your explanation so that it doesn't reflect the fundamental attribution error.

5. Use the ladder of abstraction to describe the relationships among perception, communication, and action in one interpersonal encounter in your life. First, describe the total situation as fully as you can (your descriptions won't be absolutely complete— that's impossible). Next, describe what behaviours and environmental cues you noticed. Then, identify the way you labelled what was happening and others who were present. Finally, describe how you acted in the situation. Now, consider alternative selective perceptions you might have made and how those might have influenced your labels and actions.

6. Use your InfoTrac College Edition to find articles dealing with how race is defined. Describe the controversy among scholars regarding how races are perceived. Conduct a survey to determine the most current politically correct terminology to define different ethnic groups.

Solution to the problem on page 83.

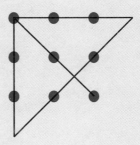

Emotions and Communication

Everyday Encounters
By Stephen Lee

Chloe? How do you feel about this relationship?

Well, I feel a little lost, somewhat queasy and a bit unsure of the next move, certainly a little fearful and a teenie bit excited.

And you?

I'm cool.

Turn off the charm, bud

Anthony's Story

My live-in partner of a year brought a kitten home. At first, we were thrilled with the new addition to "our family." Soon after, I began to feel distant. I'd sit for long periods not engaging my partner in conversation. Anxious, she would ask me what was wrong. I didn't know. I only knew that something uncomfortable was happening to me. She asked me if it was the cat. I said "No." She asked if I wanted to be alone. I said "Sometimes." Insightfully, she asked, "Is this too much like marriage?" I said "Yes." She asked if I wanted her to leave. I could only answer "Not really." It took some time and a lot of talking for me to sort out the confusing mix of feelings I was experiencing. On the one hand, she was right. This was all getting very domestic. I was panicking. On the other hand, the option of being alone again was not attractive nor was it what I wanted. I did however feel overwhelmed with what appeared like an escalation of responsibilities and commitment and yet I didn't believe I had a choice. To speak up about feeling crowded and pressured was unthinkable. I couldn't bear for her to leave. On the other hand, I wasn't sure I could put everything on hold and "start a family." The kitten was a symbol.

Emotions, or feelings, are part of our lives. We feel happiness, sadness, shame, pride, embarrassment, envy, disappointment, and a host of other emotions. And we express our emotions in interpersonal communication. We may express emotions nonverbally (smiling, trembling, blushing) or verbally ("I'm scared," "I feel anxious about the interview"). Sometimes we express emotions through complex verbal messages such as metaphors and similes (Kovecses, 1990). For instance, you might say, "I feel like a plane that's soaring," or "I am a bomb, just waiting to explode." And of course, in many situations, we communicate emotions both verbally and nonverbally, for example, saying "I'm so happy right now" while smiling.

Photo: M. Salez

Although we experience and express feelings, we don't always do so effectively. Sometimes, like Anthony, we aren't able to identify exactly what we feel. Even if we can recognize our emotions, we aren't always sure how to express them clearly and constructively. We may not realize what goal we have for expressing emotions. Do we just want to get feelings out, or do we want another person to comfort us, reassure us, or behave differently toward us? In order to communicate well, we need to develop skill in identifying and expressing our feelings in ways that support particular communication goals.

Emotions are a constant dimension of interpersonal communication. In this chapter, we'll examine how to identify and communicate emotions in healthy, effective ways. We'll begin by considering the idea that there is emotional intelligence, analogous to cognitive intelligence. Next, we will define emotions and examine the sources of emotions and expression of them. This will include examining the family scripts you learned about the expression of emotion. Third, we'll explore the difference between experiencing emotions and expressing them. Finally, we'll discuss guidelines for communicating emotions in ways that foster our individual growth and the quality of our relationships with others.

EMOTIONAL INTELLIGENCE

Emotions are intricately woven into the fabric of interpersonal communication and close relationships. By extension, how effectively and constructively we communicate emotions profoundly influences the depth and quality of our relationships. According to Daniel Goleman, emotional development and skill are critical to personal, social, and professional success. In his 1995 book *Emotional Intelligence*, Goleman claims that there is a kind of intelligence distinct from the type measured by standard IQ tests.

Goleman's book popularized an idea that Carol Saarni (1990) originated. In Saarni's early work, she emphasized a quality she called emotional competence, which includes the awareness of our own emotions, the ability to recognize and empathize with others' emotions, the realization of the impact of our expression of emotions on others, and the sensitivity to cultural rules for expressing emotions. Saarni also emphasized that we often experience several emotions simultaneously. Being aware that we sometimes feel multiple emotions at the same time is another aspect of emotional competence.

Emotional intelligence is the ability to recognize which feelings are appropriate in which situations and the skill to communicate those feelings effectively. According to Goleman (1995a, 1995b), people who have high EQs (emotional intelligence quotients) are more likely than people with lower EQs to create satisfying relationships, to be comfortable with themselves, and to succeed in careers that require skills in reading people and responding sensitively to others and situations.

Emotional intelligence includes a number of qualities that aren't assessed by conventional intelligence tests:

- being in touch with your feelings
- managing your emotions without being overcome by them (for example, not letting anger consume you)
- not letting setbacks and disappointments derail you
- channelling your feelings to assist you in achieving your goals
- having a strong sense of empathy—being able to understand how others feel without their spelling it out
- listening to your and others' feelings so you can learn from them
- having a strong yet realistic sense of optimism

Goleman notes that "so far, there's no single, well-validated paper-and-pencil test for emotional intelligence" (1995b, p. 74). However, Goleman has developed some questions (1995b, pp. 74, 75) that allow you to get an approximate measure of your EQ, which have been adapted in Apply the Idea so that you can test your EQ.

Apply the Idea

What's Your EQ?

1. Imagine you're on an airplane and it suddenly begins rolling dramatically from side to side. What would you do?

   a. Keep reading your book and ignore the turbulence.

   b. Become vigilant in case there is an emergency. Notice the flight attendants and review the card with instructions for emergencies.

   c. A little of a and b.

   d. Not sure—I never noticed an airplane's motion.

2. Imagine that you expect to earn an A in a course you are taking, but you get a C on your midterm exam. What would you do?

   a. Develop a specific plan to improve your grade and resolve to implement the plan.

   b. Resolve to do better in the future.

   c. Nurture your self-concept by telling yourself the grade doesn't really matter and focus on doing well in your other courses.

   d. Go to see the professor and try to talk him or her into raising your midterm grade.

3. While you are a passenger in a friend's car, your friend becomes enraged at another driver who just cut in front of him. What would you do?

   a. Tell your friend to let it slide—that it's no big deal.

   b. Put in your friend's favourite CD and turn up the volume to distract him.

   c. Agree with him and show rapport by talking about what a jerk the other driver is.

   d. Tell him about a time when someone cut in front of you and how mad you felt, but explain you then found out the other driver was on her way to the hospital.

4. You and your girlfriend or boyfriend have just engaged in an argument that has become a heated shouting contest. By now, you're both very upset, and each of you has started making nasty personal attacks on the other. What do you do?

   a. Suggest the two of you take a 20-minute break to cool down and then continue the discussion.

   b. Decide to put an end to the argument by not talking anymore. Just be silent and don't speak no matter what the other person says.

c. *Apologize to your partner and ask him or her to say "I'm sorry" too.*

d. *Pause to collect your thoughts, then explain your views and your side of the issue clearly.*

Scoring your EQ: Award yourself the following points for each response:

1. *a = 20, b = 20, c = 20, d = 0*
2. *a = 20, b = 0, c = 0, d = 0*
3. *a = 0, b = 5, c = 5, d = 20*
4. *a = 20, b = 0, c = 0, d = 0*

Higher scores indicate greater emotional intelligence.

Goleman insightfully notes that being aware of our emotions and being able to express them appropriately enhance our personal health and the quality of our relationships with others. Yet we are not always as effective as we might be in recognizing and expressing our emotions. Thus, developing skill in understanding and expressing your emotions will enable you to be more effective in your interpersonal communication. Understanding between people depends on their being able to know what they feel and to be able to express their feelings clearly. "Chelsey's Smile" demonstrates how important it is to be able to express emotions.

Communication Notes

Chelsey's Smile

At five years old, Chelsey Thomas was used to being ridiculed by her schoolmates. "She's ugly," they taunted. "Her face is funny." The problem was that Chelsey had a rare congenital condition called Moebius syndrome. This condition causes incomplete or absent development of muscles that control facial expressions. As a result, the corners of Chelsey's mouth perpetually sagged. She couldn't move her mouth to express the range of emotions she felt. Most important to Chelsey, she couldn't smile. Her peers thought she was unfriendly or bored because she never smiled at them. Consequently, Chelsey had few friends.

There's a happy ending to Chelsey's story. She had surgery in which muscles from her thigh were transplanted to her fifth cranial nerve. After the surgery, she could pronounce words more clearly, prevent her lower lip from drooping, and chew normally. And she could smile. People no longer perceived her as unfriendly because she had the physical ability to communicate feelings with facial expressions.

Sources: Dimmitt, B. (1997, July). Chelsey's missing smile. *Reader's Digest*, pp. 87–93; Little girl has smile surgery. (1995, December 16). *Raleigh News and Observer*, p. 14A.

Emotional intelligence is not just understanding your feelings. It also requires skill in knowing how to express your feelings constructively. To illustrate this point, let's return to the opening scenario. Once Anthony had realized that his feelings were valid and not threatening, he was able to express them to Natasha without fear of terrible reprisals. He could feel the feelings of entrapment, panic, resentment, and not act on them. He could permit himself to **feel**! What he needed to learn was to express his feelings. Anthony was able to say "You know, I'm not sure I'm up for this. I don't even know where my own career is going and caring for this kitten has made me think what it must be like to care for children in some ways. It's scaring me. But I also don't want to lose you." This couple's dilemma is not over, but they can now openly discuss and problem-solve because the feelings are not hidden behind an ambiguous silence.

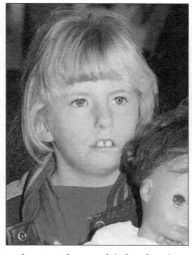

Photos: © Ut/AP (left); © Michael Tweed/AP (right)

Apply the Idea

Identifying Your Emotions

Not everyone experiences the full range of emotions, and most of us don't experience all emotions with equal frequency. Check the emotions listed below that are most familiar to you, then compare your list of familiar emotions with your classmates'. What can you conclude about yourself and others?

_____ abandonment	_____ hopelessness	_____ shame
_____ anger	_____ insecurity	_____ surprise
_____ apathy	_____ isolation	_____ suspicion
_____ depression	_____ jealousy	_____ sympathy
_____ disappointment	_____ joy	_____ tenderness
_____ embarrassment	_____ loneliness	_____ uncertainty
_____ entrapment	_____ passion	_____ used
_____ envy	_____ peacefulness	_____ vindictiveness
_____ fear	_____ pleasure	_____ weariness
_____ gratitude	_____ pressure	_____ weepiness
_____ guilt	_____ rejection	_____ woe
_____ happiness	_____ sadness	_____ yearning
_____ hope	_____ security	

What is your emotional range?

Photos: E. Matheson

The concept of emotional intelligence highlights the importance of emotions to our everyday communication and our relationships. All aspects of our lives are affected by what we feel, how skillfully we identify our feelings, and how effectively we communicate them to others.

So far, we've discussed emotions without defining exactly what they are. In the next section, we will pin down the nature of emotions by defining them and identifying their diverse components.

THE NATURE OF EMOTIONS

Although emotions are basic to human beings and communication, they are difficult to define precisely. Yet a clear definition is necessary so that we share an understanding of what we are discussing. In this section, we'll clarify what emotions are and explore different views of how we experience emotions in our lives.

BIOLOGICAL AND LEARNED EMOTIONS

Some researchers assert that humans experience two types, or levels, of emotions: those that are based in biology and, thus, instinctual and universal and others that we learn in social interaction. Theodore Kemper (1987) claims that there are only four emotions that are grounded in human physiology: fear, anger, depression, and satisfaction. He believes we experience these four emotions because we are biologically wired to do so.

Yet, scholars don't agree on which emotions are basic (Izard, 1991; Shaver, Schwartz, Kirson, & O'Connor, 1987; Shaver, Wu, & Schwartz, 1992). Also, many scholars don't believe it's useful to think of some emotions as

Kenneth:

Last year my daughter got married, and I've never felt so many things in one moment. As I walked her down the aisle and took her arm from mine and placed it on the arm of her future husband, I felt sadness and happiness, hope and anxiety about her future, pride in the woman she'd become and her confidence in starting a new life, and loss because we would no longer be her primary family.

basic and others as learned (Ekman & Davidson, 1994). In her 1989 book *Anger: The Misunderstood Emotion*, Carol Tavris argues that anger is not entirely basic or instinctual. Tavris shows that our ability to experience anger is influenced by social interaction through which we learn whether and when we are supposed to feel angry.

A majority of scholars believe that most or all emotions are socially constructed to a substantial degree. For example, we learn when and for what to feel guilty or proud. We learn from significant others and the generalized other when to feel gratitude, embarrassment, indignation, and so forth. The current consensus is that it is simplistic and not useful to draw a firm line between basic and learned emotions.

Emotions are very complex, and we experience them holistically, not individually. In many instances, we don't feel one single emotion but experience several mingled together as Anthony did. Paul Ekman and Richard Davidson (1994) surveyed research on emotions and concluded that blends of emotion are common. For instance, you might feel both sad and happy at your graduation or both grateful and frustrated when someone helps you.

DEFINITION OF EMOTIONS

Most researchers who have studied emotions agree on a definition: Emotions are processes that are shaped by physiology, perceptions, and social experiences. In addition, some scholars think that language influences the emotions we assume we are experiencing. Notice that emotions are defined as processes rather than as distinct events. Physiological, perceptual, and social influences are not independent. Instead, they blend and interact with one another in an ongoing process that shapes our experience of emotions. Although researchers vary in how much they emphasize each of these

We will examine three influences on emotions and, within those three categories, we will examine four views from scholars about the nature of emotions.

Three Influences on Emotions and Four Views

Physiological influences on emotion

- Organismic view

Perceptual influences on emotion

- Perceptual view
- Cognitive-labelling view

Social influences on emotions

- Interactive view

influences, most people who have studied emotions agree that physiology, perceptions, and social experience all play parts in our emotional lives.

Emotions provide us with the colour, texture, and richness of our lives. Without feelings, our lives would be two-dimensional. Think of any song, and you will find the language of emotions. Whole traditions of music, such as the Blues, derive from an expression of deep feelings of sorrow. Emotions are complex and sometimes paradoxical. Intense feelings can sometimes be experienced right next to each other. We laugh until we cry. There is an old Nordic saying "Love and hate are horns on the same goat." To be truly alive is to access a full range of emotions. To be an effective communicator is to express the depth and complexity of those emotions appropriately.

We'll explore each of the dimensions of emotions and the different ways they have been viewed by scholars. Our discussion should give you a foundation for understanding feelings and how you and others communicate them.

Physiological Influences on Emotions

Have you ever felt a knot in your stomach when you were anxious? Have you ever blushed when you were embarrassed? Have you ever felt a surge of physical energy when you were angry or frightened? In each case, you experienced a physiological reaction to something. Some early theorists of emotion believed that physiological changes are caused by external phenomenon. This theory is called the **organismic view of emotions,** and it is shown in Figure 4.1. For example, early theorists of emotions believed that the knot in your stomach is a direct response to a low score on an exam and blushing is a direct response to a comment someone made that called attention to you.

Organismic View of Emotions

This view of emotions was originally advanced by philosopher William James (1890) and his colleague Carl Lange (1922). The organismic view, also called the James–Lange view, proposes that when some event occurs, we respond physiologically, and only after that do we experience emotions. This perspective assumes emotions are reflexes that follow from physiological arousal. In other words, in this view emotions are both the product and the expression of what happens in our bodies.

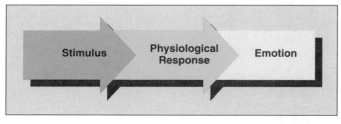

James wrote that emotional expression begins with a perception of something—perhaps seeing a gift with your name on it or noticing that someone with a weapon is running toward you. Following the perception, James believed we experience changes in our bodies: We smile on seeing the gift; adrenaline surges when we are approached by someone with a weapon. Finally, said James, we experience emotion: We feel joy at the gift, fear at the aggressor.

Figure 4.1
The Organismic View of Emotions

The organismic view of emotions regards emotions as instinctual. They are impulses that arise reflexively in response to physiological arousal caused by some external stimulus. James specifically claimed that there is none of what he called "intellectual mind stuff" (Finkelstein, 1980) that shapes our perceptions of stimuli and, by extension, our emotions. For James and others who shared his view, emotions result from physiological factors that are instinctual and beyond our conscious analysis or control. Since the time of James, the organismic view of emotions has been shown to be seriously flawed. More recent research demonstrates that physiological reactions are neither as instinctual nor as subject to conscious control as James assumed (Ekman & Davidson, 1994; Frijda, 1986).

Perceptual Influences on Emotions

Clearly, physiological experiences can be related to emotions, but James's view of the relationship between bodily states and feelings is not widely accepted by current scholars of emotions (Ekman & Davidson, 1994; Frijda, 1986; Reisenzaum, 1983). Today, most researchers think the physiological factors are less important than perceptual and social factors in shaping emotions. For these scholars, perception involves a lot more than James's idea of becoming aware of objective stimuli.

Does your body ever betray you?

Photo: M. Salez

Perceptual View of Emotions

The **perceptual view of emotions,** which is also called appraisal theory, asserts that subjective perceptions shape what external phenomena mean to us. External objects and events, as well as physiological reactions, have no intrinsic meaning. Instead, they gain meaning only as we attribute

Student Voices

Harihar:

Buddhism teaches us that our feelings arise not from things themselves, but from what we attach to them. In my life, this is true. If I find myself upset about how a conversation is going, I ask myself, "Harihar, what is it that you were expecting to happen? Can you let go of that and enter into what is actually happening here?" That helps me realize and let go of my attachment to certain outcomes of the conversation.

significance to them. In other words, events are neutral. It is only our interpretations that create meaning. We might interpret a cake as a symbol of celebration, a raised fist as a threat, and a knot in the stomach as anxiety. We act on the basis of our interpretation, not the actual cake, raised fist, or knot in our stomach.

As we will learn in Chapter 5, however, symbols are arbitrary, ambiguous, and abstract so their meanings are not fixed or clear-cut. A cake might be a symbol of freedom to a prisoner who knows there's a file hidden in it, a raised fist might be a symbol of power and ethnic pride as it was during the Mohawk uprising, and a knot in the stomach might represent excitement about receiving a major award.

The ancient Greek philosopher Epictetus observed that people are not disturbed by things, but by the views we take of them. Our view of things leads us to feel disturbed, pleased, sad, joyous, afraid, and so forth. In other words, our perceptions filter our experiences, and it is the filtered experiences that influence what we feel.

We respond differently to the same phenomenon, depending on the meaning we attribute to it. For example, if you receive a low score on a test, you might interpret it as evidence that you are not smart. This interpretation could lead you to feel shame or disappointment or other unpleasant emotions. The emotion of shame might lead you to lower your head or act in other ways that physically express your emotion. On the other hand, you might interpret the low score as the result of a tricky or overly rigorous exam, an interpretation that might lead you to feel anger at the teacher or resentment at the situation. Anger might lead you to stomp out of the room or ball up the test and throw it in a trash can.

Anger is a very different feeling than shame. Which one you feel depends on how you perceive the score and the meaning you attribute to it. In turn, the emotion you feel shapes your physiological response—slouching away in mortification or stomping belligerently out of the room. The perceptual view of emotions is represented in Figure 4.2.

Student Voices

Shinobu:

The most important lesson I learned when my family first moved to Canada was that a bad grade on a test is not a judgment that I am stupid. It is a challenge for me to do better. My English teacher taught me that. He said if I saw a bad grade as saying I am dumb or a failure that I would never learn English. He taught me to see grades as challenges that I could meet. That attitude made it possible for me not to give up and to keep learning.

Cognitive-Labelling View of Emotions

A third view of emotions is the **cognitive labelling view of emotions** (Schachter, 1964; Schachter & Singer, 1962). This perspective claims that how we label our physiological responses influences how we interpret and respond to events. Phrased another way, what we feel may be shaped by the labels we attach to physiological responses. For example, if you feel a knot in your stomach when you see that you received a low grade on an exam, you might label the knot as evidence of anxiety. Thus, what you felt would not result from either the event itself (the grade) or your perceptions of the event. Instead, it would be shaped by how you labelled your physiological response to the event. This view of emotions is represented in Figure 4.3.

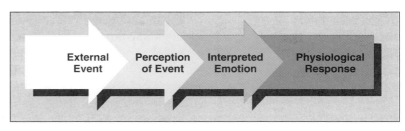

Figure 4.2
The Perceptual View of Emotions

Sometimes it's difficult to know what label to give to our physiological responses. Children often learn the labels by watching the adults around them. For example, a child might watch an adult laugh at being licked and jumped upon by a dog. The child learns that the initial feelings of elevated heart rate and trembling can be redefined as excitement. This will inform him or her how to act. How we label events (a dog's greeting) and our physiological responses (fear, surprise)

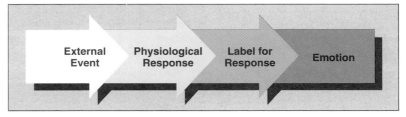

Figure 4.3
The Cognitive Labelling View of Emotions

affects how we think and act. In some cases, however, we would be wise to label our feelings as fear and to heed them. Sometimes it's difficult to know whether to trust our emotions (feeling fearful, for example) or to redefine them. Although there is no sure-fire rule for knowing when to trust emotions, one guideline is to analyze the basis for what you feel. Is there a sound basis for your emotions? Are there subtle environmental cues that alert you to be fearful? "The Gift of Fear" on page 132 explains why it is sometimes smart to trust feelings of fear.

Probably there is some validity to each view of emotions that we've explored. The organismic view calls our attention to the physiological aspects of emotions—we do have bodily responses to what happens around us. The perceptual view reminds us that how we perceive external events and our own physiological reactions influences the meanings we attach to experiences and the emotions that we think are appropriate. Finally, the cognitive labelling view emphasizes the role of language in shaping our interpretation of events and our emotions in response to them. Language may shape our feelings by providing interpretations of events, our physiological responses, appropriate emotions, or all three.

Each of the models we've considered so far helps us understand the role of particular aspects of emotions. Yet, none of these models is complete because none adequately accounts for the critical influence of culture in shaping emotions and how we communicate them.

Social Influences on Emotions

As we learned in Chapter 3, perception is influenced by the social groups to which we belong, as well as by the overall culture (generalized other). The society and communities in which we live affect what we perceive (and don't perceive) and how we interpret, organize, and respond to what we perceive. Our social circumstances also influence our beliefs about which emotions are good or bad, which emotions we should express or repress, and with whom we can appropriately communicate which emotions. Thus, a full understanding of emotions requires us to explore what our culture teaches us about emotions and how they should be expressed.

Interactive View of Emotions

Concepts at a Glance

Three Key Concepts of the Interactive View of Emotions

- Framing rules
- Feeling rules
- Emotion work

Insight into social influences on emotions and how we express them is fairly recent. Beginning in the 1970s, some scholars began advancing an **interactive view of emotions** (Hochschild, 1979), which proposes that social rules and understandings shape what individuals feel and how they do or don't express their feelings. Arlie Hochschild (1979, 1983, 1990) has pioneered in this area by conducting in-depth studies of how individuals experience and communicate feelings, as well as how they control feelings. The interactive view of emotions rests on three key concepts: framing rules, feeling rules, and emotion work. Each of these concepts helps us under-

Communication Notes

The Gift of Fear

Don't ignore your fear. That's the message of Gavin de Becker's book, *The Gift of Fear*. For years, de Becker has worked as a security consultant to celebrities. He notes that many people tend to dismiss feelings of fear by labelling them "silly" or "stupid." If you're waiting for an elevator, and when the door opens you have a strong, fearful reaction to a person in the elevator, what do you do? De Becker says many people try to talk themselves out of the fear with thoughts such as "There's nothing to be afraid of. This is a public building." Wrong, says de Becker. He advises us to wait for the next elevator. If you have a feeling that someone is lurking in a parking lot, don't dismiss it as paranoia, says de Becker. Heed it, and find someone to walk with you.

Source: de Becker, G. (1997). *The gift of fear: Survival signs that protect us from violence.* New York: Little, Brown.

Monique:

I remember the nasty things mother would say about women whose houses weren't clean. It was a mark against their character. When I first came to college, if I saw my boyfriend's apartment was dirty, I thought I was supposed to clean it up, and I did. I remember once when a boyfriend complained that I hadn't cleaned the dishes, and I felt ashamed. How I saw things started to change when I took some women's studies classes and began to think differently about women and men and what we're supposed to do. Now if I see my boyfriend's apartment is dirty, I don't think I should clean it up. If he fusses at me, I don't feel shame; now I feel angry that he would think I should do it.

stand how strongly social factors influence what we feel and how we express our emotions.

Framing Rules   **Framing rules** are guidelines for defining the emotional meaning of situations. For example, Western culture defines funerals as sad and respectful occasions and weddings as joyful events. Within any single culture, however, there are multiple social groups and resulting standpoints.

Different social groups may teach members distinct framing rules for the same situations. For example, many people of Irish descent hold wakes when a person dies. The wake is defined as a festive occasion during which people tell stories about the departed person and celebrate his or her life. Within Western culture, other groups define funerals and receptions following them as somber occasions at which any mirth or festivity would be perceived as disrespectful and inappropriate. "The Social Shaping of Grief" on page 134 explores cultural differences in framing rules for death.

Photo: © Photodisc

Feeling Rules   **Feeling rules** tell us what we have a right to feel or what we are expected to feel in particular situations. Feeling rules reflect and perpetuate the values of a specific society. For example, societies that emphasize individuality promote the feeling rule that it is appropriate to feel pride about personal accomplishments. Among many ethnic Asians, however, individuality is less esteemed than group identity, and what an individual achieves is regarded as the result of and a reflection on the larger family and community. Thus, a feeling rule might be that it is

Communication Notes

The Social Shaping of Grief

What people feel about death and how they express their feelings is not universal. Different cultures have distinct framing rules for death. In some African tribes death is regarded as a cause to celebrate a person's passage to a higher and better form of living. Among Buddhists, the death of a body is not regarded as the end of what a person is because the person is assumed to continue in other forms. In some cultures people are expected to feel deep grief over the loss of cousins to whom they have deep and lasting attachments. In contrast, there are other cultures that define cousins as distant relations whose death seldom provokes deep sadness.

Framing rules for death also vary over time in a single culture. Modern Western cultures enjoy a low infant mortality rate (approximately 9 deaths per 1,000 infants) and a long life expectancy. Today the average life expectancy for people living in Canada is 78.5 years with women having a higher life expectancy than men.

In earlier times the infant mortality rate in Western societies ranged from 50 to 400 deaths per 1,000 infants, and the life expectancy was decades shorter than today. Scholars who have studied historical and diary research from earlier times report that death was viewed as a normal, routine part of life that did not call for intense and prolonged mourning.

Source: Lofland, L. (1985). The social shaping of emotion: The case of grief. *Symbolic Interaction*, 8, 171–90; Statistics Canada (March 1999). 1996 Census catalogue: Final edition reference.

appropriate for an individual to feel gratitude to family and community for personal accomplishments. All social communities have feeling rules that specify acceptable and unacceptable ways to express feelings. "Wild Pigs Run Amok" on page 136 describes a unique cultural expression of aggression in New Guinea.

Hochschild (1979) points out that we often talk about feelings in terms of rights and duties. This tendency reveals our awareness of social expectations and responsibilities that accompany and shape our emotions and how we express them. The following phrases—all ones we commonly hear and use—highlight the language of duty and rights that infuses feeling rules:

- I'm entitled to feel sad.
- You have no right to feel unhappy. Look at all you have!
- She should be grateful to me for what I did.
- You shouldn't feel bad.
- I ought to feel happy my friend got a job.
- I shouldn't feel angry at my father.
- Men shouldn't cry.
- Women should feel nurturing toward children.

Hochschild (1979) perceives a strong connection between feeling rules and social order. She claims that one way a society attempts to control individuals is through feeling rules that uphold broad social values and structures. For example, teaching people they should feel pride in their personal accomplishments reinforces the value Western culture places on individualism. Teaching people to regard accomplishments as communal, not individual, upholds the value accorded to groups that is esteemed in many non-Western cultures.

Montreal Massacre, Dec. 6, 1989

Photo: © Ryan Remiorz/CP Picture Archive

Apply the Idea

Religions and Feeling Rules

Religions urge individuals to follow particular feeling rules. For example, Judeo-Christian commandments direct individuals to "honour thy father and thy mother" and to "not covet thy neighbour's house, nor his wife." Buddhism commands individuals to feel compassion for all living beings and to do what one can do to alleviate suffering. Hinduism commands followers to accept their place (caste) in this life.

Make a list of all the feeling rules you can identify that are proposed by your spiritual or religious affiliation. Be sure to list both what you are supposed to feel and what you are not supposed to feel.

1. _____

2. _____

3. _____

4. _____

5. _____

6. _____

Compare your responses with those from students who have different religious or spiritual beliefs. What similarities and differences among feeling rules can you identify?

A second way in which feeling rules uphold social structure is by condoning the expression of more negative feelings toward people with limited power. Hochschild's studies of people in service industries reveal that the less power employees have, the more they tend to be targets of negative emo-

Communication Notes

Wild Pigs Run Amok

Imagine you felt extremely aggressive and needed to release your tension. How would you do it? Would you go for a long, hard run? Would you work out in the gym? Would you kick a wall or closet door? Would you go on a shooting rampage?

Anthropologist Philip Newman and sociologist Susan Shott report a very different way of expressing extreme aggression. They observed that certain societies in the New Guinea highlands have a well-established custom for venting aggression. A person who feels aggressive is defined as a wild pig, or wild man, who is out of control. Because he is out of control, the individual is allowed to behave in bizarre ways that would never be condoned in a normal person.

The wild man is said to "run amok." He is able to vent aggression without being judged as deviant. After all, he's not himself—he's a wild pig. By running amok, the individual expresses aggressive feelings and can then return to normal identity. Thus, these New Guinea communities have created a safety valve for individuals who feel overcome by unruly impulses.

But the safety valve for the troubled individual may not be very safe for those who are attacked by the wild pig running amok. Sometimes people are killed by the untamed aggression. The negative effects of this custom have led some observers to regard it as a syndrome that provides an excuse for unacceptable behaviour that is not socially approved.

Sources: Newman, P. (1964, February). "Wild man" behaviour in New Guinea highlands community. *American Anthropologist, 66,* 1–19; Shott, S. (1979). Emotion and social life: A symbolic interactionist analysis. *American Journal of Sociology, 84,* 1317–34; Winzeler, R. (1990). Amok: Historical, psychological, and cultural perspectives. In W. J. Karim (Ed.), *Emotions of culture: A Malay perspective* (pp. 97–122). Oxford: Oxford University Press.

tional expressions from others. People who have greater power may learn they have a right to express anger, offence, frustration, and so forth, whereas people who have less power may learn it isn't acceptable for them to express such emotions. To test the validity of this idea, ask yourself who is the target of greater complaints and hostility: servers or restaurant managers, flight attendants or pilots, receptionists or CEOs?

Finally, Hochschild notes there are differences in the feeling rules that are taught to children in middle- and working-class families. Middle-class parents generally encourage children to control their inner feelings by **deep acting,** which is management of inner feelings. In bringing up children, the parents emphasize what they should and should not feel. Children may be taught, for instance, that they should feel grateful for gifts and should not feel angry when a sibling takes a toy.

According to Hochschild, working-class parents place greater emphasis on **surface acting,** which involves controlling the outward expression of emotions, not controlling what is felt. Parents who emphasize surface acting teach children to control their outward behaviours, not necessarily their inner feelings. Children learn, for example, that they should say thank you when they receive a gift and they should not hit a sibling who takes a toy. Expressing gratitude is emphasized more than feeling grateful, and refraining from hitting someone who takes a toy is stressed more than being willing to share toys.

In Canada, the moral teachers were always the family and the church. Now that role is shifting to schools. Many Canadian schools teach empathy at the elementary grades to improve the abilities of deep acting. Children are shown pictures that depict emotionally laden moments. The children are then asked "How would you feel if this were you?" and "What would you like people to do or say to you if this were you?" This activity allows children to learn about empathy and to expand their repertoire of feelings.

Emotion Work   The final concept that Hochschild advanced is **emotion work,** which she defines as the effort we invest to generate what we think are appropriate feelings in particular situations. Notice that emotion work concerns our effort to fashion how we feel, not necessarily the outcome of that effort. Our success at squelching feelings we think are inappropriate or at generating the feelings we think we should experience varies from occasion to occasion.

Although we do emotion work much of the time, we tend to be most aware of engaging in it when we think what we are feeling is inappropriate in a specific situation. For example, you might think it is wrong to feel gleeful when someone you dislike is hurt. Hochschild refers to this as "the pinch," which is a discrepancy between what we do feel and what we think we should feel. Typically, what we think we should feel is based on what we've learned from our social groups and the larger culture. If you feel sad at a wedding, you might engage in emotion work to make yourself feel happy.

|Student Voices|

Huang:

In my native country students are supposed to be respectful of teachers and never speak out in class. It has been hard for me to learn to feel I have a right to ask questions of a professor here. Sometimes I have a question or I do not agree with a professor, but I have to work to tell myself it is okay to assert myself. To me, it still feels disrespectful to speak up.

Emotion work involves more than outward expression of feelings—for example, smiling even though you really feel sad. It also involves efforts at deep acting by striving to generate the feeling we think we should have. We do emotion work to suppress or extinguish feelings we think are wrong (for example, feeling jealous over a friend's good fortune or happy over the misfortune of someone we dislike). We also engage in emotion work to cultivate feelings we think we should have—for example, propelling ourselves to feel joy for our friend's good fortune.

Framing rules, feeling rules, and emotion work are interrelated. Framing rules that define the emotional meaning of situations lead to feeling rules that tell us what we should feel or have a right to feel given the meaning of the situation. If we don't feel what our feeling rules designate as appropriate, we may engage in emotion work to squelch inappropriate feelings or to bring about feelings that we perceive are proper in the circumstances. We can then express our feelings by following rules for what is accepted as suitable expression of particular emotions.

The interactive view of emotions assumes that what we feel involves thinking, perceiving, and imagining while being influenced by social rules for framing situations and specifying what we should and can feel. This view of emotions emphasizes the extent to which social factors affect how we perceive, label, and respond emotionally to experiences in our lives. A noteworthy feature of this model is that it calls attention to cultural differences in feelings and how we express them. This model of emotions is represented in Figure 4.4.

Figure 4.4
The Interactive View of Emotions

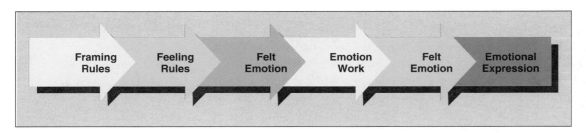

Framing Rules → Feeling Rules → Felt Emotion → Emotion Work → Felt Emotion → Emotional Expression

Apply the Idea

Identifying Feeling Rules

To become more aware of the feeling rules that influence you, write out what you think you should feel or have a right to feel in each of the following situations.

1. *You find out that the person you have been dating exclusively for two years has been dating someone else as well for the last six months.*

I Should Feel _____

I Have a Right to Feel _____

2. *You and a close friend have both been interviewing for jobs. Your friend gets a great job offer, and you still haven't received one.*

I Should Feel _____

I Have a Right to Feel _____

3. *Your roommate criticizes you for not doing your share of the cleaning, and you know you haven't been pitching in fairly.*

I Should Feel _____

I Have a Right to Feel _____

4. *Your parents tell you that they are separating.*

I Should Feel _____

I Have a Right to Feel _____

THE IMPACT OF DIFFERENT VIEWS OF EMOTIONS

Does it make a difference which view of emotions you believe? Yes, because how we view feelings affects our belief in whether we can control what we experience and express in everyday life. If you agree with William James that feelings are instinctual, then you will probably assume that feelings cannot be analyzed or controlled. Whatever you feel, you feel. That's it.

On the other hand, if you accept the interactive view of emotions, you are more likely to think you can analyze your feelings and perhaps change them and how you express them through your own emotion work. The interactive view assumes we are agents who can affect what happens to us and how we feel and act. If you agree with this perspective, you are more likely to monitor your feelings and to make choices about how to communicate them.

This isn't an all or nothing issue. The most reasonable perspective is probably that we have some control if we choose to exercise it. We may not be able to totally control what we feel, but usually we can exert some control. Further, we can exercise considerable control over how we do or don't express our feelings and to whom we express them.

There isn't a clear dividing line between what we feel and how we express feelings. The two interact in the process of emotions. What we feel influences how we express (or don't express) our emotions. It's equally true that how we express our feelings echoes back into us to affect how we interpret our feelings (Fridlund, 1994). Taking personal responsibility for when, how, and to whom you express feelings is a cornerstone of ethical interpersonal communication.

|Student Voices|

Mae:

Sometimes, during an argument with my partner, my body begins to shake out of nowhere. I know when this happens that I have tapped into deep old feelings of fear and mistrust from the past. When this happens I know that I don't feel psychologically safe. I have learned to honour this sign and to ask for some space and time to think about what is being asked of me. It's as if I have to discharge the feelings of panic and get back to the present. Sometimes I just have to leave. I tell my partner, "I don't feel comfortable right now, I'm going to leave and think about what has gone on here before continuing."

In this example, Mae is displaying a high degree of what Goleman calls "emotional intelligence" as described earlier.

OBSTACLES TO EFFECTIVE COMMUNICATION OF EMOTIONS

We've seen that emotions are not strictly personal, individual phenomena, but are profoundly social. We learn what to feel based on the values, norms, and traditions of the social groups to which we belong. We also learn from our social groups how we are expected to express or not express what we feel. How we communicate or don't communicate feelings can hurt or enrich relationships and can foster or impede understanding between people. In addition, our expression or lack of expression of our feelings can encourage or stunt personal growth.

Because many people repress emotions or express them ineffectively, it's important for us to explore obstacles to effective emotional communication. In this section, we'll consider two topics related to ineffective communication of emotions. We'll first examine common reasons that we may not express emotions. Then we'll identify some common, yet ineffective, ways of communicating feelings. Following this section, we'll conclude the chapter by focusing on ways to communicate emotions clearly and effectively.

REASONS WE MAY NOT EXPRESS EMOTIONS

We don't always express our emotions to others. This is not necessarily bad. Sometimes we make an ethical choice not to express emotions that would hurt another person. At other times, we decide not to burden another person with our feelings. There are ways to express feelings without sharing them with specific others. We might write the feelings in a personal journal or talk about them with a counsellor or friend who would not be disturbed by

Student Voices

Shae:

My best friend, Fran, is a marriage saver. When I'm really angry with my husband, I vent to her. If there's a really serious problem between me and Al, I talk with him. But a lot of times I'm upset over little stuff. I know what I'm feeling isn't going to last and isn't any serious problem in our marriage, but I may be seething anyway. Letting those feelings out to Fran gets them off my chest without hurting Al or our marriage.

them. Choosing not to express emotions in some situations or to some people can be constructive and generous.

Sometimes it is appropriate to express feelings to a particular person. When we feel something strongly, finding appropriate ways to express our emotions is important. The cost of repressing emotions or not communicating them can be high (Pennebaker, 1997). Relationships suffer when emotional connections are weak or when feelings are not understood and addressed. Individuals also experience a range of negative consequences when they deny themselves emotional outlets. They may suffer from headaches, ulcers, high blood pressure, eating disorders, and other serious problems.

Chuck's commentary is forceful testimony to the dangers of not expressing feelings. The impact of denying or repressing our emotions can be devastating to us personally and to our relationships (Schmanoff, 1985, 1987). Thus, we should understand and critically evaluate why people sometimes don't express what they feel. In this section, we'll consider four common reasons why people don't communicate emotions.

|Student Voices|

Chuck:

I guess I fell prey to the idea that real men don't whine or give in to problems. It took a nervous breakdown to teach me otherwise. Two years ago I was going to school part-time and working full-time. My company downsized, which meant that those of us who weren't fired had to pick up the work of those who were. I began putting in more hours at the job. Then I gave up my daily workout to create more time for studying and working. I just kept stuffing down all I felt—the resentment, the stress, the anxiety about getting everything done. I didn't talk to my girlfriend or brother or co-workers or anyone. I didn't want anyone to think I couldn't take the heat. One day I couldn't get up. I just couldn't get out of bed. I stayed there all day and the next day and the next. Finally, my brother hauled me to a hospital where I was diagnosed with acute stress. By that time, I also had an ulcer and my blood pressure was really elevated. My doctor said I needed counselling. I said no. He asked whether I'd rather learn how to deal with my emotions or die in the next year. Given that choice, I went into counselling. What I discovered was that I've spent my whole life stuffing emotions down. I had to learn what I should have learned as a child—that it's okay to feel things and that it really helps to talk about what I'm feeling.

Social Expectations

As we have noted, social factors shape feelings and expression of them. Gender differences in the expression of emotion are evident around us all the time. Cultural norms also dictate the expression of emotion for men and women. Generally, "men do and women discuss." These "social rules," which we will examine more closely in Chapter 5, govern the kind of emotions and the nature of their expression that is sanctioned by men and women. Research on emotion suggests these gender differences exist. Men are generally more restricted in their expression of emotions, and women are encouraged to be demonstrative. This social expectation is not universal. For example, men from Mediterranean cultures routinely express a range of emotions dramatically and openly. In Asian cultures, anyone's excessive show of emotion is considered in bad taste. It draws too much attention to the self, which is not an admired behaviour.

Men and women face different restrictions on the feelings society allows them. Men are generally expected to be emotionally restrained. Expressing hurt, fear, depression, or other "soft" emotions is not encouraged or admired in men.

Unexpressed feelings can, over time, lead to an inability to recognize feelings and result in an alienation from them. Anger has particularly strident feeling rules surrounding expression. Tavris (1989) examines how the expression of anger in women is regarded as unfeminine. This discourages many women from acknowledging legitimate anger and from expressing it assertively. Thus, many women are constrained by the feeling rule that they should not feel anger and, if they do, they should definitely not communicate it.

There are other feeling rules that influence many Western women. Most women in our society are encouraged from childhood to be caring toward others. Luise Eichenbaum and Suzie Orbach (1987) and Lillian Rubin (1985) point out that feeling rules for women make it difficult for them not

Concepts at a Glance

Four Reasons Why We May Not Express Emotions

- Social expectations
- Vulnerability
- Protecting others
- Social and professional roles

What were you taught about expressing anger?

Photos: © Corel (left); M. Salez (right)

to feel caring all the time, because not being empathic and supportive of others would be inconsistent with cultural definitions of femininity. Thus, many women engage in emotion work to make themselves feel caring when they don't naturally feel that way.

|*Student Voices*|

Sadie:

The other night I got home after working the dinner shift at my restaurant. I was dead tired. The phone rang and I almost didn't answer. Now I wish I hadn't. It was my friend Donna, and she was upset about a fight with her boyfriend. I tried to cut the call short, but she said, "I'm really hurting and I need to talk." And so I reminded myself that I do care about Donna. I told myself that my fatigue wasn't as important as Donna's problem. So we stayed on the phone for over an hour and we talked through what was happening. Sometimes I wish I could just say, "I'm not available for you now," but I'd feel like a real jerk if I did that.

What feeling rules were you taught?

Photo: © Corbis/Magma

Even more often, report researchers, women squelch feelings of jealousy toward friends and feelings of competitiveness in personal and professional relationships. Because most Western women are taught they should support others, they learn it is inappropriate to experience or express envy or competitiveness. Not being able to express or even acknowledge such feelings can interfere with honest communication in interpersonal relationships.

When women squash these taboo feelings, there can be undesirable personal and relationship effects. Denying or refusing to act on competitive feelings can limit women's career advancement. Not dealing openly with feelings of jealousy or envy in friendships can create barriers and distance. And demanding of themselves that they always be emotionally available and caring to anyone who wants their help can be overwhelming. Conversely, women in male-dominated roles or roles traditionally played by men may find that they suppress their feelings of vulnerability in favour of the more aggressive, action-oriented behaviours of their workplace, giving rise to feelings of competitiveness, detachment, and anger. Also, as men take on more care-giving and nurturing roles, so the restrictiveness of the social expectations around expression of feelings loosens. As our workplace and community roles become more gender mixed, the strict social definitions of emotional expression become more lax.

It's important for men and women to review critically the feeling rules they have been taught. This enables us to decide which ones we think are appropriate and desirable and to follow those in our communication. Equally important, critical review of social feeling rules may help us identify those that are dysfunctional and choose not to adhere to them in our personal lives.

Reflective Exercise

Examine your family's feeling rules. Which emotions were allowed expression and in what way? What gender rules for feelings were evident in your family? How did this experience prepare you for managing emotions in intimate relationships, in work relationships? Are you satisfied with the range of emotions you feel and the expression of them?

Vulnerability

A second reason we may not express our feelings is that we don't want to expose ourselves to others. Telling others how we feel or expressing feelings nonverbally may give others information that could affect how they perceive

Communication Notes

"Je t'aime Papa."

The funeral of Pierre Elliot Trudeau on October 4, 2000, transfixed a nation. The parting words of Justin Trudeau's eulogy touched everyone, regardless of political affiliation. They were the words of a son in grief: "I love you Papa." This public display of tears riveted audiences all over the country. Justin's articulate account of his father as a loving family man was profoundly moving. We all grieved for the loss of this father. As Justin painted the picture of "dad" to us all, an intimate portrait not visible in the public figure, we all grieved for the loss of the "father" in our own lives. This confident, warm, engaging son rewrote the rules of emotional expression for a nation. The wave of mourning that ensued was unprecedented in Canada. It was as if our very definition of a nation was tied up in the character of Trudeau, who advocated in his life for Canadian unity and assertiveness. His death and the words of his son took us beyond partisan politics to the human heart. Men cried openly. Foes prayed together. The nation wept.

us. We may fear that someone will like us less if we disclose that we feel angry with him or her. We may worry that someone will lose respect for us if our nonverbal behaviours show we feel weak or scared. We may be afraid that if we disclose how deeply we feel about another person, she or he will reject us. Further, we may be concerned that others could use intimate knowledge against us. To protect ourselves from being vulnerable to others, we may not express feelings verbally or nonverbally.

Protecting Others

Another reason we often choose not to express feelings is that we fear we could hurt or upset others. If you tell a friend that you feel disappointed in her, she may be hurt. If your facial expressions and body posture show that you feel depressed, those who care about you may share your pain and worry about your well-being. We may also choose not to express feelings to protect our relationships from conflicts. If a friend behaves in ways you consider irresponsible, you may refrain from verbally or nonverbally expressing your disapproval because doing so might cause tension between you.

Totally open and unrestrained expression of feeling isn't necessarily a good idea. Sometimes it is both wise and kind not to express feelings. It's often not productive to vent minor frustrations and annoyances. Romantic partners may want to deal with some issues privately—at least for a while. And if someone we care about is already overburdened with anxiety or emotional problems,

Children need to be heard.

Photo: M. Salez

| Student Voices |

Nasr:

Last week I got rejected by the law school that was my top choice. Normally, I would have gone over to Jason's apartment to hang out with him and let him boost me up. Ever since we met, we've been tight friends and we talk about everything in our lives. But right now Jason's struggling with his own stuff. His mother just got diagnosed with cancer and his father is out of work. I know we'll talk about my disappointment some time, but I figured it could wait until he gets into a better place.

we may choose to monitor our nonverbal communication so that the other person doesn't have to respond to our feelings at the moment. Thus, there can be good reasons not to show or discuss feelings, or not to show or discuss them at a specific time.

Nasr's commentary provides a good example of instances in which it is caring not to express feelings. Yet, we would be mistaken to think it's always a good idea to keep feelings to ourselves. Avoiding expression of negative or upsetting feelings can be harmful if they directly affect relationships with others or if doing so may threaten our own health. Susan Schmanoff (1987) found that intimacy wanes when couples' communication consistently lacks emotional disclosures, even unpleasant ones. If not expressing feelings is likely to create barriers in relationships or to cause us serious personal distress, then we should try to find a context and mode of expression that allows us to communicate our emotions.

Social and Professional Roles

A final reason why we may not express some feelings is that our roles make it inappropriate. An attorney who cried when hearing a sad story from a witness might be perceived as unprofessional. A doctor or nurse who talked about personal feelings to a patient might be regarded as too personally involved with the case. Police officers and social workers would probably be judged out of line if they expressed anger instead of objective detachment when investigating a crime.

When attorneys question expert witnesses at trials, they often try to ruffle the witness with personal attacks, tricky questions, or deliberate misstatements of the testimony. This is a routine and normal tactic in cross-examinations. If the witness were to respond emotionally—perhaps with an angry outburst—he or she would lose credibility with the jury. To be effective in the role of an expert witness, one has to control expression of feelings. One psychotherapist described using a formula to get through this arduous task. He called it his "ABCs." "A" reminded him to stay in his adult mode, not to retreat to a childlike response. "B" reminded him to breathe, to remember he would survive this grilling. "C" reminded him to remember the context he was in and that it was the job of the lawyer to try and discredit him. This is an effective way to manage emotions in a professional setting.

We've identified four common reasons that we may not express emotions. Although we can understand all of them, they are not equally constructive in their consequences. There is no simple rule for when to express feelings. Instead, we have to exercise judgment. We have an ethical obligation to make thoughtful choices about whether, when, and how to express our feelings. As a responsible communicator, you should strive to decide when it is necessary, appropriate, and constructive to express your feelings, keeping in mind that you, others, and relationships will be affected by your decision.

INEFFECTIVE EXPRESSION OF EMOTIONS

Concepts at a Glance

Ineffective Expression of Emotions

- Speaking in generalities
- Not owning feelings
- Counterfeit emotional language

We don't always deny or repress our emotions. Sometimes we realize we have feelings and we try to express them, but we don't communicate effectively. We'll consider three of the most common forms of ineffective expression of emotions.

Speaking in Generalities

"I feel bad." "I'm happy." "I'm sad." Statements such as these do express emotional states, but they do so ineffectively. Why? Because they are so general and abstract that they don't clearly communicate what it is the speaker feels. Does "I feel bad" mean the person feels depressed or angry or guilty or ashamed or anxious? Does "I'm happy" mean the speaker is in love, pleased with a grade, satisfied at having achieved a personal goal, delighted to be eating chocolate, or excited about an upcoming vacation? When we use highly general, abstract emotional language, we aren't communicating effectively about what we feel.

Also, our nonverbal repertoire for expressing emotions may be limited. Withdrawing from interaction may be an expression of sadness, anger, depression, or fear. Lowering our head and eyes may express a range of emotions including reverence, shame, and thoughtfulness.

There are many, many emotions that we are capable of experiencing. Yet, most of us only recognize or express the most limited number. In *Anger: The Struggle for Emotional Control in America's History* (1986), Carol Stearns and Peter Stearns report that people in the United States actually express very few emotions; in other words, many people recognize only a few of the many possible emotions humans can experience, and they express those emotions whenever they feel something. This limits insight into the self and restricts the ability to communicate feelings. There are many similarities between American and Canadian cultures in this respect.

Some people routinely describe what they feel by relying on one or a few emotions.

Apply the Idea

Enlarging Your Emotional Vocabulary

Reflect on your emotional vocabulary and how and when you use words to describe emotions. Listed below are some of the more common emotion words people use. For each one, describe three other emotion words that describe subtle distinctions in feeling.

Example: anger: resentment, outrage, offence, vindictiveness

sadness _____   *fear* _____

_____   _____

_____   _____

happiness   _____   love   _____

_____   _____

_____   _____

Extend this exercise by trying to be more precise in how you describe your feelings for the next week. Does expanding your emotional vocabulary give you and others more understanding of what you feel?

Not Owning Feelings

A second ineffective way of expressing emotions is to state feelings in a way that disowns personal responsibility for the feeling.

"You make me angry" states a feeling (although the word angry may be overly general). Yet this statement relies on you–language to suggest that somebody other than the speaker is the source or cause of the angry feeling. Nobody else can make us feel anything. We define and interpret what people say and do. We attach meaning to their actions. Thus, it's not accurate to say "You make me angry." True, others certainly say and do things that affect us; they may even do things to us. But we—not anyone else—decide what their actions mean, and we—not anyone else—decide how we feel.

Anger is a particularly charged emotion. The understanding of anger and the skills of expressing anger appropriately would do much to curb violence in relationships, in families, and more recently in our schools and communities. Anger has, for the most part, a bad reputation. "Anger management" is the first requirement of violent crime offenders in our court system. Understanding the root of one's anger response does a lot to dilute its intensity. Learning healthy expressions of anger takes the danger and fear out of it and also saves useless suffering.

Examined from the biological perspective, anger is a facilitative emotion that allows us to save ourselves under threat. Once frightened, fear is shunted into anger allowing our bodies to mobilize. *Anger generally masks fear.* The adrenaline that surges through our bodies allows for the flight or fight response. This is all very understandable when a bear is on our path or a terrifying figure threatens us. More often than not though, our anger and the fear that it masks is not so obvious to us. The expression of anger is learned from our family scripts and is culturally bound. What you experienced in your family reality around the expression of anger is the legacy that you bring forward into adulthood. This may be facilitative or destructive. Hear the voices of three students about their family experiences with anger.

As an adult, you have an opportunity to examine your family scripts and the way you currently express anger. Knowing that there are cultural and gender differences in the social expectations of emotional expression assist in this examination.

Concepts at a Glance

Key Points to Expressing Anger

- Don't damage relationships.
- Don't damage yourself.
- Don't damage property.

Annie, Takeshi, Aaron:

Annie: My mother exploded when she was angry. I became afraid of anyone's anger including my own. Anger was a dangerous emotion.

Takeshi: My parents refused to talk when they felt angry. In my family, refusing to talk, silence, is the message of anger.

Aaron: There was so much passive aggressive behaviour in my family that now as an adult when there is no apparent conflict, I am still uneasy and never feel at peace in a relationship.

Reflective Exercise

How do you usually express anger? What is the impact of expression of anger on the people around you? What are your family scripts around feeling and expressing anger? What changes, if any, would you like to make around expressing anger?

Russell Proctor (1991) studied the effects of owning and not owning feelings in emotional communication. Proctor's research indicates that failing to own feelings may be the most common obstacle to effective communication about feelings. Let's return to the example of "You make me angry." The statement would be a more effective emotional expression if the speaker said "I feel angry when you don't call when you say you will." The statement would be even more effective—more precise and clearer—if the speaker said, "I feel hurt and unimportant to you when you don't call when you say you will." And the statement would be still more effective if it included information about what the speaker wants from the other person: "I feel hurt and unimportant to you when you don't call when you say you will. Would you be willing to work on calling if we agreed that it's okay for calls to be short sometimes?" This last statement accepts responsibility for a feeling, communicates clearly what is felt, and offers a solution that could help the relationship.

Counterfeit Emotional Language

A third ineffective form of emotional communication is relying on **counterfeit emotional language.** This is language that seems to express emotions but does not actually describe what a person is feeling. For example, shouting "Why can't you leave me alone!" certainly reveals that the speaker is feeling something, but it doesn't describe what she or he is feeling. Is it anger at the particular person, frustration at being interrupted, stress at having to meet a deadline, or the need for time alone? We can't tell which of these—or other—feelings the speaker is experiencing.

To foster understanding between people, it's important to provide clear descriptions of our feelings and the connection between what we feel and others' behaviours. "I feel frustrated because when I'm working and you walk in, I lose my train of thought" is a more constructive statement than "Why can't you leave me alone!" The first statement communicates what is troubling you and states that it is situation-specific. The second comment could be interpreted to mean that you don't want the other person around at all.

It's also counterfeit and unproductive not to explain feelings. "That's just how I feel" doesn't tell a person how her or his behaviour is related to your feelings or what you would like her or him to do. Sometimes we say "That's just how I feel," because we haven't really figured out why we feel as we do or what we want from another person. In such cases, we should try to identify situations and our emotional reactions to them so that we can communicate clearly to others (Planalp, 1997).

Another form of counterfeit emotional language uses feeling words but really expresses thoughts or beliefs, for example, "I feel this discussion is getting sidetracked." The perception that a discussion is going off on tangents is a thought, not a feeling. Maybe the speaker feels frustrated that the discussion seems to be wandering, but that feeling is not communicated by the statement. "This has been a terrible day" suggests that the speaker isn't feeling too great about the day, but what the speaker feels is entirely unclear because she or he offered no description of feelings.

Avoid "I feel that———" when what you mean is "I believe that———." What follows "I feel———" should be a feeling word or description.

Apply the Idea

Avoiding Counterfeit Emotional Language

Listed below are five statements that include counterfeit emotional language. Rewrite each statement so that it describes a feeling or an emotional state. Make sure you also rely on I–language, not you–language, and you offer precise, clear descriptions, not vague ones.

1. *Shut up! I don't want to hear anything else from you.*
2. *You're a wonderful person.*
3. *I feel that we should get started on our group project.*
4. *I can't believe you were here all day and didn't even clean up the mess.*
5. *Can't you see I'm working now? Leave me alone.*

It's not surprising that many people engage in ineffective emotional communication. As we've seen in this chapter, there are many hindrances to expressing emotions authentically. The three specific forms of ineffective emotional communication we've considered give us insight into some of the more common ways we may evade—consciously or not—clear and genuine communication about our feelings. In the final section of this chapter, we consider alternatives to ineffective methods of communicating emotions. We'll see that there are specific ways to improve communicating our feelings effectively and constructively and to respond sensitively to others' communication about their emotions.

GUIDELINES FOR COMMUNICATING EMOTIONS EFFECTIVELY

In the previous section, we examined reasons people don't express emotions and ineffective ways we may express them. What we've explored so far in this chapter suggests several guidelines for becoming skilled at communicating our feelings. In this section we'll extend what we've already discussed to identify five guidelines for effective communication of emotions.

IDENTIFY YOUR EMOTIONS

You cannot communicate your feelings if you don't understand them. Thus, the first step in communicating emotions effectively is to identify what you feel. As we have seen, this isn't always easy. For reasons we've discussed, people may be alienated from their emotions—unable to recognize what they feel. Overcoming this requires giving mindful attention to your inner self. Just as some people learn to ignore their feelings, we can teach ourselves to notice and heed them.

Another challenge to identifying emotions is sorting out complex mixtures of feeling. For example, we sometimes feel both anxious and hopeful. To recognize only that you feel hopeful is to overlook anxiety. To realize only that you feel anxious is to ignore your feeling of hopefulness. Recognizing the existence of both feelings allows you to tune in to yourself and to communicate accurately to others what you are experiencing.

When sorting out intermingled feelings it's useful to identify the primary or main feeling—the one or ones that are dominant in the moment. Doing this allows you to communicate clearly to others what is most important in your emotional state. Think back to the example that opened this chapter. Anthony felt overwhelmed, trapped, and scared. But he also felt love for his partner. By deciding which one was primary, he gave her a chance to be a real support.

CHOOSE HOW TO COMMUNICATE YOUR EMOTIONS

Once you know what you feel, you are ready to decide how to express your emotions. The first choice facing you is whether you wish to communicate your emotions to particular people. As we noted in the previous section, sometimes it is both wise and compassionate to choose not to tell someone what you feel. You may decide that expressing particular emotions would hurt others and would not lead to a constructive outcome. This is not the same thing as not expressing emotions just to avoid tension, because tension between people can be healthy, leading to growth for individuals and relationships as we will see in Chapters 8 and 9.

We may also decide not to communicate emotions because we prefer to keep some of our feelings private. This is a reasonable choice if the feelings we keep to ourselves are not those that others need to know in order to understand us and be in healthy relationships with us. We don't have a responsibility to bare our souls to everyone, nor are we required to tell all of our feelings even to our intimates.

If you decide you do want to communicate your emotions, then you should assess the different ways you might do that and select the one that seems likely to be most effective. Three criteria can help guide our choice of how to express emotions. First, you should evaluate your current state. If you are agitated or enraged, you may not be able to express yourself clearly and fairly. In moments of extreme emotionality, our perceptions may be distorted, and we may say things we don't mean. Remember that communication is irreversible—we cannot unsay what we have once said. According to Daniel Goleman (1995b), it takes about 20 minutes for us to cleanse our minds and bodies of anger. Thus, if you are really angry or feeling other negative emotions, you may wish to wait until you've cooled down so that you can discuss your feelings more fruitfully.

A second criterion is to select appropriate times to discuss feelings. Timing can be very important, because most of us are more able to listen and respond when we are not preoccupied, stressed, rushed, or tired. Generally, it's not productive to launch a discussion of feelings when we or others don't have the ability to focus on the conversation. It may be better to defer discussion of a feeling until a time when you and the other person have the psychological and physical resources to engage mindfully in discussion.

A third criterion is to select a setting that is appropriate for discussing feelings. Many feelings can be expressed well in a variety of settings. It would be appropriate, for instance, while strolling with a friend through a shopping mall, walking on campus, or in a conversation in a private setting that you felt happy. However, it might not be appropriate or constructive to tell a friend in a public setting that you felt angry or disappointed in her. Doing so could make the other person feel on display, which is likely to arouse defensiveness. Thus, there's less likelihood that the two of you can have a constructive, open discussion of feelings.

OWN YOUR FEELINGS

Review

Effective Choices on Communicating Emotions

- Evaluate your current states.
- Select an appropriate time.
- Select an appropriate setting.

Owning your feelings is so important to effective communication that the guideline bears repeating. Using what is called "I–language" to express feelings has two noteworthy benefits. First, it reminds you that you—not anyone else—have responsibility for your feelings. When we rely on "you–language" ("You hurt me"), we risk misleading ourselves about our accountability for our emotions.

A second reason to avoid you–language is that it tends to make others feel defensive. When others feel on guard, they are less likely to listen thoughtfully and respond sensitively to our expression of emotion. We expand the possibility for healthy, rich interpersonal relationships when we take responsibility for our own feelings by using I–language. We visit these concepts further in Chapter 5.

MONITOR YOUR SELF-TALK

A fourth guideline for communicating feelings effectively is to monitor your self-talk. You'll recall from Chapter 2 that the ways we communicate with ourselves affect how we feel and act. **Self-talk** is intrapersonal communication, or communication we have with ourselves. We engage in self-talk to do the emotion work we discussed earlier in this chapter. We might say, "I shouldn't feel angry," or "I don't want to come across as a wimp by letting on how much that hurt." Thus, we may talk ourselves out of or into feelings and out of or into ways of expressing our feelings.

Self-talk can work for us or against us, depending on whether we manage it or it manages us. This point is stressed by Tom Rusk and Natalie Rusk in their book *Mind Traps* (1988); they assert that many people have self-defeating ideas that get in the way of their effectiveness and happiness. According to the Rusks, "feelings are the key to personal change" (p. xix). Unless we learn to manage our feelings effectively, we cannot change patterns of behaviour that leave us stuck in ruts.

Psychologist Martin Seligman (1990) agrees with this point. According to Seligman, "Our thoughts are not merely reactions to events; they change what ensues" (p. 7). In other words, the thoughts we communicate to ourselves affect what happens in our lives. Given this, it is worthwhile to develop skill in monitoring our self-talk so that we can choose how to think and feel.

Much of what we say to ourselves reflects social perspectives that we have internalized. By tuning in to your self-talk about emotions, you can make careful, informed choices about what to express and what not to express.

Apply the Idea

Tuning in to Your Self-Talk

What kinds of self-talk do you engage in when you feel emotions? To find out, describe what you think when you feel the following emotions.

Perceived Emotion	Self-Talk
helplessness	"There's nothing I can do to change things." "I'm just a little fish in this pond."
self-pity	_____
jealousy	_____
impatience	_____
sadness, verging on tears	_____

Monitoring self-talk about feelings also allows us to gain more accurate and constructive understandings of ourselves. This happens when we learn to identify and challenge irrational beliefs about ourselves and how we should feel and act. Irrational beliefs are debilitating ways of evaluating our emotions and ourselves. These **irrational beliefs** hinder our ability to manage and express emotions effectively.

Albert Ellis (1962) is a therapist who developed the **rational-emotive approach to feelings.**

This approach emphasizes using rational thinking to challenge debilitating emotions and beliefs that undermine healthy self-concepts and relationships. The rational-emotive approach to feelings proceeds through four steps, as shown in Figure 4.5. (Ellis's original ideas are discussed further in "Albert Ellis in Action.")

The first step is to monitor your emotional reactions to events and experiences that distress you. Notice what's happening in your body; notice your nonverbal behaviour. Does your stomach tighten? Do you feel lightheaded? Are you clenching your teeth? Is your heart racing? Do you feel nauseous?

The second step in Ellis's approach is to identify the events and situations to which you have unpleasant responses. Look for commonalities among situations. For example, perhaps you notice that your heartbeat races and your palms get clammy when

Figure 4.5
The Rational-Emotive Approach to Feelings

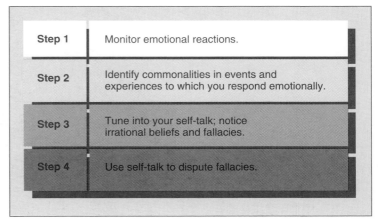

Step 1	Monitor emotional reactions.
Step 2	Identify commonalities in events and experiences to which you respond emotionally.
Step 3	Tune into your self-talk; notice irrational beliefs and fallacies.
Step 4	Use self-talk to dispute fallacies.

you talk with professors, teachers, supervisors, and academic advisers, but you don't have any of these physiological responses when you interact with friends, co-workers, or people whom you supervise. You label your emotions as insecurity in the former cases and security in the latter ones. One commonality among the situations in which you feel insecure is the power differential between you and the other person. This could suggest that you feel insecure when talking with someone who has more power than you.

The third step is to tune in to your self-talk. Listen to what's happening in your head. What is the socially conscious part of you saying? Is it telling you that you shouldn't feel certain emotions ("It's stupid to feel anxious," "Don't be a wimp")? Is it telling you to stuff your feelings ("Don't let on that you're insecure")? Is it telling you that you should feel something you don't ("You're supposed to feel confident and in command")?

Ellis places special emphasis on identifying fallacies in our self-talk about emotions. These fallacies encourage us to evaluate ourselves negatively, and the negativity is not based on logic but on invalid, unrealistic thought. Table 4.1 lists some of the most common fallacies that sabotage realistic appraisals of ourselves, our feelings, and our actions.

Communication Notes

Albert Ellis in Action

Albert Ellis was not a mild-mannered, detached sort of therapist—nor did he want to be. He was known for his dramatic style and for pushing, pushing, pushing his clients. He firmly believed that people whom many clinicians diagnosed as neurotics were really not neurotic but suffering only from irrational thinking. He often described this as stupid thinking on the part of non-stupid people. And Ellis was convinced that we can unlearn stupid behaviours in order to function more effectively.

In dealing with clients, Ellis would berate them for stupid thinking, all the while insisting that they were not stupid people. He wanted his clients to learn new and better ways of thinking. "You're living under a tyranny of shoulds. Stop shoulding yourself to death," he would demand. "Quit thinking wrong and start thinking right," he urged. And his clients responded to Ellis's unorthodox style and therapy. Many learned to think differently, and this led them to feel and act differently and more effectively in their lives.

Sources: Ellis, A. (1962). *Reason and emotion in psychotherapy.* New York: Lyle Stuart; Ellis, A., & Harper, R. (1975). *A new guide to rational living.* Englewood Cliffs, NJ: Prentice-Hall; Seligman, M.E.P. (1990). *Learned optimism: How to change your mind and your life.* New York: Simon & Schuster/Pocket Books.

Table 4.1

Common Fallacies About Emotions

Fallacy	Typical Effects
Perfectionism	Unrealistically low self-concept Stress Chronic dissatisfaction with self Jealousy and envy of others
Obsession with shoulds	Saps energy for constructive work Can make others defensive Can alienate self from feelings Unrealistic standards set the self up for failure
Overgeneralization	Perceives one failure as typical of self Generalize inadequacies in some domains to total self
Taking responsibility for others	Thinking you are responsible for others' feelings Guilt for how others feel Deprives others of taking responsibility for selves
Helplessness	Believing that there is nothing you can do to change how you feel Resignation: depression
Fear of catastrophic failure	Extreme negative fantasies and scenarios of what could happen Inability to do things because of what might happen

Therapists who teach their clients to use the rational-emotive approach to feelings emphasize learning to dispute irrational fallacies. Following this advice, we can use our self-talk to challenge the debilitating fallacies. For example, assume that Tyronne has been working well at his job and thinks his boss should give him a raise. He tunes in to his self-talk (Step 3) and hears himself saying, "Well, maybe I shouldn't ask for a raise because after all, I have made some mistakes. I could do better." This self-talk reflects the fallacy of perfectionism. Tyronne listens further to himself and hears this message: "If I ask him for a raise and he gets angry, he might fire me, and then I wouldn't have a job and couldn't stay in school. Without a degree I

The greatest gift we give is to validate another's feelings and listen to them.

Photos: J. Liburd

have no future." This self-talk exemplifies the fear of catastrophic failure.

How might Tyronne dispute these fallacies? To challenge the perfectionism fallacy, he could say, "True, I'm not perfect, but I'm doing more and better work than the other employees hired at the same time I was." To dispute the fallacy of catastrophic failure, Tyronne might say to himself, "Well, he's not likely to fire me because I do my job well and training someone new would be a headache and an expense he doesn't need. And what if he does fire me? It's not like this is the only job in the world. With my good work record I could get another job pretty fast." Instead of letting our self-talk defeat us with irrational beliefs and debilitating fallacies, we can use our self-talk to question and challenge the irrational thinking that undermines us. It is useful to remember the phrase "Catch yourself doing something right."

RESPOND SENSITIVELY WHEN OTHERS COMMUNICATE EMOTIONS

A final guideline is to respond sensitively when others express their feelings to you. Learning to communicate your emotions effectively is only half the process of communicating about emotions. You also want to become skilled in listening and responding to others when they share their feelings with you.

Many people feel inadequate when others express feelings. Often they respond with highly general statements such as "Things will look better after you get a good night's sleep," "Time heals all wounds," "You'll be fine," "Your anger is only hurting you," "You'll feel better if you get this in perspective."

Although such statements may be intended to reassure others, they can devalue others' feelings. In effect, they tell others that they aren't allowed to feel what they feel or that they will be okay (right, normal) once they stop feeling what they are feeling. This denies others the right to feel.

Another mistake many people make when responding to others' expression of feelings is to try to solve the other person's problem or to make the feeling go away. Scholars who have studied gender (Tannen, 1990; Wood, 1997) observe that the tendency to try to solve others' problems is more common in men than women. Helping another solve a problem may be appreciated, but usually it's not the first support a person needs when she or he is feeling strong emotions. What most of us need first is the freedom to feel what we are feeling and to have others accept that.

A more effective approach is to let others talk about their feelings and offer support. You don't have to try to feel as another person does to accept what she or he is feeling as legitimate. While listening, it's helpful to interject a few minimal encouragers, which we will discuss in Chapter 7. Saying "I understand" and "Go on" state that you accept the other person's feelings and invite him or her to continue talking. It is appropriate to mention your own experiences briefly to show you empathize. However, it's not advisable to refocus the conversation on you and your experiences. You may briefly offer personal information and then return to focus on the other.

Paraphrasing, which we will discuss in Chapter 7, is another way to show that you understand what another feels. When you mirror back not only the content but also the feeling of what another says, it confirms the other and what he or she feels. "So, it sounds as if you were really surprised by what happened. Is that right?" "What I'm hearing is that you are more hurt than angry. Does that sound right to you?" These examples of paraphrasing mirror the speaker's feelings and also show that you are listening actively.

The guidelines we've identified may not make emotional communication easy or comfortable in all situations. Following them, however, will give you a firm foundation for understanding and expressing your feelings and responding effectively when others discuss their feelings with you.

Review

An easy trilogy to remember is Express your emotions without causing damage to yourself, your relationships, or property.

Chapter Summary

In this chapter we explored the complex world of emotions and our communication about them. We considered different views of what's involved in experiencing and expressing emotions. From our review of theories we learned that emotions have physiological, perceptual, linguistic, and social dimensions. We also examined some of the reasons people don't express feelings or express them ineffectively. The final focus of our attention was guidelines for effective communication about emotions. We identified five guidelines that can help us be effective when expressing our feelings or responding to the feelings of others. Because these guidelines are critical to interpersonal communication, we'll close the chapter by restating them:

1. Identify your emotions.
2. Choose how to communicate your emotions.
3. Own your feelings.
4. Monitor your self-talk.
5. Respond sensitively when others communicate emotions.

Key Concepts

- cognitive labelling view of emotions
- counterfeit emotional language
- deep acting
- emotional intelligence
- emotions
- emotion work
- feeling rules
- framing rules
- interactive view of emotions
- irrational beliefs
- organismic view of emotions
- perceptual view of emotions
- rational-emotive approach to feelings
- self-talk
- surface acting

For Further Thought & Discussion

1. Do you rely on only a few emotional words to express your feelings? If so, monitor your emotional language and work to enlarge your emotional vocabulary. Can you generate more precise words to describe your feelings?

2. Use your InfoTrac College Edition to survey advice about communicating emotions that is published in popular magazines. Survey articles in magazines such as *Chatelaine* or *Maclean's*. How does advice in popular magazines compare with what you read in this chapter?

3. Review the fallacies discussed in the last section of this chapter. Do any of those fallacies show up in your intrapersonal communication? After reading about the fallacies and ways to challenge them, can you monitor and revise your intrapersonal communication?

4. We discussed different perspectives on emotions. Which of the perspectives makes most sense to you? Why? Explain how the perspective you favour gives you insight into emotions that you don't get from other perspectives.

5. Reread "Wild Pigs Run Amok." Can you identify analogous rituals for expressing emotions in Western culture? What socially accepted ways exist for expressing grief, anger, and other emotions?

6. How did you learn which emotions it was acceptable for you to express? Do you think what you were taught reflects gender and cultural expectations?

7. What ethical principles can you identify to guide when and how people express emotions to others? Is honesty always the best policy? Is it ethical for one person to decide what another should know or can handle?

The World of Words

Everyday Encounters
By Stephen Lee

Many children in Canada have heard the nursery rhyme, "Sticks and stones can break my bones, but words can never hurt me." By now, most of us have figured out that isn't true. Words can hurt us, sometimes very deeply. Words can also enchant, comfort, teach, amuse, and inspire us. We use language to plan, dream, remember, evaluate, and reflect on ourselves and the world around us. Words, in short, are powerful aspects of everyday life. "How Words Hurt Us" provides some examples of the power of words.

The human world is a world of words and meanings. Just as weavers weave individual threads together to create fabric, so do we weave words together to create meaning in our lives. We use words to express ourselves and to give meaning to our lives and activities. In this chapter, we take a close look at the verbal dimension of communication and how it affects personal identity and interpersonal interaction. We begin by defining symbols and symbolic abilities. Next, we explore different communication cultures to appreciate how various social groups communicate. We close the chapter by discussing guidelines for effective verbal communication.

THE SYMBOLIC NATURE OF LANGUAGE

As we discovered in our discussion of perception, we do not deal with raw reality most of the time. Instead, we abstract only certain parts of reality to notice and label. After we label experiences, we often respond to our labels, not to the experiences themselves. This means that our perceptions and experiences are filtered through symbols. To appreciate the importance of sym-

Communication Notes

How Words Hurt Us

To realize how powerfully words can affect us, consider how you feel about the following words:

drunk	alcoholic	problem drinker	person with a disease
nigger	Negro	coloured	Black
kike	Hebrew	Jew	Jewish person
queer	fag	homosexual	gay/lesbian
workaholic	overworker	hard worker	committed professional
chick	bimbo	girl	woman
retard	slow	handicapped	person with a disability
chug	Indian	Aboriginal	First Nations person

bols in our lives, we'll discuss what they are and how they affect us personally and interpersonally.

Symbols are arbitrary, ambiguous, abstract representations of a phenomenon. For instance, your name is a symbol that represents you. House is a symbol that stands for a particular kind of building. Love is a symbol that represents intense feelings. All language and much nonverbal behaviour is symbolic, but not all symbols are language. Art, music, and objects also are symbols that stand for feelings, thoughts, and experiences. We'll consider three key qualities of symbols: they are arbitrary, ambiguous, and abstract (see Figure 5.1).

SYMBOLS ARE ARBITRARY

Symbols are **arbitrary,** which means they are not intrinsically connected to what they represent. For instance, your name has no necessary or natural connection to you. All of our symbols are arbitrary because we could easily use other symbols as long as we all agreed on their meanings. Certain words seem right because as a society we agree to use them in particular ways, but they have no natural correspondence with their referents. Further, meanings change over time. In the 1950s, gay meant lighthearted and merry; today it is generally understood to refer to homosexuals. The majority of publishers and dictionaries no longer allow male-generic language, which uses male terms (chairman, postman, mankind) to represent both women and men. Our language also changes as we invent new words. Black communities began using "disrespect" as a verb to describe behaviours that demean someone. Now the term "disrespect" and its abbreviated form, "dis," are in the general language and are included in the newest dictionaries: In the Gage Canadian dictionary of 2000, widely used as a college dictionary of the English language, "dis" appears, along with the definition "to show disrespect or contempt for; a put-down or other show of disrespect" (deWolf et al., 2000, p. 442).

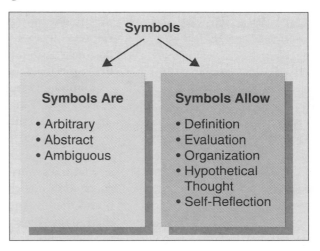

Figure 5.1
Symbols

SYMBOLS ARE AMBIGUOUS

Symbols are also **ambiguous,** which means their meanings aren't clear-cut or fixed. There are variations in what words mean. A good friend means someone to hang out with to one person and someone to confide in to another. The term "nice clothes" means different things to people in the working class and to people who are very affluent. Christmas, Hanukkah, and Thanksgiving carry distinct connotations for people who have families and for those

The symbols for food were arbitrary and ambiguous. The food, on the other hand, was fabulous.

Photo: A. Henry

who don't. Affirmative action has different meanings for people who have experienced discrimination and for those who have not. Although the words are the same, what they mean varies as a result of individuals' unique experiences.

Although words don't mean exactly the same thing to everyone, within a culture many symbols have an agreed-on range of meanings (Mead, 1934). In learning language, we learn not only words but also the meanings and values of our society. Thus, all of us know that dogs are four-footed creatures, but each of us also has personal meanings based on dogs we have known and our experiences with them.

The ambiguity of symbols explains why misunderstandings so often arise in interpersonal communication. We tend to assume that words mean the same thing to others as they do to us. But the ambiguity of symbols implies that people don't always agree on meanings. A mother tells her three-year-old daughter she needs to be more responsible about putting away her toys and later discovers that the little girl has tucked all of her stuffed animals into beds around the house. That's what being more responsible meant to her.

Ambiguity frequently surfaces in friendships and romantic relationships. For example, Pearl tells her boyfriend that he's not being attentive, meaning that she wants him to listen more closely to what she says. However, he infers she wants him to call more often and open doors for her. The word "love" means different things to people brought up in abusive and nonabusive families. Similarly, spouses often have different meanings for "doing my share" of home chores. To most women, it means doing half of the work, but to men it tends to mean doing more than their fathers, which is still less than many wives do (Hochschild with Manchung, 1989).

According to a relationship counsellor, a common problem between intimates is language that creates ambiguity (Beck, 1988). A wife asks her husband to be more loving, but she and he have different understandings of

Student Voices

Dammon:

A while ago I told my girlfriend I needed more independence. She got all upset because she thought I didn't love her anymore and was pulling away. All I meant was that I need some time with the guys and some for just myself. She said that the last time a guy said he wanted more independence, she found out he was dating others.

what being more loving means. Suggesting that a friend should be more sensitive doesn't provide a very clear idea of what you want. To minimize the problems of ambiguity, it's important to be as clear as possible when communicating. Thus, it's more effective to say "I would like you to look at me and give feedback when I'm talking" than to say "I wish you'd be more attentive."

Apply the Idea

Communicating Clearly

To express yourself clearly, it's important that you learn to translate ambiguous words into concrete language. Practice translating with the statements below.

Ambiguous language:	Clear language:
You are rude.	I don't like it when you interrupt me.
You're conceited.	_____
I want more freedom.	_____
Let's have a low-key evening.	_____
We need to be closer.	_____

SYMBOLS ARE ABSTRACT

Finally, symbols are **abstract,** which means they are not concrete or tangible. They stand for ideas, people, events, objects, feelings, and so forth, but they are not the things they represent. In Chapter 3, we discussed the process of abstraction whereby we move further and further away from concrete reality. The symbols we use vary in abstractness. "Scrambles" is the name of a cat. "Cat" is a more abstract label for her. "Animal" is even more abstract. The ladder of abstraction is a valuable way to view not only the impact our labels have on our perceptions but also the role abstract language plays in misunderstandings in communication. As our symbols become increasingly abstract, the potential for confusion mushrooms. One of the ways this happens is overgeneralization. Couple counsellor Aaron Beck (1988) reports that overly general language distorts how partners think about a relationship. They may make broad, negative statements such as "You never go along with my preferences," or "You always interrupt me." In most cases, such statements are overgeneralizations that are not entirely accurate. Yet by symbolizing experience this way, partners frame how they think about it. Researchers have shown that we are more likely to recall behaviours that are consistent with how we've labelled people than those that are inconsistent (Fincham & Bradbury, 1987). When we say a friend is always insensitive, we'll probably remember all of the occasions in which she or he was insensitive, and we'll overlook times when she or he was sensitive.

Bobby Patton and Kurt Ritter (1976), two communication scholars, suggest that misunderstandings can be minimized by using specific language. It's clearer to say "I wish you wouldn't interrupt when I'm talking" than "Don't be so dominating."

PRINCIPLES OF VERBAL COMMUNICATION

We've seen that language is symbolic, which means it consists of arbitrary, ambiguous, and abstract representations of other phenomena. Building on this understanding, we can now explore how verbal symbols work. We'll discuss four principles of verbal communication.

LANGUAGE AND CULTURE REFLECT EACH OTHER

Language and cultural life are intricately interconnected. Each reflects the other in an ongoing process. Intercultural communication scholars Larry Samovar and Richard Porter (1995) claim that communication and culture cannot be separated, because each influences the other. "Our Multicultural Language" demonstrates the various cultures reflected in Canada.

Communication reflects cultural values and perspectives. The words in a language reflect what the mainstream in a particular culture regards as worth naming. We do not name what we consider unimportant. Cultures also don't give symbolic reality to practices of which the majority of members disapprove.

Concepts at a Glance

The Four Principles of Communication

- Language and culture reflect each other.
- Meanings of language are subjective.
- Language use is rule-guided.
- Punctuation of language shapes meaning.

Communication Notes

Our Multicultural Language

Although the word "multicultural" has only recently come into popular usage, our society and our language have always been multicultural. See if you recognize the cultural origins of the following everyday words.

1. brocade
2. chocolate
3. cotton
4. klutz
5. khaki

6. silk
7. skunk
8. gingham
9. noodle
10. zombie

Answers: 1. Spanish; 2. Nahuatl (Native American); 3. Arabic; 4. Yiddish; 5. Hindi; 6. Greek; 7. Algonquian (First Nations); 8. Malay; 9. German; 10. Congo.

Source: Carnes, J. (1994, Spring). An uncommon language. *Teaching Tolerance*, 56–63.

Antagonists to same-sex marriage fight against the use of the word "marriage" to apply to enduring relationships between members of the same sex.

The mainstream values of a culture are also reflected in calendars by which social groups' important days are and are not named. Look at a calendar. Do you find the following holidays recognized: Christmas, Thanksgiving, New Year's Day, Easter? Do you find these holidays on the calendar: Hanukkah, Kwanzaa, Passover, Yom Kippur, Elderly Day, Ramadan? Standard Western calendars reflect the Christian heritage of the mainstream members of the culture.

To understand further how cultural values are woven into language, consider the adages of a culture and what they express about social values. What is meant by the common saying "Every man for himself"? Does it reflect the idea that men, and not women, are the standard? Does it reflect individualism as a value? What is meant by the phrase "The early bird gets the worm"? Compare the values in common adages in Canada with those from other cultures. In Africa, two popular adages are "The child has no owner," and "It takes a whole village to raise a child," and in China a common saying is "No need to know the person, only the family" (Samovar & Porter, 1994). What values are expressed by these sayings? How are they different from mainstream Western values and the language that embodies them?

To recognize the values woven into cultures and their languages, it's useful to compare different cultures and the ways in which they use language. For example, many Asian languages include specific words to describe particular relationships, such as my grandfather's sister, my mother's uncle, my youngest son. These words reflect traditional Asian cultures' emphasis on family relationships (Ferrante, 1995). The English language has far fewer words to represent specific kinship bonds, which suggests that Western culture places less priority on ties beyond those in the immediate family.

Scholars of language and culture maintain that the language we learn shapes how we categorize the world and even how we perceive and think about our world (Fantini, 1991; Hakuta, 1986). For example, Hopi Indians have one word for water in open space and a separate word for water in a container. The English language has only the one noun, water. In Canada, we perceive saying goodbye to guests as a single event. In contrast, in Japan, saying good-bye is a process. Hosts and guests say goodbye in the living room and again at the front door. Guests walk a distance from the house, then turn and wave goodbye to the hosts who are waiting at their gate or door to wave the third goodbye. "The Whorf-Sapir View of Language" (page 168) argues that how we perceive our world is guided by language.

Communication also changes cultures. A primary way that communication changes cultural values and perspectives is by naming things in ways that alter understandings. For example, the term "date rape" was coined in the late 1980s. Although probably many women had been forced to have sex with dates before that time, until the term was born there was no way to describe what happened as a violent and criminal act (Wood, 1992b).

Communication Notes

The Whorf-Sapir View of Language

Studies by anthropologists reveal that our perceptions are guided by language. The language of the Hopi Indians makes no distinction between stationary objects and moving processes, whereas English uses nouns and verbs respectively. The English word "snow" is the only word we have to define frozen, white precipitation that falls in the winter. In Arctic cultures where snow is a major aspect of life, there are many words to define snow that is powdery, icy, dry, wet, and so forth. The distinctions are important to designate which snows allow safe travel, hunting, and other activities.

Source: Whorf, B. (1956). *Language, thought, and reality.* New York: MIT Press/Wiley.

Cultural understandings of other sexual activities have been similarly reformed by the coining of terms such as "sexual harassment" and "marital rape," both of which characterize negatively activities that previously had been perceived as acceptable.

Language is a primary tool of social movements that change cultural life and meanings. Language has been influential in altering social views of persons with disabilities. Whereas "disabled person" was a common phrase for many years, many people are now aware that this label can offend, and they know the preferred phrase is "person with a disability" (Braithwaite, 1996). The earlier term "handicapped" reflects the British attitudes and economic realities of an earlier century where a person with a disability was relegated to begging on the street with "cap in hand." Social views of deaf people have also been altered in recent times. People with limited hearing have challenged the idea that deafness is related to intelligence. In addition, deaf, as a medical condition, has been distinguished from Deaf, as a culture with rich

Student Voices

Bryn:

It was 15 years ago when I was just starting college that a professor sexually harassed me, only I didn't know what to call it then. I felt guilty, like maybe I'd done something to encourage him, or I felt maybe I was overreacting to his kissing and touching me. But after the Clarence Thomas–Anita Hill hearings in 1991, I had a name for what happened—a name that said he was wrong, not me.

linguistic resources (Carl, 1998). Language and culture are closely related. As we learn language, we also learn the values, perspectives, and beliefs of our culture. In turn, as we use language, we often reflect and reinforce the cultural values it entails. In other cases, we use language to challenge and change taken-for-granted ideas and values in our culture.

MEANINGS OF LANGUAGE ARE SUBJECTIVE

Because symbols are abstract, ambiguous, and arbitrary, their meanings are never self-evident or absolute. Instead, we have to interpret symbols to figure out what they mean. We construct meanings in the process of interacting with others and through dialogues we carry on in our own head (Duck, 1994a, 1994b; Shotter, 1993). The process of constructing meaning is itself symbolic, because we rely on words to think about what things mean.

Photo: © Photodisc

Interpretation is an active, creative process we use to make sense of words. If we say "dinner" to a dog, the dog will respond in a predictable manner because "dinner" has a fixed, exact meaning to the dog. To us, however, the word "dinner" may mean many things—time for family talk, a romantic experience, a struggle to stick to a diet, or tension among those present at the meal. For humans, words are ambiguous and layered with multiple meanings. Although we're usually not conscious of the effort we invest to interpret words, we continuously engage in the process of constructing meanings.

What words mean depends on the self-esteem and previous experiences of the individual to whom they are directed. Individuals who are secure and have high self-esteem are not as likely to be hurt as individuals who have less self-confidence. Relationship-level meanings rely especially on understandings of the person speaking and the context of communication. Because symbols require interpretation, communication is an ongoing process of creating meanings.

Student Voices

Dirk:

It took me a long time to understand certain words in my fiancé's family. When I first met them, I heard them talk about the wife's career, but I knew she did not work. In the family, they say her career is keeping track of all the children. They also talked about the husband's hobby of being broke. I thought this meant he spent a lot of money on a hobby or something, but what they mean is he likes to give to causes and this takes a lot of money. It took several visits for me to understand the family vocabulary.

What regulative rules did you learn in school?

Photo: © Photodisc

LANGUAGE USE IS RULE-GUIDED

Verbal communication is patterned by unspoken but broadly understood rules (Argyle & Henderson, 1985; Schiminoff, 1980).

Communication rules are shared understandings of what communication means and what behaviours are appropriate in various situations. For example, we understand that people take turns speaking and that we should speak softly in libraries. In the course of interacting with our families and others, we unconsciously absorb rules that guide how we communicate and how we interpret others' communication. According to Judi Miller (1993), children begin to understand and follow communication rules by the time they are one to two years old.

There are two kinds of rules that govern communication: regulative rules and constitutive rules (Cronen, Pearce, & Snavely, 1979; Pearce, Cronen, & Conklin, 1979).

Regulative Rules

Regulative rules regulate interaction by specifying when, how, where, and with whom to talk about certain things. For instance, Westerners know not to interrupt when someone else is speaking in a formal setting, but in more casual situations, interruptions may be appropriate. In other cultures, there are strong rules against interrupting in any context. Some families have a rule that people cannot argue at the dinner table. Families also teach us rules about how to communicate in conflict situations (Honeycutt, Woods, & Fontenot, 1993; Jones & Gallois, 1989; Yerby, Buerkel-Rothfuss, & Bochner, 1990). In Chapter 4 we learned that our family experiences around emotions taught us the rules about expression of certain feelings. Regulative rules also

Concepts at a Glance

Two kinds of Communication Rules

1. Regulative Rules
2. Constitutive Rules

Student Voices

Yumiko:

I try to teach my children to follow the customs of my native Japan, but they are learning to be Canadian. I scold my daughter, who is seven this year, for talking loudly and speaking when she has not been addressed, but she tells me all the other kids talk loudly and talk when they wish to talk. I tell her it is not polite to look directly at others, but she says everyone looks at others here. She communicates as a Canadian, not a Japanese.

define when, where, and with whom it's appropriate to show affection and disclose private information. Regulative rules vary across cultures so that what is considered appropriate in one society may be regarded as impolite or offensive elsewhere.

Constitutive Rules

Constitutive rules define what communication means by specifying how certain communicative acts are to be counted. We learn what counts as respect (paying attention), affection (kisses, hugs), and rudeness (interrupting). We also learn what communication is expected if we want to be perceived as a good friend (showing support, being loyal), a responsible employee (meeting deadlines, developing strong reports), and a desirable romantic partner (showing respect and trust, being faithful, sharing confidences). We learn constitutive and regulative rules from both particular others and the generalized other. Like regulative rules, constitutive ones are shaped by cultures.

Apply the Idea

Communication Rules

Think about the regulative and constitutive rules you follow in your communication. For each item below identify two rules you learned.

Regulative Rules

List rules that regulate how you

- *Talk with elders*
- *Interact at dinner time*
- *Have first exchanges in the morning*
- *Greet casual friends on campus*
- *Talk with professors or teachers*

Constitutive Rules

How do you communicate to show

- *Respect*
- *Love*
- *Disrespect*
- *Support*

After you've identified your rules, talk with others in your class about the rules they follow. Are there commonalities among your rules that reflect broad cultural norms? What explains differences in individuals' rules?

Everyday interaction is guided by rules that tell us when to speak, what to say, and how to interpret others' communication. Our social interactions, which involve I–It and I–You relationships, tend to adhere to rules that are widely shared in our society. Interaction between intimates also follows rules, but these may not be broadly shared by members of the culture. Intimate partners negotiate private rules to guide how they communicate and what certain things mean (Wood, 1982, 1995c). Couples craft personal rules for whether and how to argue, express love, make decisions, and spend time together (Beck, 1988; Fitzpatrick, 1988).

It's important to understand that we don't have to be aware of communication rules in order to follow them. For the most part, we're not conscious of the rules that guide how, when, where, and with whom we communicate about various things. We may not realize we have rules until one is broken and we become aware that we had an expectation. A study by Victoria DeFrancisco (1991) revealed that between spouses there was a clear pattern in which husbands interrupted wives and were unresponsive to topics wives initiated. Both husbands and wives were unaware of the rules, but their communication nonetheless sustained the pattern. Becoming aware of communication rules empowers you to change those that don't promote good interaction, as Emily's commentary illustrates.

Student Voices

Emily:

My boyfriend and I had this really frustrating pattern about planning what to do. He'd say, "What do you want to do this weekend?" And I'd say, "I don't know. What do you want to do?" Then he'd suggest two or three things and ask me which of them sounded good. I would say they were all fine with me, even if they weren't. And this would keep on forever. Both of us had a rule not to impose on the other, and it kept us from stating our preferences, so we just went in circles about any decision. Well, two weekends ago, I talked to him about rules, and he agreed we had one that was frustrating. So we invented a new rule that says each of us has to state what we want to do, but the other has to say if that is not okay. It's a lot less frustrating to figure out what we want to do since we agreed on this rule.

PUNCTUATION OF LANGUAGE SHAPES MEANING

We punctuate communication to decide what it means. This isn't the kind of punctuation you study in grammar classes, although punctuation of communication is also a way of marking a flow of activity into meaningful units. In writing, we use commas, periods, and semicolons to define where ideas stop and start and where pauses are needed. Similarly, in interpersonal communication, **punctuation** defines beginnings and endings of interaction episodes (Watzlawick, Beavin, & Jackson, 1967).

To decide what communication means, we must establish its boundaries. Usually, this involves deciding who started the interaction. When we don't agree on punctuation, problems may arise. If you've ever heard children arguing about who started a fight, you understand the importance of punctuation. A common instance of conflicting punctuation is the demand–withdraw pattern (Bergner & Bergner, 1990; Christensen & Heavey, 1990; James, 1989). In this pattern, one person tries to create closeness with personal talk, and the other strives to maintain autonomy by avoiding intimate discussion (Figure 5.2). The more the first person pushes for personal talk ("Tell me what's going on in your life," "Let's talk about our future"), the further the second withdraws ("There's nothing to tell," "I don't want to talk about the future," silence). Each partner punctuates interaction as starting with the other's behaviour. Thus, the demander thinks "I pursue because you withdraw" and the withdrawer thinks "I withdraw because you pursue."

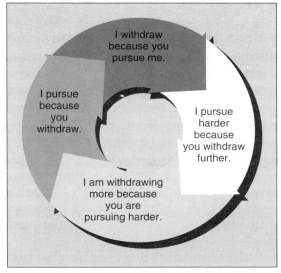

Figure 5.2
The Demand-Withdraw Pattern

|Student Voices|

Robert:

Punctuation helps me understand what happens with me and my girlfriend a lot of times. Sometimes when we first get together she's all steamed and I can't figure out why. I'm like, what's going on? How can you be mad at me when we haven't even started talking? But she's steamed about something that happened the night before or even longer ago. For me, whatever argument we might have had is over—it ended when we separated the last time. But for her, it may not be over—we're still in that episode.

Review

The meaning of verbal communication arises out of

- Cultural teachings
- Subjective interpretations
- Communication rules
- Punctuation

These four principles highlight the creativity involved in constructing meaning.

There is no objectively correct punctuation because it depends on subjective perceptions. When partners don't agree on punctuation, they don't share meanings for what is happening between them. To break out of unconstructive cycles, such as demand–withdraw, partners need, first, to realize they may punctuate differently and, second, to discuss how each of them experiences the pattern. This reminds us of a guideline discussed in Chapter 1: Dual perspective is essential to effective communication.

Apply the Idea

Punctuating Interaction

The next time you and another person get in an unproductive cycle, stop and discuss how each of you punctuates interaction.

1. *What do you define as the start of interaction?*
2. *What does the other person define as the beginning?*
3. *What happens when you learn about each other's punctuation? How does this affect understanding between you?*

Communication Notes

French Language and French-Canadian Identity

Language is a symbol of ethnic pride and distinctiveness. The fight in Quebec for French Language dominance is an issue of identity. Our linguistic journey in Canada has not been an easy one. In 1982, Canada finally established English and French as the official languages of the country. Bill 101, *The Charter of the French Language,* passed in 1977, requires that all signs in Quebec must be displayed in French. Any English words have to appear in a smaller size than the French ones. In April of 2000, the Quebec Superior Court upheld Quebec's French Language sign laws when a grocery store owner and his wife were fined for having the French and English words the same size. It was a matter of identity.

Source: The Council for Canadian Unity http://www.ccu-cuc.ca/en/library/bill_101.html (Retrieved July 3, 2001).

FUNCTIONS OF SYMBOLS

The ability to use symbols allows humans to live in a world of ideas and meanings. Instead of just reacting to our concrete environments, we think about them and sometimes transform them. Philosophers of language have identified five ways symbols affect our lives (Cassirer, 1944; Langer, 1953, 1979). As we discuss each, we'll consider how to realize the constructive power of symbols and minimize the problems they can prompt.

SYMBOLS DEFINE

We use symbols to define experiences, people, relationships, feelings, and thoughts. As we saw in Chapter 3, the definitions we impose shape what things mean to us.

Labels Shape Perceptions

When we label someone, we focus attention on particular aspects of that person and her or his activities, and we necessarily obscure other aspects of who she or he is. We might define a person as an environmentalist, a teacher, a gourmet cook, or a father. Each definition directs our attention to certain aspects of the person. We might talk with the environmentalist about wilderness legislation, discuss class assignments with the teacher, swap recipes with the chef, and exchange stories about children with the father. If we define someone as an Asian, a Buddhist, or a Canadian, then that may be all we notice about the person, although there are many other aspects of her or him. We tend to perceive and interact with people according to how we define them.

Our language reflects our subjective perceptions and, at the same time, it shapes and fixes our perceptions. If you saw a person eat a very large meal, how would you describe what you saw? If the person was a teenage boy, you might describe him as being a growing boy. If the person was a slender woman, you might describe her as having a healthy appetite. If the person was overweight, you may describe him as a glutton. Notice that the amount of food and the act of eating don't change, but our perceptions and labels do.

The labels that we apply to people and things shape how we evaluate and respond to them. According to Joel Best (1989), the impact of labels is especially evident in language about AIDS. Calling it a "moral problem" defines people with the disease as having behaved badly and suggests the solution is to change behaviour. By contrast, calling AIDS a "medical problem" defines people with the disease as having certain biological processes that are not the fault or responsibility of individuals. Consequently, the solution to AIDS as a "medical problem" lies in medical treatment.

Concepts at a Glance

Five Ways Symbols Affect Our Lives

1. Symbols define.
2. Symbols evaluate.
3. Symbols organize perception.
4. Symbols allow hypothetical thought.
5. Symbols allow self-reflection.

Indira:

I know all about totalizing. A teacher in a sociology class was referring to the immigrant population of Canada. She turned toward me and said "We have one in our class. What is it like?" I turned to see who she was talking about. I saw myself as an Indo-Canadian, female pre-med student whose family has been here for two generations. She saw me as an immigrant from India only.

Labels Can Totalize

Totalizing occurs when we respond to a person as if one label (one we have chosen or accepted from others) totally represents who he or she is. We fix on one symbol to define someone and fail to recognize many other aspects of who he or she is (Wood, 1998). Some individuals totalize gay men and lesbians as if sexual orientation is their only important facet. Interestingly, we don't totalize heterosexuals on the basis of their sexuality. Totalizing also occurs when we dismiss people by saying, "He's a Liberal," "She's old," or "He's just a jock." Totalizing is not the same as stereotyping. When we stereotype someone, we define him or her in terms of characteristics of a group. When we totalize others, we negate most of who they are by spotlighting a single aspect of their identity.

Labels Affect Relationships

The symbols we use to define experiences in our relationships affect how we think and feel about those relationships. In a study, romantic couples were asked how they defined differences between them (Wood, Dendy, Dordek, Germany, & Varallo, 1994). Some individuals define differences as positive forces that energize a relationship and keep it interesting. Others define differences as problems or barriers to closeness. The study found a direct connection between how partners defined differences and how they acted. Partners who viewed differences as constructive approached disagreements with curiosity, interest, and a hope for growth through discussion. On the other hand, partners who labelled differences as "problems" tended to deny differences and to avoid talking about them.

   A number of communication scholars have shown that the language we use to think about relationships affects what happens in them (Duck, 1985, 1994a, 1994b; Honeycutt, 1993; Spencer, 1994). People who consistently use negative labels to describe their relationships heighten awareness of what they don't like and diminish perceptions of what they do like (Cloven & Roloff, 1991). It's also been shown that partners who focus on good facets of their relationships are more conscious of virtues in partners and relationships and less bothered by imperfections (Bradbury & Fincham, 1990; Fletcher & Fincham, 1991).

These studies show us that our definitions of relationships can create self-fulfilling prophecies. Because verbal language is ambiguous, arbitrary, and abstract, there are multiple ways we can define any experience. Once we select a label, we tend to see the experience in line with our label. This suggests we should reconsider definitions that undermine healthy self-concepts and interpersonal relationships.

Communication Notes

Nondiscrimination in Housing

Whoops! Real estate ads in the United States may lead to lawsuits if they contain language that offends certain groups. "Great view" excludes persons with visual impairments; "walking distance to shops" offends people in wheelchairs; "master bedroom" suggests sexism; "family room" discriminates against child-free couples and singles; and "newlyweds" excludes gay and lesbian couples who cannot be legally wed.

In 1994, Pennsylvania's Association of Realtors, Newspaper Association, and Human Relations Commission issued a list of about 75 unacceptable words and phrases for real estate ads. Among the forbidden terms:

bachelor pad	couples	mature
children	traditional	senior citizens
private	newlyweds	exclusive

Will Canada follow this trend?

SYMBOLS EVALUATE

Symbols are not neutral or objective descriptions. They are laden with values. This is an intrinsic quality of symbols. In fact, it's impossible to find words that are completely neutral or objective.

Values in Language Reflect and Shape Perceptions

We describe people we like with language that accents their good qualities and downplays their flaws. Just the reverse is true of our descriptions for people we don't like. Restaurants use positive words to heighten the attractiveness of menu entrees. A dish described as "tender London broil gently sautéed in natural juices and topped with succulent mushrooms" sounds more appetizing than one described as "cow carcass cooked in blood and topped with fungus grown in compost and manure."

Perhaps you've seen humorous illustrations of how differently we describe the same behaviours enacted by ourselves, people we like, and people we don't like. I am casual, you are messy; she's a slob. I am organized, you are methodical, he is obsessive-compulsive. I am assertive, you are aggressive, she's a bully. Although these are funny, they also reflect our tendencies to use labels with different evaluations to describe behaviour.

Of course, there are degrees of evaluation in language. We might describe people who speak their minds as assertive, outspoken, courageous, or authoritarian. Each word has a distinct connotation. In recent years, we have become more sensitive to how symbols can hurt people. Most individuals with disabilities prefer not to be called disabled, because that totalizes them in terms of a disability. ("Nondiscrimination in Housing" discusses some forbidden terms in real estate.) Designations for homosexuals are currently in transition. The term "homosexual" has negative connotations and words such as "fairy," "dyke," and "faggot" are considered offensive (see "Reappropriating Language"). Some gays and lesbians use the term "sexual orientation" to suggest they didn't choose their sexuality. Others use the term "sexual preference" to indicate their sexuality is a matter of choice, not genetics. Still others speak of "affectional preference" to signal that their commitment concerns the entire realm of affection, not just sexual activity.

Communication Notes

Reappropriating Language

An interesting communicative phenomenon is the reappropriation of language. This happens when a group reclaims terms others use to degrade it and treats those terms as positive self-descriptions. Reappropriation intends to take the sting out of a term that others use pejoratively.

Some feminists and women musicians have reappropriated the term "girl" to define themselves and to resist the general connotations of childishness.

Some gays have reappropriated the term "queer" and are using it as a positive statement about their identity. Large people have reclaimed the word "fat."

The writer Reynolds Price developed cancer of the spine that left him paraplegic. He scoffs at terms such as "differently abled" and "physically challenged" and refers to himself as a "cripple" and others as "temporarily able-bodied."

Student Voices

Raymond:

I'm as sensitive as the next guy, but I just can't keep up with what language offends what people anymore. When I was younger, "Indian" was an accepted term, then it was "Native," and now it's "First Nations." Sometimes I forget and say "Indian," and I get accused of being racist. It used to be polite to call females "girls," but now that offends a lot of the women I work with. Just this year, I heard that we aren't supposed to say "blind" or "disabled" anymore; we're supposed to say "a person with a visual impairment" and "differently abled." I just can't keep up.

Language Can Be Loaded

Loaded language is words that strongly slant perceptions and thus meanings. For example, American radio personality Rush Limbaugh refers to feminists as Feminazis, which implies feminists are also Nazis. The city of Vancouver, B.C. gets called "Hongcouver" by those few disturbed by the increasing Asian population. Loaded language also encourages negative views of older people. Terms such as "geezers" and "raisins" or "the blue-rinse brigade" incline us to regard older people with contempt or pity. Alternatives such as "senior citizen" and "elder" reflect more respectful attitudes.

Probably many of us have sympathy with Raymond who was 54 years old when he took a communication course. It is hard to keep up with changes in language, and it's inevitable that we will occasionally offend someone unintentionally. Nonetheless, we should try to learn what terms hurt or insult others and avoid using those. It's also advisable for us to tell others when they've referred to us with a term that we dislike. As long as we speak assertively but not confrontationally, it's likely that others will respect our ideas. "Reappropriating Language" examines a trend toward defusing some loaded language.

Language Can Degrade Others

Haig Bosmajian is a scholar of communication and ethics. Throughout his career, he has been concerned with the ways in which language is used to degrade and dehumanize others. Bosmajian notes that how we see ourselves is profoundly influenced by the names we are called (1974). One form of degrading language is **hate speech,** which is language that radically dehumanizes others.

Do you speak Canadian?

Photo: © Photodisc

A malicious and abusive message scrawled on the cars and homes of minority citizens, graffiti in bathrooms and on public buildings is insulting to the social group it castigates.

Language is powerful. The values inherent in the words we use shape our perceptions and those of others. This implies that each of us has an ethical responsibility to recognize the impact of language and to guard against engaging in incivil speech ourselves, as well as not tolerating it from others.

SYMBOLS ORGANIZE PERCEPTIONS

We use symbols to organize our perceptions. As we saw in Chapter 3, we rely on cognitive schemata to classify and evaluate experiences. How we organize experiences affects what they mean to us. For example, your prototype of a good friend affects how you judge particular friends. When we place someone in the category of friend, the category influences how we interpret the friend and his or her communication. An insult is likely to be viewed as teasing if made by a friend, but a call to battle if made by an enemy. The words don't change, but their meaning varies depending on how we organize them.

Symbols Allow Abstract Thought

The organizational quality of symbols also allows us to think about abstract concepts, such as justice, integrity, and good family life. We use broad concepts to transcend specific, concrete activities and to enter the world of conceptual thought and ideals. Because we think abstractly, we don't have to consider every specific object and experience individually. Instead, we can think in general terms.

Symbols Can Stereotype

Our capacity to abstract can also distort thinking. A primary way this occurs is through stereotyping, which is thinking in broad generalizations about a whole class of people or experiences. Examples of stereotypes are "teachers are smart," "jocks are dumb," "feminists hate men," "religious people are good," and "conflict is bad." Notice that stereotypes can be positive or negative generalizations.

Common to all stereotypes is classifying an experience or person into a category based on general knowledge of that category. When we use stereotypical terms such as "WASP," "lesbian," and "working class," we may see only what members of each group have in common and not perceive differences among individuals. We may not perceive the uniqueness of the individual person if we label him or her only as a member of one group. Stereotyping is related to totalizing, because when we stereotype someone, we may not perceive other aspects of them—those not represented in the stereotype. For example, if we stereotype someone as a jock, we may see only what he has in common with other athletes or physical education students.

We may not notice his other aspects such as his political stands, individual values, ethnic background, and so forth.

Clearly, we have to generalize. We simply cannot think about each and every thing in our lives as a specific instance. However, stereotypes can blind us to important differences among phenomena we lump together. Thus, it's important to reflect on stereotypes and to stay alert to differences among people and things we place in any category. We should also remind ourselves that we place others in categories—the categories are our tools. They are not objective descriptions.

SYMBOLS ALLOW HYPOTHETICAL THOUGHT

Where do you hope to be five years from now? What would you do if you were in a friend's position? To answer these questions, you must think hypothetically, which means thinking about experiences and ideas that are not part of your concrete, present situation. Because we can think hypothetically, we can plan, dream, remember, set goals, consider alternative courses of action, and imagine possibilities.

We Can Think Beyond Immediate, Concrete Situations

Hypothetical thought is possible because we use symbols. When we symbolize, we name ideas so that we can hold them in our minds and reflect on them. We can contemplate things that currently have no real existence, and we can remember ourselves in the past and project ourselves into the future. Our ability to live simultaneously in all three dimensions of time explains why we can set goals and work toward them even though there is nothing tangible about them in the moment (Dixson & Duck, 1993). For example, you've invested many hours studying and writing papers because you have the idea of yourself as someone with a university degree. The degree is not real now, nor is the self that you will become once you have the degree. Yet the idea is sufficiently real to motivate you to work hard for many years.

We Live in Three Dimensions of Time

Hypothetical thought also allows us to live in more than just the present moment. We infuse our present lives with knowledge of our histories and plans for our futures. Both past and future affect our experience in the present. Close relationships rely on ideas of past and future. One of the strongest glues for intimacy is a history of shared experiences (Bellah, Madsen, Sullivan, Swindler, & Tipton, 1985; Wood, 1995c). Just knowing that they have weathered rough times in the past helps partners get through trials in the present. Belief in a future also sustains intimacy. We interact differently with people we don't expect to see again than with ones who are continuing parts of our lives. Talking about the future also knits intimates together because it makes real the idea that more lies ahead (Acitelli, 1993; Duck, 1990).

We Can Foster Personal Growth

Thinking hypothetically helps us improve who we are. In Chapter 2 we noted that one guideline for improving self-concept is accepting yourself as in process. This requires you to remember how you were at an earlier time, to appreciate progress you've made, and to keep an ideal image of how you want to be in the future to fuel continued self-improvement. Personal growth also requires that we symbolize a vision of ourselves that is different from how we perceive ourselves currently. If you want to become more outgoing, you imagine yourself talking easily to others, going to parties, and so forth. You rely on symbols to represent the idea of yourself as sociable, and this spurs you forward in your quest for growth.

SYMBOLS ALLOW SELF-REFLECTION

Just as we use symbols to reflect on what goes on outside us, we also use them to reflect on ourselves. Humans don't simply exist and act. Instead, we think about our existence and reflect on our actions. Mead (1934) considered self-reflection to be the basis for human selfhood. He believed that our capacity to look at ourselves and our activities was responsible for civilized society.

Writing can inspire self-reflection.

Photo: J. Todd

The ME Reflects on the I's Activities

According to Mead, there are two aspects to the self. First, there is the I, which is the spontaneous, creative self. The I acts impulsively in response to inner needs and desires, regardless of social norms. The ME is the socially conscious part of the self that monitors and moderates the I's impulses. The ME reflects on the I from the social perspectives of others. The I is impervious to social conventions and expectations, but the ME is keenly aware of them. In an argument, your I

Student Voices

Duk-kyong:

Sometimes I get very discouraged that I do not yet know English perfectly and that there is much I still do not understand about customs in this country. It helps me to remember that when I came here two years ago I did not speak English at all, and I knew nothing about how people act here. Seeing how much progress I have made helps me not to be discouraged with what I do not know yet.

Rachael:

During the first week of college, I went to a mixer and got drunk. I didn't drink in high school, so I didn't know what alcohol could do to me. I was a mess—throwing up, passing out. The next morning I hated myself for how I'd been. But in the long run, I think it was good that it happened. Whenever I feel like having more to drink than I should, I just remember what I was like that night and how much I hated myself that way, and that stops me from having anything more to drink.

may want to hurl a biting insult at someone you don't like, but your ME censors that impulse and reminds you that it's impolite to put others down.

Mead regarded the ME as the reflective part of the self. The ME reflects on the I, so we simultaneously author our lives as the I acts and reflect on our lives as the ME analyzes the I's actions. This means we can think about who we want to be and set goals for becoming the self we desire. We can feel shame, pride, and regret for our actions—emotions that are possible because we self-reflect. We can control what we do in the present by casting ourselves forward in time to consider how we might later feel about our actions.

Self-Reflection Allows Us to Monitor Communication

Self-reflection also empowers us to monitor ourselves, a skill we discussed in Chapter 1 and again in Chapter 4. When we monitor ourselves, we (the ME) notice and evaluate our (the I's) actions and may modify them based on our judgments (Phillips & Wood, 1983; Wood, 1992a). For instance, during a discussion with a friend you might say to yourself, "Gee, I've been talking nonstop about me and my worries, and I haven't even asked how she's doing." Based on your monitoring, you might inquire about your friend's life. When interacting with people from different cultures, we monitor by reminding ourselves they may not operate by the same values and communication rules that we do. Self-reflection allows us to monitor our communication and adjust it to be effective.

Apply the Idea

I—ME Dialogues

To see how the I and the ME work together, monitor your internal dialogues. These are conversations in your head as you consider different things you might say and do.

Monitor your I–ME dialogues as you talk with a professor, a close friend, and a romantic partner. What creative ideas and desires does your I initiate? What social controls does your ME impose? What urges and whims occur to your I? What social norms does your ME remind you of?

How do the I and the ME work together? Does one sometimes muffle the other? What would be lost if your I became silent? What would be missing if your ME disappeared?

Student Voices

Myrella:

I have a really bad temper that can get me into serious trouble if I'm not careful. Sometimes I feel like telling someone off or exploding or whatever, but I stop myself by thinking about how bad I'll look if I do it. I remind myself that others might see me as hysterical or crazy or something, and that helps me to check my temper.

SELF-REFLECTION ALLOWS US TO MANAGE OUR IMAGE

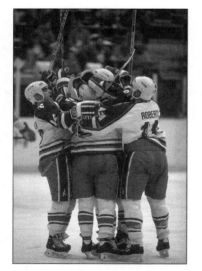

What speech communities do you belong to?

Photo: © Corel

Our image is the identity we present to others. Because we reflect on ourselves from social perspectives, we are able to consider how we appear in others' eyes. When talking with teachers, you may consciously present yourself as respectful, attentive, and studious. When interacting with parents, you may repress some of the language and topics that surface in discussions with your friends. When communicating with someone you'd like to date, you may choose to be more attentive and social than you are in other circumstances. Continuously, we adjust how we present ourselves so that we sculpt our image to fit particular situations and people.

Summing up, we use symbols to define, classify, and evaluate experiences; to think hypothetically; and to self-reflect. Each of these abilities helps us create meaning in our personal and interpersonal lives. Each also carries with it ethical responsibilities for how we use communication and the impact it has on ourselves and others.

SPEECH COMMUNITIES

Although all humans use symbols, we don't all use them in the same way. As we have seen, symbols are social conventions whose meanings we learn in the process of interacting with others. For this reason, people from different

Communication Notes

Canadianisms, eh?

Long before "The Rant," Canadians were known by their linguistic anomaly of "eh." It is a tag on a statement or a question that is as distinctive as "Y'all" is to the southern States. There are several other linguistic anomalies that identify Canada as a distinct linguistic community. Check these out:

Poutine:	A Quebecois specialty of French fries covered in cheese curds and gravy
Screech:	A Newfoundland dark rum
Loonie:	The one-dollar coin with a loon on the back
Rez:	A First Nations reservation
Robertson screw:	The square-holed screw and screwdriver invented by P.L. Robertson in 1908, highly coveted by the international market because of its resistance to being stripped
Snowbird:	A Canadian who flies south during the winter to vacation
Nanaimo bar:	A chocolate custard square originating in Nanaimo, B.C.
Skookum:	The word for "big" in Salish. Skookumchuck Narrows is a treacherous channel of water on the west coast of B.C.
Liver-in:	A Newfoundland live-in maid
Ceilidh:	A Cape Breton dance (borrowed from the Gaelic)

social groups use communication in different ways and attach different meanings to particular communicative acts.

A **speech community** exists when people share norms about how to use talk and what purposes it serves (Labov, 1972). Members of speech communities share perspectives on communication that outsiders do not have. Conversely, members of particular speech communities may not understand the ways communication is used in other speech communities. This explains why cross-cultural communication is sometimes difficult.

Speech communities are not defined by countries or geographic locations, but by shared understandings of how to communicate. In Western society there are numerous speech communities, including First Nations, gay men, lesbian women, deaf individuals, and people with disabilities. Each of these groups has distinct understandings of communication and ways of using it—ways that are not familiar to people outside the group. Some speech communities engage in more dramatic and elaborate verbal play than others. Some are very restrained, and language is minimal. Canada has a unique linguistic heritage. Our two official languages define us as distinct. See the other distinctly Canadian turns of phrase in "Canadianisms, eh?"

GENDER SPEECH COMMUNITIES

Of the many speech communities that exist, gender has received particularly intense study. Because we know more about it than other speech communities, we'll explore gender as a specific example of speech communities and the misunderstandings that surface between members of different speech communities. Researchers have investigated both the way in which women and men are socialized into different understandings of how communication functions and the way their communication differs in practice.

Socialization into Gender Speech Communities

One of the earliest studies showed that children's games are a primary agent of gender socialization (Maltz & Borker, 1982). Typically, children's play is sex-segregated, and there are notable differences between the games the sexes tend to play. These differences seem to teach boys and girls some distinct rules for using communication and interpreting the communication of others.

Games girls favour, such as house and school, involve few players, require talk to negotiate how to play (because there aren't clear-cut guidelines), and depend on cooperation and sensitivity between players. Baseball, soccer, and war, which are typical boys' games, require more players and have clear goals and rules, so less talk is needed to play. Most boys' games are highly competitive both between teams and for individual status within teams. Interaction in games teaches boys and girls distinct understandings of why, when, and how to use talk. Table 5.1 summarizes rules of feminine and masculine speech communities. These rules are generalizations of course.

Reflective Exercise

Examine Table 5.1 and identify how closely your own experience and that of your specific speech community conforms to the generalization of feminine and masculine speech rules.

Gendered Communication in Practice

Research on women's and men's communication reveals that the rules taught through childhood play remain with us. For instance, women's talk is generally more expressive and focused on feelings and personal issues, whereas men's talk tends to be more competitive and focused on doing (instrumental)(Aries, 1987; Beck, 1988; Coates & Cameron, 1989; Johnson, 1989;

Table 5.1
Rules of Gender Speech Communities

Feminine Communication Rules	Masculine Communication Rules
1. Include others. Use talk to show interest in others, and respond to their needs.	1. Assert yourself. Use talk to establish your identity, expertise, knowledge, and so on.
2. Use talk cooperatively. Communication is a joint activity, so people have to work together. It's important to invite others into conversation, wait your turn to speak, and respond to what others say.	2. Use talk competitively. Communication is an arena for proving yourself. Use talk to gain and hold attention, to wrest the talk stage from others; interrupt and reroute topics to keep you and your ideas spotlighted.
3. Use talk expressively. Talk should deal with feelings, personal ideas, and problems and should build relationships with others.	3. Use talk instrumentally. Talk should accomplish something such as solving a problem, giving advice, or taking a stand on issues.

Treichler & Kramarae, 1993; Wood, 1994c, 1994d, 1998). Notice that differences between men and women are matters of degree; they are not absolute dichotomies (Wood, 1997). Your everyday experiences will show you that men sometimes do use talk expressively and women sometimes do use talk instrumentally.

Another general difference between the sexes is what members of each sex tend to perceive as the primary foundation of close relationships. For most men, activities tend to be the primary foundation of close friendships and romantic relationships (Swain, 1989; Wood & Inman, 1993). Thus, men typically cement friendships through doing things together and for one another. For women, communication is the primary foundation of relationships. Talk is not only a means to instrumental ends but also an end in itself. Women also do things with and for people they care about, yet most women see talk as an essential foundation for intimacy. For many women, communicating is the essence of building and sustaining closeness (Aries, 1987; Becker, 1987; Riessman, 1990).

Misunderstandings between Gender Speech Communities

Given the differences between how women and men, in general, use communication, it's hardly surprising that the sexes often misunderstand each other. One clash between gender speech communities occurs when women and men discuss problems. Typically, if a woman tells a man about something that is troubling her, his response is to offer advice or a solution

Review

Men do and women talk!

(Tannen, 1990; Wood, 1994d, 1996). His view of communication as primarily instrumental leads him to show support by doing something. Because feminine communities see communication as a way to build connections with others, however, women often want empathy and discussion of feelings before advice is useful. Thus, women sometimes feel men's responses to their concerns are uncaring and insensitive. On the other hand, men may feel frustrated when women offer empathy and support instead of advice for solving problems. In general, men are also less comfortable making personal disclosures, which women regard as an important way to enhance closeness (Aries, 1987; Wood & Inman, 1993).

Another conundrum in interaction between men and women concerns different styles of listening. Socialized to be responsive and expressive, women tend to make listening noises such as "um hm," "yeah," and "I know what you mean" when others are talking (Tannen, 1990; Wood, 1996, 1998). This is how they show they are attentive and interested. Yet masculine communities don't emphasize using communication responsively, so men tend to make fewer listening noises when another is talking. Thus, women sometimes feel men aren't listening to them because men don't symbolize their attention in the ways women have learned and expect. Notice that this does not mean that men don't listen well. Rather, the ways that many men listen aren't perceived as listening carefully by some women because women and men tend to have different regulative and constitutive rules for listening. You will recall from Chapter 3 that perception shapes meaning.

Perhaps the most common complication in gender communication occurs when a woman says "Let's talk about us." To men, this can often mean trouble, because they may interpret the request as implying there is a problem in a relationship. For women, however, this is not the only—or even the main—reason to talk about a relationship. Feminine speech communities regard talking as the primary way to create relationships and build closeness (Riessman, 1990). In general, women regard talking about a rela-

Student Voices

Suzie:

Gender speech communities explain a big fight my boyfriend and I had. We've been dating for three years, and we're pretty serious, so I wanted our anniversary to be really special. I suggested going out for a romantic dinner where we could talk about the relationship. Andy said that sounded dull, and he wanted to go to a concert where there would be thousands of people. At the time, I thought that meant he didn't care about us like I do, but maybe he feels close when we do things together instead of when we just are together.

tionship as a way to celebrate and increase intimacy. Socialized to use communication instrumentally, however, men tend to think talking about a relationship is useful only if there is some problem to be resolved (Acitelli, 1988, 1993). For men, the preferred mode of enhancing closeness is to do things together. Suzie's commentary illustrates this gender difference.

OTHER SPEECH COMMUNITIES

Gender, of course, is not the only basis of speech communities, and communication between men and women is not the only kind of interaction that may be plagued by misunderstandings. Research indicates that communication patterns vary among social classes. For example, working-class people tend to use shorter, simpler sentences, less elaborate explanations, and more conventional grammar than members of the middle class (Bernstein, 1973).

Speech communities are also shaped by race and ethnicity so that different groups engage in distinct communication patterns. Imagine this scenario: A Western businessman goes to Japan to negotiate a deal. When the Westerner makes his proposal, the Japanese businessman responds, "I see you have put much thought into this idea." Assuming this indicates the Japanese executive is pleased with the proposal, the Westerner says, "Then, shall we sign the contract and be on our way?" The Japanese executive replies, "I think we have much to talk about on your good proposal." What's happening here? If you are unfamiliar with Japanese communication styles, you might assume that the Japanese businessman is being evasive or not putting his cards on the table. However, Japanese culture holds in high priority cooperation, politeness, and not causing others to lose face. The Japanese businessman's communication reflects the rules of his speech community

How have chat rooms influenced communication and relationships?

Photo: © Photodisc

Communication Notes

Ebonics

Recently, a word has been coined to identify the language of a Black community as a unique speech community. What was termed "Black English" is now called "Ebonics," a blend of the words "ebony," meaning black, and "phonics," the sounds of speech. Children from Black communities, such as the enclave in Halifax, Nova Scotia, and particularly American enclaves such as Oakland, California, are provided language support in English classes because they are regarded as coming from a different language culture. Standard English or "the Queen's English" is only a dialect.

that require him not to say no directly to another person (Cathcart & Cathcart, 1997; Dolan & Worden, 1992).

Apply the Idea

Appreciating Speech Communities

Were you socialized into a gender speech community? Are the gender communication rules we've discussed evident in how you communicate and interpret others? What about your ethnic and racial speech communities? Identify rules you learned for being polite, showing interest, and indicating disapproval.

After thinking about your own speech communities, talk with people from different speech communities. Identify differences in the rules you follow for public and private interaction. Do you recognize communication rules that explain differences between how you and others talk?

Communication Notes

Reappropriating Aboriginal Geonames

Canadian geographic names (geonames) reflect the many streams of ethnic and historical influences that comprise our country. Many aboriginal names are drawn from the landscape such as "Swift Water" (Saskatchewan) and "Where the Reeds Are" (Athabasca). They show the importance the First Nations gave to understanding the environment in order to survive. "Canada" probably comes from the Iroquois word "kanata" meaning town or settlement. In Atlantic Canada, Bouctouche, Kejimkujik and Tignish are all names used by the Mi'kmaq people. Nunavut, the newest Canadian territory, means "our land" in the Inuktitut language. Frobisher Bay became Iqaluit, the new capital of Nunavut. It means "place of fish" in Inuktitut. In Northern Quebec, many communities have adopted aboriginal names. For example, the community once called Great Whale River, then Poste-de-la-Baleine, is now officially called Kuujjuaraapik for the Inuit part of the village and Whapmagoostui for the Cree part of the village. Port Simpson, B.C., was changed to Lax Kw'alaams meaning "place of wild roses."

Sources: Geomatics Canada, Natural Resources Canada.
http://geonames.NRCan.gc.ca/english/north_comm.html (Retrieved July 3, 2001); Rayburn, Alan. (1994). *Naming Canada: Stories about place names from Canadian Geographic.* Toronto: University of Toronto Press, pp. 136–40.

Although people may use the same language, they don't all use it in the same way. Within our country, diverse speech communities exist and operate by some distinct rules about how, when, why, and with whom to talk. Recognizing and respecting different speech communities increases our ability to participate competently in a diverse culture.

GUIDELINES FOR IMPROVING VERBAL COMMUNICATION

We've explored what symbols are and how they may be used differently in distinct speech communities. Building on these understandings, we can now consider guidelines for improving effectiveness in verbal communication.

ENGAGE IN DUAL PERSPECTIVE

A critical guideline for effective verbal communication is to engage in dual perspective. This involves recognizing another person's perspective and taking that into account as you communicate. Effective interpersonal communication is not a solo performance, but a relationship between people. Awareness of others and their viewpoints should be reflected in how we speak. For instance, it's advisable to refrain from using a lot of idioms when

Concepts at a Glance

Four Guidelines for Improving Verbal Communication

- Engage in dual perspective.
- Own your own feelings and thoughts.
- Respect others' feelings and thoughts.
- Strive for accuracy and clarity.

Student Voices

Jacques:

For so long, my mother and I have argued with each other. I have always felt she was overly protective of me and tried to intrude in my life with all the questions she asked about what I'm doing, who I'm seeing, and everything. For years, almost any discussion between us wound up in an argument. I would just resist and challenge her. But for the last month, I've been trying to understand where she's coming from. When she asks who I'm seeing, I don't just say "None of your business" or "Get off my case" like I used to. Now I ask her why she wants to know. What she says is she's interested in who I hang with and why I like them. That's kind of cool, I think—that my mom is really interested in my life. That's a lot different than seeing her questions as coming from a mother hen who wants to run my life. Trying to understand her perspective has been really, really tough, but it has made an incredible difference in our relationship.

talking with someone for whom English is not a native language (see "Missing the Boat"). Similarly, instead of giving advice when a woman tells him about a problem, a man who uses dual perspective might realize empathy and supportive listening are likely to be more appreciated. The point is that competent communicators acknowledge and respect the perspectives of those with whom they interact.

We don't need to abandon our own perspectives to accommodate those of others. In fact, it would be as unconstructive to stifle your own views as to ignore those of others. Dual perspective, as the term implies, consists of two perspectives. It requires understanding both our own and another's point of view and giving voice to each when we communicate. Most of us can accept and grow from differences, but we seldom feel affirmed if we are unheard or disregarded. Understanding and heeding others' viewpoints in how you communicate paves the way for affirming relationships.

Photo: © Photodisc

OWN YOUR FEELINGS AND THOUGHTS

We often use verbal language in ways that obscure our responsibility for how we feel and what we think. For instance, people say "You made me mad," or "You hurt me," as if what they feel is caused by someone else. On a more subtle level, we sometimes blame others for our responses to what they say. "You're so demanding" really means that you feel put upon by what someone else wants or expects. The sense of feeling pressured by another's expectations is in you, not the other person. Even though others' behaviours can influence us, they can't really determine how we feel.

Communication Notes

Missing the Boat

Communication scholar Wen Shu Lee (1994) reports that one of the greatest barriers to cross-cultural communication is idioms. Although people from other cultures learn formal English, they often aren't taught slang and jargon. Examples of idioms that confuse nonnative speakers are "kick the bucket," "hang a right," "miss the boat," and "get up to speed."

Source: Lee, W. S. (1994). On not missing the boat: A processual method for intercultural understanding of idioms and lifeworld. *Journal of Applied Communication Research,* 22, 141–61.

Our feelings and thoughts result from how we interpret others' communication. Although how we interpret what others say may lead us to feel certain ways, others do not directly cause our responses. In certain contexts, such as abusive relationships, others may powerfully shape how we think and feel. Yet even in these extreme situations, we need to remember that we, not others, are responsible for our feelings. Telling others they make you feel some way is likely to arouse defensiveness, which doesn't facilitate healthy interpersonal relationships. In Chapter 4, we discussed this as the fallacy of Taking Responsibility for Others. We do not cause another's feelings.

Effective communicators take responsibility for themselves by using language that owns their thoughts and feelings. They claim their feelings and do not blame others for what happens in themselves. To take responsibility for your own feelings, rely on I–language, rather than you–language. **I–language** owns thoughts and feelings and does not blame them on others. Table 5.2 gives examples of the difference.

There are two differences between I–language and you–language. First, I–language owns responsibility, whereas **you–language** projects it onto another person. Second, I–language offers considerably more description than you–language. You-language tends to be accusations that are very abstract. This is one of the reasons they're ineffective in promoting change. I–language, on the other hand, provides concrete descriptions of behaviours that we dislike without directly blaming the other person for how we feel.

Some people feel awkward when they first start using I–language. This is natural because most of us have learned to rely on you–language. With commitment and practice, however, you can learn to communicate with I–language. Once you feel comfortable using it, you will find that I–language has many advantages. It is less likely than you–language to make others defensive, so I–language opens the doors for dialogue. I–language is also more honest. We deceive ourselves when we say "You made me feel …" because others don't control how we feel. Finally, I–language is more empowering than you–language. When we say "You did this," or "You made me feel that," we give control of our emotions to others. This reduces our personal power and, by extension, our motivation to change what is happening. Using

Table 5.2
You–Language and I–Language

You–Language	I–Language
You hurt me.	I feel hurt when you ignore what I say.
You make me feel small.	I feel small when you tell me that I'm selfish.
You're so domineering.	When you shout, I feel dominated.
You humiliated me.	I felt humiliated when you mentioned my problems in front of our friends.

I–language allows you to own your own feelings while also explaining to others how you interpret their behaviours.

Apply the Idea

Using I–Language

For the next three days, whenever you use you–language, try to rephrase what you said or thought in I–language. How does this change how you think and feel about what's happening? How does using I–language affect interaction with others? Are others less defensive when you own your feelings and describe, but don't evaluate, their behaviours? Does I–language facilitate working out constructive changes?

Now that you're tuned into I– and you–language, monitor how you feel when others use you–language about you. When a friend or romantic partner says "You make me feel …," do you feel defensive or guilty? Try teaching others to use I–language so that your relationships can be more honest and open. Remember the rule from Chapter 4: A statement that begins with "I feel that …" is not a statement of feeling but a statement of belief.

RESPECT WHAT OTHERS SAY ABOUT THEIR FEELINGS AND THOUGHTS

Has anyone ever said to you, "You shouldn't feel that way"? If so, you know how infuriating it can be to be told that your feelings aren't valid, appropriate, or acceptable. It's equally destructive to be told our thoughts are wrong. When someone says, "How can you think something so stupid?" we feel disconfirmed. Effective communicators don't disparage what others say about what

|*Student Voices*|

Neely:

I thought that the idea of I–language was kind of silly, but I did the exercise assigned in class anyway. Surprise. I found out I was using a lot of you–language, and it had the effect of letting me off the hook for what I felt and did. Like, I would say, "You pushed me to say that" when really I had control over whether to say it or not. But when I said "You pushed me," I could dismiss what I said as not my fault. I've continued to focus on not using you–language even though the assignment is over.

they feel and think. Even if you don't feel or think the same way, you can still respect another person as the expert on her or his own perspective.

One of the most disconfirming forms of communication is speaking for others when they are able to speak for themselves. Have you ever had a conversation with a couple at a party in which one person spoke for another saying things like, "She's having trouble balancing career and family," "She's really proud of sticking with her exercise program," and "She's worried about how to take care of her parents now that their health is declining." The same pattern occurs when parents speak for children by responding to questions the children could answer. Generally, it's arrogant and disempowering to speak for others.

Student Voices

Thelma:

I go crazy when someone tells me I shouldn't feel what I'm feeling. I can't help what I feel. Feelings aren't something we control. They just are. When someone tells me I should feel a certain way, I get so angry and I just shut up. I think that they're not even trying to understand me. They are just evaluating how I feel as wrong. That is totally toxic to me! There's no point in talking to someone who says (and thinks) that.

Just as we should not speak for others, we also should not assume we understand how they feel or think. As we have seen, our distinct experiences and ways of interpreting life make each of us unique. We seldom, if ever, completely grasp what another person feels or thinks. Although it is supportive to engage in dual perspective, it isn't supportive to presume we fully grasp what's happening in someone else, especially when he or she differs from us in important ways.

It's particularly important not to assume we understand people from other cultures, including those within our society. It's easy and careless to say "I know what you mean" unless we have had the exact experiences. It becomes especially poignant when someone speaks of painful experiences such as discrimination. When we claim to share what we haven't experienced, we take away from others' lives and identities.

Respecting what others say about what they feel and think is a cornerstone of effective interpersonal communication. We also grow when we open ourselves to perspectives, feelings, and thoughts that differ from our own. If you don't understand what others say, ask them to elaborate. This shows you are interested and respect their expertise or experience. Inviting others to clarify, extend, or explain their communication enlarges understanding between people.

STRIVE FOR ACCURACY AND CLARITY

Because symbols are arbitrary, abstract, and ambiguous, the potential for misunderstanding always exists. In addition, individual and cultural differences foster varying interpretations of words. Although we can't completely eliminate misunderstandings, we can minimize them.

Be Aware of Levels of Abstraction

Misunderstanding is less likely when we are conscious of levels of abstraction. Much confusion results from language that is excessively abstract. For instance, assume a professor says, "Your papers should demonstrate a sophisticated conceptual grasp of material and its pragmatic implications." Would you know how to write a paper to satisfy the professor? Probably not, because the language is very abstract and unclear. Here's a more concrete description: "Your papers should include definitions of the concepts and specific examples that show how they apply in real life." With this more concrete statement, you would have a clear idea of what the professor expected.

Apply the Idea

Using Concrete Language

Rewrite each statement below so that you replace abstract terms with some that are more concrete.

   Example: I want to be more responsible.
   (Rewrite: I want to be on time for work and classes, and I want to live within my budget each month and not run up charges on my credit card.)

1.   I get really angry when people are rude.

   _____

2.   I like teachers who are flexible and open-minded.

   _____

3.   My roommate is such a slob.

   _____

4.   I believe intimate relationships are based on unconditional love and acceptance.

   _____

5.   I think the media in this country are irresponsible.

   _____

Sometimes, however, abstract language is appropriate. As we have seen, abstract language allows us to generalize, which is necessary and useful. The goal is to use a level of abstraction that suits particular communication objectives and situations. Abstract words are appropriate when speakers and listeners have similar concrete knowledge about what is being discussed. For example, a couple who have been dating might talk about "light comedies" and "heavy movies" as shorthand ways to refer to two film genres. Because they have seen many movies together, they have shared referents for the abstract terms "lighthearted" and "heavy," so confusion is unlikely. Similarly, long-term friends can say "Let's just hang out" and understand the activities implied by the abstract term "hang out." More concrete language is useful when communicators don't have shared experiences and interpretations. For example, early in a friendship the suggestion to "hang out" would be more effective if it included specifics: "Let's hang out today—maybe watch the game and go out for pizza." In a new dating relationship, it would be clearer to give an example of a "light" movie or a "heavy" one to avoid confusion. Providing examples of general terms clarifies meanings.

Abstract language is particularly likely to lead to misunderstandings when people talk about changes they want in one another. Concrete language and specific examples help individuals have similar understandings of which behaviours are unwelcome and which ones are wanted. For example, "I want you to be more helpful around the house" does not explain what would count as being more helpful. Is it vacuuming and doing laundry? Shopping for groceries? Fixing half of the meals? It isn't clear what the speaker wants unless more concrete descriptions are supplied. Likewise, "I want to be closer" could mean the speaker wants to spend more time together, talk about the relationship, do things together, have a more adventurous sex life, or any number of other things. Vague abstractions promote misunderstanding if individuals don't share concrete referents.

Qualify Language

Another strategy for increasing the clarity of communication is to qualify language. Two types of language require qualification. First, we should qualify generalizations so that we don't mislead ourselves or others into mistaking a general statement for an absolute one. "Politicians lie" is a false statement because it overgeneralizes. A more accurate statement would be "Some politicians in the last federal election were dishonest." Qualifying reminds us of limitations on what we say.

We should also qualify language when describing and evaluating people. The term **"static evaluation"** refers to assessments that suggest something is unchanging or static. These are particularly troublesome when applied to

Concepts at a Glance

Qualify language by
- Undoing static evaluations
- Using mental indexing

Ken:

Parents are the worst for static evaluations. When I first got my license seven years ago, I had a fender-bender and then got a speeding ticket. Since then I've had a perfect record, but you'd never know it from what they say. Dad's always calling me "hot-rodder," and Mom goes through this safety spiel every time I get ready to drive somewhere. You'd think I was the same now as when I was sixteen.

people: Ann is selfish; Don is irresponsible; Bob is generous; Vy is dependent. Whenever we use the word "is," we suggest something is inherent and fixed. In reality, we aren't static but continuously changing. A person who is selfish at one time may not be at another. An individual who is irresponsible on one occasion may be responsible in other situations.

Indexing is a technique developed by early communication scholars to remind us that our evaluations apply only to specific times and circumstances (Korzybski, 1958). To index, we would say Ann on June 6, 1997 acted selfishly, Don on the task committee was irresponsible, Bob in college was generous, and Vy in her relationships with men in high school was dependent. See how indexing ties description to a specific time and circumstance? Mental indexing reminds us that we and others are able to change in remarkable ways.

Effective interpersonal communication is accurate and clear. We've considered four principles for improving the effectiveness of verbal communication. Engaging in dual perspective is the first principle and a foundation for all others. A second guideline is to take responsibility for our own feelings and thoughts by using I–language. Third, we should respect others as the experts on what they feel and think and not presume we know what they mean or share their experiences. The fourth principle is to strive for clarity by choosing appropriate degrees of abstraction, qualifying generalizations, and indexing evaluations, particularly those applied to people.

Apply the Idea

Using Qualified Language

Study the unqualified and qualified statements below.

Unqualified

Foreign cars are better than domestic ones.

Science courses are harder than humanities courses.

Television is violent.

Qualified

Hondas and Toyotas generally require less maintenance than Fords and Chevys.

Most students find chemistry tougher than music.

Many commercial programs include a lot of violence.

Practise your skill in qualifying language by providing appropriate restrictions for the overgeneralizations below.

Unqualified: Women make better doctors.
Qualified:

Unqualified: Affirmative action gives jobs to
                     unqualified people.
Qualified:

Unqualified: Men are more competitive than women.
Qualified:

Unqualified: Textbooks are boring.
Qualified:

Chapter Summary

In this chapter, we discussed the world of words and meaning—the uniquely human universe that we inhabit because we are symbol users. Because symbols are arbitrary, ambiguous, and abstract, they have no inherent meanings. Instead, we actively construct meaning by interpreting symbols based on perspectives and values that are endorsed in our culture and social groups and based on interaction with others and our personal experiences. We also punctuate to create meaning in communication.

Instead of existing only in the physical world of the here and now, we use symbols to define, evaluate, and classify ourselves, others, and our experiences in the world. In addition, we use symbols to think hypothetically, so we can consider alternatives and simultaneously inhabit all three dimensions of time. Finally, symbols allow us to self-reflect so that we can monitor our own behaviours.

Although members of a society share a common language, we don't all use it the same way. Speech communities, which exist both within and between countries, teach us rules for talking and interpreting others. Because communication rules vary among social groups based on gender, race, class, and so forth, we shouldn't assume others use words just as we do. Likewise, we shouldn't assume that others share our meanings for how we communicate.

The final section of this chapter discussed principles for improving effectiveness in verbal communication. Because words can mean different things to various people and because different social groups instill some distinct rules for interacting, misunderstandings are always possible. To minimize them, we should engage in dual perspective, own our thoughts and feelings, respect what others say about how they think and feel, and monitor abstractness, generalizations, and static evaluations. In the next chapter, we continue our discussion of the world of human communication by exploring the fascinating realm of nonverbal behaviour.

Key Concepts

- abstract
- ambiguous
- arbitrary
- communication rules
- constitutive rules
- hate speech
- I–language
- indexing
- loaded language
- punctuation
- regulative rules
- speech community
- static evaluation
- totalizing
- you–language

For Further Thought & Discussion

1. Think about different metaphors for Canadian society. Discuss the difference between the metaphors of "the cultural mosaic" and "the cultural melting pot" as they relate to the differences in Canadian and American culture. What metaphors would you propose that would capture the diversity and richness of Canadian culture?
2. Use your InfoTrac College Edition to read two articles in journals that focus on experiences and perspectives of minority groups in Canada. What does reading these articles teach you about the perspectives of minority groups in Canada? Focus on the language used in the articles to describe minority and majority culture. What definitions and evaluations are in the language?
3. To appreciate the importance of hypothetical thought, enabled by symbols, try to imagine the following: living only in the present with no memories and no anticipations of the future; having no goals for yourself; knowing only the

concrete, immediate reality. How would not having hypothetical thought affect your life?

4. In this chapter we learned that language changes. We coin new words when we feel the need to represent something that is not currently named in our language. Can you think of experiences, situations, or relationships that are not currently named? What names would you give them?

5. Check out the graffiti on your campus. Do you see examples of loaded language, stereotyping, and hate speech? Share your findings with your classmates.

6. What should be done about hate speech? Should we censor it? Would doing so violate our constitutional right to freedom of speech? Are there other,

perhaps less formal, ways to reduce hate speech?

7. What labels that you dislike have been applied to you or to groups to which you belong? Explain how the labels affect you.

8. Does your school have a code or policy on hate speech? If so, what limits does the policy impose on freedom of speech?

9. Notice how media describe Canada's ethnic and racial diversity in the news. Do television programs, newspapers, and other media spotlight race when the person is not White? How often are minorities described in terms of their races ? Are people ever described as White?

6

The World beyond Words: Nonverbal Communication

Everyday Encounters
By Stephen Lee

I don't get it, sis. I went to a good school.... graduated at the top of my class.... have a pretty good job... But still nobody takes me seriously...

Hate to tell you, little brother, it might actually be your dressing habits... Sometimes we're unaware of the impact of our clothes and the statement they make about our personality... Know what I mean, Collin?

Doctor Collin

I rest my case...

Chloe's brother is making a statement with his clothing and adornments whether he intends to or not. This chapter examines how we send messages without words. This nonverbal communication is a major dimension of human interaction. Consider the following two scenes.

Jay and Emma gaze into each other's eyes as they nibble their salads, beautifully prepared and topped with marinated mushrooms and herb croutons. They can hear only muffled sounds from people at other tables, scattered throughout the dining area. The comfortable upholstered chairs, gracious subtle lighting, and soft music add to the leisurely, intimate mood of the evening. Twenty minutes after bringing the salads, the server returns with their entrees and asks if there is anything else they would like.

Amy and Ted's eyes meet across the Formica table in the diner. They speak loudly to be heard above the clamour of rock music, conversations at other tables crowded around them, and order announcements from the grill. Within five minutes of placing their orders, the server plops loaded plates in front of them and leaves the cheque. Ted and Amy eat their burritos quickly and leave, spending less than 20 minutes total time for the meal.

Emma and Jay had a very different dining experience from Ted and Amy. Much of the reason for the difference lies in nonverbal factors. The restaurant where Jay and Emma dined featured lighting, spatial arrangements, music, and a gracious pace of service that encouraged lingering and intimate conversation. In contrast, Ted and Amy's restaurant was crowded and loud, and the service was fast and functional, all of which discouraged lingering or intimate conversation.

Nonverbal communication is the fascinating world beyond words that is central to interpersonal communication. To launch our discussion, we'll examine the nature of nonverbal communication and how it differs from verbal communication. Next we will identify four principles of nonverbal communication. The third section of the chapter discusses different types of nonverbal behaviour. We complete the chapter with guidelines for improving personal effectiveness in nonverbal communication.

Photo: © Corel

Examine the difference in the use of space and time in these eating experiences.

Photo: M. Salez

DEFINING NONVERBAL COMMUNICATION

The world beyond words is an important dimension of interpersonal communication. Scholars estimate that nonverbal behaviours account for between 65 and 93 percent of the total meaning of communication (Birdwhistell, 1970; Mehrabian, 1981). Even if we accept the lesser figure, clearly nonverbal communication is a major influence on what happens between people.

Nonverbal communication is all aspects of communication other than words themselves. It includes not only gestures and body language but also how we utter words—inflection, pauses, tone, volume, and accent. These nonverbal features affect the meanings of our words. Nonverbal communication also includes features of environments that affect interaction, personal objects such as jewellery and clothes, physical appearance, and facial expressions.

Verbal and nonverbal dimensions of interpersonal communication typically work together to create meaning in human interaction. To understand how each dimension of communication operates, we'll identify both similarities and differences between verbal and nonverbal communication, as shown in Figure 6.1.

Similarities	Differences
Both are symbolic. Both are rule-guided. Both can be intentional or unintentional. Both are culture-bound.	Nonverbal communication is usually perceived as more believable. Nonverbal can be multichanneled. Nonverbal is continuous.

Figure 6.1

Comparing Verbal and Nonverbal Communication

SIMILARITIES BETWEEN VERBAL AND NONVERBAL COMMUNICATION

Nonverbal communication is similar to verbal communication in many respects. We'll consider four similarities.

Nonverbal Communication Is Symbolic

Like verbal communication, nonverbal communication is symbolic. It consists of nonverbal representations of other things. To represent different moods, we shrug our shoulders, lower our eyes, and move away from or toward others. We smile to symbolize pleasure in seeing a friend, frown to show anger or irritation, and widen our eyes to indicate we are surprised.

Because nonverbal communication is symbolic, it, like verbal communication, is arbitrary, ambiguous, and abstract. Thus, we cannot be sure what a wink or hand movement means. Depending on the context and the people involved, a wink might express romantic interest, signal that the person winking is joking, or mean that the person winking has something in her or his eye. Also, we can't guarantee that others will perceive the meanings we intend to communicate with our nonverbal actions. You might move closer to someone to indicate you like the person, but he or she may feel you are crowding and imposing.

Nonverbal Communication Is Rule-Guided

Another similarity between the two kinds of communication is that both are rule-guided. Within particular societies, we share general understandings of what specific nonverbal behaviours are appropriate in various situations and what they mean. For example, in Canada, as well as many other countries, handshakes are the conventional method of beginning and ending business meetings. Smiles are generally understood to express friendliness, and scowls are generally perceived as indicating displeasure of some type.

We follow rules (often unconsciously) to arrange settings to create particular moods. For a formal speech, a room might be set up with a podium that is at a distance from listeners' chairs. The chairs would probably be arranged in neat rows. Flags, banners, or other ceremonial symbols might be displayed near the podium. To symbolize a less formal speaking occasion, a podium might be omitted, chairs might be arranged in a circle, and the person speaking might be seated. The different spatial arrangements symbolize different moods and set the stage for distinct kinds of interaction.

Nonverbal Communication May Be Intentional or Unintentional

Both verbal and nonverbal communication may be deliberately controlled or unintentional. For example, you may carefully select clothes to create a professional impression when you are going to a job interview. You may also deliberately control your verbal language in the interview to present yourself as assertive, articulate, and respectful. We exert conscious control over much of our nonverbal communication.

Sometimes, however, both verbal and nonverbal communication are unconscious and unplanned. Without awareness, you may wince when asked a tough question by the interviewer. Without knowing it, you may use incorrect grammar when speaking. Thus, both verbal and nonverbal communication are sometimes controlled and sometimes inadvertent.

Nonverbal Communication Is Culture-Bound

Like verbal communication, nonverbal behaviour is shaped by cultural ideas, values, customs, and history. Just as we learn the language of a culture, we also learn its nonverbal codes. In learning both language and nonverbal codes, we also learn cultural values that are embedded in communication. Many aspects of nonverbal behaviour vary across cultures. How we use implements for eating, for example, is culture bound. You might use a fork alone, a knife and fork, your hands, or chopsticks. In Canada, it is common for friends and romantic partners to sample food from each other's plate, but Germans consider this extremely rude. Dress, as we will learn, is a statement we make about ourselves. Most Westerners wear slacks, shirts, dresses, and suits for business, whereas saris are traditional dress in India. Later in this chapter we'll look more closely at cultural influences on nonverbal behaviour as one of the principles of the nonverbal communication system.

DIFFERENCES BETWEEN VERBAL AND NONVERBAL COMMUNICATION

There are also differences between the two dimensions of communication and between the meanings we attach to each. We'll consider three distinctions between the two kinds of communication.

Nonverbal Communication Is Perceived to Be More Believable

One major difference is that most people perceive nonverbal communication as more trustworthy than verbal communication, especially when verbal and nonverbal messages are inconsistent. If someone glares and says "I'm glad to see you," you are likely to believe the nonverbal message, which communicates dislike. People are particularly likely to think that nonverbal communication accurately reflects true feelings. If you are slouching, and the corners of your mouth are turned down, others will probably perceive you as unhappy or depressed.

The fact that people tend to believe nonverbal behaviours doesn't mean that nonverbal behaviours are always accurate. Although people generally trust nonverbal behaviours more than verbal ones, we need to be cautious in our interpretations. It's possible that someone whose mouth is down-turned and who is slumped over is deeply engaged in reflection or is working out a problem and isn't unhappy or depressed. It's also possible for individuals to manipulate their nonverbal communication, just as we manipulate our verbal communication.

Nonverbal Communication Is Multichannelled

A second difference between the two communication systems is that nonverbal communication often occurs simultaneously in two or more channels, whereas verbal communication tends to take place in a single channel. Nonverbal communication may be seen, felt, heard, smelled, and tasted, and we may receive nonverbal communication through several of these channels at the same time. You might touch a person while smiling and whispering an endearment—nonverbal communication occurring in three channels at once. In contrast, vocal verbal communication is received through hearing, and written verbal communication and American Sign Language are received through sight—one channel at a time.

One implication of the multichannelled nature of nonverbal communication is that selective perception is likely to operate. If you are visually oriented, you may tune in more to visual cues than to smell or touch. On the other hand, if you are touch-oriented, you may pay more attention to tactile cues than to visual ones.

Nonverbal Communication Is Continuous

Finally, nonverbal communication is more continuous than verbal communication. Verbal symbols start and stop. We say something or write something, and then we stop talking or writing. Yet, it is difficult, if not impossible, to stop nonverbal communication. As long as two people are together, they are engaging in nonverbal behaviours, deliberately or unintentionally. How we enter and leave rooms, how we move, even how we tilt our head may affect others' interpretations of us. Further, nonverbal features of environment, such as lighting or temperature, are ongoing influences on interaction and meaning. Understanding similarities and differences between verbal and nonverbal behaviour gives us insight into each form of communication and helps us appreciate how they work together in providing communication.

PRINCIPLES OF NONVERBAL COMMUNICATION

Now that we have defined nonverbal communication and compared and contrasted it with verbal communication, let's explore how nonverbal communication actually works. Four principles of nonverbal communication enhance understanding of how it affects meaning in human interaction.

NONVERBAL COMMUNICATION MAY SUPPLEMENT OR REPLACE VERBAL COMMUNICATION

Communication researchers have identified five ways in which nonverbal behaviours interact with verbal communication (Malandro & Barker, 1983). An examination of these functions of nonverbal behaviour allows us to recognize and be aware of the complexity of our communication with one another.

First, nonverbal behaviours may repeat verbal messages. For example, you might say "yes" while nodding your head. Second, nonverbal behaviours may highlight verbal communication. For instance, you can emphasize particular words by speaking more loudly, and you can indicate you mean something sarcastically by tone of voice. Third, we use nonverbal behaviour to complement or add to words. When you see a friend, you might say "I'm glad to see you" and underline the verbal message with a warm embrace. Fourth, nonverbal behaviours may contradict verbal messages, as when someone says "Nothing's wrong" in a frosty, hostile tone of voice. Finally, we sometimes substitute nonverbal behaviours for verbal ones. For instance, you might roll your eyes to indicate you disapprove of something. In all of these ways, nonverbal behaviours augment or replace verbal communication. "The Case of Clever Hans" illustrates the impact of nonverbal communication.

Concepts at a Glance

Four Principles of Nonverbal Communication

- Nonverbal communication may supplement or replace verbal communication.
- Nonverbal communication may regulate interaction.
- Nonverbal communication establishes relational-level meaning.
- Nonverbal communication reflects and expresses culture.

Concepts at a Glance

Functions of Nonverbal Communication

- Repeating
- Highlighting
- Complementing
- Contradicting
- Substituting

Communication Notes

The Case of Clever Hans

In the 1900s, Herr von Osten trained his horse Hans to count by tapping his front hoof. Hans learned quickly and was soon able to multiply, add, divide, subtract, and perform complex mathematical calculations. He could even count the number of people in a room or the number of people wearing eyeglasses. Herr von Osten took Hans on a promotional tour. At shows he would ask Hans to add 5 and 8, divide 100 by 10, and do other computations. In every case, Hans performed flawlessly, leading others to call him "Clever Hans." Because some doubters thought Clever Hans's feats involved deceit, proof of his mathematical abilities was demanded.

The first test involved computing numbers that were stated on stage by people other than von Osten. Using his hoof, Hans pounded out the correct answers. However, he didn't fare so well on the second test in which one person whispered a number into Hans's left ear and a different person whispered a number into his right ear. Hans was told to add the two numbers and pound out the sum, an answer not known by anyone present. Hans couldn't solve the problem. On further investigation, it was deduced that Hans could solve problems only if someone he could see knew the answer. When Hans was given numbers and asked to compute them, viewers leaned forward and tensed their bodies as Hans began tapping his hoof. When Hans tapped the correct number, onlookers relaxed their body postures and nodded their heads, which Hans took as a signal to stop tapping.

Hans was clever, not because he could calculate but because he could read people's nonverbal communication.

Source: Sebeok, T. A., & Rosenthal, R. (Eds.). (1981). *The Clever Hans phenomenon: Communication with horses, whales, apes and people.* New York: New York Academy of Sciences.

NONVERBAL COMMUNICATION MAY REGULATE INTERACTION

We also use nonverbal behaviours to regulate interpersonal interaction. More than verbal cues, we rely on nonverbal behaviours to know when to speak and when to let others speak, as well as how long to talk. Intricate and often unconscious nonverbal behaviours regulate the flow of communication between people.

In conversations, we generally know when someone else is through speaking and when it is our turn to talk. We also sense when a professor welcomes discussion from students and when the professor is in a lecture mode. We can even perceive when a professor or friend expects or wants us specifically to enter conversation. Seldom do explicit, verbal cues tell us when to speak and when to keep silent. When talking, friends typically don't say "Your turn to talk" or hold up signs saying "I am through now." Instead, turn-taking in conversation usually is regulated nonverbally (Malandro & Barker, 1983). We signal we don't want to be interrupted by averting our eyes or by maintaining a speaking volume and rate to thwart interruption. When we're through talking, we look back to others to signal "Okay, now somebody else can speak." We invite specific individuals to speak by looking directly at them, often after asking a question.

Although we aren't usually aware of nonverbal actions that regulate interaction, we rely on them to know when to speak and when to remain silent. Without conscious realization, we signal others they should enter a conversation or wait until we're through speaking. We send and respond to subtle nonverbal cues whenever we communicate with others.

Reflective Exercise

Watch a conversation from a distance and record the number and kind of nonverbal behaviours that speakers and listeners use to indicate the desire to speak.

NONVERBAL COMMUNICATION ESTABLISHES RELATIONAL-LEVEL MEANINGS

You'll recall that in Chapter 1 we discussed two levels of meaning that are always present in communication. To review, the content level of meaning concerns actual information or literal meaning. The relationship level of meaning defines individuals' identities and the relationships between people. More than verbal language, nonverbal communication conveys relationship-level meanings (Keeley & Hart, 1994). In fact, communication scholars refer to nonverbal communication as the "relationship language" and note that it, more than verbal messages, expresses the overall feeling of relationships (Burgoon, Buller, Hale, & deTurck, 1984; Sallinen-Kuparinen, 1992). There are three dimensions of relationship-level meanings that are conveyed primarily through nonverbal communication (Mehrabian, 1981). As we will see, how we express and interpret each of these dimensions varies among different speech communities.

Concepts at a Glance

Three Dimensions of Relational Meanings
- Responsiveness
- Liking
- Power

Responsiveness

One facet of relationship-level meaning is responsiveness. Through eye contact, facial expressions, and body posture, we indicate our interest in others' communication. Westerners signal interest by holding eye contact and assuming an attentive posture. To express lack of interest or boredom, we decrease visual contact and adopt a passive body position. Also, synchronicity, or harmony, between people's postures and facial expressions reflects how comfortable they are with each other (Berg, 1987; Capella, 1991). We're more likely to feel that others are involved with us if they look at us, nod, and lean forward than if they gaze around the room, look bored, and fiddle with papers as we speak (Miller & Parks, 1982).

|Student Voices|

Allan:

The most useful professional development seminar I've ever had was on listening. Our instructor showed us how to sit and look at people to show we were interested. We learned that most men don't show their interest with head nods and eye contact. That explained to me why some of the women I supervise complained that I never seemed interested when they came to talk to me. It wasn't that I wasn't interested. I just didn't show it with my nonverbal behaviour.

Different speech communities teach members distinct rules for showing responsiveness. Because feminine speech communities tend to emphasize building relationships by expressing interest in others, women generally display greater emotional responsiveness than men (Montgomery, 1988; Ueland, 1992). In addition to communicating their own feelings nonverbally, women are generally more skilled than men in interpreting others' emotions (Hall, 1978; Noller, 1986). There is some suggestion that those who are consistently in subordinate situations to others (women and– minorities for example) are more skilled in reading emotions than those in authority. This would suggest that decoding nonverbal language is a survival strategy. Prisoners, another subordinate group, also show strong decoding capacity (Wood, 1994e). In many ways, the well-being and sometimes physical safety of those with low power depend on being able to decipher the feelings and intentions of those with more power.

Are women more emotionally expressive than men?

Photo: © Corel

Reflective Exercise

What do you think of the notion that subordinated groups of people are more skilled at reading nonverbal communication than those in superordinate positions? In what situations would you be more likely to be vigilant of nonverbal behaviour for your safety?

Liking

A second dimension of relationship meaning is liking. Nonverbal behaviours are often keen indicators of how positively or negatively we feel toward others. Smiles and friendly touching tend to indicate positive feelings, whereas frowns and belligerent postures express antagonism (Keeley & Hart, 1994). Opening your arms to someone usually signals affection and welcome, whereas turning your back on someone indicates dislike.

In addition to these general rules shared in Western society, more specific rules are instilled by particular speech communities. Masculine speech communities tend to emphasize emotional control and independence, so men are less likely than women to use nonverbal behaviour that reveals how they feel. Reflecting the values of feminine socialization, women, in general, sit closer to others and engage in greater eye contact than men (Montgomery, 1988; Reis, Senchak, & Solomon, 1985). They are also more openly expressive of their inner feelings, because that is encouraged in feminine speech communities. Women are also more likely than men to initiate hand-holding and to touch others to show affection.

Nonverbal behaviours reflect liking between marriage partners. Happy couples sit closer together and engage in more eye contact than unhappy couples. Further, couples that like each other tend to touch more often and to orient their body postures toward each other than do couples who are less fond of each other (Miller & Parks, 1982; Noller, 1986).

Student Voices

Carla:

I swear, it's so hard to figure out what guys think of you. When you're around a guy, he's like Mr. Stone Face, so he doesn't give away anything about how he feels. I can't tell by how he acts if a guy likes me or is interested. My girlfriends say the same thing—guys are just inscrutable. Girls aren't like that at all. If we like someone, we smile and let him or her know instead of acting distant and aloof.

Why do we find this intimidating? What are the communication challenges for the officers?

Photo: Courtesy Garet Bonn, Edmonton Police Service

Power

The third dimension of relationship-level meaning is power. We rely greatly on nonverbal behaviours to assert dominance and to negotiate for status and influence (Henley, 1977). Given what we have learned about gender socialization, it is not surprising that men typically exceed women in efforts to exert control. In general, men assume greater amounts of space and use greater volume and more forceful gestures to assert their ideas than women (Hall, 1987; Major, Schmidlin, & Williams, 1990). Men are also more likely than women to use gestures and touch to symbolize control (Henley, 1977; Leathers, 1986).

Gender, however, is not the only influence on the power dimension of relationship meaning. Individuals' status is tied to how they communicate power on nonverbal levels. The prerogative to touch another reflects power, so individuals with power touch those with lesser power. For instance, bosses touch secretaries far more often than secretaries touch bosses (Spain, 1992). Time is also linked to individuals' status. People who are considered important can keep others waiting; how often have you waited for your appointment at a doctor's office? People with high status can also be late to appointments and events without risking serious repercussions. Yet, if someone with lower power is late, she or he may suffer undesirable consequences such as disapproval, penalties, or having an appointment cancelled.

As Jerry's observations indicate, space also expresses power relations. Individuals who have power usually command more space than individuals with less power. The connection between power and space is evident in the fact that most bosses have large, spacious offices whereas their administrative

Student Voices

Jerry:

Last summer I had an internship with a big accounting firm, and space really told the story on status. Interns like me worked in two large rooms on the first floor with partitions to separate our desks. New employees worked on the second floor in little cubicles. The higher up you were in the hierarchy of the firm, the higher up your office was—literally. I mean, the president and vice presidents—six of them—had the whole top floor, while there were forty or more interns crowded onto my floor.

assistants have smaller offices or workstations, even though they have to handle far more paperwork than their bosses. Office size and decor may also be tied to an individual's status in the workplace hierarchy. As people move up the organizational ladder, they tend to have larger offices with more and larger windows and more luxurious carpeting and art. Homes also reflect power differences among family members. Adults, for instance, usually have more space than children.

Reflective Exercise

Who sits at the head of the table in family dinners? Who has the most physical space in your household? How were those decisions made?

Communication Notes

"I'll Move When I'm Ready and Not Before!"

Have you ever felt that a driver was really slow in pulling out of a parking space for which you were waiting? It turns out that your imagination may not be playing tricks on you. A recent study of 400 drivers in a shopping mall found that drivers took longer to pull out of a space if someone was waiting than if nobody was there to claim the space. On average, if nobody was waiting for the space, drivers took 32.2 seconds to pull out of a spot after opening a car door. If someone was waiting, drivers took about 39 seconds. And woe to the person who honks to hurry a driver: Drivers took 43 seconds to pull out of a space when the waiting driver honked!

Source: Raphael, M. (1997, May 13). It's true: Drivers move slowly if you want their space. *Raleigh News and Observer*, p. 1A.

Power may also be exerted through silence, a forceful form of nonverbal communication. By not responding, we can discourage others from speaking and clear the way to talk about our own preferred topics. Victoria DeFrancisco (1991) found that some husbands respond with silence to their wives' communication, a behaviour that discourages wives from further interaction. Conversational control is also maintained, as we saw in the previous chapter, by a continuous flow of words and vocalizations. This forces everyone to wait for a break in the speech. This effectively maintains power over the group of listeners, as Kelly points out on the next page.

Review

Responsiveness, liking, and power are dimensions of relationship-level meanings that are often expressed through nonverbal communication.

Kelly:

A friend of mine never relinquished conversational power. It made perfect sense to me once I'd heard that term. Daryl was a great guy but he would always fill in the spaces between his sentences with a long "ah-h-h" or he'd say "and so-oo" and then he'd carry right on into his next thought. No one could get a word in edgewise. He always had the floor. Yikes, it was infuriating!

In extreme form, power is nonverbally enacted through violence and abuse, both of which reflect and sustain dominance (Wood, 1994d).

NONVERBAL COMMUNICATION REFLECTS AND EXPRESSES CULTURE

Earlier in this chapter, we noted that nonverbal communication is similar to verbal communication in expressing cultural values. Like verbal communication, nonverbal patterns reflect the values, perspectives, and heritage of specific cultures. This implies that the majority of nonverbal actions are not instinctive but are learned as we are socialized in particular cultures. We've already noted a number of differences between nonverbal behaviours encouraged in feminine and masculine speech communities. In addition to diversity among groups within our country, nonverbal behaviours vary from one country to another. As you might expect, dissimilarities reflect distinct cultural values.

Comfort with crowding: What are the cultural differences?

Photo: J. Liburd

Have you ever seen the bumper sticker "If you can read this, you're too close"? That slogan proclaims North Americans' fierce territoriality. We prize private space, and we resent, and sometimes fight, anyone who trespasses on what we consider our turf. "I'll Move When I'm Ready and Not Before!" on page 213 shows our territoriality when driving. The German culture also emphasizes private space. Germans routinely build walls and hedges to insulate themselves from neighbours. In cultures where individuality is not such a pronounced value, people are less territorial. For instance, Brazilians tend to stand close in shops, buses, and elevators, and when they bump into one another they don't apologize or draw back

(Wiemann & Harrison, 1983). In many middle Eastern countries, men often walk with their arms around other men, but in Canada touch between male friends is less common.

Student Voices

Diana:

I was so uncomfortable when I travelled to Mexico last year. People just crammed into buses even when all the seats were taken. They pushed up together and pressed against each other. I felt they were really being rude, and I was uptight about having people on top of me like that. I guess it was a learned cultural difference, but it sure made me uneasy at the time. I never knew how territorial I was until I felt my space was being invaded.

Norms for touching also reflect cultural values. In one study, North Americans, who are relatively reserved, were observed engaging in an average of only two touches an hour. The emotionally restrained British averaged zero touches per hour. Parisians, long known for their emotional expressiveness, touched 110 times per hour. Puerto Ricans touched most, averaging 180 touches an hour (Knapp, 1972).

Patterns of eye contact also reflect cultural values. In North America, frankness and assertion are valued, so meeting another's eyes is considered appropriate and a demonstration of personal honesty. Yet in many Asian and northern European countries, direct eye contact is considered abrasive and disrespectful (Hall, 1968). In Brazil, eye contact is often so intense that people from North America consider it rude. Imagine the confusion this causes in intercultural business negotiations.

Cultural training also influences how we express emotions and which emotions we express. In some ethnic groups dramatic emotional displays are typical. For example, many people raised in Italian and Jewish communities are more emotionally expressive than people raised in English or German communities. In Japan and many other Asian cultures, it is considered rude to express negative feelings toward others. Thus, the Japanese may not show dislike, disrespect, or irritation, even if they feel those emotions. In most of Canada, there is less constraint on displaying negative feelings.

Cultures also differ in their orientations toward time. Anthropologist Edward Hall (1976) distinguished between cultures that have monochronic and polychronic orientations toward time. Monochronic (one time) cultures, such as non-aboriginal Canada, view time as a valuable commodity to be saved, scheduled, and carefully guarded. Within monochronic cultures, punctuality and efficiency are valued. Thus, people are expected to be on time for appointments and classes, and they are expected to complete work quickly. In contrast, polychronic (many times) cultures take a more holistic, systemic view of time. Members of these cultures assume that many things are happening simultaneously. Thus, punctuality is seldom stressed. Meetings may start late, with people joining in after discussions begin. Tangential discussions and social conversations are part of normal meetings in polychronic cultures. People may even cancel meetings without the dramatic reasons required for politeness in monochronic cultures. The belief that time is holistic leads members of polychronic cultures to assume that the rhythms of life—working, socializing, attending to personal matters—are interrelated. This becomes especially important for teachers to remember when First Nations children do not conform to time constraints.

|*Student Voices*|

Louanne:

When I first came to the city to attend college, I thought I had come to a different planet. I had grown up on a reservation of 300 people and even though I understood there would be many adjustments, I wasn't prepared for everyone's preoccupation with time and being "on time." Everyone seemed anxious. They were always in a hurry. Coming late to a class or a meeting was unheard of. In my village, no one berated someone for being late like they do here. There was trust that everything would get done in time. I hated that first year of college.

The influence of culture on nonverbal communication will become clearer as you read the rest of this chapter. As we discuss different types of nonverbal communication, we'll highlight examples that reflect the values, traditions, and heritages of particular cultures.

We've discussed four principles that provide a foundation for understanding nonverbal communication. First, nonverbal behaviour may supplement or replace verbal communication. Second, nonverbal behaviours may regulate interaction. Third, nonverbal behaviour is more powerful than verbal behaviour in expressing relationship-level meanings. Finally, nonverbal communication reflects and expresses cultural values. Thus, much of our nonverbal communication is learned rather than instinctive. We're now ready to explore types of nonverbal behaviour that make up this intricate communication system.

Communication Notes

How to Discourage Assault

Many criminals are highly skilled at interpreting nonverbal behaviour. Their success in getting away with crimes depends on their ability to read others. Convicted thieves report that they don't pick victims randomly but instead carefully select whom to rob. They look for people whose walks signal unsureness and whose posture and face suggest passivity. Some people announce they're good targets, declared one career thief. The best way to avoid being picked as a victim is to walk confidently, hold your head upright, and meet others' eyes without staring. Above all, never appear unsure or lost—particularly if you are!

TYPES OF NONVERBAL COMMUNICATION

Because so much of our interaction is nonverbal, this system includes many types of communication. In this section, we will consider nine forms of nonverbal behaviour, and we will point out how we use each to establish relationships and to express personal identity and cultural values.

KINESICS

Kinesics is a technical term that refers to body position and body motions, including those of the face. Clearly, we signal a great deal about how we see ourselves by how we hold our bodies. Someone who stands erectly and walks confidently announces self-assurance, whereas someone who slouches and shuffles seems to be saying "I'm not very sure of myself." "How to Discourage Assault" discusses how thieves read nonverbal behaviour to choose their victims. We also communicate moods with body posture and motion. For example, someone who walks quickly with a resolute facial expression appears more determined than someone who saunters along with an unfocused gaze. We sit more rigidly when we are nervous or angry and adopt a relaxed posture when we feel at ease.

Body postures may signal whether we are open to interaction. Someone who sits with arms crossed and looks downward seems to say "Don't bother me." That's also a nonverbal strategy students sometimes use to dissuade teachers from calling on them in classes. To invite interaction, Westerners look at others and smile, signalling that conversation is welcome. Yet in many Asian societies, direct eye contact and smiling at nonintimates might

Concepts at a Glance

Nine Types of Nonverbal Communication

1. Kinesics (movement)
2. Haptics (touch)
3. Physical appearance
4. Artifacts
5. Environmental factors
6. Proxemics (space)
7. Chronemics (time)
8. Paralanguage (vocalizations)
9. Silence

Fearful body language can attract predators.

Photo: A. Potvin

be considered disrespectful. We also use gestures to signal what we think of others. We use a hand gesture to indicate okay, and a different gesture to communicate contempt. The gestures are arbitrary—ones that our culture has decided stand for particular things. This explains why gestures often don't translate into other cultures.

Our faces are intricate communication messengers. The face alone is capable of over a thousand distinct expressions that result from variations in tilt of the head and movements of the eyebrows, eyes, and mouth (Eckman, Friesen, & Ellsworth, 1971). Our eyes can shoot daggers of anger, issue challenges, or radiate feelings of love. With our faces we can indicate disapproval (scowls), doubt (raised eyebrows), admiration (warm gazes), and resistance (stares). The face is particularly powerful in conveying responsiveness and liking (Keeley & Hart, 1994; Patterson, 1992).

One of the most important interpersonal aspects of kinesics concerns how we position ourselves relative to others and what our positions say about our feelings toward them. Couples communicate dissatisfaction by increasing distance between the partners and by smiling less and looking away from each other (Miller & Parks, 1982). We also use nonverbal behaviours—such as smiles, close seating, and warm gazes—to signal we like others and are happy with them (Walker & Trimboli, 1989).

Apply the Idea

Communicating Closeness

To become more aware of subtle nonverbal behaviours that reflect intimacy, try this. Watch a television show and keep a careful record of characters' kinesic communication.

- *How close to each other do characters who are intimate stand or sit? How close do characters who are antagonistic stand or sit? What is the distance between characters who are just meeting or who have casual relationships?*
- *Watch patterns of eye contact between characters who are intimates, enemies, and casual acquaintances. How often do they look at each other? How long is eye contact maintained in each type of relationship?*
- *Notice facial expressions for characters who do and don't like each other. How often do they smile or stare?*

As a class, discuss what your observations reveal about kinesic communication and relationship-level meanings.

For good reason, poets call the eyes "the mirrors of the soul." Our eyes communicate some of the most important and complex messages about how we feel about others. If you watch infants, you'll notice that they focus on others' eyes. Babies become terrified if they can't see their mothers' eyes, but

Communication Notes

Freedom of (Nonverbal) Speech

Nonverbal communication has been costly for some sports stars. When German midfielder Stefan Effenberg made an obscene gesture to fans during a World Cup match in the summer of 1994, his coach promptly kicked him off the squad. Basketball Nova Scotia, among others, adopted a zero tolerance for disrespect to officials. This includes directing nonverbal insults at an official.

Private companies such as athletic teams can make their own rules. However, in Canada, the Canadian *Charter of Rights and Freedoms* protects nonverbal behaviour. Thus it is unlikely that we could be prosecuted for making obscene gestures in public.

Sources: Be civil. (1994, July 5). *Wall Street Journal*, p. A1; Basketball Nova Scotia Code of Conduct, http://www.basketball.ns.ca/Codeofconduct.html (retrieved 10 April 2001).

they aren't bothered when other parts of their mothers' faces are hidden (Spitz, 1965). Even as adults, we tend to look at eyes to judge emotions, honesty, interest, and self-confidence.

For years, many attorneys have used body language to sway jurors' feelings and impressions of cases. For example, to suggest that a witness is lying, attorneys sometimes roll their eyes in full sight of jurors. Standing further away from witnesses during questioning enhances the witnesses' credibility with jurors. Some attorneys look conspicuously at their watches to signal jurors that the opposition's arguments are boring or ridiculous. Recently, some judges have tried to set limits on attorneys' nonverbal behaviour. A growing number of judges now require attorneys to stand at lecterns, which restricts face and body motions that might influence jurors.

Gestures are the special interest of David McNeill, a professor of linguistics and psychology at the University of Chicago. According to McNeill, much of what we want to communicate involves imagery, and imagery is not well conveyed by words. Thus, to communicate the images we have, we rely heavily on gestures, especially hand movements. McNeill says that as much as 75 percent of the meaning of communication is conveyed by motions (McNeill, 1992). In an interview with Barbara Mahany (1997), McNeill offered the interesting observation that the gesture of an extended middle finger, which is used to convey contempt, was used for the same message over 2000 years ago by ancient Romans. "Freedom of (Nonverbal) Speech" explains how this gesture can be costly.

HAPTICS

Haptics, the sense of touch, is the first of our five senses to develop (Leathers, 1976), and many communication scholars believe touching and being touched are essential to a healthy life. Research on dysfunctional families reveals that mothers touch babies less often and less affectionately than mothers in healthy families. In disturbed families, mothers tend to push children away, nonverbally signalling rejection (Birdwhistell, 1970). In contrast, babies who are held closely and tenderly tend to develop into self-confident adults who have secure attachment styles (Main, 1981).

Touching also communicates power and status. People with high status touch others and invade others' spaces more than people with less status (Henley, 1977). Cultural views of women as more touchable than men are reflected in gendered patterns of contact. Parents touch sons less often and more roughly than they touch daughters (Condry, Condry, & Pogatshnik, 1983). These patterns early in life teach the sexes different rules for using touch and interpreting touches from others. As adults, women tend to engage in touch to show liking and intimacy (Montgomery, 1988), whereas men rely on it to assert power and control (Henley, 1977; Leathers, 1986). For example, women frequently hug others and touch the hands and arms of friends during conversation. Men are more likely than women to use touch aggressively to exert power over others or to repel physical aggression. Because many females are taught to be nice to others and preserve relationships, women may be reluctant to object to touching, even if it is unwanted. These gendered patterns contribute to sexual harassment where women are often the targets of unwelcome touch (LePoire, Burgoon, & Parrott, 1992), as Claire's commentary illustrates.

Student Voices

Claire:

There's a guy where I work who really bothers me. He doesn't really cross a clear line, but it seems like he's always brushing against me. Like when he comes to my desk, he leans over just enough that his chest presses against me. Sometimes he touches my arm or hand when he's showing me a paper, and the other day he stood behind me to show me how to run a new spreadsheet program. He had both arms around me when it would have been easier to work the mouse if he'd sat on the side. I've never said anything because I don't want to hurt his feelings or seem hysterical or something, but it really bothers me.

PHYSICAL APPEARANCE

Western culture places an extremely high value on physical appearance. For this reason, most of us notice how others look, and we form initial evaluations of others based on their appearance. We first notice obvious physical qualities such as sex and race. After interpreting these, we then form judgments of how attractive others are and make inferences about their personalities. In one study, researchers found that people associate plump, rounded bodies with laziness and weakness. Thin, angular physiques were thought to reflect youthful, hard-driven, nervous, stubborn personalities, and athletic body types were seen as indicating strong, adventurous, self-reliant personalities (Wells & Siegel, 1961). We make judgments based on these characteristics even though a person may have limited control over body features.

Does physical appearance affect what people earn? It may. According to a recent *Wall Street Journal* (1996) report, a study of 2500 male and female lawyers revealed a relationship between physical attractiveness and earning power. The attorneys who were judged more attractive earned as much as 14 percent more than attorneys who were judged less attractive ("Good-Looking Lawyers," 1996). This report is consistent with other research showing that people who are considered attractive make more money than their less attractive peers.

Reflective Exercise

What is your experience with attractiveness and earning power? Are you treated differently when you are dressed up than when you look unkempt?

Communication Notes

Help with Eating Disorders

Preoccupation with weight can rob you of vitality and, in extreme form, endanger your life. If you are obsessed with weight or have an eating disorder, help is available either from your local health centre or from the following national organization:

The National Eating Disorder Information Centre (NEDIC)
CW 1-211 Elizabeth St.
Toronto, Ontario M5G 2C4
416-340-4156
or check your province for local organizations.

Cultures stipulate ideals for physical form. Currently in the West, cultural ideals emphasize thinness and youth in women and muscularity and height in men. Women and gay men seem particularly vulnerable to cultural pressures to be thin because they are judged so keenly by their attractiveness, whereas heterosexual men are judged primarily by their accomplishments (Spitzack, 1990, 1993). The cultural emphasis on thinness is so great that many people consider being seriously overweight a greater social stigma than a criminal record, cancer, a facial scar, or a missing hand (Harris, Walters, & Waschall, 1991). These cultural pressures lead to serious problems, as "Help with Eating Disorders" explains.

What message does your body adornment send?

Photo: A. Henry

Student Voices

Andrea:

Nearly all of the girls I know have eating problems. Some constantly diet, and a lot of others binge and purge. We're all afraid to gain any weight—afraid that guys won't want to date us if we weigh even a little extra. Usually I stick to dieting, but if I eat too much I do throw it up. I hate that, but it's better than being fat.

This culture's value on thinness is qualified by ethnic identity. Take a look in high-end fashion stores across Canada where there is an ethnic concentration and compare the look of one ethnic group to another.

Class membership further modifies ethnic values concerning weight. In 1994, *Essence* magazine reported that African American women who were either affluent or poor were likely to have strong Black identities that allowed them to resist White preoccupations with thinness. On the other hand, middle-class African American women who were upwardly mobile were more inclined to de-emphasize their ethnic identities to get ahead, and they were more susceptible to obsessions with weight and eating disorders (Villarosa, 1994). Another example of how weight and ethnicity are linked is evidenced in traditional Inuit culture where a woman would not be considered good marriage material if she were too thin, because she would not have enough fat to endure the cold.

Student Voices

Iliana:

In Rio de Janeiro, large full hips on women are considered voluptuous, attractive, and are emphasized by cinched-in waistlines. The large women here in Vancouver wear loose clothes to hide their size. It's hard to get used to.

ARTIFACTS

Artifacts are personal objects we use to announce our identities and heritage and to personalize our environments. We craft our image by how we dress and what objects, if any, we carry and use. Nurses and physicians wear white and frequently drape stethoscopes around their neck; professors travel with briefcases, whereas students more often tote backpacks. White-collar professionals tend to wear tailored outfits and dress shoes, whereas blue-collar workers more often dress in jeans or uniforms and boots. The military requires uniforms that define individuals in terms of the group. In addition, stripes and medals signify rank and accomplishments.

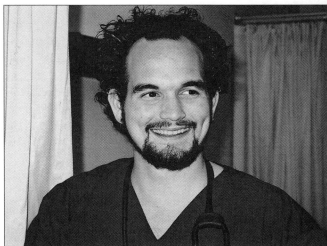

Facial piercing and the health professional: Is there an issue?

Photo: A. Henry

Artifacts may also define territories. To claim our spaces, we fill them with objects that matter to us and that reflect our experiences and values. Lovers of art adorn their homes with paintings and sculptures that announce their interests and personalize their private space. Religious families often express their commitments by displaying pictures of holy scenes and the *Bible,* the *Koran,* or other sacred texts. We exhibit artifacts that symbolize important relationships and experiences in our lives. For example, many people have pictures of family members in their offices and homes.

In her book *Composing a Life*, Mary Catherine Bateson (1990) comments that we turn houses into homes by filling them with what matters to us. We make impersonal spaces familiar and comfortable by imprinting them with our artifacts. We use mugs given to us by special people, nurture plants to enliven indoor spaces, surround ourselves with books and magazines that announce our interests, and sprinkle our world with objects that reflect what we care about.

Artifacts communicate important relationship meanings. We use them to announce our identities (see "Piercing Punishment" on page 224) and to express how we perceive and feel about others. Although clothing has become more unisex in recent years, once you venture off campus, gendered styles are evident. To declare gender, we dress to meet cultural expectations

Student Voices

Jenetta:

Whenever I move, the first thing I have to do is get out the quilt that my grandmother made. Even if it is summer and I won't use the quilt, I have to unpack it first and put it out where I can see it. She brought me up, and seeing that quilt is my way of keeping her in my life.

of men and women. Thus, women sometimes wear makeup, dresses that may have lace or other softening touches, skirts, high-heeled shoes, jewellery, and hose, all of which conform to the cultural ideal of women as decorative objects. Typically, men wear little, if any, jewellery, and their clothes and shoes are functional. Flat shoes allow a person to walk comfortably or run if necessary; high heels don't. Men's clothing is looser and less binding, and it includes pockets for wallets, keys, and so forth. In contrast, women's clothing tends to be more tailored and often doesn't include pockets, making a purse necessary.

We also use artifacts to establish racial identity. Jewellery and clothing are a common way to express a distinctive cultural heritage. Note the increase of ethnic artifacts that have reached the fashion markets in Canada.

Artifacts communicate our identity from an early age. Many hospitals still swaddle newborns in blue and pink blankets to designate sex, and even though many parents today try to be nonsexist, many still send gender messages through the toys they give their children. In general, parents, and especially fathers, give sons toys that encourage rough and active play (balls, trains) and competitiveness (baseball gloves, toy weapons), whereas they give daughters toys that cultivate nurturing (dolls, toy kitchens) and attention to appearance (makeup kits, frilly clothes) (Caldera, Huston, & O'Brien, 1989; Lytton & Romney, 1991; Pomerleau, Bolduc, Malcuit, & Cossette, 1990).

Communication Notes

Piercing Punishment

It seems not everyone appreciates the rage for body piercing. A nursing student at Camosun College in Victoria, B.C. was asked to remove three of the four earrings she wore in each ear because of the *perception* of professionalism. Restaurants seem most sensitive to piercing. Some employers set limits on which body parts can be pierced or how many piercings an employee may have. Starbucks draws the line at two piercings per ear, and those are okay only if the earrings match.

Source: Business bulletin. (1996, July 18). *Wall Street Journal*, p. A1.

Apply the Idea

Artifacts and Identity

How did artifacts in your childhood contribute to your gender identity? What kinds of toys did your parents give you? Did they ever discourage you from playing with particular kinds of toys? Did you ask for toys that aren't those society prescribes for your gender? Did your parents let you have the toys?

Now think about the clothing your parents gave you. If you're a woman, did your parents expect you to wear frilly dresses and stay clean? If you're a man, did your parents give you clothes meant for rough play and getting dirty?

Do you have artifacts that reflect your ethnic identity? What objects are part of your celebrations and spiritual observances? Do you have any jewellery or clothes that reflect your ethnic heritage?

Gifts are conventional ways to say "you matter to me." Some objects are invested with cultural meanings as well: Engagement rings and wedding bands signify commitment in ways broadly understood within Western culture. We also symbolize that we're connected to others by wearing their clothes, as when women wear male partners' shirts, or partners exchange sweatshirts.

Cultures, as well as social groups within a single culture, have artifacts that are especially important reflections of heritage and values. For example, Jewish people light candles in a menorah to symbolize sacred values. Christians rely on crosses and manger replicas to symbolize reverence for Jesus. In 1966, Kwanzaa was designated a time for African Americans to remember their African heritage and the values it entails. Now, more than 20 million people celebrate Kwanzaa in Canada, the United States, England, the Caribbean, and Africa. Kwanzaa is observed from December 26 through January 1. A kinara holds seven candles that symbolize seven distinct principles rooted in African culture. On the sixth day of Kwanzaa a magnificent feast, the karamu, draws together whole communities to celebrate their heritage and their connections (see "Kwanzaa" on page 225). Thus artifacts are an important way that we adorn not only our bodies but also our environments and make a statement about what we value.

ENVIRONMENTAL FACTORS

Environmental factors are another nonverbal influence on interpersonal interaction. Environmental factors are elements of settings that affect how we feel and act. For instance, we respond to architecture, colours (see "How Colours Affect Mood" on page 227), room design, temperature, sounds, smells, and lighting. Rooms with comfortable chairs invite relaxation, whereas rooms with stiff chairs prompt formality. Dimly lit rooms can enhance romantic feelings, although dark rooms might be depressing. We feel solemn in churches and synagogues with their sombre colours and sacred symbols.

We tend to feel more lethargic on sultry summer days and more alert on crisp fall ones. Delicious smells can make us feel hungry, even if we weren't previously interested in food. Our bodies synchronize themselves to patterns of light, so that we feel more alert during daylight than during the evening. In settings where people work during the night, extra lighting and even

Communication Notes

Kwanzaa

Kwanzaa blends a time of special celebration with friends and family with the everyday activities of keeping a home. In this way, Kwanzaa symbolizes the centrality of home and family to those of African ancestry, historically and today.

The kinara is a branched candleholder that holds seven candles, one to be lit on each day of the Kwanzaa observance. Three red candles, which symbolize struggles, are placed on the left for days two, four, and six of the celebration. The day-two candle symbolizes the principle of *kujichagulia*, or self-determination. The day four candle symbolizes *ujamma*, cooperative economics within communities. The day six candle represents *kuumba*, or creativity. On the right side of the kinara are placed three green candles to symbolize the future. The day-three candle on the far right represents *ujima*, collective work and responsibility. The day-five candle symbolizes *nio*, or purpose. The day-seven candle represents *imani*, or faith. The middle candle is black to stand for *umoja*, unity among black people.

On the sixth day of Kwanzaa there is a feast called *Karamu*. During the feast traditional African foods and family favourites are featured. Thus, Kwanzaa celebrates foods that have been passed down through generations of Africans.

Sources: Bellamy, L. (1996, December 18). Kwanzaa cultivates cultural and culinary connections. *Raleigh News and Observer*, pp. 1F, 9F; George, L. (1995, December 26). Holiday's traditions are being formed. *Raleigh News and Observer*, pp. C1, C3; Kwanzaa, http://cbc.ca/onair/specials/holidays/kwanzaa.html (retrieved 2 May 2001).

artificial skylights are used to simulate daylight so that workers stay alert. "Let the Sun Shine In" (on page 228) shows how light affects productivity.

Think about restaurants in which you've eaten. As the examples that opened this chapter illustrate, the environment of most fast-food restaurants encourages customers to eat quickly and move on, whereas more expensive restaurants are designed to promote longer stays and extra money spent on wines and desserts. For the same reason, fast-food restaurants are brightly lit and have fast music, if any. Finer restaurants tend to have dim lighting and soft, slow music, which encourages diners to linger.

The effect of restaurant atmosphere on diners was verified by an experiment. Over a 16-day period, researchers played music in a cafeteria. On the first day, the researchers played music with 122 beats per minute. The next day, they played slow instrumentals with only 56 beats per minute. On day three they played no music. The researchers repeated the sequence for 16

Communication Notes

How Colours Affect Mood

How much is mood influenced by colour? Research reports these relations between colours and moods:

red	exciting, stimulating
blue	secure, comfortable, soothing
orange	distressed, upset, disturbed
brown	dejected, unhappy, melancholy
green	calm, serene, peaceful
black	powerful, strong, defiant
yellow	cheerful, joyful, jovial
purple	dignified, stately

The effects of colour are not limited to their visual impact. Rebecca Ewing, a colour consultant, reports that she learned about the power of colour from three women—all of whom were blind. The blind women could identify different colours, a phenomenon that has been documented, by sensing distinct vibrations from different colours; these vibrations affect feeling and moods. Ewing compared the blind women's responses to colours with those of sighted people, and she found the same reactions to colours. So, how does colour affect our feelings? Says Ewing, red stimulates the appetite, blue stifles conversation, black evokes reverence, and green is calming.

Source: Varkonyi, C. (1996, June 22). Colourcode. *Raleigh News and Observer*, pp. 1E–2E; Wexner, L. B. (1954). The degree to which colours (hues) are associated with mood-tones. *Journal of Applied Psychology*, 38, 432–435.

days while they observed diners. The results confirmed the relationship between the pace of the music and the pace of eating. When no music was played, people averaged 3.23 bites per minute. When slow music was played, customers ate slightly more quickly: 3.83 bites per minute. But when the fast music with 122 beats per minute was played, diners sped up their eating to 4.4 bites per minutes (Bozzi, 1986).

An interesting illustration of cultural influences on environment is *feng shui* (pronounced "fung shway"). *Feng shui*, which stands for wind and water, is the ancient Chinese art of placement. Have you ever walked into a room and felt uncomfortable or unhappy? Have you ever entered a place and felt immediately warm and at ease? If so, you may have experienced *feng shui* in action. Dating back over 3000 years, *feng shui* is rooted in Taoism and aims to balance life energy, or *chi* (Spear, 1995). *Feng shui* consultants help homeowners and businesspeople arrange spaces to promote a smooth flow of energy and a harmony with nature. Some of the *feng shui* principles are consistent with Western research on nonverbal communication: Don't put large furniture in the path to the front door; you should never see a stairway from the front door; use green to increase good fortune; use mirrors where you want to stimulate creativity (Cozart, 1996; O'Neill, 1997).

Communication Notes

Let the Sun Shine In

Have you ever felt tired when working under fluorescent lights? Have you ever felt the need to take a break and get outside in the sunlight? If so, join the crowd. All light, it seems, is not equal. A study by the Rocky Mountain Institute in Colorado reports that increased daylight in work spaces results in less absenteeism and fewer worker errors. Wal-Mart opened a prototype daylit store. They used skylights in half of the store, with artificial lighting in the other half. Not only were workers more productive and comfortable in the areas lit by natural light, but customers were also more productive—they spent more money.

Source: Pierson, J. (1995, November 20). If sun shines in, workers work better, buyers buy more. *Wall Street Journal*, pp. B1, B8.

PROXEMICS

Proxemics refers to space and how we use it (Hall, 1968). Every culture has norms for using space and for how close people should be to one another. In Western culture, we interact with social acquaintances from a distance of 1 to 6 metres but are comfortable with 50 cm or less between us and close friends and romantic partners (Hall, 1966). When we are angry with someone, we tend to move away and to resent it if she or he approaches us. People who want to even out power in business negotiations often seek neutral territories for interaction. Gary makes this point in his commentary.

The amount of space we think we need to be comfortable is not strictly individual. There are notable cultural differences in the amount of space with which people feel comfortable. In China, for example, the average person has about 4 square metres, which amounts to a 2 metre by 2 metre room. Further, members of Chinese families often sleep in the same room and share bathrooms and kitchens with other families (Butterfield, 1982).

Space also announces status, with greater space being assumed by those with higher status (Henley, 1977). Substantial research shows that women and minorities generally have less space than white men in Western society (Spain,

Gary:

Part of our training for management was to learn how to manage turf. We were taught we should always try to get competitors into our offices—not to go to theirs. This gives us the advantage, just like playing on the home court gives a team an advantage. We also learned that we should go to subordinates' offices if we needed to criticize them so that they would feel less threatened and more willing to improve performance. The trainers also stressed the importance of meeting on neutral ground when we had to negotiate a deal with another company. They warned us never to meet on the other guys' turf because that would give them the advantage.

1992). The prerogative to invade someone else's personal space is also linked to power, with those having greater power also being most likely to trespass into others' territory (Henley, 1977). Responses to invasions of space also reflect power, with men likely to respond aggressively when their space is invaded (Fisher & Byrne, 1975). This suggests gendered socialization, which encourages women to defer and accommodate and men to vie for status. "Environmental Racism" (on page 230) reveals another connection between space and power.

How people arrange space reflects how close they are and whether they want interaction. Couples who are very interdependent tend to have greater amounts of common space and less individual space in their homes than do couples who are more independent (Fitzpatrick, 1988; Fitzpatrick & Best, 1979; Werner, Altman, & Oxley, 1985; Werner & Haggard, 1985). Similarly, families that value interaction arrange furniture to invite conversation and eye contact. Less interactive families arrange furniture to discourage conversation. Chairs may be far apart and may face televisions instead of one another (Burgoon, Buller, & Woodhall, 1989; Keeley & Hart, 1994). People also invite or discourage interaction by how they arrange office spaces. Some of your professors may have desks that face the door and a chair beside the desk for open communication with students; other professors may have desks turned away from the door and may position chairs across from their desks to preserve status and distance.

The effects of proxemics on behaviour have not gone unnoticed by companies that make money by moving people quickly. At McDonald's around the world, seats tilt forward at a 10-degree angle to discourage customers from lingering. The fast-food giant further fosters quick eating by making seats at the two-person tables only 67 cm apart when it has been established that the distance most people find comfortable for interaction is about a metre apart (Eaves & Leathers, 1991).

Apply the Idea

What Does Your Space Say?

Survey your space. Is furniture arranged to promote or discourage interaction? How much space is common and how much is reserved for individuals? Is space divided evenly among you and those who share your space, or do some people have more space than others?

Now think about a home you grew up in. How was the space arranged there? Was there a living room or family room? If so, was furniture set up to invite interaction? Was there a lot, a little, or a moderate amount of common space?

How do spatial arrangements in your home now regulate interaction and reflect the styles and status of people who live there? How is your space now different from your parents' or caregiver's?

Communication Notes

Environmental Racism

The term **"environmental racism"** arose to describe a pattern whereby toxic waste dumps and hazardous plants are disproportionately located in low-income neighbourhoods. Whether this is deliberately planned or not, many industries expose our most vulnerable communities to pollutants and carcinogens that seldom affect middle- and upper-class neighbourhoods. The pattern is very clear: The space of minorities and poor people can be invaded and contaminated, but the territory of more affluent citizens cannot. Our use of space is a statement we make about what we value and what the culture values.

Source: Cox, R., President of the national Sierra Club, 1994–96. (1995). Personal communication.

CHRONEMICS

Chronemics refers to how we perceive and use time to define identities and interaction. Nonverbal scholar Nancy Henley (1977) reports that we use time to negotiate and convey status. She has identified a cultural rule that stipulates important people with high status can keep others waiting. Conversely, people with low status are expected to be punctual in Western society. It is standard practice to have to wait, sometimes a good while, to see a physician, even if you have an appointment. This carries the message that the physician's time is more valuable than yours. Professors can be late to class, and students are expected to wait, but students may be reprimanded if they appear after a class begins. Subordinates are expected to report punctually to meetings, but bosses are allowed to be tardy.

Chronemics express cultural attitudes toward time, as illustrated in "Cultural Views of Time" (page 232). In Western societies, time is valuable, so speed is highly valued (Keyes, 1992; Schwartz, 1989). Linguists (Lakoff & Johnson, 1980) have noted many everyday Western phrases that reflect the cultural view that time is very valuable: Don't waste time; save time; spend time; can't spare time; invest time; run out of time; budget time; borrowed time; lose time; use time profitably.

The West's emphasis on speed is reflected in how we go about daily activities. We want computers, not typewriters, and we replace hardware and software as soon as faster models and programs hit the market. We often try to do several things at once to get more done, rely on the microwave to cook faster, and take for granted speed systems such as instant copying, photos, and so forth. Many other cultures have far more relaxed attitudes toward time and punctuality. It's not impolite in many South American countries to come late to meetings or classes, and it's not assumed people will leave at the scheduled time for ending. Whether time is savoured or compulsively counted and hoarded reflects larger cultural attitudes toward living.

The duration of time we spend with different individuals reflects our interpersonal priorities. When possible, we spend more time with people we like than with those we don't like or who bore us. Researchers report that increasing contact is one of the most important ways college and university students intensify relationships, and reduced time together signals decreasing interest (Baxter, 1985; Dindia, 1994; Tolhuizen, 1989). Time is also related to status in work settings. Bankers spend more time with important clients who have major accounts; brokers spend more time with clients who have a lot of money than with clients who have less; architects meet more often and for longer periods with companies that are building a series of large structures than with individuals who want to build a single home; and fundraisers invest greater amounts of time in well-off donors than in moderate contributors.

Chronemics also involve expectations of time, which are established by cultural norms. For example, you expect a class to last 50 or 75 minutes. Several minutes before the end of a class period, students often close notebooks and start gathering their belongings, signalling the teacher that time is up. Similarly, we expect weekly religious services to last approximately an hour, and we might be upset if a rabbi or minister talked beyond the time we've allowed. These expectations reflect our culture's general orientation toward time, which is that it is a precious commodity that we should not give away easily.

Communication Notes

Cultural Views of Time

North Americans and Germans differ in the time they invest in work. The typical job in Germany requires 37 hours a week, with a minimum of five weeks' paid leave annually, guaranteed by law. Stores close on weekends and four of five weeknights so that workers can have leisure time. In Canada and the United States, jobs typically require 44 to 80 hours a week, and many workers can't take more than a week's leave at a time. Further, many North Americans take second jobs even when their first jobs allow a comfortable standard of living. Germans can't understand this, remarking that "free time can't be paid for" (p. B1). Personal time is considered so precious in Germany that it is illegal to work more than one job during holidays, which are meant to allow people to restore themselves.

Source: Benjamin, D., & Horwitz, T. (1994, July 14). German view: "You Americans work too hard—and for what?" *Wall Street Journal*, pp. B1, B6.

PARALANGUAGE

Paralanguage refers to communication that is vocal but that does not use words themselves. It includes sounds, such as murmurs and gasps, and vocal qualities, such as volume, rhythm, pitch, and inflection. Paralanguage also includes how we pronounce words, the accents we use, and the complexity of our sentences. Our voices are versatile instruments that tell others how to interpret us and what we say. Vocal cues signal others to interpret what we say as a joke, threat, statement of fact, question, and so forth.

Apply the Idea

Paralinguistic Cues

Say "Oh, really" to express the following meanings:

- *I don't believe what you just said.*
- *Wow! That's interesting.*
- *I find your comment boring.*
- *That's juicy gossip!*
- *What a contemptible thing to say.*

    Now say "You love me" to convey these meanings:

- *You really do? I hadn't realized that.*
- *That ploy won't work. I told you we're through.*
- *You couldn't possibly love me after what you did!*
- *Me? I'm the one you love?*
- *You? I didn't think you loved anyone.*

Communication Notes

To Tell the Truth

Dektor Counterintelligence and Security, Inc. believes our voices reveal whether we are lying or telling the truth. Dektor invented the PSE (Psychological Stress Evaluator), a machine that measures vocal stress. The PSE is designed to detect the inaudible effect on the human voice of involuntary reactions. Dektor claims the PSE has a 94.7 percent success rate in detecting lies, and this machine has been used several times in trials.

Source: "The use of scientific methods and techniques in obtaining testimonial evidence" http://aux.lincoln.edu/departments/sociology/criminaljustice/cihypnosis.htm#admissibility (retrieved 9 June 2001).

We use our voices to communicate feelings to friends and romantic partners. Whispering, for instance, signals secrecy and intimacy, whereas shouting conveys anger. Depending on the context, sighing may communicate empathy, boredom, or contentment. Research indicates that tone of voice is a powerful clue to feelings between marital partners. Negative paralanguage, such as sneering and ridiculing by tone of voice, are closely associated with marital dissatisfaction (Gottman, Markman, & Notarius, 1977; Noller, 1987). A derisive or sarcastic tone communicates scorn or dislike more emphatically than words. The reverse is also true: A warm voice underlines feelings of love, and a playful lilt invites frolic and fun. Tone of voice and inflection are also primary gauges for interpreting honesty, as illustrated in "To Tell the Truth."

Our voices affect how others perceive us. To some extent, we control vocal cues that influence image. For instance, we can deliberately sound firm and sure of ourselves in job interviews when we want to project self-confidence. Similarly, we can consciously make ourselves sound self-righteous, seductive, and unapproachable when those images suit our purposes. In addition to the ways we intentionally use our voices to project an image, vocal qualities we don't deliberately manipulate affect how others perceive us as well. A friend might notice strain in your voice and say "Are you OK?" In the next chapter on listening, we examine more closely the nonverbal vocal clues that tell us someone may need a listener.

Reflective Exercise

Consider the distinctive sounds of Canada. What are the involuntary inflections and vocal qualities that distinguish the speech of Newfoundland, French Canada, Alberta, Caribbean Canadians, Asian Canadians, and First Nations? What assumptions do you make when you hear these sounds? How is the "paralanguage" part of the overall message being communicated?

Student Voices

Ryan:

I got an excellent job interview with Club Med eh! My teacher told me my language style might limit me. I hadn't even thought of my language before. She was right. I use a lot of slang and say "yup" and "nope" a lot. It doesn't leave the impression I wanted. I had to learn a classier language style to win my interview.

We modulate our voices to reflect our cultural heritage and to announce we are members of specific cultures. Ryan, for example, would use casual slang and tonal inflections that were part of the skateboarding culture he was familiar with.

We also use paralanguage to declare gender by behaving in a masculine or feminine manner. To appear masculine, men use strong volume, low pitch, and limited inflection, all of which conform to cultural prescriptions for men to be assertive and emotionally controlled. To enact femininity, women tend to use higher pitch, less volume, and more inflection, vocal features that reflect cultural views of women as deferential and polite. Men and women both, however, use masculine or feminine paralanguage to demonstrate control or receptivity. Consider the circumstances where you wish to sound more masculine or more feminine.

We also enact class by how we pronounce words, the accents we use, and the complexity of our sentences. Class is expressed by vocabulary (greater vocabulary is generally associated with higher education) and by grammar. Ryan discovered this in his Club Med interview. In addition to paralinguistic cues, other nonverbal behaviours communicate class. For example, artifacts generally differ in the homes of working-class and upper-class people. Affluent individuals possess more books, expensive art, and valuable jewellery than do less affluent individuals.

SILENCE

A final type of nonverbal behaviour is silence, which can communicate powerful messages. "I'm not speaking to you" actually speaks volumes. We use silence to communicate different meanings. For instance, it can symbolize contentment when intimates are so comfortable they don't need to talk. Silence can also communicate awkwardness, as you know if you've ever had trouble keeping conversation going with a new acquaintance. We feel pressured to fill the void. In some cultures, including many First Nations ones, silence indicates respect and thoughtfulness.

The positive value of silence has been proved in the case of seriously ill babies. Hospital intensive care nurseries have found that special headphones that block noise reduce the stress caused by the sounds of respirators, ventilators, and other hospital machinery. Within the headphones is a mini-microphone that detects irritating low-frequency noises and eliminates them by generating anti-noise waves. In trials of the headphones, babies who wore them had fewer sleep disturbances and less abnormal changes in blood pressure (Cyberscope, 1996).

Yet silence isn't always comforting. It is sometimes used to disconfirm others. In some families, children are disciplined by being ignored. No matter what the child says or does, parents refuse to acknowledge his or her existence. In later life, the silencing strategy may also surface. You know how disconfirming silence can be if you've ever said hello to someone and got no reply. Even if the other person didn't deliberately ignore you, you feel slighted. We sometimes deliberately freeze out intimates when we're angry with them. Organizations such as military academies and religious groups use silencing or excommunication to punish those who err or disobey. It is a powerful way to strip someone of his or her personhood.

Note the gender differences in body language.

Photo: A. Henry

Student Voices

Michael:

Silencing is the cruellest thing you can do to a person. That was how my parents disciplined all of us. They told us we were bad and then refused to speak to us—sometimes for several hours. I can't describe how awful it felt to get no response from them, to be a nonperson. I would have preferred physical punishment. I'll never use silencing with my kids.

In the final section of this chapter, we consider guidelines for improving the effectiveness of our nonverbal communication.

GUIDELINES FOR IMPROVING NONVERBAL COMMUNICATION

Nonverbal communication, like language, is symbolic and open to misinterpretation. The following two guidelines should help you avoid misunderstanding others' nonverbal behaviours and having others misperceive your actions.

ADOPT DUAL PERSPECTIVE

Before judging nonverbal behaviour or assuming you understand what is intended in the nonverbal behaviour of another, adopt dual perspective. As we discussed in Chapter 1, try to see the world from the other's perspective. This will help eliminate errors and misunderstandings.

MONITOR YOUR NONVERBAL COMMUNICATION

Concepts at a Glance

Guidelines for Improving Nonverbal Communication

1. Adopt dual perspective.
2. Monitor your nonverbal communication.
3. Be tentative when interpreting others' nonverbal communication:
   - Consider the person.
   - Consider the context.
4. Use I–language when interpreting nonverbal communication.

The monitoring skills we have stressed in other chapters are also important for competent nonverbal communication. Self-reflection allows you to take responsibility for how you present yourself and your nonverbal messages. Think about the foregoing discussion of ways we use nonverbal behaviours to announce our identities. Are you projecting the image you desire? Do your facial and body movements represent how you see yourself and how you want others to perceive you? Do friends ever tell you that you seem uninterested or far away when they are talking to you? If so, you can monitor your nonverbal actions so that you convey greater involvement and interest in conversations.

Have you set up your spaces so that they invite the kind of interaction you prefer, or are they arranged to interfere with good communication? Paying attention to nonverbal dimensions of your world can empower you to use them more effectively to achieve your interpersonal goals.

BE TENTATIVE WHEN INTERPRETING OTHERS' NONVERBAL COMMUNICATION

Although stores are filled with popular advice books that promise to show you how to read nonverbal communication, there really aren't any sure-fire formulas. It's naive to think we can precisely decode something as complex and ambiguous as nonverbal communication. When we believe that we can, we risk misjudging others.

In this chapter, we've discussed findings about the meanings people attach to nonverbal behaviours. It's important to realize these are only generalizations about conclusions people draw. We have not and cannot state what any particular behaviour ever means to specific individuals in a given context. For instance, we've said that satisfied couples tend to sit closer together than unhappy couples. As a general rule, this is true, at least in Western societies. However, sometimes very contented couples prefer autonomy and like to keep distance between them some of the time. In addition, someone may maintain distance because she or he has a cold and doesn't want a partner to catch it. In work settings, people who don't look at us and who discourage conversation may be preoccupied with solving a problem and not mean to ignore us. Also, people socialized in non-Western cultures use space in different ways and have different meanings for physical closeness and distance. Because nonverbal communication is ambiguous and personal, we should not assume we can interpret it with absolute precision. You will be more effective if you qualify interpretations of nonverbal communication with awareness of personal and contextual considerations.

Be tentative when interpreting nonverbal communication.

Photo: © Corel

Consider the Person

Generalizations about nonverbal behaviour tell us only what is generally the case. They don't tell us about the exceptions to the rule. Nonverbal patterns

Student Voices

Kincaid:

One of the most unsettling experiences of my life was trying to negotiate a deal between my company and a Japanese one. I travelled to Japan and met with a representative of the Japanese company. He wouldn't look at me when I spoke, and that made me wonder if he was being evasive. Also, he would never say "no" point blank, even if he totally disagreed with something I said or if there was no way he was going to agree to terms I proposed. His style was to say, "We will have to think about that very important idea." After two days of frustrating negotiations, I realized that the Japanese think direct eye contact is rude and refusals or disagreements make the other lose face. I had to learn how to read Mr. Watanabe.

that accurately describe most people may not apply to particular individuals. Although eye contact generally indicates responsiveness in Western culture, some individuals close their eyes to concentrate when listening. In such cases, it would be inaccurate to conclude a person who doesn't look at us isn't listening. Similarly, people who cross their arms and have a rigid posture are often expressing hostility or lack of interest in interaction. However, the same behaviours might mean a person is cold and trying to conserve body heat. Most people use less inflection, fewer gestures, and a slack posture when they're not really interested in what they're talking about. However, we all exhibit these same behaviours when we are tired.

Because nonverbal behaviours are ambiguous and vary among people, we need to be cautious about how we interpret others. *Reminder: We construct the meaning in the nonverbal behaviours we observe.*

Consider the Context

Like the meaning of verbal communication, the significance of nonverbal behaviours depends on the contexts in which they occur. How we act doesn't reflect only how we see ourselves and how we feel. In addition, our actions reflect the various settings we inhabit. We are more or less formal, relaxed, and open depending on context. Most people are more at ease on their own turf than someone else's, so we tend to be friendlier and more outgoing in our homes than in business meetings and public places. We also dress according to context.

Students who see professors in professional clothing on campus are often surprised to find them in jeans or running clothes at home or in town. Like everyone, professors costume themselves differently for various occasions and contexts.

Immediate physical setting is not the only context that affects nonverbal communication. As we have seen, all communication, including the non-

Student Voices

Mei-Ling:

I often have been misinterpreted in this country. My first semester here a professor told me he wanted me to be more assertive and to speak up in class. I could not do that, I told him. He said I should put myself forward, but I have been brought up not to do that. In Taiwan, that is very rude and ugly, and all of us are taught not to speak up to teachers. Now that I have been here for three years, I sometimes speak in classes, but I am still more quiet than Canadian students. I know my professors think I am not so smart because I am quiet, but that is the teaching of my country.

verbal dimension, reflects the values and understandings of particular cultures. We are likely to misinterpret people from other cultures when we impose the norms and rules of our own. An Arabic man who stands very close to others to talk with them is not being rude according to the standards in his culture, although he might be interpreted as pushy by Westerners. A Tibetan woman who makes little eye contact is showing respect by the norms in her country, although she might be interpreted as evasive if judged by North American rules of interaction.

USE I–LANGUAGE

A key principle to keep in mind is that nonverbal behaviours, like other symbols, have no intrinsic meaning. Meaning is something we construct and assign to behaviours. A good way to keep this distinction in mind is to rely on I–language, not you–language, which we discussed in Chapter 5. You–language might lead us to inaccurately say of someone who doesn't look at us, "You're communicating lack of interest." A more responsible statement would use I–language to say, "When you don't look at me, I think you're not interested in what I'm saying." Using I–language reminds us to take responsibility for our judgments and feelings. In addition, it reduces the likelihood we will make others defensive by inaccurately interpreting their nonverbal behaviour.

Apply the Idea

Using I–Language About Nonverbal Behaviours

I–language makes communication about nonverbal behaviours more responsible and clear. Practise the skill of translating you–language into I–language to describe nonverbal behaviour.

> Example: You–language: You're staring at me.
> I–language: When you look at me so intensely, I feel uneasy.

You–Language

You make me angry when you don't clean the kitchen after you use it.

I can tell you don't believe me by your expression.

Don't crowd me.

Your T-shirt is offensive.

Even within our own country we have diverse speech communities, and each has its own rules for nonverbal behaviour. We run the risk of misinterpreting men if we judge them by the norms of feminine speech communities. A man who doesn't make "listening noises" may well be listening intently according to the rules of masculine speech communities. Similarly, men often misperceive women as agreeing when they nod and make listening noises while someone is talking. According to feminine speech communities, ongoing feedback is a way of signalling interest, not necessarily approval. We have to adopt dual perspective when interpreting others, especially when different social groups are involved.

We can become more effective nonverbal communicators if we monitor our own nonverbal behaviours and qualify our interpretation of others by keeping personal and contextual considerations in mind. Using I–language is one way to help us avoid the danger of misreading others.

Chapter Summary

In this chapter, we've explored many facets of the fascinating world beyond words. We began by noting both similarities and differences between verbal and nonverbal communication. Next, we discussed how that nonverbal communication functions to supplement or replace verbal messages, to regulate interaction, to reflect and establish relationship-level meanings, and to express cultural membership. These four principles of nonverbal behaviour help us understand the complex ways in which nonverbal communication operates and what it may mean.

We discussed nine types of nonverbal communication. These are kinesics (face and body motion), proxemics (use of space), physical appearance, artifacts, environmental features, haptics, chronemics (use of and orientations to time), paralanguage, and silence. Each of these forms of nonverbal communication reflects cultural understandings and values and also expresses our personal identities and feelings toward others. We use nonverbal behaviours to announce and perform identities, using actions, artifacts, and contextual features to embody the rules we associate with gender, race, class, sexuality, and ethnicity. In this sense, nonverbal communication has a theatrical dimension, because it is a primary way we create and present images of ourselves.

Because nonverbal communication, like its verbal cousin, is symbolic, it has no inherent meaning that is fixed for all time. Instead, its meaning is something we construct as we notice, organize, and interpret nonverbal behaviours that we and others enact. Effectiveness requires that we use dual perspective, learn to monitor our own nonverbal communication, exercise caution in interpreting that of others, and use I–language to get clarity.

Key Concepts

- artifacts
- chronemics
- environmental racism
- haptics
- kinesics
- nonverbal communication
- paralanguage
- proxemics

For Further Thought & Discussion

1. Think about the information on attorneys' nonverbal communication (see page 219). What ethical issues are involved in attorneys' use of nonverbal behaviours in an effort to influence jurors? What ethical issues are involved in judges' restrictions of attorneys' nonverbal communication? Is this a violation of the right to free speech?

2. Visit six restaurants near your campus. Describe the seats, lighting, music (if any), distance between tables, and colours of decor. Do you find any relationship between nonverbal communication patterns and expensiveness of restaurants?

3. Describe the spatial arrangements in the family in which you grew up. How large was your home or apartment? How many people lived there? Did each member of the family have her or his own bedroom? Did anyone in the family have a separate work or hobby room or a special chair in which others did not sit? Do the proxemic patterns in your family reflect status differences among members?

4. Is it ethical to interpret others' nonverbal communication without recognizing their cultural perspective? If so, how does doing this reflect unethical behaviour and/or attitudes?

5. What does silence mean to you? Does its meaning differ in various contexts? What do you mean when you are silent? Do you ever use silence strategically?

6. What ethical issues are involved in dumping toxic wastes in poor communities? Is it fair for all citizens to enjoy the benefits of petrochemical products but for only some of them to absorb the risks of producing these products?

7. Use your Infotrac College Edition to skim articles and advertisements in two Canadian magazines. How many articles and advertisements that focus on weight (losing, controlling) do you find in each of these magazines? What can you conclude about the body image of men and women in Canada? Are there ethnic differences?

8. Use your InfoTrac College Edition to review the tables of contents for the last four issues of *Environmental Action Magazine*. Is the topic of environmental justice (also called environmental racism) discussed in any of the issues? Do you find any recent reports on patterns in location of toxic waste dumps and other environmental dangers?

Weaving Communication into Relationships

Mindful Listening

Everyday Encounters
By Stephen Lee

We've all witnessed insensitive listeners like Chloe. In this chapter, we will examine the skills, abilities, and attitudes that comprise good listening. Good listening is not only needed to navigate through our everyday lives but also a gift we give to others in need. Consider the following dialogue.

Ben: Mom just called to tell me she and Dad are divorcing. I can't believe it. My folks have been together for 23 years.

Mike: Well, half of marriages end in divorce so it's not so unusual.

Ben: Maybe half of other people's marriages, but not my parents.

Mike: Why not your parents? Divorce is pretty common. It just isn't a big deal anymore.

Ben: It's a big deal to me. Mom and Dad have always been there for me. It feels so strange to think I won't have my family anymore.

Mike: Okay, so you weren't expecting this news, but still, it's not like the end of the world. Just get on with your life.

Ben: How can I when everything my life is based on has suddenly blown up in my face?

Mike: They'll still pay for your last year of university, won't they?

Ben: I guess, but that's not the issue. The problem is that I don't have a home or family anymore.

Mike: Get a grip, man. It's not like you're a ten-year-old living at home. You left home when you came to college. Their divorce doesn't affect you or your life—not unless you let it.

How would you describe Mike's communication in the conversation? Is he being a good communicator? Does he let Ben know he understands how Ben feels? Does Mike respond sensitively to Ben's concerns?

Usually when we think about communication, we think about talking. Yet, talking is not the only or even the greatest part of communication. For people to interact and share meaning, they must also listen to one another. As obvious as this is, few of us devote as much energy to effective listening as we do to effective talking. In the example, Mike doesn't listen very well. He isn't sensitive to Ben's feelings, and he doesn't communicate support to his friend. Although most of us are probably better listeners than Mike was in this instance, few of us listen as well as we could or should.

If you think about your normal day, you'll realize that listening—or trying to—takes up about half of your waking time. Listening is the single greatest communication activity in which we engage. We spend more time listening than talking, reading, or writing. This point is well made by Marilyn Buckley, who says "Students listen to the equivalent of a book a day; talk the equivalent of a book a week; read the equivalent of a book a month; and write the equivalent of a book a year" (1992, p. 622).

Studies of people, ranging from college students to professionals, indicate that the average person spends between 45 and 53 percent of waking time listening to others (Barker, Edwards, Gaines, Gladney, & Holley, 1981; Weaver, 1972). You listen in classes, listen to acquaintances in casual

Listening is a gift.

Photo: © Photodisc

conversation, listen to your parents during phone calls, listen to clerks in stores, listen to your supervisor and customers when you're at work, and listen to friends when they talk to you about important concerns or issues in their lives. If we don't listen effectively, we're communicating poorly about half of the time! And if we don't listen well, we are diminished emotionally, intellectually, and spiritually. This point was well made in an advertisement sponsored by the Unisys Corporation: "How can we expect him to learn when we haven't taught him how to listen?" (cited in Berko, Wolvin, & Wolvin, 1995, p. 81). If we can't listen, we can't learn.

Although listening—or trying to—takes up a great deal of our time, we don't always do it as effectively as we could and should. Because listening is a vital and major form of communication, in this chapter we will explore what it is and how to listen effectively. First, we'll consider what's involved in listening, which is

Communication Notes

Signing As a Recognized Language

Canadian Sign Language (CSL), French Canadian Sign Language (FCSL), and American Sign Language (ASL) are recognized by government as real languages. Sign language interpreters are required by deaf people in the Canadian courts.

The first lesson students learn is that these sign languages are not just a visual form of English. Rather, they are complex linguistic systems with their own syntactical and grammatical structure. CSL, FCSL, and ASL are also more conceptual than spoken English. There are signs for distinct concepts such as walking quickly and walking slowly and being smart and being very smart. Spoken English relies on modifiers to make these distinctions: The word "walking" gets modified by "quickly" or "slowly"; the word "smart" gets modified by "very."

As with any language, learning ASL or its derivatives introduces students not just to words but to the values of the Deaf culture. For example, students learn that in ASL there is only one word for music—a sweeping gesture with the right hand under the left arm. Because deaf individuals cannot hear, they don't need the many terms hearing individuals use to describe different kinds of music.

Sources: Carl, W. (1998). A sign of the times. In J. T. Wood, *But I thought you meant ...: Misunderstandings in human communication* (pp. 95–208). Mountain View, CA: Mayfield; Manning, A. (1996, March 6). Signing catches on as a foreign language. *USA Today*, p. 4D.

more than most of us realize. Second, we'll discuss obstacles to effective listening and how we can minimize these. Third, we'll consider some common forms of nonlistening. The fourth section of the chapter explains different types of listening and the distinct skills required for each. To wrap up the chapter, we'll identify guidelines for improving listening effectiveness.

Concepts at a Glance

Listening

1. The listening process
2. Obstacles to effective listening
3. Forms of nonlistening
4. Adapting listening to communication goals
5. Guidelines for effective listening

THE LISTENING PROCESS

Listening is a complex process that involves far more than our ears. To listen well, we rely on our ears, minds, and hearts.

Although we often use the words listening and hearing as if they were synonyms, actually they are distinct.

Hearing is a physiological activity that occurs when sound waves hit our eardrums. People who are deaf or hearing impaired receive messages visually either through lip reading or sign language (See "Signing As a Recognized Language").

Listening has psychological and cognitive dimensions that mere hearing, or physically receiving messages, does not. The multifaceted aspects of listening are reflected in the Chinese character in Figure 7.1, which includes the symbols for eyes, ears, and heart.

Listening is not just hearing but also includes interpreting and responding to what others communicate. The International Listening Association (1995) emphasizes that listening is an active process, which means we have to exert effort to listen well. We have to be involved with our ears and hearts and minds, if we want to listen effectively. Figure 7.2 shows the listening process.

Figure 7.1
The Chinese Character for "Listening"

BEING MINDFUL

The first step in listening is making a decision to be mindful.

Mindfulness is a concept from Zen Buddhism that refers to being fully present in the moment. The Reverend Jisho Perry says that "to pay attention is to stop putting our own ideas and opinions on the situation" (1996, p. 22). To be mindful is to keep your mind on what is happening in the here and now. When we are mindful, we don't let our thoughts wander from the present situation. We don't think about what we did yesterday or plan to do this weekend, nor do we focus on our own feelings and responses. Instead, when we listen mindfully, we tune in fully to another person and try to hear that person without imposing our own ideas, judgments, or feelings on him or her. Mindfulness is symbolized by paying attention, adopting an involved posture, keeping eye contact, and indicating interest in what another person says (Bolton, 1986). These behaviours are called attending.

Review

Listening is an active, complex process that consists of being mindful, attending, hearing, selecting and organizing information, interpreting communication, responding, and remembering.

1. Mindfulness
2. Attending
3. Hearing
4. Selecting and organizing information
5. Interpreting communication
6. Responding to others
7. Remembering communication

Figure 7.2
The Listening Process

Mindfulness is the first step in effective listening, and it is the foundation for all other parts of the process.

Mindfulness enhances communication in two ways. First, attending fully to others allows us to understand them better than if we pay only superficial attention. Listening mindfully enables us to grasp the relational meanings of messages so that we have an idea of how another person feels about what she or he is saying. In other words, mindfulness fosters dual perspective, which is a cornerstone of effective communication. In addition, mindfulness enhances the effectiveness of another's communication. When people sense we are really listening, they tend to engage us more fully, elaborate their ideas, and express themselves in more depth.

Being mindful is a choice we make. It is not a talent that some people have and others don't, nor is it something that results from what others do. Instead, it is a matter of making a personal commitment to attend fully and without diversion to another person. No amount of skill will make you a good listener if you don't choose to attend mindfully to others.

Apply the Idea

Being Mindful

To develop your ability to be mindful, follow these guidelines in a situation that calls on you to listen:

- *Empty your mind of thoughts, ideas, plans, and concerns so that you are open to the other person.*

- *Concentrate on the person with whom you are interacting. Say to yourself, "I want to focus on this person and what she or he is feeling and thinking."*

- *If you find yourself framing responses to the other person, try to push those aside—they interfere with your concentration on what the other person is saying.*

- *If your mind wanders, don't criticize yourself—that's distracting. Instead, gently refocus on the person you are with and what that person is communicating to you. It's natural for other thoughts to intrude, so just push them away and stay focused on the other person.*

- *Let the other person know you are attending mindfully by giving nonverbal responses (nods, facial expressions), asking questions to encourage elaboration, and keeping eye contact.*

- *Evaluate how mindfully you listened. Did you understand the other person's thoughts and feelings? Did you feel more focused on that person than you usually do when listening to others?*

ATTENDING

The second step in the listening process is attending. **Attending** describes the specific behaviours of being mindful. These behaviours can easily be remembered by the acronym FELOR.

F = Face your speaker

E = Eye contact

L = Lean forward

O = Open posture

R = Relax

Once you have decided to be mindful, and then "attended" to your speaker, you are ready to receive messages.

Are mindfulness and technology compatible?

Photo: A. Henry

Student Voices

Talyn:

I always thought I was a good listener, until I spent two years living in Japan. In that culture there is a much deeper meaning to listening. I realized that most of the time I was only hearing others. Often I was thinking of my responses while they were still talking. I had not been listening with my mind and heart. When I spoke to a Japanese person, he listened so thoughtfully. I was embarrassed one day to realize that every time I made a noise or gesture, everyone was silent and allowed me to speak. I hadn't been giving them that same graciousness.

HEARING/RECEIVING MESSAGES

The third step involved in listening is hearing, or physically receiving messages. As we noted earlier, hearing is a physiological process in which sound waves hit our eardrums so that we become aware of noises, such as music, traffic sounds, or human voices. For individuals who have hearing impairments, messages are received in other ways—through writing, lip reading, or sign language. Whether we hear messages or receive them in other ways, the mere reception of messages is not listening. Instead, it is a passive process: If we are present when vibrations are in the air, we will hear them. If someone signs to us, we can see the signs and decode them. Hearing, or otherwise receiving messages, requires no real effort on our part.

Although receiving messages is not the same as listening, we have to receive messages in order to listen. For most of us, hearing is automatic and unhindered. However, individuals with hearing impairments may have difficulty actually receiving oral messages. When we speak with someone who has a hearing disability, we should face the person and check to make sure we are coming across clearly. In addition to physiological problems, hearing ability may decline when we are fatigued from concentrating on communication. You may have noticed that it's harder to pay attention in classes that run 75 minutes or 3 hours rather than 50 minutes. Background noise can also interfere with good hearing. If loud music is playing, a television is blaring, or others are talking in our vicinity, it's difficult to hear well. Even though this is evident, as Heather points out, we often don't control noises that interfere with effective hearing and listening.

Student Voices

Heather:

My parents are so strange! To watch them, you'd think they were deliberately trying to make it impossible to hear each other. Here's what happens: Dad will turn on the radio, and then Mom will start talking. He won't hear part of what she says, and then she'll get in a huff that he ignored her. Or sometimes Mom will have the television on, and Dad will say something from the other room. When she doesn't hear him, he'll get on her case about caring more about whatever program is on than about him. They do this all the time—no wonder they can't hear each other!

Even among people who have normal hearing, there may be physiological differences in how we hear. Women and men seem to differ in their listening styles. As a rule, women are more attentive than men to the many things that are happening around them. Thus, men tend to focus their hearing on specific content aspects of communication, whereas women are

Student Voices

Mark:

My girlfriend amazes me. We'll have a conversation, and then later one of us will bring it up again. What I remember is what we decided in the talk. She remembers that too, but she also remembers all the details about where we were and what was going on in the background and particular things one of us said in the conversation. I never notice all of that stuff, and I sure don't remember it later.

more likely to attend to the whole of communication, noticing details, tangents, and major themes (Weaver, 1972). Judy Pearson (1985), a prominent communication scholar, suggests this could be due to the brain's hemispheric specializations. Women usually have more developed right lobes, which govern creative and holistic thinking, whereas men typically have more developed left lobes, which control analytic and linear information processing.

SELECTING AND ORGANIZING MATERIAL

The fourth element of listening is selecting and organizing material. As we noted in Chapter 3, we don't perceive everything around us. Instead, we selectively attend to some messages and elements of our environments, and we disregard others. What we attend to depends on many factors, including our interests, cognitive structures, and expectations. If we realize that our own preoccupations can hamper listening, we can curb interferences. Once again, mindfulness comes into play. Choosing to be mindful doesn't necessarily mean our minds won't stray when we try to listen, but it does mean that we will bring ourselves back to the present moment. We have to remind ourselves to focus attention and concentrate on what another is saying.

We can monitor our tendencies to attend selectively by remembering that we are more likely to notice stimuli that are intense, loud, or unusual, or that otherwise stand out from the flow of communication. This implies that we may overlook communicators who speak quietly and don't call attention to themselves. Youngae, a visiting student from Taiwan, observes that most Canadian students often ignore what she says because she speaks softly and unassertively. Westerners who are accustomed to outspoken, individualistic speaking styles may not attend to speaking styles that are less bold. If we're aware of the tendency not to notice people who speak quietly, we can guard against it so that we don't miss out on people and messages that may be important. "Hard Times for Listening" (on page 253) explores the effect of our rushed lifestyles on listening.

Once we've selected what to notice, we then organize the stimuli to which we've attended. As you'll recall from Chapter 3, we organize our perceptions by relying on cognitive schemata, which include prototypes, personal constructs, stereotypes, and scripts. As we listen to others, we decide how to categorize them by asking which of our prototypes they most closely resemble—good friend, person in trouble, student, teacher, and so forth. We then apply personal constructs to define in more detail others and their messages. We evaluate whether they are smart or not smart, upset or calm, reasonable or unreasonable, open or closed to advice, and so on. Based on how we construct others, we then apply stereotypes that predict what they will do. When friends are clearly distraught, as Ben was at the beginning of this chapter, we can reasonably predict they will want to vent and may not want advice until after they have a chance to express their feelings. Finally, we apply scripts, which specify how interaction should proceed, including how we should act.

Review

We create meaning by how we select and organize communication. This reminds us to keep perceptions tentative and open to revision. In the course of interaction, we may want to modify initial perceptions.

Student Voices

Tonya:

I work as a volunteer counsellor at the women's centre, and the other day something happened that shows how wrong a script we can have. This woman came in, a student about my age, and she told me she was pregnant. She was very upset and having trouble talking, so I tried to help out by going into the discussion most pregnant women who come to the centre want. I told her a lot of people have untimely pregnancies and that it doesn't have to interfere with her life. Then I said that I could recommend several doctors who could perform abortions. By then she was crying even harder, and I started trying to tell her that abortions weren't a serious medical procedure. Finally, she managed to get out that she wanted to have the baby and needed help working out that decision. Well, that's a whole different script than abortion counselling. I had misperceived her, and that led me to adopt an inappropriate script.

The schemata we use to organize our perceptions help us figure out how to respond to others and what they say. When we decide someone is angry and needs to blow off steam, we're likely to rely on a script that tells us to back off and let the person air his or her feelings. If, on the other hand, we perceive someone as confused, we might follow a script that says we should help the person clarify her or his feelings and options. It's important to remember that we construct others and their communication when we use our schemata to organize perceptions.

Apply the Idea

Selecting and Organizing Practice

Most Canadian cities have Starbucks coffee outlets. Use the idea of ordering a specialty coffee as practice for selecting and organizing information as a listener. Choose a partner. Assign one person as the salesperson and the other as the customer. Each customer must order a specialty coffee. The salesperson must rearrange the request in the sequence of size, flavouring, milk, and then caffeine. Try several orders then change roles. The exercise forces you to empty your mind (become mindful), pay close attention (attending), and select and organize information. It is good practice for the more complicated listening activities that follow.

Communication Notes

Hard Times for Listening

Have you noticed that there's a lot more talk than listening going on these days? Television talk shows, call-in radio programs, and hot lines encourage people to talk, talk, talk. But is anyone listening?

Scholars of communication point to several factors that have reduced listening skills. First, there is the fast pace of everyday life. Hurrying is a national pastime in the West. Even when we don't need to hurry, we seem habituated to do so. In conversations, we're thinking, "Get to the point."

Another contributor to poor listening is media. Television and radio encourage passive attention, not active listening. Further, says communication consultant Sheila Bentley, the constant interruption of commercials decreases our skills in sustaining attention for periods of time.

Poor listening causes mistakes and problems, which explains why many companies now require employees to attend listening workshops. Starbucks, for instance, requires employees to learn to listen to orders and rearrange customers' requests in the sequence of size, flavoring, milk, and caffeine. That's helpful when customers often spurt out "double-shot decaf grande" or "iced, skim, cappucino, small."

Source: Crossen, C. (1997, July 10). Blah, blah, blah. *Wall Street Journal*, pp. 1A, 6A.

INTERPRETING COMMUNICATION

The fifth part of listening is interpreting others' communication. When we interpret, we put together all that we have selected and organized in a manner that makes sense of the overall situation. The most important principle for effective interpretation is to engage in dual perspective so that you interpret others in their terms. Certainly, you won't always agree with other people and how they see themselves, others, or situations. Engaging in dual perspective doesn't require you to share another's perspective; it does, however, require you to make an earnest effort to understand others.

To interpret someone on her or his own terms is one of the greatest gifts we can give another. What we give is personal regard so deep that we open our minds to how another sees the world. A genuine effort to understand others and what things mean to them is rare and very precious. Too often we impose our meanings on others, or we try to correct or argue with them about what they feel, or we crowd out their words with our own. As listening expert Robert Bolton (1986, p. 167) has observed, good listeners "stay out of the other's way," so they can learn how the speaker views his or her situation. Because fully interpersonal communication involves recognizing others as unique individuals, we must try to grasp what their experiences mean to them. Effective listening involves trying to understand others on their terms.

Student Voices

Bart:

I'd been married and working for years when I decided I wanted to come back to school and finish my degree. When I mentioned it to the guys I worked with, they all came down hard on me. They said I was looking for an easy life as a career student and trying to get above them. My dad said it would be irresponsible to quit work when I had a wife and child, and he said no self-respecting man would do that. It seemed like everyone had a view of what I was doing and why, and their views had nothing to do with mine. The only person who really listened to me was Elaine, my wife. When I told her I was thinking about going back to school, the first thing out of her mouth was, "What would that mean to you?" She didn't presume she knew my reasons, and she didn't start off arguing with me. She just asked what it meant to me, then listened for a long, long time while I talked about how I felt. She focused completely on understanding me, and that made it easy to talk. Maybe that's why we're married.

RESPONDING

The sixth step of effective listening involves **responding,** which is communicating attention and interest. As we noted in Chapter 1, interpersonal communication is not a linear process in which one person speaks at another. Rather, it is a transactive process in which we simultaneously listen and speak. Skillful listeners give outward signs that they are following and interested. In North America, signs of responsive listening include eye contact, nodding, attentive posture, and questions and comments that invite others to elaborate. These behaviours signal that we are involved in what is happening in the moment. All of us tend to communicate more clearly and interestingly when we feel others are committed to us and our communication. "The Impact of Responsive Listening" (page 256) describes an experiment that shows the power of this type of listening skill.

We don't respond only when others finish speaking; rather, we respond throughout interaction. This is what makes listening such an active process. As we saw earlier, we cannot avoid communication, so the issue is what we communicate when we are listening. Nonverbal behaviours, such as looking out a window, making notes to ourselves, and slouching, signal that we aren't involved. Disinterest is also signalled by passivity. In a book titled *Who's Listening?* psychiatrist Franklin Ernst (1973, p. 113) remarked that "to listen is to move. To listen is to be moved.... The non-moving, unblinking person can reliably be estimated to be a non-listener."

Good listeners let others know they are interested during conversation. They attend. They adopt a posture of involvement, nod their heads, make eye contact, and give vocal responses such as "um hmm," "okay," and "go on." All of these nonverbal behaviours show we are attentive, interested, and ready to hear more. These responses are used in varying degrees depending on our communication goal. Responding also includes several other very effective skills: paraphrasing, encouraging, questioning, summarizing, and supporting. We'll look more specifically at these skills when we discuss how to adapt our listening to the communication goal. On the relationship level of meaning, responsiveness communicates that we care about the other person and what she or he says.

Apply the Idea

Responsive Listening

The next time a friend starts talking with you, express disinterest by slouching, avoiding eye contact, and giving no vocal feedback. You might want to look at something else—a paper or book—while your friend is talking. Note what happens as you communicate a lack of interest. How does your friend act? What happens to her or his communication? Does she or he criticize you for not listening?

Now reverse the experiment. When somebody starts talking to you, show interest. Put aside what you were doing, incline your body slightly forward, make eye contact, and give vocal feedback to indicate you are following. Note what happens as you listen responsively. Does your friend continue talking? Does she or he become more engaging?

Finally, try varying your listening style during a single conversation. Begin by listening responsively, then lapse into a passive mode that expresses disinterest. What happens when you vary your listening style?

REMEMBERING

The seventh and final part of listening is **remembering,** which is the process of retaining what you have heard. According to communication scholars Ron Adler and Neil Towne (1993), we remember less than half a message

Communication Notes

The Impact of Responsive Listening

Two researchers decided to test the impact of responsive listening on a speaker. They taught students in a college psychology course to respond with nonverbal communication cues. The professor in the class was a boring lecturer who read his notes in a monotone voice, seldom gestured, and did little to engage students. After the first few minutes of class, the students who had been trained in responsiveness began to show interest in the lecturer. They changed their postures, kept greater eye contact, nodded their interest, and so forth. Within half a minute after the students began to respond, the lecturer started to use gestures, his speaking rate and inflection increased, and he began to interact with students visually and verbally. Then, at a prearranged signal, the students stopped responding and communicated disinterest. For a few awkward minutes the lecturer sought responses, but then he lapsed back into his monotone lecture, not engaging the students. Simply by demonstrating interest in the teacher's communication, the students were able to make him more effective and the class more exciting for everyone.

Source: Bolton, R. (1986). Listening is more than merely hearing. In J. Stewart (Ed.), *Bridges, not walls* (4th ed., pp. 159–179). New York: Random House.

Listening is the gift we give to those we respect.

Photo: © Corel

immediately after we hear it. As time goes by, retention decreases further so that we recall only about 35 percent of a message eight hours after hearing it. Because we forget about two-thirds of what we hear, it's important to make sure we hang on to the most important third. Effective listeners let go of a lot of details in order to retain basic ideas and general impressions (Fisher, 1987). By being selective about what to remember, we enhance our listening competence. Later in this chapter, we'll discuss more detailed strategies for retaining material.

Effective listening is a complex process that involves being mindful, attending, hearing, selecting and organizing, interpreting, responding, and remembering. Next we'll consider hindrances to our ability to enact the seven processes that make up effective listening.

OBSTACLES TO EFFECTIVE LISTENING

Now that we've seen how much is involved in listening, it's easier to understand why we don't listen effectively to all the communication in our lives. There are two broad types of obstacles to good listening—obstacles related to the communication situation and obstacles that are inside us. (Did you notice that a series of ideas to be discussed were organized into two broad classes to aid your retention of the basic idea?) See Figure 7.3 for the description of these obstacles.

EXTERNAL OBSTACLES

Much of what interferes with effective listening has to do with communication situations themselves. Although we can't always control external obstacles, knowing what situational factors hinder effective listening can help us guard against them or compensate for the noise they create.

External Obstacles	Internal Obstacles
• Message overload	• Preoccupation
• Message complexity	• Prejudgment
• Noise (physical, psychological, and semantic)	• Lack of effort
	• Not recognizing diverse listening styles
	• Our desire to fix

Figure 7.3
The External and Internal Obstacles to Listening

Message Overload

The sheer amount of communication we engage in makes it difficult to listen fully all of the time. We simply aren't able to be mindful and totally involved in all of the listening we do, because it consumes up to 53 percent of our total communication activity. Think about your typical day. Perhaps you go to class for three hours. How much you learn and how well you do on examinations depends on your ability to listen mindfully to material that is often difficult. After listening for 50 minutes in a history class, you listen for 50 minutes in a communication class, and 50 more minutes in a business class. A great deal of information came your way in those three lectures. Then you go to work, and your supervisor tells you there will be some new procedures you are expected to follow. The supervisor, feeling a need to get on to other matters, describes the changes quickly, and you are expected to understand and remember them immediately. Obviously, we can and do experience message overload at times. We may feel overwhelmed by the amount of information we are supposed to understand and retain. Clearly, we can't give equal attention to all that

Is this an example of message overload or psychological noise?

Photo: A. Henry

Desmond:

I've been married nearly thirty years, so I've figured out when I have to listen sharply to Edna and when I can just let her talk flow in one ear and out the other. She's a talker, but most of what she talks about isn't important to me. But if I hear code words, I know to listen up. If Edna says, "I'm really upset about such and such," or if she says, "We have a problem," my ears perk up and I listen carefully. It's not very fair to Edna, but it's the only way I can cope sometimes with her constant talk.

information. Instead, we screen the talk around us, much as we screen calls on our answering machines, to decide when to listen carefully.

Message Complexity

Listening is also impeded by messages that are complex. The more detailed and complicated ideas are, the more difficult it is to follow and retain them. People for whom English is a second language often find it hard to understand English speakers who use complex sentences that have multiple clauses or that include slang expressions. Even native speakers of English often feel overwhelmed by the complexity of some communication. It's tempting to tune out people who use technical vocabularies, focus on specifics, and use complex sentences. Yet we might miss interesting or important messages if we disregard complex ones.

There are ways to manage complex messages in ways that maximize how much we understand and retain. When we have to listen to messages that are dense with information, we should summon up extra energy. In addition, taking notes may help us understand and retain difficult information. A third strategy is to group material as you listen—organize the ideas in ways that will be easy for you to recall later.

Noise

A third impediment to effective listening is noise. Sounds around us can divert our attention or even make it difficult to hear clearly. Perhaps you've been part of a crowd at a rally or a game. If so, you probably had to shout to the person next to you just to be heard. Although most noise is not as overwhelming as the roar of crowds, there is always some noise in communication situations. It might be music or television in the background, other conversations nearby, or muffled traffic sounds from outside. From our discussion in Chapter 1, we know this as physical noise. The other two kinds of noise, psychological and semantic, are examples of internal obstacles. We'll examine them later.

Review

Managing Complex Messages

- Summon up extra energy.
- Take notes.
- Group information for easier recall.

|*Student Voices*|

Gregory:

I've been a salesman for a long time, and I know when clients are really interested and when they're not. When someone answers a phone when I'm in his or her office, I know he or she is not really focused on what I'm saying. Taking calls or leaving the door open for people to drop in communicates that they're not interested in me or the service I represent.

Gregory makes an important point by reminding us that allowing distractions communicates the relationship-level meaning that we're not interested. Good listeners do what they can to create nondistracting environments. It's considerate to turn off a television or lower the volume on music if someone wants to talk with you. Professionals often instruct secretaries to hold their calls when they want to give undivided attention to a conversation with a client or business associate. It's also appropriate to suggest moving from a noisy area in order to cut down on distractions. Even if we can't always eliminate noise, we can usually reduce it or change our location to one that is more conducive to good communication.

INTERNAL OBSTACLES

In addition to external interference, listening is hindered by things we do or don't do. In other words, some of the obstacles to effective listening are those we can control. We'll discuss five psychological obstacles to effective listening.

Preoccupation

A common hindrance to listening is preoccupation. When we are absorbed in our own thoughts and concerns, we can't focus on what someone else is saying. Perhaps you've attended a lecture right before you had a test in another class and later realized you got virtually nothing out of the lecture. That's because you were distracted by thoughts and anxieties about the upcoming test, which was of more immediate concern to you than what was being discussed in the lecture. Or maybe you've been in conversations with friends and realized after a few minutes that you weren't listening at all because you were thinking about your own concerns.

When we are preoccupied with our own thoughts, we can't be present for others. In other words, we're not being mindful. One method of enhancing mindfulness is to call our minds back to the present situation and the listening we want to do. It's natural for our thoughts to wander occasionally, especially if something is worrying us. However, we don't have to be passive

Dawn:

I think my biggest problem as a listener is preoccupation. Like my friend Marta came to me the other day and said she wanted to talk about her relationship with her boyfriend. I followed her for a few minutes, but then I started thinking about my relationship with Ted. After a while—I don't know how long—Marta said to me, "You're not listening at all. Where is your head?" She was right. My head was in a totally different place.

when our thoughts roam. Instead, we may actively call our minds back by reminding ourselves to focus on the person who is speaking and the meaning of his or her message.

Prejudgment

Another reason we don't always listen effectively is that we prejudge others or their communication. Sometimes we think we already know what is being said and don't need to listen carefully. In other cases, we decide in advance that others have nothing to offer us, so we tune them out. When you are talking to people with whom you disagree, do you listen mindfully to them? Do you assume you might learn something, or do you prejudge their communication as not worth your attention?

A third kind of prejudgment occurs when we impose our preconceptions about a message on the person who is communicating. When this happens, we assume we know what another feels, thinks, and is going to say, and we then assimilate her or his message into our preconceptions. In the workplace, we may not pay close attention to what a co-worker says because we think we already know what is being expressed. Recalling our earlier discussion of mindreading, you'll realize that it's not wise to assume we know what others think and feel. When we mindread, misunderstandings are likely. We may misinterpret what the person means because we haven't really listened on her or his terms.

Prejudgments disconfirm others, because we deny them their own voices. Instead of listening openly to them, we force their words into our own preconceived mind set. This devalues others and their messages. When we impose our prejudgments on others' words at the relational level of meaning, we express a disregard for them and what they say.

Prejudgments also reduce what we can learn in communication with others. If we decide in advance that another person has nothing to say that interests us, we foreclose the possibility of learning something from that person. This diminishes the richness of our own perspective.

Student Voices

Dustin:

My boyfriend drives me crazy. He never listens, I mean really listens, to what I am saying. He always listens through his own version of what I think and mean. Yesterday I said to him that I was having trouble deciding about wanting to come to summer school. Before I could even explain what the trouble was, he said, "Yeah it's expensive. Tap your parents up. Get them to pay for summer school." Well, as it so happens, money wasn't the issue at all. I wanted to do an internship to get some practical experience in my field before I continued with school, so Jake's advice is totally irrelevant.

Lack of Effort

It takes considerable effort to listen carefully, and sometimes we don't invest the necessary energy. It is hard work to be mindful—to focus closely on what others are saying, to grasp their meanings, to ask questions, and to give responses so that they know we are interested and involved. In addition to these activities, we also have to control distractions inside ourselves, monitor external noise, and perhaps fight against fatigue, hunger, or other physiological conditions that can impede listening.

Because active listening requires so much effort, we're not always able or willing to do it well. Sometimes we make a decision not to listen fully, perhaps because the person or topic is not important to us. In other cases, we really want to listen, but have trouble marshalling the energy required. When this happens, an effective strategy is to ask the other person to postpone interaction until a time when you will have the energy and mindfulness to listen with care. If you explain that you want to defer communication because you really are interested and want to be able to listen well, she or he is likely to appreciate your honesty and commitment to listening.

Failing to invest the necessary effort in listening also occurs in classrooms. You may feel tired when you go to a class. As a result, you may sit passively and not work to understand what your instructor is teaching. If you don't involve yourself actively in listening, you cannot get much out of the class.

Not Recognizing Diverse Listening Styles

A fourth way in which we sometimes hinder our listening effectiveness is by not realizing and adjusting to different listening styles. How we listen differs for two reasons. First, different skills are required when we listen for information, to support others, and for pleasure. We'll discuss these kinds of listening later in the chapter.

A second basis for diverse listening styles is differences in what we learn about listening in our speech communities. The more we understand about different people's rules for listening, the more effectively we can signal our attention in ways others understand. For example, Nepalese citizens give little vocal feedback when another is speaking. In that culture it would be considered rude and disrespectful to make sounds while someone else is talking. Cultures also vary in what they teach members about eye contact. In the West, it is considered polite to make frequent, but not constant, eye contact with someone who is speaking. In other cultures, continuous eye contact is normative, and still others frown on virtually any eye contact.

Even within Canada, there are differences in listening rules based on membership in gender, racial, and other speech communities. Because feminine socialization emphasizes talking as a way to form and develop relationships, responsive listening is emphasized. Thus, women, in general, make more eye contact, give more vocal and verbal feedback, and use nodding and facial expressions to signal interest (Tannen, 1990; Wood, 1994d, 1998). Masculine culture, with its more instrumental orientation and focus on emotional control, deemphasizes obvious responsiveness. For this reason, men typically provide fewer verbal and nonverbal clues about their interest and attentiveness. If you understand these general differences between the genders, you can adapt your listening style to provide appropriate responses to both women and men. Men can provide more vocal and verbal feedback when listening to women, and women, as Jennifer discovers, can recognize listening in their male partners even though it may not be very animated.

Listening competence includes being sensitive to differences in listening and speaking styles. Because others may speak and listen differently than we do, we shouldn't automatically impose our rules and interpretations on them. Instead, we should try to understand and respect their styles. By exercising dual perspective, we are more likely to listen effectively to others on their terms.

Student Voices

Jennifer:

I used to get irritated at my boyfriend because I thought he wasn't listening to me. I'd tell him stuff, and he'd just sit there and not say anything. He didn't react to what I was saying by showing emotions in his face or anything. Several times, I accused him of not listening, and he said back to me exactly what I'd said. He was listening, just not my way. I've learned not to expect him to show a lot of emotions or respond to what I say as I'm talking. That's just not his way, but he is listening.

Our Desire to Fix

The final way we hinder our listening effectiveness comes from our desire to fix what is wrong with those who share with us. Too quickly, we can fall into advising, directing, and taking charge when what is needed is our attentive, mindful, empathic listening. Our desire to "fix" frequently comes from our own discomfort with witnessing someone in distress. We'd rather do something than watch someone go through pain or anguish. Yet, when we step in unbidden, we give a very clear message that we don't trust the other person to solve his or her own problems. Our help becomes a hindrance by disempowering the people we care about. Consider that it is likely our own pain we wish to avoid.

Concepts at a Glance

Six Kinds of Nonlistening
- Pseudolistening
- Monopolizing
- Selective listening
- Defensive listening
- Ambushing
- Literal listening

FORMS OF NONLISTENING

Now that we've discussed obstacles to effective listening, let's consider forms of nonlistening. We refer to these patterns as nonlistening because they don't involve real listening. We will discuss six kinds of nonlistening that may seem familiar to you, because we all engage in these at times.

PSEUDOLISTENING

Pseudolistening is pretending to listen. When we pseudolisten, we appear to be attentive, but really our minds are elsewhere. We engage in pseudolistening when we want to appear conscientious, although we really aren't interested. Sometimes we pseudolisten because we don't want to hurt someone who is sharing experiences, even though we are preoccupied with other things.

There are many forms of nonlistening.

Photo: © Corbis/Magma

|Student Voices|

Renee:

Pseudolistening should be in the training manual for flight attendants. I had that job for six years, and you wouldn't believe the kinds of things passengers told me about—everything from love affairs to family problems. At first I tried to listen, because I wanted to be a good attendant. After a year, though, I learned just to appear to be listening and to let my mind be elsewhere.

We also pseudolisten when communication bores us, but we have to appear interested. Superficial talk in social situations and dull lectures are two communication situations in which we may consciously choose to pseudolisten so that we seem polite even though we really aren't involved. Although it may be appropriate to decide consciously to pseudolisten in some situations, there is a cost: We run the risk of missing information because we really aren't attending.

Student Voices

Bellino:

I get in a lot of trouble because I pseudolisten. Often I slip into pretending to listen in classes. I'll start off paying attention and then just drift off and not even realize I've stopped listening until the teacher asks me a question and I don't even know what we're discussing. That's humiliating!

Pseudolisteners often give themselves away by revealing that they haven't been attending to communication. Common indicators of pseudolistening are responses that are tangential, irrelevant, or impervious to what was said. For example, if Martin talks to Charlotte about his interviews for a new job, she might respond tangentially by asking about the cities he visited: "Did you like Winnipeg or Thunder Bay better?" Although this is related to the topic of Martin's job interviews, it is tangential to the main issue. An irrelevant response would be "Where do you want to go for dinner tonight?" An impervious response such as "You're lucky to have a job that suits you" indicates that Charlotte didn't listen to what Martin said.

MONOPOLIZING

Monopolizing is continuously focusing communication on ourselves instead of the person who is talking. Two tactics are typical of monopolizing. One is conversational rerouting, in which a person shifts the topic back to him or herself. For example, if Ellen tells her friend Marla that she's having trouble with her roommate, Marla should respond by showing interest in Ellen's problem and feelings. Instead, however, Marla might reroute the conversation by saying, "You think that's bad. My roommate is a real slob." Then Marla would go off on an extended description of her own roommate problems. Rerouting takes the conversation away from the person who is talking and focuses it on the other.

Another monopolizing tactic is interrupting to divert attention to ourselves or to topics that interest us. Interrupting can occur in combination with rerouting, so that a person interrupts and then directs the conversation to a new topic. In other cases, diversionary interrupting involves questions and challenges that are not intended to support the person who is speaking (see "Doctor, Are You Listening?" on page 266). Monopolizers may fire questions that express doubt about what a speaker says ("What makes you think that?" "How can you be sure?" "Did anyone else see what you did?") or prematurely offer advice to establish their own command of the situation and possibly to put down the other person ("What you should do is ...," "You really blew that," "What I would have done is ..."). Both rerouting and diversionary interrupting are techniques to monopolize a conversation. They are the antithesis of good listening.

The following transcript illustrates monopolizing in action and also shows how disconfirming of others it can be:

Chuck: I'm really bummed about my econ class. I just can't seem to get the stuff.

Sally: Well, I know what you mean. Econ was a real struggle for me too, but it's nothing compared to the stat course I'm taking now. I mean this one is going to destroy me totally.

Chuck: I remember how frustrated you got in econ, but you finally did get it. I just can't seem to, and I need the course for my major. I've tried going to review sessions, but—

Sally: I didn't find the review sessions helpful. Why don't you focus on your other classes and use them to pull up your average?

Chuck: That's not the point. I want to get this stuff.

Sally: You're blowing this all out of proportion. Do you know that right now I have three papers and one exam hanging over my head?

Chuck: I wonder if I should hire a tutor.

Sally: I don't want you to take any of our time away. This weekend we are getting together with Sam and Lucy, remember? I've really been looking forward to that.

In this transcript, Sally shows she is not interested in Chuck's concerns, and she pushes her conversational agenda. Chances are good that she doesn't even understand what he is feeling because she is not focusing on what he says.

Monopolizing is costly not only to those who are neglected but also to the monopolizers. A person who dominates communication has much less opportunity to learn from others than a person who listens to what others think and feel. We already know what we think and feel, so there's little we can learn from hearing ourselves!

It's important to realize that not all interruptions are attempts to monopolize communication. We also interrupt the flow of others' talk to show interest, voice support, and ask for elaboration. Interrupting for these reasons doesn't divert attention from the person speaking; instead, it affirms that person and keeps the focus on her or him. Research indicates that women tend to interrupt to show interest and support, whereas men tend to

Communication Notes

Doctor, Are You Listening?

If you've ever been frustrated by doctors who didn't listen well, you're not alone. Communication researcher Michael Nyquist studied doctor-patient interaction. He found that, on average, patients had only 18 seconds to describe their problems before doctors interrupted them. Once the doctor interrupted, she or he tended to ask specific, closed questions that discouraged patients from explaining symptoms, life situations, and so forth that might affect diagnosis and treatment. Once interrupted, only 1 of 52 patients asserted themselves to complete what they had originally wanted to tell the doctor.

Sheila Bentley presents communication workshops to medical practitioners. Listening is a primary focus in her training because she has found that many of the mistakes doctors make—ones that often lead to expensive malpractice suits—result from poor listening on the part of doctors.

Sources: Crossen, C. (1997, July 10). Blah, blah, blah. *Wall Street Journal*, pp. 1A, 6A; Nyquist, M. (1992, Fall). Learning to listen. *Ward Rounds*. Evanston, IL: Northwestern University Medical School, pp. 11–15.

interrupt to control conversations and capture the talk stage (Aries, 1987; Beck, 1988; Mulac, Wiemann, Widenmann, & Gibson, 1988; Stewart, Stewart, Friedley, & Cooper, 1990). Because masculine communication cultures emphasize using talk to compete for attention, men more than women engage in diversionary interrupting. Consistent with the rules of feminine communication cultures, women tend to interrupt to support and affirm others and what they are saying. Thus, women may make supportive interruptions such as "I know what you mean," "I really feel for you," or "I've had the same problem."

SELECTIVE LISTENING

A third form of nonlistening is **selective listening**, which involves focusing on only particular parts of communication. We listen selectively when we screen out parts of a message that don't interest us or with which we disagree; conversely, we listen selectively when we rivet attention on topics that do interest us or with which we do agree. For example, if you are worried about a storm, you will selectively listen to weather reports while disregarding news, talk, and music on the radio. Students often become highly attentive in classes when

Part 2
Weaving Communication into Relationships

NTL

266

teachers say "This will show up on the test," because they regard information about testing as particularly important. We also listen selectively when we give only half an ear to a friend until the friend mentions spring break, and then we zero in because that topic interests us.

Selective listening also occurs when we reject communication that bores us or makes us uncomfortable. Many smokers, for instance, selectively block out reports on the dangers of smoking and of secondhand smoke. Taking in that information would be upsetting. We may also choose not to hear certain requests. For instance, you might conveniently not hear your partner's request to help more in the cleanup while your partner might similarly not hear your appeal to spend more time together. Neither of you wants to do what the other asks, so you screen out communication on those topics.

Many people listen selectively to criticism. We may screen out communication from others that calls attention to our weaknesses or pushes us to change in ways we find uncomfortable. For example, a friend may selectively listen to your attempts to help her with money management if the topic brings up uncomfortable feelings and a sense of failure. We all have subjects that bore us or disturb us, and we may selectively avoid listening to communication about them. What is important is to avoid listening selectively when doing so could deprive us of information or insights that could be valuable to us.

DEFENSIVE LISTENING

Defensive listening involves perceiving personal attacks, criticisms, or hostile undertones where none are intended. When we listen defensively, we assume others don't like, trust, or respect us, and we read these motives into whatever they say, no matter how innocent their communication actually is. Some individuals are generally defensive, expecting insults and criticism from all quarters. They hear threats and negative judgments in almost anything said to them. Thus, an innocent remark such as "Isn't that a new shirt?" may be perceived as a veiled suggestion that the shirt is ugly or that all the other shirts in the person's wardrobe are tacky.

In other instances, defensive listening is confined to specific topics or vulnerable times when we judge ourselves to be inadequate. A man who is defensive about money may perceive phone solicitations as reproaches for his lack of earning power; a woman who fears she is selfish may interpret offers of help as proof others don't think of her as helpful; a woman who feels unattractive may hear genuine compliments as false; a student who has just failed a test may hear questioning of his intelligence in benign comments. Defensive listening can deprive us of information and insights that might be valuable, even if not pleasant. Defensive listening also tends to discourage others from giving us honest feedback. If stating genuine thoughts and feelings leads to quarrels and anger, others may learn not to be honest with us.

Dan:

I remember a time when I was a defensive listener. I had just gotten laid off from work—the recession, you know—and I felt like nothing. I couldn't support my family, and I couldn't stand the idea of going on unemployment. Nobody in my family ever did that. Once when my son asked me for a few bucks for a school outing, I just lit in to him about how irresponsible he was about money. My wife mentioned the car needed some repair work, and I shouted at her that I wasn't a money machine. I'd never been like that before, but I was just so sensitive to being out of work that I had a chip on my shoulder. You couldn't talk to me about money without my taking it as a personal attack.

AMBUSHING

Ambushing is listening carefully for the purpose of attacking a speaker. Unlike the other kinds of nonlistening we've discussed, ambushing involves very careful listening, but it isn't motivated by openness and interest in another. Instead, ambushers listen intently to gather ammunition they can use to attack a speaker. They don't mind bending or even distorting what a speaker says in order to advance their combative goals. One of the most common instances of ambushing is public debates between political candidates. Each person listens carefully to the other for the sole purpose of later undercutting the opponent. There is no openness, no effort to understand the other's meaning, and no interest in genuine dialogue.

Kralyn:

My first husband was a real ambusher. If I tried to talk to him about a dress I'd bought, he'd listen just long enough to find out what it cost and then attack me for spending money. Once I told him about a problem I was having with one of my co-workers, and he came back at me with all of the things I'd done wrong and didn't mention any of the things the other person had done. Talking to him was like setting myself up to be assaulted.

Not surprisingly, people who engage in ambushing tend to arouse defensiveness in others. Few of us want to speak up when we feel we are going to be attacked. In Chapter 8 we'll look more closely at communication that fosters defensiveness in others.

LITERAL LISTENING

The final form of nonlistening is **literal listening,** which involves listening only to the content level and ignoring the relationship level of meaning. As we have seen, all communication includes both content or literal meaning and relationship meaning, which pertains to the power, responsiveness, and liking between individuals. When we listen literally, we attend to only the content meaning and overlook what's being communicated about the other person or our relationship with that person. When we listen only literally, we are insensitive to others' feelings and to our connections with them.

Perhaps the greatest danger of literal listening is that it may disconfirm others. When we listen literally, we don't make the effort to understand how others feel about what they say and how it affects their self-concepts. As a result, any responses we make are unlikely to confirm their identities and worth.

We have seen that there are many obstacles to effective listening. Those in messages and situations include message overload, difficulty of messages,

Student Voices

Cammy:

My sister is a literal listener. I swear, she just doesn't get all of the meaning that is between words. The last time we were home together, Mom was talking about how bad she felt that she didn't seem to have the interest in cleaning the house as it should be and making elaborate meals. Lannie heard that, and her response to Mom was that the house wasn't clean, and Mom needed to either devote more time to it or hire someone. Then Lannie told her she ought to plan the week's dinners on Sunday so that she could shop and set aside time to make nice meals. Give me a break! Mom just had a double radical mastectomy a month ago, and she's really depressed. She feels bad about losing her breasts, and she's worried that they didn't get all of the cancer. Who would feel like scrubbing floors and fixing gourmet food after going through that? What Mom needed was for us to hear that she was worried and unhappy and for us to tell her the house and fancy meals didn't matter. Anybody with an ounce of sensitivity could figure that out.

and external noise. In addition to these, there are five potential interferences inside us: preoccupation, prejudgment, lack of effort, failure to recognize and adapt to diverse expectations of listening, and our desire to fix people. The obstacles to effective listening combine to create six types of nonlistening. These are pseudolistening, monopolizing, listening selectively, listening defensively, ambushing, and listening literally. Learning about hindrances to mindful listening and learning to recognize forms of nonlistening enable you to exercise greater control over your listening and, thus, your relationships with others. To test your understanding of internal obstacles, take a look back at the beginning of the chapter, where Chloe is demonstrating nonlistening. What kind of nonlistening is she using?

Apply the Idea

Identifying Your Ineffective Listening

Apply the material we've just discussed by identifying times when you listen ineffectively.

- *Describe a situation in which you pseudolistened.*
- *Describe an instance in which you monopolized communication.*
- *Report on a time when you listened defensively.*
- *Discuss an example of ambushing someone else.*
- *Describe an instance when you listened selectively.*
- *Identify a time when you listened literally.*

   Now repeat this exercise, but this time focus on examples of others who engage in each of the six types of ineffective listening.

ADAPTING LISTENING TO COMMUNICATION GOALS

Now that you recognize some of the common pitfalls to effective listening, let's focus on how to listen well. The first requirement is to determine your reason for listening. We listen differently when we listen for pleasure, to gain information, and to support others. We'll discuss the specific attitudes and skills that contribute to effective listening of each type.

LISTENING FOR PLEASURE

Often the goal is **listening for pleasure** or enjoyment. Rather than trying to learn something or to support someone else, we're listening for sheer enjoyment. Often we listen to music for entertainment. We may also listen to television shows and nightclub routines for enjoyment.

Be Mindful

Because listening for pleasure doesn't require us to remember or respond to communication, there are few guidelines for effective listening for enjoyment. Being mindful is important for all types of listening. Just as being mindful in lectures allows us to gain information, being mindful when listening for pleasure allows us to derive the full enjoyment from what we hear.

Control Obstacles

Controlling interferences is also important when we are listening for pleasure. A beautifully rendered Mozart concerto can be wonderfully satisfying, but not if a television is on in the background.

LISTENING FOR INFORMATION

Much of the time we are **listening for information**, to gain and evaluate information. We listen informationally in classes, at political debates, when important news stories are reported, and when we need guidance on everything from medical treatments to directions to a new place. In all of these cases, the primary purpose of listening is to gain and understand information in order to act appropriately or be successful. To do this, we need to use skills for critical thinking and for organizing and retaining information.

Be Mindful

Our discussion of obstacles to listening suggests some important clues for how we can listen critically to information. First, it's important to make a decision to be mindful, choosing to attend carefully even if material is complex and difficult. Don't let your mind wander if information gets complicated or confusing. Instead, stay focused on your goal and take in as much as you can. Later you may want to ask questions about material that isn't clear even when you listen mindfully.

Control Obstacles

You can also minimize noise in communication situations. You might shut a window to block out traffic noises or adjust a thermostat so that room temperature is comfortable. In addition, you should try to minimize psychological distractions by emptying your mind of the many concerns and ideas that can divert your attention from the communication at hand. This means you should try to let go of preoccupations as well as prejudgments that can interfere with effective listening.

Concepts at a Glance

Snapshot of Listening for Pleasure

- Be mindful.
- Control obstacles.

Concepts at a Glance

Snapshot of Listening for Information

- Be mindful.
- Control obstacles.
- Ask questions.
- Use aids to recall.
- Organize information.

Ask Questions

Also important is posing questions to speakers. Asking speakers to clarify or elaborate their message allows you to gain understanding of information you didn't grasp at first and enhances insight into content that you did comprehend. "Could you explain what you meant by ...?" "I didn't follow your explanation of ..." and "Can you clarify the distinction between ...?" are questions that allow listeners to gain further information to clarify content. Questions compliment a speaker because they indicate you are interested and want to know more.

Use Aids to Recall

To understand and remember important information, we can apply the principles of perception we discussed in Chapter 3. For instance, we learned that we tend to notice and recall stimuli that are repeated. To use this principle in everyday communication, repeat important ideas to yourself immediately after hearing them. This moves the ideas from short-term to long-term memory (Estes, 1989). Repetition can save you the embarrassment of having to ask people you just met to repeat their names.

Another way to increase retention is to use mnemonic (pronounced "new-monic") devices, which are memory aids that create patterns for what you've heard. You probably already do this in studying. For instance, you could create the mnemonic MAHSIRR, which is made up of the first letter of each of the seven parts of listening (Mindfulness, Attending, Hearing, Selecting and organizing, Interpreting, Responding, Remembering). You can also invent mnemonics to help you recall personal information in communication. For example, PAL is a mnemonic to remember that Peter from Alberta is going into Law. Likewise, random letters and numbers that you need to remember like a license plate can be easily remembered by adding detail to each letter or number. For example, a B.C. license plate of BTR430 can be remembered by "Big Trouble at 4:30."

Organize Information

A third technique to increase retention is to organize what you hear. When communicating informally, most people don't order their ideas carefully. The result is a flow of information that isn't coherently organized, and so is hard to retain. We can impose order by regrouping what we hear. For example, suppose a friend tells you he's confused about long-range goals, then says he doesn't know what he can do with a math major, wants to locate in the North, wonders if graduate school is necessary, likes small towns, needs some internships to try out different options, and wants a family eventually. You could regroup this stream of concerns into two categories: academic information (careers for math majors, graduate school, internship opportunities) and lifestyle preferences (North, small town, family). Remembering those two categories allows you to retain the essence of your friend's concerns, even if you forget many of the specifics. Repetition, mnemonics to create patterns, and regrouping are ways to enhance what we remember.

Apply the Idea

Improving Recall

Apply the principles we've discussed to enhance memory.

- *The next time you meet someone, repeat his or her name to yourself three times in a row after you are introduced. Do you find you remember the name better when you do this?*

- *After your next interpersonal communication class, take 15 minutes to review your notes. Try reading them aloud so that you hear as well as see the main ideas. Does this increase your retention of material covered in class?*

- *Invent mnemonics to help you remember basic information in communication.*

- *Organize complex ideas by grouping them into categories. Try this first in relation to material in classes. To remember the main ideas of this chapter, you might use major subheadings to form categories: the listening process, obstacles to listening, forms of nonlistening, listening goals, and guidelines. The mnemonic PONAG (Process, Obstacles, Nonlistening, Adapting, Guidelines) could help you remember those categories. You can also group ideas in interpersonal interactions.*

Review

By choosing to be mindful, minimizing distractions, asking questions, repeating and organizing ideas, and using mnemonic devices, we can increase our abilities to understand and remember informational communication.

Communication Notes

Listening Totally

Gerald Egan has studied listening extensively. In his view of mindful relationship listening, we don't just listen with our ears; we also listen with our eyes and sense of touch, with our minds, hearts, and imaginations. Total listening is more than attending to another person's words. According to Egan, total listening entails listening to the meanings that are buried in the words and between the words and in the silences in communication.

Source: Egan, G. (1973). Listening as empathic support. In J. Stewart (Ed.), *Bridges, not walls*. Reading, MA: Addison-Wesley.

LISTENING TO SUPPORT OTHERS

Listening for information focuses on the content level of meaning in communication. Yet, often we're more concerned with the relationship level of meaning, which involves another's feelings and perceptions. We engage in

Concepts at a Glance

Snapshot of Listening to Support

- Be mindful.
- Control obstacles.
- Attend.
- Suspend judgment.
- Understand the other's perspective:
  - paraphrase;
  - use minimal encouragers;
  - question;
  - summarize.
- Express support.

relationship listening, **listening to support others,** when we listen to a friend's worries, hear a romantic partner discuss our relationship, or help someone work out a problem. Our primary interest is the other person and our relationship, rather than information. Specific attitudes and skills enhance relationship listening.

Be Mindful

The first requirement for effective relationship listening is to be mindful. You'll recall this was also the first step in listening for information and pleasure. When we're interested in relationship-level meanings, however, a different kind of mindfulness is needed. Instead of focusing our minds on informational content, we need to concentrate on understanding feelings that may not be communicated explicitly. Thus, mindful relationship listening calls on us to pay attention to what lies between the words, the subtle clues to feelings and perceptions. The essence of mindfulness is to listen to the other and focus on what he or she is feeling, thinking, and wanting in the conversation. Mindful listening is described in "Listening Totally."

Control Obstacles

It is particularly important to control the external and internal obstacles when we are called upon to listen empathically to someone. Our decision to turn off a TV or stereo, not answer a phone, or ask someone to watch the children are important acts of respect to our speaker. If it is not a convenient time for you to be completely mindful, it is more honest and kind to reschedule so you can be an undistracted listener.

Attend

Once you've controlled the obstacles to your ability to listen, it is time to let your speaker know that you are paying attention and that her or his thoughts and feelings are important to you. We do this by using the attending behaviours described earlier, FELOR. Turn and face your speaker, maintain appropriate eye contact, lean forward as opposed to lounging back so there is not a great distance between your faces, open your posture, and relax.

Suspend Judgment

When listening to help another person, it's important to avoid judgmental responses, at least initially. Although Western culture emphasizes evaluation, often we don't need to judge others or what they feel or do. Making judgments clutters communication by adding our evaluations to the others' experiences. When we do this, we are one step removed from them and their feelings. We've inserted something between us. To curb evaluative tendencies, we can ask whether we really need to pass judgment.

Yet there are times when it is appropriate and supportive to offer opinions and to make evaluative statements. Sometimes people we care about genuinely want our judgments, and in those cases we should be honest about how we feel. Particularly when others are confronting ethical dilemmas, they may seek the judgments of people they trust.

Student Voices

Margaret:

Once my friend Cordelia was asked to work for an MLA, but she had agreed to take a job at a large law firm. She talked to me about her quandary and asked me what I thought she should do. Although it was clear to me that Cordelia wanted to renege on the job and join the MLA's team, I couldn't honestly approve of that. I told her that I think it is dishonourable to go back on one's word. After a long talk, Cordelia told me that I was the only friend who cared enough about her to have been so honest. Part of being a real friend as it turned out was making a judgment.

Even positive evaluations ("That's a good way to approach the problem!") may seem to indicate we think we have the right to pass judgment on others and their feelings. If someone asks our opinion, we should try to present it in a way that doesn't disconfirm the other person or interfere with decision-making. Many times people excuse critical comments by saying, "Well you asked me to be honest," or "I mean this as constructive criticism." Too often, however, the judgments are not constructive and are more harsh than candour requires. If we are committed to helping others, we respond in ways that support them rather than tear them down.

Student Voices

Logan:

I hate the term "constructive criticism." Every time my dad says it, what follows is a put-down. By now I've learned not to go to him when I have problems or when I'm worried about something in my life. He always judges what I'm feeling and tells me what I ought to feel and do. All that does is make me feel worse than I did before.

Apply the Idea

Practising Suspending Judgment

It is very difficult to refrain from giving advice or judging. Remember our discussion earlier about wanting to "fix" the dilemmas in our friends and partners? In the following statements, avoid advising and judging. Try and turn the focus back onto the speaker to encourage her or him to find her or his own solutions. As a guideline, don't advise or judge until the other has asked three times for help.

Your friend is talking about breaking up a long-term relationship. *"What should I do?"*
Your response:

_____

"You've been through this before, tell me what you did."
Your response:

_____

"I have no idea what to do."
Your response:

_____

_____

Understand the Other Person's Perspective

One of the most important principles for effective relationship listening is to concentrate on grasping the other person's perspective. This means we have to step outside of our own point of view, at least long enough to understand another's perceptions. We can't respond feelingly to others until we understand their perspective and meanings. To do this, we must put aside preconceptions about issues and how others feel and try to focus on their words and nonverbal behaviours for clues about how they feel and think. There are four skills that help us do that: paraphrasing, using minimal encouragers, asking questions, and summarizing what we have heard.

Review

Listening Skills for Understanding the Other's Perspective

- Paraphrase
- Use minimal encouragers
- Ask questions
- Summarize

Paraphrase

Paraphrasing is a method of clarifying others' meaning or needs by reflecting our interpretations of their communication back to them. For example, a friend might confide, "I think my kid brother is messing around with drugs." We could paraphrase this way: "So you're really worried that your brother's experimenting with drugs." This paraphrase allows us to clarify whether the friend has any evidence of the brother's drug involvement. The response might be, "No, I don't have any real reason to suspect him, but I just worry, because drugs are so pervasive in high schools now."

This clarifies by telling us the friend's worries are more the issue than any evidence that the brother is experimenting with drugs. Paraphrasing also helps us figure out what others feel. If a friend screams, "This situation is making me crazy," it's not clear whether your friend is angry, hurt, upset, or going insane. We could find out which emotion prevails by saying, "You seem really angry." If anger is the emotion, your friend would agree; if not, she would clarify what she is feeling.

Apply the Idea

Learning to Paraphrase

Practise effective listening by paraphrasing the following statements.

- *I've got so many pressures closing in on me right now.*
- *I'm worried about all of the money I've borrowed to get through school.*
- *I'm nervous about telling my parents I'm gay when I see them next weekend.*
- *I don't know if Kim and I can keep the relationship together once she moves away for her job.*

Use Minimal Encouragers

Minimal encouragers prompt the speaker to go on. Minimal encouragers increase understanding of the other's thoughts and feelings by soliciting more information. These communications gently invite another person to elaborate by expressing interest in hearing more. Examples of minimal encouragers are "Tell me more," "Really?" "Go on," "I'm with you," "Then what happened?" "Yeah?" and "I see." We can also use nonverbal minimal encouragers such as a raised eyebrow to show involvement, a head motion to indicate we understand, or widened eyes to indicate we're fascinated. Minimal encouragers indicate we are listening, following, and interested. They encourage others to keep talking so that we can more fully understand what they mean. Keep in mind that these are minimal encouragers. They should not interrupt or take the talk stage away from another. Instead, effective minimal encouragers are very brief interjections that prompt, rather than interfere with, the flow of another's talk.

Apply the Idea

Using Minimal Encouragers

Practise encouraging others to elaborate their thoughts and feelings by developing minimal encouragers in response to each of these comments:

- *I'm feeling really worried about getting into grad school.*
- *My boss is driving me crazy.*
- *I think my girlfriend is cheating on me.*

- *I'm having a lot of trouble making my classes when the kids are so sick.*
- *I'm so excited about how this relationship is going. I've never been with someone as attentive and thoughtful as Pat.*

Question

Asking questions is a third way to enhance understanding of what another feels or needs. Sometimes it's helpful to ask questions that yield insight into what a speaker thinks or feels. For instance, we might ask "How do you feel about that?" "What do you plan to do?" or "How are you working this through?" Another reason we ask questions is to find out what a person wants from us. Sometimes it isn't clear whether someone wants advice, a shoulder to cry on, or a safe place to vent feelings. If we can't figure out what's wanted, we can ask the other person: "Are you looking for advice or a sounding board?" "Do you want to talk about how to handle the situation or just air the issues?" Asking direct questions signals that we want to help and allows others to tell us how we can best do that. Try and avoid "why" questions like "Why did you do that?" They tend to force someone to defend their position instead of exploring it. As well, a question like "Why do you think she did that?" calls for too much speculation about a third party. It takes away from the speaker's feelings.

Summarize

Summarizing is the fourth skill of understanding and helping. When we offer a summary of what we have heard others say, it is as if we are holding a mirror up for them to see themselves in a new way. A summary is a long paraphrase that captures all the thoughts, feelings, and actions that the speaker has shared. A good summary can lay out the complexities of what the speaker is struggling with and perhaps provide him or her with some insight into feelings and wants. We might say something like "It sounds like you have a lot on your plate right now. You are trying to make a decision about university in the fall, manage a part-time job, four courses and a full-time relationship. You describe feeling overwhelmed, pressured, and a little resentful. Am I right?" Summarizing assists others to sort through and put into priority what is most important to them. It allows them to feel truly heard and understood. Notice how the example does not try to "fix" the dilemma, it just provides good listening.

Are there gender differences in the way we listen?

Photos: A. Henry (top); © Photodisc (bottom)

Express Support

Once understanding of another's meanings and perspective is shown, relationship-level listeners should focus on communicating support. This doesn't necessarily require us to agree with the other person's perspective or feelings, but it does require that we communicate support for the person. To illustrate how we can support a person even if we don't agree with his or her position, consider the following dialogue:

Janice: I just don't see how I can have a baby right now.

Elaine: Tell me more about what you're feeling. (minimal encourager)

Janice: I feel trapped. I mean, I've still got two years of school, and we're not ready to get married.

Elaine: So? (minimal encourager)

Janice: (silence, then) I hate the thought, but I guess I'll have to get an abortion.

Elaine: Sounds as if you don't feel very comfortable with that choice. (paraphrase)

Janice: I'm not, but it seems like the only answer.

Elaine: What other options have you considered?

Janice: Well, I guess I really don't know of any other answers. Do you?

Elaine: You could have the baby and place it for adoption or maybe even work out an arrangement with a couple that can't have a baby of their own. (advising)

Janice: No, I really can't afford to give up nine months of my life right now. Besides, I don't think I could give away a baby after carrying it all that time. Don't you think I should have an abortion?

Elaine: Gee, I don't want to tell you what to do. I'm not comfortable endorsing abortion for myself, but you may not feel the same way. (judging, supporting)

Janice: I don't endorse abortion either, but I don't feel like I have a realistic choice.

Elaine: I respect you for the way you're going about making this choice. It's a good idea to talk with people like we're doing now. (supporting)

Janice: I just hate the idea of having an abortion.

Elaine: It sounds like you're not very sure that's the right answer for you, either. (paraphrase)

Janice: I don't know.

Elaine: Let's talk a little more. How do you think you'd feel if you did have an abortion? (minimal encourager, open question)

This dialogue illustrates several principles of effective relationship listening. First, notice that Elaine's first two comments are minimal encouragers, designed to nudge Janice to elaborate her perspective. Elaine's third response is a paraphrase to make sure she understands what Janice is feeling. Elaine then tries suggesting alternatives to abortion, but when Janice rejects those, Elaine doesn't push her. Advising can roadblock the flow of speaking and listening. Elaine then validates Janice's feelings by expressing support. Elaine makes her own position on abortion clear—she doesn't condone it— but she separates her personal stance from her respect for Janice and the way Janice is thinking through the decision.

Particularly important in this conversation is Elaine's effort to collaborate with Janice in problem-solving. By showing that she's willing to talk further and that she wants to help Janice work out the problem, Elaine behaves as an active listener and a committed friend. Elaine's listening style allows Janice to talk through a very tough issue without Elaine imposing her own judgments. Sometimes it's difficult to listen openly and nonjudgmentally, particularly if we don't agree with the person speaking. However, if your goal is to support another person, then sensitive, responsive involvement including collaboration, if appropriate, is an ideal listening style.

|Student Voices|

Sheryl:

I think the greatest gift my mother ever gave me was when I told her I was going to marry Bruce. He isn't Jewish, and nobody in my family has ever married out of the faith before. I could tell my mother was disappointed, and she didn't try to hide that. She asked me if I understood how that would complicate things like family relations and rearing kids. We talked for a while, and she realized I had thought through what it means to marry out of the faith. Then she sighed and said she had hoped I would find a nice Jewish man. But then she said she supported me whatever I did, and Bruce was welcome in our family. She told me she'd raised me to think for myself, and that's what I was doing. I just felt so loved and accepted by how she acted.

GUIDELINES FOR EFFECTIVE LISTENING

To develop pragmatic strategies for effectiveness, let's summarize what we've learned about listening. Three guidelines integrate and extend information already covered.

1. Be mindful.
2. Adapt listening appropriately.
3. Listen actively.

BE MINDFUL

By now you've read this suggestion many times. Because it is so central to effective listening, however, it bears repeating. Mindfulness is a choice to be wholly present in an experience. It requires that we put aside preoccupations and preconceptions in order to attend fully to what is happening in the moment. Mindful listening is a process of being totally with another person in communication. It is one of the highest compliments we can pay to others, because it conveys the relationship-level meaning that they matter to us. Being mindful is a choice, not a knack or a natural aptitude. It is a matter of discipline and commitment. We have to discipline our tendencies to judge others, dominate the talk stage, and let our minds wander away from what another is saying. Mindfulness also requires commitment to another person and the integrity of the interpersonal communication process. Being mindful is the first and most important principle of effective listening.

ADAPT LISTENING APPROPRIATELY

Like all communication activities, listening varies according to goals, situations, and individuals. What we've discussed in this chapter makes it clear that there is no one best way to listen. What's effective depends on our purpose for listening, the context in which we are listening, and the needs and circumstances of the other person.

The purpose for listening is a primary influence on what skills are appropriate. When we listen for pleasure, we simply need to be mindful and minimize distractions so that we derive as much enjoyment as possible from listening. When we listen for information, a critical attitude, evaluation of material, and a focus on the content level of meaning are desirable listening behaviours. Yet, when we engage in relationship listening, very different skills are needed. We want to communicate openness and caring, and the relationship-level meaning is more important than the content-level meaning. Thus, we need to adapt our listening styles and attitudes to different goals.

Effective listening is also adapted to individuals. Some people need considerable prompting and encouragment to express themselves, whereas others need only for us to be silent and attentive. Paraphrasing helps some individuals clarify what they think or feel, whereas others don't need that kind of assistance. Because people respond to different kinds of listening, we need to be skillful in using a variety of listening behaviours and to know when each is appropriate. Recall from Chapter 1 that the ability to employ a range of skills and knowledge of when each is called for are two of the foundations of effective interpersonal communication.

Although fully interpersonal communication requires us to interact with others as unique individuals, there are some generalizations that can guide our choices for how to listen. We've noted, for instance, that men and women have generally different listening styles. As a rule, women provide a good deal of vocal and visual response to speakers to indicate that they are interested and following. Men generally make fewer listening noises, providing less overt feedback on their involvement and their feelings about what is being said. Because our listening styles reflect the rules we learned in our communication cultures, they also reflect our expectations of how others should listen to us. Knowing this, we might remind ourselves to give more overt responses when listening to women than when listening to men. Conversely, if we have feminine listening inclinations, we might want to curb some of our responsiveness. In masculine speech communities, nodding and saying "yes" or "um hmm" are interpreted to mean agreement, not just involvement, so a feminine listening style can be misinterpreted by a masculine speaker. Of course, there are exceptions to these generalizations. Some women don't provide a great deal of feedback, and some men do. Thus, our best bet is to treat generalizations as hypotheses, not truths. This allows us to act on the basis of what is generally appropriate, but at the same time to stay open to the possibility that we may need to revise our behaviours in particular cases.

LISTEN ACTIVELY

We've seen that effective listening is an active process that requires substantial effort. When we realize all that's involved in listening, we appreciate how active an effort it is. Hearing is a physiological process that is passive; we don't have to do anything but be in the vicinity of sound waves to hear. Listening, however, is a highly active process. To do it effectively, we have to be willing to focus our minds, organize and interpret others' ideas and feelings, generate responses that signal our interest and that enhance both content and relationship levels of meaning, and retain what we have learned in the process of listening. In some situations, we also become active partners by listening collaboratively and engaging in problem-solving. Doing all of this is hard work! Recognizing that genuine listening is an active process prepares us to invest the amount of effort required to do it effectively.

Chapter Summary

Zeno of Citium was an ancient philosopher who once remarked that "we have been given two ears and but a single mouth, in order that we may hear more and talk less." Thousands of years later, the wisdom of that comment is still relevant. Listening is a major and vital part of communication, yet too often we don't consider it as important as talking. In this chapter, we've explored the complex and demanding process of listening. We began by distinguishing hearing and listening. Hearing is a straightforward physiological process that doesn't require effort on our part. Listening, in contrast, is a complicated process involving mindfulness, attending, hearing, selecting and organizing, interpreting, responding, and remembering. Doing it well requires commitment and skill.

To understand what interferes with effective listening, we discussed external obstacles that are in situations and messages and internal obstacles that are in ourselves. Listening is complicated by message overload, complexity of material, and external noise in communication contexts. In addition, listening can be hampered by our preoccupations and prejudgments, by a lack of effort, by our not recognizing differences in listening styles, and our desire to fix. These obstacles to careful listening give rise to various types of ineffective listening, including pseudolistening, monopolizing, selective listening, defensive listening, ambushing, and literal listening. Each form

of nonlistening signals that we aren't fully present in the interaction.

We also discussed different purposes for listening and identified the skills and attitudes that advance each. Listening for pleasure is supported by mindfulness and efforts to minimize distractions and noise. Informational listening requires us to adopt a mindful attitude and to think critically, organize and evaluate information, clarify understanding through asking questions, and develop aids for retention of complex material. Relationship listening also requires mindfulness, but it calls for different listening skills: controlling obstacles, attending, suspending judgment, paraphrasing, giving minimal encouragers, questioning, summarizing, and expressing support enhance the effectiveness of relationship listening.

The ideas we've discussed yield three guidelines for improving listening effectiveness. First, we need to be mindful—to be fully present in communication and focused on what is happening between us and others. Second, we should adapt our listening skills and style to accommodate differences in listening purpose and individuals. Finally, we must remember that listening is an active process and be prepared to invest energy and effort in doing it skillfully. Because listening is important in all speech communities, we will revisit some of the ideas covered here as we discuss dynamics in relationships in the following chapters.

Key Concepts

- attending
- ambushing
- defensive listening
- hearing
- listening
- listening for information

- listening for pleasure
- listening to support others
- literal listening
- mindfulness
- minimal encouragers
- monopolizing

- paraphrasing
- pseudolistening
- remembering
- responding
- summarizing
- selective listening

For Further Thought & Discussion

1. Review the six types of nonlistening discussed in this chapter. Are any of them common in your communication? Select one of your nonlistening practices and work to reduce its occurrence.

2. What ethical principles can you identify to guide the three kinds of listening? Are different ethical principles appropriate when listening for information and listening to support others?

3. Keep a record of your listening for the next two days. How much time do you spend listening for information, listening to support others, and listening for pleasure?

4. Use your InfoTrac College Edition to read pamphlets and articles published by professional associations. Also skim articles in recent issues of the *Globe and Mail* or *Business Quarterly*. Is the importance of listening mentioned in these publications? Discuss your findings with others in your class.

5. Apply the strategies for remembering that we discussed in this chapter. Create mnemonics, organize material as you listen, and review material immediately after listening. Do you find that using these strategies increases your listening effectiveness?

6. Who is your prototype, or model, for an effective listener? Describe what the person does that makes him or her effective. How do the person's behaviours fit with guidelines for effective listening discussed in this chapter?

Communication Climate: The Foundation of Personal Relationships

Everyday Encounters
By Stephen Lee

*The tension in this cartoon tells us something about the "climate" in the rela-*tionship. As you work through this chapter, you will be able to identify the elements that contribute to the creation of that climate. Let's begin by examining what defines climate.

Do you feel foggy-headed or down when the sky is overcast and upbeat when it's sunny? Does your mood ever shift as the weather changes? Most of us do respond to the climate. We feel more or less positive depending on the conditions around us. In much the same way that we react to physical weather, we also respond to **interpersonal climates.**

Sunshine or clouds, warmth and cold, fog or clear skies contribute to the climate in outdoor contexts. In the same way, how we communicate with others establishes the climate in personal relationships. Interpersonal climate is the overall feeling or emotional mood between people. Interpersonal climate is not something we can see or measure objectively, and it's not made up of things people do together. Instead, climate is the dominant feeling between people who are involved with each other. Two couples might live in the same apartment complex, have similar jobs, and distribute responsibilities for cleaning, cooking, and shopping in the same way. Yet in one of the relationships there is constant tension, marked by short and sometimes cutting remarks and frequent flares of temper. In the other relationship, the pervasive feeling is comfortable and friendly. Although the two couples do similar things, the climates of their relationships differ dramatically. Similarly, in the workplace, interpersonal climates make some of our relationships easy and comfortable and others difficult and defensive.

Because interpersonal climate concerns the overall feeling between people, it is the foundation of personal relationships. Friendships, romantic relationships, and collegial work relationships develop climates that reflect and establish emotional moods. In this chapter, we focus on climate as a cornerstone of satisfying interpersonal relationships. We'll begin by discussing the elements of healthy interpersonal relationships. Next, we'll examine confirming and disconfirming climates and identify kinds of communication that foster each. The third section of the chapter identifies guidelines for creating and sustaining healthy interpersonal climates. In the next chapter, we'll see how building confirming climates assists us in managing conflict effectively.

Photo: A. Henry

ELEMENTS OF SATISFYING PERSONAL RELATIONSHIPS

Personal relationships are basic to our lives. As we saw in Chapter 1, we relate to others to fulfill human needs for survival, safety, belonging, esteem, self-actualization, and participation in a diverse social world. People who lack friends are more depressed and have lower self-esteem than people who have satisfying friendships (Hojat, 1982; Jones & Moore, 1989). Just having relationships, however, doesn't necessarily enhance us. To feel good about ourselves and our connections with others, we need to build relationships that are confirming and satisfying.

Building good relationships depends not only on others but also on ourselves—especially our perceptions and attributions that shape how we feel about others and relationships. Communication scholars report that some lonely people are locked into a "negativity cycle" in which they focus on negative aspects of interaction and discount positive aspects. This leads them to feel more pessimistic about their relationships and themselves, which, in turn, heightens their awareness of negative features (Duck, Pond, & Leatham, 1994). The converse is also true: When we are involved in satisfying relationships, we feel more positive about ourselves and life. Researchers have shown that people who fall in love see the world through "rose-coloured glasses" (Hendrick & Hendrick, 1988).

Many people feel as Fiona does. Research indicates that loneliness during the first year of college depends more on whether a person has friends than on good family ties and romantic relationships (Cutrona, 1982). It seems that we look primarily to friends to satisfy our needs for belonging and acceptance, especially after we have moved away from home.

Because personal relationships make such a difference in our lives, we need to understand what makes relationships healthy and gratifying. Four

Student Voices

Fiona:

The worst time in my whole life was my first semester here. I felt so lonely being away from my family and all my friends at home. Back there we were really close, and there was always somebody to be with and talk to, but I didn't know anybody on this campus. I felt all alone and like nobody cared about me. I became depressed and almost left school, but then I started seeing a guy, and I made a couple of friends. Everything got better once I had some people to talk to and be with.

Concepts at a Glance

Four Features of Close Relationships

- Investment
- Commitment
- Trust
- Comfort with relational dialectics

features characterize satisfying close relationships: investment, commitment, trust, and comfort with relational dialectics (Wood, 1995c). We'll discuss each of these. As we do, realize that members of different speech communities may have distinct rules for what each feature is and how it is communicated. For example, in general, Westerners rely heavily on verbal disclosures to build trust, whereas most Asians are less verbally revealing and depend on actions to build trust. Caucasians tend to regard commitment as a tie between two people, whereas other ethnic groups often perceive commitment more as a broad tie that links families and communities (Gaines, 1995). Although people may experience and express these four features in diverse ways, they appear to be cornerstones of closeness for most of us. Taken together, these four features create a strong nucleus for a relationship and confirm the value of each partner.

INVESTMENT

Good relationships grow out of **investment,** which is what we put into relationships and what we could not retrieve if the relationship were to end. When we care about another person, we invest time, energy, thought, and feelings into interaction. In doing this, we invest ourselves in others. Investment is powerful because it consists of personal choices. Further, investment cannot be recovered, so the only way to make good on it is to stick with a relationship (Brehm, 1992). We can't get back the time, feelings, and energy we invest in a relationship. We cannot recover the history we have shared with another person. Thus, to leave is to lose the investment we've made.

What challenges do you face in personal relationships?

Photo: © Corel

Apply the Idea

Your Investment in Relationships

Choose two important relationships in your life. You might consider a friend, a romantic partner, a sibling, or a parent for example. Answer the following questions in regards to person A and then again for person B.

- *How much time have you spent?*
- *How many decisions have you made to accommodate the other?*
- *How much money have you spent?*
- *How much is your history entwined with the history of the other?*
- *How much trust have you given?*
- *How much support have you given?*
- *Do your investments roughly equal the investments of the other?*

Finally, ask yourself, "Is this a satisfying relationship?" Consider how your investments have influenced the satisfaction you experience.

Perceived equality of partners' investment affects satisfaction with relationships. Researchers report that in the happiest dating and married couples, partners feel they invest equally (Fletcher, Fincham, Cramer, & Heron, 1987; Hecht, Marston, & Larkey, 1994). When we feel we are investing more than a partner, we tend to be dissatisfied and resentful. When it seems our partner is investing more than we are, we may feel guilty. Because imbalance of either sort is disconfirming, perceived inequity erodes satisfaction (Brehm, 1992). Not surprisingly, communication is affected by perceived inequity. Partners who feel they are investing unequally tend to communicate limited support to each other and to minimize major disclosures (Brehm, 1992).

|*Student Voices*|

Tris:

I dated this one guy for a long time before I finally had to cut my losses. He said he loved me, but he wouldn't put anything in the relationship. I gave so much—always accommodating him, doing things for him, loving him, but there just wasn't any reciprocity. It was a one-way street with him, and I felt like he didn't value me very much at all.

COMMITMENT

Closely related to investment is **commitment,** which is a decision to remain with a relationship. Notice that commitment is defined as a decision, not a feeling. The hallmark of commitment is the assumption of a future. In committed relationships, partners assume they will continue together. Unlike passion or attraction, which exist in the present, commitment links partners together in the future. Because partners in committed relationships view their connection as continuing, they are unlikely to bail out during the inevitable rough times. Instead, they weather those, confident that they will stay together. Communication between committed partners reflects the assumed continuity of the relationship. Problems and tensions that inevitably arise aren't seen as reasons to end a relationship. Instead, partners try to work through their conflicts. We'll discuss ways to manage conflicts in detail in Chapter 9.

Whereas love is a feeling we can't necessarily control, commitment is a decision, as explained in "Love and Commitment: Different Matters," on page 290. It is a personal choice to maintain a relationship. Partners who make this choice strive for dual perspective and commit to listening and speaking effectively to each other. Aaron Beck (1988), a counsellor, believes

Love and Commitment: Different Matters

To find out what holds a relationship together, Mary Lund studied 129 heterosexual college students. She measured their commitment and love for partners in February and in the summer following graduation. She found that the continuation of relationships depended more on commitment than love. Couples who had high levels of love but low commitment to a shared future were less likely to remain together than couples who were highly committed to a joint future. Thus, the intention to stay together is a more powerful glue than positive feelings between partners.

Lund's study also showed that commitment is more strongly linked to making investments than to perceptions that a relationship is rewarding or that love exists. Investments increase commitment because they are personal choices, whereas loving and being loved are not acts of will.

Summarizing her findings, Lund said that although love usually accompanies commitment, commitment and investment have more to do with whether a relationship lasts than do love and rewards.

Source: Lund, M. (1985). The development of investment and commitment scales for predicting continuity of personal relationships. *Journal of Social and Personal Relationships, 2,* 3–23.

that the decision to commit injects responsibility into relationships. When partners make a commitment, they take responsibility for continuing to invest in and care for their bond. Without responsibility, relationships are subject to the whims of feeling and fortune, which are hardly a stable basis for enduring intimacy.

TRUST

A third cornerstone of healthy personal relationships is a high degree of trust between partners.

Trust involves believing in another's reliability (he or she will do what is promised) and emotionally relying on another to care about and protect our welfare (Brehm, 1992). Trust doesn't come automatically in relationships. Instead, it is earned. Individuals earn each other's trust by communicating honestly and by honouring each other's perspective. They show that they

Part 2
Weaving Communication into Relationships

NTL

290

Erin:

I've been married for six years, and it has been a very difficult relationship. We were married right out of high school because I was pregnant. This set our marriage off to a rocky start. We separated twice, which tells you that we weren't totally committed. The last time we separated and got back together, we agreed this would be our last try at making the marriage work. We decided that if it was going to have a chance of working, both of us had to put everything we have into it. We also decided to get the words "separation" and "divorce" out of our vocabulary. I can't believe the change that we have had in our relationship since we decided to put everything into it and not to talk about breaking up. We now have a true commitment.

care about each other and are willing to make the investments necessary to understand how each other thinks and feels. When we trust someone, we count on her or him to be loving and respectful. These feelings allow us to feel psychologically safe.

One reason that trust is so important to close friendships and romantic relationships is that it allows us to take risks with others. For intimacy to grow, we have to risk ourselves. We have to be willing to let another into our hearts and heads, and that requires trust. We only open ourselves to others if they have earned our trust and if we feel we can count on them to protect our confidences and to care about us and our feelings. Trust develops as people do what they say they will and as they provide support and safety to each other.

Student Voices

Terry:

I was really crazy about this girl my first year, but I just didn't trust that she really cared about me. I was always doing little things to show her I cared, like taking her a flower or changing the oil in her car. But she never did little things for me. As long as I was taking care of her, she was great. But when I needed to feel she was there for me, things didn't work very well. I just didn't trust her to look out for me.

Self-Disclosure

One clear influence on trust is self-disclosure, which can both build and reflect trust between people.

Self-disclosure is revealing personal information about ourselves that others are unlikely to discover in other ways. According to researchers who have studied communication between intimates, self-disclosure is a key gauge of closeness, at least among Westerners (Derlega & Berg, 1987; Hansen & Schuldt, 1984). Self-disclosure should take place gradually and with appropriate caution. It's unwise to tell anyone too much about ourselves too quickly, especially if revelations could be used against us. We begin by disclosing relatively superficial information ("I'm from a small town," "I love Mexican food," "I'm afraid of heights"). If a person responds with empathy to early and limited disclosures, we're likely to reveal progressively more intimate information ("I just found my biological parents," "I am gay," "I go through periods of real depression"). These disclosures have a great deal more emotional risk attached to them. If they are also met with understanding and confidentiality, trust continues to grow.

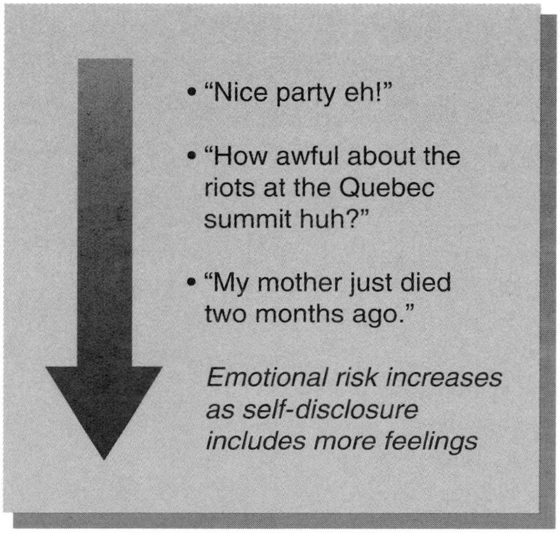

In the early stages of relationship development, it is important that there be reciprocity of disclosures. We're willing to make disclosures of our private feelings only so long as the other person is also revealing personal information (Cunningham, Strassberg, & Haan, 1986). The need for reciprocity exists because trust is still developing and being earned. When a relationship is just beginning, we feel vulnerable—the other could betray a confidence or reject us because we disclose something negative. Our feeling of vulnerability is reduced if the other person is also trusting us with self-disclosures.

The need to match disclosures recedes in importance once trust is established. Partners in stable relationships don't feel the need to reciprocate disclosures immediately. Unlike beginning acquaintances, they have the time to reciprocate on a more leisurely schedule. Thus, disclosure between established intimates is more likely to be greeted with a response to what has been revealed than with an equivalent disclosure. Of course, there are exceptions to these general patterns. People vary in how much they want to self-disclose, so an absolute amount of disclosure is not a sure-fire measure of closeness. Also, people vary in their perceptions of the link between disclosure and intimacy, so we need to respect individual differences.

Although all of us disclose some personal information in close relationships, not everyone discloses equally or in the same ways. Cultural differences shape our tendencies to self-disclose. People raised in traditional Chinese society disclose less personal information than most Westerners.

- "Nice party eh!"

- "How awful about the riots at the Quebec summit huh?"

- "My mother just died two months ago."

Emotional risk increases as self-disclosure includes more feelings

Figure 8.1
Increasing Risk in Self-Disclosure

Among Pakistanis, disclosures between parents and children are much more rare than among Canadian-born residents. Gender also seems to affect how and how much people disclose, as discussed in "Different Modes of Closeness." In general, women make more verbal disclosures both to other women and to men. Women also tend to place greater value on verbal disclosures than most men (Floyd & Parks, 1995). Men are generally less inclined to talk about personal feelings, even to intimates. Many men disclose feelings through their actions rather than through words. Sorell's comments make this point.

Student Voices

Sorell:

When I really need some support from my girlfriend, I don't just come out and say, "I need you." What I do is go over to her place or call her to see if she wants to come to my place. Sometimes we just sit together watching TV or something. And that helps. I know she knows that I am down and need her, but I don't have to say it. I do the same thing when I think she is feeling low. It's hard for me to say "I love you and am sorry you feel bad." But I can be with her, and I can hug her and let her know through my actions that I care.

Although self-disclosing is important early in relationships, it is not a primary communication dynamic over the long haul. When we're first getting to know another, we have to reveal ourselves and learn about the other, so disclosures are necessary and desirable. In relationships that endure, however, disclosures make up very little of the total communication between partners. Although disclosure wanes over time, partners continue to reap the benefits of the trust and depth of personal knowledge created by early disclosures. Also, partners do continue to disclose new experiences and insights to each other; however, there is less disclosure as a relationship matures. Radical decreases in disclosures, other than explosions of negative feelings, are key signals of trouble in a relationship (Baxter, 1987). We are reluctant to entrust others with our secrets and personal emotions when intimacy is fading or gone.

COMFORT WITH RELATIONAL DIALECTICS

A final quality of healthy relationships is understanding and being comfortable with **relational dialectics.** These are opposing forces, or tensions, that are normal parts of all relationships. Leslie Baxter, a scholar of interpersonal com-

Communication Notes

Different Modes of Closeness

Research indicates that women generally disclose more frequently and more deeply than men. This difference was interpreted to mean that men are less interested in or comfortable with intimacy. However, recent work suggests instead that the sexes do not differ in how much they value closeness; they merely create it in different ways.

Feminine speech communities emphasize using personal talk to create and sustain closeness. Thus, in general, women learn to disclose personal thoughts and feelings as a primary way of enhancing intimacy. This is called *closeness in dialogue*.

Because masculine speech communities place less emphasis on personal talk, men typically don't regard intimate conversation and self-disclosure as a path to closeness. Instead, they usually learn to bond with others through doing things together. Their mode is called *closeness in the doing*.

These two modes of closeness, although related to gender, aren't dichotomized by sex. Recent studies indicate that both women and men do things for people they care about. Instrumental shows of affection, or closeness in the doing, seems less gender-bound than closeness in dialogue. Research also indicates that men sometimes express closeness through dialogue, just not as frequently as most women.

Both modes of closeness are ways for people to connect. The two ways of expressing and experiencing closeness are equally valid, and both should be respected.

Sources: Canary, D., & Dindia, K. (Eds.). (1998). *Sex differences and similarities in communication,* Mahwah, NJ: Erlbaum; Floyd, K., & Parks, M. (1995). Manifesting closeness in the interactions of peers: A look at siblings and friends. *Communication Reports,* 8, 69–76; Wood, J. T., & Inman, C. C. (1993). In a different mode: Masculine styles of communicating closeness. *Journal of Applied Communication Research,* 21, 279–295.

munication, has identified three dialectics of relationships (Baxter, 1988, 1990, 1993; Baxter & Simon, 1993). We'll discuss the three, shown in Table 8.1, to clarify how they operate as normal, productive processes in relational life.

The Opposing Forces

Autonomy/Connection

All close friends and romantic partners experience tension between wanting to be autonomous, or individual, and wanting to be close, or connected. Because we want to be deeply linked to others, we seek intimacy and

Table 8.1
Relational Dialectics

Autonomy/Connection	I want to be close. I need my own space.
Novelty/Predictability	I like the familiar rhythms we have. We need to do something new and different.
Openness/Closedness	I like sharing so much with you. There are some things I don't want to talk about with you.

Student Voices

Kalen:

I think what first clued me in that Shelby was losing interest was that she stopped telling me private stuff about herself. For the first couple of months we dated, she shared so much about her dreams, plans, and fears. The more she told me about herself and the more I told her, the closer I felt. But then she seemed to withdraw and not want to share her private thoughts. That was really the start of the end.

sharing. Friends and lovers want to spend time with each other, have joint interests, and talk personally. At the same time, each of us needs a sense of independent identity. We want to know that our individuality is not swallowed up by relationships. We need our own space, so we seek distance even from our intimates.

Relationship counsellors agree that the most central and continuous friction in most close relationships arises from the contradictory impulses for autonomy and connection (Beck, 1988; Scarf, 1987). Both autonomy and closeness are natural human needs. The challenge is to preserve individuality while also creating unity in a relationship.

Novelty/Predictability

The second dialectic is the tension between wanting routine, or familiarity, and wanting novelty in a relationship. All of us like a certain amount of routine to provide security and predictability to our lives. For example, you may have a friend with whom you meet regularly at the same time. It may be breakfast or lunch on a particular day or a workout at a gym or studio. This

|Student Voices|

Max:

Dialectics explains something that has really confused me. I've never understood how I could want so much to be with Ashley for a while and then feel suffocated and need to get away. I've worried that it means I don't love her anymore or there is something wrong between us. But now I see how both needs are normal and okay.

predictability would then become something that defines your relationship. Yet too much routine becomes boring, so it's also natural to seek novel experiences. Every so often you may seek that novelty by varying your customary routine.

Openness/Closedness

The third dialectic is a tension between wanting open communication and needing a degree of privacy, even with intimates. With our closest partners, we want to share our inner selves and be open with no holds barred. Even so, we also desire a zone of privacy, and we want our partners to respect that. Some partners agree not to talk about certain topics, such as money or religion. Although they are open about other matters, these topics are respected as off-limits. It's also normal to be temporarily closed after we have revealed something highly personal.

Although intimate relationships are sometimes idealized as totally open and honest, in reality completely unbridled expressiveness would be intolerable (Baxter, 1993; Petronio, 1991). There is nothing wrong when we seek privacy; it doesn't mean a relationship is in trouble. It means only that we need both openness and closedness in our lives.

The three dialectics create ongoing tensions in healthy relationships. This is a problem only if partners don't understand that dialectics and the tension

|Student Voices|

Kira:

Most of the time I like how Michael and I are. We've worked out some nice, comfortable routines for time together, so we don't have to figure out what we're going to do all the time. But every now and then I get bored, and I want to break out of the routines. I want something that stimulates me—something new and different in our relationship. I think that's healthy.

Andy:

My girlfriend has trouble accepting the fact that I won't talk to her about my brother Jacob. He died when I was eight, and I still can't deal with all my feelings, especially with feeling guilty that he died and I'm alive. I just can't talk about that to anybody. With my girlfriend, I talk about lots of personal stuff, but Jacob is just too private and too hard.

they generate are natural parts of relational life. If we think it's wrong to be closed at times or not to want togetherness always, then we'll misinterpret our feelings and what they mean. Once we realize that dialectics are normal in all relationships, we can accept and grow from the tensions they generate.

Dialectics do not operate in isolation. Instead, they interact and affect one another within the overall system of a relationship. Thus, friends who are highly open are also likely to be very connected, whereas a more closed couple tends to favour greater autonomy (Aries, 1987). Relational dialectics also interact with other facets of interpersonal communication. For instance, partners who prefer a high amount of individu-

Respectful negotiation is crucial to resolving differences.

Photo: J. Liburd

ality tend to create more individual spaces and fewer common ones in their homes than do partners who favour greater connection (Fitzpatrick, 1988; Fitzpatrick & Best, 1979). Frequent and in-depth disclosures are most likely in relationships that are highly open and connected. Like all aspects of interpersonal communication, relational dialectics operate systemically.

Responding to Dialectics

There is no single correct method of responding to relational dialectics. Baxter (1990) has identified four ways partners deal with the tension generated by opposing needs.

Neutralization is a negotiation of balance between the two poles of a dialectic. This involves striking a compromise in which each need is met to an extent, but neither is fully satisfied. A couple that does this might have a fairly consistent equilibrium between the amount of novelty and the amount of routine in their relationship.

A second response is selection in which we give priority to one of the needs in a dialectic and neglect the other. For example, friends might focus on novelty and suppress their needs for ritual and routine. Some partners

Concepts at a Glance

Responding to Dialectics

- Neutralize the two poles.
- Prioritize dialectics.
- Separate dialectics.
- Reframe needs.

cycle between competing poles of dialectics, so that they favour each one alternately. A couple could be open and continuously together for a period and then be autonomous and closed for a time.

A third way to manage dialectics is called separation. When we separate dialectics, we assign one dialectical need to certain spheres of interaction and the opposing dialectical need to other aspects of interaction. For instance, friends might be open about many topics but respect each other's privacy in one or two areas. A couple might have rigid daily schedules and patterns of socializing but be very spontaneous on vacations. Many dual-career couples are autonomous about their work, relying little on each other for advice, although they are very connected about family, collaborating, and being close in that area.

The final method of dealing with dialectics is called reframing. This is a complex and transformative strategy in which partners redefine contradictory needs as not in opposition. In other words, they reframe their perceptions by redefining what is happening. One study examining differences between intimate partners discovered examples of reframing (Wood et al., 1994). Some partners in the study transcended the opposition between autonomy and connection by defining differences and disagreements as enhancing intimacy. Another example of reframing is deciding that novelty and predictability are not opposites, but allies. Similarly, routine and spontaneity can be regarded as supporting each other. Routines make novelty interesting, and novelty makes routines comforting.

Student Voices

Beverly:

My folks are so funny. They plod along in the same old rut for ages and ages, and my sister and I can't get them to do anything different. Mom won't try a new recipe for chicken because "we like ours like I always fix it." Dad won't try a new style of shirt because "that's not the kind of shirt I wear." Dynamite wouldn't blow them out of their ruts. But then all of a sudden they'll do a whole bunch of unusual things. Like once they went out to three movies in a day, and the next day they went for a picnic at the zoo. This kind of zaniness goes on for a while, then it's back to hum-drum for months and months. I guess they get all of their novelty in occasional bursts.

Apply the Idea

Applying Relational Dialectics

How do relational dialectics operate in your life? To find out, select three of your relationships: a very close friendship, a current or past romantic relationship, and a friendly but not really intimate relationship. For each relationship answer these questions:

- *How are needs for autonomy expressed and satisfied?*
- *How are needs for connection expressed and met?*
- *How are needs for novelty expressed and met?*
- *How are needs for predictability expressed and met?*
- *How are needs for openness expressed and satisfied?*
- *How are needs for closedness expressed and met?*

Now think about how you manage the tension between opposing needs in each dialectic. When do you rely on neutralization, selection, separation, and reframing? How satisfied are you with your responses? Experiment with new ways of managing the tensions.

Dialectics can be effectively managed in a variety of ways. However, research indicates that, in general, the least effective and least satisfying response is to honour one need and repress the opposing one (Baxter, 1990). Squelching any natural human impulse diminishes us. The challenge is to find ways to accommodate all of our needs, even when they seem contradictory.

Healthy relationships exist when partners create a climate in which each feels valued and comfortable with the other. This tends to happen when partners make commitments and investments, build trust, and effectively manage dialectical tensions. Underlying all the elements we've discussed is confirmation, which is at the heart of fulfilling interpersonal relationships. Because confirmation is so important to relationships, the next section of the chapter explores how communication influences confirming climates.

Review

Establishing confirming climates in a relationship ensures the health of that relationship.

CONFIRMING AND DISCONFIRMING CLIMATES

The philosopher Martin Buber (1957) believed that each of us needs confirmation to be healthy and to grow. Buber also emphasized that full humanness can develop only when people confirm others and are confirmed by them. The essence of confirmation is valuing. We all want to feel we are

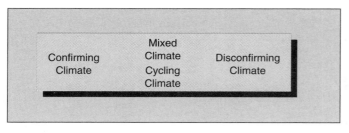

Figure 8.2
Continuum of Interpersonal Climates

valued, especially by our intimates. When others confirm us, we feel cherished and respected. When they disconfirm us, we feel discounted and less contented with ourselves.

Interpersonal climates exist on a continuum from confirming to disconfirming (Figure 8.2). Of course, few relationships are purely confirming or disconfirming. In reality, most fall in between the two extremes of the continuum. In these, some messages are confirming, whereas other messages are disconfirming, or communication cycles between being basically confirming and basically disconfirming.

Relationships also don't usually move abruptly and completely from being at one spot on the continuum to being in a different spot. Usually, one level of confirmation flows into the next in a gradual way. You might feel less than confirmed by a person you are just getting to know. As the two of you talk and interact more, the other person may communicate that he or she values you and your ideas, so you begin to feel more confirmed. Over time, you move to feeling that the relationship is basically confirming.

LEVELS OF CONFIRMATION AND DISCONFIRMATION

Concepts at a Glance

Elements of Confirming Climates

- Recognition
- Acknowledgment
- Endorsement

Building on Buber's ideas, as well as those of psychiatrist R. D. Laing (1961), communication scholars have extended insight into confirming and disconfirming climates (Cissna & Sieburg, 1986). They have identified specific kinds of communication that confirm or disconfirm others on three levels.

Recognition

The most basic form of confirmation is recognizing that another person exists. We do this with nonverbal behaviours (a smile, hug, or touch) and verbal communication ("Hello," "Good to meet you," "I see you're home").

Student Voices

Kingston:

Canadians like to claim that there is no discrimination here. It just isn't so. Discrimination and racism is alive and well in Canada. It's just not as obvious as in the States. At least in the States you know where you stand. In Canada, there is a blanket of politeness on everything. I still get regarded as a second-class citizen, just not to my face. I feel invisible, which is pretty funny when I'm the only black face in a white room.

We disconfirm others at a fundamental level when we don't acknowledge their existence. For example, you might not speak to or look at a person when you enter a room. Not responding to someone's question also disconfirms their presence. Parents who punish a child by refusing to speak to her or him disconfirm the child's existence. A person who uses the silent treatment disconfirms another's existence.

Acknowledgment

A second and more positive level of confirmation is acknowledgment of what another feels, thinks, or says. We acknowledge others nonverbally by nodding our heads or by making strong eye contact to indicate we are listening. Verbal acknowledgments are direct responses to others' communication. If a friend says, "I'm really worried that I blew my final," you could acknowledge that by responding, "So you're scared that you didn't do well on it, huh?" This paraphrasing response acknowledges both the thoughts and the feelings of the other person.

A disconfirming climate is established in this scene by the act of turning away.

Photo: A. Henry

We disconfirm others when we don't acknowledge their feelings or thoughts. For instance, if you respond to your friend's statement about doing poorly on the exam by saying, "Want to go out and shoot some darts tonight?" that would be an irrelevant response that ignores the friend's comment. It is also disconfirming when we deny our friend's feelings and communication: "You did fine on the exam."

Lori makes an important point. We shouldn't assume we know what others will perceive as confirming. You may recall that in Chapter 5 we emphasized that we shouldn't presume to speak for others. It is fundamentally disconfirming to be made voiceless when others ignore what we say and

|Student Voices|

Lori:

You'd be amazed by how often people refuse to acknowledge what differently abled people say. A hundred times I've been walking across campus and someone has come up and offered to guide me. I tell them I know the way and don't need help, and they still put an arm under my elbow to guide me. I may be blind, but there's nothing wrong with my mind. I know if I need help. Why won't others acknowledge that?

think. Especially when we deal with people who differ from us in important ways, we should take time to learn what they perceive as confirming and disconfirming. This idea is illustrated in "Guidelines for Communicating with Persons with Disabilities" on page 304.

Endorsement

The final level of confirmation is endorsement. Endorsement involves accepting another's feelings or thoughts as valid. In the foregoing example, you could endorse by saying, "It's natural to be worried about your exam when you have so much riding on it." We disconfirm others when we don't accept their thoughts and feelings. If you respond to the friend by saying, "That's crazy," or "How can you worry about a psych exam when people are starving in Rwanda?" you reject the validity of the expressed feelings.

Endorsement isn't always possible if we are trying to be honest with others. Sometimes we cannot accept what another feels or thinks, so we can't make an endorsing response. University of Victoria researcher Sibylle Artz, in her landmark research on violence in school girls (1998; in press), makes an important distinction between judgment and condemnation. Because so many of the girls she researched had poor models around them for moral reasoning, Artz found it important to judge a violent act without condemning the person. In this way, she could provide a moral response and yet still maintain the confidence of the girls. Artz could *acknowledge* the fears but not necessarily *endorse* the behaviour. This is a very important approach in dealing with youth at risk.

Table 8.2 illustrates the different levels on which confirmation and disconfirmation occur. The most essential confirmation we can give is to recognize another exists. Conversely, the most basic kind of disconfirmation is to deny someone exists. When we don't speak to others, or when we look away when they approach us, we disconfirm their existence. We say, "You aren't there." On the second level, we confirm others by acknowledging their ideas and feelings, which carries the relationship-level meaning that they matter to us. In essence, we say "I am paying attention because your feelings and ideas matter to me." We disconfirm others on this level when we communicate that they don't matter to us, that we don't care what they feel or think. The highest form of confirmation is acceptance of others and what they communicate. We feel validated when others accept us as we are and accept what we think and feel. Disconfirmation is not mere disagreement. Disagreements, after all, can be productive and healthy, and they imply that people matter enough to each other to argue.

When we understand that confirmation is basic for all of us and that it is given or withheld on different levels, we gain insight into relationships. If you think about what we've discussed, you'll probably find that the relationships in which you feel most valued and comfortable are those with a high degree of confirmation.

Review

What is disconfirming is to be told that we or our ideas are crazy, wrong, stupid, or deviant.

Table 8.2

Confirming and Disconfirming Messages

	Confirming Messages	Disconfirming Messages
Recognition	You exist. "Hello."	You don't exist. Silence
Acknowledgment	You matter to me. We have a relationship. "I'm sorry you're hurt."	You don't matter. We are not a team. "You'll get over it."
Endorsement	What you think is true. What you feel is okay. "You have every right to feel that way."	You are wrong. You shouldn't feel what you do. "Your feeling doesn't make sense."

Student Voices

Wayne:

I've gotten a lot of disconfirmation since I came out. When I told my parents I was gay, Mom said, "No, you're not." I told her I was, and she and Dad both said I was just confused, but I wasn't gay. They refuse to acknowledge I'm gay, which means they reject who I am. My older brother isn't any better. His view is that I'm sinful and headed for hell. Now what could be more disconfirming than that?

Reflective Exercise

Analyzing Your Relationships

Think about two relationships in your life. One should be a relationship in which you feel good about yourself and safe in the connection. The second relationship should be one in which you feel disregarded or not valued. Identify instances of each level of confirmation in the satisfying relationship and instances of each level of disconfirmation in the unpleasant one. Recognizing confirming and disconfirming communication should give you insight into why these relationships are so different.

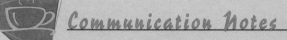

Communication Notes

Guidelines for Communicating with Persons with Disabilities

- When talking with someone who has a disability, speak directly to the person, not to a companion or interpreter.
- When introduced to a person with a disability, offer to shake hands. People who have limited hand use or who have artificial limbs can usually shake.
- When meeting a person with a visual impairment, identify yourself and anyone who is with you. If a person with a visual impairment is part of a group, preface comments to him or her with a name.
- You may offer assistance, but don't provide it unless your offer is accepted. Then ask the person how you can best assist (ask for instructions).
- Treat adults as adults. Don't patronize people in wheelchairs by patting them on the shoulder or head; don't use childish language when speaking to individuals who have no mental disability.
- Respect the personal space of persons with disabilities. It is rude to lean on a wheelchair because that is part of an individual's personal territory.
- Listen mindfully when talking with someone who has difficulty speaking. Don't interrupt or supply words to others. Just be patient and let them finish. Don't pretend to understand if you don't. Instead, explain what you didn't understand and ask the person to respond.
- When you talk with persons who use a wheelchair or crutches, try to position yourself at their eye level and in front of them to allow good eye contact.
- It is appropriate to wave your hand or tap the shoulder of persons with hearing impairments as a way to get their attention. Look directly at the person and speak clearly, slowly, and expressively. Face those who lip-read, place yourself in a good light source, and keep hands, cigarettes, and gum away from your mouth.
- Relax. Don't be afraid to use common expressions such as "See you later" to someone with a visual impairment or "Did you hear the news?" to someone with a hearing difficulty. They're unlikely to be offended and may turn the irony into a joke.

Source: Adapted from AXIS Centre for Public Awareness of People with Disabilities, 4550 Indianola Avenue, Columbus, OH 43214.

Confirming and disconfirming messages are important influences on the climate of personal relationships. In addition, other kinds of communication contribute to the overall feeling of a relationship. We'll now consider specific forms of communication that shape the interpersonal atmosphere between friends and romantic partners.

DEFENSIVE AND SUPPORTIVE CLIMATES

Communication researcher Jack Gibb (1961, 1964, 1970) studied the relationship between communication and interpersonal climates. He began by noting that with some people we feel defensive and on guard, so we are unlikely to communicate openly with them. Gibb called these defensive climates. Gibb also noted that with some other people we feel supported and comfortable, so we are likely to communicate freely with them. Gibb referred to these as supportive climates. The two kinds of feelings, and the interpersonal climates that foster them, are not typically pure in form. Even in the most healthy and supportive relationships there are usually some defensive moments and some situations in which we don't feel comfortable. Yet, most established relationships have a fairly stable climate.

Being ignored is the most disconfirming message of all.

Photo: M. Salez

Gibb believed that the different feelings we have around various people are due largely to communication that promotes feeling defensive or feeling supported. Gibb identified six types of communication that promote defensive climates and six opposite types of communication that foster supportive climates, as shown in Table 8.3.

Table 8.3
Communication and Climate

Defensive Communication	Supportive Communication
Evaluation	Description
Certainty	Provisionalism
Strategy	Spontaneity
Control	Problem orientation
Neutrality	Empathy
Superiority	Equality

Evaluation Versus Description

We tend to become defensive when we feel that others are evaluating us. Few of us feel what Gibb called "psychologically safe" when we are the targets of judgments. Other communication researchers report that evaluative communication evokes defensiveness (Eadie, 1982; Stephenson & D'Angelo, 1973). It's not surprising that Wayne in the last commentary felt judged by his family when he told them he was gay. His parents and brother made evaluations—very negative ones of him and of being gay. As we noted in Chapter 7, even positive evaluations can sometimes make us defensive because they carry the relationship meaning that another person feels entitled to judge us. Here are several examples of evaluative statements: "You have no discipline," "It's dumb to feel that way," "You shouldn't have done that," "You did the right thing," "That's a stupid idea."

Descriptive communication doesn't evaluate others or what they think and feel. Instead, it describes behaviours without passing judgment. I–language, which we learned about in Chapter 5, describes what the person speaking feels or thinks, but it doesn't evaluate another (you–language does evaluate). For example, "I wish you hadn't done that" describes your feelings, whereas "You shouldn't have done that" evaluates another's behaviour. Descriptive language may also refer to another, but it does so by describing, not evaluating, the other's behaviour: "You seem to be sleeping more lately" versus "You're sleeping too much"; "You've lost your temper three times today" versus "Quit flying off the handle"; "You are running late" versus "You shouldn't have kept me waiting."

Is your criticism filled with You–language?

Photo: A. Henry

Apply the Idea

Using Descriptive Language

To develop skill in supportive communication, translate the following evaluative statements into descriptive ones.

For example,

Evaluative: This report is poorly done.

Descriptive: This report doesn't include background information.

Evaluative

You're lazy. _____

_____

I hate the way you dominate conversations with me. _____

_____

Stop obsessing about the problem. _____

_____

You're too involved. _____

_____

Your work isn't up to par. _____

_____

Certainty Versus Provisionalism

Certainty language is absolute and often dogmatic. It suggests there is one and only one answer, valid point of view, or reasonable course of action. Because communication laced with certainty proclaims an absolutely correct position, it slams the door on further discussion. There's no point in talking with people whose minds are made up and who demean any point of view other than theirs. Sometimes certainty is expressed by restating a position over and over, instead of responding to alternate ideas from others (Alexander, 1979).

Perhaps you've been in a conversation with someone who says "I don't want to hear it," "You can't change my mind," "I've already figured out what I'm going to do, so just save your breath." These comments reflect certainty and an unwillingness to engage in interaction with others. When confronted with such statements, we're likely to follow the advice and "save our breath." We're also likely to be uninterested in communicating with people who imply that our ideas are wrong because they don't agree with their ideas. "I know what I'm talking about; you don't" is a disconfirming comment that squelches motivation to continue interacting.

One form of certainty communication is **ethnocentrism**, which is the assumption that our culture and its norms are the only right ones. If a speaker assumes that Western Anglo communication styles are the only correct ones, he or she makes a serious communication error. Dogmatically asserting "It's disrespectful to be late" reveals a lack of awareness of cultures that are less obsessed with speed and efficiency than white Canadian culture. Aboriginal cultures, for example, have a much more relaxed notion of time. Additional examples of certainty statements are "This is the only idea that makes sense," "My mind can't be changed because I'm right," and "Only a fool would vote for that person."

An alternative to certainty is provisionalism, which communicates openness to other points of view. When we speak provisionally, or tentatively, we suggest we have a point of view, yet our minds aren't sealed. We signal we're

Student Voices

Monika:

My father is a classic case of closed-mindedness. He has his ideas, and everything else is crazy. I told him I was majoring in communication studies, and he hit the roof. He said there was no future in learning to write speeches, and he told me I should go into business so that I could get a good job. He never even asked me what communication studies is. If he had, I would have told him it's a lot more than speech writing. He starts off sure that he knows everything about whatever is being discussed. He has no interest in other points of view or learning something new. He just locks his mind and throws away the key. We've all learned just to keep our ideas to ourselves around him—there's no communication.

willing to consider alternative positions, and this encourages others to voice their ideas. Provisional communication includes statements such as "The way I tend to see the issue is ...," "One way to look at this is ...," and "Probably what I would do in that situation is ..." Notice how each of these comments signals that the speaker realizes there could be other positions that are also reasonable. Tentativeness signals an open mind, which is why it invites continued communication.

It is much more facilitative to include "I might be wrong but ..." or "I thought we'd agreed upon ..." in our speech behaviours than the destructive certainty of "You're wrong!"

Strategy Versus Spontaneity

Most of us feel on guard when we think others are manipulating us or being less than upfront about what's on their minds. Defensiveness is a natural response to feeling that others are using strategies in an effort to control us. Strategic communication doesn't allow openness between people, because one person is keeping something from another (Eadie, 1982). An example of strategic communication is this: "Would you do something for me if I told you it really matters?" If the speaker doesn't tell us what we're expected to do, it feels like a setup.

We're also likely to feel that another is trying to manipulate us with a comment such as "Remember when I helped you with your math last term and when I did your chores last week because you were busy?" With a preamble like that, we can smell a trap. We also get defensive when we suspect others of using openness to manipulate how we feel about them. For instance, people who disclose intimate personal information early in a relationship may be trying to win our trust and to trick us into revealing details of our own personal life. Nonverbal behaviours may also convey strategy, as when a person pauses a long time before answering or refuses to look at us when he or she speaks. A sense of deception pollutes the communication climate.

Spontaneity is the counterpoint to strategy. Spontaneous communication feels open, honest, and unpremeditated. "I really need your help with this computer glitch" is a more spontaneous comment than "Would you do something for me if I told you it really matters?" Likewise, it is more spontaneous to ask for a favour in a straightforward way ("Would you help me?") than to preface a request with a recitation of all we've done for someone else. Whereas strategic communication comes across as contrived and devious, spontaneous interaction feels authentic and natural.

Strategy or spontaneity? What do you choose when you are in conflict?

Photo: J. Liburd

Control Versus Problem-Orientation

Controlling communication is also likely to trigger defensiveness. Similar to strategies, controlling communication more overtly attempts to manipulate others. A common instance of controlling communication is when a person insists her or his solution or preference should prevail. Whether the issue is trivial (what movie to see) or serious (where to locate after college), con-

Student Voices

Maja:

A guy I dated last year was a real con artist, but it took me a while to figure that out. He would look me straight in the eye and tell me he really felt he could trust me. Then he'd say he was going to tell me something he'd never told anyone else in his life, and he'd tell me about fights with his father or how he didn't make the soccer team in high school. The stuff wasn't really that personal, but the way he said it made it seem that way. So I found myself telling him a lot more than I usually disclose and a lot more than I should have. He started using some of the information against me, which was when I started getting wise to him. Later on, I found out he ran through the same song and dance with every girl he dated. It was quite an act!

trollers try to impose their point of view on others. This disconfirms and disrespects others. Defensiveness arises because the relational meaning is that the person exerting control thinks she or he has greater power, rights, or intelligence than others. It's disconfirming to be told our opinions are wrong, our preferences don't matter, or we aren't smart enough to have good ideas. Controlling communication is particularly objectionable when it combines with strategies. For example, a wife who earns a higher salary might say to her husband, "Well, I like the Honda more than the Ford you want, and it's my money that's going to pay for it." The speaker not only pushes her preference but also tells her husband that she has more power than he does because she makes more money.

Problem-oriented communication is less likely than control to generate defensiveness. Rather than imposing a preference, problem-oriented communication focuses on finding answers that satisfy everyone. The goal is to come up with a solution that all parties find acceptable. Here's an example of problem-oriented communication: "It seems that we have really different ideas about how to spend our vacation. Let's talk through what each of us wants and see if there's a way for both of us to have a good vacation." Notice how this statement invites collaboration and emphasizes the goal of meeting both people's needs. According to communication researchers, problem-oriented behaviours tend to reduce conflict and keep lines of communication open (Alexander, 1979; Civickly, Pace, & Krause, 1977).

One of the benefits of problem-oriented communication is that the relationship level of meaning emphasizes the importance of the relationship between communicators. When we convey that we want to collaborate with another person to resolve some mutual problem, we let the other know that we care more about the relationship than getting our own way. In contrast, controlling behaviours aim for one person to triumph over the other, an outcome that undercuts interpersonal harmony.

Student Voices

Pat:

My roommate last year was a real jerk. Her goal in life was to control me and everyone else around her. Sometimes she'd say she felt like going out for dinner, and I'd agree and then she'd ask me where I wanted to go. Even if I picked her favourite place, she would insist on going somewhere else. She just had to be in charge. Once I moved things around in the room, and she fussed a lot and moved them back. Later, she moved things the way I had, but then it was her choice. She didn't care about issues or working things through. All she cared about was being in control.

Neutrality Versus Empathy

Gibb's (1961, 1964, 1970) observations of group interaction revealed that people tend to become defensive when others act in a neutral, or detached, manner. It's easy to understand why we might feel uneasy with people who seem distant and removed, especially if we are talking about personal matters. Research on interview climates indicates that defensiveness arises when an interviewer appears withdrawn and distant (Civickly, Pace, & Krause, 1977). Neutral communication implies a lack of regard and caring for others. Consequently, it disconfirms their worth.

In contrast to neutrality, expressed empathy confirms the worth of others and our concern for their thoughts and feelings. Empathic communication is illustrated by these examples: "I can understand why you feel that way," "It sounds like you really feel uncomfortable with your job," "You seem to feel very secure in the relationship." Gibb stressed that empathy doesn't necessarily mean agreement; instead, it conveys acceptance of other people and recognition of their perspectives. Especially when we don't agree with others, it's important to communicate that we respect them as persons. Doing so fosters a supportive communication climate, even if differences exist.

Superiority Versus Equality

Like many of the other communication behaviours we've discussed, the final pair of behaviours affecting climate is most pertinent to the relationship level of meaning. Communication that conveys superiority says "I'm better" or "You are inadequate." We feel understandably on guard when talking with people who act as if they are better than we are. When others act as if they are superior to us, it disconfirms our worth by making us feel inadequate in their eyes.

Consider several messages that convey superiority: "I know a lot more about this than you," "You just don't have my experience," "Is this the best you could do?" "I can't believe you did that," "You really should go to my hairdresser." Each of these messages clearly says "You aren't as good (smart, savvy, competent, attractive) as I am." Predictably, the result is that we protect our self-esteem by defensively shutting out the people and messages that belittle us.

Student Voices

Faye:
My brother never responds to what I say. He listens, but he just gives me nothing back. Sometimes I push him and ask, "What do you think?" or "Does what I'm saying make sense to you?" All he does is shrug or say, "Whatever." He simply won't show any involvement. So I say, why bother talking to him?

Communication that conveys equality is confirming and fosters a supportive interpersonal climate. We feel more relaxed and comfortable when communicating with people who treat us as equals. At the relationship level of meaning, expressed equality communicates respect and equivalent status between people. This promotes an open, unguarded climate in which interaction flows freely. Communicating equality has less to do with actual skills and abilities, which may differ between people, than with interpersonal attitudes. We can have outstanding experience or ability in certain areas and still show regard for others and what they have to contribute to interaction. Creating a climate of equality allows everyone to be involved without fear of being judged inadequate.

Apply the Idea

Assessing Communication Climate in Your Relationships

When communicating with someone, we either use language and behaviours that are likely to solicit a defensive response or a supportive response. Use the checklist below to examine and improve your communication behaviours.

When speaking to or giving feedback to someone, I have been …

Evaluative (judged or name-called)____

    Example: _____

    Rewrite as Descriptive (describing observable behaviour) _____

    _____

Certain (inflexible, overly definitive) ____

    Example: _____

    Rewrite as Provisional (being tentative)_____

    _____

Strategical (plotted, schemed, or guarded) ____

    Example: _____

    Rewrite as Spontaneous (revealing feelings and thoughts in the moment)

    _____

Controlling (instead of trying to solve the problem)____

    Example: _____

    Rewrite as Problem-Orientation _____

    _____

Neutral (showing no empathy) _____

    Example: _____

    Rewrite as Empathy (using dual perspective) _____

    _____

Superior ("I am better than you") _____

    Example: _____

    Rewrite as Equality (believing and acting as equals, forgiving) _____

    _____

Review

To improve defensive climates, try modelling supportive communication. Resist the normal tendencies to respond defensively when a climate feels disconfirming. Instead, focus on being empathic, descriptive, and spontaneous; showing equality and tentativeness; and solving problems.

We've seen that confirmation, which may include recognizing, acknowledging, and endorsing others, is the basis of healthy communication climates. Our discussion of defensive and supportive forms of communication enlightens us about the specific behaviours that tend to make us feel confirmed or disconfirmed. Now that we understand how communication creates interpersonal climates, we're ready to consider guidelines for communicating to create healthy, positive climates for your relationships.

GUIDELINES FOR CREATING AND SUSTAINING HEALTHY CLIMATES

We've seen that communication plays a vital role in creating the climate of relationships. To translate what we've learned into pragmatic information, we'll discuss six guidelines for building and sustaining healthy climates.

ACTIVELY USE COMMUNICATION TO SHAPE CLIMATES

The first principle is to use what you've learned in this chapter to enhance climates in your relationships. Now that you know what generates defensive and supportive climates, you can monitor your communication to make sure it contributes to open, positive interaction. You can identify and stifle disconfirming patterns of talk such as evaluation and superiority. In addition, you can actively work to use supportive communication such as problem orientation and tentativeness.

    Active management of communication climate also involves accepting and growing from the tension generated by relational dialectics. Although friction between contradictory needs can naturally make us uncomfortable,

Concepts at a Glance

Guidelines for Creating and Sustaining Healthy Climates

- Actively use communication to shape climates.
- Accept and confirm others.
- Affirm and assert yourself.
- Self-disclose when appropriate.
- Respect diversity in relationships.
- Respond to criticism constructively.

we should recognize its constructive potential. Communication scholars who have studied dialectics point out that such tension can generate growth and change in relationships (Baxter, 1990, 1993; Wood et al., 1994).

The discomfort of tension pushes us to transform our relationships by changing the dynamics in them. When a couple feels bored, they are motivated to inject novelty into their relationship; when there is too much innovation, they crave rituals and find ways to increase predictability. Our growth as individuals and as partners in relationships depends on honouring our needs for both autonomy and connection, both novelty and routine, and both openness and closedness. When any of these needs is not met, we experience tension that leads to change. Thus, the friction of dialectics keeps us aware of our multiple needs and the importance of fulfilling each of them.

ACCEPT AND CONFIRM OTHERS

Throughout this chapter, we've seen that confirmation is an ethical cornerstone of healthy climates and fulfilling relationships. Although we can understand how important it is, it isn't always easy to give confirmation. Sometimes we disagree with others or don't like certain things they do. Being honest with others is important because it enhances trust between people. Communication research indicates that, in fact, people expect real friends to be sources of honest feedback, even if it isn't always pleasant to hear (Rawlins, 1994). This implies that we should express honest misgivings about our friends' behaviours or other aspects of their identity. False friends tell us only what we want to hear. Deceit, no matter how well intentioned, diminishes personal growth and trust between people. We can offer honest feedback within a context that assures others we value and respect them, as Houston's commentary explains.

It can be difficult to accept and affirm others when we find their needs taxing or discover conflicts between our preferences and those of others. It's not unusual for one partner to desire more closeness than another or for partners to differ in the paths they travel to achieve closeness. These are

Student Voices

Houston:

The best thing my friend Jack ever did for me was to get on my case about experimenting with drugs. He told me it was stupid to play with my mind and to risk my health just for kicks, and he kept at me until I tapered off. What made it work was that Jack was clear that he thought too much of me to stand by when I was hurting myself. A lot of my other so-called friends just stood by and said nothing. Jack is the only one who was a real friend.

common problems, and partners need to discuss them in order to work out mutually agreeable solutions.

For a relationship to work, both partners must be confirmed. Confirmation begins with accepting others and the validity of their needs and preferences. This doesn't mean that you feel the same way or that you defer your own needs. Instead, the point is to recognize and respect others' needs just as you wish them to respect yours. Dual perspective is a primary tool for accepting others because it calls on us to consider them on their own terms. Although intimate talk may be what makes you feel closest to your partner, your partner may experience greater closeness by doing things together. To meet both of your needs, you could take turns honouring each other's preferred paths to closeness. Alternatively, you might combine the two styles of intimacy by doing things together that invite conversation. For example, backpacking is an activity in which talking naturally occurs.

AFFIRM AND ASSERT YOURSELF

It is just as important to affirm and accept yourself as to do that for others. You are no less valuable; your needs are no less important; your preferences are no less valid. It is a misunderstanding to think interpersonal communication principles we've discussed concern only how we behave toward others. Equally, they pertain to how we should treat ourselves. Thus, the principle of confirming people's worth applies just as much to yourself. Likewise, we should respect and honour both our own and others' needs, preferences, and ways of creating intimacy.

Although we can't always meet the needs of all parties in relationships, it is possible to give voice to everyone, including yourself. If your partner favours greater autonomy than you do, you need to recognize that preference and also assert your own. If you don't express your feelings, there's no way others can confirm you. Thus, you should assert your feelings and preferences while simultaneously honouring different ones in others.

Student Voices

Laquanda:

It took me a long time to learn to look out for myself as well as I look out for others. I was always taught to put others first, probably because I'm a girl. I mean, neither of my brothers had that drilled into them. But I did, and for years I would just muffle my needs and whatever I wanted. I concentrated on pleasing others. I thought I was taking care of relationships, but really I was hurting them, because I felt neglected and I resented that. What I'm working on now is learning to take care of myself and others at the same time.

Unlike aggression, assertion doesn't involve putting your needs above those of others. At the same time, assertion doesn't subordinate your needs to those of others, as does deference.

Assertion is a matter of clearly and nonjudgmentally stating what you feel, need, or want (see Table 8.4). This should be done without disparaging others and what they want. You should simply make your feelings known in an open, descriptive manner.

Table 8.4
Aggression, Assertion, and Deference

Aggression	Assertion	Deference
We're going to spend time together.	I'd like to create more time for us.	It's okay with me not to spend time with each other.
Tell me what you're feeling; I insist.	I would like to understand more of how you feel.	If you don't want to talk about how you feel, okay.
I don't care what you want; I'm not going to a movie.	I'm really not up for a movie tonight.	It's fine with me to go to a movie if you want to.

Because relationships include more than one person, they must involve acceptance and affirmation of more than one. Good relationships develop when partners understand and respect each other. The first requirement for this to happen is for each person to communicate honestly how she or he thinks and feels and what she or he wants and needs. A second requirement is for each person to communicate respect for the other's feelings and needs.

Apply the Idea

Communicating Assertively

The statements below are deferential or aggressive. Revise each one so that it is assertive.

1. *I guess your preference for going to the party is more important than my studying.*
2. *I don't need your permission to go out. I'll do what I please.*
3. *I suppose I could work extra next week if you really need a loan.*
4. *I don't like it when you spend time with Tim. Either stop seeing him or we're through.*

We should remember that the meaning of assertion varies among different cultures. For instance, openly asserting your own ideas is considered disrespectful in Korea and parts of China. Even if Koreans or Chinese don't want to do something, they seldom directly turn down another's request. Thus, people with diverse cultural backgrounds may have different ways of affirming and asserting themselves. To communicate effectively with others, we need to learn how they affirm themselves and how they express their feelings directly or indirectly.

We can tolerate sometimes not getting what we want without feeling personally devalued. However, it is far more disconfirming to have our needs go unacknowledged. Even when partners disagree or have conflicting needs, each person can state his or her feelings and express awareness of the other's perspective. Usually there are ways to acknowledge both viewpoints, as Eleanor illustrates.

Student Voices

Eleanor:

About a year after George and I married, he was offered a promotion if he'd move to Halifax. We were living in Calgary at the time, and that's where our families and friends were. I didn't want to move, because I was rooted with my people, but we could both see how important the move was to George's career. The week before we moved, George gave me the greatest present of our lives. He handed me two tickets—one for a round-trip flight from Halifax to Calgary so that I could visit my family, and a second ticket he'd gotten for my best friend so that she could visit me after we moved. I felt he really understood me and had found a way to take care of my needs. I still have the ticket stubs in my box of special memories.

SELF-DISCLOSE WHEN APPROPRIATE

As we noted earlier, self-disclosure allows people to know each other in greater depth. For this reason, it's an important communication skill, especially in the early stages of relationships. Research indicates that appropriate self-disclosure tends to increase trust and feelings of closeness (Cosby, 1973). In addition, self-disclosure can enhance self-esteem and security in relationships because we feel that others accept the most private parts of us. Finally, self-disclosure is an important way to learn about ourselves. As we reveal our hopes, fears, dreams, and feelings, we get responses from others that give us

Self-disclosure can deepen a relationship.

Photo: J. Liburd

new perspectives on who we are. In addition, we gain insight into ourselves by seeing how we interact with others in new situations.

Although self-disclosure has many potential values, it is not always advisable. As we have seen, self-disclosure necessarily involves risks—the risk that others will not accept what we reveal or that they might use it against us. Appropriate self-disclosure minimizes these risks by proceeding slowly and in climates where sufficient trust has been proved. It's wise to test the waters gradually before plunging into major self-disclosures. Begin by revealing information that is personal but not highly intimate or able to damage you if exploited. Before disclosing further, observe how the other person responds to your communication and what she or he does with it. You might also pay attention to whether the other person reciprocates by disclosing personal information to you. Because self-disclosures involve risk, we need to be cautious about when and to whom we reveal ourselves. When trust exists and we want to intensify a relationship, self-disclosure is one of many communication practices that can be healthy. Table 8.5 lists key benefits and risks of self-disclosing communication.

A number of years ago, Joseph Luft and Harry Ingham created a model of different sorts of knowledge that affect self-development. They called the model the Johari Window (Figure 8.3), which is a combination of their first names, Joe and Harry.

The Johari Window

Four types of information are relevant to the self. Open, or public, information is known to both us and others. Your name, height, major, and tastes

Table 8.5
Benefits and Risks of Self-Disclosing Communication

Benefits	Risks
May increase trust	Others may reject us
May increase closeness	Others may think less of us
May enhance self-esteem	Others may violate our confidences
May increase security	
May enhance self-growth	

in music are probably free information that you share easily with others. The blind area contains information that others know about us, but we don't know about ourselves. For example, others may see that we are insecure even though we think we've hidden that well. Others may also recognize needs or feelings that we've not acknowledged to ourselves. The third area includes hidden information, which we know about ourselves but choose not to reveal to most others. You might not tell many people about your vulnerabilities or about traumas in your past because you consider this private information. The unknown area is made up of information about ourselves that neither we nor others know. This consists of your untapped resources, your untried talents, and your reactions to experiences you've never had. You don't know how you will manage a crisis until you've been in one, and you can't tell what kind of parent you would be unless you've had a child.

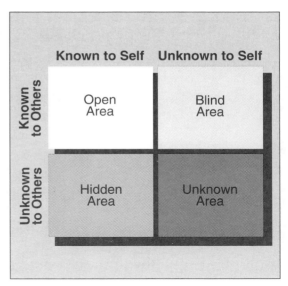

Figure 8.3
The Johari Window

Because a healthy self-concept requires knowledge of ourselves, it's important to gain access to information in our blind and unknown areas. One way to do this is to expand our experiences by entering unfamiliar situations, trying novel things, and experimenting with new kinds of communication. Another way to increase self-knowledge is to interact with others to learn how they see us. We can gain insight into ourselves by reflecting on their perceptions. Others are likely to offer us insights into ourselves only if we make it safe for them to do so. If a friend states a perception of you that you dislike and you become defensive, the friend may not risk sharing other perceptions in the future. If we learn to respond nondefensively to others' perceptions of us, including criticism, then we pave the way for honest appraisals from them.

RESPECT DIVERSITY IN RELATIONSHIPS

Just as individuals differ, so do relationships. There is tremendous variety in what people find comfortable, affirming, and satisfying in interpersonal interaction. It's counterproductive to try to force all people and relationships to fit into a single mode. For example, you might have one friend who enjoys a lot of verbal disclosure and another who prefers less. There's no reason to try to persuade the first friend to disclose less or the second one to be more revealing. Similarly, you may be comfortable with greater closeness in some of your relationships and more autonomy in others. The differences between people create a rich diversity of relationships we can experience.

Even a single relationship varies over time, and we should accept this as normal. Because dialectics generate constant tension, partners continuously shift their patterns and ways of honouring contradictory needs. It's natural to

Josephie:

Communication has a lot to do with climate in work relationships too. When I first came here from Davis Inlet, I had many job interviews. People would say to me, "We've never hired one of you," like Innu are not normal people. They also would say I would have to work hard and was I ready to do that, which told me they assumed I was lazy. When I did get a job, my supervisor watched me much more closely than he watched the local workers. He was always judging.

want more closeness at some times and more distance at others in the life of a relationship. It's also advisable to experiment with different responses to dialectical tensions. You may find it's effective to compromise between closeness and autonomy and to satisfy your desire for openness by sharing certain topics while meeting your need for privacy by not discussing other topics.

Because people and relationships are diverse, we should strive to respect a range of communicative choices and relationship patterns. In addition, we should be cautious about imposing our meaning on others' communication. People from various cultures, including those within Canada, have learned different communication styles. What Westerners consider openness and healthy self-disclosure may feel offensively intrusive to people from some Asian societies. A dramatic, assertive speaking style of some can be misinterpreted as abrasive by others. The best way to understand what others' behaviour means is to ask. This conveys the relational message that they matter to you, and it allows you to gain insight into the interesting diversity around us.

RESPOND TO OTHERS' CRITICISM CONSTRUCTIVELY

A sixth guideline is to learn to respond effectively when others offer constructive criticism. Sometimes others communicate criticism in language that fosters defensiveness: "You are so inconsiderate!" "You're selfish." We tend to react defensively to such judgmental language, and we may dismiss the criticism—think that it isn't true—or just think the other person is being mean. These are natural and understandable responses, but they aren't necessarily constructive ways to deal with criticism. The problem with denying or dismissing criticism is that it deprives us of a chance to learn more about how others see us and to reevaluate our own actions. Refusing to acknowledge others' criticism is also likely to erect barriers in relationships.

We have discussed giving feedback in a respectful manner that confirms the relationship climate. Now, let's examine how to receive feedback in a nondefensive manner. There are four steps.

Count to 10

A good response to criticism is to begin by counting to 10. This little reminder helps you edit out your first response, which may not be facilitative. If, when criticized, your first response is to cry or get "stony-faced," you create a barrier. Conversely, if your first response is an aggressive sarcastic remark, you can create more conflict than is already present. Counting to 10 lets you calm yourself and become mindful.

Seek More Information

The second step is seeking more information: "What do you mean I'm inconsiderate?" "What do I do that you see as selfish?" Asking these questions allows you to get concrete information. Remember that others may not have your understanding of how to communicate effectively. Thus, they may use abstract terms that you can help them translate into specifics to be addressed. They may also use you–language ("You hurt me") that you can explore to determine if there is something that you do to which they respond by feeling hurt.

Consider Criticism Thoughtfully

The third step in responding constructively to criticism is to consider it thoughtfully. Is the criticism valid? Are you inconsiderate in some ways? Are you selfish in some respects? If after reflection you don't think the criticism is accurate, offer your interpretation of the behaviours the other perceived as inconsiderate or selfish. You might say, "I can see how you might feel it's selfish of me to go out with my friends so often, but to me it's because I care about them, just like I spend time with you because I care about you." Or you might say, "I can see where it would seem inconsiderate that I didn't call, but the battery on my cell phone was dead, and I didn't want to delay getting here by stopping to call. I wanted to be with you as soon as possible."

Notice that both of the responses above not only offer an alternative interpretation of particular behaviour but also affirm the other person and his or her worth to you.

If you decide that the criticism is valid, then consider whether you want to change how you act. Do you want to be perceived by others as inconsiderate or selfish? If not, you can choose to change how you act. For suggestions on how to bring about changes in yourself, you may want to review the guidelines offered at the end of Chapter 2.

Concepts at a Glance

Responding to Criticism

1. Count to 10.
2. Seek more information.
3. Consider criticism thoughtfully.
   - Own your behaviour.
   - Offer an interpretation.
   - Affirm the critic.
4. Thank the critic.

Frieda:

I didn't appreciate it when my roommate called me a slob. But because of what I've learned in this course, I didn't just ignore what Marie said or fire back an insult to her. Instead, I asked her what she meant. She told me she hated coming home to our apartment and finding my clothes on the bathroom floor and dishes in the sink. Well, I could deal with that. So I resolved to pick my clothes up and wash my dishes before I left each day. Before, if this had happened, I would have felt hurt and probably wouldn't have done anything different. But I felt less hurt and more in control because of how I responded to Marie's criticism, and I know she's a lot happier living with me now!

Thank the Critic

The final step is to thank the person who offered the criticism. At first, this may seem absurd. After all, criticism doesn't feel good, so it's hard to be grateful. But on second thought, you may realize that criticism is a gift. It offers us opportunities to see ourselves through others' eyes. In addition, it gives us insight into how others feel about us and what we do. Both of these effects of criticism can foster personal growth and healthy relationships that allow honest expression of feelings. Even if we disagree with a criticism, we should let others know we are glad they shared their perceptions of us. This keeps the door open for communication in the future.

The guidelines we've discussed combine respect for self, others, and relationships with communication that fosters healthy, affirming climates for connections with others. We can transform our relationships when we take responsibility for shaping interpersonal climates and when we develop the knowledge and communication skills to do so.

Chapter Summary

In this chapter, we've explored personal relationships and the communication climates that make them more or less satisfying. Four elements of healthy interpersonal connections are investment, commitment, trust, and comfort with relational dialectics. Even though love is important for intimacy, it alone is insufficient. To it we must add personal choices to invest ourselves, to make enduring commitments to remain with others even in hard times, to develop trust, and to learn to manage the ongoing dialectical tensions that promote change and growth.

Perhaps the most basic requirement for healthy communication climates is confirmation. Each of us wants to feel valued, especially by those for whom we care most deeply. When partners recognize, acknowledge, and endorse each other, they give the important gift of confirmation. They communicate "You matter to me." We discussed particular kinds of communication that foster supportive and defensive climates in relationships. Defensiveness is bred by evaluation, certainty, superiority, strategies, control, and neutrality. More supportive climates arise from communication that is descriptive, provisional, equal, spontaneous, empathic, and problem-oriented.

To close the chapter, we considered six guidelines for building healthy communication climates. The first one is to assume responsibility for communicating in ways that actively enhance the mood of a relationship. Second, we should accept and confirm our friends and romantic partners, communicating that we respect them, even though we may not always agree with them or feel the same as they do. The third guideline is a companion to the second one: We should accept and confirm ourselves just as fully as we do others. Each of us is entitled to assert our own thoughts, feelings, and needs. Doing so allows us to honour ourselves and to help our partners understand us. A fourth guideline is to self-disclose when appropriate so that we increase our security in relationships and add to the information we have about ourselves. Fifth, we should realize that diversity in relationships is a source of personal and interpersonal growth. People vary widely, as do the relationship patterns and forms they prefer. By respecting differences among us, we all expand our insights into the fascinating array of ways that humans form and sustain intimate relations. Finally, personal growth and healthy relationships are fostered by dealing constructively with criticism.

In the next three chapters, we'll look in greater detail at personal relationships. Chapter 9 extends our discussion of climate by examining how we can create constructive relationship contexts for dealing effectively with conflict. Chapter 10 discusses friendships and romantic relationships, and Chapter 11 examines relationships in the workplace. In each chapter, we consider what these relationships are, how communication affects them, and how we might cope with some of the inevitable problems and challenges of sustaining these different relationships over time. What we have learned about climate, as well as what we've learned about other facets of interpersonal communication in earlier chapters, will serve as a foundation for a more in-depth look at the dynamics of both close relationships and workplace relationships.

Key Concepts

- assertion
- commitment
- ethnocentrism
- interpersonal climate
- investment
- relational dialectics
- self-disclosure
- trust

For Further Thought and Discussion

1. Have you found it difficult to confirm others when you disagree with them? If so, does reading this chapter help you distinguish among recognition, acknowledgment, and endorsement? Can you distinguish between confirming others as persons and endorsing particular ideas or behaviours?

2. What ethical principles are implied in communication that confirms and disconfirms others? Is it wrong to disconfirm others? All others? Intimates?

3. To what extent do you honour yourself and others in communication situations? Do you give equal attention to both your needs and those of others? If not, focus on balancing your efforts to confirm yourself and others in future interactions.

4. Think of an interaction in which you felt disconfirmed and defensive. Describe how others in the situation communicated toward you. How many of Gibb's defensive-producing communication behaviours can you identify as present in the situation?

5. How often are you deferential, assertive, and aggressive in your communication? What are the situations and relationships in which each kind of behaviour is most likely for you? Do the behaviours you select advance your own goals and your relationships?

6. Use your InfoTrac College Edition to locate recent reports on assertion. How do researchers define assertion? Do they advocate any guidelines for when assertiveness is appropriate and inappropriate?

7. Practise following the guidelines in this chapter for responding to criticism. What happens when you listen to criticism without becoming angry and when you let others know you appreciate their perceptions of you and your behaviour?

9

Managing Conflict in Relationships

Everyday Encounters
By Stephen Lee

Just as Chloe has observed, there are many responses to conflict, and our response to conflict determines the comfort and health of our relationships. Managing conflict in relationships will require all the skills and attitudes we have discussed so far. Consider the following dialogue.

Dave: You really made me angry when you flirted with other guys at the party last night.

Pam: Yeah, well you made me angry that you didn't know when to stop drinking.

Dave: Well, maybe I was drinking a lot because my girlfriend was too busy dancing with other guys to pay any attention to me.

Pam: Well, maybe I'd pay more attention to you if you'd clean up your act. Why don't you get serious about graduate school and start acting responsible?

Dave: I'll do that right after you quit smoking and spend some time with me instead of always burying yourself in readings for your classes.

Pam: You just say that because you're jealous that I'm in a graduate program and you're not.

Dave: I wouldn't exactly call social work much of a graduate program.

Pam: At least it's a graduate program. That's more than you have.

Dave: You never do anything but complain, complain, complain. You really are a drag.

Pam: It takes one to know one.

Clearly Dave and Pam are having trouble. The real problem isn't the issues they're discussing, but how they manage conflict. Dave and Pam are not communicating constructively. What we've learned in previous chapters helps us understand how negative communication fuels discord between them. For example, Dave launched the conversation with you–language. Instead of owning his anger, he blamed Pam for it. In turn, she didn't own her anger. Dave may also have misidentified what he was feeling. Is he really feeling angry at Pam, or is he hurt that she spent more time with others than him? Both Dave and Pam disconfirmed the other with personal attacks. Further, neither of them really recognized and acknowledged the other's point of view. Each of them listened defensively and engaged in ambushing the other. Pam and Dave pursued their individual agendas and failed to connect with each other. The result is that Pam and Dave clash. Their argument did nothing for either of them or the relationship.

Let's start the conversation over and see how more positive communication might improve what happens.

Dave: I felt hurt when you flirted with other guys at the party last night, and then I felt angry. *Dave identifies hurt as the more basic feeling. He also owns his feelings.*

Photo: © Photodisc

Pam: I can understand that. I know you don't like it when I pay attention to other men. *She acknowledges Dave's feelings.* I got upset when you drank too much, and I want you to understand how I feel about that. *Pam owns her feelings and asserts her needs in the situation.*

Dave: You're right. I know you hate it when I drink a lot. *He acknowledges and endorses her concern.*

Pam: Well, I guess neither of us was at our best last night. *She shares responsibility for what happened.* I was really tired, so I probably got more irritated than I usually would.

Dave: And I've been feeling kind of down because you're so focused on your graduate program, and I can't seem to get started. *Because an affirming climate has been created, Dave can disclose his deeper worries to Pam.*

Pam: I know you feel discouraged right now. *She again acknowledges his feelings.* I would too. *She shows empathy.* But you're so smart, and you'll do great once you settle on a course of action. *She confirms him by showing that she believes in him.* Why don't we put our heads together to sort through some of the options and try to figure out how you can proceed. *She offers support and shows commitment to his welfare.*

Dave: That would really help me. I just need to talk through a lot of possibilities. *He acknowledges her offer of help.* I'd really like to get your perspective on some ideas I've got. *He shows he values her viewpoint.*

Pam: I've got all the time you want. *She confirms his value and her commitment to the relationship. Her comment also addresses Dave's relationship-level concern that she may not want to spend time with him.*

Dave: (smile) Okay, and I promise I won't drink while we're talking. *He uses humour to restore good climate. On the relationship-level of meaning, he is asking, "Are we okay now?"*

Pam: (smile) And I promise I won't flirt with other guys while we're talking. *She responds to his relationship-level message by signalling that she too feels friendly again.*

The conflict proceeded very differently in the second instance. Both Pam and Dave owned their feelings and confirmed each other by acknowledging expressed concerns. The supportive climate they established enabled Dave to reveal deeper worries that lay below his opening complaint about flirting, and Pam responded supportively to his disclosure. They also came up with a plan to address Dave's worries. Especially important, they communicated effectively at the relationship level of meaning. The relationship probably will be strengthened by how they managed their conflict in the second scenario.

Not all conflicts can be turned around as effectively as this one. There is no magic bullet for handling conflict constructively. Even skillful communication is not a remedy for all of the tensions that come up in relationships. However, communication is one of the most important influences on how conflict affects relationships. Skillful speaking and listening help us manage conflict, regardless of the difficulties we face. Research shows that communication problems contribute to dissatisfaction with relationships and

The expressed struggle is the "topic" but not always the "issue" in a relationship. What topics do you argue about? What might the real issues be?

Photo: © Photodisc

Photo: © Photodisc

breakups (Dindia & Fitzpatrick, 1985). We also know that positive communication is one of the strongest influences on long-term satisfaction (Markman, 1981). Communication powerfully sculpts conflict and its consequences.

In this chapter, we'll explore how communication and conflict weave together in interpersonal relationships. We'll begin by defining conflict. Next, we'll consider principles of conflict so that we understand what it is and the roles it plays in our relationships. Third, we'll consider basic orientations to conflict and the ways in which individuals' approaches to conflict are shaped by their membership in various social groups. The fourth section of the chapter focuses on specific communication patterns that enhance or impede constructive management of conflict. We'll conclude by identifying guidelines for communicating effectively when engaging in conflict.

DEFINING CONFLICT

We've all experienced conflict in our relationships, so we have a general idea of what it is. Yet, our general ideas may not help us zero in on what conflict involves and how it operates in relationships. A clear definition of **conflict** is that it exists when individuals who depend on each other express different views, interests, or goals and perceive their views as incompatible or oppositional. We'll look more closely at each part of this definition.

EXPRESSED DISAGREEMENT

Conflict is expressed disagreement, struggle, or discord. Thus, it is not conflict if we don't recognize disagreement or anger or if we repress it completely so that it is not expressed at all. Conflict involves some means of expressing disagreements or tensions.

We express disagreement both verbally and nonverbally. Shooting daggers with your eyes communicates anger and discord every bit as clearly as saying "I'm angry with you." Walking out on a conversation and slamming a door express hostility, as does refusing to talk to someone. Often we express conflict with both verbal and nonverbal communication. For instance, you might shout, "I'm so angry with you" while slamming your fist on a desk. The verbal communication—the words themselves—states the anger, while the nonverbal communication—volume and kinesics—emphasizes the extent of the anger.

Although all conflict is expressed, how it is expressed varies. Some means of expressing disagreement are overt, such as saying "I'm furious with you." Other modes of communicating conflict are more covert, such as

Concepts at a Glance

Three Elements of Conflict

- Expressed disagreement
- Interdependence
- Opposition

deliberately not answering the phone because you don't want to talk to someone. In both cases, the individuals realize they have differences and they both express their disagreements, although in distinct ways.

INTERDEPENDENCE

Conflict can occur only between people who depend on each other. Differences don't have to be resolved between people who don't affect each other. You may not like the way your neighbour landscaped his yard but you wouldn't necessarily be in conflict with him. You and your in-laws may have differing preferences about dogs, but those preferences don't interfere with your relationship as long as you each leave your dog home when you visit. Because you are not dependent on your in-laws or your neighbours on matters of dogs and landscaping, you don't have conflicts over these issues.

Conflict occurs because people depend on each other and need each other's agreement or approval. If you and your partner disagreed on pets, then there might be conflict because you live together and your pets affect both of you. Two friends who have agreed to spend the evening together could have conflict if they disagreed on what to do or which film to see. Couples often experience disagreements about money. If one person wants to save money or pay off bills and the other wants to splurge on a vacation, conflict is likely to arise.

We may disagree with others and even make negative judgments of them, but that alone doesn't mean conflict will occur. Conflict exists only when it is expressed by individuals who affect one another. Lenore, a 20-year-old student, explains that conflict assumes connection.

|Student Voices|

Lenore:
It's kind of strange, but you really don't fight with people who don't matter. With a lot of guys I dated, if I didn't like something they did, I'd just let it go because they weren't important enough for the hassle. But Rod and I argue a lot, because we do affect each other. Maybe fighting is a sign that people care about each other.

OPPOSITION

Conflict is more than just having differences. We disagree with many people about many things, but this doesn't invariably lead to conflict. Conflict involves opposition, which is a tension between goals, preferences, or decisions that are perceived as incompatible. If you are in a student work group and you want an A on your assignment, but one of your group members is happy with a C, you would be in conflict. The goals are incompatible. Likewise, if there is only one position of employment available and you and a friend both apply, you are in direct competition. Similarly, if two friends are attracted to the same person, there is a perceived lack of resources, namely affection. This can create conflict. In other words, conflict involves two perceptions: (1) the perception that our concerns are at odds with those of another and (2) the perception that we and another must reconcile our differences. When those two perceptions exist, so does conflict.

PRINCIPLES OF CONFLICT

Concepts at a Glance

Four Principles of Conflict

- Conflict is natural.
- Conflict may be overt or covert.
- Conflict may be managed well or poorly.
- Conflict may be good.

Many people fear conflict and view it as negative. That is a misunderstanding of what conflict is and how it operates. To address that and other misunderstandings, we'll discuss four principles of conflict.

CONFLICT IS A NATURAL PROCESS IN ALL RELATIONSHIPS

Conflict is a normal, inevitable part of all interpersonal relationships. When people matter to each other and affect each other, disagreements are unavoidable. You like meat, and your friend is a strict vegetarian. You prefer to rent a condo and avoid the hassles of home ownership, but your mate's fondest dream is to own a home. You like to work alone, and your co-worker likes to interact on teams. You believe money should be enjoyed, and your partner lives by the philosophy of saving for a rainy day. You want to move where there's a great job for you, but the location has no career prospects for your partner. Again and again, we find ourselves seemingly at odds with people who matter to us. When this happens, we have to resolve the differences, preferably in a way that doesn't harm the relationship.

The presence of conflict does not indicate a relationship is unhealthy or in trouble, although how partners manage conflict does influence relational health. Actually, conflict indicates that individuals are involved with each other. If they weren't, there would be no need to resolve differences. This is a good point to keep in mind when conflicts arise because it reminds us that a strong connection underlies even disagreement.

Ron's insight is important. He has realized that conflict is an undercurrent in his family, but it remains unresolved because people won't discuss tensions. Most of us have attitudes about conflict that reflect scripts we learned in our families. Like Ron, some of us were taught that conflict is bad and should be avoided, whereas others learned that airing differences is healthy.

Student Voices

Ron:

It sounds funny, but the biggest thing my fiancée and I fight about is whether it's okay to fight. I was brought up not to argue and to think that conflict is bad. In her family, people did argue a lot, and she thinks it is healthy. What I'm coming to realize is that there is a lot of conflict in my family but it's hidden, so it never gets dealt with very well. I've seen her and her parents really go at it, but, I have to admit, they work through their differences, and people in my family don't.

Apply the Idea

Understanding Your Conflict Script

What conflict script did you learn in your family? Think back to your childhood and adolescence and try to remember what implicit rules for conflict your family modelled and perhaps taught.

- *Did people disagree openly with each other?*
- *What was said or done when disagreements surfaced? Was it verbal? Was it physical? Was it respectful? Did your parents encourage open discussion of differences?*
- *How do you currently reflect your family's conflict script? Now that you can edit family scripts and author your own, how would you like to deal with conflict?*

Read on in this chapter to consider ways you might write a conflict script that is constructive and reflects your values.

Is your conflict style overt or covert?

Photo: M. Salez

Although conflict itself is inevitable, how we manage it is not predetermined. We can deal with differences more or less effectively, and our choices have personal and relational impact.

CONFLICT MAY BE OVERT OR COVERT

When we defined conflict, we noted that disagreement could be expressed either overtly or covertly. We'll now elaborate that point. Overt conflict is out in the open and explicit. It exists when individuals deal with their differences

Is this an example of overt or covert conflict?

Photo: © Photodisc

Concepts at a Glance

Destructive Games

- Blemish
- NIGYYSOB
- Mine is Worse Than Yours
- Yes, But

in a straightforward manner. They might calmly discuss their disagreement in a responsible assertive way, intensely argue about ideas, or engage in a shouting match. Overt conflict may also involve directly aggressive acts such as physical or verbal attacks, which are usually destructive to the relationship! **Assertion** and **aggression** are forms of overt conflict.

Yet, much conflict isn't overt. Covert conflict is hidden and often unacknowledged to others. It may be expressed as **nonassertion** by silence or complaining to a third party. Partners may also camouflage disagreements and express their feelings indirectly. When angry, a person may deliberately do something to hurt or upset a partner. For instance, Janet is annoyed because her roommate Myra has rearranged Janet's half of the apartment, so when Myra is studying, Janet turns the stereo on at high volume. Knowing that Elliott hates to be kept waiting, his son intentionally arrives 20 minutes late for a dinner date. These individuals expressed their anger indirectly, and conflict was covert. This is the most common form of covert conflict called passive aggression.

Passive aggression is aggression that is denied or disguised by the aggressor. This allows someone who is angry to vent the anger while also denying that she or he is doing so. If Dedra doesn't call her mother every week, her mother forgets to send Dedra a cheque for spending money. When Charles has obnoxious customers at the restaurant where he waits tables, he accidentally spills something on them. When Takeshi won't forgo studying to go out, Yumiko coincidentally decides to call friends and talk to them in the room adjacent to Takeshi. Passive aggressive behaviours are efforts to punish another person without accepting responsibility for the punishment. They undercut the possibility of honest, healthy relationships.

Much covert conflict takes place in **games,** which Eric Berne (1964) catalogued in a fascinating book titled *Games People Play.* Games often involve passive aggression, but they can be much more complicated than that. According to Berne, games are highly patterned interactions in which the real conflicts are hidden or denied, and a counterfeit excuse is created for arguing or criticizing. In addition to being highly patterned, games also require two players if they are to continue. In contrast, passive aggression doesn't require significant cooperation from the target of aggression.

The nature of games will become clear if we analyze a few.

In the game called "Blemish," one person pretends to be complimentary but actually puts another down. If Ann asks her friend if she looks okay for an important interview, the friend could respond, "Gee, you look really great with the new suit and hair style. There's just this one little thing. You seem to be kind of overweight lately. Your stomach and hips look big, and that suit doesn't hide the extra pounds." The friend is playing "Blemish" because she focuses on one thing that is wrong and downplays all that is right. Her unexpressed anger or resentment surfaces covertly.

Another game is "NIGYYSOB" ("Now I've Got You, You Son of a Bitch"). In this one, an individual deliberately sets another person up for a fall.

Staci:

I was recently in a relationship that I thought was the greatest ever strictly because we never fought. I've had relationships with lots of arguments, so I thought it was fabulous that Steve and I never fought. I grew up with a twice-divorced mom, and I've seen her and my father and stepfather really go at it. All I ever wanted was a conflict-free relationship because I thought that would be a good relationship. One time Steve called me to say he had to break our date to cover at work for another guy. All I did was sigh and say, "Fine, if that is what you need to do." But it wasn't fine with me; I resented his putting the other guy ahead of me. A little later he called me back to say he'd changed his mind and would join me and two friends of ours. So, what happened? He sat at the table all night and barely said two words. I was so mad, but I didn't say a word about the evening and neither did he. Just a month later we broke up. Even then, there was no overt conflict.

Knowing that his partner has poor taste in furniture, Kevin asks him to pick out a new chair for their home. When it arrives and predictably is ugly, Kevin criticizes his partner. He worked to find a way to make him fail and then pounced on him when he did. Another game is "Mine Is Worse than Yours." Suppose you tell a friend that you are overloaded with two tests and a paper due next week, and your friend says, "You think that's bad? Listen to this: I have two tests, three papers, and an oral report all due in the next two weeks." Your friend expressed no concern for your plight; rather, he told you that his situation is worse. In this game, people try to monopolize rather than to listen and respond to each other.

"Yes, But" is a game in which a person pretends to be asking for help but then refuses all help that's offered. Doing this allows the player to make the other person feel inadequate for being unable to help. Lorna asks her boyfriend to help her figure out how to better manage her money. When he suggests she should spend less, Lorna says, "Yes, but I don't buy anything I don't need." When he suggests she might work extra hours at her job, she responds, "Yes, but that would cut into my free time." When he mentions she could get a job that pays more per hour, Lorna says, "Yes, but I really like the people where I work now." When he points out that she could save a lot by packing lunches instead of buying them, she replies, "Yes, but I'd have to get up earlier." "Yes, But" continues until the person trying to help finally

Chuck:

My parents specialize in games. Dad likes to set Mom up by asking her to take care of some financial business or get the car fixed. Then he explodes about what she does. I think he is just trying to find excuses for chewing her out. Mom also plays games. Her favourite is Blemish. She always finds something wrong with an idea or a paper I've written or a vacation or whatever. Then she just harps and harps on the defect. Sometimes being around them is like being in a minefield.

gives up in defeat. Then the initiator of the game can complain, "You didn't help me."

Games and passive aggression are ineffective ways to manage conflict. Both approaches are dishonest, because they camouflage the real issues behind counterfeit communication. As long as conflict remains hidden or disguised, it's virtually impossible for friends and romantic partners to resolve the real problems.

Apply the Idea

Identifying Games in Your Communication

Apply what you've read about covert conflict to your own life. Describe an example of when you or someone you have a relationship with played each of these games:

Blemish

NIGYYSOB

Mine Is Worse than Yours

Yes, But

What was accomplished by playing the game? Were the real conflicts addressed?

Review

Conflict may be overtly expressed as assertion (responsible, active behaviour) or aggression (threatening behaviour) or it may be covertly expressed as nonassertion (silence or complaining) or passive aggression (game-playing and sabotage).

CONFLICT MAY BE MANAGED WELL OR POORLY

The third principle is that conflict may be managed more or less constructively. Because conflict is natural and inevitable, we need to learn to deal with it in ways that benefit both our relationships and us as individuals. People respond to conflict in a variety of ways, ranging from physical attack to verbal aggression to reflective problem-solving. Although each method may resolve differences, some are clearly preferable to others. Depending on how we handle disagreements, conflict can either promote continuing attachment or split a relationship apart.

One of the main reasons that conflict is handled poorly is because it often involves intense feelings that many people do not know how to identify or express. We may feel deep disappointment, resentment, or anger toward someone we care about, and this is difficult to manage. Our discussion in Chapter 4 should help you recognize what you are feeling and choose effective means of communicating your emotions in conflict situations. Other skills we've discussed—such as using I–language and monitoring the self-serving bias—will also help you manage the feelings that often accompany conflict.

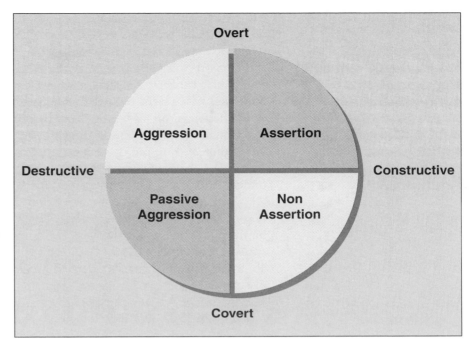

Figure 9.1
Overt and Covert Conflict Styles

Communication skills are especially important when dealing with differences. We need to know how particular behaviours affect interpersonal conflict so that we can make intelligent decisions about how to act. Without a base of good information about communication and conflict, we can only follow scripts that we have learned from previous interactions and observations. Unfortunately, not all of us have learned constructive scripts for managing conflict. Later in this chapter, we'll identify specific kinds of communication that foster healthy and unhealthy conflict.

Some forms of communication can actually enhance relationships as well as resolve disagreements effectively. Other kinds of communication can erode trust, climate, and the self-esteem of partners. Learning how different kinds of communication affect relationships, individuals, and resolution of conflict empowers you to make informed choices about how to deal with conflict in your relationships. The ideas and skills we cover in this chapter should give you a better understanding of how to manage conflict effectively so that it cultivates personal growth and relationship maturity.

CONFLICT MAY BE GOOD

Although we tend to think of conflict negatively, actually it can be beneficial in a number of ways. When managed constructively, conflict can help us grow as individuals and strengthen our relationships. We can enlarge our

Danger   Opportunity

Figure 9.2
Chinese Character for "Crisis"

perspectives when we engage in conflicts that propel personal growth and learning (see Figure 9.2). We deepen insight into our ideas and feelings when we have to express them and consider critical responses. Sometimes this supports our own identity by clarifying how we differ from others. Romantic partners indicated that one value of differences was strengthening awareness of partners' individuality (Wood et al., 1994).

Differences can also prompt personal growth by helping us see when it's appropriate to change our minds. Conflict allows us to consider points of view different from our own. Based on what we learn, we may change our opinions, behaviours, or goals. As Jens points out, conflict can enhance understanding and spur positive personal growth.

Conflict can also benefit relationships. In fact, a book titled *The Intimate Enemy: How to Fight Fair in Love and Marriage* states that verbal conflict between intimates is highly constructive and desirable if it is managed constructively (Bach & Wyden, 1973). One potential benefit of conflict is its ability to expand partners' understandings of each other. What begins as a discussion of some particular issue usually winds up providing broader information about why partners feel as they do and what meanings they attach to the issue. In the example that opened this chapter, the original complaint about Pam's flirting led to the discovery that Dave felt insecure about his identity and Pam's respect for him, because she was succeeding in graduate work and he wasn't. Once his concern emerged, the couple could address the real issue.

Ron Arnett (1986), a scholar of communication ethics, points out that lack of conflict isn't necessarily a symptom of a healthy relationship. It's at least as likely that low levels of conflict reflect lack of emotional depth between partners or repression of disagreements. Researchers report that there is no association between the number of arguments spouses have and marital happiness (Howard & Dawes, 1976). Some of the respondents in the study mentioned previously (Wood et al., 1994) said differences energized their relationships by providing zest and excitement. This may explain the inter-

Student Voices

Jens:
We were arguing in class about whether nursing and teaching should be declared essential services in Canada and therefore exempt from strikes. I was very opposed to strikes and job action, especially in health care, but after listening to two of the nursing students in my class talk about inequity, I really saw a different point of view. I thought our positions were irresolvable, but the argument was actually pretty enlightening.

esting finding that sexual activity and arguments are positively related. It seems that partners who argue more also have livelier sex lives (Howard & Dawes, 1976). One group of researchers refers to this as "keeping a positive balance in the marital bank account" (Gottman et al, 1976b). When conflict is managed well, it can be constructive for both individuals and relationships.

|*Student Voices*|

Jana:

Geoff and I have a pretty intense relationship. We fight a lot, and we fight hard. Some of my friends think this is bad, but we don't. Nothing is brushed under the carpet in our relationship. If either of us is angry or upset about something, we hash it out then and there. But we are just as intense in positive ways. Geoff lets me know all the time that he loves me, and I am always hugging and kissing him. I guess you could just say our relationship is passionate—in bad moments and good ones.

To review, we've discussed four basic principles of conflict. First, we noted that conflict is both natural and inevitable in interpersonal relationships. Second, we discovered that conflict may be overtly communicated or covertly expressed through indirect communication or games that camouflage real issues. The third principle is that how we manage conflict influences its resolution and its impact on interpersonal climates. Finally, we saw that conflict can be constructive for both individuals and relationships. We can now build on these principles by discussing diverse ways people think about and respond to conflict.

APPROACHES TO CONFLICT

We've noted that conflict can be managed in various ways, some more effective than others. We now want to look at three distinct orientations toward conflict. Each orientation has fairly predictable consequences on how interaction proceeds.

A Mohawk warrior punches a Canadian soldier during a fight that took place on the Kanasehtake Reserve Sept. 18, 1990.

Photo: © CP Picture Archive

Our orientations toward conflict affect how we approach conflict situations. Based on what we've learned from social groups and personal experiences, we approach conflict from one of three basic orientations. Each is appropriate in some relationships and situations; the challenge is to know when a particular approach is constructive.

LOSE–LOSE

A **lose–lose** orientation assumes that conflict results in losses for everyone. Behind this approach to conflict is the belief that expressing disagreement is unhealthy and destructive for everyone. A wife might feel that conflicts over money hurt her, her husband, and the marriage. Similarly, a person may not argue with a friend, believing the result would be wounded pride for both of them. The lose–lose view presumes that conflict cannot produce winners or benefits.

Student Voices

Theo:

I hate to fight with friends. I do just about anything to avoid an argument. But sometimes what I have to do is sacrifice my preferences or even my rights just to avoid conflict. And sometimes I have to go along with something I don't believe in or think is right. I'm starting to think that maybe conflict would be better than avoiding it—at least in some cases.

Theo's insight is worth our attention. When we seek to avoid conflict at all costs, the costs may be high indeed. We may have to defer our own needs or rights, and we may feel unable to give honest feedback to others. Avoiding conflict doesn't necessarily avoid undesirable consequences, as Theo has discovered.

Although the lose–lose orientation is not usually beneficial in dealing with conflicts in close relationships, it has merit in some circumstances. One obvious value of this approach is that it prompts us to ask whether we want or need to engage in conflict. Some issues aren't worth the energy and the discomfort that conflict arouses. We might have a more peaceful planet if national leaders believed that war produces only losers, regardless of whether one side officially wins.

Communication Notes

Japanese and American Styles of Negotiation

The differences between Japanese and American views of conflict shape specific communication patterns during business negotiations. Consider how each of the following negotiation strategies reflects values typical of Japanese or U.S. society.

Japanese Style	American Style
Understate your own initial position or state it vaguely to allow the other room to state his or her position.	Overstate initial position to establish a strong image.
Find informal ways to let the other person know your bottom line in order to move agreement forward without directly confronting the other with your bottom line.	Keep your bottom line secret from the other person to preserve your power and gain the most.
Look for areas of agreement and focus talk on them.	Where there are differences, assert your position and attempt to win the other's assent.
Avoid confrontation.	Be adversarial.
Work to make sure that neither you nor the other person fails.	Work to win all you can.

Source: Weiss, S. E. (1987). The changing logic of a former minor power. In H. Binnendijk (Ed.), *National negotiating styles.* Washington, DC: Department of State, (pp. 44–74).

WIN–LOSE

Win–lose orientations assume one person wins at the expense of the other. A person who sees conflict as a win–lose matter thinks disagreements are battles that can have only one victor. What one person gains is at the other's loss; what one person loses benefits the other. Disagreements are seen as zero-sum games in which there is no possibility for everyone to benefit.

The win–lose orientation is cultivated in cultures that place value on individualism, self-assertion, and competition. We know that Canada is largely an individualistic society that values those qualities. Other cultures, such as Japan, place priority on quite different values: cooperation, keeping others from failing, and finding areas of agreement. Not surprisingly, the win–lose orientation to conflict is more common in the West than in Japan. Examine the interesting American account of "Japanese and American Styles of Negotiation."

Reflective Exercise

In what way are Canadians different from and similar to Americans in the approach to business abroad? What assumptions do you make when you are in another country?

Partners who disagree about whether to move to a new location might adopt a win–lose orientation. In turn, this would lock them into a yes–no view in which only two alternatives are seen: move or stay put. The win–lose orientation virtually guarantees that the individuals won't make a strong effort to find or create a mutually acceptable solution, such as moving to a third place that meets both partners' needs or having a long-distance relationship so that each person can have the best individual location. The more person A argues for moving, the more person B argues for not moving. Eventually one of them "wins" but at the cost of the other and the relationship. A win–lose orientation toward conflict tends to undermine relationships, because someone has to lose. There is no possibility that both can win, much less that the relationship can.

Before you dismiss win–lose as a totally unconstructive view of conflict, let's consider when it might be effective. Win–lose can be appropriate when we have low commitment to a relationship and little desire to take care of the person with whom we disagree. When you're buying a car, for instance, you want the best deal you can get, and you have little concern for the dealer's profit. Similarly, if a member of your family needed medical care and you disagreed with the doctor's approach, you might well ignore the doctor's feelings and reputation in order to win the care you want for your loved one.

WIN–WIN

Win–win orientations assume there are usually ways to resolve differences so that everyone gains. For people who view conflict as win–win, the goal is to come up with a resolution that everyone involved can accept. Ideally, the solution might be that everyone felt was the best possible one. When both people are committed to finding a solution that pleases both, a win–win resolution to conflict is possible.

Consider this example. Two close friends worked through a conflict using the win–win orientation. After three years of renting a house, Becker and Shelly wanted to build their own home. The conflict arose because Shelly was willing to borrow heavily to pay for construction of the home, and Becker was not willing to take on a serious debt. Becker wanted to save money before they built their home; Shelly wanted to borrow and not wait. For several months they talked and talked, neither willing to defer to the other, and neither willing to force a position. One day Becker jokingly reminded Shelly that she had done some construction work in the past. Becker suggested that maybe Shelly could build their house herself. After initially laughing, Shelly took the idea seriously and realized she could do some of the building and be the general contractor for the rest of the construction. With Shelly in charge, the couple would have to borrow far less money to build. Becker volunteered to take a second job so that Shelly could take time off from work during the building. Shelly was able to keep a daily check on the construction and to incorporate special touches that reflect her and Becker's lifestyle. When the house was finished, both Becker and Shelly loved it and agreed it was more their kind of house than one that strangers would have built. Because they kept talking and kept looking for a solution both could celebrate, they were able to create a plan that was better than either of their original ideas.

Student Voices

Tess:

One of the roughest issues for Jerry and me was when he started working most nights. The time after dinner had always been "our time." When Jerry took the new job, he had to stay in constant contact with the Vancouver office. Jerry and I used to do something together at 6 p.m., but because of the time difference, it's only 3 p.m. on the West Coast, and the business day is still going. I was hurt that he no longer had time for us, and he was angry that I wanted time he needed for business. We kept talking and came up with the idea of spending a day together each weekend, which we'd never done. Although my ideal would still be to share evenings, this solution keeps us in touch with each other.

As Tess's story illustrates, not all win–win solutions maximize each person's preferences. Sometimes people can't find or create a solution that is each person's ideal. In those cases, each person may be able to redefine his or her priorities. Each individual may make some accommodations in order to build a solution that lets the other win also. When partners adopt win–win views of conflict, they often discover solutions that neither had thought of previously. This happens because they are committed to their own and the other's satisfaction. Sometimes win–win attitudes result in compromises that satisfy enough of each person's needs to provide confirmation and to protect the health of the relationship.

Apply the Idea

Identifying Orientations toward Conflict

For each statement below, decide which of the three orientations to conflict it reflects.

_____ 1. We can't both be satisfied on this issue.
_____ 2. Since we disagree about which movie to see, let's just not go out tonight.
_____ 3. We're never going to see eye to eye on this, so I'll just defer to you.
_____ 4. If we keep talking, I think we'll figure out something that will work for both of us.
_____ 5. I can't stand fighting. Nobody ever wins.
_____ 6. No matter what you say, I'm not giving any ground on this issue. I feel very strongly about it, so you'll just have to go along with me.
_____ 7. We may not have a solution yet, but I think we're finding some areas of agreement. Let's try to build on those.

Key: 1 = win–lose; 2 = lose–lose; 3 = win–lose; 4 = win–win; 5 = lose–lose; 6 = win–lose; 7 = win–win

Lose–lose, win–lose, and win–win are basic ways individuals think about conflict. What we learned in Chapter 3 reminds us that how we perceive something has a powerful impact on what it means to us and on the possibilities of resolution that we imagine. Remember how you couldn't solve the nine dots problem in Chapter 3 if you perceived it as a square? In a similar way, we're unlikely to find a win–win solution if we perceive conflict as win–lose or lose–lose.

Apply the Idea

Identifying Your Conflict Tendencies

Could you identify your orientation to conflict from this discussion? To check, answer these questions:

1. When conflict seems about to occur, do you
    a. marshal arguments for your solution
    b. feel everyone is going to get hurt
    c. feel there's probably a way to satisfy everyone
2. When involved in conflict, do you
    a. feel competitive urges
    b. feel resigned that everyone will lose

c. feel committed to finding a mutual solution
3. When you disagree with another person, do you
    a. assume the other person is wrong
    b. assume neither of you is right
    c. assume there are good reasons for what each of you thinks and feels

Key: (a) answers indicate a win–lose orientation; (b) answers suggest a lose–lose orientation; (c) answers reflect a win–win orientation.

RESPONSES TO CONFLICT

In addition to orientations toward conflict, most individuals have fairly consistent patterns for responding to conflict. A series of studies identified four distinct ways North Americans respond to relational distress (Rusbult, 1987; Rusbult, Johnson, & Morrow, 1986; Rusbult & Zembrodt, 1983; Rusbult, Zembrodt, & Iwaniszek, 1986). These are represented in Figure 9.3. According to this model, responses to conflict can be either active or passive, depending on how emphatically they address problems. Responses can also be constructive or destructive in their capacity to resolve tension and to preserve relationships.

As we discuss four common responses to conflict, you'll notice their connection to the orientations toward conflict we discussed in the prior section. This reminds us of the systemic character of interpersonal communication: Each part of communication is connected to all other parts.

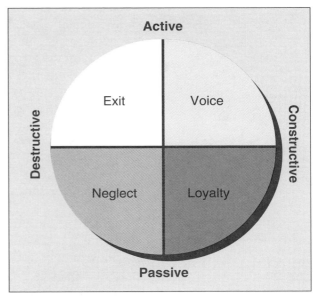

Figure 9.3
Responses to Conflict in Relationships

EXIT RESPONSE

The **exit response** involves leaving a relationship by either physically walking out, psychologically withdrawing, or using verbal or physical tactics to avoid discussing problems and to force resolutions. Refusing to talk about a problem is an example of psychological exit. Ending a relationship rather than dealing with a conflict is an example of literal exit. Because exit doesn't address problems, it is destructive. Because it is a forceful way to avoid conflict, it is active.

Exit responses are associated with lose–lose and win–lose orientations toward conflict. Individuals who have a lose–lose orientation assume that nobody can benefit if conflict takes place, so they see no point in engaging in conflict and prefer to avoid it. For different reasons, the

When is an exit response appropriate?

Photo: © Photodisc

win–lose orientation may promote the exit response. A person who sees conflicts as win–lose situations may exit physically or psychologically if she or he perceives she or he will lose if the conflict is allowed to take place.

NEGLECT RESPONSE

The **neglect response** occurs when an individual denies or minimizes problems, disagreements, anger, tension, or other matters that could lead to overt conflict. Individuals communicate that they prefer to neglect conflicts by making statements such as "There isn't a disagreement here," "You're creating a problem where none exists," or "You're making a mountain out of a molehill." These statements either deny a problem exists or deny that a problem is important. Neglect is generally destructive, because it doesn't promote any resolution of tension. It is passive because it avoids discussion. In some specific situations, however, neglect may be an effective response to conflict. For instance, if an issue can't be resolved, discussing it may further harm a relationship. Also, if a conflict isn't important to you, it may be appropriate not to deal with it.

Which orientations toward conflict would you think foster a neglect response? Either lose–lose or win–lose may prompt the neglect response for the same reasons each of those orientations is associated with the exit response. That's not surprising because both exit and neglect are destructive responses to conflict. Either the person thinks escalating disagreement will harm everyone, or the person perceives she or he will lose if conflict is allowed to progress.

LOYALTY RESPONSE

The **loyalty response** is staying committed to a relationship despite differences. In other words, the person who adopts loyalty as a response to conflict decides to stay committed to the relationship and tolerate the differences. Loyalty often involves deferring to another in order to preserve a relationship. This may be desirable if the deference doesn't cost too much, but deferring your own needs and goals may be too high a price for harmony. In other cases, loyalty is enacted by focusing on what is good and desirable about the relationship and by deemphasizing problems in it. Loyalty is silent allegiance that doesn't actively address conflict, so it is a passive response. Because it doesn't end a relationship and it preserves the option of addressing tension later, loyalty is constructive.

Loyalty is most likely to spring from a lose–lose orientation toward conflict. Believing that engaging in overt disagreement only hurts everyone, individuals may choose to remain loyal to the relationship and not express anger, resentment, disappointment, and disagreement.

Zondomoni:

In South Africa, the tradition is for women not to speak out against their husbands. Women are supposed to support whatever the husband says or does. A woman who speaks out or who disagrees with her husband or any male relative is considered bad; she is behaving inappropriately.

But some of us are now challenging this custom. I disagreed with my father about my marriage, and he did not speak to me for many months after. Now he speaks to me again. I also sometimes disagree with my husband. Life is changing in South Africa.

VOICE RESPONSE

Finally, the **voice response** is an active, constructive strategy for dealing with conflict by talking about problems and trying to resolve them. Individuals who respond with voice identify problems or tensions and assert a desire to deal with them. Voice implies that people care enough about a relationship to notice when something is wrong and to want to do something to improve the situation. Thus, voice is often the most constructive strategy for enduring intimate relationships.

The voice response is most likely to be fostered by a win–win orientation toward conflict. It requires belief in yourself and the other person to give voice to problems and disagreements. Voicing concerns also expresses belief in the relationship. We're unlikely to give voice to disagreements unless we believe a relationship can withstand conflict and that the partners will work to resolve the tension in ways that both people find acceptable.

Although each of us has developed a preferred response, we can become skillful in other responses if we choose. Constructive strategies (voice and loyalty) are advisable for relationships that matter to you and that you want to maintain. Of those two, voice is stronger, because it actively intervenes to resolve conflict. Exit may be useful as an interim strategy when partners need time to reflect or cool off before dealing with conflict directly. Loyalty may be appropriate in situations where conflict is temporary and provoked by external pressures. For example, if you want more time with a friend who is under a lot of pressure at work, it may be wise not to assert your preferences and to quietly accept the short-term disappointment. Developing skill in using a range of responses to conflict increases your ability to communicate sensitively and effectively.

Apply the Idea

Enlarging Your Responses to Conflict

Identify two responses to conflict that you do not currently use much. For each one, specify two strategies for increasing your skill in using that response.

Example: Response to Conflict	Strategies for Achieving Competence
Voice response: I have trouble talking about conflict.	1. When I feel like avoiding conflict, I will remind myself that avoiding has never made problems go away.
	2. When friends ask what's wrong, I will stop saying "nothing's wrong."

SOCIAL INFLUENCES ON CONFLICT

Our orientations toward conflict and our typical ways of responding to conflict aren't random. They reflect many social influences. We've already noted that our views of conflict reflect personal experiences, especially ones in our families. Along with personal experiences, our membership in social groups affects how we view and respond to conflict. In this section, we'll examine the relationship between conflict and membership in social groups defined by culture, gender, and sexual orientation.

CULTURAL BACKGROUND

As we have seen throughout this book, cultures vary in the attitudes, values, and communication practices they approve and disapprove. This is especially true concerning conflict. Different cultures have distinct attitudes toward conflict and what it means (constitutive rules). The majority of Mediterranean cultures regard conflict as a normal and valuable part of everyday life. Within these cultures, people routinely argue and wrangle, and nobody gets upset or angry. Customers haggle with merchants over prices; neighbours argue, sometimes quite dramatically, over community issues; people bargain with one another for favours. In France and Arabic countries, men routinely debate one another for the sheer fun of it. It doesn't matter who wins the argument—the process of arguing is itself enjoyable (Copeland & Griggs, 1985).

Mediterranean cultures also regard conflict as both normal and interesting. Because Hispanic cultures tend to value emotionalism, they perceive conflict as an opportunity to be emotionally expressive and dramatic. The calm, reserved, rational style of discussion prized in many Western societies is perceived as boring and unimaginative.

In the West, assertiveness and individuality are emphasized, so native citizens tend to be more active and competitive in responding to conflict. More than many peoples, Westerners adopt an exchange view of relationships in which each person expects (and sometimes demands) to get her or his fair share. As a people, we are reluctant to give in, defer, or be passive.

In more communal societies such as the Netherlands, people have less individualistic perspectives and are less likely to focus on winning at conflict (Vanyperen & Buunk, 1991). Similarly, in Japan and many other Asian cultures, open disagreement is strongly condemned. Japanese society teaches people to accommodate or appear to do so and not to express disagreement openly. In line with this cultural norm, Japanese persons tend to favour the exit approach to conflict (Ting-Toomey, 1991).

The attitude toward conflict that tends to prevail in Japan and China, as well as many other Asian cultures, places high value on interpersonal harmony and cooperation. Any overt conflict is considered in very bad taste and is regarded as disrespectful of others. Rather than trying to win at another's expense, the goal is to find points of agreement and build from those to a solution that benefits everyone and that sustains harmony. Great effort is made to avoid disagreement and to avoid winning at the cost of causing another person to lose face (Rowland, 1985; Weiss, 1987). Avoiding embarrassment or causing another to lose face is also found in sports, as "Win–Win Athletics" explains.

Student Voices

Roberto:

One of the hardest adjustments for me in Canada has been keeping my voice down. In Italy, people shout all the time and wave their arms. No one avoids conflict there. It is the normal way of communicating where I come from. When my girlfriend visits my family, she is always alarmed at the shouting and thinks everyone is fighting. I tell her that we just disagree noisily and 10 minutes later we will be singing or laughing.

Communication Notes

Win–Win Athletics

North Americans view sports as competitions in which one person or team wins and the other loses. This perspective is in dramatic contrast to the Japanese attitude toward athletics. In baseball, for instance, the goal is not for one team to win, but for a tie to be achieved. The Japanese play for ties because that way nobody loses face. Everyone plays hard and competitively, yet nobody loses—no face is lost. That's a perfect game! When the Japanese win a championship, they try to win by only slim margins. One team may be ahead by many games at a point in the season, but by the end of the season that team will have trimmed its lead to one or two games. This preserves the face of the other teams, because they don't lose by an embarrassing degree.

Source: American games, Japanese rules. (1988). Frontline documentary. National Public Television. Cited in Ferrante, J. (1992). *Sociology: A global perspective*. Belmont, CA: Wadsworth.

GENDER

There are some general differences in how women and men respond to conflict. In general, women are more likely to enact loyalty and voice, both of which have constructive implications for relationships. Men, on the other hand, respond more often with exit and neglect. These differences in response tendencies make sense in light of what we know about gendered socialization. As we noted in Chapter 4, women are taught to place a priority on relationships and to use talk to create and sustain closeness. Thus, it's natural for women to want to talk about problems. Women are also more likely than men to defer and compromise, which reflects gendered prescriptions for women to accommodate others (Wood 1986, 1992b).

The different response tendencies of women and men pave the way for misunderstandings in relationships (Wood, 1998). Men sometimes feel

Student Voices

Kristo:
My girlfriend drives me crazy. She thinks anytime the slightest thing is wrong in our relationship, we have to have a long, drawn-out analysis of it. I just don't want to spend all that time dissecting the relationship.

overwhelmed by the number of issues women want to discuss and resolve. Women sometimes feel that men are unwilling to discuss anything about relationships. Of course, neither perception is likely to be accurate. Both are very broad generalizations that probably overstate how men and women act. Nonetheless, women and men often find themselves responding very differently to relationship tensions and not understanding each other's perspective.

|Student Voices|

Genevieve:

My boyfriend is a world-class avoider. When something is wrong between us, I naturally want to talk about it and get things right again. But he will evade, tell me everything's fine when it's not, say the problem is too minor to talk about, and use any other tactic he can come up with to avoid facing the problem. He seems to think if you don't deal with problems they somehow solve themselves.

Masculine socialization places less emphasis on talk as a means to intimacy, so as a group, men are less likely than women to see discussion as a good way to handle conflict in personal relationships. In professional situations and athletics, however, men may be very vocal in dealing with conflict. Yet in their personal lives, men often deny or minimize problems rather than deal openly with them. However, research indicates that in Western relationships, avoiding discussion seldom helps matters, and it often compounds tension between partners in a relationship. Long-term studies of marriage indicate that husbands are more inclined than wives to withdraw from conflict and that stonewalling by husbands is a strong predictor of divorce (Bass, 1993). The other response preferred by men, exit, is a unilateral show of power, which is part of masculine socialization. Men, more than women, use coercive tactics, both verbal and physical, to avoid discussing problems and to force their resolutions on others (Snell, Hawkins, & Belk, 1988; White, 1989).

Before leaving our discussion of gender, we should note one other important finding. Psychologist John Gottman (1993) reports that men experience greater and longer-lasting physical responses to interpersonal conflict. Compared to women, during conflict men's heart rate rises more quickly and to higher levels, and it stays elevated for a longer period of time. Thus, engaging in conflict generally may be more physically and psychologically painful to men than to women. This may offer a partial explanation of why men are more likely than women to deny or minimize issues that could cause conflict.

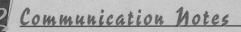

Communication Notes

The White Ribbon Campaign (WRC)

In Canada, the White Ribbon Campaign was begun by a group of men deeply concerned about violence against women. Most violent acts are committed by men. From November 25th to December 6th, the anniversary of the 1989 Montreal Massacre, men and boys are encouraged to wear white ribbons to symbolize their opposition to violence against women. Today, the White Ribbon Campaign is celebrated by both men and women across Canada.

For more information contact:
White Ribbon Campaign
365 Bloor Street East, Suite 203
Toronto, Ontario, M4W 3L4
Or check out the Web site at www.whiteribbon.ca

Apply the Idea

Gendered Styles of Conflict

Reflect on responses to conflict used by you and two women and two men you know well. Do your observations indicate that women are more likely than men to defer and accommodate and to want to talk about problems? Do the men you observe tend to avoid problems or exit when they arise?

SEXUAL ORIENTATION

Do gays and lesbians respond to conflict differently than heterosexuals? Actually, sexual orientation doesn't seem to be a major influence on how individuals see and deal with conflict. Caryl Rusbult and her colleagues (1986) found that gay men were much like heterosexual men, and lesbians were similar to heterosexual women, in their responses to conflict. Similarly, a major national study reported that gender explains far more of the differences between partners than does affectional preference (Blumstein & Schwartz, 1983; Wood, 1986, 1994b).

At first this finding seems surprising, because sexual orientation is such a core part of identity. On closer examination, however, it makes sense that gays and lesbians don't approach conflict differently than heterosexuals. The majority of children, regardless of sexual orientation, are socialized on the basis of their sex. Thus, boys, both gay and straight, tend to learn masculine orientations toward interaction, whereas lesbian and straight girls are socialized toward feminine styles of interaction.

Although gays, lesbians, and heterosexuals seem similar in how they think about and respond to conflict, sexual orientation is linked to some differences in relationship tensions. First, gays and lesbians appear to have fewer sexual conflicts and to talk more openly about sexual issues than heterosexuals (Masters & Johnson, 1979). This can be significant, because sexual tensions can poison overall satisfaction with a relationship (Cupach & Comstock, 1990).

On the whole, gay and lesbian couples may have less overall conflict than heterosexuals. It's possible that gay and lesbian partners have an intragender empathy that heterosexual couples lack (Masters & Johnson, 1979). Because most homosexual partners were socialized in the same gender culture, they often share views of the importance of talk and activities in relationships. Of all couples, lesbians most often rely on voice to talk through tensions. Because both partners usually view communication as the primary path to intimacy, they are similarly inclined to engage in process talk. Gay male couples, in contrast, talk less about relationship issues than other couples and are more likely than other partners to exit when problems arise (Wood, 1994b). Heterosexual couples talk more than gays and less than l esbians about their relationship, reflecting a combination of gendered socialization.

In this section, we've seen that people differ in how they view and respond to conflict. Although lose–lose and win–lose perceptions of conflict are appropriate in situations where there is low commitment to relationships and others, the win–win view is generally ideal when partners care about each other and want to stay together.

People respond to conflict either actively (voice, exit) or passively (neglect, loyalty) and in ways that either help (voice, loyalty) or harm (exit, neglect) relationships. How we think about and respond to conflict is learned, not innate. It reflects our cultural background, gender, and sexual orientation. The fact that conflict orientations are learned suggests that we can develop skills for managing tension constructively. In the next section, we discuss specific communication behaviours that affect the process of conflict and its impact on relationships.

COMMUNICATION PATTERNS DURING CONFLICT

Marriage counsellors have particularly keen insight into how conflict dynamics affect relationships. Communication scholar Anita Vangelisti (1993) reports that counsellors stress communication training for couples who manage conflict unproductively. Therapeutic training teaches partners to recognize destructive and constructive patterns of communication and to use constructive patterns in their relationships. In this section, we discuss specific kinds of communication that foster or impede effective conflict (Gottman, 1979, 1993; Gottman et al., 1976a, 1976b).

UNPRODUCTIVE CONFLICT COMMUNICATION

Ineffective communication can have serious consequences. It damages efforts to resolve problems, harms individuals, and jeopardizes relational health. The communication that creates unproductive patterns in conflict reflects a preoccupation with self and a disregard for the other. This is not genuine interpersonal communication, because partners don't recognize and engage each other as unique individuals.

Specific communication behaviours make up the syndrome of destructive conflict communication.

Early Stages

The foundation for destructive conflict is established by communication that fails to confirm individuals. If John says "I want us to spend more time together," Shannon may reply, "That's unreasonable." This disconfirms John's feeling and request. Shannon could also disconfirm him by not replying at all, which would be a refusal to acknowledge him. During early stages, partners tend not to listen well. They may listen selectively, taking in only what they expect or want to believe. In addition, partners display little mindfulness. They don't show that they are interested in what the other is saying. Instead, they may give feedback that disconfirms the other. For instance, Shannon could roll her eyes to tell John his request is outrageous, or she might shrug and turn away to signal she doesn't care what he wants. Poor listening is also demonstrated when partners don't respond to each other.

Cross-complaining occurs when one person's complaint is met by a countercomplaint. Shannon could respond to John's request for more time by saying, "Yeah, well what I want is a little more respect for what I do." That response doesn't address John's concern; it is an attempt to divert the conversation and to switch the fault from Shannon to John. Poor listening and disconfirmation establish a climate in which dual perspective is low and defensiveness is high.

Negative climates tend to build on themselves. As partners continue to talk, mindreading is likely. Instead of asking John to clarify or explain his feelings, Shannon assumes she knows his motives. Perhaps she thinks he wants to divert her from her work so that she doesn't succeed. If Shannon makes this assumption, she discounts what John wants. Mindreading in distressed relationships has a distinctively negative tone. Partners assume the worst motives and feelings of each other. The negative assumptions they make fuel hostility and mistrust.

Middle Stages

Once a negative climate has been set, it is stoked by other unconstructive communication. Focusing on specific issues is one of the clearest differences between partners who resolve conflicts constructively and those who don't. In unproductive conflict interaction, partners engage in **kitchensinking,** in which everything except the kitchen sink is thrown into the argument. John may add to his original complaint by recalling all sorts of other real and imagined slights from Shannon. In turn, she may reciprocate by hauling out her own laundry list of gripes. The result is such a mass of grievances that partners are overwhelmed. They can't solve all of the problems they've dragged into the discussion, and they may well forget what the original issue was. Kitchensinking is particularly likely to occur when partners have a host of concerns they've repressed for some time. Once a conflict begins, everything that has been stored up is thrown in.

The middle stages of unproductive conflict are also marked by frequent interruptions that disrupt the flow of talk. These interruptions aren't efforts to clarify ideas or feelings. Instead, they are objections to what a partner says: "How dare you say I don't know how to manage money!" Interruptions may also be attempts to derail a partner's issues and reroute discussion: "I have no interest in talking about time together. What I'd like to discuss is your responsibility for this house." Cross-complaining frequently continues in this middle stage of the syndrome. Because neither partner is allowed to develop thoughts fully (or even to finish a sentence), discussion never focuses on any topic long enough to make headway in resolving it.

Later Stages

Even if partners make little progress in solving their problems, limited time and energy guarantee an end to an episode of conflict. Solutions become the focus in the final stage of unproductive conflict. Unfortunately, preceding stages didn't lay the groundwork for effective discussion of solutions. As a result, each person's proposals are met with **counterproposals**. The self-preoccupation that first surfaced in the early phase persists now so that each person is more interested in pushing his or her solution than in considering that of the other. John proposes, "Maybe we could spend two nights together each week." Shannon counterproposes, "Maybe you could assume responsibility for half of the chores around here." Her counterproposal fails to recognize and acknowledge his suggestion, so her communication does not confirm him. Compounding self-preoccupation is **self-summarizing,** which is when a person keeps repeating what she or he has said. This is egocentric communication. It is not genuine interpersonal communication, because it ignores the other person and simply restates the speaker's feelings and perspective.

A final form of negative communication in the middle and later phases of unproductive conflict is **excessive metacommunication.** Metacommunication is communication about communication. For example, John might say, "I think maybe we're getting sidetracked in this discussion," or Shannon might say, "I think we're avoiding talking about the real issue here." Both of these are comments about the communication that is happening. Gottman and his associates (1976a, 1976b, 1977) have found that both distressed and satisfied couples engage in metacommunication. However, they do so in very different ways.

Couples who manage conflict effectively use metacommunication to keep discussion on track, and then they return to the topics at hand. For instance, during a disagreement, Aaron might comment that Norma doesn't seem to be expressing her feelings and invite her to do so. Then he and Norma would return to their discussion. In contrast, couples who manage conflict ineffectively often become embroiled in metacommunication and can't get back to the issues. For example, Norma and Aaron might get into an extended argument about whether she's expressing feelings and not return to the original topic of conflict. Excessive metacommunication is more likely to block partners than to resolve tensions cooperatively.

These forms of communication that make up the unproductive conflict syndrome reflect and promote egocentrism and dogmatism because negative communication tends to be self-perpetuating. When one becomes dogmatic, he or she asserts opinion as if it is authority. Unproductive conflict doesn't involve dual perspective, and it seals off awareness of common grounds as well as potential avenues of compromise.

You may recall that in Chapter 1 we described interpersonal communication as systemic, because all aspects of communication interact and affect one another. This is clearly the case in the unproductive conflict syndrome.

Each negative form of communication feeds into the overall negative system. Unproductive communication fosters a defensive, negative climate, which makes it virtually impossible to resolve conflicts. When egocentrism prevails, each partner is more interested in getting his or her own way than in creating a solution that both can accept. In addition, unconstructive communication is so disconfirming that it damages individual partners and the long-term health of the relationship. "How to Fight" compares fair and unfair conflict tactics.

Review

Egocentrism leads to poor listening, which promotes disconfirmation, which fuels defensiveness, which stokes dogmatism, which leads to hostile mindreading and kitchensinking, which pave the way for self-summarizing.

CONSTRUCTIVE CONFLICT COMMUNICATION

According to relationship counsellors, healthy, constructive communication during conflict is open, nonjudgmental, confirming, and nonstrategic. In addition, it reflects dual perspective by focusing on both partners and the relationship even when tension is high. Constructive communication creates a supportive, positive climate that increases the possibility of resolving conflict without harming the relationship. Let's look at how constructive communication plays out in the three phases of the conflict syndrome.

Communication Notes

How to Fight

Rules for Fighting Dirty

Apologize prematurely.

Refuse to take the fight seriously.

Chain-react by piling on all the issues and gripes (kitchensinking).

Hit below the belt. Use intimate knowledge to humiliate the other person.

Withdraw and avoid confrontation: walk out, be silent.

Withhold affection, approval, recognition, or material things.

Encourage others to side with you against your partner.

Play demolition derby with your partner's character—tell her or him what's wrong with her or him, what she or he thinks, feels, means, and so on (mindreading).

Demand more—nothing is ever enough. Push to have everything your way.

Attack a person, activity, value, or idea that your partner holds dear.

Rules for Fighting Clean

Fully express your positive and negative feelings.

Define your out-of-bounds areas of vulnerability.

Paraphrase the other's arguments in your own words and allow the other to do likewise.

Think before fighting, not after fighting. Try not to let your feelings undermine reason and fair play.

Consider the merit of the other person's opinions of you before rejecting or accepting them.

Focus on the other person's behaviour and ideas.

Define what the fight is about and stay within limits.

Look for where you and your partner agree, as well as where you disagree.

Decide how each of you can help the other resolve the issue in a way that satisfies her or him.

Avoid discussing a problem or conflict when you are emotionally raw.

Source: Adapted from Bach, G. R., & Wyden, P. (1973). *The intimate enemy: How to fight fair in love and marriage.* New York: Avon.

Early Stages

The foundation for constructive management of conflict is established long before a specific disagreement is aired. Climate, which is the foundation for both the overall relationship and conflict, sets the tone for communication during conflict. To establish a good climate, partners confirm each other by recognizing and acknowledging each other's concerns and feelings. Returning to our example, when John says "I want us to spend more time together," Shannon could confirm him by replying, "I wish we could too. It's nice that you want us to have more time together." That simple act on Shannon's part communicates to John that she is listening and that she cares about his concerns and about him. After she says that, a different conversation unfolds. It might go like this:

John: Yeah, it just seems that we used to spend a lot more time together, and we felt closer then. I miss that.

Shannon: I do too. It sounds as if what's really on your mind is how close we are, not specifically the amount of time we spend together. Is that right?

John: Yeah, I guess that is more what's bothering me, but I kind of think they're connected, don't you?

Shannon: I see what you mean. But we won't feel closer just by spending more time together. I think we also need some shared interests like we used to have.

John: I'd like that. Do you have any ideas?

Let's highlight several things in this conversation. First, notice that when Shannon began by reflecting John's opening statement, he elaborated and clarified what was troubling him. Instead of time per se, the issue is closeness. Listening sensitively, Shannon picks up on this and refocuses their conversation on closeness. We should also notice that Shannon doesn't mindread; instead, she asks John whether she understood what he meant. When he asks Shannon whether she thinks time and closeness are related, John shows openness to her perceptions; thus, he confirms her and doesn't mindread. The openness they create clears the way for effective discussion of how to increase closeness. Once a supportive climate is established, the couple can proceed to the middle stages of conflict knowing they are not fighting each other but working together to solve a problem.

Middle Stages

The positive groundwork laid in the early phase of conflict supports what happens as partners dig into issues. The middle stages of constructive conflict are marked by what Gottman (1993) calls "agenda building," which involves staying focused on the main issues. Kitchensinking is unlikely to derail discussion, because partners keep communication on target. It's not that other issues might not come up as they do in unproductive conflict. However, partners who have learned to communicate effectively control digressions. One useful technique is **bracketing,** which is noting that an issue that comes up in the course of conflict is important and needs to be discussed at a later time. Bracketing allows partners to stay effectively focused on a specific issue at one time, but to agree to deal with other issues later. Bracketing confirms partners' feelings that issues brought up are important by promising to deal with them later. Yet by bracketing topics that are peripheral to the current discussion, partners are able to stay on track and make progress in resolving the immediate issue.

Constructive fighting models good relationship management.

Photo: A. Bradley

During the middle stage of constructive conflict, partners continue to show respect for each other by interrupting infrequently. Any interruptions that occur are to clarify meanings ("Before you go on, could you explain what you mean by closeness?") or to check perceptions ("So you think time together leads to closeness?"). Unlike disruptive interruptions, those that clarify ideas and check perceptions confirm the person speaking by showing that the listener wants to understand the meaning. In this stage, partners continue to recognize and acknowledge each other's points of view. Rather than the cross-complaining that characterizes unproductive conflict, partners acknowledge each other's feelings, thoughts, and concerns. This doesn't mean they don't put their own concerns on the table. Constructive conflict requires that we assert our own feelings and needs as part of engaging in honest dialogue. There is no conflict between honouring ourselves and others; doing both is the essence of good interpersonal communication.

Final Stages

The opening phase of constructive conflict establishes a supportive climate for discussion. The focus of the middle stages is to elaborate issues and feelings so that partners understand all that is involved. In the culminating phase, attention shifts to resolving the tension between partners. Whereas in unproductive conflict this involves meeting proposals with counterproposals, in constructive conflict partners continue to operate cooperatively. Keeping in mind that they share a relationship, they continue using dual perspective to remain aware of both individuals' perspectives. Instead of countering each other's proposals, partners engage in **contracting,** which is building a solution through negotiation and acceptance of parts of proposals. The difference between counterproposals and contracting is illustrated in this example:

Counterproposals

John: I want us to spend three nights a week doing things together.

Shannon: I can't do that right now, because we're short-handed at work, and I am filling in nights. Get a hobby so you aren't bored nights.

John: Not being bored isn't the same as our being close. I want us to spend time together again.

Shannon: I told you, I can't do that. Don't be so selfish.

John: Aren't we as important as your job?

Shannon: That's a stupid question. I can't take three nights off. Let's take more vacations.

Contracting

John: I want us to spend three nights a week doing things together.

Shannon: I'm all for that, but right now we're short-handed at work. How about if we use your idea but adjust it to my job? Maybe we could start with one night each week and expand that later.

John: Okay, that's a start, but could we also reserve some weekend time for us?

Shannon: That's a good idea. Let's plan on that. I just can't be sure how much I'll have to work on weekends until we hire some new people. What if we promise to give ourselves an extra week's vacation to spend together when we have full staff?

John: Okay, that's a good back-up plan, but can we take weekend time when you don't work?

Shannon: Absolutely. How about a picnic this Sunday? We've haven't gone on a picnic in so long.

In the counterproposal scenario, John and Shannon were competing to get their own ways. Neither tried to identify workable parts of the other's

Student Voices

Bettina:

My son and I used to argue all the time, and we never got anywhere because we were each trying to get our own way, and we weren't paying attention to the other. Then we went into family counselling, and we learned how to make our arguments more productive. The most important thing I learned was to be looking for ways to respond to what my son says and wants. Once I started focusing on him and trying to satisfy him, he was more willing to listen to my point of view and to think about solutions that would satisfy me. We still argue a lot—I guess we always will—but now it's more like we're working things through together instead of trying to tear each other down.

proposals or to find common ground. Because each adopts a win–lose view of the conflict, it's likely that both of them and the relationship will be losers. A very different tone shows up in the contracting scenario. In it, both partners look for ways to agree with each other, while also asserting their own concerns. Neither partner represses personal needs, but each is committed to finding what might be workable in the other's proposals.

Specific differences between unproductive and productive conflict can be summarized as the difference between confirming and disconfirming communication. The particular kinds of communication that generate unproductive conflict share the quality of disconfirming the partner, the relationship, or both. On the other hand, the communication in constructive conflict consistently confirms both partners and the relationship. This reminds us of the importance of supportive, confirming climates, which we explored in Chapter 8. The climate, or emotional mood, of interpersonal relationships is created by communication. Our discussion of specific skills highlights communication that fosters affirming climates in which conflicts can be productively resolved without damage to relationships.

Let us now summarize the many elements presented in this discussion of unproductive and constructive conflict communication in Table 9.1, adapted from Gottman, (1993); Gottman et al., (1976a).

Table 9.1
Summary of Constructive and Unproductive Communication

Constructive	Unproductive
Mindfulness	Mindlessness
Confirming messages and validations	Disconfirming messages
Sensitive listening	Poor listening
Dual perspective	Egocentrism
Recognize other's concerns	Cross-complaining
Asking for clarification	Hostile mindreading
Infrequent interruptions	Frequent interruptions
Bracketing	Kitchensinking
Compromises and contracts	Counterproposals
Useful metacommunication	Excessive metacommunication
Summarizing the concerns	Self-summarizing of both partners
Grace	Mean-spiritedness

Source: Gottman, J. (1993). The roles of conflict engagement, escalation, or avoidance in marital interaction: A longitudinal view of five types of couples. *The Journal of Consulting and Clinical Psychology*, 61, 6–15; Gottman, J., Notarious, C., Gonso, J., & Markman, H. J. (1976a). A Couple's Guide to Communication. Champaign, IL: Research Press.

Photo: © Corbis/Magma

GUIDELINES FOR EFFECTIVE COMMUNICATION DURING CONFLICT

Our study of conflict, along with many of the ideas we've considered in previous chapters, suggests five guidelines for dealing with conflict. Following these should increase your ability to handle conflicts effectively.

FOCUS ON THE OVERALL COMMUNICATION SYSTEM

Conflict does not occur in a vacuum. Instead, it takes place in the context of relationships and the overall communication climate established over time. As we noted in Chapter 1, communication is systemic, which means it occurs in contexts, and it is composed of many interacting parts. Applying the principle of systems to conflict, we can see that how we deal with conflict is shaped by factors beyond an immediate disagreement. This means that we must attend to the overall systems of relationships and communication if we wish to make conflict constructive.

Couples who have developed negative interpersonal climates cannot argue constructively simply by practising "good conflict techniques" such as focusing talk and not interrupting. Those techniques occur within larger contexts that affect how they are interpreted. Partners who have learned to be generally defensive and distrustful are unlikely to respond openly to even the best conflict methods. By the same reasoning, in climates that are generally supportive and confirming, even unconstructive conflict communication is unlikely to derail relationships. Conflict, like all interaction, is affected by its contexts.

To make conflict more constructive in your relationships, you should apply the information and guidelines discussed throughout this book. These will allow you to create positive, affirming interpersonal climates in which conflict can be managed most constructively. Engaging in mindful listening, which we discussed in Chapter 7, is essential to effective management of conflict. Also important is creating confirming climates, which we examined in Chapter 8. In addition, it's a good idea to apply the guidelines for effective verbal and nonverbal communication that we considered in Chapters 5 and 6. What you've learned about self-concept and perception should also help you control the multiple factors that influence how you deal with conflict in your relationships. In other words, conflict is part of a larger whole, and we must make that whole healthy in order to create a context in which conflict can be resolved without jeopardizing partners or relationships. Keep in mind that conflict always has three parties: you, another person, and the relationship between the two of you. Healthy conflict communication honours all three. In Chapter 4, we discussed how to manage difficult emotions. It is worth reviewing the simple rule of ABC's created by psychotherapist David Stewart as we discuss managing conflict.

Table 9.2
The ABCs of Managing Conflict

A		**Adult:** Stay in your adult behaviours. It is easy under conflict to believe you are in a fight for survival, which stimulates child behaviours.
B		**Breathe:** Conflict is not necessarily bad. Under stress, we frequently hold our breath.
C		**Context:** Remember the context you are in. The relationship may be more important than winning small battles. Also, as in the context of a courtroom, for example, combativeness is expected.

As discussed earlier, our response to conflict is heavily influenced by our childhood scripts. ABCs becomes a valuable tool to aid conflict resolution.

TIME CONFLICT EFFECTIVELY

Timing affects how we communicate about conflicts. There are three ways to use chronemics so that conflicts are most likely to be effective.

First, try not to engage in serious conflict discussions at times when one or both people will not be fully present psychologically. Most of us are more irritable when we are sick or stressed. We're also less attentive and less mindful listeners when we are tired. It's generally more productive to discuss problems in private rather than in public settings. If time is limited, or we are rushing, we're less likely to take the time to deal constructively with differences. It's impossible to listen well, develop ideas, and respond thoughtfully when a stopwatch is ticking in our minds. One guideline to keep in mind, then, is to time when you have conflicts.

Concepts at a Glance

Three Time Considerations for Resolving Conflict:

1. Wait until both parties are fully mindful.

2. Wait until the more urgent needs are met.

3. Bracket less urgent issues.

A second guideline for timing is to be flexible about when you deal with differences. Constructive conflict is most likely when everyone's needs are accommodated. If one partner feels ready to talk about a problem but the other doesn't, it's probably wise to delay discussion. This works, of course, only if the person who isn't ready agrees to talk about the issue at a later time. Because research indicates that men are more likely than women to avoid discussing relationship conflicts, they may be especially reluctant to talk about disagreements without first gaining some distance (Beck, 1988; Rusbult, 1987). Some individuals prefer to tackle problems as soon as they arise, whereas others need time to percolate privately before interacting. It's generally a good idea not to discuss conflict in the heat of anger. The danger is that anger may provoke us to hurl cruel words and insults that we cannot take back later. Constructive, healthy conflict communication is more likely when tempers aren't flaring.

Student Voices

Stephanie:

I have a really hot temper, so I can cut someone to pieces if I argue when I'm mad. I have hurt a lot of friends by attacking them before I cooled off, and I hate myself when I act like that. I have finally figured out that I can handle fights constructively if I cool down. Now when I'm hot, I tell my friends or my boyfriend that I can't discuss it right then. Later, when I'm calm, I can talk without saying things that hurt them and that I feel bad about.

A third way to use chronemics to promote positive conflict is bracketing, which we discussed earlier in this chapter. It is natural that a variety of issues needing attention come up in the course of conflict. If we try to deal with all the sideline problems that arise, however, we can't focus on the immediate problem. For example, during an argument about cleaning their apartment Eddy may say to Brian, "I know I sometimes dump my clothes on the floor, but I don't keep you awake talking to people at all hours of the night." Eddy's comment is a countercomplaint that could sidetrack the conversation from a focus on cleaning. Brian might respond, "Fair enough. We do need to talk about my telephone calls, but let's resolve the issue of cleaning first. Then we can talk about late-night phone calls." Bracketing other concerns for later discussion lets us keep conflict focused productively. Keep in mind, however, that bracketing works only if partners return to the issues they set aside.

AIM FOR WIN–WIN CONFLICT

How you approach conflict shapes what will happen in communication. As we have seen in this chapter, each orientation to conflict can be appropriate in certain circumstances. When conflict exists between two people who care about each other and want to sustain a good relationship, however, the win–win style is most desirable. Thus, we should aim to manage conflict so that both we and the other person come out ahead. If you enter conflict with the assumption that you, the other person, and the relationship can all benefit from conflict, it's likely that you will bring about a resolution that benefits everyone. Adopting a win–win orientation to conflict reflects a commitment to honouring yourself and your needs, the other person and her or his needs, and the integrity of your shared relationship.

To maximize the chance of a win–win resolution of conflict, begin by identifying your feelings and your needs or desires in the situation. You may want to review Chapter 4 to remind yourself of ways to clarify your emotions. Understanding what you feel and want is essential to productive conflict communication. Once you figure out what you feel and need, express yourself in clear language. It's not effective to make vague or judgmental statements such as, "I don't like the way you ignore me, and I want you to be more sensitive." It would be more effective to say, "I feel hurt when you don't call, and I want us to find some way that I can be assured of your feelings about me without making you feel handcuffed."

The second step is to identify what the other person feels, needs, or wants. If you don't already know what the other person wants and feels, don't mind read. Instead, ask the other person what she or he is feeling and what she needs or wants in terms of a resolution to the conflict. When the other person expresses his or her feelings and preferences, listen mindfully. Resist the temptation to countercomplain or argue. Just listen and try to understand the other person's perspective as fully as you can. Minimal encouragers and paraphrasing are valuable because they let the other person know you are listening closely and are committed to understanding her or his perspective.

Focus on language that promotes cooperation and mutual respect. To do this, rely on supportive communication and monitor any communication that might foster a defensive climate. You should also use I–language to own your thoughts and feelings.

Third, negotiate a solution that benefits both. Strive for the ideal but settle for a workable compromise. Remember that bracketing here will be very helpful in keeping focused on the important issues.

1. **Express your needs:** Identify your own feelings, needs, or desires. Then express yourself clearly, letting your partner know what behaviour is troublesome, how you feel about it, and what you want.

2. **Solicit the needs of the other:** Be mindful, ask questions, paraphrase, encourage, and support to fully understand the needs and feelings of the other.

3. **Negotiate a solution:** Strive for a high-quality solution. Settle for a workable compromise. Be flexible.

4. **Follow-up:** Check in to make sure the solution fits both parties.

Figure 9.4
Steps to Win–Win Conflict

Fourth, plan to follow up on your solution to make any needed adjustments or to share insights that may arise as you both experience the changes.

Throughout conflict communication, mindful listening is critical. Being fully present in the discussion and focusing on the other achieve two important goals: First, those skills allow you to gain the maximum understanding of the other person's perspective and feelings; second, by modelling mindfulness in your own communication you foster mindfulness in the other's.

Throughout conflict communication, keep reminding yourself that win–win solutions are usually possible when both people balance concerns for themselves and each other. On the relationship level of meaning you want to communicate this message: "I care about you and your feelings and desires, and I know you care about me and how I feel and what I want." If that message underlies your conflict communication, chances are good that you will attain a win–win resolution.

Psychologists Arthur Lange and Patricia Jakubowski (1978) in their definition of responsible assertion, identify the rights we have in any situation. We have the right to the use of our space, our time, and our bodies. We have the right to express ourselves and to be treated with respect. These rights become a very helpful guideline in approaching conflict. Acting responsibly means that you do not violate the rights of another in dealing with conflict. So, for example, even though you have the right to express yourself, if your expression is aggressive and disrespectful, you have violated the other's right to be treated with respect. Similarly, if your insistence on dealing with an issue right now is not appropriate or convenient for the other, you have violated the other's right to the use of his or her time.

Concepts at a Glance

The Five Human Rights

- The right to the use of your space
- The right to the use of your time
- The right to the use of your body
- The right to express yourself
- The right to be treated with respect

HONOUR YOURSELF, YOUR PARTNER, AND THE RELATIONSHIP

Figure 9.5
The Parties Involved in Conflict

The guidelines we've discussed so far share a key principle: Effective interpersonal communication attends to each person and the relationship between them (see Figure 9.5). Throughout this book we've emphasized the importance of honouring yourself, others, and relationships. It's important to keep all three in balance, especially when conflicts arise.

Healthy, constructive conflict communication is impossible if we disregard the other person's needs, rights, and feelings. Doing so disconfirms the other and sets a win–lose tone for conversation. Being sensitive to others, however, is not enough. Just as it is ineffective to disregard others' concerns, it is also unwise to muffle your own. In fairness to yourself and the other person, you should express your feelings and needs clearly. For conflicts to be resolved in truly satisfying ways, each person must put her or his ideas, feelings, and needs on the table in a way that does not violate the rights of the other. Only then can partners engage in informed, open efforts to generate workable solutions to their problems.

In addition to attending to ourselves and our friends and romantic partners, we must remember that relationships are affected by how we handle conflict. For this reason, win–lose orientations toward conflict should really be called win–lose–lose, because when one person wins, both the other person and the relationship lose. Win–win orientations and constructive forms of communication make it possible for both individuals and the relationship to be winners.

Children "let go" and "show grace" more readily than adults.

Photo: © Photodisc

SHOW GRACE WHEN APPROPRIATE

Finally, an important principle to keep in mind during conflict is that grace is sometimes appropriate. Although the idea of grace has not traditionally been discussed in communication texts, it is very much a part of spiritual and philosophical thinking, which should influence how we interact with others. You don't have to be religious to show grace, nor do you have to have a knowledge of philosophy. All that's required is a willingness to sometimes excuse someone who has no formal right to expect your compassion.

By definition, **grace** is granting forgiveness or putting aside our own needs when there is no standard that says we should or must do so. Rather than being prompted by rules or expectations, grace springs from a generosity of personal spirit. Grace is not forgiving when we should—for instance, excusing people who aren't responsible for their actions. Also, grace isn't allowing others to have their way when we have no choice. Instead, grace is unearned and unnecessary kindness. For instance, two roommates agree to split chores, and one doesn't do her share because she has three tests in a week. Her roommate might do all the chores even though there is no agreement or expectation of this generosity. This is an act of grace. It's also an act of grace to defer to another person's preference when you could hold out for your own. Similarly, when someone hurts us and has no right to expect forgiveness, we may choose to forgive anyway. We do so not because we have to, but because we want to. Grace is a matter of choice.

Grace involves the Zen concept of **letting go,** which is to free ourselves of anger, blame, and judgments about another and what she or he did. When we let go of these feelings, we release both ourselves and others from their consequences. Sometimes we tell a friend we forgive him for some offense, but then later we remind him of it. We might say we'll forget a transgression by our romantic partner, but later hold it against her. When we continue to hang on to blame and judgment, we haven't really let go, so we have not really shown grace. There's no grace when we blackmail others for kindness or hang on to hostile feelings. An act of grace must also be done gracefully. It is not grace if we yield to a friend and snap, "Okay, have it your own darned way." Grace doesn't create feelings of debt in others. Grace involves letting go of hostile feelings and blame with a style that is as graceful as what we actually do.

Grace is given without strings. Arthur Osborne (1996), who believes grace is essential in loving relationships, makes this point clearly when he says, "the person who asks for a reward is a merchant, not a lover" (p. 6). We show kindness, defer our needs, or forgive a wrong without any expectation of reward. Grace isn't doing something nice to make a friend feel grateful or indebted to us. It's also not acting in grace when we do something with the expectation of a payback. To do a favour for your partner because you want a reciprocal favour is a matter of bargaining, not grace. For an act to be one of grace, it must be done without conditions or expectations of return.

Grace is not always appropriate, and it can be exploited by individuals who take advantage of kindness. Some people repeatedly abuse and hurt others, confident that pardons will be granted. When grace is extended and then exploited, it may be unwise to extend it again. However, if you show grace in good faith and another takes advantage, you should not fault yourself. Kindness and a willingness to forgive are worthy moral precepts. Those who abuse grace, not those who offer it, are blameworthy.

Because Western culture emphasizes assertion and protection of self-interests, grace is not widely practised or esteemed. We are told to stand up for ourselves, not let others walk all over us, not put up with being hurt, and not tolerate transgressions. It is important to honour and assert ourselves, as we've emphasized throughout this book. However, self-interest and self-assertion alone are insufficient principles for creating rich interpersonal relationships.

None of us is perfect. We all make mistakes, hurt others with thoughtless acts, and occasionally do things we know are wrong. Sometimes there is no reason others should forgive us when we wrong them; we have no right to expect exoneration. Yet, in human relations there has to be some room for redemption, for the extension of grace when it is not required or earned. Clearly we should not always forgive others if they betray or hurt us, and certainly we should be cautious of granting grace repeatedly to someone who exploits it. At the same time, the richest relationships allow room for grace occasionally.

Chapter Summary

This chapter focused on conflict as a natural, inevitable, and potentially constructive aspect of interpersonal life. Because conflicts are normal and unavoidable in any relationship of real depth, the challenge is to learn to manage conflicts effectively. Patterns of conflict are shaped by how individuals view conflict. We discussed lose–lose, win–lose, and win–win approaches to conflict, and explored how each affects interaction. In addition, conflict patterns are influenced by how individuals respond to tension. Inclinations to exit, neglect, show loyalty, or voice conflict vary in how actively they deal with tension and how constructive they are for relationships. In most cases, voice is the preferred response because only voice allows partners to intervene actively and constructively when conflicts arise.

Communication is particularly important in influencing the process of interpersonal conflict. Research by communication scholars as well as clinicians indicates that patterns of interaction that promote constructive management of conflict include being mindful, confirming others, showing dual perspective, listening sensitively, focusing discussion, contracting solutions, and avoiding mindreading, interrupting, self-summarizing, and cross-complaining.

Finally, we considered five guidelines for increasing the constructiveness of interpersonal conflict. First, we need to remember that conflicts occur within overall systems of communication and relationships. To be constructive, conflict must take place within supportive, confirming climates in which good interpersonal communication is practised. Second, it's important to time conflicts so that all individuals have the time they need for private reflection and for productive discussion. A third principle is to aim for win–win solutions to conflict. Consistent with these four guidelines is working to balance commitments to yourself, others, and relationships in a respectful manner when conflict arises. It is unwise to squelch any of these four, because all are affected by how we manage disagreements. Finally, we saw that it is sometimes appropriate to show grace in our personal relationships. Although grace can be exploited, it can also infuse relationships with kindness and make room for inevitable human errors. It's important to balance the tensions inherent in the notion of grace so that we recognize both its potential values and its dangers.

In the next two chapters, we'll explore the worlds of friendship and romance and the workplace. As we do so, we'll carry forward the information and guidelines we've considered in this chapter, because how we manage conflicts affects the health of our friendships, romantic relationships, and relationships with our co-workers and employers.

Key Concepts

- aggression
- assertion
- bracketing
- conflict
- contracting
- counterproposals
- cross-complaining
- excessive metacommunication
- exit response
- games
- grace
- kitchensinking
- letting go
- lose–lose
- loyalty response
- neglect response
- nonassertion
- passive aggression
- self-summarizing
- voice response
- win–lose
- win–win

For Further Thought and Discussion

1. What ethical principles are implicit in lose–lose, win–lose, and win–win orientations toward conflict? Some styles of conflict emphasize fairness, whereas other styles place greater value on cooperation. Do you identify more strongly with either of these value orientations?

2. Think about the ways that you typically respond to conflict. Do you tend to rely on one or two of the four responses we discussed (exit, voice, loyalty, neglect)? Are your response tendencies consistent with research findings about women and men, in general?

3. Have you ever been in a relationship in which conflict was stifled? Using the concepts you learned in this chapter, can you now describe how the conflict was repressed? Can you now think of ways you might have engaged in more effective conflict communication in that relationship?

4. Identify one situation in your life in which each orientation to conflict was, or would have been, appropriate. When would lose–lose have been appropriate? When would win–lose have been a reasonable approach? When would win–win have been the best approach?

5. Use your InfoTrac College Edition to review the table of contents for the five most recent issues of *Journal of Family Practice* and *Journal of Comparative Family Studies*. Do you find articles that discuss how conflicts affect families or how families can handle conflicts productively?

6. This chapter emphasizes aiming for a win–win approach to conflict in personal relationships. Do you believe that in most cases both people can benefit (or win) if each is committed to honouring self and other?

7. Have you been in relationships in which you felt there was grace? How was grace communicated? What was the impact of grace? Have you extended grace to others?

Friendships and Romantic Relationships

Everyday Encounters
By Stephen Lee

Recall Anthony and Natasha from Chapter 4? They began their relationship as friends. Anthony lived in the same building as Natasha's girlfriend. What began as mutual attraction grew into a close friendship and matured into a committed romantic relationship. As a committed cohabiting couple, Anthony and Natasha are now navigating through the challenges of sustaining their relationship.

Much has been written on close relationships. In this chapter, we will examine both friendships and committed romantic relationships and the communication challenges posed by each. We will begin by considering the nature of close relationships and the elements that distinguish these relationships. Then we will explore the rules of friendship, the different styles of loving and the stages of relationship development. We will conclude with the challenges of sustaining close relationships and guidelines for effective communication.

For most of us, friends and lovers are important. Friends help us pass time, grow personally, celebrate moments of joy, and get through the trials and tribulations of everyday life. Romantic partnerships involve romantic and sexual feelings in addition to the sort of love we feel for our friends and family. The intricate design of our lives is made richer by the friendships and intimacies that thread through them.

Across differences in race, gender, class, and sexual preference, most of us expect friends and lovers to invest in us, to provide intimacy, acceptance, trust, practical assistance, support, and in romantic relationships, passion and commitment. These are common threads in diverse close relationships. However, people differ in how they express these elements.

Friendship is essential to our well-being.

Photo: M. Salez

THE NATURE OF CLOSE RELATIONSHIPS

We don't pick our relatives, neighbours, or work associates. Biology or legal bonds establish relationships among family members, and proximity defines neighbours and co-workers. In Western cultures our friendships and romantic intimates, however, are people we choose. Most of our social relationships are I–You bonds. Committed romantic relationships and deep friendships are I–Thou bonds. Friendships and committed romantic relationships share many of the same features. Committed romantic relationships usually have the added inclusion of sexual intimacy and legal and financial bonds that friendships are not usually tethered with. Let's examine the similarities and differences of friendships and committed romantic relationships.

THE NATURE OF FRIENDSHIP

Friendship is a unique relationship. In contrast to most relationships, friendship is voluntary. Friendships are also unique in lacking institutionalized structure or guidelines. There are legal and religious ceremonies for marriage, and social and legal rules for governing marital relationships. However, we have no parallel ceremonies to recognize friendships and no formal standards to guide interaction among friends. The lack of social standards and recognition makes friendship a particularly challenging and exciting relationship.

Even though there are no formal standards for friendship, we have generated some fairly consistent ideas about what a friend is and what happens between friends. Regardless of race, sexual orientation, gender, age, and class, Westerners share some basic expectations of what friends do and what friendship is.

THE NATURE OF COMMITTED ROMANTIC RELATIONSHIPS

Committed romantic relationships, in Western culture at least, are also voluntary relationships that exist between unique individuals—ones who cannot be replaced. We assume most often that the relationships will be primary and continuing parts of our lives. We invest heavily of ourselves and come to know the other as a completely distinct individual.

Committed romantic relationships are distinct from other close relationships in two ways. First, they involve romantic and sexual feelings in addition to the sort of love we feel for friends and family. Another distinctive quality of romantic relationships is that they are considered primary and permanent in our society. We expect to move away from friends and family, but we assume we'll be permanently connected to a romantic partner. Current divorce rates in Canada, according to the 1998 census, indicate that roughly a third of those who marry will separate. Even so, we think of romantic commitment (though not every romantic relationship) as permanent, and this makes romantic commitments unique.

Cultural Shaping of Romantic Ties

Views of romantic relationships vary across cultures. In some countries, marriages are arranged by families, and spouses may get to know each other only after the wedding ceremony. In other cultures, some polygamy is practised, although typically only men have multiple mates (Werner, Altman, Brown, & Ginat, 1993). In Western societies, marriage is an autonomous choice of two individuals who live relatively independently of families. In many other societies, however, marriage joins two families, and couples are intricately connected to both families.

Student Voices

Mansoora:

I find it very odd that Canadians marry only each other and not whole families. In South Africa, people marry into families. The parents must approve of the choice or marriage does not happen. After marriage, the wife moves in with the husband's family. To me this is stronger than a marriage of only two people.

Even within a single country, views of committed romantic relationships vary over time. Whereas traditional marriage was once the only socially recognized form of romantic commitment, today we have a smorgasbord of relationship forms. Commuter marriages are increasingly common (Rohlfing, 1995), as are cohabiting arrangements (Cunningham & Antill, 1995). Every society recognizes and gives privileges to approved relationships and withholds legitimacy from those of which it disapproves. Although gay and lesbian marriages and spousal rights of gay and lesbian partners are undergoing rapid change in Canada, commitments between gays and lesbians are still not yet widely accepted. The cultural bias against homosexual relationships is enforced by denying gays and lesbians privileges that heterosexual couples enjoy. Thus, gays and lesbians can't file joint tax returns, have next-of-kin visiting privileges, insure each other as family, or will each other

Student Voices

Peggy:

I get so burned up about how society treats gay and lesbian couples. My mom and Adrienne have lived together since Mom and Daddy divorced when I was two. We've always been a family. We eat together, work out problems together, vacation together, make decisions together—everything a heterosexual family does. But my mom and Adrienne aren't accepted as a legitimate couple. We've had to move several times because they were "queers," which is what a neighbour called them. Mom's insurance company won't cover Adrienne, so they have to pay for two policies. It goes on and on. I'll tell you, though, I don't know many heterosexual couples as close or stable as Adrienne and Mom.

Divorce and Disobedience

In China, the family has traditionally been considered sacred, and divorces occurred only if a spouse denounced ancestors or killed someone in his mate's family. Marriages were regarded as enduring social ties that did not depend on love.

Wang Wanli encountered the strong pressure not to divorce when he sought to end his marriage in 1981. Chinese traditions often require an individual to get the approval of the work unit for a divorce. In Mr. Wang's case, his unit didn't approve; in fact, they reassigned him to work in the village where he and his wife had grown up in the hope that the community would fortify the marriage. When Wang refused to work there, he was dismissed for disobeying orders.

In the 1980s, the Chinese marriage law was amended to state that love is the most important element for marriage and that the demise of love is justification for divorce. In response to that change, divorces skyrocketed. Between 1980 and 1990, divorces more than doubled, rising from 341,000 to 800,000.

Source: WuDunn, S. (1991, April 17). Romance, a novel idea, rocks marriages in China. *The New York Times*, pp. B1, B12.

tax-free property. In addition, homosexual couples often face discrimination when they wish to rent or buy property or raise children (Issacson, 1989; Weston, 1991).

Social acceptance of divorce, remarriage, and single-parent families has increased. "Divorce and Disobedience" examines the growing acceptance of divorce in China. The traditional Western ideal of the family consisted of a male breadwinner, a female homemaker, and 2.4 children. That solitary ideal has given way to multiple family forms. We have dual-earner couples with children, child-free marriages, single-parent families, and couples in which men are homemakers and women are the primary or sole wage earners. A collage of romantic relationships makes up the contemporary scene.

DIMENSIONS OF CLOSE RELATIONSHIPS

There are seven dimensions of close relationships that bear examination.

Concepts at a Glance

The Seven Dimensions of Close Relationships

1. Willingness to invest
2. Intimacy
   - Closeness through dialogue
   - Closeness through doing
3. Acceptance
4. Trust
5. Support
6. Passion
7. Commitment

WILLINGNESS TO INVEST

Most people assume friendships and romantic relationships require personal investments (Duck & Wright, 1993; Monsour, 1992). We expect to invest time, effort, energy, thought, and feeling in our relationships. Women and men of both homosexual and heterosexual orientations report that having friends is important for a fulfilling life (Mazur, 1989; Nardi & Sherrod, 1994; Sherrod, 1989). Although people differ in how they build and experience close relationships, most of us agree they are important.

Student Voices

Lakisha:

I don't know what I'd do without my friends. More than once they've held me together when I had a fight with my mom or broke up with a guy. When something good happens, it's not quite real until I share it with my friends. I don't think I could be happy without friends.

Student Voices

Dennis:

I really count on my buddies to be there for me. Sometimes we talk or do stuff, but a lot of times we just hang out together. That might not sound important, but it is. Hanging out with friends is a big part of my life.

INTIMACY

We also expect **intimacy** or emotional closeness with lovers and friends. We want those close to us to know our inner selves and to let us know theirs. In addition, intimacy implies that friends like or love each other and care about each other's happiness. Yet the shared view that friendship includes intimacy isn't paralleled by shared ideas about what intimacy is. Research on friendship suggests that how we experience and express intimacy with friends depends on our backgrounds.

There are two ways in which we establish and maintain emotional closeness. One is through dialogue, the other is through doing.

Your Style of Friendship

Before reading further, answer the following questions about how you experience and express closeness with friends.

With your closest or best friends, how often do you:

1. *talk about family problems*
2. *exchange favours (provide transportation, lend money)*
3. *engage in sports (shoot hoops, play tennis, and so forth)*
4. *try to take their minds off problems with diversions*
5. *disclose your personal anxieties and fears*
6. *talk about your romantic relationships and family relationships*
7. *do things together (camp, go to a game, shop)*
8. *confide secrets you wouldn't want others to know*
9. *just hang out without a lot of conversation*
10. *talk about small events in your day-to-day life*
11. *provide practical assistance to help friends*
12. *talk explicitly about your feelings for each other*
13. *discuss and work through tensions in your friendship*
14. *physically embrace or touch to show affection*
15. *ignore or work around problems in the friendship*

Items 1, 5, 6, 8, 10, 12, 13, and 14 have been found to be more prominent in women's friendships; items 2, 3, 4, 7, 9, 11, and 15 tend to be more pronounced in men's friendships.

Closeness through Dialogue

One way to build and express intimacy is through communication. For many people, communication is the centrepiece of intimate relationships. This is especially true for people socialized in feminine speech communities, which emphasize talk as a primary path to intimacy. In general, women see talking and listening as the main activities that create and sustain feelings of closeness (Aries, 1987; Becker, 1987; Rubin, 1985). Talk between women friends tends to be disclosive and emotionally expressive (Brehm, 1992). Women discuss not only major events and issues but also day-to-day activities. This small talk isn't really small at all, because it allows friends to understand the rhythms of each other's life. Intimacy is created as friends talk about themselves and their relationships and as they reveal personal feelings and information. Out of intimate conversation friends weave their separate worlds into a shared mosaic. This builds a strong and deep sense of connection.

Photo: © Corel

Reflecting feminine socialization, communication between women friends is typically responsive and supportive (Wright & Scanlon, 1991). Friends use facial expressions and head movements to show involvement. In addition, they ask questions and give feedback that signals they are following and want to know more. Women friends also offer generous emotional support to one another. They do this by accepting one another's feelings and staying involved in the other's dreams, problems, and lives.

Closeness through Doing

A second way to create and express closeness is by sharing activities. Friends enjoy doing things together and doing things for one another. Activities and companionship are the centre of friendship for some individuals. Closeness through doing is often the primary, although not the only, emphasis in men's friendships (Swain, 1989; Wood & Inman, 1993). As we have seen in previous chapters, masculine speech communities pivot on activities such as sports. This may be why men, in general, find it more natural to build intimacy through doing things than through talking. Sharing activities and working toward common goals (winning the game or battle) build a sense of camaraderie (Sherrod, 1989).

Josh has a good insight. We do reveal ourselves and learn about others in the process of doing things together. In the course of playing hockey or soccer, teammates learn a lot about one another's courage, reliability, willingness to take risks, and security. Soldiers who fight together also discover one another's strengths and weaknesses. Strong emotional bonds and personal knowledge can develop without verbal interaction (Rubin, 1985).

|Student Voices|

Josh:

The thing I like about my buddies is that we can just do stuff together without a lot of talk. Our wives expect us to talk about every feeling we have as if that's required to be real. I'm tight with my buddies, but we don't have to talk about feelings all the time. You learn a lot about someone when you hunt together or coach the Little League.

Intimacy through doing also involves expressing care by doing things for friends. Scott Swain (1989) says men's friendships typically involve a give and take of favours. Jake helps Matt move into his new apartment, and Matt later assists Jake with a glitch in his computer. As a rule, men perceive giving and receiving practical help as expressions of caring and closeness. Perhaps because masculine socialization emphasizes instrumental activities, men are more likely than women to see doing things for others as a primary way to say they care. Notice that the gender difference is a matter of degree, not exclusively one way or the other. Although men tend to place more emphasis on instrumental expressions of care (doing) than women, most men also value and engage in expressive communication (talking) with close friends. Similarly, although women tend to place more emphasis on expressive shows of care than men, most women value and engage in instrumental expressions of caring.

Student Voices

Kaya:
My husband's life centres on doing things for me and our kids. He looks for things to do for us. Like when our son came home over break, he tuned up his car and replaced a tire. I hadn't even noticed the tire was bad. When I wanted to return to school, he took a second job to make more money. One day he came home with a microwave to make cooking easier for me. All the things he does for us are his way of expressing love.

Sometimes the different emphases men and women place on instrumental and expressive behaviours leads to misunderstandings. If Myra sees intimate talk as the crux of closeness, she may not interpret Ed's practical help in fixing her computer as indicating that he cares about her.

Let's repeat a key point that is often overlooked: It would be a mistake to conclude that women and men differ entirely in how they create intimacy; they are actually more alike than we often think (Canary & Dindia, 1998). Recent studies reveal that the sexes are not as different as they are sometimes stereotyped to be (Duck & Wright, 1993). Although women generally place a special priority on communication, men obviously talk with their friends. Like women, men disclose personal feelings and vulnerabilities. They simply do it less, as a rule, than women. Similarly, although men's friendships may be more instrumental, women friends also do things with and for one another and count these as important in friendship (Duck & Wright, 1993).

Review

Many of the differences between how women and men create and express intimacy are matters of degree, not absolute contrasts. Both talking and doing are legitimate ways to show you care about others.

Apply the Idea

Appreciating Talking and Doing in Friendships

For each scenario described below, write out one thing you might say and one thing you might do to show you cared about the person described.

1. *Your best friend has just broken up with his/her long-term boyfriend/girlfriend. Your friend calls you and says, "I feel so lonely."*

   You say _____

   You do _____

2. *A good friend of yours tells you he/she has been fired from an important job.*

You say _____

You do _____

3. *Your best friend tells you his or her grandparent has just died.*

You say _____

You do _____

4. *A close friend stops you on campus and excitedly says, "I just found out I'm pregnant at last. Can you believe it?"*

You say _____

You do _____

LOVE AND FRIENDSHIP

Intimacy includes feelings of closeness, connection, and tenderness. Unlike passion and commitment, which are distinct dimensions of romance, intimacy seems to underlie both passion and commitment (Acker & Davis, 1992). Intimacy is related to passion because both dimensions involve feelings. The link between intimacy and commitment is connectedness, which joins partners in romantic relationships not only in the present but also through the past and into the future.

Intimacy is abiding affection and warm feelings for another person. It is why romantic partners are comfortable with each other and enjoy being together even when fireworks aren't exploding. When asked to evaluate various features of love, people consistently rate companionate features such as getting along and friendship as most important. Although passionate feelings also matter, they are less central to perceptions of love than caring, honesty, respect, friendship, and trust (Fehr, 1993; Luby & Aron, 1990).

Love and friendship

Photo: © Photodisc

ACCEPTANCE

A third common expectation of friends and lovers is that they will accept us. We expect those close to us to like us for who we are and to accept us, warts and all. Each of us has shortcomings and vices, but we count on our intimates and friends to accept us in spite of these. The essence of acceptance is feeling that we are okay as human beings. As we saw with Maslow's hierarchy of human needs in Chapter 1, being accepted by others is important to our sense of self-worth. Most of us are fortunate enough to gain acceptance from family as well as friends and romantic partners. However, this is not always true for lesbians and gays. Sadly, some parents reject sons and daughters who are homosexual. They refuse to validate the basic worth of a child who isn't heterosexual. Parental rejection echoes Western culture's general hostility to homosexuality. Because social and familial acceptance is sometimes lacking for them, gays and lesbians may count on friends for acceptance even more than heterosexuals do (Nardi & Sherrod, 1994). Friendships may have heightened importance because they often substitute for families, as reflected in the book title *Families We Choose* (Weston, 1991).

Student Voices

Doug:

About a year ago, I came out to my parents, and they acted like I was from another planet. It was like once I said I was gay, nothing else about me mattered. Just being gay made me less than human. They shouted and cried and threatened and begged me to get therapy. The only thing they didn't do was consider that maybe I didn't need therapy—maybe it's okay to be gay. The gay community became my family. They are the people who accept me and support who I am. I still hope Mom and Dad will come around one day, but in the meantime I've made another family for myself.

Notice in Doug's commentary that he felt judged by his parents, which probably made him feel defensive. Doug's experience also illustrates the damage done by totalizing—focusing on a single aspect of a person's identity and ignoring many others. Doug is still a student, a loving son, a person who has dreams, ambitions, hopes, and fears. Yet, he feels that his parents see only his sexual orientation and disregard everything else about him.

Although lesbians and gays may depend more heavily than heterosexuals on friends and lovers for acceptance, there are few other differences in how their close relationships operate. Like heterosexuals, gays and lesbians value friendship and distinguish among casual, close, and best friends. Also like heterosexuals, gays and lesbians rely on both communication and activities as paths to intimacy.

TRUST

A key component of close relationships is trust, which has two dimensions. First, trust involves confidence in others to be dependable. We count on them to do what they say and not to do what they promise they won't. Second, trust assumes emotional reliability, which is the belief that a friend or intimate cares about us and our welfare. When we feel both dimensions of trust, we don't need to preface private information with warnings not to tell anyone, and we don't have to have detailed knowledge about what our friends do and who they talk with to believe that they will not hurt us. In committed romantic relationships, trust takes on an added dimension of faithfulness. We will discuss this more closely under the topic of commitment.

Like most qualities of friendship, trust is something that develops gradually and in degrees. We learn to trust people over time as we interact with them and discover they do what they say they will and they don't betray us. As trust develops, friends increasingly reveal themselves to one another. If each new disclosure is accepted and kept confidential, trust continues to grow. When a high level of trust develops, friends and lovers feel less of the uncertainty and insecurity that are natural in early stages of relationships (Boon, 1994).

The level of trust that develops between friends depends on a number of factors. First, our individual histories influence our capacity to trust others. Recalling the discussion of attachment styles in Chapter 2, you'll remember that early interactions with caregivers shape our beliefs about others. For those of us who got consistently loving and nurturing care, trusting others is not especially difficult. On the other hand, some children do not receive that kind of care. For them, caregivers were sometimes available and nurturing and at other times caregivers were absent or not nurturing. If caring is either absent or inconsistent, the capacity to trust others withers. Researchers think the tendency to trust or not to trust is relatively enduring unless later experiences change the early lessons about relationships (Bartholomew, 1993).

Family scripts also influence how much and how quickly we trust others. Some of us were taught that people are good and we should count on them, whereas others learned that people are untrustworthy and that we shouldn't

|Student Voices|

James:
It's tough for me to really trust anybody, even my closest friends or my girlfriend. It's not that they aren't trustworthy. The problem's in me. I just have trouble putting full faith in anyone. When my parents had me, Dad was on the bottle, and Mom was thinking about divorce. He got in Alcoholics Anonymous and they stayed together, but I wonder if what was happening between them meant they weren't there for me. Maybe I learned from the start that I couldn't count on others.

ever turn our back on anyone. Families also influence the importance we attach to friends. Did your parents have many friends? Did you see them enjoying being with their friends? Were their friends often in your home? Or did you seldom see your parents spending time with friends, and were there few occasions when any of their friends were in your home? How many friends your parents had and how much they seemed to value them may have taught you an early lesson about the importance of close relationships in our lives. Basic scripts from families, although not irrevocable, often affect the ease and extent of our ability to trust and our interest in maintaining good friendships and romantic attachments.

Willingness to take risks also influences trust in relationships. There is considerable risk in trusting a friend with our secrets, fears, and flaws. The friend could always use the information against us or share our most private disclosures with others (Boon, 1994). We can never know for sure what friends will do with private information, but we trust them not to use it to exploit or expose us. In this sense, trust is a leap into the unknown. To emphasize the risk in trusting, it has been said that "trust begins where knowledge ends" (Lewis & Weigert, 1985, p. 462). The risk involved may explain why we trust only selected people.

SUPPORT

Communication scholars Brant Burleson and Wendy Samter (1994) report that support is a basic expectation of close relationships. We expect friends to support us in times of personal stress. Once individuals leave home for work or college, friends often become the primary people to whom they turn for help and comfort (Adelman, Parks, & Albrecht, 1987).

There are many ways to show support. What is common among the various types of support is the relationship message "I care about you." Often we support friends by listening to their problems. The more mindfully we listen, the more support we provide. How we respond also shows support. For example, it's supportive to offer to help a friend with a problem or to talk through options. Another way we support friends is by letting them know they're not alone. When we say "I've felt that way too," or "That must be awful for you!" we signal that we understand their feelings. Having the grace to accept friends when they err or hurt us is also a way to show support. To comfort friends in difficult times, we can validate their worth and help them place problems in a larger perspective that includes positive outlooks (Burleson, 1984).

Another important form of support is being available. Sometimes we can't do or say much to ease a friend's unhappiness. Breaking up with a partner, losing a parent, or being rejected by a graduate program are not matters we can change by our words or deeds. However, we can offer ourselves. We show we care by standing by friends so that at least they have company in their sadness. In one study, young adults said the essence of real

José:

Last year my father died back in Mexico, and I wasn't with him when he died. I felt terrible. My friend Alex spent a lot of time with me after my father died. Alex didn't do anything special, and we didn't even really talk much about my father or how I felt. But he was there for me, and that meant everything. I knew he cared even though he never said that.

Is your closeness through dialogue or through doing?

Photo: © Comstock

Photo: © Corbis/Magma

friendship was "being there for each other" (Secklin, 1991). It is a great comfort to know someone is there for us no matter what.

Women and men tend to differ somewhat in how they support friends. Because feminine socialization emphasizes personal communication, women generally provide more verbal emotional support than men (Aries, 1987; Becker, 1987; Duck & Wright, 1993). Women are likely to talk in detail about feelings, dimensions of emotional issues, and fears that accompany distress. By talking in depth about emotional troubles, women help one another identify and ventilate feelings. In addition, intimate talk weaves friends closely together. This exemplifies closeness through dialogue.

Men tend to rely less than women on emotional talk to support friends. Instead, they often engage in **"covert intimacy,"** a term Swain (1989) coined to describe the indirect ways men support one another. Instead of an intense hug, which women might use to support a hurting friend, men are more likely to clasp a shoulder or playfully punch an arm. Instead of engaging in direct and sustained emotional talk, men tend to communicate support more instrumentally. This could mean giving advice on how to solve a problem or offering assistance, such as a loan or transportation. Finally, men are more likely than women to support friends by coming up with diversions (Cancian, 1987; Tavris, 1992). If you can't make a problem any better, at least you can take a friend's mind off it. "Let's go for a run" and "Let's check out the new movie" are offers to support a friend by providing diversions. These ways of supporting others are consistent with the masculine mode of closeness.

Ethnicity also influences orientations toward friendship. In a study of Japanese and Western friendships, Dean Barnlund (1989) found both similarities and differences. Both ethnic groups preferred friends who were similar to them in age and ethnic heritage, and both groups agreed on many of the qualities that describe friends. Commonly valued qualities in friends included understanding, respect, trust, and sincerity. Yet Japanese and Western friends differed in the priority they assigned the qualities. Japanese respondents said togetherness, trust, and warmth were the most important qualities in friendship, whereas Westerners listed understanding, respect, and sincerity as the top qualities. The differences in rankings reflect distinctions between Japanese and Western culture. Interpersonal harmony and collective orientation are central values in Japan, and these are reflected in the qualities Japanese consider most important in friends. Western culture emphasizes individuality, candor, and respect—the very qualities Canadians most prize in friends.

The last two dimensions of close relationships are found predominantly in committed romantic relationships. Passion and commitment combined with intimacy form a triangle that represents the different facets of what researchers define as love (Acker & Davis, 1992; Hendrick & Hendrick, 1989; Sternberg, 1986). See Figure 10.1.

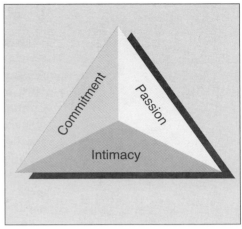

Figure 10.1
The Triangle of Love

PASSION

For most of us, **passion** is what first springs to mind when we think about romance. Passion is intensely positive feelings and desires for another person. Passion is not equivalent to sexual or sensual emotions, although these are types of passion. In addition to erotic feelings, passion may involve intense emotional, spiritual, and intellectual attraction. The sparks and emotional high of being in love stem from passion. It's why we feel butterflies in the stomach and fall head over heels.

As much fun as passion is, it isn't the primary foundation for enduring romance. In fact, research consistently shows that passion is less central to how we think about love than intimacy and commitment. This makes sense when we realize that passion can seldom be sustained for a lifetime. Like other intense feelings, it ebbs and flows. Because passion comes and goes and is largely beyond our will, it isn't a strong basis for long-term relationships. In other words, passion may set romance apart from other relationships, but it isn't what holds romance together. To build a lasting relationship, we need something more durable.

COMMITMENT

The something else needed is **commitment,** the second dimension of romantic relationships. Commitment is an intention to remain with a relationship. As we noted earlier, commitment is not the same thing as love. Love is a feeling based on rewards we get from being involved with a person. Commitment, in contrast, is a decision based on investments we put into a relationship (Lund, 1985). We choose to entwine our life and future with another person's.

In an important study of Western values, Robert Bellah and his colleagues (1985) found that most Westerners want both passion and commitment in long-term romantic relationships. We desire the euphoria of passion, but we know that it won't weather rough times or ensure compatibility and comfort on a day-in, day-out basis. We also want commitment as a stable foundation for a life together. Commitment is a determination to stay together in spite of trouble, disappointments, sporadic restlessness, and lulls in passion. Commitment involves responsibility, not just feeling (Beck, 1988). The responsibilities of commitment are to make a relationship a priority and to invest continuously in it.

Review

Passion is a feeling. Commitment is a choice. Passion may fade, commitment remains steadfast.

Student Voices

Wade:

I've been married for 15 years, and we would have split a dozen times if love was all that held us together. A marriage simply can't survive on love alone. You can't count on feeling in love or passionate all the time. Lucy and I have gone through spells where we were bored with each other or where we wanted to walk away from our problems. We didn't because we made a promise to stay together "for better or for worse." Believe me, a marriage has both.

Apply the Idea

Measuring Love and Commitment

Think of a current or past romance to answer these questions:

1. *Do you think your relationship will be permanent?*
2. *Do you feel you can confide in your partner about virtually anything?*
3. *Are you attracted to other potential partners or to a single lifestyle?*
4. *Would you be miserable if you couldn't be with your partner?*
5. *Would you find it personally difficult to end your relationship?*

6. *If you felt lonely, would your first thought be to seek your partner?*
7. *Do you feel obligated to continue this relationship?*
8. *Would you forgive your partner for virtually anything?*
9. *In your opinion, do you think your partner intends to continue this relationship?*
10. *Is one of your primary concerns your partner's welfare?*

Commitment is measured by odd-numbered items; love is measured by even-numbered items.

Based on: Lund, M. (1985). The development of investment and commitment scales for predicting continuity of personal relationships. *Journal of Social and Personal Relationships*, 2, 15.

Communication Notes

The Prototype of Love

Westerners appear to have a fairly specific prototype of what love is. Research repeatedly reveals that we regard feeling valued by and comfortable with another as more important than passion. Love is typified by feelings such as closeness, caring, and friendship, and by commitment, as defined by features such as trust and respect. Intimacy and commitment eclipse passion in importance. Even when people are asked what's most important for "being in love," companionate features have priority.

Do women and men differ in how important they consider the dimensions of love? Although women and men don't differ significantly in what they consider typical of love in general, they do diverge in their personal ideals for love. For both sexes, passion is less salient than companionate features. However, features linked to intimacy and commitment are even more prominent in women's personal ideals of love than in men's. The only feature that men rate higher than women is fantasy. No differences have been found among heterosexuals, gays, and lesbians.

Sources: Button, C. M., & Collier, D. R. (1991, June). A comparison of people's concepts of love and romantic love. Paper presented at the Canadian Psychological Association Conference, Calgary, Alberta; Fehr, B. (1993). How do I love thee: Let me consult my prototype. In S. W. Duck (Ed.), Understanding relationship processes, 1: *Individuals in relationships* (pp. 87–122). Newbury Park, CA: Sage; Luby, V., & Aron, A. (1990, July). A prototype structuring of love, like, and being in love. Paper presented at the Fifth International Conference on Personal Relationships, Oxford, England; Rousar, E. E., III, & Aron, A. (1990, July). Valuing, altruism, and the concept of love. Paper presented at the Fifth International Conference on Personal Relationships, Oxford, England.

Although close relationships reflect the influence of personal experience, gender, and ethnic heritage, there is also much common ground in what people expect and value in these relationships. We expect friends and romantic partners to invest in our relationship and to provide intimacy, acceptance, trust, support, and in romantic relationships, passion and commitment. As a result of gender, race, ethnicity, economic class, age, and sexual orientation, we may differ in how we experience and express deep feelings. However, it seems that these seven common expectations transcend differences among us. Yet, it's not enough for us to have these feelings; we must also communicate them. Skills in verbal and nonverbal communication, listening, building climate, and managing conflict contribute to effective expression of friendship and love.

THE DEVELOPMENT OF CLOSE RELATIONSHIPS

Researchers in the development of close relationships in Western society identify three broad phases that relationships evolve through: growth, navigation, and deterioration (Duck, 1994a, 1994b, 1992; Rawlins, 1981). Table 10.1 identifies the distinctiveness and similarity between the development of friendships and the development of romantic relationships.

Table 10.1

The Developmental Course of Close Relationships

Phase	Friendships	Romantic Relationships
Growth	Role-Limited Interaction	Attraction without Interaction
	Friendly Relations	Invitational Communication
	Moving toward Friendship	Explorational Communication
	Nascent Friendship	Intensifying Communication
		Revising Communication
		Commitment
Navigating	Stabilizing	Managing Relational Dialectics
		Rules & Rituals
		Placemaking
		Everyday Interactions
Deterioration	Waning	Dyadic Breakdown
		Intrapsychic Phase
		Dyadic Phase
		Social Phase
		Social Support
		Grave Dressing

THE DEVELOPMENTAL COURSE OF FRIENDSHIP

Most friendships develop over time in fairly patterned ways. Although intense bonds are sometimes formed quickly in unusual circumstances such as crises, the majority of friends work out their relationship in a series of stages. Bill Rawlins (1981), an interpersonal communication researcher who focuses on communication between friends, developed a six-stage model of how friendships develop (Table 10.1).

Role-Limited Interaction

Friendships begin with an encounter in two individuals' social circle. We might meet a new person at work, through membership on an athletic team, in a club, or by chance in an airport, store, or class. The initial meeting is the first stage of interaction and, possibly, friendship. During this stage, we tend to rely on standard social rules and roles. We are polite, and we are less than fully open and disclosive, because we aren't ready to reveal our private selves. In early meetings, people don't have enough personal knowledge of each other to engage in dual perspective. Instead, they rely on more general scripts and stereotypes. Also, early interactions are often awkward and laced with uncertainty, because individuals haven't worked out their own patterns for relating to each other.

Friendly Relations

The second stage of friendship is **friendly relations**, in which individuals check out the other to see whether common ground and interests exist. Jean tries to start a conversation with Paula by commenting on the teacher in a class they share. If Paula responds with her impressions of the teacher, she conveys the relationship-level message that she's interested in interacting. A businessperson may joke or engage in small talk to see if an associate wants to move beyond the acquaintance level of relating. Although friendly exchanges are not dramatic, they are useful. Through them, we explore the potential for a more personal relationship with another person.

Moving toward Friendship

During the third stage of interaction, we start making serious moves to create a friendship. Until this stage, we stick pretty closely to social rules and norms, and we interact in contexts where we naturally meet. **Moving toward friendship** involves stepping beyond social roles. We might make a small self-disclosure or comment that we're angry about something to signal we'd like to personalize the relationship. We also move toward friendship when we meet outside of contexts that naturally occur. Emily might ask her associate Sam if he wants to stop at a bar for a drink before leaving for the day. Ben might ask his classmate Drew if he wants to get together to study. Sometimes we involve others to lessen the potential awkwardness of being with someone we don't yet know well. For instance, Amy might invite Tsering to a party where others will be present. As we interact more personally with others, we begin to talk about feelings, values, interests, and attitudes. This personal knowledge forms the initial foundation of friendship.

Nascent Friendship

If individuals continue to interact and to like what they discover in each other, they begin to think of themselves as friends or as becoming friends. This is the stage of **nascent,** or embryonic, friendship. At this point, social rules and standards become less important, and friends begin to work out their own private rules for regulating interaction. Friends might agree to reserve a specific day for lunch or breakfast with each other. Some friends settle into patterns of getting together for specific things (watching games, shopping, racquetball, going to movies) and don't ever expand those boundaries. Other friends share a wider range of times and activities. Although friends are working out rules for their relationship during the nascent stage, often they aren't aware of the rules until later. The milestones of this stage are that individuals begin to think of themselves as friends and to work out their own patterns for interaction. "Maintaining Friendships" discusses how much time we invest in various types of friendships.

Communication Notes

Maintaining Friendships

Do we spend more time with casual friends or best friends? The answer might surprise you. A recent study indicates that frequent interaction is more important for casual friendships than for close or best friendships. When casual friends don't see each other, they aren't sure the friendship still exists.

Lack of interaction doesn't appear to threaten relationships between best friends. Close and best friendships depend more on assurances of affection, though these need not be frequent. The best explanation is that close and best friends feel more secure in their connection than do casual friends. Because they assume they're continuing parts of each other's life, best friends don't need regular interaction.

Source: Rose, S., & Serafica, F. (1986) Keeping and ending casual, close and best friendships. *Journal of Social and Personal Relationships, 3,* 275–288.

Stabilized Friendship

When friends feel established in each other's life, the friendship is stabilized. A key benchmark of this stage of **stabilized friendship** is the assumption of continuity. Whereas in earlier stages individuals didn't count on getting together unless they made a specific plan, stabilized friends assume they'll continue to see each other. We no longer have to ask if a friend wants to get together again. We take future encounters for granted because we consider the relationship ongoing.

Another criterion of this stage is trust, which stabilizes the friendship. Throughout earlier stages of interaction, individuals make limited disclosures to build and test trust. A close friendship is unlikely to stabilize until there is a mutually high level of trust. Once friends have earned each other's trust, many of the barriers to fully interpersonal communication disintegrate. It now feels safe to share intimate information and to reveal vulnerabilities that we normally conceal from others. As we communicate more openly, our friendships become more honest and personal. We remove social masks we wear with most people and enter into I–Thou relationships by engaging friends in their unique individuality. Stabilized friendships may continue indefinitely, in some cases lasting a lifetime.

Waning Friendship

As we have seen, a common expectation of friendship is investment. **Waning friendship** is likely to occur when one or both individuals stop investing in a friendship. Sometimes friends drift apart because each is pulled in different

Student Voices

Marlene:

Martha and I go way, way back—all the way to childhood when we lived in the same housing complex. As kids we made mud pies and ran a lemonade stand together. In high school, we double-dated and planned our lives together. Then we both got married and stayed in touch, even when Martha moved away. We still sent each other pictures of our children, and we called a lot. When my last child entered college, I decided it was time for me to do that too, so I enrolled in college. Before I did that, though, I had to talk to Martha and get her perspective on whether I was nuts to go to college in my thirties. She thought it was a great idea, and she's thinking about that for herself now. For nearly forty years we've shared everything in our lives.

directions by career and family demands. In other cases, friendships deteriorate because they've run their natural course and become boring. A third reason friendships end is violations of trust or other rules friends establish for themselves. Saying "I don't have time for you now" may violate friends' tacit agreement to always make room for each other. Criticizing a friend or not sharing confidences may also breach unspoken rules between friends.

When friendships deteriorate or suffer serious violations, communication changes in predictable ways. Defensiveness and uncertainty rise, causing individuals to be more guarded, less spontaneous, and less disclosive than they were in the stage of stabilized friendship. Communication may also become more controlling and strategic as waning friends try to protect themselves from further exposure and hurt. Yet the clearest indication that a friendship is fading may be reductions in the quantity and quality of communication. As former friends drift apart or experience hurt from each other, they are likely to interact less often and to talk about less personal and consequential topics.

Even when serious violations occur between friends, relationships can sometimes be repaired. Sometimes friends hurt us when they are under serious stress. If we attribute something we don't like to factors beyond their control, we may be willing to forgive them and continue the friendship. We may also be more willing to stay with a friend who has hurt us unintentionally than one who deliberately harmed us. For a friendship that has waned to be revived, however, requires both friends to be committed to rebuilding trust and intimacy. They must be willing to work through their feelings in open, constructive discussion.

The ways friendship grows and operates are not random. Although we're usually not aware of patterns, friendships tend to follow rules in how they develop and function. See "The Rules of Friendship."

THE DEVELOPMENTAL COURSE OF ROMANTIC RELATIONSHIPS

Like friendships, romantic relationships tend to follow a developmental course. Initially, scholars thought relationships move through stages as a result of objective activities such as self-disclosing. More recently, however, we have realized that romance progresses based on how we perceive interaction, not on interaction itself (Honeycutt, 1993). For example, if Terry discloses personal information to Janet, then the relationship will escalate if Janet and Terry interpret self-disclosure as a move toward greater intimacy. If Janet doesn't perceive Terry's disclosure as personal, she's unlikely to feel he has made a move toward greater closeness. It is the meaning they assign to self-disclosing, not the actual act of self-disclosing, that determines how they perceive their level of intimacy.

The Rules of Friendship

When researchers asked people to describe their ideas about what is needed to maintain a good friendship, they found high consistency on a number of rules for keeping friendship intact:

1. Stand up for a friend when she or he isn't around.
2. Share your successes and how you feel about them.
3. Give emotional support.
4. Trust and confide in each other.
5. Help a friend when he or she is needy.
6. Respect a friend's privacy.
7. Try to make friends feel good when you are together.

People were just as consistent in what they described as "anti-rules," or ways to end a friendship:

1. Fail to tolerate your friend's friends.
2. Criticize a friend in front of others.
3. Share a friend's confidences with other people.
4. Fail to show a friend you like him or her.
5. Fail to support a friend.
6. Nag a friend, or get on his or her case.
7. Fail to confide in a friend.
8. Fail to help a friend when she or he is needy.
9. Act jealous or critical of a friend's other friends.

Source: Argyle, M., & Henderson, M. (1985). The rules of relationships. In S. W. Duck & D. Perlman (Eds.), *Understanding personal relationships: An interdisciplinary approach* (pp. 63–84). Beverly Hills, CA: Sage.

As we learned in Chapter 3, perceiving is an active process in which we notice, organize, and interpret what goes on around us. We use cognitive schematas and information from past experiences to decide what things mean. The meanings we assign to romance, however, are not entirely individualistic. They also reflect broad cultural beliefs that we internalize as we are socialized. Because members of a society share many views, there are strong consistencies in how we perceive what happens in romantic relationships. Research shows that Western college students agree on the script for first dates (Pryor & Merluzzi, 1985). They also share ideas about how men and women should act. The majority of college students think men should initiate and plan dates and make decisions about most activities, but women control sexual activity (Rose & Frieze, 1989). In other cultures, different rules prevail. For example, in India, marriages are often arranged by parents; love is understood to be something couples develop after they wed. In Nepal, ritualistic dancing and celebrations are an important part of courtship. Although views of romantic relationships vary among cultures, every culture has shared understandings of what love is and how love develops.

Research on the evolution of romantic relationships has focused on Western society, so we know little about the developmental course of romance in other cultures. Let's now examine the three phases of growth, navigation, and deterioration as they relate to romantic relationships.

Growth Stages

In moving toward romantic commitment, researchers have identified six stages of interaction that mark progressive intimacy within the three phases. Usually, although not always, these stages occur in sequence.

Attraction without Interaction

The first stage is individuals who aren't interacting. We are aware of ourselves as individuals with particular needs, goals, love styles, and qualities that affect what we look for in relationships. Our choices of people with whom to start romance may also be influenced by aspects of ourselves of which we are unaware—for example, attachment styles and the hidden area of the Johari window. We can call this stage attraction without interaction.

Invitational Communication

The second growth stage is **invitational communication** in which individuals signal they are interested in interacting and respond to invitations from others. "Want to dance?" "Where are you from?" "I love this kind of music," "Hi, my name's Shelby" are examples of bids for interaction. Invitational communication usually follows a conventional script for initial interaction. The meaning of invitational communication is found on the relationship level, not the content level. "I love this kind of music" literally means a person likes the music. On the relationship level of meaning, however, the message is "I'm available and interested. Are you?"

Apply the Idea

Relationship Meanings of Invitations

Go to a place where people are likely to meet for the first time. Observe how individuals extend and respond to invitations for interaction. What are the content meanings of invitations and responses? What do you perceive as the relationship meaning of invitations and responses?

Of all the people we meet, we are attracted to only a few. The three greatest influences on initial attraction are self-concept, proximity, and similarity. How we see ourselves affects the people we consider candidates for romance. Heterosexuals, lesbians, bisexuals, and gays seek romance with others who share their sexual orientation. "Bases of Romantic Attraction" summarizes research on heterosexual, gay, and lesbian attraction. Social class also influences whom we notice and consider appropriate for us. Most people pair with others of their race and social class. Even with all of the attention to diversity in our era, research indicates that people still seek others who are similar to them. In fact, social prestige influences dating patterns now more than in the 1950s (Whitbeck & Hoyt, 1994). Most college students seek to date people who share their social and class backgrounds.

In addition to personal identity, proximity and similarity influence initial attraction. We can interact only with people we meet, so where we live,

Communication Notes

Bases of Romantic Attraction

Gay men tend to desire very specific physical characteristics, including an extremely attractive face, a slim and well-conditioned body, and good grooming. In addition, they want partners who are self-sufficient and have prestigious careers that yield good incomes.

Straight men also state that physical attractiveness is very important to them in romantic partners. They report looking for women who are slim and beautiful. Intelligence, status, and personality matter less than physical beauty.

Lesbians generally stress emotional and personal qualities in partners and care little about physical appearance or dress. Although some lesbians admire a "butch" look, others prefer traditional feminine beauty. Lesbians value economic independence in partners, though less so than gays.

Straight women emphasize personal qualities in romantic partners. Warmth, honesty, kindness, and personal integrity are among the qualities straight women consider important. They also value ambition and status in partners.

Sources: Based on Huston, M., & Schwartz, P. (1995). Relationships of lesbians and gay men. In J. T. Wood & S. W. Duck (Eds.), Understanding relationship processes, 6; *Off the beaten track: Understudied relationships* (pp. 89–121). Thousand Oaks, CA: Sage; Sprecher, S. (1989). The importance to males and females of physical attractiveness, earning potential, and expressiveness in initial attraction. *Sex Roles*, 21, 591–607.

work, and socialize affects the possibilities for relationships. Nearness to others, however, doesn't necessarily increase liking.

Environmental spoiling describes situations in which proximity breeds ill will. This happens when we're forced to be around others whose values, lifestyles, or behaviours conflict with our own. For the most part, we seek romantic partners who are like us. "Birds of a feather" seems more true than "Opposites attract." In general, we are attracted to people whose values, attitudes, and lifestyles are similar to ours. Similarity of personality is also linked to long-term marital happiness (Caspi & Harbener, 1990).

Explorational Communication

Explorational communication is the third stage in the escalation of romance, and it involves exchanging information to explore the possibilities for a relationship. We use communication to announce our identities and to learn about others. In this stage, individuals fish for common interests and grounds for interaction: Are you from the Territories? Do you like blues? What kind of family did you come from? Have you been following the political debates? As we continue to interact with others, both breadth and depth of information increase. Because we perceive self-disclosure as a sign of trust, it tends to escalate intimacy (Berger & Bell, 1988). At this early stage of interaction, reciprocity of disclosure is expected so that one person isn't more vulnerable than the other (Duck, 1992; Miell & Duck, 1986).

Intensifying Communication

If early interaction increases attraction, then individuals may dramatically escalate the relationship. During the fourth growth stage, **intensifying communication,** the partners increase the depth of their relationship by increasing personal knowledge; this allows the couple to begin creating a private culture. During this stage, partners spend more and more time together, and they rely less on external structures such as movies or parties. Instead, they immerse themselves in the budding relationship and may feel they can't be together enough. Further disclosures are exchanged, personal biographies are filled in, and partners increasingly learn how each other feels and thinks. As personal knowledge expands, dual perspective is possible. "The Chemistry of Love" explores the biological basis of attraction between people.

Also characteristic of the intensifying stage are idealizing and personalized communication. Idealizing involves seeing a relationship and a partner as more wonderful, exciting, and perfect than he or she really is (Hendrick & Hendrick, 1988). During euphoria, partners often exaggerate each other's virtues, downplay or fail to perceive vices, and overlook problems in the relationship. It is also during euphoria that partners begin to develop relationship vocabularies made up of nicknames and private codes. Most relationship vocabularies include terms that symbolize important experiences partners have shared. Relationship vocabularies both reflect and fuel intimacy.

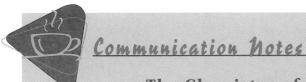

Communication Notes

The Chemistry of Love

People often talk about the chemistry they have with certain others. Recent research suggests there may be a factual, biological basis to the idea that there is chemistry between people. Consider:

The cuddle chemical is oxytocin, which is stimulated by either physical or emotional cues. Oxytocin is released when babies nurse, making mothers nuzzle and cuddle them. Oxytocin also pours out during sexual arousal and lovemaking, making lovers want to caress and cuddle one another.

The infatuation chemical is phenylethylamine (PEA). Like amphetamines, PEA makes our bodies tremble when we're attracted to someone and makes us feel euphoric, happy, and energetic when we're in love.

The attachment chemical is really a group of morphine-like opiates that calm us and create feelings of relaxed comfort. This allows couples to form more peaceful, steady relationships than the speedlike PEA does. Opiates of the mind promote abiding commitment.

Source: Ackerman, D. (1994). *A natural history of love.* New York: Random House.

Apply the Idea

Intimate Talk

Do you and your partner have a private language in your relationship?

- *Do you have special nicknames for each other that others don't have and use?*
- *Do you have special words that you made up to describe experiences, activities, and feelings?*
- *Do you have codes that allow you and your partner to send messages in public that other people don't understand?*
- *How does your special relationship language reflect your relationship? How does it affect the bond?*

Revising Communication

Revising communication, although not part of escalation in all romantic relationships, is important. During this fifth stage, partners come down out of the clouds to look at their relationship more realistically. Problems and dissatisfactions are recognized as partners evaluate the relationship's potential to survive. With the rush of euphoria over, partners consider whether this relationship is one they want for the long run. If it is, they work through obstacles to long-term viability. Many couples that fall in love and move through the intensifying stage choose not to stay together. It is entirely possible to love a person with whom we don't want to share our life or to decide that it's better to stay together without formalizing the relationship. Some older couples make this choice, because marrying can decrease their Social Security benefits.

Student Voices

Esther:

Breaking up with Ted was the hardest thing I ever did. I really loved him, and he loved me, but I just couldn't see myself living with a Christian. My whole heritage is Jewish—it's who I am. I celebrate Hanukkah, not Christmas. Seder, Passover, and Yom Kippur are very important to me. Those aren't part of Ted's heritage, and he wouldn't convert. I loved him, but we couldn't have made a life together.

Commitment

The final growth stage is **commitment,** which is a decision to stay with a relationship permanently. This decision transforms a romantic relationship from one based on past and present experiences and feelings into one with a future. Prior to making a commitment, partners don't view the relationship as continuing forever. With commitment, the relationship becomes a given, around which they arrange other aspects of their lives. The unique qualities of surrendering and co-mingling that are part of this stage are expressed in the poem "The Wisdom of Porcelain" on pages 398–99.

Navigating

Navigating is a long-term process. Ideally, a relationship stabilizes in navigating once a commitment has been made. Navigating is the ongoing process of staying committed and living a life together, despite ups and downs and pleasant and unpleasant surprises. Although we hope to stabilize in navigating, the stage itself is full of movement. Couples continuously adjust, work through new problems, revisit old ones, and accommodate to changes in their individual and relational lives. During navigation, partners also continuously experience tension from relational dialectics, which are never resolved once and for all. As partners respond to dialectical tensions, they revise and refine the nature of the relationship itself.

In relationships that do endure, ongoing navigation helps partners avoid dangerous shoals and keep their intimacy on a good course. To use an automotive analogy, navigating involves both preventive maintenance and periodic repairs (Canary & Stafford, 1994). The goals of navigating are to keep intimacy satisfying and healthy and to remedy any serious problems that arise. To understand the navigating stage, we'll discuss how relational culture is created by managing relational dialectics, rules and rituals, placemaking, and everyday interaction.

Managing Relational Dialectics

The nucleus of intimacy is **relational culture,** which is a private world of rules, understandings, meanings, and patterns of acting and interpreting that partners create for their relationship (Wood, 1982, 1995c). Relational culture includes **managing relational dialectics.** Jan and Byron may negotiate a lot of autonomy and little togetherness, whereas Louise and Teresa emphasize connectedness and minimize autonomy. Bobby and Cassandra are very open and expressive, whereas Mike and Zelda preserve more individual privacy in their marriage. There are not right and wrong ways to manage dialectics, because individuals and couples differ in what they need. What is most important is for couples to agree on how to deal with tensions between autonomy and connection, openness and privacy, and novelty and routine (Fitzpatrick & Best, 1979; Wood, 1995c).

Rules and Rituals

Relational culture includes **rules and rituals** that partners work out. Couples develop constitutive rules, usually unspoken, about how to show anger, love, sexual interest, and so forth. They also develop routines for contact. Couples reserve weekends for staying in touch. Couples also develop rules for commemorating special times such as birthdays and holidays.

Romantic couples develop rituals to structure interaction. Carol Bruess and Judy Pearson (1997) identified seven rituals that are common among married couples. The couples they studied had established rituals for couple time, celebrations and play, daily routines and tasks, expressing intimacy, communicating, dealing with habits and mannerisms, and spiritual engagement. The rules and rituals that partners develop and follow provide a predictable rhythm for intimate interaction. See Figure 10.2.

Placemaking

Placemaking is the process of creating a personal environment that is comfortable and that reflects the values, experiences, and tastes of a couple (Werner et al., 1993). We see placemaking evident in the poem "The Wisdom of Porcelain."

1. Couple time rituals (activities, togetherness, escapes)

2. Symbolic rituals (private codes, play, celebration)

3. Daily routines and tasks

4. Intimacy expressions

5. Communication rituals

6. Patterns, habits, and mannerisms

7. Spiritual rituals

Figure 10.2
The Seven Rituals of Couples

The Wisdom of Porcelain
(or Entry into Tandem)
by T.E. Henry

It wasn't until they went to Ikea and he
bought a toothbrush holder for his bathroom
while asking her what colour coffee mugs to buy
that she realized that they were *going out* and
this was the part where the bachelor decides to
add detail to his life because the topography of his singularity
(dirty underwear rejected to the corners of the bedroom,
endless empty milk cartons and hollow boxes of honey nut
cheerios stacked like elaborate bee hives in the kitchen) now
had a witness.

She began
examining lingerie
debating contour and texture—
critical of her own sexiness
knowing full well that a new interpretation would be present
when the soft straps were revealed.
It wasn't until the pronoun *we* entered her sentence that
her singular pride was forced to retreat,
to live in the plural,
and acknowledge the relief of defeat.

Loneliness was tampered with.
Her mouth began to form the words "I lo …"
her head closed in,
pinning the phrase to her tongue—stopping the syllables
from spattering
blood, letting
her
heart out.
Out
in the open
vulnerable to the tempest
of reciprocity.

Somehow their egos managed to adapt to the way the two
toothbrushes

leaned towards the edge of the cup,
heads touching,
succumbing to each other's weight.
The sink was forgiving of the match,
years of grooming,
many round shoulders bending to strike the shave,
the whisper of mascara being brushed on lashes—
the preparations for sleep,
the separate rituals involving face cream, dialogues with the
mirror, diaphragm gel and floss
rendered the white porcelain sink wise,
and accepting
of the kind weaknesses
that time altered by two can reveal.

Everyday Interactions

Another important dimension of relational culture is **everyday interaction**. Partners weave the basic fabric of their relationship in day-to-day conversations that realize their togetherness. "Absence Makes the Words Grow Fonder" explores the importance of everyday interaction for couples. Most

Love comes in many forms.

Photos: © Photodisc

conversations between intimates aren't dramatic or noteworthy; actually, the majority of interaction is fairly routine and mundane. Yet everyday talk is more important than major celebrations and big crises in creating and sustaining intimacy (Duck, 1994b; Spencer, 1994). Ordinary talk between partners nourishes their interpersonal climate by continuously recognizing and affirming each other.

Communication Notes

Absence Makes the Words Grow Fonder

Couples who have long-distance or commuter relationships face many challenges. Yet what long-distance partners say is most difficult is the loss of daily routines and conversation about everyday matters. What they miss most is sharing trivial details of their lives and small talk.

Source: Gerstel, N., & Gross, H. (1985). *Commuter marriage*. New York: Guilford.

Deterioration

Steve Duck, a scholar of communication in personal relationships, proposed a six-phase model of relational decline.

Dyadic Breakdown

Dyadic breakdown is the first phase of relational decay, and it involves degeneration of established patterns, understandings, and routines that make up a relational culture. Partners may stop talking after dinner, no longer bother to call when they are running late, and in other ways neglect the little things that tie them together. As the fabric of intimacy weakens, dissatisfaction intensifies.

There are general gender differences in the causes of dyadic breakdown. For women, unhappiness with a relationship most often arises when communication declines in quality, quantity, or both. Men are more likely to be dissatisfied by specific behaviours. For instance, men report being dissatisfied when their partners don't greet them at the door and make special meals (Riessman, 1990). For many men, dissatisfaction also arises if they have domestic responsibilities, which they feel aren't a man's job (Gottman & Carrère, 1994). Many women regard a relationship as breaking down if "We don't really communicate with each other anymore," whereas men tend to be dissatisfied if "We don't do fun things together anymore." Another gender difference is in who notices problems in a relationship. As a rule, women are more likely than men to perceive declines in intimacy.

Because women are socialized to take care of relationships, they are more likely than men to notice tensions and early symptoms of problems (Cancian, 1989; Tavris, 1992).

Intrapsychic Phase

The **intrapsychic phase** involves brooding about problems in the relationship and dissatisfactions with a partner (Duck, 1992). Women's brooding about languishing relationships tends to focus on perceived declines in closeness and intimate communication, whereas men's reflections more often centre on lapses in joint activities and acts of consideration between partners. It's easy for the intrapsychic phase to become a self-fulfilling prophecy: As gloomy thoughts snowball and awareness of positive features of the relationship ebb, partners may actually bring about the failure of their relationship. During the intrapsychic phase, partners may begin to think about alternatives to the relationship.

Dyadic Phase

The **dyadic phase** is the third stage in relational decline, and it doesn't always occur (Duck, 1992). As we saw in Chapter 9, women are more likely to respond to conflict by initiating discussion of problems, and men often deny problems or exit rather than talk about them. Communication scholars report that many people avoid talking about problems, refuse to return calls from partners, and in other ways evade confronting difficulties (Baxter, 1984; Metts, Cupach, & Bejlovec, 1989). Although this is understandable, because it is painful to talk about the decline of intimacy, avoiding problems does nothing to resolve them and may, in fact, make them worse. In formal relationships such as marriage, partners must negotiate matters such as division of property and child custody, but they may choose to talk through lawyers rather than directly to each other. What happens in the negotiation phase depends on how committed partners are, whether they perceive attractive alternatives to the relationship, and whether they have the communication skills to work through problems constructively.

Social Phase

If partners lack commitment or the communication skills needed to resuscitate intimacy, they enter the fourth stage, the **social phase** of disintegration, which involves figuring out how to tell outsiders they are parting. Either separately or in collaboration, partners decide how to explain their breakup to friends, children, in-laws, and social acquaintances. When partners don't cooperatively craft a joint explanation for breaking up, friends may take sides, gossip, and disparage one or the other partner as the "bad guy"(La Gaipa, 1982).

Social Support

Social support is a fifth phase in which partners look to friends and family for support during the breakup. Others can provide support by being available and by listening mindfully. Partners may give self-serving accounts of the breakup in order to save face and secure sympathy and support from others. Thus, Beth may portray Janine as at fault and herself as the innocent party in a breakup. During this phase, partners often criticize their exes and expect friends to take their side (Duck, 1992). Although self-serving explanations of breakups are common, they aren't necessarily constructive. It's a good idea to monitor communication during this period so that we don't say things we'll later regret.

Student Voices

Samantha:

I really hate it when couples in our social circle divorce. It never fails that we lose one of the two of them as a friend, because each of them wants us to take sides. They each blame the other and expect us to help them do that, and you can't do it for both spouses. One of them won't be a friend anymore.

Grave Dressing

Grave dressing is the sixth phase in relational decline, and it involves burying the relationship and accepting its end. Like individuals, relationships deserve a proper burial (Duck, 1992). During grave dressing, we work to make sense of the relationship—what it meant, why it failed, and how it affected us. Usually, individuals need to mourn intimacy that has died. Even if we initiate a breakup, we are sad about the failure to realize what seemed possible at one time. Grave dressing completes the process of relational dissolution by putting the relationship to rest so that partners can get on with their individual lives.

The stages we have discussed describe how most people perceive the course of romance. However, not all couples follow the standard pattern. Some partners skip one or more stages in the typical sequences of escalation or deterioration, and many of us cycle more than once through certain stages. For example, a couple might soar through euphoria, work out some tough issues in revising, then go through euphoria a second time. It's also normal for long-term partners to depart navigation periodically to experience both euphoric seasons and intervals of dyadic breakdown. Further, because relationships are embedded in larger systems, it's likely that romantic intimacy follows different developmental paths in other cultures.

To add to our understanding of romance, let's now consider the different styles of loving that individuals exhibit.

STYLES OF LOVING

- Does real love grow out of long friendship?
- Should you love someone whose background is similar to yours?
- Would you rather suffer yourself than have someone you love suffer?
- Is love at first sight possible?
- Is the real fun of love getting someone to fall for you rather than becoming seriously involved?

If you were to survey everyone in your class, you'd discover different answers to the above questions. For every person who thinks love grows out of friendship, someone else believes love at first sight is possible. For each of us who considers love the most important focus of life, another person views love as a game.

Although we accept varied tastes in everything from clothes to lifestyle, we seem less open-minded about diversity in love. Whatever we have experienced as love is what we consider "real love." Anything else we discount as "just infatuation," "a sexual fling," or "being a doormat." Yet, it appears people differ in how they love (Lee, 1973, 1988).

Just as there are three primary colours, there are three primary styles of loving. In addition, just as purple is created by blending the primary colours of blue and red, secondary love styles are made by blending primary ones. Secondary styles are as vibrant as primary ones, just as purple is as lovely as red or blue. Figure 10.3 illustrates the colours of love.

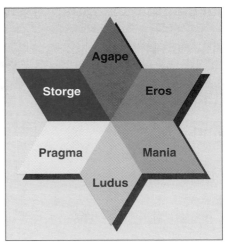

Figure 10.3
The Colours of Love

Primary Styles of Love

The three primary styles of love are *eros*, *storge*, and *ludus*.

Eros

Eros is a powerful, passionate style of love that blazes to life suddenly and dramatically. It is an intense kind of love that may include sexual, spiritual, intellectual, or emotional attraction. Erotic love is the most intuitive and spontaneous of all styles, and it is also the fastest moving. Erotic lovers are

|Student Voices|

Rosa:
When I fall for someone, I fall all the way—like, I mean total and all that. I can't love halfway, and I can't go gradually, though my mother is always warning me to slow down. That's just not how I love. It's fast and furious for me.

likely to self-disclose early in a relationship, be very sentimental, and fall in love hard and fast. Although folk wisdom claims women are more romantic than men, research indicates that men are more likely than women to be erotic lovers (Hendrick & Hendrick, 1996).

Storge

Storge (pronounced "store-gay") is a comfortable, even-keeled kind of love based on friendship. Storgic love tends to grow gradually and to be peaceful and stable. In most cases, it grows out of common interests, values, and life goals (Lasswell & Lobsenz, 1980). Storgic relationships don't have the great highs of erotic love, but neither do they have the fiery conflict and anger that erotic people often experience. Steadiness is *storge*'s standard mood.

Student Voices

Stephen:

Lisa and I have been together for 15 years now, and it's been easy and steady between us from the start. I don't remember even falling in love way back when. Maybe I never did fall in love with Lisa. I just gradually grew into loving her and feeling we belonged to each other.

Ludus

The final primary style of love is *ludus*, which is playful love. Ludic lovers see love as a game. It's a lighthearted adventure full of challenges, puzzles, and fun, and love is not to be taken seriously. For ludics, commitment is poison. Instead, they like to play the field and enjoy falling in love; they don't seek commitment. Many people go through ludic periods but are not true ludics. After ending a long-term relationship, it's natural and healthy to avoid serious involvement for a while. Dating casually and steering clear of heavy entanglement may be wise and fun. Ludic loving may also suit people who enjoy romance but aren't ready to settle down. Research indicates that more men than women have ludic inclinations when it comes to love (Hendrick & Hendrick, 1996).

Student Voices

Vijay:

I'm not ready to settle down, and I may not ever be. I really like dating and seeing if I can get a girl to fall for me, but I'm not out for anything permanent. To me, the fun is in the chase. Once somebody falls for me, I kind of lose interest. It's just not challenging anymore.

Secondary Styles of Love

There are three secondary styles of love: *pragma*, *mania*, and *agape*.

Pragma

Pragma, as the name suggests, is pragmatic or practical love. *Pragma* blends the conscious strategies of *ludus* with the stable, secure love of *storge*. Pragmatic lovers have clear criteria for partners such as religious affiliation, career, and family background. Although many people dismiss *pragma* as coldly practical and not really love, this is a mistake. Pragmatic lovers aren't necessarily unfeeling or unloving at all. For them, though, practical considerations are the foundation of enduring commitments, so these must be satisfied before they let themselves fall in love. Pragmatic considerations also guide arranged marriages in which families match children for economic and social reasons.

Student Voices

Ranchana:

I have to think carefully about who to marry. I must go to graduate school, and I must support my family with what I earn when I finish. I cannot marry someone who is poor, who will not help me get through school, or who won't support my family. For me, these are very basic matters.

Mania

Mania derives its name from the Greek term *theia mania*, which means "madness from the gods" (Lee, 1973). Manic lovers have the passion of *eros*, but they play by ludic rules with results that can be disturbing to them and those they love. Typically unsure that others really love them, manics may devise tests and games to evaluate a partner's commitment. They may also think obsessively about a relationship and be unable to think about anyone

Student Voices

Pattie:

I never feel sure of myself when I'm in love. I always wonder when it will end, when my boyfriend will walk away, when he will lose interest. Sometimes I play games to see how interested a guy is, but then I get all upset if the game doesn't work out right. Then I just wallow in my insecurities, and they get worse the more I think about them.

or anything else. In addition, manic lovers often experience emotional extremes, ranging from euphoric ecstasy to bottomless despair.

Agape

The final style of love is *agape*, which is a blend of *storge* and *eros*. The term agape comes from Saint Paul's admonition that we should love others without expectation of personal gain or return. Agapic lovers feel the intense passion of *eros* and the constancy of *storge*. Generous and selfless, agapic lovers will put a loved one's happiness ahead of their own without any expectation of reciprocity. For them, loving and giving to another is its own reward. Agapic love sounds more possible for saints than for mere mortals. Research bears out this insight, because the original studies of love styles found no individuals who were purely agapic. However, many people have agapic tendencies in their style of loving.

|Student Voices|

Keenan:

My mother is agapic. She has moved more times than I can count because my father needed to relocate to advance. She agreed to the house he wanted and went on the vacations he wanted, even when she had other ideas. There's nothing she wouldn't do for him. I used to think she was a patsy, but I've come to see her way of loving as very strong.

In thinking about styles of love, you should keep several points in mind. First, most of us have a combination of styles (Hendrick, Hendrick, Foote, & Slapion-Foote, 1984). So you might be primarily storgic with strong agapic inclinations or mainly erotic with an undertone of ludic mischief. Second, your style of love is not necessarily permanent. Recent studies indicate we learn how to love (Maugh, 1994), so our style of loving may change as we have more experiences in loving. Third, remember that your love style is part of an overall interpersonal system, so it is affected by all other aspects of your relationship (Hendrick & Hendrick, 1996). Your partner's style of love may influence your own. If you are primarily erotic and in love with a strong ludic, it's possible manic tendencies will be evoked. Finally, we should realize that individual styles of love are not good or bad in an absolute sense; what matters is how partners' styles fit together. An erotic partner's intensity might overwhelm a calm storgic; an agapic person might be exploited by a true ludic; the extremes of *mania* would clash with the serene steadiness of *storge*.

"What is that you express in your eyes? It seems to me more than all the words I have read in my life."
—Walt Whitman

Photos: B. Lemley

Romantic relationships are highlighted by intimacy, passion and commitment. They tend to follow a developmental course and individuals experience and express romantic intimacy in various styles of loving. Now let's consider the challenges facing friends and couples in sustaining relationships for the long haul.

CHALLENGES TO SUSTAINING CLOSE RELATIONSHIPS

Like all human relationships, friendships and committed romantic relationships experience pressures and difficulties. Many of the challenges are natural, even inevitable. To understand the strains friends and lovers face, we'll consider the internal tensions and the external constraints that tug at relationships.

INTERNAL TENSIONS

Close relationships, like all personal connections, are vulnerable to tensions inherent in being close. **Internal tensions** are relationship stresses that grow out of individuals and their interaction. We'll consider four of these.

Relational Dialectics

In earlier chapters, we discussed relational dialectics, which are opposing human needs that create tension and propel change in close relationships. The three dialectics are tension between connection and autonomy, openness and privacy, and novelty and familiarity. These three dialectics punctuate

Concepts at a Glance

Internal Tensions and External Constraints of Close Relationships

Internal Tensions:

- Relational Dialectics
- Diverse Communication Styles
- Managing Sex
- Avoiding Violence and Abuse

External Constraints:

- Competing Demands
- Personal Change
- Surviving Distance
- Ensuring Equity

Chapter 10
Friendships and Romantic Relationships

407

What are the challenges of cyber-relationships?

Photo: © Photodisc

friendships and committed romantic relationships, prompting us to adjust continuously to natural yet contradictory needs.

Dialectics may strain relationships when individuals differ in their needs. For instance, there could be tension if Harry is bored and needing novelty, but his partner Andy is overstimulated and seeking calming routines. Similarly, if Clint has just broken up with a woman, he may seek greater closeness with his friend Joe. When needs collide, we should talk. It's important to be upfront about what you need and to be sensitive to what your friend or partner needs. Doing this simultaneously honours yourself, the other, and the relationship. The goal is for friends to express themselves honestly and to engage in dual perspective and sensitive listening within a supportive communication climate. When this occurs, we can usually work out ways to meet each other's needs or at least to understand that differing needs don't reflect unequal commitment to the relationship.

Student Voices

Lana:

My girlfriends and I are so often in different places that it's hard to take care of each other. If one of my friends isn't seeing anyone special, she wants more time with me and wants to do things together. If I'm in a relationship with a guy, her needs feel demanding. But when I've just broken up, I really need my friends to fill time and talk with. So I try to remember how I feel and use that to help me accept it when my friends need my time.

Lana highlights the importance of dual perspective in dealing with tensions caused by relational dialectics. She draws on her own experience of breakups to understand her friends' perspective when they've broken up. This motivates Lana to make time to be with her friends. If she communicates her understanding and acceptance, her friends will feel she supports and cares about them.

Relational dialectics are natural and constructive forces in friendship. They keep us aware of multiple, sometimes clashing needs. In addition, because we find tension uncomfortable, dialectics motivate us to fine-tune friendships continuously. The strains dialectics spark can be managed by revising friendships and by accepting dialectical tensions as normal, ongoing relationship processes.

Diverse Communication Styles

Friendships may also be strained when friends misinterpret each other's communication. The potential for misunderstanding mushrooms as our society becomes increasingly diverse, making it more likely that some of our friends will have cultural backgrounds different from our own. Because how we communicate reflects the understandings and rules of our culture, misinterpretations are likely between friends from different cultures (Wood, 1995a). For instance, in many Asian societies, individuals are socialized to be unassuming and modest, whereas in the West, we encourage assertion and we celebrate ourselves. Thus, a native Japanese might perceive a friend from Ottawa as arrogant for saying "Let's go out to celebrate my acceptance to law school." A Thai woman might not get the support she wants from a friend from Calgary because she was taught not to assert her needs and the Calgary friend was taught that people should speak up for themselves. "Japanese Friendships" explores some of the cultural differences in friendship.

Misunderstandings also arise from differences among social groups. As a rule, Asian cultures are more communal than Western ones, so taking care of extended family members is a priority over individual needs and desires. Similarly, feminine and masculine communication rules may cause misunderstandings. For example Ellen may feel that her friend Jed isn't being supportive when instead of empathizing with her problems, he offers advice or suggests they go out to take her mind off her troubles. Yet, he is showing support according to masculine rules of communication. Jed, on the other hand, may feel that Ellen is intruding on his autonomy when she pushes him to talk about his feelings. According to feminine rules of communication, however, Ellen is showing interest and concern.

Differences themselves aren't usually the cause of problems in friendship. Instead, how we interpret and judge others' communication is the root of tension and hurt. What Jed and Ellen did wasn't the source of their frus-

Communication Notes

Japanese Friendships

The Japanese distinguish between two types of friendships. *Tsukiai* are friendships based on social obligation. These usually involve neighbours or work associates and tend to have limited life spans. Friendships based on affection and common interests usually last a lifetime: Personal friendship is serious business. The number of personal friends is very small and stable, in contrast to friendship patterns in the West. Friendships between women and men are rare in Japan. Prior to marriage, only 20 percent of Japanese say they have close friends of the opposite sex.

Sources: Atsumi, R. (1980). Patterns of personal relationships. *Social Analysis*, 5, 63–78; Mochizuki, T. (1981). Changing patterns of mate selection. *Journal of Comparative Family Studies*, 12, 318–328.

trations. Jed interpreted Ellen according to his communication rules, not hers, and she interpreted Jed according to her communication rules, not his. Notice that the misunderstandings result from our interpretations of others' behaviours, not the behaviours themselves. This reminds us of the need to distinguish between fact and inference.

Gary Chapman describes in his book *The Five Love Languages* (1995) how people express love differently. Most people look to receive love in the same way they give it, resulting in misunderstandings. Chapman claims that if partners understand each other's love language, they can give and receive love more effectively. Chapman's five love languages are

- Quality Time
- Words of Affirmation
- Acts of Service
- Physical Touch
- Giving Gifts

For example, if your primary love language is Acts of Service, you might make a special dinner for your partner. If your partner's primary love language is Words of Affirmation, she may not view the special dinner as an act of love. She will be wondering why you never tell her how you feel. You must learn to give love in the way your partner understands it and to teach your partner your love language.

Apply the Idea

Identify your love languages and those of your romantic partner in order of importance. Choose from Quality Time, Words of Affirmation, Acts of Service, Physical Touch, and Giving Gifts.

You	Your Partner
#1 Language _____	#1 Language _____
#2 Language _____	#2 Language _____
#3 Language _____	#2 Language _____

Now examine what you need to do to speak the language of love spoken by your partner.

Managing Sex

Managing sex in relationships can pose challenges. Sexual attraction can cause difficulty between friends. Friendships between heterosexual men and women, or gay men, or lesbians often include sexual tensions. Because Western culture so strongly emphasizes gender and sex, it's difficult not to perceive people in sexual terms (Johnson, Stockdale, & Saal, 1991; O'Meara, 1989). Even if there is no sexual activity between friends, sexual undertones may ripple beneath the surface of their friendships.

Sexual attraction or invitations can be a problem between friends who have agreed not to have a sexual relationship. Tension over sexual attraction or interest can be present in friendships between heterosexual women and men (West, Anderson, & Duck, 1996) as well as in friendships between lesbians and between gay men (Nardi & Sherrod, 1994). Trust may be damaged if someone we consider a friend makes a pass. Further, once a friend transgresses the agreed-upon boundaries of the friendship, it's hard to know how to act with each other or to feel completely comfortable unless the relationship has shifted to a romantic one.

In the HIV/AIDS era, sexual activities pose serious, even deadly, threats to romantic relationships. See "Safe Sex Still Safest Approach" on page 413.

Despite vigorous public education campaigns, many individuals still don't practise safer sex, which includes abstaining, restricting sexual activity to a single partner who has been tested for HIV, and/or using latex condoms (Reel & Thompson, 1994). Not practising safer sex puts both partners at grave risk for early death.

Why don't people who know about Sexually Transmitted Diseases (STDs) consistently follow safer sex techniques? Communication scholars have discovered two primary reasons. First, many individuals find it more embarrassing to talk about sex than to engage in it. They find it awkward to ask direct questions of partners ("Have you been tested for HIV?" "Are you having sex with anyone else?") or to make direct requests of partners ("I want you to wear a condom," "I would like for you to be tested for HIV before we have sex"). Naturally, it's difficult to talk explicitly about sex and the dangers of HIV/AIDS. However, it is far more difficult to live with HIV or the knowledge you infected a lover.

A second reason people sometimes fail to practise safer sex is that their rational thought and control are debilitated by drugs, alcohol, or both. In a series of studies of college students' sexual activities, communication researchers Sheryl Bowen and Paula Michal-Johnson (1995) found that safer sex precautions are often neglected when individuals drink heavily. Alcohol and other drugs loosen inhibitions, including appropriate concerns about personal safety. "Reasons Good Enough to Die For?" on page 412 examines why people do not practise safer sex.

Discussing and practising safer sex may be embarrassing, but there is no other sensible option. Principles of effective interpersonal communication we've discussed help ease the discomfort of negotiating safer sex. I–language that owns your feelings is especially important. It is more constructive to say "I feel unsafe having unprotected sex" than to say "Without a condom, you could give me HIV." A positive interpersonal climate is fostered by relational language, such as "we," "us," and "our relationship," to talk about sex (Reel

Communication Notes

Reasons Good Enough to Die For?

When students and members of singles organizations were asked about their sexual activities, these were the top five reasons they reported for not practising safer sex:
1. I knew my partner. We'd discussed our past sexual experiences.
2. I use another form of birth control.
3. A condom wasn't available at the time.
4. Things happened too fast.
5. I didn't feel I was at risk.

Source: Reel, B. W., & Thompson, T. L. (1994). A test of the effectiveness of strategies for talking about AIDS and condom use. *Journal of Applied Communication Research, 22,* 127–141.

& Thompson, 1994). Individuals who care about themselves and their partners are honest about their sexual histories and careful in their sex practices.

Avoiding Violence and Abuse

Although we like to think of romantic relationships as loving, many are not. Violence and abuse are unfortunately common between romantic partners, and they cut across lines of class, race, and ethnicity (French, 1992; West, 1995). Violence is high not only in heterosexual marriage but also in heterosexual cohabitation. In fact, cohabiting couples have the highest incidence of violence of all couples (Cunningham & Antill, 1995; White & Bondurant, 1996). Cohabiting women suffer one and one-half to two times more physical abuse than married women, perhaps because their partners are less committed than husbands (Ellis, 1989). Gay and lesbian relationships are also not immune to abuse.

The majority of detected violence and abuse in intimacy is committed by men against women. Currently in Canada, according to a *Family Violence Report* by Statistics Canada in 2001, over a million women reported violence by a spouse, with aboriginal women reporting more than twice as many violent episodes per population than other Canadian women. Marital separation does not necessarily mark the end of a violent relationship (p. 2). Rape and date rape are escalating, especially when individuals have been drinking ("What Teens Say," 1994). Verbal and emotional abuse cause deep and lasting scars (Vachss, 1994). And dysfunctional relationships, often called toxic connections, seem to be rising (Wright & Wright, 1995).

Safe Sex Still Safest Approach

One of the leading researchers in the world in sexually transmitted diseases is Canada's Dr. Robert Brunham, Director of the British Columbia Centre for Disease Control. Brunham asserts that frank knowledge about safe sex still offers the best protection for sexually transmitted diseases. Brunham reports that HIV/AIDS continues to be the greatest public health challenge in the world today. While infection rates in Canada are substantially lower than in other parts of the world, it still remains a very serious disease. Sexually transmitted HIV still poses the greatest risk for gay men and women who have sex with HIV infected men. Brunham goes on to say that among other STDs, chlamydia continues to be the most common, with 200,000 new infections occurring in Canada each year. Chlamydia commonly produces asymptomatic infection for prolonged periods of time. Because of this, it can be transmitted unknowingly to sex partners. Screening for infection still remains the best approach to prevention of chlamydia. New infectious agents are being recognized as sexually transmitted ones. The most important of these is the Human Papilloma Virus (HPV) which is demonstrated to be the cause of cervical cancer. It is difficult to recognize and treat. In light of these findings, says Brunham, safe sex is still the best approach to disease prevention. For current reports and more information, check out www.bccdc.org

Source: Personal communication with Dr. Robert Brunham, August 7, 2001.

Mental health counsellors who specialize in violence have come to the conclusion that relationships in which men abuse women are not rare but exemplify in extreme form the traditional power dynamics that structure relationships between women and men (Goldner, Penn, Sheinberg, & Walker, 1990). Men are taught to use power to assert themselves and to compete with others, whereas women are socialized to defer and preserve relationships. When these internalized patterns combine in heterosexual relationships, a foundation exists for men to abuse women and for women to tolerate it, rather than be disloyal (West, 1995).

Violence seldom stops without intervention. Instead it follows a predictable cycle, just as Katrina describes: Tension mounts in the abuser, the abuser explodes by being violent, the abuser then is remorseful and loving, the victim feels loved and that the relationship is working, and then tension mounts up and the cycle begins again (see Figure 10.4 on page 415).

Katrina:

It's hard for me to believe now, but I was in an abusive relationship, and it took me a long time to get out of it. The first time Ray hit me, I was so surprised I didn't know what to do, so I didn't do anything. The next time, I told him to stop or I'd leave. He said how sorry he was and promised never to hit me again, and then he was real sweet for a long time. I felt like he really did love me, and I felt I should stand by him. And then it happened again. I went to talk to my minister, and he told me my Christian duty was to honour the marriage vows I made before God, so I went back again. Each time Ray beat up on me, he'd follow it with being romantic and sweet, so I'd get sucked back in. I didn't finally leave him until he threw me down some stairs and dislocated my shoulder.

Being loyal in the face of abuse, a response to conflict that we discussed in Chapter 9, is inappropriate because it doesn't protect a victim's safety. Relationships that are violent and abusive are unhealthy for everyone involved. They obviously jeopardize the comfort, health, and sometimes the survival of victims of violence. Less obvious is the damage experienced by abusers. Using physical force against others is a sign of weakness—an admission that a person can't exercise power in intellectual or emotional ways and must resort to the crudest and least imaginative methods of influence. Further, abusers can destroy relationships that they need and want.

Reflective Exercise

Resisting Violence

Think about your experience with violence, both directly and indirectly. No one should tolerate violence, especially from a person who claims to love her or him. If you are being abused, seek counselling to discover and think through your options. If you suspect someone you care about is being abused, be a real friend and talk with the person. Too often, signs of abuse are ignored because we find it awkward to talk about violence between intimates. However, standing by and doing nothing is a kind of abuse in itself. If you are abusing someone you care about, get professional help.

Relational dialectics, misinterpretations of different communication styles, sexual tensions, and coping with abuse are sources of internal tension in many close relationships. Usually, straightforward communication, although not always easy, is the best way to deal with these problems and to restore ease. See the guidelines for effective communication at the end of the chapter for ways to improve relationships.

EXTERNAL CONSTRAINTS

In addition to internal tensions, close relationships may encounter pressures from outside sources. Four of these **external tensions** are competing demands, changes, surviving distance, and equity.

Competing Demands

Close relationships exist within larger social systems that affect how they function (Allan, 1994). Because our lives are complex, we continuously struggle to balance competing demands for our time and energy. Our important relationships can be easily neglected. Our work and even our romantic relationships tend to be woven into our everyday lives, ensuring they will get daily attention. Time with friends, however, isn't reserved in what we must do each day. We have to make room in our lives, plan meetings, and set aside time to interact. When all that we must do overwhelms us, we may not get to what we want to do.

We may also neglect important relationships because of other relationships. When a new romance is taking off, we may be totally immersed in it and we may neglect our friends. The excitement of getting to know a new person can absorb all of our time and thoughts. When other important relationships in our lives are in crisis, we may neglect others. If one of our parents is ill or another friend is having trouble, we may need all of our energy to cope with the acute situation. When we are wrapped up in other relationships in happy or anxious ways, we have little of ourselves left to give to those we care about the most. To avoid hurtful feelings, we should let friends and lovers know when we need a leave of absence from the relationship to deal with immediate priorities. If we don't explain our inattention to others, they may feel hurt or rejected (Wood, 1995c).

Personal Changes

Our relationships change as our lives do. Although a few friendships are lifelong, most persist for shorter periods. If you think about your experiences, you'll realize that many of your friends changed as you made major transitions in your life (Allan, 1994). The people you spent time with and counted as friends shifted when you started high school, entered college, or moved to a new town. They'll change again when you leave college, move for career or family reasons, and perhaps have children. Because one base of friendship is common interests,

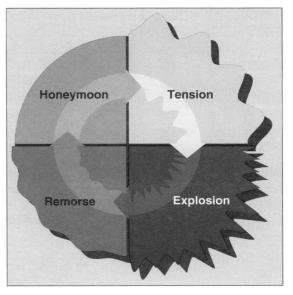

Figure 10.4
The Cycle of Abuse

Ruth:

Sandi and I had been friends for years when I had my first baby. Gradually, we saw less of each other and couldn't find much to talk about when we did get together. She was still doing the singles scene, and I was totally absorbed in mothering. I got to know other mothers in the neighbourhood, and soon I thought of them as my friends. What's funny is that last year Sandi had a baby, and it was so good to get together and talk. We reconnected with each other.

established friends may not be able to share new interests we develop. Our friends change over the course of life as we and our interests continually evolve.

Because our romantic partners are also our friends, many of the same stressors surrounding change in our lives apply to our intimate relationships. Couples often experience strain in their relationships when one goes back to school, starts a new job, or takes on new interests. The new stimulus upsets the equilibrium of the dyad.

Surviving Distance

Most close relationships face the challenge of distance, and many won't survive it. Currently, as many as 90 percent of North Americans have at least one long-distance friendship (Rohlfing, 1995). In our highly mobile society, friendships are continuously in flux.

Whether friends and romantic partners survive distance depends on several factors. Perhaps the most obvious influence is how much individuals care about continuing to be close. The greater the commitment, the more likely a relationship will persist despite separation. Geographic distance is the reason the majority of high school friendships dissolve when individuals begin college (Rose, 1984). Yet, the likelihood of sustaining a long-distance friendship also depends on other factors, such as socioeconomic class and gender.

Because socioeconomic class profoundly affects who we are and how we live, it's not surprising that it influences the prospect that long-distance friendships will endure. The reason is simple: money. Friendships that survive distance involve frequent phone calls and letters and visits every so often. It takes money to finance trips and long-distance calls. Thus, friends with greater economic resources are better able to maintain their relationships than are friends with less discretionary income (Willmott, 1987). Thus, people in middle and upper socioeconomic classes have a greater chance of bridging distance with friends. A second way in which socioeconomic class affects the endurance of long-distance friendships is flexibility in managing work and family. Middle and upper-class individuals usually have generous vacations and flexibility in work schedules, so they can make time to travel. Working-class citizens tend to have less personal control over when they work and how much vacation time they get. Income also affects our ability to pay for babysitters who may make it possible for a parent to visit a friend for a weekend.

Apply the Idea

Maintaining Friendship at a Distance

Do you have a long-distance friendship? If so, which of the following strategies do you use to maintain it?

- *Call at least once a week.*
- *Call at least once a month.*
- *Communicate by electronic mail at least weekly.*
- *Call once or twice a year.*
- *Write letters.*
- *Visit weekly.*
- *Visit monthly.*
- *Visit occasionally.*
- *Have conversations in your head with the friend.*

Now identify three ways you might strengthen the closeness between you and your friend.

Gender also affects the endurance of long-distance friendships. There appear to be two reasons why women are more likely than men to sustain ties with friends who live at a distance. First, the sexes differ in how much they value same-sex friendships and how much they give to and get from them. Compared to women, men place less value on their same-sex relationships and invest less in them (Duck & Wright, 1993). This is especially true of married men who often name their wives as their best friends (Rubin, 1985). Women are also more willing than men to adjust schedules and priorities to make time for friends (Rubin, 1985), and they are more willing to tolerate less than ideal circumstances for being with friends. For example, mothers who sustain long-distance friendships report that when they visit, they are seldom alone, because their children need attention and care. Even though these mothers say they miss the intimacy of uninterrupted conversations, they value each other enough to sustain friendships under the terms that are possible (Rohlfing, 1995). Women also report getting more out of their friendships with women than men report getting out of their friendships with men (Duck & Wright, 1993). For women more than men, friendships are a primary and important thread woven through their lives.

Women can and do sustain ties with important friends by talking on the phone and writing. Men, on the other hand, are more likely to replace friends who have moved away with others who can share activities they enjoy (Rohlfing, 1995). Lillian Rubin's (1985) studies led her to say that women tend to develop **friends of the heart,** who remain close regardless of distance and circumstances. Rubin also noted that many men have **friends of the road,** who change as they move along the road of life and develop new interests and find themselves in new situations. It is easier to replace a friend who was a tennis partner than one with whom we shared intimate feelings and details of our life.

Geographic separation can be even more difficult for romantic couples because Western culture teaches us to expect to live with our partners. The assumption of living together permanently, however, isn't universal. Many immigrants to Canada work several years before bringing spouses and children to join them. Westerners facing long-distance relationships might take heart from the fact that couples in other cultures manage to stay together despite long periods of living apart.

Many of us will be involved in long-distance romantic relationships because they are increasingly common. The number of long-distance romantic relationships will increase further as more partners pursue independent careers and as extended travel becomes part of more people's jobs. Many couples who share the same home will still be apart a great deal of the time. Researchers have identified three problems, or tensions, commonly experienced in long-distance relationships; loss of daily routines, unrealistic expectations of time together, and unequal investments into the relationship.

Perhaps the greatest problem is the lack of daily sharing of small events and unrealistic expectations about time together. Not being able to share small talk and daily routines is a major loss. As we have seen, sharing the ordinary comings and goings of days helps partners keep their lives woven together. The routine conversations of romantic partners form and continuously reform the basic fabric of their relationship. Everyday talk is how couples connect in countless little moments that shape the overall climate of the relationship.

The lack of routine contact leads to the second problem faced by couples who live apart: unrealistic expectations for time together. Based on 25 years of studying marriages, psychologist and marriage counsellor John Gottman (1997) reports that the mundane, ordinary moments couples share are what build love and establish a positive emotional climate between people. Because partners have so little time together, they often believe every moment must be perfect. They feel that there should be no harsh words or conflict and that they should be happily focused on each other for all the time they have together. Yet, this is an unrealistic expectation. Conflict and needs for autonomy are natural and inevitable in all romantic relationships. They may be even more likely in reunions of long-distance couples, because partners are used to living alone and have established independent rhythms that may not mesh well.

A third common problem in long-distance relationships is unequal effort that the two partners invest in maintaining the connection. According to Vicki Helgeson (1994), one of the major reasons that long-distance couples break up

---

Concepts at a Glance

Three Problems in Long-Distance Relationships

- Loss of daily routines
- Unrealistic expectations of time together
- Unequal investments into the relationship

Françoise:

When Maurice found a good job outside Quebec, he moved, and both of us thought our relationship would survive. We had talked about marrying when I finished school, so we were pretty serious. At first we did okay, even though it was hard. I would write every day, and he wrote me once or twice each week. One of us called the other every week. Then his letters got less frequent. Then it seemed I was always the one who called him. I told him he was acting like he wasn't committed anymore, but he said he was just busy. I think that was true, but it didn't matter after a while. The upshot is that he was too busy for us, and I couldn't keep the relationship going on my own.

is that one partner is doing most of the work to sustain contact and to take care of the relationship. The inequity in investment creates resentment in the person who is assuming the majority of the work to keep the relationship alive.

The good news is that these problems don't necessarily sabotage long-distance romance. Most researchers report that partners can maintain satisfying commitments despite geographic separation (Rohlfing, 1995). In fact, there are some noteworthy advantages of long-distance relationships. James Reske and Laura Stafford (1990) report that the very everydayness that geographically separated partners miss is a boon to romance. Because couples aren't together continuously, they tend to be more loving when they are together and to feel more passionately about each other. Also, partners who live apart are able to focus on their individual projects and ambitions without the distraction of a constant companion.

The strategies devised by college students (see "Coping with Geographic Separation") are sound guidelines for sustaining intimacy across distance. Notice that these strategies reflect many of the communication principles we've discussed in this and previous chapters. Because partners don't have the comfort of everyday interaction, it is especially important to build climates that are trusting, open, and honest in long-distance relationships. It's also critical that couples who live apart focus on what is positive and good about the relationship and even the separation. One important advantage of living apart is that each partner can concentrate more fully on work, school, or other priorities (Gross, 1980). This may allow partners to advance in their careers so that when they are reunited they have secure jobs and better than average resources.

Ensuring Equity

The last external constraint that challenges close relationships, especially romantic relationships, is ensuring equity within the relationship. Friends may

Communication Notes

Coping with Geographic Separation

College students report nine coping strategies they use to sustain intimacy across long distances:

1. Recognize that long-distance relationships are common; you're not alone.
2. Create more social support systems (friends) while separated from a romantic partner.
3. Communicate creatively—send video- and audiotapes.
4. Before separating, work out ground rules for going out with friends, phoning, visiting, and writing.
5. Use time together "wisely" to be affectionate and to have fun together. Being serious all the time isn't constructive.
6. Maintain honesty. Especially when partners live apart, they need to be straight with each other.
7. Build an open, supportive communication climate so that you can talk about issues and feelings.
8. Maintain trust by abiding by ground rules that were agreed on, phoning when you say you will, and keeping lines of communication open.
9. Focus on the positive aspects of separation.

Source: Westefield, J. S., & Liddell, D. (1982). Coping with long-distance relationships. *Journal of College Student Personnel, 23,* 550–551.

keep a "loose tally" of whose turn it is to do what. In committed romantic relationships, however, perceived equity is very important. **Equity** means fairness, based on the perception that both partners invest relatively equally in a relationship and benefit similarly from their investments. We all want to feel that our partners are as committed as we are and that we gain equally from being together. Although few partners demand moment-to-moment equality, most of us want our relationships to be equitable over time. Inequity tends to breed unhappiness, which lessens satisfaction and commitment and sometimes prompts affairs (Walster, Traupmann, & Walster, 1978).

Equity has multiple dimensions. We may evaluate the fairness of financial, emotional, physical, and other contributions to a relationship. One area that strongly affects relationship quality is perceived equity in housework and child care, as discussed in "The Second Shift." Inequitable division of domestic obligations fuels dissatisfaction and resentment, both of which harm intimacy (Gottman & Carrère, 1994). Marital stability is more closely linked to perceptions of equitable divisions of child care and housework

Communication Notes

The Second Shift

In 80 percent of dual-worker families, men work one job and women work two—the second shift begins when they come home. Not only do women do more domestic work than men but also work that is less satisfying and more stressful. Women tend to do the day-in, day-out jobs such as cooking, shopping, and helping children with homework. Men more often do domestic work that they can schedule to suit themselves. Mowing the lawn can be scheduled flexibly, whereas fixing meals must be done on a tight timetable. Men also are more likely to take care of occasional and fun child-care activities, such as visiting the zoo, whereas women manage the daily grind of bathing, dressing, and feeding children.

As a rule, women assume **psychological responsibility,** which involves remembering, planning, and coordinating domestic activities. Parents may alternate who takes children to the doctor, but it is usually the mother who remembers when checkups are needed, makes appointments, and reminds the father to take the child. Birthday cards and gifts are signed by both partners, but women typically assume the psychological responsibility for remembering when birthdays are and for buying cards and gifts.

Source: Based on Hochschild, A., with Machung, A. (1989). *The second shift.* New York: Viking Press.

than to income or sex life (Fowers, 1991; Suitor, 1991). Beginning with the Industrial Revolution, men were assigned responsibility for earning income and women for caring for children and a home. A gendered division of labour no longer makes sense, because most marriages today include two wage earners (Wilkie, 1991). Unfortunately, divisions of family and home responsibilities have not changed in response to changing employment patterns. Even when both partners in heterosexual relationships work outside the home, the vast majority of child care and homemaking is done by women (Nussbaum, 1992; Okin, 1989). In only 20 percent of dual-worker families do men assume equal domestic responsibilities (Hochschild with Machung, 1989). Although many men with partners who work outside the home do contribute, they do less than a fair share. Since the 1950s, the amount of housework and child care that husbands do has risen a scant 10 percent—from 20 to 30 percent (Pleck, 1987).

How are domestic responsibilities managed when both partners are the same sex? Lesbian couples create more egalitarian relationships than either

Cora May:

I said, "Either things are going to change around here or I'm leaving." He didn't believe me, but I stood my ground. For 20 years I had done all of the housework, the cooking, and the child care, while he did none of these. Walter just went to his job each day and came back home for me to wait on him. Well, I went to my job each day too. I worked hard, and I was tired when I got home. You'd think he could figure that out, wouldn't you? It got really bad when I started taking night courses. I need to study at night, not fix meals and do laundry, so I asked him to help out. You'd think he'd been stung by a bee. He said no, so I just quit fixing his meals and left his laundry when I washed my clothes. Finally, he got with the program.

heterosexuals or gays. More than any other type of couple, lesbians are likely to share decision-making and domestic work (Huston & Schwartz, 1995). Consequently, lesbians are least likely to perceive inequity in contributions to home life (Kurdek, 1993). Gay men, like their heterosexual brothers, use the power derived from income to authorize inequitable contributions to domestic life. In gay couples, the man who makes more money has and uses more power, both in making decisions that affect the relationship and in avoiding housework (Huston & Schwartz, 1995). This suggests that power is the basis of gendered divisions of labour and that men, more than women, seek the privileges of power, including evasion of domestic work.

The perception of inequity damages romantic relationships. It creates resentment and anger and erodes love. As resentment eclipses positive feelings, dissatisfaction mushrooms. In addition, there are health consequences. Women who work a second shift are stressed, starved for sleep, and susceptible to illness because they are continuously doing double duty (Hochschild with Machung, 1989). Successful long-term relationships in our era require more equitable divisions of home responsibilities than have been traditional.

GUIDELINES FOR SUSTAINING CLOSE RELATIONSHIPS

The principles for healthy communication with friends and romantic partners echo the basic principles of good interpersonal communication that we've discussed in preceding chapters. You should be aware that your self-concept and your perceptions influence how you interpret interaction with intimates. It's also important to create a confirming climate by being open, spontaneous, empathic, equal, and nonevaluative. Keeping love and commitment alive for a lifetime is one of the greatest challenges we all face. In addition, you should keep in mind what you have learned about using verbal and nonverbal communication effectively, including when you discuss emotions. Finally, managing conflict constructively is important in all relationships. In addition to these general principles, we can identify six specific guidelines for satisfying communication between friends and romantic partners.

ENGAGE IN DUAL PERSPECTIVE

As in all interpersonal relationships, dual perspective is important. To be a good friend and partner we must understand and accept the other's perspectives, thoughts, and feelings. As we've noted before, accepting another person's perspective is not the same as agreeing with it. The point is to understand what the other feels and thinks and to accept that as his or her reality. Dual perspective helps us to understand others on their terms, not ours.

Two communication principles help us avoid misinterpreting our friends and lovers. First, it's useful to ask questions to find out what others mean. You might ask of a friend, "Why would you want to go out when I said I needed support?" This would allow your friend to explain that he or she was trying to support you in his or her own way by coming up with an activity to divert you from your problems. Second, we should explain, or translate, our own feelings and needs so that our partners understand what would feel supportive to us. You could say, "What would help me most right now is to have a sympathetic ear. Could we just stay in and talk about the problem?" If we make our needs clear, we're more likely to get the kind of support we value.

Concepts at a Glance

Six Guidelines for Sustaining Close Relationships

- Engage in dual perspective.
- Communicate honestly.
- Grow from differences.
- Show respect and consideration.
- Make choices that enhance the relationship.
- Don't sweat the small stuff.

Apply the Idea

Communicating Needs Clearly

Below are three scenarios that describe interactions in which a friend or lover does not initially give the desired response. For each one, write out what you could say to clarify what is wanted.

1. *You just found out that your car needs two new tires and alignment, and you don't have any extra cash. Worrying about money is the last thing you want to do now, with everything else on your mind. You see a friend and tell him what's happened. He says, "Sit down, let's talk about it." You don't want to talk—you want to get your mind off the problem.*

   You say _____

2. *You are unhappy because your romantic partner is transferring to a university 600 km away. You know that you'll miss him or her and you're also worried that*

the relationship might not survive distance. A friend calls and you mention your concerns. In response, she says, "You can handle this. Just make sure that the two of you have e-mail accounts, and you'll be fine." Although you'd like to believe this, it seems like empty reassurance to you. You'd rather have some help sorting through your feelings.

You say _____

3. *Your live-in partner tells you that he or she is really worried about the job market. As he or she talks, you hear several things: worry about making a living, uncertainty about where you will be living, and doubts about self-worth. You say to your partner, "Sounds as if you are feeling pretty overwhelmed by all of this. Maybe it would help if we took one piece of the problem at a time." Your partner lets out a frustrated sigh and replies, "I don't want to analyze every bit and piece!" You're not sure what it is that your partner wants and how to help.*

You say _____

COMMUNICATE HONESTLY

Honesty is one of the most important gifts friends can give each other. Even when honesty is less than pleasant or not what we think we want to hear, we count on it from friends and loving partners. In fact, people believe that honest feedback is what sets real friends apart from others (Burleson & Samter, 1994). Sometimes it's difficult to be honest with friends and partners. Yet, if we can't count on our friends for honest feedback, then where can we turn for truthfulness? The following three guidelines are helpful for communicating honestly on difficult issues. Firstly, describe your true feelings without condemning the other. Secondly, tell your friend or partner that you will support and love him or her whatever the decision. Lastly, suggest that there may be more options than the ones he or she sees.

Many people make the mistake of confusing support with saying only nice things that others want to hear. Yet, this is not the essence of support. The key

Photo: © Photodisc

is caring enough about a person to look out for her or his welfare. Parents discipline children and set limits because they care about their children's long-term welfare. Colleagues who want to help each other give honest, often critical, feedback on work so that others can improve. Romantic partners who are committed tell each other when they perceive problems or when the other isn't being his or her best self. We can be supportive and loving while being honest, but to be less than honest is to betray the trust placed in us. Honesty is part of what it means to care genuinely about another. Although it may be easier to tell friends or lovers what they want to hear or only nice things, genuine friendship and intimacy include honest feedback and candid talk.

GROW FROM DIFFERENCES

A third principle for forming rich relationships is to be open to diversity in people. As we learned in Chapter 5, Western culture encourages polarized thinking. We have been socialized to think in either–or terms: Either she's like me or not; either he acts like I do or he's wrong; either they support me as I want to be supported or they're not real friends. The problem with this either–or thinking is that it sharply limits interpersonal growth.

Egocentric mind-sets and either–or thinking limit our horizons. We can't learn and grow if we reject what and who is different simply because they're different. Most of us tend to choose friends and romantic partners who are like us. We feel more immediately comfortable with those who share our values, attitudes, backgrounds, and communication rules. But if we restrict our close relationships to people like us, we miss out on the fascinating variety of people and relationships that are possible. It does take more time and effort to understand and become comfortable with individuals who differ from us, but the dividends of doing so can be exceptional. Forming friendships and entering committed romantic relationships with diverse people facilitates both your growth as an individual and the richness of your interpersonal world.

SHOW RESPECT AND CONSIDERATION

For friendship and romantic intimacy to remain healthy and satisfying, partners need to demonstrate continuously that they value and respect each other. As obvious as this guideline seems, many people don't follow it. Sometimes we treat strangers with more respect and kindness than we offer our closest friends and romantic partners. It's easy to take for granted a person who is a continuing part of our life and to be less loving, respectful, and considerate than we should be.

Communication scholars Gottman et al (1996) identify four behaviours that can damage a relationship. They are contempt for the other, constant criticism, defensiveness, and stonewalling or withdrawal.

Concepts at a Glance

Four Damaging Behaviours in Close Relationships

- Contempt
- Criticism
- Defensiveness
- Stonewalling

Student Voices

Jackson:

One of the things I love most about Meleika is the way she starts each day. Before getting out of bed, she reaches over and kisses my cheek. Then she gets up and showers while I sneak a little more shut-eye. When I get up, the first thing she always says is, "Morning, love." That is such a great way to start each day. Even after five years of marriage she starts each day by letting me know I matter.

Gottman and his colleagues focused their research largely on married couples, but the damaging behaviours carry over to friendships and as we will see in the next chapter, to work relationships.

Consideration and respect don't magically infuse relationships just because we know about interpersonal communication skills, such as those we've discussed in this book. For a respectful, confirming climate to exist, partners must practise effective interpersonal communication in the relationship. We should be as mindful of good communication when we enter a dialogue with close friends and established romantic partners as when we talk with casual acquaintances.

Friends and romantic partners should be respectful of each other, particularly when discussing problems and complaints. Disagreement is natural and often constructive, but how we disagree with a friend or partner is critical. Studies of marriages reveal differences between how satisfied and dissatisfied spouses talk about complaints and problems. Satisfied couples assert grievances and express anger and disagreement. Dissatisfied couples, however, communicate criticism, contempt, and sometimes disgust (Gottman & Carrère, 1994). It would be appropriate for Mary to tell Simon, "I feel angry when you smoke in the house because the smell bothers me." However, it would be personally disrespectful for Mary to say, "Smoking is a filthy, repulsive habit. Every time you light a cigarette you look revolting." The first statement is a civil complaint about a behaviour; the second statement is a vicious attack on Simon's personal worth.

Both our relationships and our self-respect are at stake in how we act toward close friends and intimate partners. As we learned in Chapter 1, communication is irreversible. Harsh words and personal insults cannot be taken back once we've said them. Neither can we retract sneers, scowls, and other nonverbal behaviours that express contempt. Because we cannot undo communication or its impact, we need to be mindful of what we say and how we say it.

MAKE DAILY CHOICES THAT ENHANCE CLOSENESS AND INTIMACY

Perhaps the most important guideline for sustaining close relationships is to be aware that they are creative projects that reflect the choices partners make. Relationships are not things we enter but processes we create and continuously refine. Realizing that we are choice makers enables us to take responsibility for our choices and how they chart the course of intimacy.

The relationships we create reflect a series of personal choices. Although we are not always aware that we are making choices, we continuously choose who we will be and what kind of relationships we will fashion. Intimate partners and close friends choose to sustain closeness or let it wither, to build climates that are open or closed and defensive, to rely on constructive or destructive communication to deal with conflict, to fulfill or betray trust, and to enhance or diminish each other's self-concept.

Too often we focus on large choices such as whether to commit, how to manage a serious conflict, or how to celebrate an anniversary. As important as major choices are, they don't make up the basic fabric of a relationship (Wood, 1995c). Instead, undramatic, day-to-day choices sculpt the quality of intimacy. Do you listen mindfully to a partner or friend when you are tired? Do you continue to invest in intimacy after the initial euphoria has waned? Do you care enough about a relationship to work through crises and conflicts? Do you neglect your partner when you've had a rough day? Do you exert the effort to use dual perspective so that you can understand your friend on her or his terms? Seemingly small choices like these shape the quality of intimacy and the individuals in it. Although they appear small and insignificant, our ordinary, daily choices weave the basic fabric of our close relationships. By being aware of the impact of our "small" choices, we can make ones that continuously enhance the quality of intimacy.

DON'T SWEAT THE SMALL STUFF

Samuel Johnson once remarked that most friendships die not because of major violations and problems but because of small slights and irritations that slowly destroy closeness. Johnson's point is well taken. Certainly, we are going to be irritated by a number of qualities and habits of others. If you are a punctual person, you might be annoyed by a friend who is chronically late. If you are a tidy person (or a neatness fanatic), you might be bothered by your live-in partner's leaving the toothpaste cap off the tube. Feeling annoyance is normal in all relationships. What we do with that feeling, however, can make the difference between sustaining a relationship and suffocating it.

One insight into how to let go of small irritations comes from what we've learned about perception. Knowing that perceptions are subjective, you might remind yourself not to fixate on aspects of a friend or intimate that you dislike or find bothersome. There's a big difference between acknowledging irritations and letting them preoccupy us. Is the lateness really more significant than all that you value in your friend? Do your lover's good qualities compensate for the toothpaste mess in the bathroom? You can exercise some control over your perceptions and the weight you attach to them.

Monitoring attributions can also help us avoid sweating the small stuff. You will feel very differently about your best friends or romantic partners if you define irritating behaviour as beyond their control instead of something they are doing to annoy you. It is also important to consider that you may be projecting the very qualities in your own personality that you do not like onto your friends or partners. Perhaps it is your own lateness or your own messiness that bothers you. Accepting our own failings and those of our partners and responding with grace to small irritations goes a long way to creating harmony in relationships. A valuable practice when the "small stuff" is the focus of conflict between friends and especially live-in partners is to consider that the real issues are not identified yet and the fighting over the toothpaste is simply a cover-up for what is really troubling you.

Chapter Summary

In this chapter, we focused upon the dynamics of two kinds of close relationships, friendships and committed romantic relationships. We have seen that close relationships are typified by a willingness to invest, intimacy that is established through dialogue and intimacy that is established through doing, acceptance, trust, support, and, in the specific case of romantic relationships, passion and commitment. We considered the rules of friendship that are often unspoken and culturally bound. We then examined the development of close relationships through three stages; growth stages, navigation, and finally deterioration stages. Our discussion then focused on six styles of loving; the primary styles of *eros*, *storge*, and *ludus* followed by the secondary styles of *pragma*, *mania*, and *agape*. This led us to examine the challenges inherent in sustaining close relationships. These challenges were identified as either internal or external tensions. The internal tensions were relational dialectics, diverse communication styles, managing sex, and avoiding violence and abuse. The external tensions included competing demands, personal change, surviving distance, and ensuring equity.

We then concluded the chapter with guidelines for communicating effectively with friends and romantic partners. The behaviours for effective communication fell into six helpful categories: engaging in dual perspective, communicating honestly, appreciation for differences, showing respect and consideration, making choices that enhance relationships, and finally ignoring the small irritations in our relationships. Following these guidelines as well as others identified in previous chapters should enhance your ability to create satisfying friendships and romantic relationships that can stand the test of time.

Key Concepts

- *agape*
- committed romantic relationships
- commitment
- covert intimacy
- dyadic breakdown
- dyadic phase
- environmental spoiling
- equity
- *eros*
- everyday interactions
- explorational communication
- external tensions
- friendly relations
- friends of the heart
- friends of the road
- grave dressing
- intensifying communication
- internal tensions
- intimacy
- intrapsychic phase
- invitational communication
- *ludus*
- *mania*
- moving toward friendship
- nascent friendship
- navigating
- passion
- placemaking
- *pragma*
- psychological responsibility
- relational culture
- revising communication
- role-limited interaction
- social phase
- social support
- stabilized friendship
- *storge*
- waning friendship

For Further Thought & Discussion

1. Think about a friendship you have with a person of your sex and a friendship you have with a person of the other sex. To what extent does each friendship conform to the gender patterns described in this chapter?

2. Review the rules of friendship presented in this chapter. Do these rules show up in your friendships? Are there other rules that you would add based on your personal experiences with friendship?

3. Do you have any long-distance friends? How far away are they? How often do you see them in person? How do you manage to maintain the friendship across the distance?

4. Use your InfoTrac College Edition to read the table of contents for the last year's issues of *Sex Roles*. Read studies that focus on differences and similarities in how women and men engage in close relationships. Are the findings from articles you read consistent with what you've learned in this chapter?

5. Use your InfoTracCollege Edition to look up current information on marriages and divorces in Canada. Access the most recent census of Statistics Canada. Can you find statistics on how many people married in the most recent year for which there is a report? What was the average age of women and men who married? How many marriages were first, second, or third marriages? How many divorces were reported in the most recent year for which information is available? Is there information on the average length of marriages that end in divorce?

6. If you have a current romantic partner, can you identify her or his love style? How does it fit with your own love style? Does understanding love styles give you any new insights into dynamics in your relationship?

7. This chapter discussed some gender differences in romantic relationships. Do the differences identified by researchers apply to your own relationships? How do you see gender operating in your romantic relationships?

Relationships at Work

Everyday Encounters
By Stephen Lee

Chloe is navigating one of the communication demands that are present in the workplace. She is trying to maintain a warm interpersonal style with someone she will likely not meet or deal with again. This is one of the many challenges of workplace relationships. Most of us will spend a large portion of our lives at work. Almost all of those jobs will require us to relate to and communicate with others. The people that inhabit our workplace can include employers, colleagues and co-workers, clients, patients or customers, and the people of other organizations or agencies related to our place of business. We may develop close personal connections with some of these people that approximate the I–Thou relationships we discussed in Chapter 1. We may develop cordial I–You relationships with people we interact with daily, and we may have impersonal I–It relationships with others. Each of these relationships is managed differently. Many of the principles of good interpersonal relationships we have discussed so far will apply to the workplace. There are however some important differences.

In this chapter we will examine the communication skills required in the Canadian workplace, the nature of workplace relationships and how they differ from other interpersonal relationships, how communication is established through climate and culture, and the particular challenges and skills of working in teams. Our discussion will then focus on the challenges of communicating effectively in the workplace with particular focus on the conflict issues of dealing with difficult people and harassment. We will conclude with guidelines for improving communication in the workplace to ensure a satisfying work environment.

....

THE IMPORTANCE OF COMMUNICATION IN THE WORKPLACE

The concept of work can encompass an extremely broad range of tasks and responsibilities, but there is one activity that is common to virtually every job you might think of: communication.

In most jobs, communication is an essential part of day-to-day activity, as well as a defining feature of the settings where work takes place. We interact with others to obtain information, to offer our products and provide services, to share ideas, to make decisions, and to coordinate our activities with others. Even in highly technical positions, the need to interact with others is a critical aspect of getting the work done. For almost all of us, therefore, interpersonal communication is one of the most important work-related skills we can develop. Leadership scholar Stephen Covey highlights

Even monotonous work is tolerable when there is a climate of respect and team support.

Photo: © Corel

communication skills as critical to effectiveness in the workplace (1991). Indeed, employers increasingly insist that communication skills are a basic requirement for most jobs, and that demonstrations of communication expertise particularly in teamwork are a key basis for professional advancement. An examination of the Employability Skills Profile of the Canadian Workforce (Table 11.1) highlights the importance of communication skills in the modern workplace.

THE NATURE OF WORKPLACE RELATIONSHIPS

Relationships in the workplace are unique. Unlike romantic relationships or friendships, the investments are more about keeping your job and making a satisfying work environment than about sustaining a long-term relationship. People who report having the most satisfying work relationships describe many of the qualities that we have come to enjoy and value in our close relationships. But good working relationships, because of the common focus of accomplishing tasks and striving for the same goal, can be simply civil and still satisfying. There are also elements in our work relationships that are not present in our other relationships. We will examine four elements that affect communication in the workplace: power, fear of reprisals, task demands, and technology.

ELEMENTS AFFECTING COMMUNICATION IN THE WORKPLACE

Concepts at a Glance

Four Elements of the Workplace That Influence Communication

- Power
- Fear of reprisals
- Task demands
- Technology

Work relationships are not always equal. Regardless of your personal feelings for your boss or your out of work relationship with him or her, you are responsible to that boss and he or she has power over you. Similarly, others may report to you and regardless of your relationship with them, you have power over them. We don't give or get performance appraisals from our friends, lovers, family members, or neighbours. This difference in power affects our behaviour. We may be reluctant to be assertive, for example, for fear of reprisals or job loss. Other times, we recognize the impact of power when decisions are made without our input. The workplace is not always democratic or egalitarian. Thirdly, tasks sometimes demand that our personal feelings be submerged or our issues bracketed in order to meet deadlines. Fourth, technology has affected our workplace relationships by increasing isolation and reliance on electronic means for communicating.

Power

Researchers in leadership and power identify different kinds of power that occur in groups (Brown, 1998; Johnson & Johnson, 1991; Jordan, 1996).

Table 11.1

Employability Skills Profile: The Critical Skills Required of the Canadian Workforce

Academic Skills

Those skills that provide the basic foundation to get, keep, and progress on a job and to achieve the best results.

Canadian employers need a person who can:

Communicate
- Understand and speak the languages in which business is conducted
- Listen to understand and learn
- Read, comprehend, and use written materials, including graphs, charts, and displays
- Write effectively in the languages in which business is conducted

Think
- Think critically and act logically to evaluate situations, solve problems, and make decisions
- Understand and solve problems involving mathematics and use the results
- Use technology, instruments, tools, and information systems effectively
- Access and apply specialized knowledge from various fields (e.g., skilled trades, technology, physical sciences, arts, and social sciences)

Learn
- Continue to learn for life

Personal Management Skills

The combination of skills, attitudes and behaviours required to get, keep, and progress on a job and to achieve the best results.

Canadian employers need a person who can demonstrate:

Positive Attitudes and Behaviours
- Self-esteem and confidence
- Honesty, integrity, and personal ethics
- A positive attitude toward learning, growth, and personal health
- Initiative, energy, and persistence to get the job done

Responsibility
- The ability to set goals and priorities in work and personal life
- The ability to plan and manage time, money, and other resources to achieve goals
- Accountability for actions taken

Adaptability
- A positive attitude toward change
- Recognition of and respect for people's diversity and individual differences
- The ability to identify and suggest new ideas to get the job done creatively

Teamwork Skills

Those skills needed to work with others on a job and to achieve the best results.

Canadian employers need a person who can:

Work with Others
- Understand and contribute to the organization's goals
- Understand and work within the culture of the group
- Plan and make decisions with others and support the outcomes
- Respect the thoughts and opinions of others in the group
- Exercise "give and take" to achieve group results
- Seek a team approach as appropriate
- Lead when appropriate, mobilizing the group for high performance

Reprinted with permission of the Corporate Council on Education: The National Business and Education Centre, The Conference Board of Canada, 255 Smyth Road, Ottawa, Ontario K1H 8M7. Copies in English or French can be obtained by calling (613) 526-3280 or faxing (613) 526-4857.

The most common kinds of **power** that a leader or group member has are coercive, reward, expert, legitimate, referent, networking, and helplessness (see Table 11.2).

Table 11.2
Kinds of Power

Kind of Power	Description
Coercive	The ability to punish or withhold resources
Reward	The ability to reward
Expert	Owning special knowledge or expertise
Referent	Having personal charisma and charm
Helplessness	Ability to get others to do one's bidding by claiming helplessness or inability
Networking	Knowing the right people
Legitimate	Having authority by virtue of position

Source: Adapted from French J. and Raven, B. (1959). The bases of social power, in D. Cartwright (Ed.), *Studies in social power.* Ann Arbor: University of Michigan. Reprinted with permission.

We are often not aware of the power we hold over others. It is sometimes not power we wish to have. For example, teachers must give grades. This is at the same time both reward and coercive power. A co-worker with great technical skill is suddenly a leader in an electrical blackout. This is expert power.

Fear of Reprisals

As we discussed in Chapter 9, the most appropriate response to conflict is assertiveness. This ensures the best possibility for a win–win solution for both parties. In the workplace, however, it may not be wise to be assertive if speaking your mind endangers your job. You are then forced to make an ethical decision about what you are willing to live with and at what price. This is a key difference between workplace relationships and other interpersonal relationships. Sometimes, because of the power of unions and collective agreements, your job may not be threatened but the quality of your workplace may be altered. A disgruntled boss could give you the least desirable tasks or "forget" to invite you to the staff party. This kind of passive aggressive conflict style would be unpleasant to be around but not a breach of a contract.

Task Demands

It isn't always appropriate to bring up irritations or inequities when the tasks required of a work team have strident restrictions on them. It isn't always timely to engage your team members in discussion about how you feel or where the team is going when task demands are very heavy. In these circumstances, you must bracket personal issues until the task is completed. This is not usually the case in our close relationships. Indeed, the sooner we clear the air on issues that concern us with our friends and partners, the better. In the workplace, we must balance the needs of the people with the demands of the tasks. We'll discuss this in greater length later.

Technology

The increase in new kinds of communication technologies means that the work space and the work day has changed considerably (see "Virtually Networking"). Many workers are in constant contact with their offices with the aid of computers, laptops, e-mail, fax machines, telephones, and scanners. This has created a large workforce of "telecommuters" who on the one hand enjoy the freedom of being able to work from home or while travelling but who on the other hand experience isolation and an invasion of privacy by being on call all the time. The loss of the human element of the workplace, the sense of belonging to a team with shared visions and goals led

Communication Notes

Virtually Networking

In addition to formal and informal communication networks in physical workplaces, an increasing number of workers are part of virtual networks. Made possible by new technologies, telecommuting allows millions of people to work out of their homes or from mobile offices. Hooked up to computers, e-mail, and faxes, these telecommuters work and maintain contact with their colleagues—all without going to the physical job site. Telecommuting raises the productivity and morale of many employees, and employers like it because it reduces the cost of office space.

Source: Sue Shellenbarger. (1995, August 23). Telecommuter Profile. *Wall Street Journal*, p. B1.

futurist John Naisbitt to entitle his current book *High Tech High Touch: Technology and Our Search for Meaning* (1999).

COMMUNICATION CLIMATE AND CULTURE

Organizational scholars have long believed that the overall quality of communication and working relationships in a company has a major impact on both individual and organizational performance. In studying this idea, two concepts have been advanced to help characterize the overall nature of these environments: communication climate and organizational culture.

Climate

The overall character and quality of the communication environment of an organization is called the communication **climate.** It is similar to the concept of relationship climates discussed in Chapter 8, although in this case it applies to a larger social group. The climate of a workplace will decide the quality of the communication that takes place there. Interpersonal climate is either confirming, that is, positive, respectful, and supportive or disconfirming, that is, negative, sometimes punitive, disrespectful, or overly critical. Remember that recognition, acknowledgment, and endorsement are the three key behaviours that establish a confirming climate. A confirming climate can be established in the ways we greet, involve, and acknowledge the contributions of others. For example, Jack might say to Jane as she enters a meeting, "Jane, glad you could join us. We were just talking about tomorrow's plans" (recognition). Further evidence of a positive climate is found in statements like "I think Jane was trying to say something. Go ahead, Jane" (acknowledgment) and "That's a very interesting idea. It's an inspired solution. I'm with Jane" (endorsement).

According to Gerald Goldhaber (1993), the communication climate of an organization is most strongly affected by (1) supportiveness: the degree to which communication relationships foster a sense of personal worth and importance; (2) participation: the degree to which employees feel they can influence decisions that affect them; (3) trust: the extent to which information sources are reliable and believable; (4) openness: the degree to which supervisors and co-workers are both open to participate in communication; and (5) **goal clarity:** the prospect of clear, attainable goals. Where these qualities exist to a high degree, employees tend to have higher levels of job satisfaction. It is unclear if positive climates always lead to increased performance; however, research does indicate that this is true in many cases.

More stress is created in the workplace by interpersonal conflict than by hard work.

Photo: © Corel

Without these five qualities, stressors build. Stressors in the workplace are rarely from the hard work demanded of us. The greatest stressors come from interpersonal conflict with those with whom we are forced to interact. See "The Cost of Conflict in the Workplace."

Communication Notes

The Cost of Conflict in the Workplace

According to the December 2000 edition of the Northern Ontario Business Editorial Archives, workplace stress is on the rise and the most common source is attributed to the person assigning the work not the workload itself. Debbie West, a mental health therapist reports more incidents of interpersonal conflict as the source of job-related stress than any other stressor in the workplace. One study conducted by the Canadian information technology consulting firm called Convoke, suggests that absenteeism has tripled over the last 15 years and almost one-third of it can be attributed to disorders linked to stress. Another study by the Toronto-based Business and Economic Roundtable on Mental Health reports mental health disorders globally have increased about 200 per cent over the past five years costing an estimated $124 billion CDN per year.

Source: Gouliquer, Dianne. (December 2000). When the boss is the problem. Northern Ontario business Editorial Archives. www.nob.on.ca/archives/dec00story/bossprob.html (Retrieved June 17, 2001)

Organizational Culture

The concept of **organizational culture** provides an alternative way of characterizing the overall quality of an organization. Adapted from anthropology, the concept of culture refers to the overall pattern of beliefs, values, and practices that uniquely characterize a specific social group. Just as individual societies can have unique cultures, organizations have distinct ways of doing things that allow us to identify each as having a unique character. Some companies have a family culture that is expressed by employees' interest in each other's lives. Other organizations have a down-to-business culture reflected by a lot of task communication and little social talk. In each case, the organizational culture is both a reflection and a product of the communication that takes place.

Photo: © ITP Nelson 1997

Communication and organizational culture are intertwined. Communication creates, sustains, and sometimes alters organizational culture. At the same time, the culture of business shapes how employees communicate (Pacanowsky, 1989; Van Maanen & Barley, 1985). Let's examine three kinds of communication that express organizational cultures: vocabulary, rites and rituals, and soul in the workplace.

Notice Institutional Culture

What is the culture of your school? Does it portray itself as an institution of higher learning, a place for personal and intellectual growth, or a school devoted to technical excellence? Can you locate documents that express the proclaimed identity of your school?

Now, identify specific practices that you and other students engage in that reflect and sustain the identity your school claims to maintain. Going to classes, making notes, studying, taking exams, and so forth are all activities that support a campus's identity as a place in which learning is the preeminent goal.

Vocabulary

Just as the language of an ethnic culture reflects and expresses its history, norms, values, and identity, so does the language of an organization. We will examine the impact of two kinds of language that influence the culture of an organization, hierarchical and masculine language.

Hierarchical Language   Many organizations and professions have vocabularies that distinguish levels of status among members. The military, for example, relies on language that continuously acknowledges rank ("Yes sir,"

Canadian peacekeepers en route to Zagreb, October 5, 1993. The military poses unique communication challenges.

Photo: © Jaques Boissinot/CP Picture Archive

Student Voices

Daria:

Language really communicates status in the medical world. I worked six years as a nurse in a large hospital, and I never had a doctor call me Ms. Jenkins or address me as Nurse Jenkins. The doctors always used our first names or referred to us as "nurse." But all of us had to call them Dr. So-and-So. And the doctors didn't even bother to learn the names of orderlies and technicians—they just called them "hey you."

"chain of command"), which reflects that status, respect, and privilege connected to official rank. Rank is also communicated by unequal terms of address. For instance, a corporate CEO may use first names ("Good morning, Jan") when speaking to employees, but unless given permission to use the CEO's first name, lower status members of a company typically refer to the CEO as Mister, Miss, Sir, or Ma'am. Instructors generally use students' first names, whereas students tend to use titles to address their teachers: Dr. Armstrong, Ms. Armstrong, Mr. Armstrong, or Professor Armstrong.

Masculine Language   Perhaps because men have historically outnumbered women in the workplace, language in many organizations emphasizes interests and experiences more typical of men than women. Consider the number of phrases in the working world that are taken from sports (home run, ballpark estimate, touchdown, game plan, team player, starting line-up), military life (battle plan, mount a campaign, plan of attack, under fire, the big guns, defensive move, offensive strike), and sexual activities initiated by men (hit on a person, screw someone, stick it to them, a person has real balls). Because masculine language legitimizes men's experiences more than those of women, it may foster cultures in which some women feel unwelcome or uncomfortable.

Language in the workplace may also normalize sexist behaviour, including sexual harassment. Calling women "hon" and "sweetheart" or commenting repeatedly on a woman's appearance spotlights women's sexuality and obscures their professional abilities and status. Sexualized language also contributes to cultures in which sexist behaviour is regarded as normal and acceptable (Bingham, 1994, 1996; Taylor & Conrad, 1992; Wood, 1992b, 1997c).

Much has been done to de-sex the language in the workplace. See Table 11.3 for some of the changes that have improved the language of the workplace.

Table 11.3
De-Sexing the Language of the Workplace

Sexist Language	De-Sexed Language
Man the desk	Staff the desk
Chairman	Chairperson, Chairwoman/Chairman
Postman	Letter-carrier
Waiter/Waitress	Server
Steward/Stewardess	Flight Attendant
Secretary	Administrative Assistant
Foreman	Charge-hand
Policeman	Officer
Fireman	Firefighter

|Student Voices|

Evangeline:

I had always had male supervisors in the agency I worked for until Julie was hired. On my first visit to her office, I expected the usual light-hearted banter and down-to-business attitude I had engaged in with all my supervisors. But instead, Julie asked me how I was doing and waited for an answer. I replied "Fine," as was our custom in the office. No one really wanted to know the answer. But Julie persisted and said, "No, how are you really doing?" I burst into tears. No one had ever asked me how I was really doing before and waited with interest for the answer. It was a breath of fresh air. I realized that feminine communication style was OK in the workplace.

Concepts at a Glance

Four Rites of an Organization

- Rites of passage
- Rites of integration
- Rites of degradation
- Rites of enhancement

Rites and Rituals

Rites and rituals are communication practices that express organizational values and identity. **Rites** are dramatic, planned activities that bring together aspects of cultural ideology into a single event. Harrison Trice and Janice Beyer (1984) identify several kinds of organizational rites.

Rites of passage mark entry into different levels in organizations. For example, promotions may be symbolized by larger offices with nicer artwork. Retirements may be acknowledged with banquets and laudatory speeches. Rites of integration affirm and enhance the sense of community in an organization. Holiday parties and annual picnics are common rites of integration.

Organizational cultures include rites that blame or praise individuals and teams. Rites of degradation punish employees and proclaim that the company does not approve of certain identities or activities. Firings and demotions are the most common degradation rites. Conversely, rites of enhancement praise individuals or teams who represent the organization's self-image. Schools that value teaching, for instance, bestow awards upon faculty who are especially gifted teachers. Many sales companies give awards for productivity (most sales of the month, quarter, year).

Rituals are forms of communication that occur regularly and that employees perceive as familiar and routine parts of organizational life. Rituals are less dramatic and more frequently performed than rites and don't bring together a number of aspects of organizational ideology into a single event. Rather, rituals are repeated communications that express a particular value or role definition.

Personal, social, and task rituals are common in organizations.

Personal Rituals **Personal rituals** are activities that individuals routinely engage in to define themselves. In their study of organizational cultures, Michael Pacanowsky and Nick O'Donnell-Trujillo (1983) noted that Lou Polito, the owner of a car company, opened all of the company's mail himself each day. Whenever possible, Mr. Polito hand-delivered mail to the divisions of his company to communicate his openness and his involvement with the day-to-day business.

Social Rituals **Social rituals** are standardized performances that affirm relationships among members of organizations. Some organizations have a company dining room to encourage socializing among employees. Others permit informal interaction during breaks. Tamar Katriel (1990) identified a social ritual of griping among Israelis. *Kiturim,* the name Israelis give to their griping, most often occurs during Friday night social events called *mesibot kiturim,* which means gripe sessions. Some Jewish families engage in ritualized *kvetching,* which is personal griping that aims to air frustrations but not necessarily to resolve them. The point of the ritual is to complain, not to feel better.

Concepts at a Glance

Three Rituals of an Organization

- Personal rituals
- Social rituals
- Task rituals

Student Voices

Sharon:
We spend the first half hour or so at work every Monday complaining about what we have to get done that week. Even if we don't have a rough week ahead, we go through the motions, moaning and groaning. It's kind of like a bonding ceremony for us.

Task Rituals   **Task rituals** help members of an organization perform their jobs. A special conference room may be reserved for strategy meetings. In their study of police, Pacanowsky and O'Donnell-Trujillo (1983) identified a ritual that officers are trained to perform when they stop traffic violators. The officers ask questions ("May I see your licence? Do you know why I stopped you? Do you know how fast you were going?") to size up motorists and to decide whether to give them a break.

Student Voices

Eileen:

Our whitewater kayak instructor began every open water session with a series of rituals that we all came to love. She would "raft us up" in a group and then each one of us would try our rolls. If successful, the group would all thump the tops of their boats and whoop loudly to signal support. Then we would pass a hug along the line of kayaks. This had an amazing effect of discharging some of our anxiety and making us laugh. The final ritual was a prayer to the "River God" to allow us safe passage over the surface. All of us, regardless of our religious beliefs, took part in this symbolic ritual because it focused our attention to the risks of the sport but also to the respect we owed the river.

Working in outdoor recreation presents many unusual challenges.

Photo: A. Henry

Eileen points out how effective the rituals are prior to taking part in risk sports. The rituals became the vehicle to pass on values, acknowledge each member of the group, and cheer on the work ahead.

In a number of ways, then, organizational cultures provide an important means of shaping communication in the workplace. Cultures provide a common set of rituals and practices that help to give voice to shared beliefs, values, and understanding. They help to define the relational environment of the organization, and to give shape to interactions within it. At the same time, everyday interactions within the organization contribute to the continued shaping and renewal of the culture itself. So, in a sense, communication is shaped by an organization's culture, but it is also the means by which the culture itself is expressed and continuously renewed.

Soul in the Workplace

Much has been written recently about bringing soul back to the workplace (Briskin, 1998; Canfield, 1996; McDargh, retrieved June 19, 2001; Taylor, retrieved June 19, 2001). **Soul** can be defined as a sense of connectedness and meaning in one's life. In the workplace, it means having a deeper purpose than just receiving a paycheque; being regarded as a whole person with a brain, a heart, and a soul. The dilemma of the modern workplace is to not succumb to a world that ignores soul. If we do, we permit our jobs to drain and exhaust our human energies. Ways to bring soul into the workplace include seizing an opportunity for meaningful contribution, innovation, and learning. When the workplace allows for creativity and flexibility, when the communication between the working team is respectful and energetic, when there is opportunity to work with and relate to others in meaningful ways, when we can take part in shaping and actualizing a vision, then we have a sense of soul in our work.

COMMUNICATING IN GROUPS AND TEAMS

Groups and teams are central to professional life. Whether you are an attorney working with a litigation team, a health care professional in a health delivery unit, or a factory worker in a group assigned to reduce production time, working with others will probably be a part of your career. Your raises and advancement will likely depend significantly on how effectively you communicate in groups.

Defining Groups and Teams

What is a group? Are six people standing in line for tickets a group? Are five individuals studying individual materials in a library a group? No—these examples describe collections of individuals, but not groups.

Chapter 11
Relationships at Work
443

For a group to exist, there must be interaction and interdependence among individuals. So, we can define a **group** as three or more individuals who interact over time, who depend on one another, and who communicate to reach a common goal. A **team** is a special kind of group that is brought together for a very specific task, and is normally characterized by the distinct and complementary resources of members and by their strong sense of collective identity. Like all groups, teams involve interaction, interdependence, shared rules, and common goals. However, because they are formed with a particular purpose in mind, teams tend to consist of people with specialized and unique skills, and may develop a stronger sense of identity than is typical of most groups (Lumsden & Lumsden, 1997).

Why Organizations Rely on Groups

Organizations have increasingly turned to the use of groups because they offer a number of potential advantages over individuals working alone. For example, compared with individuals' work, groups can bring a far greater range of resources to a task. They have the potential to think through issues more thoroughly, bring heightened creativity to solutions, and often provide enhanced commitment to decisions (Wood, 1992, 1997a).

A group obviously exceeds any individual in terms of the ideas, perspectives, experiences, and expertise it has to solve a problem. While one member may know technical aspects of a product, another may understand market psychology, a third may be talented in advertising, and so forth. Health care teams consist of doctors, nurses, social workers, and other specialists who combine their knowledge to provide a better level of patient care.

Groups also tend to be more thorough than individuals, probably because members act as a check and balance system for each other. Issues one member doesn't understand, another member does; the details of a plan that bore one person interest another; the holes in a proposal that some members overlook are caught by others. Greater thoroughness by groups isn't simply the result of more people working, but reflects interaction among members. Discussion can promote critical and careful analysis because members are stimulated by each other's thinking (Wood, 1997a). **Synergy** is a special kind of energy that enlarges the efforts, talents, and strengths of individual members (Lumsden & Lumsden, 1997).

A third value of groups is that they are generally more creative than individuals. Again, the reason lies in the synergy of groups. When members know how to communicate effectively, they spark good ideas, integrative thinking, and creativity. Any individual eventually runs out of new ideas, but groups have an almost infinite generative ability. As members talk, they build upon each other's ideas. They refine proposals and see new possibilities in each other's comments. The result is often a greater number of overall ideas and more creative solutions.

Concepts at a Glance

Four Advantages of Groups over Individuals

- Groups bring a greater range of resources.
- Groups are more thorough.
- Groups bring more creativity to solutions.
- Groups provide enhanced commitment to decisions.

Student Voices

Laura:

When the supervisor said all of us in my department were to meet together to come up with ideas for cutting costs, I thought it was silly. I thought it would be more efficient for each person to submit suggestions individually. But I was wrong. When my group started, each of us had one or two ideas. But the six of us came up with over 25 ideas after we'd talked awhile.

A final strength of groups is their ability to generate commitment to outcomes. The greater commitment fostered in groups arises from two sources. First, participation enhances loyalty to decisions. Thus, groups with balanced participation build commitment among members, which is especially important if members will be involved in implementing the decision. Second, groups are more likely than individuals to consider the points of view of various people needed to implement a decision. This is critical, since a decision can be sabotaged if the people affected feel their opinions were ignored.

Many of the strengths that groups offer are the result of members' abilities to combine their knowledge, their efforts, and their creativity into a single effort. The synergy that is created by group interaction is available, however, only when group members effectively communicate, share, and merge their ideas. The highest quality outcomes from groups are always the result of the highest quality communication.

The Limitations of Groups

Groups enjoy many advantages, but they also have very important limitations, and at times can even generate negative outcomes for organizations. Two of the most significant limitations of group discussion are the time required for group processes and the potential of the pressures of conformity that can interfere with critical, high-quality discussion.

Operating alone, a person can think through ideas efficiently and choose the one he or she considers to be best. In group discussion, however, time is needed so that all members have an opportunity to voice their ideas and respond to ideas put forward by others. Groups also need time to deliberate alternative courses of action. As a result, group discussion is not a wise choice for routine or trivial decisions, where the time required by a group would be wasted. When creativity and thoroughness are important, however, the time that groups require is well spent.

Groups also have the potential to suppress individuals and to encourage conformity. This can happen in two ways. First, pressure for conformity may exist when a majority of members have an opinion different than a minority of members or a single member. It is hard to maintain a point of view when most or all of your peers have a different one. In effective groups, however, all members understand and resist conformity pressures. They realize that the majority is sometimes wrong and the minority, even a single person, is sometimes right. Members have an ethical responsibility to encourage expression of diverse ideas and to foster open debate about different viewpoints.

Conformity pressures may also arise when one member is extremely charismatic or has greater power or prestige than other members. Even if that person is alone in a point of view, other members may conform. President Kennedy's advisers, for example, regarded him so highly that in some cases they suspended their individual critical thinking and agreed with whatever he said (Janis, 1977). Conformity can occur even in the absence of a high-status person. Janis's work on the phenomenon of *groupthink* has shown that ordinary decision-making groups can make extremely poor decisions, even with the presence of top quality participants and information, when they allow conformity to override common sense.

Student Voices

Lance:

I used to belong to a creative writing group where all of us helped each other improve our writing. At first all of us were equally vocal, and we aired different ideas. But then one member of the group had a story accepted by a big magazine, and suddenly we thought of her as a better writer than any of us. She didn't act any different, but we saw her as more accomplished, so when she said something everybody listened and nobody disagreed. It was like a wet blanket on our creativity because her opinion just carried too much weight once she got published.

Concepts at a Glance

Group Characteristics

- Groups manage task and maintenance functions.
- Groups go through specific stages of development.
- Members exhibit positive and negative group roles.
- Groups make decisions and solve problems.
- Leadership emerges.

Group Process

What happens when groups go to work? Researchers have found that group processes tend to have several stable characteristics, though the action is sometimes fast and furious. Groups experience both attention to task and attention to the maintenance of the people of the group. Groups tend to go through predictable stages of development. Group members exhibit specific group roles that are both productive and counterproductive to group functioning. Finally, decision-making, problem-solving, and leadership are all characteristics of groups. Let's examine each one of these group characteristics.

Task and Maintenance

One very consistent finding that students of group behaviour have found is a tendency for the focus of communication to shift back and forth between the **task** and the **maintenance** of the group itself. Clearly, in order for a group to work effectively, a good part of its energy has to be directed toward accomplishing its defined goals. However, group members also need to feel that they are included, that their contributions are valued, and that the group as a whole is functioning smoothly (Schutz, 1958). Although attention to the needs of group maintenance may not appear at first to contribute to the task, these needs permit individuals to develop trust toward the group as a whole, and help the group to function smoothly. Groups that fail to look after maintenance needs tend to become ineffective, and often have to return to these important concerns before moving on with a task. Effective group leaders recognize the importance of balancing task and maintenance needs, and often intervene to ensure that these needs are equally met.

Communication Notes

Stages in Group Development

Bruce Tuckman reviewed research on therapy, learning, and task groups. The groups followed a four-phase sequence of development.

Forming is the initial stage of group life in which members define a purpose and become acquainted. *Storming* is typically marked by conflict about goals, personalities, information, and so forth. There may also be struggles for power among members. *Norming* is a phase in which members work out norms, rules, and roles to regulate how they interact.

Performing occurs when members settle down to business after resolving conflicts and establishing norms.

Source: Tuckman, B. (1965). Developmental sequences in small groups. Psychological Bulletin, 63, 384–399.

Stages of Group Development

Another consistent observation of group research is that groups pass through regular stages as they mature over time. Although several different formulations have been proposed, the general pattern demonstrates an initial period in which individuals feel each other out and assess if and how they will decide to accept group membership, typically followed by a stage of conflict, when individuals vie for control of group topics and procedures; resolution of the conflict finally leads to a period of productive operation, when the group agrees upon its own procedures and norms of interaction and is able to work together effectively. These stages are often revisited whenever the group encounters a difficulty or accepts a new member.

Knowledge of these stages of development can help group leaders and members through difficult transitions. In each stage, the group must ensure that certain task or maintenance needs are met. An effective leader can recognize these needs and provide what the group needs to effectively focus its energy and move forward (Sept, 1981).

Effective Member Roles

Throughout its life cycle, each group requires its members to contribute actively and positively to both task and maintenance needs. Of course, every person will make that contribution according to her or his own skills, abilities, and interests. As a result, group members often perform a variety of different roles in order to assist the group to effectively meet its goals.

Several different kinds of member roles have been observed in groups, some of which contribute positively to the groups' progress while others detract. Participation in groups has been classified into four distinct categories, each of which can be associated with a specific type of communication. The first three, task, procedural, and climate communication, are constructive because they foster healthy working relationships and productivity. The fourth category, egocentric communication, detracts from a healthy culture and good decision-making. Figure 11.1 illustrates several communication behaviours in each of these categories. **Task communication** focuses on the problem, issue, or information. It provides ideas and information, clarifies understanding, and critically evaluates ideas. Task contributions may include initiating ideas, responding to others' ideas, or providing critical evaluation of information. Task comments also include asking for ideas and criticism from others.

If you've ever participated in a disorganized group, you understand the importance of **procedural communication,** which helps a group get organized and stay on track in its decision-making. Procedural contributions establish an agenda, coordinate comments of different members, and record group progress. In addition, procedural contributions may curb digressions and tangents, summarize progress, and regulate participation so that everyone has opportunities to speak and nobody dominates.

Climate communication focuses on creating and maintaining a constructive climate that encourages people to contribute freely and to evaluate ideas critically. Climate comments emphasize strengths and progress, recognize others' con-

What roles do you play in groups?

Photo: © Photodisc

tributions, reconcile conflicts, and build enthusiasm for the organization and its work.

The final kind of communication is not recommended, but it sometimes surfaces in organizational contexts. **Egocentric communication,** or dysfunctional communication, is used to block others or to call attention to oneself. Examples of egocentric talk include devaluing another person's ideas, trivializing group efforts, acting aggressively toward others, bragging about personal accomplishments, dominating, disrupting group work, and pleading for special causes that don't advance organizational goals.

Task, procedural, and climate communication work together to foster productive and comfortable interaction. Egocentric communication, if not checked, can damage an organization's climate and hinder goal achievement. As an illustration, "Analyzing Communication in Groups" shows how various contributions to a group discussion can be coded in terms of the kinds of communication just discussed. Notice how the combination of task, procedural, and climate communication helps to move the group forward in its task.

Apply the Idea

Analyzing Communication in Groups

The following excerpt from a group discussion allows you to assess your understanding of the four kinds of communication we've discussed:

Ed: Let's start by talking about our goals. **[procedural]**

Jan: That's a good idea. **[climate]**

Bob: I think our goal is to come up with a better meal plan for students on campus. **[task]**

Ed: What do you mean by "better"? Do you mean cheaper, or more variety, or more tasteful? **[task]**

Ann: I think it's all three. **[task]**

Ed: Well, we probably do care about all three, but maybe we should talk about one at a time so we can keep our discussion focused. **[procedural]**

Bob: Okay, I vote we focus first on taste—like it would be good if there were some taste to the food on campus! **[task and climate (humour)]**

Jan: Do you mean taste itself or quality of food, which might also consider nutrition? **[task]**

Bob: Pure taste! When I'm hungry, I don't think about what's good for me, just what tastes good. **[task]**

Jan: Well, maybe we want the food service to think about nutrition since we don't. **[task]**

Task Communication
Initiates ideas
Seeks information
Elaborates ideas
Gives information
Evaluates, offers critical analysis

Procedural Communication
Establishes agenda
Provides orientation
Curbs digression
Guides participation
Coordinates ideas
Records group progress
Summarizes others' contributions

Climate Communication
Establishes and maintains healthy climate
Energizes group process
Recognizes others
Harmonizes ideas
Reconciles conflicts
Builds enthusiasm for group

Egocentric Communication
Aggresses toward others
Blocks ideas
Seeks personal recognition
Dominates interaction
Pleads for special interests
Disrupts the task
Devalues others
Trivializes group's work
Confesses, self-discloses, seeks personal help

Figure 11.1
Communication Roles in Groups

Bob: If you're a health food nut, that's your problem. I don't think nutrition is something that's important in the food service on campus. [task; possibly also egocentric if his tone toward Jan was snide]

Ed: Let's do this: Let's talk first about what we would like in terms of taste itself. [procedural] Before we meet next time, we can talk with staff of the cafeteria to see if they have to meet any nutritional guidelines in what they serve. [task]

Ann: I'll volunteer to do that. [task]

Ed: Great. Thanks, Ann. [climate]

Bob: I'll volunteer to do taste testing! [climate (humour)]

Jan: With your weight, you'd better not. [egocentric]

Bob: Yeah, like you have a right to criticize me. [egocentric]

Ann: Look, none of us is here to criticize anyone else. We're here because all of us care about food service on campus. [climate] We've decided we want to focus first on taste [procedural], so who has an idea of how do we go about studying that? [task]

Decision-Making and Problem-Solving

Most groups in the workplace concentrate on solving problems or making decisions—that is, after all, what they do best. We have already said that groups can produce highly creative decisions and solutions. But to do so, their communication must provide for an orderly and coherent working process in order to harness a group's creative power and apply it effectively to the problem at hand. Decisions are made and problems solved by using steps similar to the problem-solving model used for interpersonal conflict. First, the problem must be defined, then analyzed and assessed, solutions are generated and evaluated, an action plan is implemented and followed up (Dewey, 1910, Wood 1997a). This works exceedingly well as long as interpersonal conflict is not part of the mix. We'll discuss this more thoroughly when we examine conflict.

Leadership

To be effective, groups and organizations need leadership. For decades, it was assumed that leaders were individuals with special qualities. Research, however, shows that leadership can be provided by one or more people. Strong leadership exists when one person (or more) communicates to establish a good working climate, organizes collective efforts, ensures that discussion is substantive, and controls disruptive people. You may have noticed that leadership parallels types of participation we just discussed. Leadership, in that sense, is effective participation.

When a single person provides leadership, she or he takes responsibility for managing everything. In other cases, several people share leadership responsibilities. Sometimes one person provides guidance on a task and another person leads in building a healthy climate. Different people may

|Student Voices|

Krystal:

The most effective group I've ever been in had three leaders. I understood our task best, so I led the way in analyzing information. Belinda kept us organized. She could get us off tangents and move us from one stage of work to the next. She also pulled our ideas together. Kevin was the climate leader. He could tell a joke if things got tense, and he was the best person I've ever seen for recognizing everyone's contributions. I couldn't point to any one leader in that group, but we sure did have good leadership.

provide leadership at different times. The individual who guides at the outset may not be the one who is most effective in bringing a project to conclusion. Even when an official leader exists, other people may contribute much of the communication that provides leadership. The most effective group members are those who can identify what the group needs at any given time and provide the skills or information that will help move the group forward.

Whether provided by one or several people, effective leadership involves communication that advances tasks, organizes deliberations, controls disruptions, and fosters a constructive climate.

CHALLENGES TO COMMUNICATING IN THE WORKPLACE

The workplace poses many challenges. We will examine three that cause much stress for employees and employers alike. The most distressing and conversely the most exhilarating challenge in the workplace is managing conflict. Certainly, dealing with difficult people can create much stress in our lives. Successfully resolving differences on the other hand can be very satisfying and creative. Inherent in the discussion of conflict in the workplace is the issue of harassment. We will also visit alternate communication approaches. Our discussion will then move to the two areas of managing intimacy and managing diversity and change in the workplace.

MANAGING CONFLICT IN THE WORKPLACE

Our discussion in Chapter 9 on managing conflict provides us with the basis of sound conflict resolution. There are some changes we will make to the

Concepts at a Glance

Challenges in the Workplace

- Managing conflict
  - Conflict resolution style
  - Dealing with difficult people
  - Harassment
  - Tactical communication
- Managing intimacy
- Managing diversity and change

approach to conflict that take into account the various people we deal with and our investment in those relationships.

Conflict is natural and can be productive. In the workplace, conflict can also have a number of positive spinoffs if it is managed effectively. For example, the presence of mild conflict can stimulate thinking, help people search for more information, and seek better solutions to problems. The challenge of conflict often spurs people to be more creative in addressing issues in order to come up with the best possible solution. Mild conflict also gives voice to diverse perspectives on issues, and allows minority views to be expressed in ways that otherwise might not be possible. To the extent that conflict brings about a more open sharing and discussion of issues, it can lead to increased understanding of problems, assignments, and decisions.

To achieve these goals, however, conflict must be managed carefully so that it enriches an organization's ability to achieve its goals rather than getting in the way. Conflict can be allowed to exist as a creative tension between individuals or groups, but it must be carefully monitored to ensure that it does not get out of hand. Opposing groups or individuals should be encouraged to seek positive means of addressing the issue—seeking new information, clearly expressing viewpoints, seeking creative solutions, and so on—rather than attempting to harm or undermine the other person. Conflicts that begin to cross the line and become destructive may require intervention, such as some form of mediation or third-party settlement, so that they do not negatively affect others in the organization.

Troy's commentary is instructive. Although many of us don't enjoy conflict, we can nonetheless recognize its value—even its necessity—in the workplace. The challenge is to harness the positive potentials of conflict. To encourage constructive conflict, communication should demonstrate openness to different ideas, willingness to alter opinions when good reasons exist, and respect for the integrity of other people and the views they express. Construc-

|Student Voices|

Troy:

I used to think conflict was terrible and hurt groups, but last year I was on a committee that had no—I mean, zero—conflict. A couple of times I brought up a reservation about what the committee was doing, but the others squelched my ideas. Everyone was determined to agree and to get along. When our recommendation was put into practice, it bombed. We could have foreseen and avoided the failure if we had been willing to argue and disagree in order to develop a sound proposal.

tive conflict allows people to broaden their understanding and to subject their ideas to careful, cooperative analysis. Constructive conflict is most likely to occur when the appropriate groundwork has been established by creating a supportive and open climate of communication. A positive climate is built throughout the life of a group, beginning with the first meeting among members. Thus, it is important to communicate in ways that build a strong climate from the start so that it has been established when conflict arises.

Conflict Resolution Model

As we discussed in Chapter 9, sometimes it is not worth resolving conflict because we have little investment in a relationship. A server in a restaurant for example, although irritated or frustrated with an insensitive diner, is not likely to invest in resolving conflict in the same manner that he or she does with a co-worker. Similarly, a merchant who relies heavily on word of mouth for business is going to shrug off or accommodate behaviour that he or she would not tolerate from an intimate partner or a friend. A police officer or youth worker might use humour or might ignore troublesome behaviour in order to diffuse hostility. Let's examine the similarities and differences in conflict resolution of interpersonal relationships and workplace relationships (see Table 11.4). As we discussed earlier, the basic process of problem-solving is defining, analyzing, generating solutions, implementing, and following up. Note the variations when more difficult interpersonal conflict is encountered.

A conversation about conflict might sound something like this: "I am concerned about …" (raise the issue). "When this happens, the result is …" and "How do you see the situation?" and "Then, from your perspective …" (describe your experience, solicit response from the other, paraphrase). "In the future, how can we …" (request a change in behaviour). "OK, so I'll … and you'll …" (agree on an action plan). "When can I expect to see some change?" (make plans to follow up). There is certainly much similarity in style between the two relationship approaches, but there is evidence of the power differences in the workplace scenario.

Table 11.4
Comparison of Conflict Resolution Styles

Interpersonal Relationship Conflict Resolution Model	Workplace Relationship Conflict Resolution Model
Step One: Express your needs	Step One: Raise the issue
Step Two: Solicit the needs of the other	Step Two: Describe the specifics
Step Three: Negotiate a solution	Step Three: Request a change in behaviour
Step Four: Follow up	Step Four: Agree on an action plan
	Step Five: Make plans to follow up

Dealing with Difficult People

Sometimes our best conflict-resolution efforts do not resolve conflict because the people with whom we are in conflict are not invested in a win–win solution. Usually difficult people are invested in a win–lose solution. Table 11.5 identifies six types of personalities that frequently present conflict for us and some suggested responses.

Tactical Communication

Police officers and mediators have long been acquainted with tactical communication to diffuse potentially hostile situations. Communication scholars use the term "verbal judo" or "tongue fu" (Thompson, 1994; Horn, 1996) to describe this alternative to the common conflict resolution approach of voice or assertiveness. Because our work lives bring us into contact with people we might never choose to have a relationship with, it is valuable to have some alternative communication abilities for difficult situations. Horn identifies four behaviours to diffuse, deflect, or disarm verbal conflict; agree, apologize, act, appreciate. For example, a salesperson might say to a complaining abusive customer, "You're right, those shoes should have lasted longer" (agree). "I'm sorry you have had so much trouble with them" (apologize). "I'll personally get the rep to send you a new pair" (act). "I'm so glad you would come back and let us straighten this out. We appreciate your business" (appreciate).

The above tactic works very well in the customer service domain, but there are some situations when clear limits need to be set with hostile people. The respectful I–language that is so important in civil interpersonal interchanges might need to be replaced with stronger You–language to stop abusive people. So instead of saying "I'm uncomfortable with you shouting like that" you might need to use the stronger language of "You need to lower your voice when you are speaking to me." Abusive people frequently do not hear the subtle language cues of civil speech. Try the exercise below to practise deciding what kind of tactical communication might be most effective. Remember that the goal is to diffuse conflict and open the door to conflict resolution.

Apply the Idea

Diffusing Conflict

Examine the four scenarios on page 456 and decide whether to use the four steps of agree, apologize, act, and appreciate, or the stronger You–language to create suitable responses to the following situations. Once you have written your responses, choose a partner and put into practice your new verbal behaviours.

Table 11.5
Dealing with Difficult People

Type	Problem	Action	Sample Responses
Procrastinators and Perfectionists	They get paralyzed by a belief that work must be perfect. They miss deadlines.	• Encourage • Create the structure they lack • Help break down tasks • Validate the good work they do	Try: "There are two standards; acceptable and excellence. Maybe this task can be just acceptable." "Not everything has to be perfect." "You do such good work that your acceptable will be excellent to others."
Verbally Abusive People	They violate others' rights: • the right to be treated with respect • the right to express oneself • the right to one's body, time, and space	• Set limits • Remove yourself if unsafe • Listen, let them vent a bit • Ask them what they want • Agree with any truth in their rantings	Try: "You don't have to yell at me to make me listen to you. I want to hear what you have to say but not when you abuse me with your words." "I am going to leave if you don't lower your voice and take your hand off my shoulder." "What exactly do you want?" (After you've talked) "Your concerns are important to me, but the next time something's bothering you, please discharge some of that anger before you walk in here. Do not yell at me, shake your fist at me, poke my shoulder, or stand too close. It makes me very uncomfortable."
Complainers and "Yes but-ters"	They focus on the negative and are not committed to solving problems. By complaining, they don't have to endorse a project or policy. They undermine the climate of the workplace.	• Make the distinction between complaining and problem-solving • Identify your desire to hear about problems and to engage in problem-solving • Model good problem-solving • Teach problem-solving skills	Try: "I'm not interested in your complaints. I am very interested in solving problems. Let's define the problem." "I want to hear your good ideas, not complaints."
Ego-centric Self-summarizers	They have difficulty with dual perspective. They constantly bring issues, topics around to their needs, wants. They are insensitive to time-sharing. They often lead discussion off topic.	• Interrupt their monologues • Set time limits on self-disclosures • Ask for dual perspective • Get them to bracket irrelevant or tangential issues	Try: "We need to move on, who else would like to speak?" "I think I understand your point (short paraphrase). I'd like to hear from others." "I see your position, could you summarize others' positions for us?" "That issue will have to wait for another time. Let's confine our discussion to this issue."
Non-committal "I don't know" People	They are often afraid to voice opinion. They may be approval-seeking. They may be sabotaging the efforts of the team by covert fighting.	• Force commitment to one side of the issue or the other • Validate their position on the team	Try: "If you did know, what would it be?" "Use the 49/51 rule; be on one side or the other. You cannot choose 50/50." "I really want to know what you want, your thoughts are important to me."
Smarmy, Manipulative People	They believe they cannot be straightforward in getting what they want so they use flattery or hinting. They want to catch you off-guard. Their orientation to conflict is win–lose.	• Set limits • Call out their indirect hinting behaviour	Try: "You seem to want something, what might that be?" "I get the feeling something else is bothering you, that we're not talking about the real issue yet. Would you be more direct please." "It's hard for me to accept your kind words when there's a 'but' coming. What is it you want?"

Scenario One:

You are the receptionist at a community recreation centre, and a hostile mother comes in claiming to have been bumped off the waiting list for a set of lessons for her child.

You say: _____

Scenario Two:

You are a nurse on a ward with restricted visiting privileges to patients. A distraught family member has been refused entry into his loved one's room.

You say: _____

Scenario Three:

You are a cashier in a college cafeteria, and an angry student demands money back from a vending machine that ran out of his selection.

You say: _____

Scenario Four:

You are a teacher in an elementary school, and an angry parent demands to be able to sit in on his or her child's classes even though his or her presence is disruptive.

You say: _____

There is not a magic solution to dealing with difficult people. The situation, the goals you wish to achieve, the state of mind of the adversarial person, and the resources you have at hand will determine whether you act assertively, with humour, aggressively, or by simply ignoring the situation. Sometimes the high ground in a difficult situation is to walk away.

Harassment

Concepts at a Glance

Dealing with Harassment

- Tell the harasser to stop.
- Keep notes.
- Seek assistance of a supervisor, counsellor, or union representative.
- File a human rights claim.

Harassment is a common problem in the workplace. Harassment can be based upon a person's race, colour, place of origin, sexual orientation, religion, or ability. The outcome of harassment in the workplace is costly. It contributes to increased absenteeism, lack of productivity, and personal health deterioration. Sexual harassment has become recognized as one of the most common barriers to equality experienced by women in the workplace. Sexual harassment is also experienced by men, but less often. **Harassment** is any uninvited, unwelcome conduct that poisons the work environment. Harassment is an abuse of power, and the person who is harassed frequently suffers personal feelings of anger, frustration, and loss of self-esteem. If you experience harassment in your workplace, follow this four-step response.

Harassment is a serious issue in the workplace. Not only for the one being harassed but also for anyone who feels falsely accused of harassing. The first line of defence against a poisoned workplace is clear, respectful communication. Remember that we all have the right to our bodies, to our time, to our space, to express ourselves, and to be treated with respect. When our actions violate the rights of another, conflict results.

Harassment in the workplace: What do you do?

Photo: © Photodisc

Student Voices

Kirk:

Everyone thinks that harassment just happens to women, gay men or visible minorities. But I'm a married man working in a sheet metal shop, and I have to put up with disgusting crude behaviours from the guys I work with, including the boss, all day long. They are constantly making sexist derogatory remarks about women. To get along, I laugh with them and just try to keep separate from it all. But it takes a toll on me. When I come home to my beautiful wife and three little daughters, I feel irritated and angry and depressed. My wife has stopped asking me how my day was or what is wrong with me. She knows I need to be alone for a good half-hour to let the grunge of my work fall off me before I feel human enough to interact with her and the girls. I feel harassed!

MANAGING INTIMACY IN THE WORKPLACE

A second challenge of communication in the workplace involves participating in relationships that are simultaneously personal and professional. In a study titled "Bosses and Buddies," Ted Zorn (1995) noted that close relationships between people who work together are commonplace. Since most adults work at least 40 hours a week, personal relationships on the job are inevitable.

Friendships between co-workers or between supervisors and subordinates can be difficult. A supervisor may have trouble fairly evaluating a subordinate who is also a friend. The supervisor might overrate the subordinate's strengths or might be overly harsh to compensate for personal affection. Friendship may also make it difficult to give negative feedback, which is essential to effective performance on the job (Larson, 1984). On the positive side, personal relationships may enhance commitment to a job and communication between co-workers (Zorn, 1995).

Romantic relationships between people who work together involve many of the tensions that operate in friendships between co-workers. In addition, romantic relationships may especially cause resentment and discomfort for others in the workplace. Romantic breakups also tend to be more dramatic than ended friendships. Thus, when a romance dies, there may be repercussions in workplace relationships and climate (Dillard & Witteman, 1985).

It's unrealistic to think we won't form personal relationships with co-workers. The challenge is to manage those relationships so that the workplace doesn't interfere with the personal bond, and the intimacy doesn't jeopardize professionalism. Friends and romantic partners may need to

Mandy:

It's hard for me now that my best friend has been promoted over me. Part of it is envy, because I wanted the promotion, too. But the hardest part is that I resent her power over me. When Billie gives me an assignment, I feel that as my friend she shouldn't dump extra work on me. But I also know that as the boss she has to give extra work to all of us sometimes. It just doesn't feel right for my best friend to tell me what to do and to evaluate my work.

Eugene:

Once, I got involved with a girl where I was working. We were assigned to the same team and really hit it off, and one thing led to another and we were dating. The problem came when we broke up. It's impossible to avoid seeing your ex when you work together in a small office, and everyone else walked on eggshells around us. When she quit, I could feel tension drain out of everyone in our office.

separate personal and work roles so that on-the-job communication doesn't reflect favouritism and privileges that could cause resentment in co-workers. When away from the job, they may have to curb shop talk.

MANAGING DIVERSITY AND CHANGE

Consider the following descriptions of individuals who work in one company:

- Eileen is a 28-year-old, single, bilingual Jewish woman who is the primary caregiver for her disabled mother.
- Frank is a 37-year-old, married European-Canadian man whose wife is a full-time homemaker and mother for their two children. He is especially skilled in collaborative team-building.
- Denise is a 30-year-old European-Canadian single mother of a 4-year-old daughter. Denise has expertise as a public speaker.
- Sam is a 59-year-old African-Canadian who has two grown children, and whose wife is an accountant. He is widely regarded as supportive and empathic.

- Ned is a divorced First Nations man who is 42 years old and who just had a heart-bypass operation.
- Vinh is a 23-year-old Asian-Canadian. He and his wife, who works full time, are expecting their first child.

Eileen, Frank, Denise, Sam, Ned, and Vinh illustrate the diversity of people, life situations, and needs that characterizes the modern workplace. Organizations need to adapt to the needs of an increasingly diverse workforce. Eileen and Denise need flexible working hours so that they can manage care-giving responsibilities. Eileen may also expect her employer to allow her to respect Rosh Hashanah, Yom Kippur, and Hanukkah. Ned may need extended disability leave and a period of part-time work while he recuperates from his heart surgery. Vinh may want family leave when his child is born.

Other changes are also revolutionizing work life. As more people telecommute, managers will need to learn how to lead employees who work in different locations and at different hours. Project teams may interact through e-mail bulletin boards as often or more often than they interact face to face. The organizations that survive and thrive in the years ahead will be those that adapt effectively to meet the expectations and needs of different workers. By extension, individuals who succeed will be comfortable with a stream of changes in people and in ways of working.

GUIDELINES FOR EFFECTIVE WORKPLACE COMMUNICATION

In this chapter we have discussed the nature of relationships in the workplace and the specific challenges that surround our communication with others in this specialized context. To conclude our discussion, we will examine several guidelines that help improve and maintain effective communication in the workplace. Several of the guidelines will now look familiar as they have occurred in many of the preceding chapters. This underscores the basic elements of interpersonal communication. The contexts may change, but the abiding principles of good communication remain.

PARTICIPATE EFFECTIVELY

We have seen how organizations rely very heavily on communication to perform all of their complex functions. Participating effectively in such an environment has several dimensions. First, it is important to realize that, despite all the complexity of the organization, most work is accomplished through basic interpersonal exchanges—the kind we have been exploring throughout

---

Concepts at a Glance

Four Guidelines for Effective Workplace Communication

1. Participate effectively
   - Use dual perspective
   - Listen mindfully
   - Avoid damaging relationship behaviours
   - Monitor self
   - Provide leadership
2. Use celebration and humour
3. Be equally responsible for task and people
4. Bring soul to the workplace

this book. You can enhance your workplace communication—and your value to the organization—by honing your own personal communication skills. Use dual perspective in your dealings with others, practise mindful listening, be clear and precise in your spoken communication, and watch and understand nonverbal cues. Understanding is the prelude to action (Covey, 1991). You cannot make accurate effective decisions if you have not first understood the needs of others. All of the basic skills of interpersonal communication touched upon earlier in this book are the basic tools of effective workplace communication. Use them.

Practising effective interpersonal communication may also help your co-workers to become clear about their own information and communication needs on the job, and may provide a model for others to follow. Being clear and effective in your interpersonal communication can help others understand the benefits of high-quality communication, and may inspire them to improve their own communication skills. In group settings, effective participation often includes monitoring yourself by being aware of the roles that you play. Knowing your own strengths as a communicator, as well as the strengths of others, will help you to know when to actively step in and when to sit back and allow others to contribute. Understanding the key aspects of group process can help you contribute more positively as an equal member.

Critical to the smooth functioning of relationships in the workplace is avoiding damaging relationship behaviours. Recall in Chapter 10 that the four most damaging behaviours to relationships according to Gottman et al. (1996) are contempt, criticism, defensiveness, and stonewalling. Just as these behaviours stress and damage friendships and romantic relationships, so do they damage workplace relationships. Hear Don's words on the next page as he recognizes the impact of his damaging behaviours in a meeting.

Beyond participating as an individual, you may also be called upon to provide leadership. We have seen that, especially in group settings, leadership may come from a number of sources, and it does not always require a formal title or position. Occasionally, contributing effectively as a group member may mean that you take charge and offer your own ideas about how to approach a task, suggest procedures, assist other members to bring forth their contributions, and so on. By being aware of roles that are not being fulfilled, and by stepping in to provide the needed action, you can provide helpful leadership for the group, even if you are not designated as a leader. In interview settings, either as interviewer or interviewee, you can assist others by recognizing how the communication process is unfolding and offering information or other help to move the process forward. Whenever you use your knowledge of communication to facilitate more effective working relationships, you will be exercising effective leadership. And if your boss is paying attention, you may be rewarded with recognition and opportunities for advancement.

Don:

I realized all too late that I fell into all four of the damaging relation-ship behaviours. I was irritated when I went to one of our team meet-ings because we were behind schedule. I began the meeting by saying sarcastically "How hard can it be to get a two-page report in?" (con-tempt). Then I criticized and challenged everyone's work commitment (criticism). When people tried to explain why there had been holdups in the schedule and how they needed more support, I became defen-sive (defensiveness) and then I withdrew and got silent, refusing to participate in further discussion (stonewalling). Needless to say, the meeting didn't go well. Back at my office, I realized how ineffective I had been and how damaging my behaviour had been to the team. I had lots of repairing to do.

USE CELEBRATION AND HUMOUR

As we have discussed earlier in the chapter, the culture of an organization affects communication. If there is a culture of celebration, where small and large accomplishments are recognized, where personal events are punctuated (birthdays and anniversaries, etc.), where even creative acts that fail are acknowledged, then there is a climate of acceptance, openness, and support. When we are encouraged by humour instead of punished by criticism, there is a climate of risk-taking and ingenuity. These are worth cultivating in the workplace.

BE EQUALLY RESPONSIBLE FOR TASK AND PEOPLE

Every group is charged with completing tasks and managing the people of the working team. With increased emphasis in our modern work life to work in teams, each member must become responsible for contributing to the health of the team. That is accomplished when there is equal attention to the demands of the tasks and to the needs of the people. This does not happen simultaneously. Sometimes it is necessary to stop working toward comple-tion of a task in order to sort through group members' feelings or concerns that are getting in the way. Sometimes, this requires leaving the workplace and truly having a break. At other times, it is evident that everyone must bracket their personal issues and needs for the sake of making a pressing deadline. The important communication imperative is to watch that both task and people are being attended to. To be completely task oriented would result in bullying. To be completely people oriented would result in work stoppage. Balance and self-monitoring is the key.

BRING SOUL TO THE WORKPLACE

The final guideline to the chapter and fittingly, to the book, is to bring soul to the workplace. Our earlier discussion of soul identifies the need to treat individuals as whole people with minds, bodies, hearts, and souls. This requires the employer to make opportunities for flexibility, innovation, connectedness, vision, and contribution. This requires the employee to seek ways to create meaning in the workplace and to respect and honour relationships. Our connectedness to ourselves, the people around us, and the physical environment we inhabit is the essence of soul.

The face of the Canadian workplace is changing.

Photos: L. Stubel (left); © Corbis/Magma (right)

Chapter Summary

Our examination of communication in the workplace has led us to identify the importance of communication in creating satisfying work relationships and in creating effective organizations. Communication skills and the ability to work in teams ranks highest in the sought-after employability skills of the Canadian workforce. We then defined the nature of the relationships we create and sustain in the workplace. Four elements that affect these relationships are power, the fear of reprisals, task demands, and technologies. We focused our discussion on the climate and culture of organizations and how each is created. A positive climate is typified by supportiveness, participation, trust, openness, and goal clarity. Culture is created by the vocabulary we use, which has been influenced by a hierarchical and masculine language style. Modern workplaces require a de-sexing of that language. Culture is also created by the rites and rituals that take place in an organization. Finally, infusing the workplace with soul creates a positive, healthy work environment. The last of the topics under the nature of relationships in the workplace explored teamwork and groups. We discussed the nature of groups and the roles individuals play in groups. We then focused our discussion on the several challenges that are inherent in communicating in the workplace. Three specific challenges were identified; managing conflict, managing intimacy, and managing diversity and change. The discussion of conflict embraced differing conflict-resolution styles, dealing with difficult people, tactical communication and harassment. The chapter concluded with four guidelines for effective communication in the workplace. Participating effectively by using dual perspective, mindful listening, avoiding damaging relationship behaviours, monitoring self, and providing leadership was the first guideline. This was followed by the power of celebration and humour. Thirdly, we emphasized the responsibility of each to manage equally both tasks and people. We concluded the chapter with the need to bring soul to the workplace.

Key Concepts

- climate
- climate communication
- egocentric communication
- goal clarity
- group
- harassment
- organizational culture
- personal rituals
- power
- procedural communication
- rites
- rituals
- social rituals
- soul
- synergy
- task communication
- task rituals
- team

For Further Thought and Discussion

1. Visit your local police academy and interview officers on their specialized training in tactical communication. Identify the ways in which police officers defuse difficult situations with verbal communication skills.

2. Use your InfoTrac College Edition to look up current information on soul in the workplace.

3. Use your InfoTrac College Edition to look up current information on the changing shape of the North American workforce. What is the impact of immigration patterns and the aging baby boomers on the future of work in Canada?

4. Search your province's Human Rights Commission for the latest publications on harassment in the workplace. Look up a recent decision by your Human Rights Tribunal and determine the nature and implications of communication practice in the workplace.

5. Examine two groups to which you belong in terms of the roles you and others play in maintaining or sabotaging the task and people functions of the group. Choose one group that is largely cooperative in nature and the second that is largely competitive in nature. Compare the two.

6. Examine the rites and rituals of one of the places in which you have worked. How do these behaviours contribute or detract from a healthy communication climate in that workplace?

Epilogue

CONTINUING THE CONVERSATION

Although *Everyday Encounters* is drawing to a close, the conversation we've launched in these pages will continue. Interpersonal communication will be central to your life in the years ahead. There have been three predominant themes in the 11 chapters: communication creates and reflects identity; interpersonal communication is central to relationships; and interpersonal communication takes place in a diverse world.

COMMUNICATION CREATES AND REFLECTS IDENTITY

Communication is both an important source of personal identity and a primary means by which we express who we are. Our sense of personal identity grows directly out of interpersonal communication. We enter the world without any clear sense of self, and we look to others to tell us who we are. Parents, grandparents, siblings, and others who are significant in the first years of our life provide us with reflected appraisals that express how they see us and our value. Family members also shape our attachment styles and the scripts we follow in dealing with conflict, expressing emotions, and engaging in other forms of interpersonal communication. As we venture beyond the confines of family, we continue to learn from others and to see ourselves through the eyes of others. Peers, teachers, friends, and romantic partners communicate their views of us, and those become part of how we see ourselves and how we define our paths of personal growth. They also provide us with additional scripts and perspectives that we may rely on in our interpersonal communication.

Identity not only grows out of interpersonal communication but also is expressed in communication. How we communicate expresses who we are. Verbally and nonverbally, we announce that we are dominant or deferential, outgoing or introverted, caring or indifferent, emotionally expressive or reserved, egotistical or interested in others, assertive or passive, accepting or judgmental, and so forth.

INTERPERSONAL COMMUNICATION IS CENTRAL TO RELATIONSHIPS

Communication is the heart of personal relationships. The health and endurance of personal relationships depends in large measure on our ability to communicate effectively. For relationships to be satisfying, we need to know how to express our feelings, needs, and ideas in ways that others can understand. We also need to know how to listen sensitively and responsively to people in our lives so that they feel safe being open and honest with us. Interpersonal communication skills also allow us to create climates that are supportive and affirming so that our relationships are healthy. Communication is the basis of meaning in human relationships, and it is the primary way we build, refine, sustain, and transform close connections with others.

INTERPERSONAL COMMUNICATION TAKES PLACE IN A DIVERSE WORLD

A third theme of this book is that social diversity shapes and is reflected in communication. We've seen that our social standpoints affect how we communicate and how we interpret the communication of others. What is normal or desirable in one social group may be offensive or odd in other communities. Once we understand that standpoints shape communication, we are able to see that there are no absolutely right or wrong styles of communicating. Our ways of communicating, then, reflect not only our individual identities but also standpoints that are shaped by the social groups to which we belong.

Diverse cultures and the communication styles they cultivate offer rich opportunities to learn about others and ourselves. The more we interact with people whose backgrounds, beliefs, and communication styles differ from our own, the more we will grow as individuals and as members of a common world.

What you've studied about interpersonal communication should give you insight into how each of these themes applies in your current life. Let's now consider how they pertain to our personal and collective future.

THE ROAD AHEAD

Interpersonal communication will be as much a part of your everyday life in the future as it is today, although it may assume different forms and functions in the years ahead. The skills and perspectives we've discussed in this book will serve you well in meeting the challenges that will accompany changes in yourself, relationships, and society.

In the coming years, your interpersonal relationships will change both in anticipated and surprising ways. Some of the friends you have today will still be close in years to come, whereas others will fade away and new people will assume importance in your life. Some romances of the moment will flourish and endure, and others will wither. New people will come into your life, and familiar ones will leave. Each person who enters or exits your life will affect your personal identity.

There will also be changes and surprises in how people go about the process of forming and sustaining relationships. The trend toward long-distance romances and friendships will grow as more individuals who care about each other find they cannot live and work in the same location. Technology will also alter how we communicate with friends and romantic partners. Increasingly, we will rely on electronic forms of communication to sustain important personal relationships. Most of us rely on e-mail to communicate daily with parents, siblings, friends, partners, work associates, and leisure groups. In the future, friends, romantic partners, and family members will make increasing use of the Internet to stay in touch.

Finally, interpersonal communication and relationships will evolve in response to changes in the larger society. Medical advances will stretch the average life span further, so that a promise to stay together "'til death do us part" will involve a greater time commitment than it does today. Longer lives will also increase the number of older people in society and the opportunities for them to be part of our friendships and families. Relationship forms that are not recognized or approved of today may be accepted in the future. Interaction with an increasing diversity of people will change our perspective on what relationships are and how to sustain them. In addition, diversity will broaden the options we recognize for creating our own relationships.

We cannot foresee what lies ahead for us and for our world. However, we can predict with assurance that there will be changes in us, others, and cultural life. Whatever changes we experience, we can be sure that interpersonal communication will continue to be central to our happiness and effectiveness.

In *Everyday Encounters* and the course it accompanies, you have learned a good deal about interpersonal communication. The understandings you've gained and the skills you've acquired will be valuable to you in the years ahead. If you commit to practising and continuously enlarging the principles and skills introduced in this book, then you are on the threshold of a life-long journey that will enrich you and your relationships with others.

Glossary

A

abstract Removed from concrete reality. Symbols are abstract because they are inferences and generalizations abstracted from a total reality.

agape A secondary style of loving that is selfless and based on giving to others, not receiving rewards or returns from them. *Agape* is a blend of *eros* and *storge*.

aggression Form of overt conflict expressed in an act or attitude of hostility.

ambiguous Unclear meaning. Symbols are ambiguous because their meanings vary from person to person, context to context, and so forth.

ambushing Listening carefully for the purpose of attacking a speaker.

anxious/resistant attachment style This style tends to develop when a caregiver behaves inconsistently toward a child—sometimes being loving and other times being rejecting or neglectful.

arbitrary Random or unnecessary. Symbols are arbitrary because there is no necessary reason for any particular symbol to stand for a particular referent.

artifacts Personal objects we use to announce our identities and personalize our environments.

assertion Clearly and nonjudgmentally stating what we feel, need, or want. Assertion is not synonymous with aggression because aggression involves putting our needs ahead of, and sometimes at the cost of, others' needs.

attachment styles Patterns of parenting that teach children who they are, who others are, and how to approach relationships.

attending Non-verbal listening behaviours that let the speaker know we are being mindful. Captured by the acronym of FELOR.

attributions Causal accounts that explain why things happen and why people act as they do.

B

bracketing Noting an important issue that comes up in the course of discussing other matters and that needs to be discussed at a later time. Bracketing allows partners to stay effectively focused on a specific issue at one time but to agree to deal with other issues later.

C

chronemics A type of nonverbal communication concerned with how we perceive and use time to define identities and interaction.

climate The dominant feeling between people who are involved with each other.

climate communication Group communication that focuses on creating and maintaining a constructive climate that encourages people to contribute freely and to evaluate ideas critically.

cognitive complexity Determined by the number of constructs used, how abstract they are, and how elaborately they interact to create perceptions.

cognitive labelling view of emotions Theory that claims what we feel is shaped by how we label physiological responses.

commitment A decision to remain with a relationship. Commitment is one of three dimensions of enduring romantic relationships, and it has more impact on relationship continuity than does love alone. It is also an advanced stage in the process of escalation in romantic relationships.

committed romantic relationships Voluntary connections we presume will be primary and continuing parts of our lives. Committed romantic relationships include three dimensions: intimacy, passion, and commitment.

communication climate The overall character and quality of the communication investment of an organization.

communication rules Shared understandings of what communication means and what behaviours are appropriate in various situations.

conflict Exists when individuals who depend on each other express different views, interests, or goals and perceive their differences as incompatible or as opposed by the other.

constitutive rules Communication rules that define what communication means by specifying how certain communicative acts are to be counted.

constructivism Theory that states that we organize and interpret experience by applying cognitive structures called schemata.

content level of meaning Refers to the content or denotative information in communication. Content-level meanings are literal.

contracting Building a solution through negotiation and acceptance of parts of proposals for resolution. Contracting is usually present in the later stages of constructive conflict.

counterfeit emotional language Communication that seems to express feelings but doesn't actually describe what a person is feeling.

counterproposals A proposal made in response to another proposal instead of serious consideration of the first.

covert intimacy A term Swain (1989) coined to describe the indirect ways men support one another.

cross-complaining Occurs when one person's complaint is met by a counter-complaint; unproductive conflict response.

culture Beliefs, understandings, practices, and ways of interpreting experience that are shared by a number of people.

D

deep acting Management of inner feelings.

defensive listening Perceiving personal attacks, criticisms, or hostile undertones in communication when none are intended.

direct definition Communication that explicitly tells us who we are by specifically labelling us and reacting to our behaviours. Direct definition usually occurs first in families and also in interaction with peers and others.

dismissive attachment style Promoted by caregivers who are disinterested, rejecting, or abusive toward children. Unlike people who develop fearful attachment styles, those experiencing a dismissive style do not accept the caregiver's view of them as unlovable. Instead, they dismiss others as unworthy and thus do not seek close relationships.

downers People who communicate negatively about us and reflect negative appraisals of our self-worth.

dual perspective The ability to understand both your own and another's perspective, beliefs, thoughts, and feelings.

dyadic breakdown The first stage of relational decay. Dyadic breakdown involves degeneration of established patterns, understandings, and routines that make up a relational culture and that sustain intimacy on a day-to-day basis.

dyadic phase Stage of relational deterioration that involves discussing problems and negotiation.

E

ego boundaries Define where an individual stops and the rest of the world begins.

egocentric communication Dysfunctional group communication that blocks others and calls attention to the individual. Egocentric communication aggresses toward others, disrupts the task, devalues others, trivializes the group's work, and is self-serving.

emotional intelligence The ability to recognize which feelings are appropriate in which situations and the skill to communicate those feelings effectively.

emotions Processes that are shaped by physiology, perceptions, social experience, and language.

emotion work Effort invested to make ourselves feel what our culture defines as appropriate and to not feel what our culture defines as inappropriate in particular situations.

empathy Ability to feel with another person; to feel what she or he feels in a situation.

environmental spoiling Process by which proximity breeds ill will.

environmental racism A pattern whereby toxic waste dumps and hazardous plants are disproportionately located in lower-income neighbourhoods.

equity Fairness, based on the perception that both partners invest relatively equally in a relationship and benefit similarly from their investments. Perceived equity is a primary influence on satisfaction with relationships.

eros A powerful, passionate style of love that blazes to life suddenly and dramatically. *Eros* is one of the three primary styles of loving.

ethics Branch of philosophy that deals with moral principles and codes of conduct. Interpersonal communication involves ethical issues.

ethnocentrism The assumption that our culture and its norms are the only right ones. Ethnocentric communication reflects certainty, which tends to create defensive communication climates.

everyday interaction The way in which partners weave the basic fabric of their relationship in day-to-day conversations that realize their togetherness.

excessive metacommunication A behaviour in conflict situations where discussion gets sidetracked onto how communication occurs instead of an examination of the issues.

exit response One of four ways of responding to conflict. The exit response is to leave conflict either psychologically (by tuning out disagreement) or physically (by walking away or even leaving the relationship). The exit response is active and generally destructive.

external tensions Relationship stresses derived from competing demands, personal change, surviving distance, and ensuring equity.

explorational communication The third stage in relational escalation, which involves exchanges of information to check out the possibilities of a relationship.

F

fearful attachment style Cultivated when the caregiver in the first bond communicates in consistently negative, rejecting, or even abusive ways to a child.

feedback Responses to messages. Feedback may be verbal, nonverbal, or both; it may be intentional or unintentional.

feeling rules Culturally based guidelines that tell us what we have a right to feel or are expected to feel in specific situations.

framing rules Culturally based guidelines that define the emotional meaning of situations and events.

friendly relations Second stage of the growth phase of friendship development.

friends of the heart Friends who remain close, regardless of distance and changes in individuals' lives.

friends of the road Friends who are temporary and with whom intimacy is not sustained when one of the friends moves or changes occur.

fundamental attribution error Overestimating the internal causes of others' behaviour and underestimating the external causes.

G

games Interactions in which the real conflicts are hidden or denied and a counterfeit excuse is created for arguing or put-downs.

goal clarity The prospect of clear attainable goals.

grace Granting forgiveness or putting aside personal needs when it is not required or expected. Grace reflects generosity of spirit.

grave dressing The final phase in relational decline, it involves burying the relationship and putting it to rest.

group Three or more individuals who interact over time.

H

haptics The sense of touch and what it means. Haptics is one form of nonverbal communication.

harassment Any uninvited, unwelcome conduct that poisons the work environment.

hate speech Language that radically dehumanizes others.

hearing A physiological activity that occurs when sound waves hit our eardrums. Unlike listening, hearing is a passive process.

I

identity scripts Guides to action based on rules for living and identity. Initially communicated in families, scripts define our roles, how we are to play them, and basic elements in the plot of our lives.

I–It communication Impersonal communication in which individuals are treated as objects or instruments for our purposes.

I–language Language that takes personal responsibility for feelings by using words that own the feelings and do not project the responsibility for feelings onto others.

implicit personality theory Assumptions about which qualities fit together in human personalities. Implicit personality theories are often unconscious.

indexing Technique to remind us that evaluations are not static, not unchanging. Indexing links evaluations to specific times and/or circumstances.

intensifying communication Stage in the escalation of romantic relationships that increases the depth of a relationship by increasing personal knowledge and allowing a couple to begin creating a private culture. Also called euphoria.

interactive models Models that represent communication as a process in which listeners are involved in sending messages back to speakers through feedback.

interactive view of emotions Claims that social rules and understandings shape what people feel and how they do or don't express feelings.

internal tensions Relationship stresses that grow out of individuals and their interaction.

interpersonal climate The overall feeling, or emotional mood, of a relationship.

interpersonal communication A selective, systemic, ongoing process in which unique individuals interact to reflect and build personal knowledge and to create meanings.

interpersonal communication competence Communication that is interpersonally effective and appropriate. Competence includes abilities to monitor oneself, engage in dual perspective, enact a range of communication skills, and adapt communication appropriately.

interpretation The subjective process of evaluating and explaining perceptions.

intimacy Includes feelings of closeness, connection, and tenderness between lovers. Intimacy is one of three dimensions of committed romantic relationships.

intrapsychic phase The second phase in disintegration of romantic relationships, this involves brooding about problems in the relationship and dissatisfactions with a partner.

investment Something put into a relationship that cannot be recovered should the relationship end. Investment, more than rewards and love, increases commitment.

invitational communication The second stage in the escalation phase of romantic relationships. In this stage, individuals signal they are interested in interacting and respond to invitations from others.

irrational beliefs Debilitating ways of evaluating our emotions and ourselves. Irrational beliefs hinder our ability to manage and express emotions effectively.

I–Thou communication Fully interpersonal communication in which individuals acknowledge and deal with each other as unique individuals who meet fully in dialogue.

I–You communication Interaction that is midway between impersonal and interpersonal communication. In I–You relationships, communicators acknowledge each other as human beings but do not know and act toward each other as unique individuals in their totalities.

K

kinesics Body position and body motions, including those of the face.

kitchensinking Unproductive form of conflict communication in which everything except the kitchen sink is thrown into the argument.

L

letting go To free ourselves of anger, blame, and judgments about another and what she or he did. Letting go of these feelings is part of showing grace.

linear models Models that represent communication as a one-way process that flows in one direction—from sender to receiver. Linear models do not capture the dynamism of communication or the active participation of all communicators.

listening A complex process that consists of being mindful, hearing, selecting and organizing information, interpreting communication, responding, and remembering.

listening for information One of three goals of listening. Listening for information focuses on gaining and evaluating ideas, facts, opinions, reasons, and so forth.

listening for pleasure One of three goals of listening. Listening for pleasure is motivated by a desire to enjoy rather than to gain information or support others.

listening to support others One of three goals of listening. Listening to support others focuses more on the relationship level of meaning than on the content level of meaning. It aims to understand and respond to others' feelings, thoughts, and perceptions in ways that affirm them.

literal listening Listening only to the content level of meaning and ignoring the relationship level of meaning.

loaded language An extreme form of evaluative language that relies on words that strongly slant perceptions and, thus, meanings.

lose–lose An orientation toward conflict in which it is assumed that nobody can win and everyone loses from engaging in conflict.

loyalty response One of four ways of responding to conflict. The loyalty response consists of silent allegiance to a relationship and a person when conflict exists. Loyalty is passive and tends to be constructive.

ludus One of three primary styles of love. *Ludus* is playful love in which the goal is not commitment but to have fun at love as a game or a series of challenges and maneuvres.

M

maintenance-related behaviours Behaviours that focus a group's energy on the survival and smooth functioning of the group itself.

mania One of three secondary styles of loving made up of *eros* and *ludus*. *Mania* is passionate, sometimes obsessive love that includes emotional extremes.

metacommunication Communication about communication. When excessive, as in unproductive conflict interaction, metacommunication becomes self-absorbing and diverts partners from the issues causing conflict.

mindfulness A concept from Zen Buddhism that refers to being fully present in the moment. Being mindful is the first step of listening and the foundation for all others.

mindreading Assuming we understand what another person thinks or how another person perceives something.

minimal encouragers Communication that gently invites another person to elaborate by expressing interest in hearing more.

models Representations of what something is and how it works.

monitoring The capacity to observe and regulate your own communication.

monopolizing Continuously focusing communication on ourselves instead of on the person who is talking.

moving toward friendship The third stage of the growth phase of friendship development.

N

nascent friendship The stage of embryonic friendship.

navigating After relationships have escalated to commitment, partners navigate continuously, adjusting and reworking interaction to keep a relationship satisfying and healthy. Ideally, this stage lasts a lifetime.

neglect response One of four ways of responding to conflict. The neglect response is to deny or minimize problems. The neglect response is passive and tends to be destructive.

noise Anything that distorts communication so that it is more difficult for individuals to understand each other.

nonassertion A conflict resolution choice not to act, to ignore conflict, similar to loyalty.

nonverbal communication All forms of communication other than words themselves. Nonverbal communication includes inflection and other vocal qualities as well as several other behaviours.

O

organismic view of emotions Theory that external phenomena cause physiological changes that lead us to experience emotions. Also called James-Lange view of emotions.

organizational culture The overall pattern of beliefs, values, and practices that are uniquely characteristic of a specific organization.

P

paralanguage Communication that is vocal but not verbal.

paraphrasing A method of clarifying another's meaning by reflecting our interpretations of his or her communication back to him or her.

particular others One source of social perspectives that individuals use to define themselves and guide how they think, act, and feel. The perspectives of particular others are the viewpoints of specific individuals who are significant to the self.

passion Intensely positive feelings and desires for another person. Passion is based on rewards from involvement and is not equivalent to commitment. It is one of three dimensions of enduring romantic relationships.

passive aggression Attacking while denying doing so. Passive aggression is a means of covertly expressing conflict, anger, or both.

perception An active process of selecting, organizing, and interpreting people, objects, events, situations, and activities.

perceptual view of emotions Theory that claims subjective perceptions shape what external phenomena mean and what emotions we associate with external phenomena. Also called appraisal theory.

personal constructs Bipolar mental yardsticks that allow us to measure people and situations along specific dimensions of judgment.

personal rituals Activities that individuals routinely engage in to define themselves.

person-centredness Ability to perceive individuals as unique and to differentiate them from social roles and generalizations based on membership in social groups.

perspective of the generalized other The collection of rules, roles, and attitudes endorsed by the whole social community in which we live.

physical noise external and physiological influences that interfere with communication.

placemaking Process of creating a physical environment that is comfortable and that reflects the values, experiences, and tastes of individuals. Physical environment is part of relational culture, which is the nucleus of intimacy.

power Influence and control that one person has over another.

pragma A secondary style of loving that is pragmatic or practical in nature. *Pragma* is a blend of *storge* and *ludus*.

procedural communication Group communication that helps keep a group organized and on track. Procedural communication establishes the agenda, provides orientation, curbs digression, guides participation, coordinates ideas, records group process, and summarizes contributions.

process An ongoing, continuous, dynamic flow that has no clear-cut beginnings or endings and that is always evolving and changing. Interpersonal communication is a process.

prototypes Knowledge structures that define the clearest or most representative examples of some category.

proxemics A type of nonverbal communication that includes space and how we use it.

pseudolistening Pretending to listen.

psychological noise Beliefs, perceptions, feelings that interfere with communication and affect how we interpret others.

psychological responsibility Responsibility to remember, plan, and coordinate domestic work and child care. In general, women assume psychological responsibility for child care and housework, even if both partners share in the actual tasks.

punctuation Defining the beginning and ending of interaction or interaction episodes.

R

rational-emotive approach to feelings Approach that emphasizes using rational thinking to challenge and change debilitating emotions that undermine self-concept and self-esteem.

reflected appraisal Process of seeing and thinking about ourselves in terms of the appraisals of us that others reflect.

regulative rules Communication rules that regulate interaction by specifying when, how, where, and with whom to talk about certain things.

relational culture A private world of rules, understandings, and patterns of acting and interpreting that partners create to give meaning to their relationship. Relational culture is the nucleus of intimacy.

relational dialectics Opposing forces, or tensions, that are normal parts of all relationships. The three relational dialectics are autonomy/intimacy, novelty/routine, and openness/closedness.

relational level of meaning Refers to what communication expresses about the relationship between communicators. Three dimensions of relationship-level meanings are liking or disliking, responsiveness, and power (control).

remembering The process of recalling what you have heard. This is the sixth part of listening.

responding Symbolizing your interest in what is being said with observable feedback to speakers during the process of interaction. This is the fifth of six elements in listening.

revising communication A stage in the escalation of romantic relationships that many, but not all, couples experience. Revising involves evaluating a relationship and working out any obstacles or problems before committing for the long term.

rites Communication practices that express organizational values and identity through dramatic, planned activities that bring together aspects of cultural ideology into a single event.

rituals Communication practices that express organizational values and identity. They occur regularly, and members of an organization perceive them as familiar and routine parts of organizational life.

role-limited interaction During the first stage of friendship, we tend to rely on standard social rules and roles.

S

scripts One of four cognitive schemata. Scripts define expected or appropriate sequences of action in particular settings.

secure attachment style The most common and most positive attachment style. This style develops when the caregiver responds in a consistently attentive and loving way to a child.

selective listening Focusing on only selected parts of communication. We listen selectively when we screen out parts of a message that don't interest us or with which we disagree, and also when we rivet attention on parts of communication that do interest us or with which we agree.

self A multidimensional process that involves forming and acting from social perspectives that arise and evolve in communication with others and ourselves.

self-disclosure Revealing personal information about ourselves that others are unlikely to discover in other ways.

self-fulfilling prophecy Acting in ways that bring about expectations or judgments of ourselves.

self-sabotage Self-talk that communicates we are no good, we can't do something, we can't change, and so forth. Self-sabotaging communication undermines belief in ourselves and motivation to change and grow.

self-serving bias Tendency to attribute our positive actions and successes to stable, global, internal influences that we control, and to attribute negative actions and failures to unstable, specific, external influences beyond our control.

self-talk Ways that we communicate with ourselves that affect how we feel and act. Self-talk is intrapersonal communication.

semantic noise When words themselves are not mutually understood.

social comparison Involves comparing ourselves with others to form judgments of our own talents, abilities, qualities, and so forth.

social phase Part of relational disintegration in which partners figure out how to inform outsiders that the relationship is ending.

social rituals Standardized performances that affirm relationships among members of organizations.

social support Phase of relational decline in which partners look to friends and family for support during the trauma of breaking up.

soul A sense of connectedness and meaning in one's life.

speech community Group of people who share norms, regulative rules, and constitutive rules for communicating and interpreting the communication of others.

stabilized friendship The middle stage of friendship development in the navigating phase.

standpoint theory Claims that a culture includes a number of social groups that offer particular material, symbolic, and social conditions that distinctively shape the perceptions, identities, and opportunities of members of those groups.

static evaluation Assessments that suggest something is unchanging. "Bob is impatient" is a static evaluation.

stereotypes Predictive generalizations about people and situations.

storge A comfortable, friendly kind of love, often likened to friendship. It is one of three primary styles of loving.

summarizing A paraphrase that captures all the thoughts, feelings, and actions that the speaker has shared.

surface acting Controlling outward expression in inner feelings.

symbols Abstract, arbitrary, and ambiguous representations of other phenomena, including feelings, events, ideas, relationships, situations, and individuals.

synergy A special kind of energy that enlarges the efforts, talents, and strengths of individual group or team members.

systemic A quality of interpersonal communication that means it takes place within multiple systems that influence what is communicated and what meanings are constructed. Examples of systems affecting communication are physical context, culture, personal histories, and previous interactions between people.

T

task communication Group communication that focuses on the problem, issues, or information needed to accomplish group business. Task communication initiates ideas, seeks information, elaborates ideas, gives information, and offers critical analysis.

task-related behaviours Behaviours that focus a group's energy on accomplishing the defined project.

task rituals Behaviours that help members perform the tasks of their jobs.

team A special kind of group that is brought together for a special task and is characterized by distinct and complementary resources of members, and by a strong sense of collective identity.

totalizing Responding to a person as if one aspect of him or her is the total of who he or she is.

transactional models Models that represent communication as a dynamic process that changes over time and in which participants assume multiple roles.

trust Entails two factors: (1) belief in another's reliability (he or she will do what is promised); (2) emotional reliance on another to care about and protect our welfare. Trust is believing that private information about us is safe with another person because she or he cares for us and will look out for our welfare.

U

uppers People who communicate positively about us and who reflect positive appraisals of our self-worth.

V

voice response One of four responses to conflict. The voice response involves communicating about differences, tensions, and disagreements. Voice responses are active and can be constructive for individuals and relationships.

vultures An extreme form of downers. They not only communicate negative images of us but also attack our self-concepts.

W

waning friendship When one or both individuals stop investing in a friendship, it is likely to wane.

win–lose An orientation toward conflict that assumes one person wins at the expense of another person whenever conflict arises.

win–win An orientation toward conflict that assumes everyone can win, or benefit, from engaging in conflict and that it is possible to generate resolutions that satisfy everyone.

Y

you–language Language that projects responsibility for feelings or actions onto other people. You–language is not recommended for interpersonal communication.

References

Acitelli, L. (1988). When spouses talk to each other about their relationship. *Journal of Social and Personal Relationships*, 5, 185–199.

Acitelli, L. (1993). You, me, and us: Perspectives on relationship awareness. In S. W. Duck (Ed.), *Understanding relationship processes, 1: Individuals in relationships* (pp. 144–174). Newbury Park, CA: Sage.

Acker, M., & Davis, M. H. (1992). Intimacy, passion and commitment in adult romantic relationships: A test of the triangular theory of love. *Journal of Social and Personal Relationships*, 9, 21–51.

Ackerman, D. (1994). *A natural history of love*. New York: Random House.

Adelman, M. B., Parks, M. R., & Albrecht, T. L. (1987). Supporting friends in need. In T. L. Albrecht, M. B. Adelman, & Associates (Eds.), *Communicating social support* (pp. 105–125). Beverly Hills, CA: Sage.

Adler, R., & Towne, N. (1993). *Looking out/looking in* (7th ed.). Fort Worth, TX: Harcourt Brace Jovanovich.

Ainsworth, M. D. S., Blehar, M. C., Waters, E., & Wall, S. (1978). *Patterns of attachment: A psychological study of the strange situation*. Hillsdale, NJ: Erlbaum.

Alexander, E. R., III. (1979). The reduction of cognitive conflict: Effects of various types of communication. *Journal of Conflict Resolution*, 23, 120–138.

Allan, G. (1994). Social structure and relationships. In S. W. Duck (Ed.), *Understanding relationship processes, 3: Social context and relationships* (pp. 1–25). Newbury Park, CA: Sage.

Allen, S., Waton, A., Purcell, K., & Wood, S. (1986). *The experience of unemployment*. Basingstoke: Macmillan.

American games, Japanese rules. (1988). Frontline documentary. National Public Television. Cited in Ferrante, J. (1992). *Sociology: A global perspective* (p. 102). Belmont, CA: Wadsworth.

Anders, G. (1997, September 4). Doctors learn to bridge cultural gaps. *Wall Street Journal*, pp. B1, B4.

Andersen, M. L., & Collins, P. H. (Eds.). (1992). *Race, class, and gender: An anthology*. Belmont, CA: Wadsworth.

Anderson, S., Russell, C., & Schumm, W. (1983). Perceived marital quality and family life cycle categories: A further analysis. *Journal of Marriage and the Family*, 45, 127–139.

Annual report on Americans' health "a wealth of good news." (1997, September 12). *Raleigh News and Observer*, p. 8A.

Argyle, M., & Henderson, M. (1985). The rules of relationships. In S. W. Duck & D. Perlman (Eds.), *Understanding personal relationships: An interdisciplinary approach* (pp. 63–84). Beverly Hills, CA: Sage.

Aries, E. (1987). Gender and communication. In P. Shaver (Ed.), *Sex and gender* (pp. 149–176). Newbury Park, CA: Sage.

Arnett, R. C. (1986). The inevitable conflict and confronting in dialogue. In J. Stewart (Ed.), *Bridges, not walls* (4th ed., pp. 272–279). New York: Random House.

Artz, Sibylle. (1998). *Sex, power and the violent school girl*. Toronto: Trifolium Books.

Artz, Sibylle. (in press). Violence in the schoolyard: Girls' use of violence revisited. In Alder, C. and Worall, A. (Eds.) *Girls' Violence*. New York, NY: Suny Press.

Atsumi, R. (1980). Patterns of personal relationships. *Social Analysis*, 5, 63–78.

AXIS Center for Public Awareness of People with Disabilities, 4550 Indianola Avenue, Columbus OH 43214.

Bach, G. R., & Wyden, P. (1973). *The intimate enemy: How to fight fair in love and marriage*. New York: Avon.

Bachen, C., & Illouz, E. (1996). Imagining romance: Young people's cultural models of romance and love. *Critical Studies of Mass Communication*, 13, 279–308.

Barker, L., Edwards, R., Gaines, C., Gladney, K., & Holley, F. (1981). An investigation of proportional time spent in various communication activities by college students. *Journal of Applied Communication Research*, 8, 101–109.

Barnlund, D. (1989). *Communication styles of Japanese and Americans: Images and reality*. Belmont, CA: Wadsworth.

Bartholomew K., & Horowitz, L. M. (1991). Attachment styles among young adults: A test of a four-category model. *Journal of Personality and Social Psychology*, 61, 226–244.

Bartholomew, K. (1993). From childhood to adult relationships: Attachment theory and research. In S. W. Duck (Ed.), *Understanding relationship processes, 2: Learning about relationships* (pp. 30–62). Newbury Park, CA: Sage.

Bass, A. (1993, December 5). Behavior that can wreck a marriage. *Raleigh News and Observer*, p. 8E. Bates, E. (1994, fall). Beyond black and white. *Southern Exposure*, pp. 11–15.

Bateson, M. C. (1990). *Composing a life*. New York: Penguin/Plume.

Baxter, L. A. (1984). Trajectories of relationship disengagement. *Journal of Social and Personal Relationships*, 7, 141–178.

Baxter, L. A. (1985). Accomplishing relational disengagement. In S. Duck & D. Perlman (Eds.), *Understanding personal relationships: An interdisciplinary approach* (pp. 243–265). Beverly Hills, CA: Sage.

Baxter, L. A. (1987). Self-disclosure and relationship disengagement. In V. Derlega & J. H. Berg (Eds.), *Self-disclosure: Theory, research, and therapy* (pp. 155–174). New York: Plenum.

Baxter, L. A. (1988). A dialectical perspective on communication strategies in relationship development. In S. W. Duck, D. F. Hay, S. E. Hobfoll, W. Iches, & B. Montgomery (Eds.), *Handbook of personal relationships* (pp. 257–273). London: Wiley.

Baxter, L. A. (1990). Dialectical contradictions in relational development. *Journal of Social and Personal Relationships, 7*, 69–88.

Baxter, L. A. (1993). The social side of personal relationships: A dialectical perspective. In S. Duck (Ed.), *Understanding relationship processes, 3: Social context and relationships* (pp. 139–165). Newbury Park, CA: Sage.

Baxter, L. A., & Simon, E. P. (1993). Relationship maintenance strategies and dialectical contradictions in personal relationships. *Journal of Social and Personal Relationships, 10*, 225–242.

Be civil. (1994, July 5). *Wall Street Journal*, p. A1.

Beck, A. (1988). *Love is never enough.* New York: Harper & Row.

Becker, C. S. (1987). Friendship between women: A phenomenological study of best friends. *Journal of Phenomenological Psychology, 18*, 59–72.

Begley, S. (1997, Spring/Summer special issue). How to build a baby's brain. *Newsweek*, pp. 27–30.

Bellah, R., Madsen, R., Sullivan, W., Swindler, A., & Tipton, S. (1985). *Habits of the heart: Individualism and commitment in American life.* Berkeley, CA: University of California Press.

Bellamy, L. (1996, December 18). Kwanzaa cultivates cultural and culinary connections. *Raleigh News and Observer*, pp. 1F, 9F.

Belsky, J., & Pensky, E. (1988). Developmental history, personality, and family relationships: Toward an emergent family system. In R. A. Hinde & J. Stevenson-Hinde (Eds.), *Relationships within families: Mutual influences* (pp. 193–217). Oxford: Clarendon.

Belsky, J., & Rovine, M. (1990). Patterns of marital change across the transition to parenthood: Pregnancy to three years postpartum. *Journal of Marriage and the Family, 52*, 5–19.

Benjamin, D., & Horwitz, T. (1994, July 14). German view: "You Americans work too hard—and for what?" *Wall Street Journal*, pp. B1, B6.

Berg, J. H. (1987). Responsiveness and self-disclosure. In V. J. Derlega & J. H. Berg (Eds.), *Self-disclosure: Theory, research, and therapy.* New York: Plenum.

Berger, C. R., & Bell, R. A. (1988). Plans and the initiation of social relationships. *Human Communication Research, 15*, 217–235.

Bergner, R. M., & Bergner, L. L. (1990). Sexual misunderstanding: A descriptive and pragmatic formulation. *Psychotherapy, 27*, 464–467.

Berko, I. (1987, June 2). The coloring of bird. *The New York Times*, p. D27.

Berko, R., Wolvin, A., & Wolvin, D. (1995). *Communicating: A social and career focus.* Boston: Houghton Mifflin.

Berne, E. (1964). *Games people play.* New York: Grove.

Bernstein, B. (1974). *Class, codes, and control: Theoretical studies toward a sociology of language* (rev. ed.). New York: Shocken.

Bernstein, B. (Ed.). (1973). *Class, codes, and control* (vol. 2). London: Routledge and Kegan Paul.

Best, J. (1989). *Images of issues: Typifying contemporary social problems.* New York: Aldine de Gruyter.

Birdwhistell, R. (1970). *Kinesics and context.* Philadelphia: University of Pennsylvania Press.

Blieszner, R., & Adams, R. (1992). *Adult friendship.* Newbury Park, CA: Sage.

Blumstein, P., & Schwartz, P. (1983). *American couples: Money, work, and sex.* New York: William Morrow.

Bolton, R. (1986). Listening is more than merely hearing. In J. Stewart (Ed.), *Bridges, not walls* (4th ed., pp. 159–179). New York: Random House.

Boon, S. (1994). Dispelling doubt and uncertainty: Trust in romantic relationships. In S. W. Duck (Ed.), *Understanding relationship processes, 4: Dynamics of relationships* (pp. 86–111). Thousand Oaks, CA: Sage.

Borovilos, John, ed., (1990). *Breaking through: A Canadian literary mosaic.* Scarborough, ON: Prentice Hall, 181–182.

Bosmajian, H. (1974). *The language of oppression.* Washington, DC: Public Affairs Papers.

Bowen, S. P., & Michal-Johnson, P. (1995). Sexuality in the AIDS era. In S. W. Duck & J. T. Wood (Eds.), *Understanding relationship processes, 5: Relationship challenges* (pp. 150–180). Thousand Oaks, CA: Sage.

Bowlby, J. (1973). *Separation: Attachment and loss* (Vol. 2). New York: Basic.

Bowlby, J. (1988). *A secure base: Parent–child attachment and healthy human development.* New York: Basic.

Boyd, R. (1996, October 9). Notion of separate races rejected. *Raleigh News and Observer*, pp. 1A, 15A.

Bozzi, V. (1986, February). Eat to the beat. *Psychology Today*, p. 16.

Bradbury, T. N., & Fincham, F. D. (1990). Attributions in marriage: Review and critique. *Psychological Bulletin, 107*, 3–33.

Braithwaite, D. (1996). "Persons first": Exploring different perspectives on the communication of persons with disabilities. In E. B. Ray (Ed.), *Communication and disenfranchisement: Social health issues and implications* (pp. 449–464). Hillsdale, NJ: Erlbaum.

Brazelton, T. B. (1997, Spring/Summer special issue). Building a better self-image. *Newsweek*, pp. 76–77.

Brehm, S. (1992). *Intimate relations* (2nd ed.). New York: McGraw-Hill.

Briskin, Alan. (1998). *The stirring of the soul in the workplace.* New York: Berrett-Koehler Pub.

Brock-Utne, B. (1989). *Feminist perspectives on peace and peace education.* New York: Pergamon.

Brown, R. (1988). *Group processes: Dynamics within and between groups.* Cambridge, MA: Basil Blackwell, Inc.

Bruess, C., & Pearson, J. (1997). Interpersonal rituals in marriage and adult friendship. *Communication Monographs, 64,* 25–46.

Buber, M. (1957). Distance and relation. *Psychiatry, 20,* 97–104.

Buber, M. (1970). *I and thou* (Walter Kaufmann, Trans.). New York: Scribner.

Buckley, M. (1992). Focus on research: We listen a book a day; we speak a book a week: Learning from Walter Loban. *Language Arts, 69,* 622–626.

Bumpass, L. L., & Sweet, J. A. (1989). National estimates of cohabitation. *Demography, 26,* 615–625.

Burgoon, J. K., Buller, D. B., & Woodhall, G. W. (1989). *Nonverbal communication: The unspoken dialogue.* New York: Harper & Row.

Burgoon, J. K., Buller, D. B., Hale, J. L., & deTurck, M. A. (1984). Relational messages associated with nonverbal behaviors. *Human Communication Research, 10,* 351–378.

Burleson, B. R. (1984). Comforting communication. In H. E. Sypher & J. L. Applegate (Eds.), *Communication by children and adults: Social cognitive and strategic processes* (pp. 63–104). Beverly Hills, CA: Sage.

Burleson, B. R. (1987). Cognitive complexity. In J. C. McCroskey & J. A. Daly (Eds.), *Personality and interpersonal communication* (pp. 305–349). Newbury Park, CA: Sage.

Burleson, B. R., & Samter, W. (1994). A social skills approach to relationship maintenance: How individual differences in communication skills affect the achievement of relationship functions. In D. J. Canary & L. Stafford (Eds.), *Communication and relational maintenance.* Orlando: Academic.

Business bulletin. (1996, July 18). *Wall Street Journal,* p. A1.

Butterfield, F. (1982). *China: Alive in the bitter sea.* New York: Times Books.

Button, C. M., & Collier, D. R. (1991, June). A comparison of people's concepts of love and romantic love. Paper presented at the Canadian Psychological Association Conference, Calgary, Alberta.

Caldera, Y. M., Huston, A. C., & O'Brien, M. (1989). Social interactions and play patterns of parents and toddlers with feminine, masculine, and neutral toys. *Child Development, 60,* 70–76.

Campbell, S. M. (1986). From either-or to both-and relationships. In J. Stewart (Ed.), *Bridges, not walls* (4th ed., pp. 262–270). New York: Random House.

Canary, D., & Dindia, K. (eds.). (1998). *Sex differences and similarities in communication.* Mahwah, NJ: Erlbaum.

Canary, D., & Stafford, L. (Eds.). (1994). *Communication and relational maintenance.* New York: Academic.

Cancian, F. (1987). *Love in America.* Cambridge, MA: Cambridge University Press.

Cancian, F. (1989). Love and the rise of capitalism. In B. Risman & P. Schwartz (Eds.), *Gender in intimate relationships* (pp. 12–25). Belmont, CA: Wadsworth.

Canfield, Jack, ed. (1996). Chicken soup for the soul at work: 101 stories of courage, compassion and creativity in the workplace. *Health Communications,* Nov.

Capella, J. N. (1991). The biological origins of automated patterns of human interaction. *Communication Theory, 1,* 4–35.

Carl, W. (1998). A sign of the times. In J. T. Wood, *But I thought you meant ...: Misunderstandings in human communication* (pp. 195–208). Mountain View, CA: Mayfield.

Carnes, J. (1994, spring). An uncommon language. *Teaching Tolerance,* pp. 56–63.

Caspi, A., & Harbener, E. S. (1990). Continuity and change: Assortive marriage and the consistency of personality in adulthood. *Journal of Personality and Social Psychology, 58,* 250–258.

Cassirer, E. (1944). An essay on man. New Haven, CT: Yale University Press.

Cate, R. M., Huston, T. L., and Nesselroade, J. R. (1986). Premarital relationships: Toward the identification of alternative pathways to marriage. *Journal of Social and Clinical Psychology, 4,* 3–22.

Cathcart, D., & Cathcart, R. (1997). The group: A Japanese context. In L. Samovar & R. Porter (Eds.), *Intercultural communication: A reader* (8th ed., pp. 329–339). Belmont, CA: Wadsworth.

Chapman, Gary. (1995). *The five love languages: How to express heartfelt commitment to your mate.* Chicago: Northfield Pub.

Cherlin, A. (1992). *Marriage, divorce, remarriage.* Cambridge, MA: Harvard University Press.

Chodorow, N. (1989). *Feminism and psychoanalytic theory.* New Haven, CT: Yale University Press.

Christensen, A., & Heavey, C. (1990). Gender and social structure in the demand/withdraw pattern in marital conflict. *Journal of Personality and Social Psychology, 59,* 73–81.

Cissna, K. N. L., & Sieburg, E. (1986). Patterns of interactional confirmation and disconfirmation. In J. Stewart (Ed.), *Bridges, not walls* (4th ed., pp. 230–239). New York: Random House.

Civickly, J. M., Pace, R. W., & Krause, R. M. (1977). Interviewer and client behaviors in supportive and defensive interviews. In B. D. Ruben (Ed.), *Communication yearbook, 1* (pp. 347–362). New Brunswick, NJ: Transaction.

Clements, M. (1994, August 7). Sex in America today. *Parade,* pp. 4–6.

Clements, M., & Markman, H. (1996). The transition to parenthood: Is having children hazardous to marriage? In N. Vanzetti & S. Duck (Eds.), *A lifetime of relationships* (pp. 290–310). Pacific Grove, CA: Brooks/Cole.

Cloven, D. H., & Roloff, M. E. (1991). Sense-making activities and interpersonal conflict: Communicative cures for the mulling blues. *Western Journal of Speech Communication, 55,* 134–158.

Coates, J., & Cameron, D. (1989). *Women in their speech communities: New perspectives on language and sex.* London: Longman.

Code of Conduct, www.basketball.ns.ca/Codeofconduct.html (retrieved April 10, 2001).

Collier, M. J. (1996). Communication competence problematics in ethnic friendships. *Communication Monographs, 63,* 314–336.

Condry, S. M., Condry, J. C., & Pogatshnik, L. W. (1983). Sex differences: A study of the ear of the beholder. *Sex Roles, 9,* 697–704.

Conover, T. (1987). *Coyotes: A journey through the secret world of America's illegal aliens.* New York: Vintage.

Cooley, C. H. (1912). *Human nature and the social order.* New York: Scribner.

Cooley, C. H. (1961). The social self. In T. Parsons, E. Shils, K. D. Naegele, & J. R. Pitts (Eds.), *Theories of society* (pp. 822–828). New York: Free Press.

Copeland, L., & Griggs, L. (1985). *Going international.* New York: Random House.

Cosby, P. (1973). Self-disclosure: A literature review. *Psychological Bulletin, 79,* 73–91.

Covey, Stephen R. (1991). *Principle-centered leadership.* New York: Fireside.

Cowan, C., Cowan, P., Heming, G., & Miller, N. (1991). Becoming a family: Marriage, parenting, and child development. In P. A. Cowan & M. Hetherington (Eds.), *Family transitions* (pp. 79–109). Hillsdale, NJ: Erlbaum.

Cox, R. (1995). President of the National Sierra Club, 1994–1996. Personal communication.

Cozart, E. (1996, November 1997). Feng Shui. *Raleigh News and Observer,* p. D1.

Crockett, W. (1965). Cognitive complexity and impression formation. In B. A. Maher (Ed.), *Progress in experimental personality research, 2.* New York: Academic.

Cronen, V., Pearce, W. B., & Snavely, L. (1979). A theory of rule-structure and types of episodes and a study of perceived enmeshment in undesired repetitive patterns ("URPs"). In D. Nimmo (Ed.), *Communication yearbook, 3.* New Brunswick, NJ: Transaction.

Crossen, C. (1997, July 10). Blah, blah, blah. *Wall Street Journal,* p. 1A, 6A.

CRTC Canadian Content, www.media-awareness.ca/eng/issues/cultural/issues/cancon.htm (retrieved April 10, 2001).

Cuber, J. F., & Harroff, P. B. (1965). *Sex and the significant Americans.* Baltimore: Penguin.

Cunningham, J. A., Strassberg, D. S., & Haan, B. (1986). Effects of intimacy and sex-role congruency on self-disclosure. *Journal of Social and Clinical Psychology, 4,* 393–401.

Cunningham, J. D., & Antill, J. K. (1995). Current trends in nonmarital cohabitation: The great POSSLQ hunt continues. In J. T. Wood & S. W. Duck (Eds.), *Understanding relationship processes, 6: Off the beaten track: Understudied relationships* (pp. 148–172). Thousand Oaks, CA: Sage.

Cupach, W. R., & Comstock, J. (1990). Satisfaction with sexual communication in marriage: Links to sexual satisfaction and dyadic adjustment. *Journal of Social and Personal Relationships, 7,* 179–182.

Cutrona, C. E. (1982). Transitions to college: Loneliness and the process of social adjustment. In L. A. Peplau & D. Perlman (Eds.), *Loneliness: A sourcebook of current theory, research, and therapy* (pp. 291–309). New York: Wiley Interscience.

Cyberscope, (1996, December 23). *Newsweek,* p. 10.

Davis K. (1947). A final note on a case of extreme isolation. *American Journal of Sociology, 52,* 432–437.

Davis, K. (1940). Extreme isolation of a child. *American Journal of Sociology, 45,* 554–565.

Davis, V. T., & Singh, R. (1989). Attitudes of university students from India toward marriage and family life. *International Journal of Sociology of the Family, 19,* 43–57.

de Becker, G. (1997). *The gift of fear: Survival signals that protect us from violence.* New York: Little Brown.

de Frane, Gordon. (2000). Spirituality and generosity: An understanding of the sacred men and women in aboriginal societies of the Americas. Unpublished manuscript.

de Wolf, G., Gregg, R., Harris, B., and Scargill, M. Eds. (2000). *Gage Canadian dictionary.* Vancouver: Gage Educational Publishing Co.

DeFrancisco, V. (1991). The sounds of silence: How men silence women in marital relations. *Discourse and Society, 2,* 413–423.

Delia, J., Clark, R. A., & Switzer, D. (1974). Cognitive complexity and impression formation in informal social interaction. *Speech Monographs, 41,* 299–308.

Derlega, V. J., & Berg, J. H. (1987). *Self-disclosure: Research, theory, and therapy.* New York: Plenum.

Dewar, H. (1997, May 11). Threads of a new nation. *Raleigh News and Observer,* pp. 23A–24A.

Dewey, J. (1910). *How we think.* Boston: D.C. Heath

Dews, B., & Law, C. (Eds.). (1995). *This fine place so far from home: Voices of academics from the working class.* Philadelphia: Temple University Press.

Dickens, W. J., & Perlman, D. (1981). Friendship over the life-cycle. In S. Duck & R. Gilmour (Eds.), *Personal relationships, 2: Developing personal relationships.* London: Academic.

Dickson, F. (1995). The best is yet to be: Research on long-lasting marriages. In J. T. Wood & S. Duck (Eds.), *Understanding relationship processes, 6: Understudied relationships* (pp. 22–50). Thousand Oaks, CA: Sage.

Dillard, J.P., & Witteman, G. (1985). Romantic relationships at work: Organizational and personal influences. *Human Communication Research, 12,* 99–116.

Dimmitt, B. (1997, July). Chelsey's missing smile, *Reader's Digest,* 87–93.

Dindia, K. (1994). A multiphasic view of relationship maintenance strategies. In D. Canary & L. Stafford (Eds.), *Communication and relational maintenance* (pp. 91–112). New York: Academic.

Dindia, K., & Fitzpatrick, M. A. (1985). Marital communication: Three approaches compared. In S. Duck & D. Perlman (Eds.), *Understanding personal relationships: An interdisciplinary approach* (pp. 137–157). Newbury Park, CA: Sage.

Divorces, www.statcan.ca/english/Pgdb/People/Families/famil02.htm (retrieved August 12, 2001).

Dixson M., & Duck, S. W. (1993). Understanding relationship processes: Uncovering the human search for meaning. In S. W. Duck (Ed.), *Understanding relationship processes, 1: Individuals in relationships* (pp. 175–206). Newbury Park, CA: Sage.

Dolan, R. E., & Worden, R. L. (Eds.). (1992). *Japan: A country study.* Washington, DC: Library of Congress.

Duck, S. W. (1985). Social and personal relationships. In M. L. Knapp & G. R. Miller (Eds.), *Handbook of interpersonal communication* (pp. 655–686). Beverly Hills, CA: Sage.

Duck, S. W. (1990). Relationships as unfinished business: Out of the frying pan and into the 1990s. *Journal of Social and Personal Relationships, 7,* 5–24.

Duck, S. W. (1992). *Human relationships* (2nd ed.). Newbury Park, CA: Sage.

Duck, S. W. (1994a). *Meaningful relationships.* Thousand Oaks, CA: Sage.

Duck, S. W. (1994b). Steady as (s)he goes: Relational maintenance as a shared meaning system. In D. Canary & L. Stafford (Eds.), *Communication and relational maintenance* (pp. 45–60). New York: Academic.

Duck, S. W., & Wright, P. H. (1993). Reexamining gender differences in same-gender friendships: A close look at two kinds of data. *Sex Roles, 28,* 709–727.

Duck, S. W., Pond, K., & Leatham, G. (1994). Loneliness and the evaluation of relational events. *Journal of Social and Personal Relationships, 11,* 253–276.

Duck, S. W., Rutt, D. J., Hurst, M. H., & Strejc, H. (1991). Some evident truths about conversation in everyday relationships: All communications are not created equal. *Human Communication Research, 18,* 228–267.

Eadie, W. F. (1982). Defensive communication revisited: A critical examination of Gibb's theory. *Southern Speech Communication Journal, 47,* 163–177.

Eaves, M., & Leathers, D. (1991). Context as communication: McDonalds vs. Burger King. *Journal of Applied Communication, 19,* 263–289.

Eckman, P., Friesen, W., & Ellsworth, P. (1971). *Emotion in the human face: Guidelines for research and an integration of findings.* Elmsford, NY: Pergamon.

Egan, G. (1973). Listening as empathic support. In J. Stewart (Ed.), *Bridges, not walls.* Reading, MA: Addison-Wesley.

Eichenbaum, L., & Orbach, S. (1987). *Between women: Love, envy, and competition in women's friendships.* New York: Viking.

Ekman, P. & Davidson, R. (Eds.) (1994). *The nature of emotions: Fundamental questions.* New York: Oxford University Press.

Ellis A., & Harper, R. (1975). *A new guide to rational living.* Englewood Cliffs, NJ: Prentice-Hall.

Ellis, A. (1962). *Reason and emotion in psychotherapy.* New York: Lyle Stuart.

Ellis, D. (1989). *Male abuse of a marriage or cohabiting female partner.* Violence and Victims, 4, 235–255.

Ernst, F., Jr. (1973). *Who's listening? A handbook of the transactional analysis of the listening function.* Vallejo, CA: Addresso'set.

Essig, David. (1998). High Ground. On *Redbird Country and High Ground* [CD] Appaloosa.

Estes, W. K. (1989). Learning theory. In A. Lessold & R. Glaser (Eds.), *Foundations for a psychology of education.* Hillsdale, NJ: Erlbaum.

Faludi, S. (1991). *Backlash: The undeclared war against American women.* New York: Crown.

Fantini, A. E. (1991). Bilingualism: Exploring language and culture. In L. Malave & G. Duquette (Eds.), *Language, culture, and cognition: A collection of studies on first and second language acquisition* (pp. 110–119). Bristol, PA: Multilingual Matters, Ltd.

Fehr, B. (1993). How do I love thee: Let me consult my prototype. In S. W. Duck (Ed.), *Understanding relationship processes, 1: Individuals in relationships* (pp. 87–122). Newbury Park, CA: Sage.

Fehr, B., & Russell, J. A. (1991). Concept of love viewed from a prototype perspective. *Journal of Personality and Social Psychology, 60,* 425–438.

Ferrante, J. (1992). *Sociology: A global perspective.* Belmont, CA: Wadsworth.

Ferrante, J. (1995). *Sociology: A global perspective* (2nd ed.). Belmont, CA: Wadsworth.

Fincham, F. D., & Bradbury, T. N. (1987). The impact of attributions in marriage: A longitudinal analysis. *Journal of Personality and Social Psychology, 53,* 510–517.

Fincham, F. D., Bradbury, T. N., & Scott, C. K. (1990). Cognition in marriage. In F. D. Fincham & T. N. Bradbury (Eds.), *The psychology of marriage: Basic issues and applications* (pp. 118–119). New York: Guilford.

Finkelstein, J. (1980). Considerations for a sociology of emotions. *Studies in Symbolic Interaction, 3,* 111–121.

Fisher, B. A. (1987). *Interpersonal communication: The pragmatics of human relationships.* New York: Random House.

Fisher, J. D., & Byrne, D. (1975). Too close for comfort: Sex differences in response to invasions of personal space. *Journal of Personal and Social Psychology, 32,* 15–21.

Fitzpatrick, M. A. (1988). *Between husbands and wives: Communication in marriage.* Newbury Park, CA: Sage.

Fitzpatrick, M. A., & Best, P. (1979). Dyadic adjustment in relational types: Consensus, cohesion, affectional expression and satisfaction in enduring relationships. *Communication Monographs, 46,* 167–178.

Fletcher, G. J., & Fincham, F. D. (1991). Attribution in close relationships. In G. J. Fletcher & F. D. Fincham (Eds.), *Cognition in close relationships* (pp. 7–35). Hillsdale, NJ: Erlbaum.

Fletcher, G. J., Fincham, F. D., Cramer, L., & Heron, N. (1987). The role of attributions in the development of dating relationships. *Journal of Personality and Social Psychology, 51*, 875–884.

Floyd, K., & Parks, M. (1995). Manifesting closeness in the interactions of peers: A look at siblings and friends. *Communication Reports, 8*, 69–76.

Fowers, B. J. (1991). His and her marriage: A multivariate study of gender and marital satisfaction. *Sex Roles, 24*, 209–221.

Fox-Genovese, E. (1991). *Feminism without illusions.* Chapel Hill: University of North Carolina Press.

French Language Bill, www.ccu-cuc.ca/en/library/bill_101.htm (retrieved July 3, 2001)

French, J.R.P. and Raven, B. (1959). The bases of social power, in D. Cartwright (Ed.), *Studies in social power,* Ann Arbor: University of Michigan.

French, M. (1992). *The war against women.* New York: Summit.

Fridlund, A. J. (1994). *Human facial expression.* San Diego: Academic.

Frijda, N. H. (1986). *The emotions.* Cambridge, England: Cambridge University Press.

Gaines, S., Jr. (1995). Relationships among members of cultural minorities. In J. T. Wood & S. W. Duck (Eds.), *Understanding relationship processes, 6: Off the beaten track: Understudied relationships* (pp. 51–88). Thousand Oaks, CA: Sage.

Gans, H. (1995). *The war against the poor: The underclass and antipoverty policy.* New York: Basic.

Garner, T. (1994). Oral rhetorical practice in African American culture. In A. González, M. Houston, & V. Chen (Eds.), *Our voices: Essays in culture, ethnicity, and communication* (pp. 81–91). Los Angeles: Roxbury.

Gelles, R. (1987). *Family violence* (2nd ed.). Newbury Park, CA: Sage.

Geonames, geonames.NRCan.gc.ca/english/north_comm.html (retrieved July 3, 2001).

George L. (1995, December 26). Holiday's traditions are being formed. *Raleigh News and Observer,* pp. C1, C3.

Gerstel, N., & Gross, H. (1985). *Commuter marriage.* New York: Guilford.

Gibb, J. (1961). Defensive communication. *Journal of Communication, 11*, 141–148.

Gibb, J. R. (1964). Climate for trust formation. In L. Bradford, J. Gibb, & K. Benne (Eds.), *T-group theory and laboratory method* (pp. 279–309). New York: Wiley.

Gibb, J. R. (1970). Sensitivity training as a medium for personal growth and improved interpersonal relationships. *Interpersonal Development, 1*, 6–31.

Gibbs, J. T. (1992). Young black males in America: Endangered, embittered, and embattled. In M. L. Andersen & P. H. Collins (Eds.), *Race, class, and gender: An anthology* (pp. 267–276). Belmont, CA: Wadsworth.

Goldhaber, G.M. (1993). *Organizational communication* (6th ed). Dubuque, IA: Wm. C. Brown & Benchmark.

Goldner, V., Penn, P., Sheinberg, M., & Walker, G. (1990). Love and violence: Gender paradoxes in volatile attachments. *Family Process, 19*, 343–364.

Goleman, D. (1995a). *Emotional intelligence.* New York: Bantam.

Goleman, D. (1995b, November–December). What's your emotional intelligence? *Utne Reader,* pp. 74–76.

Good-looking lawyers make more money, says a study by economists. (1996, January 4). *Wall Street Journal,* p. A1.

Gottman, J. (1979). *Marital interaction: Experimental investigations.* New York: Academic.

Gottman, J. (1993). The roles of conflict engagement, escalation or avoidance in marital interaction: A longitudinal view of five types of couples. *Journal of Consulting and Clinical Psychology, 61*, 6–15.

Gottman, J. (1997, May). Findings from 25 years of studying marriage. Paper presented at the Conference of the Coalition of Marriage, Family and Couples Education, Arlington, VA.

Gottman, J., & Carrère, S. (1994). Why can't men and women get along? Developmental roots and marital inequities. In D. J. Canary & L. Stafford (Eds.), *Communication and relational maintenance* (pp. 203–229). New York: Academic.

Gottman, J., Markman, H. J., & Notarius, C. (1977). The topography of marital conflict: A sequential analysis of verbal and nonverbal behavior. *Journal of Marriage and the Family, 39*, 461–477.

Gottman, J., Notarius, C., Gonso, J., & Markman, H. J. (1976a). *A couple's guide to communication.* Champaign, IL: Research Press.

Gottman, J., Notarius, C., Markman, H., Banks, S., Yoppi, B., & Rubin, M. E. (1976b). Behavior exchange theory and marital decision making. *Journal of Experimental Social Psychology, 34*, 14–23.

Gottman, J., Katz, L., and Hooven, C. (1996). *Meta-emotions: How families communicate emotionally.* Hillsdale, NJ: Lawrence Erlbaum Assoc.

Gouliquer, Dianne. (December 2000). When the boss is the problem. Northern Ontario Business Editorial Archives. www.nob.on.ca/archives/dec00story/bossprob.html (retrieved August 2, 2001).

Greenberg, S. (1997, Spring/Summer special issue). The loving ties that bind. *Newsweek,* pp. 68–72.

Griffin, D., and Bartholomew, K. (1994). The metaphysics of measurement: The case of adult attachment. *Advances in Personal Relationships, 5*, 17–52.

Gross, H. E. (1980). Couples who live apart: Time/place disjunctions and their consequence. *Symbolic Interaction, 3,* 69–82.

Hakuta, K. (1986). *Mirror of language: The debate on bilingualism.* New York: Basic.

Hall, E. (1976). *Beyond culture.* New York: Doubleday.

Hall, E. T. (1966). *The hidden dimension.* New York: Anchor.

Hall, E. T. (1968). Proxemics. *Current Anthropology, 9,* 83–108.

Hall, J. A. (1978). Gender effects in decoding nonverbal cues. *Psychological Bulletin, 85,* 845–857.

Hall, J. A. (1987). On explaining gender differences: The case of nonverbal communication. In P. Shaver & C. Hendricks (Eds.), *Sex and gender* (pp. 177–200). Newbury Park, CA: Sage.

Hamachek, D. (1992). *Encounters with the self* (3rd ed.). Fort Worth: Harcourt Brace Jovanovich.

Hansen, J. E., & Schuldt, W. J. (1984). Marital self-disclosure and marital satisfaction. *Journal of Marriage and the Family, 46,* 923–926.

Haraway, D. (1988). Situated knowledges: The science question in feminism and the privilege of partial perspective. *Signs, 14,* 575–599.

Harding, S. (1991). Whose *science? Whose knowledge? Thinking from women's lives.* Ithaca, NY: Cornell University Press.

Harris, M., Walters, L., & Waschall, S. (1991). Gender and ethnic differences in obesity-related behaviors and attitudes in a college sample. *Journal of Applied Social Psychology, 21,* 1545–1566.

Harris, T. J. (1969). *I'm OK, you're OK.* New York: Harper & Row.

Hayakawa, S. I. (1962). *The use and misuse of language.* New York: Fawcett.

Hayakawa, S. I. (1964). *Language in thought and action* (2nd ed.). New York: Harcourt, Brace & World.

Hecht, M. L., Marston, P. J., & Larkey, L. K. (1994). Love ways and relationship quality in heterosexual relationships. *Journal of Social and Personal Relationships, 11,* 25–44.

Hegel, G. W. F. (1807). *Phenomenology of mind* (J. B. Baillie, Trans.). Germany: Wurzburg & Bamburg.

Heider, F. (1958). *The psychology of interpersonal relations.* New York: Wiley.

Helgeson, V. (1994). Long-distance romantic relationships: Sex differences in adjustment and breakup. *Personal and Social Psychology Bulletin, 20,* 254–266.

Hendrick, C., & Hendrick, S. (1988). Lovers wear rose-colored glasses. *Journal of Social and Personal Relationships, 5,* 161–184.

Hendrick, C., & Hendrick, S. (1989). Research on love: Does it measure up? *Journal of Personality and Social Psychology, 56,* 784–794.

Hendrick, C., & Hendrick, S. (1996). Gender and the experience of heterosexual love. In J. T. Wood (Ed.), *Gendered relationships.* Mountain View, CA: Mayfield.

Hendrick, C., Hendrick, S., Foote, F. H., & Slapion-Foote, M. J. (1984). Do men and women love differently? *Journal of Social and Personal Relationships, 2,* 177–196.

Henley, N. M. (1977). *Body politics: Power, sex and nonverbal communication.* Englewood Cliffs, NJ: Prentice-Hall.

Henry, Tasha E. (2001) *The Wisdom of Porcelain.* Unpublished manuscript.

Higginbotham, E. (1992). We were never on a pedestal: Women of color continue to struggle with poverty, racism, and sexism. In M. L. Andersen & P. H. Collins (Eds.), *Race, class, and gender: An anthology* (pp. 183–190). Belmont, CA: Wadsworth.

Hochschild, A. (1979). Emotion work, feeling rules, and social structure. *American Journal of Sociology, 85,* 551–575.

Hochschild, A. (1983). *The managed heart.* Berkeley: University of California Press.

Hochschild, A. (1990). Ideology and emotion management: A perspective and path for future research. In T. Kemper (Ed.), *Research agendas in the sociology of emotions* (pp. 117–142). New York: State University of New York Press.

Hochschild, A., with Machung, A. (1989). *The second shift.* New York: Viking.

Hojat, M. (1982). Loneliness as a function of selected personality variables. *Journal of Clinical Psychology, 38,* 136–141.

Honeycutt, J. M. (1993). Memory structures for the rise and fall of personal relationships. In S. W. Duck (Ed.), *Understanding relationship processes, 1: Individuals in relationships* (pp. 30–59). Newbury Park, CA: Sage.

Honeycutt, J. M., Woods, B., & Fontenot, K. (1993). The endorsement of communication conflict rules as a function of engagement, marriage and marital ideology. *Journal of Social and Personal Relationships, 10,* 285–304.

Horn, Sam. (1996). *Tongue Fu!* New York, NY: St. Martin's Griffin.

Houston, M. (1994). When black women talk with white women: Why dialogues are difficult. In A. González, M. Houston, & V. Chen (Eds.), *Our voices: Essays in culture, ethnicity, and communication* (pp. 133–139). Los Angeles: Roxbury.

Houston, M., & Wood, J. T. (1996). Difficult dialogues, expanded horizons: Communicating across race and class. In J. T. Wood (Ed.), *Gendered relationships* (pp. 39–56). Mountain View, CA: Mayfield.

Howard, J. W., & Dawes, R. M. (1976). Linear prediction of marital happiness. *Personality and Social Psychology Bulletin, 2,* 478–480.

Huston, M., & Schwartz, P. (1995). Relationships of lesbians and gay men. In J. T. Wood & S. W. Duck (Eds.), *Understanding relationship processes, 6: Off the beaten track: Understudied relationships* (pp. 89–121). Thousand Oaks, CA: Sage.

Huston, T. L., McHale, S. M., & Crouter, A. C. (1985). When the honeymoon is over: Changes in the marriage relationship over the first year. In R. Gilmour & S. Duck (Eds.), *The emerging field of personal relationships* (pp. 109–132). Hillsdale, NJ: Erlbaum.

ILA (1995, April). An ILA definition of listening. *ILA Listening Post*, 53, p. 4.

Issacson, W. (1989, November 20). Should gays have marriage rights? *Time*, pp. 101–102.

It doesn't add up. (1997, May 19). *Newsweek*, n. p.

Izard, C. E. (1991). *The psychology of emotions*. New York: Plenum.

James, C. (1999). *Seeing ourselves: Exploring race, ethnicity and culture*. (2nd ed.). Toronto: Thompson Ed. Pub.

James, K. (1989). When twos are really threes: The triangular dance in couple conflict. *Australian and New Zealand Journal of Family Therapy*, 10, 179–186.

James, W. (1890). *Principles of psychology*, 2 vols. New York: Henry Holt Company.

James, W., & Lange, C. B. (1922). *The emotions*. Baltimore: Williams and Wilkins.

Janis, I.L. (1977). *Victims of group-think*. Boston: Houghton-Mifflin.

Johnson, C. B., Stockdale, M. S., & Saal, F. E. (1991). Persistence of men's misperceptions of friendly cues across a variety of interpersonal encounters. *Psychology of Women Quarterly*, 15, 463–465.

Johnson, D. and Johnson, F. (1991). *Joining together: Group theory and group skills* (4th ed.). Englewood Cliffs, NJ: Prentice Hall.

Johnson, F. L. (1989). Women's culture and communication: An analytic perspective. In C. M. Lont & S. A. Friedley (Eds.), *Beyond the boundaries: Sex and gender diversity in communication* (pp. 301–316). Fairfax, VA: George Mason University Press.

Jones, A. (1994). *Next time she'll be dead: Battering and how to stop it*. Boston: Beacon.

Jones, E., & Gallois, C. (1989). Spouses' impressions of rules for communication in public and private marital conflicts. *Journal of Marriage and the Family*, 51, 957–967.

Jones, G. P., & Dembo, M. H. (1989). Age and sex role differences in intimate friendships during childhood and adolescence. *Merrill-Palmer Quarterly of Behavior and Development*, 35, 445–462.

Jones, W. H., & Moore, T. L. (1989). Loneliness and social support. In M. Hojat & R. Crandall (Eds.), *Loneliness: Theory, research, and applications* (pp. 145–156). Newbury Park, CA: Sage.

Jordan, D. J. (1996). *Leadership in leisure services: Making a difference*. State College, PA: Venture Publishing, Inc.

Kaye, L. W., & Applegate, J. S. (1990). Men as elder caregivers: A response to changing families. *American Journal of Orthopsychiatry*, 60, 86–95.

Keeley, M. P., & Hart, A. J. (1994). Nonverbal behavior in dyadic interaction. In S. W. Duck (Ed.), *Understanding rela-tionship processes, 4: Dynamics of relationships* (pp. 135–162). Thousand Oaks, CA: Sage.

Kelley, H. H. (1967). Attribution theory in social psychology. In D. Levine (Ed.), *Nebraska symposium on motivation* (vol. 15, pp. 192–238). Lincoln: University of Nebraska Press.

Kelly, C., Huston, T. L., & Cate, R. M. (1985). Premarital relationship correlates of the erosion of satisfaction in marriage. *Journal of Social and Personal Relationships*, 2, 167–178.

Kelly, G. A. (1955). *The psychology of personal constructs*. New York: Norton.

Kemper, T. (1987). How many emotions are there? Wedding the social and autonomic components. *American Journal of Sociology*, 93, 263–289.

Keyes, R. (1992, February 22). Do you have the time? *Parade*, pp. 22–25.

Kilpatrick, J. (1996, June 1). An odd word or two—but don't dis the dictionary. *Raleigh News and Observer*, p. 15A.

Knapp, M. L. (1972). *Nonverbal communication in human interaction*. New York: Holt, Rinehart & Winston.

Kohlberg, L. (1958). The development of modes of thinking and moral choice in the years 10 to 16. Unpublished doctoral dissertation, University of Chicago.

Korzybski, A. (1958). *Science and sanity* (4th ed.). Lakeville, CT: International Non-Aristotelian Library Publishing Company.

Kovecses, Z. (1990). *Emotion concepts*. New York: Springer-Verlag.

Kozol, J. (1995). *Amazing grace: The lives of children and the conscience of a nation*. New York: Crown.

Kurdek, L. A. (1993). The allocation of household labor in gay, lesbian, and heterosexual married couples. *Journal of Social Issues*, 49, 127–139.

Kwanzaa, cbc.ca/onair/specials/holidays/kwanzaa.html (retrieved May 2, 2001).

La Gaipa, J. J. (1982). Rituals of disengagement. In S. W. Duck (Ed.), *Personal relationships, 4: Dissolving personal relationships*. London: Academic.

Labor letter. (1994, July 16). *Wall Street Journal*, p. A1.

Labov, W. (1972). *Sociolinguistic patterns*. Philadelphia: University of Pennsylvania Press.

Laing, R. D. (1961). *The self and others*. New York: Pantheon.

Lakoff, G., & Johnson, M. (1980). *Metaphors we live by*. Chicago: University of Chicago Press.

Landale, N., & Fennelly, K. (1992). Informal unions among mainland Puerto Ricans: Cohabitation or an alternative to legal marriage? *Journal of Marriage and the Family*, 54, 269–280.

Lange, A., and Jakubowske, P. (1978). *Responsible Assertion* (videorecording). Champaign, Ill.; Waterloo, ON: Research Press.

Langer, S. (1953). *Feeling and form: A theory of art*. New York: Scribner.

Langer, S. (1979). *Philosophy in a new key: A study in the symbolism of reason, rite, and art* (3rd ed.). Cambridge, MA: Harvard University Press.

Langston, D. (1992). Tired of playing monopoly? In M. L. Andersen & P. H. Collins (Eds.), *Race, class, and gender: An anthology* (pp. 110–119). Belmont, CA: Wadsworth.

Larson, J.R. (1984). The performance feedback process: A preliminary model. *Organizational Behavior and Human Performance, 33*, 42–76.

Lasswell, M., & Lobsenz, N. M. (1980). *Styles of loving.* New York: Doubleday.

Laswell, H. (1948). The structure and function of communication in society. In L. Bryson (Ed.), *The communication of ideas.* New York: Harper & Row.

Leathers, D. G. (1976). *Nonverbal communication systems.* Boston: Allyn & Bacon.

Leathers, D. G. (1986). *Successful nonverbal communication: Principles and applications.* New York: Macmillan.

Lee, J. A. (1973). *The colours of love: An exploration of the ways of loving.* Don Mills, Ontario, Canada: New Press.

Lee, J. A. (1988). Love-styles. In R. J. Sternberg & M. L. Barnes (Eds.), *The psychology of love* (pp. 38–67). New Haven, CT: Yale University Press.

Lee, W. S. (1994). On not missing the boat: A processual method for intercultural understanding of idioms and lifeworld. *Journal of Applied Communication Research, 22,* 141–161.

Leland, J., & Beals, G. (1997, May 5). In living color. *Newsweek,* pp. 58–60.

LePoire, B. A., Burgoon, J. K., & Parrott, R. (1992). Status and privacy restoring communication in the workplace. *Journal of Applied Communication Research, 4,* 419–436.

Lewis, J. D., & Weigert, A. J. (1985). Social atomism, holism and trust. *Sociological Quarterly, 26,* 455–471.

Liang, S. (1997, Summer). Mix: A multiethnic women's dialogue. *Hues,* pp. 22–23, 56.

Life Expectancy, www.statcan.ca/english/freepub/89F0123XIE/04.htm (retrieved August 12, 2001).

Little girl has smile surgery. (1995, December 16). *Raleigh News and Observer,* p. 14A.

Lofland, L. (1985). The social shaping of emotion: The case of grief. *Symbolic Interaction, 8,* 171–190.

Lorde, A. (1992). Age, race, class, and sex: Women redefining difference. In M. L. Andersen & P. H. Collins (Eds.), *Race, class, and gender: An anthology* (pp. 495–502). Belmont, CA: Wadsworth.

Luby, V., & Aron, A. (1990, July). A prototype structuring of love, like, and being in-love. Paper presented at the Fifth International Conference on Personal Relationships, Oxford, England.

Lumsden, G., & Lumsden, D. (1997). *Communicating in groups and teams.* Belmont, CA: Wadsworth.

Lund, M. (1985). The development of investment and commitment scales for predicting continuity of personal relationships. *Journal of Social and Personal Relationships, 2,* 3–23.

Lytton, H., & Romney, D. M. (1991). Parents' differential socialization of boys and girls: A meta-analysis. *Psychological Bulletin, 109,* 267–296.

Mahany, B. (1997, August 7). A hands-on study of language. *Raleigh News and Observer,* pp. 1E, 3E.

Main, M. (1981). Avoidance in the service of attachment. In K. Immelmann, G. Barlow, L. Petrenovich, & M. Main (Eds.), *Behavioral development: The Beilfield interdisciplinary project.* New York: Cambridge University Press.

Major, B., Schmidlin, A. M., & Williams, L. (1990). Gender patterns in social touch: The impact of setting and age. In C. Mayo & N. M. Henley (Eds.), *Gender and nonverbal behavior* (pp. 3–37). New York: Springer-Verlag.

Malandro, L. A., & Barker, L. L. (1983). *Nonverbal communication.* Reading, MA: Addison-Wesley.

Maltz, D. N., & Borker, R. (1982). A cultural approach to male–female miscommunication. In J. J. Gumpertz (Ed.), *Language and social identity* (pp. 196–216). Cambridge, England: Cambridge University Press.

Manning, A. (1996, March 6). Signing catches on as a foreign language. *USA Today,* p. 4D.

Mares, M. (1995). The aging family. In M. Fitzpatrick & A. Vangelisti (Eds.), *Explaining family interactions.* Thousand Oaks, CA: Sage.

Markman, H. (1990). Advances in understanding marital distress. Unpublished manuscript. University of Denver.

Markman, H. J. (1981). Prediction of marital distress: A 5-year follow-up. *Journal of Consulting and Clinical Psychology, 49,* 760–762.

Markman, H., Clements, M., & Wright, R. (1991, April). Why father's pre-birth negativity and a first-born daughter predict marital problems: Results from a ten-year investigation. Paper presented at a symposium at the biennial meeting of the Society for Research in Child Development, Seattle.

Maslow, A. H. (1968). *Toward a psychology of being.* New York: Van Nostrand Reinhold.

Masters, W. H., & Johnson, V. E. (1979). *Homosexuality in perspective.* Boston: Little, Brown.

Maternity leave, www.hrdc-drhc.gc.ca/ae-ei/pubs/in201_e.shtml#new (retrieved January 31, 2001).

Maugh, T., II. (1994, November 26). Romantics seem to be bred, not born. *Raleigh News and Observer,* pp. 1A, 4A.

Mayes, Linda, Cohen, Donald. (2002). *The Yale child study center guide to understanding your child.* Little, Brown & Co.

Mazur, E. (1989). Predicting gender differences in same-sex friendships from affiliation motive and value. *Psychology of Women Quarterly, 13,* 277–291.

McCormick, J., & Begley, S. (1996, December 9). How to raise a tiger. *Newsweek,* pp. 52–59.

McDargh, E. (n.d.). Uncovering soul in the workplace. www.refresher.com/!soul.html (retrieved June 19, 2001).

McDowell, D. (1989, July 17). He's got to have his way. *Time*, pp. 92–94.

McGurl, M. (1990, June 3). That's history, not black history. *The New York Times Book Review*, p. 13.

McNeill, D. (1992). *Hand and mind: What gestures reveal about thought.* Chicago: University of Chicago Press.

Mead, G. H. (1934). *Mind, self, and society.* Chicago: University of Chicago Press.

Mehrabian, A. (1981). *Silent messages: Implicit communication of emotion and attitudes* (2nd ed.). Belmont, CA: Wadsworth.

Metts, S., Cupach, W. R., & Bejlovec, R. A. (1989). "I love you too much to ever start liking you": Redefining romantic relationships. *Journal of Social and Personal Relationships, 6,* 259–274.

Miell, D. E., & Duck, S. W. (1986). Strategies in developing friendship. In V. J. Derlega & B. A. Winstead (Eds.), *Friendship and social interaction* (pp. 129–143). New York: Springer-Verlag.

Miller, G. R., & Parks, M. R. (1982). Communication in dissolving relationships. In S. W. Duck (Ed.), *Personal relationships, 4: Dissolving personal relationships* (pp. 127–154). London: Academic.

Miller, J. B. (1993). Learning from early relationship experience. In S. W. Duck (Ed.), *Understanding relationship processes, 2: Learning about relationships* (pp. 1–29). Newbury Park, CA: Sage.

Mochizuki, T. (1981). Changing patterns of mate selection. *Journal of Comparative Family Studies, 12,* 318–328.

Monkerud, D. (1990, October). Blurring the lines. Androgyny on trial. *Omni,* pp. 81–86.

Monsour, M. (1992). Meanings of intimacy in cross- and same-sex friendships. *Journal of Social and Personal Relationships, 9,* 277–295.

Montgomery, B. M. (1988). Quality communication in personal relationships. In S. W. Duck (Ed.), *Handbook of personal relationships* (pp. 343–366). New York: Wiley.

Morris, D. (1997, March–April). The civility wars: Is poverty more vulgar than profanity? *Utne Reader,* pp. 15–16.

Mosley-Howard, S., & Evans, C. (1997). Relationships in the African American family. Paper presented at the 1997 Conference of the International Network on Personal Relationships, Oxford, Ohio.

Mulac, A., Wiemann, J. M., Widenmann, S. J., & Gibson, T. W. (1988). Male/female language differences and effects in same-sex and mixed-sex dyads: The gender-linked language effect. *Communication Monographs, 55,* 315–335.

Multiculturalism Act, laws.justice.gc.ca/en/c-18.7/28210.html (retrieved October 5, 2000).

Mustard, F. (1994). The contribution of the community to the competence and resilience of children. *Bulletin of the Sparrow Lake Alliance,* Vol. 5, No. 1, 8–10.

Naisbitt, J. (1999). *High tech high touch: Technology and our search for meaning.* New York, NY: Broadway Books.

Nardi, P. M., & Sherrod, D. (1994). Friendship in the lives of gay men and lesbians. *Journal of Social and Personal Relationships,* 11, 185–199.

Narem, T. R. (1980). Try a little TLC. *Science,* 80, 15.

National Center for Health Statistics, (1993). *Births, marriages, divorces, and deaths for 1992.* Monthly vital statistics report 41 (no. 12). (DHHS Publication No. PHS 83–1120). Hyattsville, MD: Public Health Service.

National survey results of gay couples in long-lasting relationships. (1990). *Partners: Newsletter for Gay and Lesbian Couples,* pp. 1–16.

New York public library desk reference (pp. 189–191). (1989). New York: Simon & Schuster/Songstone Press.

Newman, P. (1964, February). "Wild man" behavior in New Guinea Highlands community. *American Anthropologist,* 66, 1–19.

Noller, P. (1986). Sex differences in nonverbal communication: Advantage lost or supremacy regained? *Australian Journal of Psychology,* 38, 23–32.

Noller, P. (1987). Nonverbal communication in marriage. In D. Perlman & S. Duck (Eds.), *Intimate relationships: Development, dynamics, and deterioration* (pp. 149–176). Newbury Park, CA: Sage.

Notarius, C. I. (1996). Marriage: Will I be happy or will I be sad? In N. Vanzetti & S. Duck (Eds.), *A lifetime of relationships* (pp. 265–289). Pacific Grove, CA: Brooks/Cole.

Nussbaum, J. E. (1992, October 18). Justice for women! *New York Review of Books,* pp. 43–48.

Nyquist, M. (1992, Fall). Learning to listen. *Ward Rounds* (pp. 11–15). Evanston, IL: Northwestern University Medical School.

O'Connor, P. (1992). *Friendships between women.* London: Harvester Wheatsheaf.

O'Meara, J. D. (1989). Cross-sex friendship: Four basic challenges of an ignored relationship. *Sex Roles,* 21, 525–543.

O'Neill, M. (1997, January 12). Asian folk art of feng shui hits home with Americans. *Raleigh News and Observer,* p. 6E.

Okin, S. M. (1989). *Gender, justice, and the family.* New York: Basic.

Olien, M. (1978). *The human myth.* New York: Harper & Row.

Olson, D., & McCubbin, H. (1983). *Families: What makes them work?* Thousand Oaks, CA: Sage.

Orange County Health Department (1997, September 5). Informational material provided at the Community Solutions to Family Violence Conference, Chapel Hill, NC.

Osborne, A. (1996, Summer). The paradox of effort and grace. *Inner Directions,* pp. 4–6.

Pacanowsky, M. (1989). *Creating and narrating organizational realities.* In B. Dervin, L. Grossberg, B. O'Keefe, & E. Wartella (Eds.), *Rethinking communication: Paradigm exemplars.* Newbury Park, CA: Sage. 250–257.

Pacanowsky, M., & O'Donnell-Trujillo, N. (1983). Organizational communication as cultural performance. *Communication Monographs, 30*, 126–147.

Park M. (1979). *Communication styles in two different cultures: Korean and American*. Seoul: Han Shin.

Patterson, M. L. (1992). A functional approach to nonverbal exchange. In R. S. Feldman & B. Rime (Eds.), *Fundamentals of nonverbal behavior* (pp. 458–495). New York: Cambridge University Press.

Patton, B. R., & Ritter, K. (1976). *Living together ... female/male communication*. Columbus, OH: Merrill.

Pearce, W. B., Cronen, V. E., & Conklin, F. (1979). On what to look at when analyzing communication: A hierarchical model of actors' meanings. *Communication, 4*, 195–220.

Pearson, J. C. (1985). *Gender and communication*. Dubuque, IA: Brown.

Pennebaker, J. W. (1997). *Opening up: The healing power of expressing emotions* (rev. ed.). New York: Guilford.

Perry, J., the Rev. (1996, Summer). Applying meditation to everyday life. *Inner Directions*, pp. 21–23, 26.

Persons Case, www.swc-cfc.gc.ca/persons/case-e.html (retrieved April 10, 2001).

Petersen, A. (1996, December 20). One person's "geometric pattern" can be another's sacred saying. *Wall Street Journal*, p. B1.

Petersen, W. (1997). *Ethnicity counts*. New York: Transaction.

Petronio, S. (1991). Communication boundary management: A theoretical model of managing disclosure of private information between married couples. *Communication Theory, 1*, 311–335.

Pettigrew, T. F. (1967). Social evaluation theory: Consequences and applications. In D. Levine (Ed.), *Nebraska symposium on motivation* (pp. 241–311). Lincoln: University of Nebraska Press.

Phillips, G. M., & Wood, J. T. (1983). *Communication and human relationships*. New York: Macmillan.

Piaget, J. (1932/1965). *The moral judgment of the child*. New York: Free Press.

Pierson, J. (1995, November 20). If sun shines in, workers work better, buyers buy more. *Wall Street Journal*, pp. B1, B8.

Planalp, S. (1997, September). Personal correspondence.

Pleck, J. H. (1987). American fathering in historical perspective. In M. S. Kimmel (Ed.), *Changing men: New directions in research on men and masculinity* (pp. 83–97). Englewood Cliffs, NJ: Prentice-Hall.

Politically correct monikers are labeled incorrect. (1995, November 7). *Wall Street Journal*, p. A1.

Pomerleau, A., Bolduc, D., Malcuit, G., & Cossette, L. (1990). Pink or blue: Environmental stereotypes in the first two years of life. *Sex Roles, 22*, 359–367.

Popenoe, D. (1996). *Life without father*. New York: Free Press.

Proctor, R. (1991). An exploratory analysis of responses to owned messages in interpersonal communication. Doctoral dissertation, Bowling Green University, Bowling Green, Ohio.

Pryor, J. B., & Merluzzi, T. V. (1985). The role of expertise in processing social interaction scripts. *Journal of Experimental Social Psychology, 21*, 362–379.

Psychological Stress Evaluator, aux.lincoln.edu/departments/sociology/criminaljustice/cihypnosis.htm#voice (retrieved June 9, 2001).

Public pillow talk. (1987, October). *Psychology Today*, p. 18.

Raphael, M. (1997, May 13). It's true: Drivers move slowly if you want their space. *Raleigh News and Observer*, p. 1A.

Raspberry, W. (1994, July 5). Major gains in minorities' grades at Tech. *Raleigh News and Observer*, p. 9A.

Rawlins, W. K. (1981). Friendship as a communicative achievement: A theory and an interpretive analysis of verbal reports. Doctoral dissertation, Temple University, Philadelphia.

Rawlins, W. K. (1994). Being there and growing apart: Sustaining friendships during adulthood. In D. Canary & L. Stafford (Eds.), *Communication and relational maintenance* (pp. 275–294). New York: Academic.

Reel, B. W., & Thompson, T. L. (1994). A test of the effectiveness of strategies for talking about AIDS and condom use. *Journal of Applied Communication Research, 22*, 127–141.

Reis, H. T., Senchak, M., & Solomon, B. (1985). Sex differences in the intimacy of social interaction: Further examination of potential explanations. *Journal of Personality and Social Psychology, 48*, 1204–1217.

Reisenzaum, R. (1983). The Schachter theory of emotion: Two decades later. *Psychological Bulletin, 94*, 239–264.

Reske, J., & Stafford, L. (1990). Idealization and communication in long-distance premarital relationships. *Family Relations, 39*, 274–290.

Ribeau, S. A., Baldwin, J. R., & Hecht, M. L. (1994). An African-American communication perspective. In L. Samovar & R. Porter (Eds.), *Intercultural communication: A reader* (7th ed., pp. 140–147). Belmont, CA: Wadsworth.

Riessman, C. (1990). *Divorce talk: Women and men make sense of personal relationships*. New Brunswick, NJ: Rutgers University Press.

Robertson, R. and Jacobson, L. (1992). *Pygmalion in the classroom: Teacher expectation and pupils' intellectual development*. Irvington Pub.

Rohlfing, M. (1995). Doesn't anybody stay in one place anymore? An exploration of the understudied phenomenon of long-distance relationships. In J. T. Wood & S. W. Duck (Eds.), *Understanding relationship processes, 6: Off the beaten track: Understudied relationships* (pp. 173–196). Thousand Oaks, CA: Sage.

Root, M. P. P. (1990). Disordered eating habits in women of color. *Sex Roles, 22*, 525–536.

Rose, S. M. (1984). How friendships end: Patterns among young adults. *Journal of Social and Personal Relationships, 1,* 267–277.

Rose, S., & Frieze, I. H. (1989). Young singles' scripts for a first date. *Gender and Society, 3,* 258–268.

Rose, S., & Serafica, F. (1986). Keeping and ending casual, close and best friendships. *Journal of Social and Personal Relationships, 3,* 275–288.

Rosenberg, M. (1979). *Conceiving the self.* New York: Basic.

Rousar, E. E., III, & Aron, A. (1990, July). Valuing, altruism, and the concept of love. Paper presented at the Fifth International Conference on Personal Relationships, Oxford, England.

Rowland, D. (1985). *Japanese business etiquette.* New York: Warner.

Ruberman, T. R. (1992, January 22–29). Psychosocial influences on mortality of patients with coronary heart disease. *Journal of the American Medical Association, 267,* 559–560.

Rubin, L. (1985). Just friends: The role of friendship in our lives. New York: Harper & Row.

Rubinson, L., & De Rubertis, L. (1991). Trends in sexual attitudes and behaviors of a college population over a 15-year period. *Journal of Sex Education and Therapy, 17,* 32–42.

Ruddick, S. (1989). *Maternal thinking: Towards a politics of peace.* Boston: Beacon.

Rusbult, C. (1987). Responses to dissatisfaction in close relationships: The exit–voice–loyalty–neglect model. In D. Perlman & S. W. Duck (Eds.), *Intimate relationships: Development, dynamics, and deterioration* (pp. 109–238). London: Sage.

Rusbult, C. E., & Zembrodt, I. M. (1983). Responses to dissatisfaction in romantic involvement: A multidimensional scaling analysis. *Journal of Experimental Social Psychology, 19,* 274–293.

Rusbult, C. E., Johnson, D. J., & Morrow, G. D. (1986). Impact of couple patterns of problem solving on distress and nondistress in dating relationships. *Journal of Personality and Social Psychology, 50,* 744–753.

Rusbult, C. E., Zembrodt, I. M., & Iwaniszek, J. (1986). The impact of gender and sex-role orientation on responses to dissatisfaction in close relationships. *Sex Roles, 15,* 1–20.

Rusk, T., & Rusk, N. (1988). Mind traps: Change your mind, change your life. Los Angeles: Price, Stern, Sloan.

Saarni, C. (1990). Emotional competence: How emotions and relationships become integrated. In R. A. Thompson (Ed.), *Socioemotional development: Nebraska symposium on motivation* (pp. 115–182). Lincoln: University of Nebraska Press.

Sallinen-Kuparinen, A. (1992). Teacher communicator style. *Communication Education, 41,* 153–166.

Samovar, L., & Porter, R. (Eds.). (1994). *Intercultural communication: A reader.* Belmont, CA: Wadsworth.

Samover, L., & Porter, R. (1995). *Intercultural communication: A reader* (7th ed.). Belmont, CA: Wadsworth.

Scarf, M. (1987). *Intimate partners.* New York: Random House.

Schachter, S. (1964). The interaction of cognitive and physiological determinants of emotion states (pp. 138–173). In P. Leiderman & D. Shapiro (eds.), *Psychobiological approaches to social behavior.* Stanford, CA: Stanford University Press.

Schachter, S., & Singer, J. (1962). Cognitive, social, and physiological determinants of emotional state. Psychological Review, 69, 379–399.

Schiminoff, S. B. (1980). *Communication rules: Theory and research.* Newbury Park, CA: Sage.

Schmanoff, S. (1985). Expressing emotions in words: Verbal patterns of interactions. *Journal of Communication, 35,* 16–31.

Schmanoff, S. (1987). Types of emotional disclosures and request compliance between spouses. *Communication Monographs, 54,* 85–100.

Schmitt, R. (1997, September 11). Judges try curbing lawyers' body language antics. *Wall Street Journal,* pp. B1, B7.

Schneider, D. (1997). Implicit personality theory: A review. *Psychological Bulletin, 27,* 294–309.

Schramm, W. (1955). *The process and effects of mass communication.* Urbana: University of Illinois Press.

Schutz, W. (1958*). The interpersonal communication underworld.* Palo Alto, CA: Science and Behavior Books.

Sebeok, T. A., & Rosenthal, R. (Eds.). (1981). *The Clever Hans phenomenon: Communication with horses, whales, apes and people.* New York: New York Academy of Sciences.

Secklin, P. (1991, November). Being there: A qualitative study of young adults' descriptions of friendship. Paper presented at the Speech Communication Association Convention, Atlanta.

Secord, P. F., Bevan, W., & Katz, B. (1956). The Negro stereotype and perceptual accentuation. *Journal of Abnormal and Social Psychology, 54,* 78–83.

Seligman, M. E. P. (1990). *Learned optimism: How to change your mind and your life.* New York: Simon & Schuster/Pocket Books.

Sept, R. (1981). *Bridging theory and practice in laboratory education: An heuristic model for intervention in human relations training groups.* Unpublished thesis, Simon Fraser University, Vancouver, BC.

Shannon, C, & Weaver, W. (1949). *The mathematical theory of communication.* Urbana: University of Illinois Press.

Shattuck, T. R. (1980). *The forbidden experiment: The story of the wild boy of Aveyron.* New York: Farrar, Straus & Giroux.

Shaver, P., Schwartz, J., Kirson, D., & O'Connor, C. (1987). Further explorations of a prototype approach. *Journal of Personality and Social Psychology, 52,* 1061–1086.

Shaver, P., Wu, S., & Schwartz, J. (1992). Cross-cultural similarities and differences in emotion and its representation: A prototype approach. In M. S. Clark (Ed.), *Emotion* (pp. 175–212). Newbury Park, CA: Sage.

Shellenbarger, S. (1995, August 23). Telecommuter profile: Productive, efficient, and a little weird. *Wall Street Journal*, B1.

Sher, T. G. (1996). Courtship and marriage: Choosing a primary partner. In N. Vanzetti & S. Duck (Eds.), *A lifetime of relationships* (pp. 243–264). Pacific Grove, CA: Brooks/Cole.

Sherrod, D. (1989). The influence of gender on same-sex friendships. In C. Hendrick (Ed.), *Close relationships* (pp. 164–186). Newbury Park, CA: Sage.

Shott, S. (1979). Emotion and social life: A symbolic interactionist analysis. *American Journal of Sociology*, 84, 1317–1334.

Shotter, J. (1993). *Conversational realities: The construction of life through language*. Newbury Park, CA: Sage.

Simon, S. B. (1977). *Vulture: A modern allegory on the art of putting oneself down*. Niles, IL: Argus Communications.

Smitherman, G. (1994). *Black talk: Words and phrases from the hood to the amen corner*. Boston: Houghton Mifflin.

Snell, W. E., Jr., Hawkins, R. C., II, & Belk, S. S. (1988). Stereotypes about male sexuality and the use of social influence strategies in intimate relationships. *Journal of Clinical and Social Psychology*, 7, 42–48.

Spain, D. (1992). *Gendered spaces*. Chapel Hill: University of North Carolina Press.

Spear, W. (1995). *Feng shui made easy: Designing your life with the ancient art of placement*. New York: HarperCollins.

Spencer, T. (1994). Transforming relationships through ordinary talk. In S. W. Duck (Ed.), *Understanding relationship processes, 4: Dynamics of relationships* (pp. 58–85). Thousand Oaks, CA: Sage.

Spitz, R. (1965). *The first year of life*. New York: International Universities Press.

Spitzack, C. (1990). *Confessing excess*. Albany: State University of New York Press.

Spitzack, C. (1993). The spectacle of anorexia nervosa. *Text and Performance Quarterly*, 13, 1–21.

Spousal Violence, www.statcan.ca/english/freepub/85-224-XIE/free.htm (retrieved August 13, 2001).

Sprecher, S. (1989). The importance to males and females of physical attractiveness, earning potential, and expressiveness in initial attraction. *Sex Roles*, 21, 591–607.

Stacey, J. (1996). *In the name of the father: Rethinking family values in a postmodern age*. Boston: Beacon.

Statistics Canada. (2001). *Family Violence in Canada: A statistical profile 2001*. www.statcan.ca/english/freepub/85-224-XIE/free.htm (retrieved August 13, 2001).

Statistics Canada. (March, 1999). *Life expectancy at birth by sex*. www.statcan.ca/English/freepub/89F0123XIE/04.htm (retrieved August 20, 2001).

Statistics Canada. (n.d.). *1996 Census: Divorce*. www.statcan.ca/english/Pgdb/People/Families/famil02.htm (retrieved August 6, 2001).

Stearns, C., & Stearns, P. (1986). *Anger: The struggle for emotional control in America's history*. Chicago: University of Chicago Press.

Stephenson, S. J., & D'Angelo, G. (1973). The effects of evaluative/empathic listening and self-esteem on defensive reactions in dyads. Paper presented to the International Communication Association. Montreal, Quebec, Canada.

Sternberg, R. J. (1986). A triangular theory of love. *Psychological Review*, 93, 119–135.

Stewart, J. (1986). *Bridges, not walls* (4th ed.). New York: Random House.

Stewart, L. P., Stewart, A. D., Friedley, S. A., & Cooper, P. J. (1990). *Communication between the sexes: Sex differences and sex role stereotypes* (2nd ed.). Scottsdale, AZ: Gorsuch Scarisbrick.

Stone, R. (1992). The feminization of poverty among the elderly. In M. L. Andersen & P. H. Collins (Eds.), *Race, class, and gender: An anthology* (pp. 201–214). Belmont, CA: Wadsworth.

Strege, J. (1997). *Tiger: A biography of Tiger Woods*. New York: Bantam Doubleday.

Suitor, J. J. (1991). Marital quality and satisfaction with the division of household labor across the family life cycle. *Journal of Marriage and the Family*, 53, 221–230.

Surra, C. (1987). Mate selection as social transition. In D. Perlman & S. Duck (Eds.), *Intimate relationships: Development, dynamics and deterioration* (pp. 88–120). Newbury Park, CA: Sage.

Surra, C., Arizzi, P., & Asmussen, L. (1988). The association between reasons for commitment and the development and outcome of marital relationships. *Journal of Social and Personal Relationships*, 5, 47–64.

Swain, S. (1989). Covert intimacy: Closeness in men's friendships. In B. Risman & P. Schwartz (Ed.), *Gender and intimate relationships* (pp. 71–86). Belmont, CA: Wadsworth.

Sypher, B. (1984). Seeing ourselves as others see us. *Communication Research*, 11, 97–115.

Tannen, D. (1990). *You just don't understand: Women and men in conversation*. New York: William Morrow.

Tavris, C. (1989). *Anger: The misunderstood emotion*. New York: Simon & Schuster.

Tavris, C. (1992). *The mismeasure of woman*. New York: Simon & Schuster.

Taylor, B., & Conrad, C. (1992). Narratives of sexual harassment: Organizational dimensions. *Journal of Applied Communication Research*, 4, 401–418.

Templin, N. (1994, October 17). Wanted: Six bedrooms, seven baths for empty nesters. *Wall Street Journal*, pp. B1, B7.

Thomas, V. G. (1989). Body-image satisfaction among black women. *Journal of Social Psychology*, 129, 107–112.

Thompson, G., and Jenkins, J. (1993). *Verbal judo: The gentle art of persuasion*. New York, NY: William Morrow.

Three million around the world contracted AIDS in last year. (1994, August 9). *Raleigh News and Observer*, p. 5A.

Ting-Toomey, S. (1991). Intimacy expressions in three cultures: France, Japan, and the United States. *International Journal of Intercultural Relations, 15*, 29–46.

Toffler, A. (1970). *Future shock.* New York: William Morrow.

Toffler, A. (1980). *The third wave.* New York: William Morrow.

Tolhuizen, J. H. (1989). Communication strategies for intensifying dating relationships: Identification, use, and structure. *Journal of Social and Personal Relationships, 6*, 413–434.

Townsend, P. (1962). Quoted on p. 146 in A. Fontana, *The last frontier: The social meaning of growing old.* Beverly Hills, CA: Sage.

Trainor, B. (1996, May 20). Commit suicide over a medal? An ex-general gives his view. *The New York Times*, p. A8.

Treichler, P. A., & Kramarae, C. (1983). Women's talk in the ivory tower. *Communication Quarterly, 31*, 118–132.

Trice, H., & Beyer, J. (1984). Studying organizational cultures through rites and ceremonials. *Academy of Management Review, 9*, 653–669.

Trotter, R. J. (1975, October 25). The truth, the whole truth, and nothing but .... *Science News, 108*, 269.

Tuckman, B.W. (1965). Developmental sequences in small groups. *Psychological Bulletin, 63*, 384–399.

U. S. Bureau of the Census. (1994). *Current population reports, geographic mobility.* Washington, DC: U.S. Government Printing Office.

U.S. Bureau of the Census. (1992). *Current population reports, geographical mobility* (pp. 20–463). Washington, DC: U.S. Government Printing Office.

Ueland, B. (1992, November/December). Tell me more: On the fine art of listening. *Utne Reader*, pp. 104–109.

Vachss, A. (1994, August 28). You carry the cure in your own heart. *Parade*, pp. 4–6.

Van Maanen, J., & Barley, S. (1985). *Cultural organization; Fragments of a theory.* In P.J. Frost, et al. (Eds.) Organizational culture. Beverly Hills, CA: Sage, 31–54.

Vangelisti, A. (1993). Couples' communication problems: The counselor's perspective. *Journal of Applied Communication Research, 22*, 106–126.

Vanyperen, N. W., & Buunk, B. P. (1991). Equity theory and exchange and communal orientation from a cross-national perspective. *Journal of Social Psychology, 131*, 5–20.

Varkonyi, C. (1996, June 22). Color code. *Raleigh News and Observer*, pp. 1–2E.

Villarosa, L. (1994, January). Dangerous eating. *Essence*, pp. 19–21, 87.

Walker, M. B., & Trimboli, A. (1989). Communicating affect: The role of verbal and nonverbal content. *Journal of Language and Social Psychology, 8*, 229–248.

Walster, E., Traupmann, J., & Walster, G. W. (1978). Equity and extramarital sexuality. *Archives of Sexual Behavior, 7*, 127–141.

Watzlawick, P., Beavin, J., & Jackson, D. D. (1967). *Pragmatics of human communication.* New York: Norton.

Weaver, C. (1972). *Human listening: Processes and behavior.* Indianapolis: Bobbs-Merrill.

Weber, S. N. (1994). The need to be: The socio-cultural significance of black language. In L. Samovar & R. Porter (Eds.), *Intercultural communication: A reader* (7th ed., pp. 221–226). Belmont, CA: Wadsworth.

Weiner, N. (1997). *The human use of human beings.* New York: Avon.

Weiss, S. E. (1987). The changing logic of a former minor power. In H. Binnendijk (Ed.), *National negotiating styles* (pp. 44–74). Washington DC: U.S. Department of State.

Wellman, B. (1985). Domestic work, paid work, and net work. In S. W. Duck & D. Perlman (Eds.), *Understanding personal relationships.* Beverly Hills, CA: Sage.

Wells, W., & Siegel, B. (1961). Stereotyped somatypes. *Psychological Reports, 8*, 77–78.

Werner, C. M., & Haggard, I. M. (1985). Temporal qualities of interpersonal relationships. In G. R. Miller & M. L. Knapp (Eds.), *Handbook of interpersonal communication* (pp. 59–99). Beverly Hills, CA: Sage.

Werner, C. M., Altman, I., Brown, B. B., & Ginat, J. (1993). Celebrations in personal relationships: A transactional/dialectical perspective. In S. W. Duck (Ed.), *Understanding relational processes, 3: Social context and relationships* (pp. 109–138). Newbury Park, CA: Sage.

Werner, C., Altman, I., & Oxley, D. (1985). Temporal aspects of homes: A transactional perspective. In I. Altman & C. M. Werner (Eds.), *Home environments: Vol. 8. Human behavior and environment: Advances in theory and research* (pp. 1–32). Beverly Hills, CA: Sage.

West, J. (1995). Understanding how the dynamics of ideology influence violence between intimates. In S. W. Duck & J. T. Wood (Eds.), *Understanding relationship processes, 5: Confronting relationship challenges* (pp. 129–149). Thousand Oaks, CA: Sage.

West, L., Anderson, J., & Duck, S. (1996). Crossing the barriers to friendship between men and women. In J. T. Wood (Ed.), *Gendered relationships.* Mountain View, CA: Mayfield.

Westefield, J. S., & Liddell, D. (1982). Coping with long-distance relationships. *Journal of College Student Personnel, 23*, 550–551.

Weston, K. (1991). *Families we choose: Lesbian, gays, kinship.* New York: Columbia University Press.

Wexner, L. B. (1954). The degree to which colors (hues) are associated with mood-tones. *Journal of Applied Psychology, 38*, 432–435.

Whan, K. (1997, August 10). UNC study observes link between health, loving support. *The Chapel Hill Herald*, p. 7.

What teens say about drinking. (1994, August 7). *Parade*, p. 9.

Whitbeck, L. B., & Hoyt, D. R. (1994). Social prestige and assortive mating: A comparison of students from 1956 and

1988. *Journal of Social and Personal Relationships, 11,* 137–145.

White Ribbon Campaign, www.whiteribbon.ca (retrieved April 16, 2001).

White, B. (1989). Gender differences in marital communication patterns. *Family Process, 28,* 89–106.

White, J., & Bondurant, B. (1996). Gendered violence in intimate relationships. In J. T. Wood (Ed.), *Gendered relationships.* Mountain View, CA: Mayfield.

Whitman, Walt. (1855/1983). *Leaves of Grass.* New York, NY: Bantam Books, lines 226–227.

Whorf, B. (1956). *Language, thought, and reality.* New York: MIT Press/Wiley.

Wiemann, J. M., & Harrison, R. P. (Eds). (1983). *Nonverbal interaction.* Beverly Hills, CA: Sage.

Wilkie, J. R. (1991). The decline in men's labor force participation and income and the changing structure of family economic support. *Journal of Marriage and the Family, 53,* 111–122.

Williams, D. G. (1985). Gender, masculinity–femininity, and emotional intimacy in same-sex friendship. *Sex Roles, 12,* 587–600.

Willmott, P. (1987). *Friendship networks and social support.* London: Policy Studies Institute.

Wilson, J. A. R., Robick, M. C., & Michael, W. B. (1974). *Psychological foundations of learning and teaching* (2nd ed.). New York: McGraw-Hill.

Winzeler, R. (1990). Amok: Historical, psychological, and cultural perspectives. In W. J. Karim (Ed.), *Emotions of culture: A Malay perspective* (pp. 97–122). Oxford, England: Oxford University Press.

Wolf, N. (1991). *The beauty myth.* New York: William Morrow.

Woo, E. (1995, December 18). Stereotypes may psych out students. *Raleigh News and Observer,* pp. 1A, 10A.

Wood, J. T. (1982). Communication and relational culture: Bases for the study of human relationships. *Communication Quarterly, 30,* 75–84.

Wood, J. T. (1986). Different voices in relationship crises: An extension of Gilligan's theory. *American Behavioral Scientist, 29,* 273–301.

Wood, J. T. (1992a). *Spinning the symbolic web.* Norwood, NJ: Ablex.

Wood, J. T. (1992b). Telling our stories: Narratives as a basis for theorizing sexual harassment. *Journal of Applied Communication Research, 4,* 349–363.

Wood, J. T. (1993). Engendered relations: Interaction, caring, power, and responsibility in intimacy. In S. W. Duck (Ed.), *Understanding relationship processes, 3: Social context and relationships* (pp. 26–54). Newbury Park, CA: Sage.

Wood, J. T. (1994a). Engendered identities: Shaping voice and mind through gender. In D. Vocate (Ed.), *Intrapersonal communication: Different voices, different minds* (pp. 145–167). Hillsdale, NJ: Erlbaum.

Wood, J. T. (1994b). Gender and relationship crises: Contrasting reasons, responses, and relational orientations. In J. Ringer (Ed.), *Queer words, queer images: The construction of homosexuality* (pp. 238–265). New York: New York University Press.

Wood, J. T. (1994c). Gender, communication, and culture. In L. Samovar & R. Porter (Eds.), *Intercultural communication: A reader* (7th ed., pp. 155–164). Belmont, CA: Wadsworth.

Wood, J. T. (1994d). *Gendered lives: Communication, gender, and culture.* Belmont, CA: Wadsworth.

Wood, J. T. (1994e). *Who cares? Women, care, and culture.* Carbondale: University of Southern Illinois Press.

Wood, J. T. (1995a). Diversity in dialogue: Communication between friends. In J. Makau & R. Arnett (Eds.), *Ethics of communication in an age of diversity.* Urbana: University of Illinois Press.

Wood, J. T. (1995b). Feminist scholarship and research on relationships. *Journal of Social and Personal Relationships, 12,* 103–120.

Wood, J. T. (1995c). *Relational communication.* Belmont, CA: Wadsworth.

Wood, J. T. (1997). Clarifying the issues. *Personal Relationships, 4,* 221–228.

Wood, J. T. (1997c). *Gendered lives,* 2nd ed. Belmont, CA: Wadsworth.

Wood, J. T. (1998). *But I thought you meant ...: Misunderstandings in human communication.* Mountain View, CA: Mayfield.

Wood, J. T. (Ed.). (1996). *Gendered relationships.* Mountain View, CA: Mayfield.

Wood, J. T., & Inman, C. C. (1993). In a different mode: Masculine styles of communicating closeness. *Journal of Applied Communication Research, 21,* 279–295.

Wood, J. T., Dendy, L., Dordek, E., Germany, M., & Varallo, S. (1994). Dialectic of difference: A thematic analysis of intimates' meanings for differences. In K. Carter & M. Presnell (Eds.), *Interpretive approaches to interpersonal communication* (pp. 115–136). New York: State University of New York Press.

Wood, J.T. (1997a). *Communication in our lives.* Belmont, CA: Wadsworth.

Wren, C. S. (1990, October 16). A South Africa color bar falls quietly. *The New York Times,* pp. Y1, Y10.

Wright, P. H., & Scanlon, M. B. (1991). Gender role orientations and friendship: Some attenuation but gender differences still abound. *Sex Roles, 24,* 551–566.

Wright, P. H., & Wright, K. (1995). Codependency: Personality syndrome or relationship process? In S. Duck & J. T. Wood (Eds.), *Understanding relationship processes, 5: Confronting relationship challenges* (pp. 109–128). Thousand Oaks, CA: Sage.

WuDunn, S. (1991, April 17). Romance, a novel idea, rocks marriages in China. *The New York Times,* pp. B1, B12.

Yerby, J., Buerkel-Rothfuss, N., & Bochner, A. (1990). *Understanding family communication.* Scottsdale, AZ: Gorsuch Scarisbrick.

Zorn, T. (1995). Bosses and buddies: Constructing and performing simultaneously hierarchical and close friendship relationships. In J. T. Wood & S. W. Duck (Eds.), *Understanding relationship processes, 6: Off the beaten track: Understudied relationships* (pp. 122–147). Thousand Oaks, CA: Sage.

Copyright Acknowledgments

Grateful acknowledgment is made to the copyright holders who granted permission to reprint previously published material.

Page 364 (The Five Human Rights): Lange, A., and Jakubowske, P. (1978). Responsible Assertion (video-recording). Champaign, Ill.; Waterloo, ON: Research Press. Reprinted with permission.

Page 410 (Five love languages): Chapman, Gary. (1995). The five love languages: How to express heartfelt commitment to your mate. Chicago: Northfield Pub. Reprinted with permission.

Page 425 (Four Damaging Behaviours in Close Relationships): Gottman, J., Katz, L., and Hooven, C. (1996). *Meta-emotion: How families communicate emotionally.* Hillsdale, NJ: Lawrence Erlbaum Assoc. Reprinted with permission.

Index

NOTES

NOTES